MW01538973

Authentic Christianity

An Exposition of the Theology and Ethics of the Westminster Larger Catechism

AUTHENTIC CHRISTIANITY

An Exposition of the Theology and Ethics of the Westminster Larger Catechism

VOLUME FIVE

JOSEPH C. MORECRAFT, III

MINKOFF FAMILY PUBLISHING
AMERICAN VISION PRESS
POWDER SPRINGS, GEORGIA

AUTHENTIC CHRISTIANITY:

An Exposition of the Theology and Ethics of the Westminster Larger Catechism • Volume Five

by Joseph C. Morecraft, III

Published by:

American Vision Press in cooperation with
Minkoff Family Publishing

The American Vision, Inc.
3150 Florence Road
Powder Springs, Georgia 30127-5385
www.AmericanVision.org • 1-800-628-9460

Printed in The United States of America.

Cover and interior layout design by Luis D. Lovelace

ISBN13: 978-0-9840641-3-7 (5 Volume Set)

ABOUT THE COVER: *The Assertion of Liberty of Conscience By the Independents at the Westminster Assembly of Divines* by John Rogers Herbert (1810–1890). The Westminster Assembly of Divines was appointed by the Long Parliament in 1643 for the work of restructuring the Church of England. The Assembly met for six years (1643 through 1649), and in the process produced the major Confessional Standards of the Presbyterian faith, including the *Westminster Confession of Faith*, the *Westminster Larger Catechism*, the *Westminster Shorter Catechism*, and the *Directory of Public Worship*.

CONTENTS *of* VOLUME FIVE

CHAPTER THIRTY-THREE

The Tenth Commandment 1

The Relation of the Tenth Commandment to the Other Nine Commandments (4) • The Language of the Tenth Commandment (4) • The Purpose of the Tenth Commandment (8) • The Roman Catholic Splitting of the Tenth Commandment (12) • The Effect of the Tenth Commandment on the Apostle Paul (12) • The Promise of the Tenth Commandment (13) • The Accompaniments of Covetousness (14) • **(Q. 147) The Duties Required in the Tenth Commandment** (17) • The Exhortations to Contentment With Our Condition (20) • **(Q. 148) The Sins Forbidden by the Tenth Commandment** (33) • The Application of the Tenth Commandment to 21st Century America (47)

CHAPTER THIRTY-FOUR

Man's Inability, the Degrees and Desert of Sin and Escape from the Wrath of God 55

(Q. 149) The Inability of Man to Keep God's Law Perfectly (60) • **(Q. 150) The Degrees & Aggravations of Sin** (69) • **(Q. 151) The Aggravations That Make Some Sins Worse Than Others** (72) • **(Q. 152) The Desert of Every Sin** (127) • The Three Required Means of Escape From God's Wrath (136) • **How Does Larger Catechism Q. 70 Relate to Larger Catechism Q. 153?** (148)

CHAPTER THIRTY-FIVE

The Saving Power of the Reading and Preaching of God's Word 153

The Vital Importance of the Reading and Preaching of the Bible (157) • **(Q. 154) The Diligent Use of the Means of Grace** (159) • **(Q. 155) The Saving Effects of the Reading and Preaching of the Bible** (161) • The Reading of the Bible (178) • **(Q. 156) The Persons Who Should Read the Bible** (181) • **(Q. 157) The Manner in Which the Bible Should Be Read** (184) • The Preaching of the Bible (192) • **(Q. 158) The Preachers of the Bible** (192) • **(Q. 159) The Manner in Which The Bible is to Be Preached** (196) • **(Q. 160) The Hearing of the Bible Preached** (200) • The Power of Preaching (206) • **Appendix: The Preaching of the Word of God According to the Westminster Directory for the Publick Worship of God** (218)

CHAPTER THIRTY-SIX

The Sacraments in the Worship of God 225

(Q. 161) THE EFFECTIVENESS OF THE SACRAMENTS AS MEANS OF GRACE AND SALVATION (234) • The Meaning of "Effectual Means of Salvation" (235) • **THE SOURCE OF THE SACRAMENTS' POWER** (237) • The Spirit of Christ (237) • The Word of God (240) • **(Q. 162) The Definition and Purpose of A Sacrament** (242) • The Definition of a Sacrament (243) • The Purpose of a Sacrament (247) • The Biblical Basis for This Viewpoint (247) • The Believer's Mystical Union with Christ (251) • To *Seal* to Covenant Members the Benefits of Christ's Redemptive Work (256) • **(Q. 163) The Parts of a Sacrament** (270) • **(Q. 164) The Number of Sacraments** (284) • **(Q. 165) The Sacrament of Baptism** (294) • The Ordinance of Christ (295) • The Mode of Baptism by John the Baptist (304) • The Purpose of Baptism (312) • The Exposition of Galatians 3:26–27 (319) • The Corroboration of Romans 6:3–5 & Colossians 2:12 (323) • A Public Initiation and A Public Confession (340) • **(Q. 166) The Recipients of Baptism** (347) • **THE BIBLICAL BASIS FOR THE BAPTISM OF CHILDREN OF BELIEVERS** (355) • The Summary of the Basic Pillars of Infant Baptism (355) • The Case for the Baptism of Children of Believers (356) • The Unity of the Covenantal Structure of the Bible (358) • The Unity and Continuity of the Church (363) • The Unity and Continuity of the Sign of the Covenant (370) • The Solemnity and Sanctity of the Baptism of the Children of Believers (380) • **(Q. 167) The "Improvement" of Baptism** (382) • **(Q. 168) THE SACRAMENT OF THE LORD'S SUPPER** (384) • The Ordinance of Christ (386) • The Purpose of the Lord's Supper (389) • The Presence of Christ in the Lord's Supper (398) • **(Q. 169) The Administration of the Lord's Supper** (405) • The Method of Administering the Lord's Supper (407) • The Elements to be Used in the Lord's Supper (421) • **(Q. 170) The Meaning of "Feeding Upon the Body and Blood of Christ"** (423) • **THE NATURE OF EATING THIS BREAD** (428) • **THE NECESSITY OF EATING JESUS' FLESH AND DRINKING JESUS' BLOOD TO RECEIVE ETERNAL LIFE** (428) • **(Q. 171) The Preparation for Receiving the Lord's Supper** (436) • The Preparation for Receiving the Lord's Supper (442) • **(Q. 172) The Question of the Doubter: Should He Partake?** (448) • **(Q. 173) The Question of the Ignorant or Scandalous: Should They Partake?** (450) • **(Q. 174) The Attitude of Heart and Mind During the Receiving of the Lord's Supper** (452) • **(Q. 175) The Duties of Christians After They Have Received the Lord's Supper** (461) • The Responsibilities of One Who Upon Reflection Concludes That, As An Unworthy Eater, He Was Not Blessed of God in the Lord's Supper, After He Has Partaken of the Supper (468) • **(Q. 176) The Similarities of Baptism and the Lord's Supper** (473) • **(Q. 177) How Baptism and the Lord's Supper Differ** (474)

CHAPTER THIRTY-SEVEN

The Reality of Prayer 487

(Q. 178) The Essence of Prayer: An Offering Up of Our Desires to God (493) • **(Q. 179) The Object of Prayer: An Offering Up of Our Desires unto God** (496) • The Presuppositions of Prayer (496) • The Perfections of God and Prayer (501) • **(Q. 180) The Necessity of Praying in Jesus' Name** (503) • **(Q. 181) The Reason for Praying in the Name of Christ** (507) • **(Q. 182) The Necessity of Praying with the Help of the Holy Spirit** (509) • The Kinds of Prayer (515) • The Purpose of Prayer in the Plan of God (522) • **(Q. 183) THE PEOPLE AND CONCERNS FOR WHICH WE ARE TO PRAY** (525) • **(Q. 184) The Concerns for Which We Should Pray** (533) • **(Q. 185) The Manner in Which We Are to Pray** (535) • **(Q. 186) THE RULE THAT GOVERNS PRAYER: THE WORD OF GOD** (552) • The Comprehensive Rule and The Special Rule Governing Prayer (555) • Stonewall Jackson: Man of Prayer (559) • Eleven Directions for Praying by Richard Baxter, 17th Century English Presbyterian (567) • Ten Directions for Family Prayers by Richard Baxter (569) • Six Directions for Secret Prayer by Richard Baxter (570) • Advice from Richard Baxter on How We May Know When Our Prayers Are Heard and When They Are Not (571)

CHAPTER THIRTY-EIGHT

The Lord's Prayer 573

(Q. 186–187) THE SPECIAL RULE OF PRAYER (581) • The Context of the Lord's Prayer in the Sermon on the Mount (583) • **(Q. 188) The Divisions of the Lord's Prayer** (586) • **(Q. 189) The Preface of the Lord's Prayer** (589) • **(Q. 190) The First Petition of the Lord's Prayer** (598) • The Wise Instruction of our Catechism Q. 190 on Hallowing God's Great Name (604) • **(Q. 191) The Second Petition of the Lord's Prayer** (622) • **(Q. 192) The Third Petition of the Lord's Prayer** (671) • The Two Parts of the Third Petition of The Lord's Prayer (672) • The Reasons for Making This Petition (677) • **(Q. 193) The Fourth Petition of the Lord's Prayer** (693) • The Specific Requests of the Fourth Petition (702) • The Manner in Which the Fourth Petition Must be Made to God (711) • **(Q. 194) The Fifth Petition of the Lord's Prayer** (715) • The Reasons for the Fifth Petition (720) • The Basis and Prerequisites for a Prayer for Forgiveness (724) • **APPENDIX: HOW TO FORGIVE: LUKE 17:1–10** (745) • **THE WORDS FOR "FORGIVENESS" IN THE BIBLE** (749) • **(Q. 195) The Sixth Petition of the Lord's Prayer** (751) • The Means By Which This Goal will be Reached (767) • **(Q. 196) The Conclusion of the Lord's Prayer** (800) • The Enforcing of Petitions With Arguments (804)

BIBLIOGRAPHY 821

Chapter Thirty-Three

The Tenth Commandment

Exodus 20:17

"Here in the Tenth Commandment we come to the heart of what it means to face God's demand upon the whole of our life. Here at the end of the Commandments, we find out where God expects us to begin to serve Him."
~ *Ronald Wallace*

He that spared not His own Son, but delivered Him up for us all, how shall He not with Him also freely give us all things?
Romans 8:32

The Tenth Commandment

Exodus 20:17

Q. 146: Which is the tenth commandment?

A.: The tenth commandment is, *Thou shalt not covet thy neighbour's house, thou shalt not covet they neighbour's wife, nor his man-servant, nor his maid-servant, nor his ox, nor his ass, nor any thing that is thy neighbour's.*

Q. 147: What are the duties required in the tenth commandment?

A.: The duties required in the tenth commandment are, such a full contentment with our own condition, and such a charitable frame of the whole soul toward our neighbour, as that all our inward motions and affections touching him, tend unto, and further all that good which is his.

Q. 148: What are the sins forbidden in the tenth commandment?

A.: The sins forbidden in the tenth commandment are, discontentment with our own estate; envying and grieving at the good of our neighbour, together with all inordinate motions and affections to any thing that is his.

The Relation of the Tenth Commandment to the Other Nine Commandments

God in the First Commandment makes a total demand upon the heart and soul and strength and life of His people. Then in the next eight Commandments, He defines all the areas of life in which He seeks for them to express this devotion and commitment. Then, in the last Commandment, He makes another total and radical demand, reminding us that if we are going to serve God at all in these areas of life on which He has laid His hand, we must serve Him with the heart as well as with the outward life, we must obey Him in spirit as well as in letter. Therefore, though this Commandment adds nothing new to what has been already implied in all the other Commandments, it brings out everything that is most important in the sight of God, and sends us back again to the other Commandments with a new understanding of their meaning. It keeps us from becoming superficial.[1]

The Language of the Tenth Commandment

> You shall not covet your neighbor's house; you shall not covet your neighbor's wife or his male servant or his female servant or his ox or his donkey or anything that belongs to your neighbor (Ex. 20:17).

> You shall not covet your neighbor's wife, and you shall not desire your neighbor's house, his field or his manservant, his ox or his donkey or anything that belongs to your neighbor (Deut. 5:21).

In order to understand the meaning of the Tenth Commandment, we must ascertain: (1) The meaning of "covet;" (2) The mean-

1. Ronald Wallace, *The Ten Commandments: A Study of Ethical Freedom* (Grand Rapids, MI: William B. Eerdmans Publishing Co., 1965), 174.

ing of "your neighbor's house"; and (3) The reason for the repetition not to covet in this Commandment.

The Meaning of the Word "Covet"

First, the word "covet" in the Tenth Commandment has two meanings: "to covet or to desire strongly" and "to take or defraud" (Mark 10:19). The Hebrew word for covet, *chamad*, signifies "an *earnest* and *strong* desire after a matter, on which all the affections are concentrated and fixed" [Clarke],[2] and which leads to "the attempt to attach something to oneself illegally. The commandment therefore deals with all possible undertakings which involve gaining power over the goods and possessions of a 'neighbor,' whether through theft or through all kinds of dishonest machinations" [Martin Noth].[3]

> The Hebrew *hāmad*, "desire," is in itself a neutral word. It is only when misdirected to that which belongs to another that such "desire" becomes wrong. It is sometimes claimed that this is the only one of the ten commandments which prohibits an attitude of mind rather than an outward act: but to make this distinction is probably to misunderstand Hebrew thought. As in the case of "loving" and "hating", "desiring" is an activity, almost equivalent to "seeking to acquire."... Ultimately to desire, and to try to obtain, the property of another is to be dissatisfied with what God has given, and thus to show lack of faith in His love. Further, the envy which this encourages will lead sooner or later to the hurt of one's neighbour, and this is inconsistent with the primary duty of love.[4]

So then, "covet" has a comprehensive meaning. Not only are we forbidden to deprive our neighbor of anything that belongs to him

2. Rousas J. Rushdoony, *The Institutes of Biblical Law* (Nutley, NJ: The Craig Press, 1973), 633.

3. Quoted in Rushdoony, *The Institutes of Biblical Law*, 632.

4. R. Alan Cole, *Exodus: An Introduction and Commentary* (Downers Grove, IL: InterVarsity Press, 1973), 161.

in any of our dealings with him, but we are to repent of the very inward thought and desire from which our sinful actions spring.

The words "covet" and "desire" used in Exodus 20:17 and Deuteronomy 5:21 denote

> an *earnest* and *strong* desire after a matter, on which all the affections are concentrated and fixed, whether the thing be *good* or *bad*. This is what we commonly term *covetousness*, which word is taken both in a *good* and *bad* sense. So when the Scripture says, that *covetousness is idolatry*: yet it also says, *covet earnestly the best things* [1 Corinthians 12:31]; so we find that this disposition is sinful or holy, according to the object on which it is fixed. In this command, the *covetousness* which is placed on forbidden objects, is that which is prohibited and condemned. To covet in this sense, is intensely to long after, in order to enjoy as *property*, the *person*, or *thing* coveted. He breaks this command, who by any means endeavours to deprive a man of his *house*, or *farm*, by some *underhand* and *clandestine* bargain with the original landlord; what is called in some countries, *taking a man's house and farm over his head*. He breaks it also, who lusts after his neighbour's wife, and endeavours to ingratiate himself into her affections, by striving to lessen her husband in her esteem:—and he breaks it, who endeavours to possess himself of the servants, cattle, &c. of another, in any clandestine or unjustifiable way. This is a most excellent moral precept, the observance of which will prevent all public crimes: for he who feels the force of the law which prohibits the inordinate desire of any thing that is the property of another, can never make a breach in the peace of society by an act of *wrong* to any of even its feeblest members.[5]

The Bible makes a distinction between "good coveting" and "evil coveting." We have already defined coveting in an evil sense. 1 Corinthians 12:31 uses the word in a positive sense: "But earnestly desire [covet] the greater gifts." In this text "covet" (KJV)

5. Adam Clarke, quoted in Rushdoony, *The Institutes of Biblical Law*, 633–34.

means "earnestly desire, aim hard for, work earnestly and zealously for the best gifts."

The Significance of the Phrase "Your Neighbor's House"

Second, "your neighbor's house" refers to a man's household or family, and all that is in it, with primary reference to his wife (Deut. 5:21), his servants and employees, his animals, means of production and possessions, his land and property, and "anything that belongs to your neighbor." A "house" is not merely a dwelling place, it includes the entire household (Gen. 15:2; Job 8:15), either including the wife, or exclusive of her.

> In the text before us [Ex. 20:17] she is included [in the 'house']; in Deuteronomy [5:21] she is not, but is placed first as the crown of the man, and a possession more costly than pearls (Prov. xii:4; xxxi:10). In this case, the idea of the "house" is restricted to the other property belonging to the domestic economy, which is classified in Deuteronomy as fields, servant cattle, and whatever else a man may have; whereas in Exodus the "house" is divided into wife, servants, cattle, and the rest of the possessions.[6]

The Repetition of the Forbidding of Coveting in the Tenth Commandment

Third, the repetition of the forbidding of coveting in the Tenth Commandment is for emphasis.

> The repetition merely serves to strengthen and give the greater emphasis to that which constitutes the very kernel of the command, and is just as much in harmony with the simple and appropriate language of the law, as the employment

6. C. F. Keil and F. Delitzsch, *Biblical Commentary on the Old Testament: The Pentateuch*, trans. by Rev. James Martin, 3 vols (Grand Rapids, MI: William B. Eerdmans Publishing Co., 1971), 2:125.

> of a synonym in the place of the repetition of the same word is with the rhetorical character of Deuteronomy.[7]

The Tenth Commandment as expressed in Deuteronomy 5:21 contains two words prohibiting coveting: "covet" and "desire." These are synonyms.

> The only difference between them being, that 'the former denotes the desire as founded upon the perception of beauty, and therefore excited from without; the latter, desire originating at the very outset in the person himself, and arising from his own want or inclination.'[8]

The Purpose of the Tenth Commandment

According to John Calvin

> The purpose of this commandment is: since God wills that our whole soul be possessed with a disposition to love, we must banish from our hearts all desire contrary to love. To sum up, then: no thought should steal upon us to move our hearts to a harmful covetousness that tends to our neighbor's loss. To this corresponds the opposite precept: whatever we conceive, deliberate, will or attempt is to be linked to our neighbor's good and advantage.[9]

According to Wilhelmus á Brakel

> Man is not self-sufficient; he cannot satisfy himself with himself. He is but an empty vessel, only capable of receiving something. He must find his fulfillment by matters which are exterior to himself—both according to soul and body. He must have food, drink, air, and light, will it be well with his

7. Keil and Delitzsch, *Biblical Commentary on the Old Testament: The Pentateuch*, 2:125.

8. Schultz, quoted in Keil and Delitzsch, *Biblical Commentary on the Old Testament: The Pentateuch*, 2:125.

9. John Calvin, *Institutes of the Christian Religion*, ed. by John T. McNeill, trans. by Ford Lewis Battles, 2 vols. (Philadelphia: Westminster Press, 1960), 1:413.

body. According to his soul, he must have something spiritual and infinite—that is God Himself—in order for his infinite desire to be satisfied.

In order to be fulfilled, God has created an innate desire within man. This desire, considered in and of itself, was a perfect desire. As long as man was in the state of perfection, that desire was directed toward the right objects in a right manner. In regard to the soul, his desire was only directed toward God in order to be continually satisfied in having fellowship with and finding delight in Him—and as far as the body was concerned, his desire was directed toward that which it needed. It was the food of Christ's soul to do the will of His Father (John 4:34), and according to the body He had a desire for temporal food and drink. He hungered (Matt. 4:2), and He thirsted (John 19:28).

However, after man had sinned, desire remained but it has been distorted and corrupted, both as to the manner in which it functions, as well as relative to its objects. He has no desire after God and his desires are therefore not directed toward God as being the satisfaction of his soul. His desire is after this world, whereby he seeks to satisfy his spiritual soul, and according to the body he has unlawful desires toward that which is lawful in and of itself. These desires furthermore extend themselves toward forbidden objects. This is the sin forbidden in this commandment.[10]

According to the Heidelberg Catechism Q. 113–115

Q. 113: What doth the tenth commandment require of us?

A.: That even the smallest inclination or thought, contrary to any of God's commandments never

10. Wilhelmus á Brakel, *The Christian's Reasonable Service*, trans. by Bartel Elshout, 4 vols. (Pittsburgh, PA: Soli Deo Gloria, 1994), 3:238.

rise in our hearts; but that at all times we hate all sin with our whole heart, and delight in all righteousness.

Q. 114: But can those who are converted to God perfectly keep these commandments?

A.: No: but even the holiest men, while in this life, have only a small beginning of this obedience; yet so, that with a sincere resolution they begin to live, not only according to some but all the commandments of God.

Q. 115: Why will God then have the ten commandments so strictly preached, since no man in this life can keep them?

A.: First, that all our lifetime we may learn more and more to know our sinful nature, and thus become the more earnest in seeking the remission of sin, and righteousness in Christ; likewise, that we constantly endeavor and pray to God for the grace of the Holy Spirit, that we may become more and more conformable to the image of God, till we arrive at the perfection proposed to us, in a life to come.

The Heidelberg Catechism connects Q. 113 with Q. 114 and Q. 115 because it understands the deep, inner meaning of the Tenth Commandment. It "openly and directly points the finger to our inner life when it forbids us to covet."[11] It points the finger directly at the

11. Herman Hoeksema, *The Triple Knowledge*, 3 vols. (Grand Rapids, MI: Reformed Free Publishing House, 1972), 3:422.

> inner life of the Christian, at his thoughts and desires, at his will, and at his deepest heart.... The tenth commandment in its very form, in its literal expression, very clearly claims the whole inner life of man.... It is for that reason that the Heidelberg Catechism correctly sees in this tenth commandment the manifestation of the perfection of the law.... And it is because of that character of the tenth commandment that the Catechism with it joins the question: can anyone keep that law perfectly; can the Christian keep that law of God without fail? And of course, for the same reason the next question follows: what, then, is the use to preach the law of God, if no one can keep it perfectly anyway?[12]

The Westminster Larger Catechism's understanding of the Tenth Commandment is similar to that of the Heidelberg Catechism. Question 146–148 explain the duties and sins involved in the meaning of the Tenth Commandment. Question 149 then asks: *Is any man able perfectly to keep the commandments of God?* And answers: *No man is able, either of himself, or by any grace received in this life, perfectly to keep the commandments of God; but doth daily break them in thought, word, and deed.* Therefore, the interpretation of the Tenth Commandment by the Westminster Larger Catechism and the older Heidelberg Catechism is all-embracing and profound.

The Roman Catholic Splitting of the Tenth Commandment

> Rome,... having suppressed the 2nd commandment, divides the 10th in order to make out the requisite number. Her 9th commandment is, "Thou shalt not covet thy neighbor's house;"and her 10th , "Neither shalt thou desire his wife," etc. Her plea is, that houses are typical of property; and wives of those things which excite sensual desire. The 9th commandment therefore forbids covetousness; the 10th , lust and ap-

12. Hoeksema, *The Triple Knowledge*, 3:422–23.

petite. But unfortunately, the "ox and ass," obvious "property" are in the latter part; and in Deut. v:21, where Moses recites the Decalogue literally, he puts the wife first, and the property second. There is no basis for the distinction. For what is property craved by sinners? Only for its instrumentality to satisfy some appetite or sensual desire.[13]

The Effect of the Tenth Commandment on the Apostle Paul

> What shall we say then? Is the Law sin? May it never be! On the contrary, I would not have come to know sin except through the Law; for I would not have known about coveting if the Law had not said, "You shall not covet" (Rom. 7:7).

When the apostle Paul measured his life against the Tenth Commandment, he was brought to a state of deep despair. In his pursuit for eternal life before his conversion,

> he felt he had achieved success and made progress, until the true meaning of the Tenth Commandment dawned on him. "Thou shalt not covet." He had not kept that, and with no amount of effort could he come anywhere near to keeping that!... It was when he faced this Commandment and began to see that God demanded the whole obedience of the heart and of the desire as well as the whole obedience of the outward life, that he realised just how great a sinner he was. "Though he was able to prevent his evil desires from realising themselves in outward acts of hatred, or impurity or greed or slander, he was powerless to check, and still more powerless to destroy, the growing fount of lawless desire within him, or free himself from inward longings after the sins in which he refused to indulge outwardly" [Charles].... In taking us in this way to the heart of God's demand upon

13. Robert L. Dabney, *Lectures in Systematic Theology* (Grand Rapids, MI: Zondervan Publishing House, [1878] 1975), 426.

us, the Tenth Commandment helps us all to discover that we are, and will ever remain while this life lasts, sinners before God.[14]

The Promise of the Tenth Commandment

The promise of the Lord's help in curing coveting in us is found in the heart of the Tenth Commandment itself. "You shall not covet" also means "You shall not need to covet."

> It is a promise that God Himself will provide for us in everything we think we lack.... It takes us to the heart of the answer given by God to the Apostle Paul, when he besought the Lord twice for the deliverance from the particular "thorn in the flesh" which he was bound to feel as his own peculiar privation in life, and under the burden of which he was bound to covet the freedom of other men. "My grace is sufficient for thee; for My strength is made perfect in weakness" (2 Cor. xii:9). "I have learned," Paul can say later, "in whatsoever state I am, therewith to be content. I know both how to be abased, and I know how to abound: everywhere and in all things I am instructed both how to be full and how to be hungry, both to abound and to suffer need" (Phil. iv:11–12).[15]
>
> Is there not something very rich here that we have to discover? God has given us so much in Jesus Christ that we need no longer make comparisons between ourselves and others with regard to possessions or talents or privileges or sufferings. Paul was never weary of asserting this emphatically. "All things are yours; whether Paul, or Apollos, or Cephas, or the world, or life, or death, or things present, or things to come; all are yours, and you are Christ's; and Christ is God's" (1 Cor. iii:22–3). "He that spared not His own Son, but delivered Him up for us all, how shall He not with Him also freely give us all things?" (Rom. viii:32). How can any of us who

14. Wallace, *The Ten Commandments*, 176, 175.
15. Wallace, *The Ten Commandments*, 179–80.

> believe this promise, and have grasped anything of its reality, now look round from what it holds out to us, give way to the spirit of covetousness, or nurse gloom or bitterness or envy even for one moment?[16]

In other words, the preventative of and remedy for covetousness is: (1) Faith in the promises of God in Christ; (2) Contentment with God's will, revealed and unrevealed (Deut. 29:29); and (3) Discipline, restraint and control of the mind. (4) Ultimately, the cure for covetousness in the heart and for its inevitable self-centeredness is the work of God alone: "A new heart also will I give you, and a new spirit will I put within you; and I will take away the stony heart out of your flesh, and I will give you an heart of flesh" (Ezek. 36:26).

The Accompaniments of Covetousness

Covetousness and Immorality

Covetousness is the love of irresponsible wealth and power that makes us envious of anyone who has what we want.[17] Because a covetous person is committed to satisfying all his desires and wants, the New Testament brings out the close connection between immorality (Heb. 13:4) and covetousness (Heb. 13:5).

> I wrote to you not to associate with any so-called brother, if he is an immoral person or covetous, not even to eat with him (1 Cor. 5:11).

> Do not let immorality or any impurity or greed even be named among you (Eph. 5:3).

---

16. Wallace, *The Ten Commandments*, 180.

17. "Covetousness is an inordinate desire with a suitable endeavour after the enjoyment of more riches than we have, or than God is pleased to give unto us, proceeding from an undue valuation of them, or love unto them" (John Owen, *Hebrews: The Epistle of Warning* [Grand Rapids, MI: Kregel Publications, (1953) 1968], 270).

> Consider the members of your body as dead to immorality, impurity, passion, evil desire, and greed, which amounts to idolatry (Col. 3:5).
>
> As Moffat has said: "The love of luxury and the desire for wealth open up opportunities of sensual indulgence."

Covetousness and Gossip

Gossip could be the most common outworking of covetousness and envy. The love of irresponsible wealth and power makes a person envious of those who have or are what we don't have or are not, so we try to destroy them with *verbal bullets.*

Covetousness and Wealth

Material and financial wealth is often a blessing of God. It is to be received with gratitude and used for His glory: "Praise the LORD! How blessed is the man who fears the LORD, who greatly delights in His commandments. His descendants will be mighty on earth; the generation of the upright will be blessed. Wealth and riches are in his house, and his righteousness endures forever." The Bible does not say that wealth and luxury lead to sin; but rather man's sinful heart uses wealth and luxury at times to increase its ability and opportunity to sin. "Profit" is not a four-letter word, and the desire for a profit is a godly desire, if the intent is to use it faithfully for the Lord. It is not money, but the love of it that is the root of all evil, *i.e.*, the love of irresponsible wealth and power.

Covetousness and Inflation

Covetousness and envy destroy a production-oriented society and create a consumer-oriented society, where people live for consumption and leisure. This kind of people will demand a social order which produces more money for them to spend, *i.e.*, an inflationary money supply unbacked by silver and gold. All segments of society will demand financial "hand-outs" from the state, *e.g.*, transfer payments, entitlements, food stamps, subsidies for industries, tariffs, inflated money, etc. The society that lusts for wealth quickly destroys wealth. It liquidates productive wealth for consumer wealth. It sells the future for the present.

Covetousness and Socialism

Covetousness and envy are the basis for Marxism, Socialism, Fascism, and the big government we have in the U.S. today. When someone is dominated by larceny in the heart, he looks at his neighbor's property and says to himself: "I wish I had that. If I could get my hands on it, I'd be happy. Maybe I can steal it. Maybe I can get someone to loan me the money to buy it. Or maybe I can get Congress to confiscate it and give it to me." The civil government's legalized plundering is motivated by covetousness.

Envy says: "He has what I want. I don't have it. I want it, but I know I can never get it. Nobody ought to be allowed to have it if everyone can't have one just like it. I'll destroy it. I'll have the government make it illegal to own one. I'll make sure nobody ever has one like it again." Envy is destructive.

> Envy demands the leveling of all things [and the redistribution of the wealth], because the envious man finds superiority in others intolerable. He sees it as better to turn the world into hell rather than to allow anyone to prosper more than himself, or to be superior to him.... Envy creates a conflict society in which the evil men are held to be precisely the most successful and advanced members of society. Their crime is their success.[18]

They must be punished. They must be regulated and taxed.

Covetousness and the IRS

The IRS fuels envy and protects it. A graduated income tax that progressively rises with income is based on envy, but it calls envy a social virtue that transfers the wealth from the rich to the poor. However, in reality, it transfers the wealth from the productive middle class to the bureaucrats and consumers.

---

18. R. J. Rushdoony, *The Roots of Inflation* (Vallecito, CA: Ross House Books, 1982), 33–34.

Covetousness (Envy) and Arson

The arson resents the prosperity of others. He gets joy from fire, not simply because the flames are pretty, but because the arsonist gets joy from seeing the property, hopes and success of others being destroyed by flames. Many people are arsonists at heart, who love to see the rich fall, justly or unjustly.

Covetousness and Terrorism

Terrorism does not make sense unless you define it in terms of covetousness and envy. The professional terrorist is not ultimately governed by the belief that his terrorism will bring peace on earth. He uses terror to create a loss of faith and to strike out at leaders of a society. The act of terrorism is useful only if your political philosophy makes the destruction of society itself a blessing. If you resent the economic or social superiority of others, then terrorism is a way of striking at what you resent. It is not that the terrorist believes that his violence will better society, but that it will burn it down and level it, which is his goal.

The Duties Required in the Tenth Commandment

Q. 147: What are the duties required in the tenth commandment?

A. The duties required in the tenth commandment are, such a full contentment with our own condition, and such a charitable frame of the whole soul toward our neighbour, as that all our inward motions and affections touching him, tend unto, and further all that good which is his.

A Full Contentment With Our Own Condition

The only cure for covetousness is faith in Christ and contentment with His will. Contentment is the result of the surrender of the heart and life to the care and rule of God in Christ. "Contentment is an inner, quiet satisfaction and peace of mind which moves us to freely submit to and take pleasure in God's control, management and disposal of life in every condition and circumstance."[19] Contentment is a frame of mind which keeps us from being mastered and controlled by circumstances. If you can improve your circumstances by godly means, do it; but if you cannot, and if you must remain in a trying and difficult position, do not be mastered by it, do not let it get you down, do not let it control you. Do not let circumstances determine whether you will be happy or sad, because you have committed your life to a sovereign God who is the Author of all circumstances in terms of Romans 8:28!

> Contentment is a Christian virtue consisting in a correspondence between the desire[20] of God's children and their present condition—this being true because it is the will of their God in Christ and according to His sovereign determination. In this they rest with delight, in quiet confidence, joyfully, and with gratitude, trusting that the Lord will cause the present and the future to turnout to their advantage. This causes them to utilize their present condition to the advancement of their spiritual life and to the glory of God.[21]

---

19. Jeremiah Burroughs, *Rare Jewel of Christian Contentment* (Grand Rapids, MI: Sovereign Grace Publishers, 1971), 12.

20. "We must not eliminate all desires—as if the absence of desire would constitute true contentment. That would be to dehumanize man and to make him less than an animal. Our desires must be contrary to that which is evil.... That which is good must be desirable to us and our desires must be focused on its enjoyment. We must pursue these desires by using those means which are subservient to this. Thus, contentment neither excludes the having of desires nor the use of the means, but it excludes all those desires which are focused on sinful matters. This relates to all desires for all that which exceeds our needs; all vehement and passionate desires for something which normally could be lawfully desired; all mental anguish, heartache, and pouting if things do not go our way; and the use of all evil means for the fulfillment of our desire—whereby all lawful means are neglected, and God is tempted" (Brakel, *The Christian's Reasonable Service*, 3:381).

21. Brakel, *The Christian's Reasonable Service*, 3:379–80.

Notice in this definition of contentment the following points: (1) The object of contentment is our *present condition.* (2) The nature of contentment consists in the harmony of our desires and our present condition. (3) The foundation of contentment is the sovereign will of God in Christ (Rom. 8:28). And (4) The effects of contentment include: delight with our circumstances (2 Cor. 12:10), a quiet confidence in the Lord (Ps. 39:9), a joyful heart (James 1:2), gratitude to God (Job 1:21), rest in God's providence (Ps. 91:1–2), spiritual growth (Rom. 5:3–4; Ps. 94:12), and the glorifying of God by us (1 Pet. 1:7; 4:16).

Contentment replaces covetousness when we: (1) Believe the promises of God (Deut. 31:6, 8; Josh. 1:5; Ps. 118:6). If God's omnipotence is our defense, God's wisdom our guide, God's righteousness our standard, God's sovereignty our security and God's love our portion, why should we ever covet and be anything other than fully content in Him? (2) Understand the nature and use of wealth (Prov. 3). (3) Do not desire anything but what the Bible says is permissible. (4) Find a calling (vocation). (5) Remember the brevity of life and that eternity is straight ahead. (6) Learn to find pleasure and satisfaction only in Christ and always in Christ. (7) Learn to reason Biblically.[22] (8) Covetousness and envy in a society can be defeated and controlled, and a society can survive and prosper, only when there are decades of faithful preaching on the nature and dan-

22. "1. Conditions are always changing, therefore I must obviously not be dependent upon conditions. 2. What matters supremely and vitally is my soul and my relationship to God—that is the first thing. 3. God is concerned about me as my Father, and nothing happens to me apart from God. Even the very hairs of my head are all numbered. I must never forget that. 4. God's will and God's ways are a great mystery, but I know that whatever He wills or permits is of necessity for my good. 5. Every situation in life is the unfolding of some manifestation of God's love and goodness. Therefore my business is to look for this peculiar manifestation of God's goodness and kindness and to be prepared for surprises and blessings because 'His ways are not my ways, neither His thoughts my thoughts.' 6. I must regard circumstances and conditions, not in and of themselves therefore, but as a part of God's dealings with me in the work of perfecting my soul and bringing me to final perfection. 7. Whatever my conditions may be at this present moment they are only temporary, they are only passing, and they can never rob me of the joy and the glory that ultimately await me with Christ" (Martyn Lloyd-Jones, *Spiritual Depression: Its Causes and Cures* [Grand Rapids, MI: William B. Eerdmans Publishing Co., 1965], 284–85).

ger of envy and encouraging contentment in Christ and His will for us. The West's original commitment against the sin of envy made it the wealthiest culture in man's history.

The Exhortations to Contentment With Our Condition

> But godliness actually is a means of great gain, when accompanied by contentment. For we have brought nothing into the world, so we cannot take anything out of it either. And if we have food and covering, with these we shall be content. But those who want to get rich fall into temptations and a snare and many foolish and harmful desires which plunge men into ruin and destruction. For the love of money is a root of all sorts of evil, and some by longing for it have wandered away from the faith and pierced themselves with many a pang (1 Tim. 6:6–10).

The main points of this text are these: (v. 6) A statement of fact; (v. 7) A reason for the statement; (v. 8) An inference drawn from the statement; (v. 9) A warning for those who disregard the statement; and (v. 10) The reason for the warning.

(v. 6) A Statement of Fact: Godliness is a Means of Great Gain, When Accompanied By Contentment

Cultivating godliness of life merely for financial, material or social advancement is a perversion of godliness. But, godliness with contentment, with submission to God and His will is "a means of great gain," that is, "godliness cultivated for its own sake, not as a stepping-stone to wealth or worldly consideration," brings its own good with it and makes the believer satisfied in the sufficiency of Christ.

What is this "great gain?" 1 Timothy 4:8 explains: "bodily discipline is only little profit, but godliness is profitable for all things, since it holds promise for the present life and also for the life to come." Here Paul is saying that physical training and gymnastics, with which the ancient Greeks were so preoccupied, is "only little profit," in that it conditions the physical body, but the sincere and strenuous cultivation of godliness is vastly more important since it is "profitable for all things." Its value and benefits are comprehensive in that those benefits enrich all of life—spiritual, physical, intellectual, social, eternal—"since it holds promise for the present life and also for the life to come." As John Calvin said, "godliness is a very great gain to us, because, by means of it, we obtain the benefit, not only of being heirs of the world, but likewise of enjoying Christ and all His riches."[23] As the psalmist says: "O fear the LORD, you His saints; for to those who fear Him, there is no want. The young lions do lack and suffer hunger; but they who seek the LORD shall not be in want of any good thing" (Ps. 34:9–10, *e.g.*, Prov. 3:1–12).

(v. 7) A Reason for the Statement: For We Have Brought Nothing into the World, So We Cannot Take Anything Out of it Either

The lasting happiness of a person is not to be found in the abundance of material possessions, because

> we brought nothing with us of earthly treasure when we were ushered into life here, because neither could we take [anything] with us when we leave it; thus having a lesson embodied in our very birth, in order that we might keep in view the solemn exemplification it was to find at the hour of death.[24]

(v. 8) An Inference From the Statement: And If We Have Food and Covering, With These We Shall be Content

Therefore, in the light of verses six and seven, we should be content with what God provides us for nourishment and shelter, thank-

23. John Calvin, *Commentaries on the Epistles to Timothy, Titus, and Philemon*, trans by Rev. William Pringle (Edinburgh: Calvin Translation Society, 1843; reprint Grand Rapids, MI: Baker Book House, 1979), 157.

24. Patrick Fairbairn, *Commentary on the Pastoral Epistles: I and II Timothy, Titus* (T & T Clark, 1874; reprint Grand Rapids, MI: Zondervan Publishing House, 1956), 236.

fully receiving any other gifts of God's providence beyond those of necessity, and using them for His glory.

(v. 9) A Warning Against Disregarding the Statement: But Those Who Want to Get Rich Fall into Temptation and A Snare and Many Foolish and Harmful Desires Which Plunge Men into Ruin and Destruction

But, in verse nine, after exhorting us to contentment with God's providence, he warns us of the danger of craving riches and of living to "get rich," not because riches are evil, as we have seen, but because the craving of them, instead of the craving of spiritual blessings, destroys us. It causes that person to "fall" into a perilous, downward and ruinous course.

First, he falls "into temptation" to deny or disobey the Lord which will be too strong for him to resist in his spiritually weakened condition. Second, he falls into "a snare," *i.e.*, entanglements with money, business and society in which it is impossible for him to work his way through with a good conscience. He is trapped! Third, he falls into "many foolish and harmful desires which plunge men into ruin and destruction," or "which *sink men into destruction and perdition.*"[25]

> Sin never walks alone. The desire to become rich causes the man...to fall into numerous cravings. One kind of craving easily leads to another. The person who craves riches generally also yearns for honor, popularity, power, ease, the satisfaction of the desires of the flesh, etc. All spring from the same root, selfishness [self-love], which, being the worst possible method of *really* satisfying the 'self,' is both senseless and hurtful.... Instead of the *gain* which they were seeking... the men whose hearts are set on riches experience only *loss.*[26]

They plunge themselves into "ruin and destruction."

---

25. Fairbairn, *Commentary on the Pastoral Epistles,* 238.

26. William Hendriksen, *Exposition of the Pastoral Epistles* (Grand Rapids, MI: Baker Book House, 1957), 199–200.

(v. 10) The Reason for the Warning: For the Love of Money is a Root of All Sorts of Evil, and Some By Longing for it Have Wandered Away from the Faith, and Pierced Themselves with Many a Pang

Verse ten answers the question: why is the craving for riches so destructive? Its answer is in two parts:

First, "the love of money is a root of all sorts of evil." Remember what the inordinate love of money, of the market place, and of what money can buy, did to: the man who stole a poor man's one little lamb in the prophet Nathan's parable, the rich young ruler who turned away from Christ, the rich fool in Christ's parable who deceived himself into thinking all is well, the rich man, in another story by Jesus, who neglected poor Lazarus and went to hell, Judas, who betrayed Christ and committed suicide, Ananias and Sapphira whom God struck dead, and the rich oppressors of James' epistle who exploited their employees. "The desire for riches... has been the cause of innumerable frauds, dollar-sign marriages, divorces, perjuries, robberies, poisonings, murders, and wars."[27]

Second, "some by longing for it have wandered away from the faith, and pierced themselves with many a pang." Craving for riches makes shipwreck of one's Christian principles, departing from the faith; and it makes shipwreck of his happiness, transfixing him with many "pangs."

> What precisely these were we are left to infer; but the expression seems to point to inward rather than to outward troubles—to sorrows of heart, the pungent rebukes of conscience, which came upon the individuals referred to when they saw, and had time to reflect on, the shameful course they had pursued.[28]

Therefore, in verse eleven, in contrast to those who idolatrously pursue riches, Paul exhorts ministers: "But flee from these things,

27. Hendriksen, *Exposition of the Pastoral Epistles*, 201.
28. Fairbairn, *Commentary on the Pastoral Epistles*, 239.

you man of God; and pursue after righteousness, godliness, faith, love, perseverance, and gentleness."

> Let your way of life be free from the love of money, being content with what you have; for He Himself has said, "I will never desert you, nor will I ever forsake you," so that we confidently say, "The Lord is my Helper, I will not be afraid. What shall man do to me?" (Heb. 13:5–6).

The greedy and covetous person is never content with God's will and providence,

> ungenerous and grasping, he always wants more and is always afraid of losing what he has. How different from the serenity of the true Christian who knows that, having Christ, he lacks nothing that is essential for his well-being (cf Ps. 23:1). Paul, destitute of worldly possession, sublimely speaks of himself "as having nothing, and yet possessing everything" (2 Cor. 6:10).[29]

Paul learned these things from the example and teaching of Christ, who on earth had no place to lay his head (Matt. 8:20), who taught that "a man's life does not consist in the abundance of his possessions" (Luke 12:15), and who exhorted his disciples to lay up treasures in heaven rather than on earth, Matthew 6:19–21. It is better to be poor in the sight of men and "rich toward God" than to be rich in the sight of men and poor toward God (Luke 12:21).

Because the Bible promises that "the Lord is [our] helper" who "will never leave [us] nor forsake [us]"—no matter how destitute our material resources or bitter our circumstances—we need not fear what man can do to us, nor have we any basis for complaint or covetousness.

---

29. Philip E. Hughes, *A Commentary on the Epistle to the Hebrews* (Grand Rapids, MI: Wm. B. Eerdmans Publishing Co., 1977), 567.

The Example of the Apostle Paul: Philippians 4:11–13

> (11) Not that I speak from want; for I have learned to be content in whatever circumstances I am. (12) I know how to get along with humble means, and I also know how to live in prosperity; in any and every circumstance I have learned the secret of being filled and going hungry, both of having abundance and suffering need. (13) I can do all things through Him who strengthens me.

In Philippians 4:10, Paul thanks the Philippians for their kindness and generosity in sending him some kind of gift in his imprisonment. Then, in 4:11–13, he tells them that

> he had not been waiting impatiently for, or expecting, this expressing of their kindness, and still more that he was in no sense dependent upon their goodness and generosity… he has to express his thanks to the members of the church at Philippi, and yet he has to do it in a way which will not in any sense detract or derogate from the reality of his experience as a Christian man, dependent upon God.[30]

Paul is explaining to the Philippians about the Lord's all-sufficient grace even in circumstances that he was experiencing in prison. He is saying, in effect: "I have learned in whatever circumstances I find myself to be Christ-sufficient, independent of his surroundings, circumstances and outward conditions." Of course, this did not mean that Paul was indifferent to his circumstances. He was not a stoic. He is simply saying that he is not mastered and controlled by his circumstances and if he can improve his circumstances by God-honoring means, he will most definitely do so. But if that cannot be done, if he has to remain in this trying situation, he will not let it rob him of his joy in the Lord and his confidence that God has a purpose for his being in prison unjustly (Phil. 1:12–14). Paul does not depend upon his outward conditions for his happiness and joy in the Lord (Phil. 4:4). He says that whether he is in dire

---

30. Lloyd-Jones, *Spiritual Depression*, 276.

straits or enjoying wealth and luxury, he has learned how to be completely content in the Lord and dependent on Him in everything. In every situation and in all the details of life, Paul has learned to be content with the Lord's will for His life.

> What helped him most to learn this lesson [of being content with the all-sufficiency of Christ in all circumstances] was his looking at the great and perfect example of Christ Himself. "Looking unto Jesus...who for the joy that was set before Him endured the Cross, despising the shame" (Heb. 12:1–4). Paul "looked unto Him" and saw Him and His perfect example. And he applied it to his own life.[31]

Six Reasons Why We as Christians Should be Content with Our Condition

These following reasons are from Thomas Boston quoted by Buddy Hanson in *God's Ten Words.*

First,

> Let the discontented person answer that question which God proposes to sinners to silence their murmurings. "Is it not lawful for Me to do what I will with mine own?" (Matt. 20:15). "Must the clay be allowed to say to the potter, Why have you made me like this? Should it be according to your mind?" (Job 34:33).

Second,

> Your condition is ordered by Infinite Wisdom. There is nothing that befalls us without the providence of God; and that is no blind chance, but a wise disposal of all according to the counsel of God's will. If the product of Infinite Wisdom content us not, we do but show ourselves headstrong fools. He that numbers the hairs of our heads (Matt. 10:30), no doubt keeps an exact account of all the crosses in our lot, and of

31. Lloyd-Jones, *Spiritual Depression,* 285.

every ingredient in our cross, and gives them all out by weight and measure, as may most suit his infinitely-wise ends. And it is the height of folly to impeach the conduct of Infinite Wisdom.

Third,

Your condition, whatever it is, is for God's honor; for it is ordered by Him who does all for that end, and cannot fail of His design. Though you do not see how it is so, you may believe that it is so, upon this ground. Providence runs much under ground, so as weak man cannot see how the means answer the end: but God sees it, and that is enough. This is a contenting consideration to a gracious soul, that will be pleased with that which may glorify God, (Phil. 1:20) "according to my earnest expectation and hope that in nothing I shall be ashamed, but with all boldness, as always, so now also Christ will be magnified in my body, whether by life or by death."

Fourth,

Consider that those things in your lot which you are so ready to be discontented with, are truly necessary for you (Lam. 3:33).... For God takes no pleasure merely in making His creatures miserable. If your lot be afflicted, know that strong diseases must have strong remedies; blame not the physician for that, but the disease. The willful child would live without the rod, but the parent sees it necessary to chastise him. If God withdraw any thing from you, it is but to starve a lust that would feed on it; if He lay on you what you would not, it is but to bear down a lust, that otherwise would carry you headlong. Give providence a fair hearing, it will answer for itself.

Fifth,

All the good that is in our lot is undeserved (Lam. 3:22). The bitterest lot that any has in the world is mixed with mercy;

and mercy is still predominant in our cup. It is true, discontented persons are like wasps and flies that look not near the sound parts, but swarm together on the sore place.... But let there be fair count and reckoning between us and providence, we shall find we are in God's debt, and every mercy we enjoy we have it freely and undeservedly from God's hand (Job 2:10).

Sixth,

All the evil that we meet with in our lot, we deserve it,we have ourselves to thank for it (Lam. 3:39). Shall men's hearts rise against God for what they have procured to themselves? Is it not a reasonable resolve, "I will bear the indignation of the Lord, because I have sinned against Him?" (Micah 7:9). A discontented spirit will always be found in an un-humbled spirit, insensible of its ill deservings at God's hand.... Let us remember we are in the world as on a stage, where one must represent a king and another a beggar. It is God's part to choose what part we shall act, and it is our business contentedly to act the part allotted for us.[32]

Such a Charitable Frame of the Whole Soul Toward our Neighbour, As That All Our Inward Motions and Affections Touching Him, Tend Unto, and Further All that Good Which is His.

This charitable frame of spirit ought to be exercised towards those who excel us in gifts or graces. These they receive from the hand of providence, as talents to be improved. Hence, if they have a greater share of them than ourselves, more is required of them in proportion [Luke 12:48]. If they excel us in grace, we ought rather to rejoice that, though we bring but little glory to God, others bring more; and it will afford us an evidence of the truth of grace, if, while we are humbled under

32. Hanson, *God's Ten Words*, 253–54.

> a sense of our own defects, we are thankful for the honour which is brought to God by others [Gal. 1:23, 24].
>
> Again we ought to exercise a charitable frame of spirit towards those who are in more prosperous circumstances in the world; not envying, grieving, or repining at the providence of God, because their condition is better than ours. We are, therefore, to consider that the most flourishing and prosperous condition in the world is not always the best; and that it is not without many temptations which often attend it. Besides, if it be not improved to the glory of God, it will bring a greater weight of guilt on their consciences. If, on the other hand, we enjoy communion with God, and the blessings of the upper springs, we have what is much more desirable than the most prosperous condition in the world, without it [Ps. 16:5–6].[33]

> Have I rejoiced at the extinction of my enemy, or exulted when evil befell him? (Job 31:29).

Job, in the midst of affliction, showed this *charitable frame* of heart in these words.

> Although men did bear [Job] ill will and endeavored to hurt him and to put him at loss, yet notwithstanding he rendered not like for like, nor... nourished any secret hatred in his heart. And this protestation is well worthy to be noted, because it is one of the hardest things that God commands us.... For if Job had not loved his enemies, surely he would have rejoiced at their misfortune. So then let us learn, not only to keep our hearts locked up, that they be not provoked against such as offend us; but let us learn to bear them such an affection of friendship, as we may be sorry when any evil happens to them, and also have pity and compassion on them; and if this seems too hard for us to do, was not Job a man subject to affections as we are and yet did God get the

33. Thomas Ridgeley, *Commentary on the Larger Catechism* 2 vols. (Edmonton, Canada: Still Waters Revival Books, [1855] 1993), 2:419.

> upper hand of them…we must strain ourselves, howbeit not upon trust of our own strength, but with praying unto God to give us the spirit of meekness to bring us thither as we see His word leads us.[34]

> Rejoice with those who rejoice, and weep with those who weep (Rom. 12:15).

Christians, who share a mutual love and affection for each other, are to consider each other's condition as their own. In fact, Paul exhorts us: "with humility of mind let each of you regard one another as more important than himself" (Phil. 2:3). We are to rejoice with the rejoicing and weep with the weeping. This is the nature of Christian love, "one prefers to weep with his brother, rather than to look at a distance on his grief, and to live in pleasure or ease."[35] Furthermore, this means that the believer does not covet the blessings of another believer. The weeping believer still rejoices with the rejoicing believer, even while his own circumstances are hard. And, while the weeping believer is rejoicing with the rejoicing believer, the rejoicing believer is weeping with the weeping believer.

> We, as much as possible, ought to sympathize with one another, and that, whatever our lot may be, each should transfer to himself the feeling of another, whether of grief in adversity, or of joy in prosperity. And, doubtless, not to regard with joy the happiness of a brother is envy; and not to grieve for his misfortunes in inhumanity.[36]

> Pray for the peace of Jerusalem: "May they prosper who love you. May peace be within your walls, and prosperity within

---

34. John Calvin, *Sermons on Job*, trans. by Arthur Golding (1574; facsimile reprint Edinburgh: The Banner of Truth Trust, 1993), 546, 547.

35. John Calvin, *Commentaries on the Epistle of Paul the Apostle to the Romans*, trans. by Christopher Fetherstone, ed. by Henry Beveridge, (Edinburgh: Calvin Translation Society, 1843; reprint Grand Rapids, MI: Baker Book House, 1979), 469.

36. Calvin, *Commentaries on the Epistle of Paul the Apostle to the Romans*, 469–70.

> your palaces." For the sake of my brothers and my friends, I will now say, "May peace be within you." For the sake of the house of the LORD our God I will seek your good (Ps. 122:6–9).

Here is a beautiful and earnest prayer for the welfare and prosperity of the church of God. Each of us individually should utter these petitions before God for the whole church and everyone in it: that those who truly love the Lord will enjoy peace and prosperity. Unless our hearts are full of covetousness, when we see our prayer answered in the prospering of other believers far beyond what we ourselves are experiencing, we will rejoice for them without an envious spirit, fully content with what God's providence has given us, honestly agreeing with Proverbs 30:7–9:

> Two things I asked of Thee, do not refuse me before I die: keep deception and lies far from me, give me neither poverty nor riches, feed me with the food that is my portion, lest I be full and deny Thee and say, 'Who is the LORD?' Or lest I be in want and steal, and profane the name of my God.

Not only does the psalmist pray for the peace and prosperity of the whole church of God on earth, he also seeks her welfare and prosperity: "For the sake of the house of the LORD our God I will seek your good" (Ps. 122:9). A true Christian loves the church of God, therefore he cannot be indifferent about her condition in this world. He knows that because she is "'the pillar and foundation of truth,' the inevitable consequence of her destruction must be the extinction of true piety. And if the body is destroyed, how can each of the members fail to be involved in destruction?"[37] Therefore, he does not remain passive, but actively and diligently strives for the purity and peace of the church and for the enhancement of her prosperity and glory in the world.

> Love...is not jealous (1 Cor. 13:4–7).

---

37. John Calvin, *Commentary of the Book of Psalms*, trans. by Rev. James Anderson, 5 vols. (Edinburgh, Calvin Translation Society, 1843; reprint Grand Rapids, MI: Baker Book House, 1979), 5:79.

Love is the exact opposite of envy. Envy feels disappointment, dissatisfaction and jealousy when another person prospers, advances, or is honored, rather than he and his family. There are two levels of jealousy/envy: (1) A superficial and immature level that says: "I want what you have." (2) A deep, wicked and destructive level that says: "I wish you did not have what you have." This is a trait a welfare state encourages: "If I can't have it, I don't want anybody to get it."

The Greek word for envy means "to boil," referring to the inner boiling, seething, steaming over something someone else has, which you do not have. The first sin was envy (Gen. 3:5). And the second sin recorded in the Bible was Cain's envy over Abel's sacrifice that led to his murdering of Abel.

The only cure for envy is confession of sin, repentance and learning to be content with what God has dealt out to you, knowing that your circumstances are full of expressions of His love for you as a Christian, if you would only look for them (Phil. 4).

> Wrath is fierce and anger is a flood, but who can stand before jealousy? (Prov. 27:4).

When jealousy is rooted in love it is a healthy response to threats to that love (Ex. 20:5, Prov. 6:34, 35); but when it grows out of suspicion, distrust, and envy, it is an expression of a lack of love. Then it is a destructive thing. As cruel and as destructive as "wrath" can be, it can be appeased (Gen. 27:41; 33:4); but "envy is an implacable [*i.e.*, cold-hearted, ruthless and merciless] passion. The native principle, with a fearful train of evils. *Anger* is stirred up by offence; *envy* by godliness [Dan. 6:3–5], prosperity, [Ps. 73:3], or favor, [Gen. 4:5–8]."[38] Envy works its way into every dimension of a person's life. It destroys the insides of a person and makes him destructive on the outside in all his relations with other people (James 3:14–16).

---

38. Charles Bridges, *An Exposition of Proverbs* (Marshallton, DE: The National Foundation for Christian Education, n.d.), 503.

The Sins Forbidden by the Tenth Commandment

Q. 148: What are the sins forbidden in the tenth commandment?

A.: The sins forbidden in the tenth commandment are, discontentment with our own estate; envying and grieving at the good of our neighbour, together with all inordinate motions and affections to any thing that is his.

Discontentment With Our Own Estate

Both the Old Testament and the New Testament view discontentment with what God has providentially apportioned out in one's life as a sin that not only is destructive in one's life, but as a sin that is an insult to God, which He has severely punished.

> Now it came about after these things, that Naboth the Jezreelite had a vineyard which was in Jezreel beside the palace of Ahab king of Samaria. And Ahab spoke to Naboth, saying, "Give me your vineyard, that I may have it for a vegetable garden because it is close beside my house, and I will give you a better vineyard than it in its place; if you like, I will give you the price of it in money." But Naboth said to Ahab, "The LORD forbid me that I should give you the inheritance of my fathers." And he lay down on his bed and turned away his face and ate no food. But Jezebel his wife came to him and said to him, "How is it that your spirit is so sullen that you are not eating food?" So he said to her, "Because I spoke to Naboth the Jezreelite, and said to him, 'Give me your vineyard for money; or else, if it pleases you, I will give you a vineyard in its place.' But he said, 'I will not give you my vineyard.'" And Jezebel his wife said to him, "Do you now reign over Israel? Arise, eat bread, and let your heart be joyful; I will give you the vineyard of Naboth the Jezreelite." So she wrote let-

> ters in Ahab's name and sealed them with his seal, and sent letters to the elders and to the nobles who were living with Naboth in his city. Now she wrote in the letters, saying, "Proclaim a fast, and seat Naboth at the head of the people; and seat two worthless men before him, and let them testify against him, saying, 'You cursed God and the king.' Then take him out and stone him to death."... So they took him outside the city and stoned him to death with stones.... And it came about when Ahab heard that Naboth was dead, that Ahab arose to go down to the vineyard of Naboth the Jezreelite, to take possession of it. Then the word of the LORD came to Elijah the Tishbite, saying, "Arise, go down to meet Ahab king of Israel, who is in Samaria; behold he is in the vineyard of Naboth where he has gone down to take possession of it. And you shall speak to him, saying, 'Thus says the LORD, "Have you murdered, and also taken possession?"' And you shall speak to him, saying, 'Thus says the LORD, "in the place where the dogs licked up the blood of Naboth the dogs shall lick up your blood, even yours"'" (1 Kings 21:1–19).

Ahab's discontentment with the riches, property and power God had given him as king of Israel, and his envy of Naboth's vineyard, proved fatal to Ahab, Jezebel and Naboth. Naboth was a godly man, grateful to the inheritance God had allotted to his family in the Land of Promise. Being duty-bound before God to cultivate his land and keep it in his family, Naboth could not sell it to Ahab, because he must obey God rather than man. Ahab knew the Law, or should have known it, and therefore should never have asked Naboth to do what was sinful.

Because of Ahab's discontentment and envy and Naboth's refusal, "he lay down on his bed and turned away his face and ate no food" (v. 4). His spirit had become "so sullen" that he would not eat. His proud spirit could not bear the disappointment of Naboth's refusal. And so he secretly planned revenge with Jezebel to kill Naboth and confiscate his property.

> Note: (1). Discontent is a sin that is its own punishment and makes men torment themselves; it makes the spirit sad, the body sick, and all the enjoyments sour; it is the heaviness of the heart and the rottenness of the bones. (2). It is a sin that is its own parent. It arises not from the condition, but from the mind. As we find Paul contented in a prison, so Ahab discontent in a palace. He had all the delights of Canaan, that pleasant land… [He had] command [of] the wealth of a kingdom, the pleasures of a court, and the honours and powers of a throne; and *yet all this avails him nothing* without Naboth's vineyard. Inordinate desires expose men to continual vexations, and those that are disposed to fret, be they ever so happy, will always find something or other to fret at.[39]

Furthermore, the pathetic deaths of Ahab and Jezebel were performed by the Lord in judgment on their audacious discontentment with His provisions for their lives and the resulting envy that killed Naboth.

> Nor [let us] grumble, as some of them did, and were destroyed by the destroyer (1 Cor. 10:10).

This admonition grows out of an incident in the Old Testament recorded in Numbers 16:41–50. Here, because the children of Israel dared to complain ungratefully about God's providential provisions and arrangements for them in the wilderness, God sent a plague on them and over 14,000 died, being "destroyed by the destroyer." Once again Israel is taught that God will not tolerate discontentment with His providential ordering of things among His people. Refusing to trust His promise and submit to His will, and then casting aspersion on that divine will, are equally intolerable sins to God. Since Paul refers to this text from Numbers in 1 Corinthians 10:10, this applies to the church today as well.

---

39. Matthew Henry, *Matthew Henry's Commentary on the Whole Bible*, 6 vols. (Peabody, MA: Hendrickson Publishers, [1991] 1992), 2:539.

Envying... at the Good of Our Neighbour

> Let us not become boastful, challenging one another, envying one another (Gal.5:26).

A conceited person tends to both challenge or provoke others and envy others. This is because "our conduct to others is determined by our opinion of ourselves. It is when we have 'self-conceit' that we provoke and envy other people."[40] "Provoking" and "challenging" other people implies

> that we are so sure of our superiority that we want to demonstrate it. So we challenge people to dispute it in order to give ourselves a chance to prove it. Secondly, we envy one another, being jealous of one another's gifts or attainments.... We are motivated by feelings either of inferiority or superiority. If we regard ourselves as superior to other people we challenge them, for we want them to know and feel our superiority. If, on the other hand, we regard them as superior to us, we envy them.... Very different is that love which is the fruit of the Spirit, which Christians exhibit when they are walking by the Spirit. Such people have no self-conceit, or rather are continuously seeking by the Spirit to subdue it. They do not think of themselves more highly that they ought to think.... People with such love regard others as "more important" and seek every opportunity to serve them.[41]

> But if you have bitter jealousy and selfish ambition in your heart, do not be arrogant and so lie against the truth.... For where jealousy and selfish ambition exist, there is disorder and every evil thing (James 3:14, 16).

In James 3:13–18, the author is contrasting "wisdom [that] is not come down from above" (v. 14–16), and "the wisdom from above" (v. 17–18). The purpose of this contrast is to prove who is

---

40. John R. W. Stott, *The Message of Galatians* (London: Inter-Varsity Press, 1968), 156.

41. Stott, *The Message of Galatians*, 156–57.

truly "wise and understanding" (v. 13). "Earthly wisdom" is distinguished from "the wisdom from above" by: (1) Its evidences in life (v. 14); (2) Its distinctive trait (v. 15). and (3) Its destructive consequences (v. 16). Among its evidences in life is "bitter jealousy and selfish ambition in your heart"; and the consequence of the existence of jealousy and selfish ambition in the heart is "disorder and every evil thing."

"Jealousy" in this text is literally translated "zeal," not a good zeal but an evil one. Here it is a strong desire to promote oneself even if it means stepping on other people and depriving other people of wealth and happiness, in order to enhance one's own. Such zeal is "bitter," *i.e.*, harsh and resentful, "originating in bitter (resentful) feelings and manifests itself in bitter (resentful) actions.... Resentment, jealousy, selfish ambition—these then are the sure marks of a life dominated by worldly wisdom."[42]

The destructive consequence of such heart-sins is confusion and every kind of sinful action. "Disorder" denotes disturbance and unruliness and confusion. One commentator renders it "anarchy." "Every evil thing" denotes all kinds of evil and base deeds that are produced by *envying...at the good of our neighbor.*

Grieving... at the Good of Our Neighbour

> He has given freely to the poor;
> His righteousness endures forever;
> His horn will be exalted in honor.
> The wicked will see it and be vexed;
> He will gnash his teeth and melt away;
> The desire of the wicked will perish (Ps. 112:9–10).

God promises to exalt the prosperity of those righteous people who are generous in their contributions to help the truly poor. When wicked people see the righteous prosper and generous, the wicked are "vexed," grieve, gnash their teeth and melt away be-

---

42. Curtis Vaughan, *James: A Study Guide* (Grand Rapids, MI: Zondervan Publishing Co., 1969), 76.

cause of their covetousness and envy. They will be disappointed in all their desires.

> Let them harden themselves as they choose, yet he declares that the honour, which God confers upon his children, shall be exhibited to them, the sight of which shall make them gnash with their teeth, and shall excite an envy that shall consume them by inches.... They are never content, but are continually thirsting after something, and their confidence is as presumptuous as their avarice [love of money] is unbounded. And hence, in their foolish expectations, they do not hesitate at grasping at the whole world. But the prophet tells them that God will snatch from them what they imagined was already in their possession, so that they shall always depart destitute and famishing.[43]

Together With All Inordinate Motions and Affections to Anything That is His

> What shall we say then? Is the Law sin? May it never be! On the contrary, I would not have come to know sin except through the Law; for I would not have known about coveting [lust] if the Law had not said, "You shall not covet [lust]" (Rom. 7:7).

The Tenth Commandment focuses on the heart where lusting and coveting take place: "But I say to you, whoever looks on a woman to lust after her has committed adultery with her already in his heart" (Matt. 5:28). It goes to the root of all sin,

> habitual lust, or corruption of nature, together with its very first motions, and especially as these are contrary to the love of our neighbour; whereas, other commandments chiefly respect such secret and heart sins as are actually committed, though not known to the world. Q. How does it appear that this commandment is leveled particularly at habitual lust, or

---

43. Calvin, *Commentary on the Book of Psalms*, 4:330.

> at the root of all sin? A. Because, since other commandments chiefly forbid heart sins actually formed, this commandment must forbid the very rise of them, or the least bias and inclination to evil; otherwise it would not be distinct from the rest, nor would the law be absolutely perfect.[44]

Therefore *all inordinate motions and affections to anything that is [our neighbor's]* include "not only the unlawful purposes, intentions, and desires, that are actually formed in the heart, but even the first risings and stirrings of corruption in the soul, which are antecedent to the consent of the will Gen. vi:5."[45]

> Q. If the first motions of corruption are not entertained, but immediately curbed and restrained, why are they prohibited as sinful? A. Because, however soon they are curbed or restrained, yet having once been in the soul, they cannot but leave a stain and pollution behind them, contrary to the holiness and purity required in the law [But each one is tempted when he is carried away and enticed by his own lust] James i:14.[46]
>
> Q. Who are they that are sensible of these inordinate motions and affections of the heart, and are humbled for the same? A. None properly but the regenerate; as is evident from the instance of the apostle, who says of himself, after his conversation: 'I had not known lust, except the law had said, Thou shalt not covet' (Rom. 7:7).
>
> Q. What is the apostle's meaning in these words? A. It is, as if he had said, I had not known this strong propensity that is in my heart to all manner of sin, even before it be consented to, or deliberately committed; unless the Spirit of God had [revealed] it to me, in this precept of the law forbidding the same.

---

44. James Fisher, *Fisher's Catechism* (Presbyterian Board of Publishing and Sabbath School Work, 1911), 135.
45. Fisher, *Fisher's Catechism*, 135.
46. Fisher, *Fisher's Catechism*, 136.

> Q. How does the propensity to sin evidence itself? A. In that no sooner is the object presented, than instantly there is an inordinate motion and affection of the heart after it. The combustible matter within catches fire at the very first spark of temptation, Josh. vii:21.[47]

Therefore, we must guard our heart with all diligence for the basic issues of life and conduct flow from it. As Jesus said, it is not what goes into a person from his environment that makes him what he is, it is what flows from his heart (Mark 7). A person lives like he lives, because he thinks like he thinks.

> Owe nothing to anyone except to love one another; for he who loves his neighbor has fulfilled the law. For this, "You shall not commit adultery, You shall not murder, You shall not steal, You shall not covet," and if there is any other commandment, it is summed up in this saying, "You shall love your neighbor as yourself." Love does no wrong to a neighbor; love therefore is the fulfillment of the law (Rom. 13:8–10).

God not only forbids acts of adultery, murder and theft, he also forbids coveting our neighbor's wife, life and property.

> But there are other lusts to which we neither adhere nor give consent, which nevertheless excite and lure us and make us aware of an evil inclination within [ourselves] which is contrary to God and rebellious against the righteousness which the law contains. Such lusts are forbidden in this passage. Thus we see that God, having condemned every evil will and affection, quite reasonably adds that this does not yet constitute the perfection which he requires, rather it is necessary for us to recognize every affection that excites us toward evil, even though in ourselves we may not resolve [to do] anything. For we must not stop there. If a lust is only passed up by us for [lack] of courage, that is still a committed sin, [and] we are guilty before God. Thus we see the [level of] integrity that is required in this passage. For after forbidding evil in-

47. Fisher, *Fisher's Catechism*, 136–37.

> tentions, our Lord adds that it is necessary for minds and senses to be so enclosed by his fear and aflame with a love and desire to walk in all holiness that we may not be lured or pushed about here and there by [any] passion to covet either another man's property or his wife.... Let us realize that in order to serve God well, it is not simply a matter of our desiring to do good and to derive profit from it, rather we have to purge ourselves of all wicked affections and all corrupt thoughts to the extent that everything within us directs us toward the goal of fully surrendering ourselves to God.[48]

> Therefore consider the members of your earthly body as dead to immorality, impurity, passion, evil desire, and greed, which amounts to idolatry. For it is on account of these things that the wrath of God will come, and in them you also once walked, when you were living in them (Col. 3:5–7).

Because Christ is the believer's life by virtue of his vital union with Him, that believer is to recognize what he is in Christ—a new creation with old things passing and new things coming—he is to reckon himself dead to sin and alive to God and righteousness, having been spiritually raised with Christ to newness of life. And drawing strength from his new state, he is to consider himself as dead to the dominion of sins, such as "immorality, impurity, passion [inordinate affection], evil desire [concupiscence], and greed [covetousness], which amounts to idolatry," and effectively resist them by the power of the Spirit of Christ (Rom. 6:1–23; Gal. 5:16–21). Covetousness here is linked here with sexual immorality, impurity, inordinate affection, concupiscence and idolatry, in heart and life. Covetousness is not only a mother-sin that gives birth to many others, it is "idolatrous, for it concentrates the whole being upon something other than God."[49]

---

48. John Calvin, *Calvin's Sermons on the Ten Commandments*, ed. and trans. by Benjamin W. Farley (Grand Rapids, MI: Baker Book House, 1980), 220–21, 225.

49. Herbert Carson, *The Epistles of Paul to the Colossians and Philemon: An Introduction and Commentary* (Grand Rapids, MI: William B. Eerdmans Publishing Co., [1960] 1972), 82.

It is on account of these things that the wrath of God will come.[50] The point is that "God does not stand as a spectator viewing the consequences which man's sin brings upon him; but rather intervenes in a judgment which may manifest itself in leaving men to wallow in the filth of their own lusts, so that they are worthy objects of the final condemnation."[51]

Application:

It is sad to say that even true Christians are sometimes troubled with discontentment and envy. How can this be? Wilhelmus á Brakel gives us the answer:

> (1) Their eyes and heart look too much to that which is of the world...as if that could yield them any satisfaction.
>
> (2) They also want to have their way, and if this does not occur and men do not yield to them, they are sorrowful, fretful, and angry.
>
> (3) They eat their bread with discontentment since the quantity and the taste is not such as they would desire it to be.
>
> (4) They tremble and quiver as far as the future is concerned...
>
> (5) Anxiety troubles the heart, and concerns take away the joy of life.
>
> (6) They waver in regard to God's providence.
>
> (7) They immediately perceive God as being angry with them.
>
> (8) They reject their spiritual state.

---

50. This verb in Greek is in a present tense suggesting that judgment is not merely a future event, but a present reality.

51. Carson, *The Epistles of Paul to the Colossians and Philemon*, 82.

> (9) They make themselves vulnerable to the assaults of the devil who then easily gets hold of them, tossing them to and fro.
>
> (10) Spiritual life will lose its vigor, and if the Lord were not faithful and immutable, they would be corrupted in body and soul—so severely can worldly tribulations injure them. In such a condition they delight in being pitied and desire to be comforted, but in a manner concurring with the receipt of their desire—then they would be encouraged. Sorrow must first disappear, the matter must first be attained, they must first see and possess that from which they will live, and then comfort will have an effect. Then they would be able to live carefree and serve the Lord.[52]

The response to discontentment in Christians is this:

> Shall I pity you? That I shall do, but in such a manner that I shall neither harm nor encourage you in your sin. Rather, I shall do so by stirring you up to over come these unproductive anxieties, this wicked discontentment, and these concerns which drag you down.
>
> First, as we uncover all this, you yourself will perceive that you are yet very carnal and that you focus your attention upon things which are insignificant.... Why should there be more concern for your body than for your soul?
>
> Secondly, do you not perceive that this is idolatry? There is a secret departure from God, a neglect of depending upon Him, and a secret denial of God's providence. There is a secret accusation of cruelty and unwillingness on His part to care for you.... Under pretense of being concerned about necessities, there is a desire to rely upon temporal things and a living by bread alone... Do you serve God in order that He would give you temporal things?... How far removed this [disposition] is from Asaph's disposition—"Whom have I in heaven but Thee? And there is none upon earth that I desire beside Thee. My flesh and my heart fai-

52. Brakel, *The Christian's Reasonable Service*, 3:386–87.

leth; but God is the strength of my heart and my portion forever" (Ps. 73:25–26).

Thirdly, these concerns and anxieties which cause one to tremble issue forth from a proud heart—relative both to God and to man. It is pride *relative to God*, as it implies that one is worthy of something and that God is obligated to serve us according to our wishes.... It is also a manifestation of pride *relative to our neighbor*, for we look toward those who are superior to us and ask, "Why not I as well as he?"... God wishes to humble us and keep us humble. Therefore, concealed under the cover of being concerned about necessities...is pride.... The will of God must be our delight in whatever circumstances we are. Discouragement about being in a lower position is nothing but pride. Therefore, become humble and you will be delivered from many unprofitable cares.

Fourthly, all your concerns are in vain and you will not gain one penny by them. God has already decreed from eternity how much you will have.... "Therefore I say unto you, Take no thought for your life, what ye shall eat, or what ye shall drink; nor yet for your body, what ye shall put on. Is not the life more than meat, and the body than raiment? Which of you by taking thought can add one cubit to his stature?" (Matt. 6:25, 27, 32).

Fifthly, you dishonor God and harm yourself, for by way of these nagging concerns you show that it does not suffice you to have God alone as your portion and that you cannot be satisfied with Him unless you have as many temporal goods as you deem necessary.... [By this attitude] you bring yourself into continual unrest, apprehension, fear and anxiety. You rob yourself of delighting and rejoicing in God.

Sixthly, after the Lord will have delivered you from your perplexity—which He certainly will do in His time—then, due to your previous dissatisfaction and grumbling, you will have made yourself incapable of being truly grateful to the Lord, and a sense of shame about your prior distrust will cause your soul new grief.[53]

Therefore, children of God—either rich, of the middle class, of limited means, insignificant, poor, oppressed, or tossed with tempest—whoever you may be and whatever your circumstances may be, you are all in need of an exhortation, for no circumstances in and of themselves yield contentment. Learn to adjust your desires to your circumstances—regardless of what they may be—and do not endeavor to adjust your circumstances to your desires, for there would be no end to that. Cast dissatisfaction far away from you as being a harmful pestilence for your spiritual life, and possess your soul in contentment.[54]

Commit your way to the Lord; trust also in Him;
And He shall bring it to pass (Ps. 37:5).

Cast your burden on the LORD, and He shall sustain you;
He shall never allow the righteous to be moved (Ps. 55:22).

Be content with such things as you have; for He has said, "I will never leave you nor forsake you" (Heb. 13:5).

Therefore take no thought...for your heavenly Father knows that you have need of all these things (Matt. 6:31–32).

Casting all your cares upon Him; for He cares for you (1 Pet. 5:7).

He who spared not His own Son, but delivered Him up for us all, how shall He not with Him also freely give us all things? (Rom. 8:32).

What is this world to you anyway? What is it that you are coveting that makes you so discontent with God? Is not all this transito-

53. Brakel, *The Christian's Reasonable Service*, 3:386–89.
54. Brakel, *The Christian's Reasonable Service*, 3:390.

ry? Why then do you trouble yourself about it? Has a godly person ever lacked anything necessary for their service to God?

> Better is the little of the righteous than the abundance of many wicked. For the arms of the wicked will be broken; but the LORD sustains the righteous.... The steps of a man are established by the LORD; and He delights in his way.... I have been young, and now I am old; yet I have not seen the righteous forsaken, or his descendants begging bread (Ps. 37:16, 17, 23, 25).

Here are some guidelines for learning how to be content and how to avoid discontentment:

> (1) Always consider what you deserve, and you will then be happy that you are not yet in hell. (2) Look at others, and you will not want to exchange your condition with theirs.... (3) Live only by the day.... Sufficient to the day is the evil thereof. (4) Your difficulty is perhaps not as great as you make it out to be—this in consequence of your desire being excessive. You must therefore make more of an effort to adjust your desire to your circumstances—considering it to be the will of God—rather than seeking to improve your circumstances in accordance with your desire. (5) Make use of the means with all diligence and faithfulness so that your conscience will not accuse you, and leave the outcome to the Lord. Trust in His promise and He will make it well. (6) Let your focus continually be upon heaven...he that doeth the will of God shall abide forever.[55]

55. Brakel, *The Christian's Reasonable Service,* 3:395.

The Application of the Tenth Commandment to 21st Century America

The Signs of Covetousness

The following signs are from Richard Baxter quoted by Buddy Hanson, *God's Ten Words.*

- When our needs [and wants] overshadow our thoughts of our sins and God's displeasure.
- When worldly cares and concerns shut out all serious service for God regarding our own and others' souls.
- When worldly matters cause us to quarrel with our neighbor.
- When in our trouble and distress we receive comfort from the thoughts of our provisions in the world.
- When we are more thankful to God or man for outward riches, or any gift for the provision of the flesh, than for hopes or helps regarding salvation.
- When we are pleased if we prosper, and have plenty in the world, though our soul be miserable, unsanctified, and unpardoned.
- We are more careful to provide a worldly than a heavenly portion, for children and friends, and rejoice more in their bodily than their spiritual prosperity.
- When we will venture upon sinful means for gain, as lying, overreaching, deceiving, flattering, or going against our consciences, or the commands of God.
- When the riches we have, are used but for the pampering of our flesh, and superfluous provision for our posterity, and nothing but some inconsiderable crumbs are employed for God and His servants.[56]

56. Hanson, *God's Ten Words*, 250.

Coveting and Freedom

Thus, what is clearly condemned by the tenth commandment is every attempt to gain by fraud, coercion, or deceit that which belongs to our neighbor. On this principle, alienation of affection suits were once a part of the law of the land. Their abuse by a lawless age led to their abolition, but the principle is sound. A person who works systematically to alienate the affections of a husband or wife in order to gain him or her for himself, sometimes together with his monetary assets, is guilty of violating this law.

This law thus forbids the expropriations by fraud or deceit of that which belongs to our neighbor. The tenth commandment therefore does sum up commandments six through nine and gives them an additional perspective. The other commandments deal with obviously illegal acts, *i.e.*, clear-cut violations of law. The Tenth Commandment can be broken within these laws.... Thus, a variety of laws in Western civilization are based on this principle of the fraudulent use of the law to defraud or to harm. Many of these laws legislate against the conspiracy aspect of fraud. They legislate against the covetous seizure of our neighbor's possessions by evil although sometimes legal means....

This law against dishonest gain is directed by God, not merely to the individual, but to the state and all institutions. The state can be and often is as guilty as are any individuals, and the state is often used as the legal means whereby others are defrauded of their possessions. The law against evil covetousness is thus an especially needed one in the 20th century.[57]

If all desiring and taking by force or by law what is our neighbor's is strictly against God's law, it follows that the organization of such covetousness into a system is the creation of an anti-God society. A welfare economy—socialism, commu-

57. Rushdoony, *The Institutes of Biblical Law*, 634–35.

nism or any form of social order which takes from one group to give to another—is thus lawlessness organized into a system. In such a society, this lawless seizure can lay hold of what belongs to our neighbor by asking the state to serve as our instrument of seizure; to covet by law is no less a sin.[58]

The names for the society whereby men can covet everything that is their neighbor's may vary: socialism, communism, a welfare economy, rugged individualism, fascism, and national socialism are a few of the names common to history. Their goal is the same: under a façade of morality, a system is created to seize what is properly our neighbor's. Not surprisingly, such a system shows a general decline in morality. Theft, murder, adultery, and false witness all increase, because man is a unity. If he can legalize and "justify" seizing his neighbor's wealth or property, he will then legalize and justify taking his neighbor's wife.[59]

Covetousness and Trade

The tenth commandment groups together several forms of coveted property: a neighbor's wife, manservant, maidservant, and work animals. The problem here is *trade*. How can men come together and trade if they are not desirous of purchasing each other's goods?

The sale of a wife is obviously illegal. A man is not permitted to lust after another man's wife. No exchange here is legitimate. But why should the same prohibition restrict the exchange of, say, gold for work animals? Why should it be immoral to offer to buy the services of work animals on a permanent basis? True the manservant or maidservant may be permanently associated with a particular family. The permanent slave in the Old Testament voluntarily decided to undergo the pierced ear ritual (the shedding of blood) in or-

58. Rushdoony, *The Institutes of Biblical Law*, 640.
59. Rushdoony, *The Institutes of Biblical Law*, 649.

der to become part of a family (Deut. 15:16–17). He was unsalable. But other servants could be sold. Why, then, the prohibition against coveting these others?

Since bargains are made constantly...what sense can we make of the commandment? The passage in Micah throws light on the usage of the Hebrew word for coveting.[60] Covetousness involves *uncontrolled lusting,* a desire that can be satisfied only by possessing the other man's property. It is the kind of lusting that is involved in adultery, where the desire cannot legitimately be fulfilled, yet it persists. It is the desire that results in lawlessness when it is thwarted, the desire which cannot take "no" for an answer.... It is the kind of desire that resulted in Ahab's unlawful confiscation of Naboth's vineyard (1 Kgs 21). The man with power uses that power, despite the protection given to the original owner by the biblical laws regarding property.[61]

Covetousness and Downward Mobility

Another aspect of this jealousy is overlooked by most commentators. *Covetousness can also be directed downward,* toward those who have fewer goods, and therefore fewer responsibilities. This can be seen in the social phenomenon known as the *drop-out mentality....* Those with wealth and responsible callings became "primitive" in an attempt to escape the burdens associated with economic stewardship. They wanted others to take the risks and bear the responsibilities.[62]

The Bible prohibits men from escaping lawful callings, unless they are upgrading their responsibilities. A slave is au-

60. Micah 2:1–2: "Woe to those who scheme iniquity, who work out evil on their beds! When morning comes, they do it, for it is in the power of their hands. They covet fields and then seize them, and houses, and take them away. They rob a man and his house, a man and his inheritance."

61. Gary North, *The Sinai Strategy* (Tyler, TX: Institute for Christian Economics, 1986), 196–97.

62. North, *The Sinai Strategy,* 198.

thorized to take his freedom, if and when it is voluntarily offered by his master, either free of charge or by sale (1 Cor. 7:21). The idea is to extend God's rule into every area of life, and men are not to turn their backs on this task simply because a particular calling looks as though it would involve too much responsibility. *It is important for each person involved to evaluate his own capabilities accurately, and then to match those capabilities with his calling before God—his highest, most productive calling....* This kind of steady improvement involves *upward mobility*: spiritual improvement, at the very least, but also economic and social mobility. The individual may not see himself advancing economically, but over generations, the spiritual heirs of a man will advance. The wealth of the wicked is laid up for the just (Prov. 13:22). Upward mobility must be in terms of God's calling—service to God—and not simply in terms of amassing wealth (1 Tim. 6:6–10).[63]

Covetousness and Politics

The commandment has implications beyond the local neighborhood. *When covetousness becomes widespread, the next step is political coercion.* The very usage of the words, "to covet," implies violence. The covetous man will not limit his attempt to gain control of another man's property to an offer to purchase. Like Ahab, who was determined to gain control of Naboth's vineyard when Naboth refused to sell, the covetous man seeks to coerce his neighbor. When this cannot be done with the connivance of the police—outright oppression or theft—then he seeks to gain control of the civil government. Covetous men can join forces and encourage the civil government to adopt policies of wealth redistribution. The *monopoly of legal violence* possessed by the civil government can then be turned against property owners. Those within the civil government can gain control over people's assets.

63. North, *The Sinai Strategy,* 198–99.

They can then use them personally, or inside a government bureau, or distribute them to political special-interest groups. Political covetousness is a manifestation of *unrestrained desire* and the *threat of violence.* When the civil government becomes an instrument of covetousness, its monopoly of violence increases the danger of theft. A new commandment is adopted: "Thou shalt not covet, except by majority vote." What private citizen can effectively defend his property against unjust magistrates? Naboth died in his attempt to keep that which was his by law—God's law.

The misuse of the civil government in this way is doubly evil. First, it violates the principle of responsible stewardship. Second, it misuses the office of magistrate. *The spread of covetousness cannot be restrained by the magistrate when the structure of civil government is deeply influenced by political covetousness.* The old warning against putting the foxes in charge of the chicken coop is accurate: when the State becomes the agent of widespread covetousness, the whole society is threatened. *Waves of power struggles ensue, for each special-interest group recognizes that it must gain control of the primary agency of wealth redistribution.* The more power is offered to the controllers by means of statist coercive mechanisms, the more ferocious is the struggle to gain access to the seats of power. Central planning rewards ruthlessness. Hayek[64] has spoken plainly concerning the awful implications of unlimited State power: *the worst get on top....*

Thus, the power to redistribute wealth in accordance to some preconceived statist program eventually destroys human freedom and therefore thwarts personal responsibility to act as a steward under God. *Covetousness, when legislated, becomes a major foundation of totalitarianism.*[65]

64. F. A. Hayek, *The Road to Serfdom* (University of Chicago Press, 1944), 150–151.

65. North, *The Sinai Strategy*, 199–201.

As is evident in the tax system of the United States, along with its welfare programs and wealth distribution, we have seen in the twentieth century

> the creation of a universal system of *legislated covetousness.* Biblical law has been ignored, even as Christians have ignored the principle of the tithe.... Steadily, political freedoms have been removed; the after-tax income of the citizenry has been reduced systematically, leaving men with fewer resources to use in stewardship programs of voluntary charity. The civil government has steadily supplanted churches and voluntary associations as the primary agent of charity—a compulsory charity which is in fact a form of State-operated serfdom. The difference is this: the non-working servants (welfare recipients) are controlled by the State, and the working servants who support them are also controlled by the State. *Massive, unrelenting political covetousness has led to universal enslavement.*[66]

Covetousness and Social Cooperation

> When men do not trust their neighbors, it becomes expensive for them to cooperate in projects that would otherwise be mutually beneficial to them. They hesitate to share their goals, feelings, and economic expectations with each other. After all, if a man is known to be economically successful in a covetous society, he faces the threat of theft, either by individuals or bureaucrats. He faces the hostility of his associates. He faces others on a regular basis who are determined to confiscate what he has. The obvious response is to conceal one's success from others. But this also means concealing one's economic expectations. *Planning becomes clothed in secrecy.* The planning agency of the family limits its goals. Disputes between families increase, since families cannot easily cooperate under such circumstances.[67]

---

66. North, *The Sinai Strategy,* 202.
67. North, *The Sinai Strategy,* 203.

Chapter Thirty-Four

Man's Inability, The Degrees and Desert of Sin, and Escape from the Wrath of God

"God is pleased to deny his people that perfection of holiness here which they shall attain to hereafter, that he may give them daily occasion to exercise the duties of self-denial, mortification of sin, faith and repentance, which redound to his own glory and their spiritual advantage."
~ *Thomas Ridgeley*

INDEED, THERE IS NOT A RIGHTEOUS MAN ON EARTH WHO CONTINUALLY DOES GOOD AND WHO NEVER SINS.

ECCLESIASTES 7:22.

Man's Inability, The Degrees and Desert of Sin, and Escape from the Wrath of God

---

Q. 149: Is any man able perfectly to keep the commandments of God?

A.: No man is able, either of himself, or by any grace received in this life, perfectly to keep the commandments of God; but doth daily break them in thought, word, and deed.

Q. 150: Are all transgressions of the law of God equally heinous in themselves, and in the sight of God?

A.: All transgressions of the law of God are not equally heinous; but some sins in themselves, and by reason of several aggravations, are more heinous in the sight of God than others.

Q. 151: What are those aggravations that make some sins more heinous than others?

A.: Sins receive their aggravations,

1. From the persons offending; if they be of riper age, greater experience or grace, eminent for profession, gifts, place, office, guides to others, and whose example is likely

to be followed by others.

2. From the parties offended: if immediately against God, his attributes, and worship; against Christ, and his grace; the Holy Spirit, his witness, and workings; against superiors, men of eminency, and such as we stand especially related and engaged unto; against any of the saints, particularly weak brethren, the souls of them, or any other, and the common good of all or many.

3. From the nature and quality of the offence: if it be against the express letter of the law, break many commandments, contain in it many sins: if not only conceived in the heart, but breaks forth in words and actions, scandalize others, and admit of no reparation: if against means, mercies, judgments, light of nature, conviction of conscience, publick or private admonition, censures of the church, civil punishments; and our prayers, purposes, promises, vows, covenants, and engagements to God or men: if done deliberately, wilfully, presumptuously, impudently, boastingly, maliciously, frequently, obstinately, with delight, continuance, or relapsing after repentance.

4. From circumstances of time and place: if on the Lord's day, or other times of divine worship; or immediately before or after these, or other helps to prevent or remedy such miscarriages: if in public, or in the presence of

others, who are thereby likely to be provoked or defiled.

Q. 152: What doth every sin deserve at the hands of God?

A.: Every sin, even the least, being against the sovereignty, goodness, and holiness of God, and against his righteous law, deserveth his wrath and curse, both in this life, and that which is to come; and cannot be expiated but by the blood of Christ.

Q. 153: What doth God require of us, that we may escape his wrath and curse due to us by reason of the transgression of the law?

A.: That we may escape the wrath and curse of God due to us by reason of the transgression of the law, he requireth of us repentance toward God, and faith toward our Lord Jesus Christ, and the diligent use of the outward means whereby Christ communicates to us the benefits of his mediation.

The Inability of Man to Keep God's Law Perfectly

Q. 149: Is any man able perfectly to keep the commandments of God?

A.: No man is able, either of himself, or by any grace received in this life, perfectly to keep the commandments of God; but doth daily break them in thought, word, and deed.

The Impossibility of Perfect Obedience

Having considered our duty to keep all the commandments of God, (Q. 91–148), the Catechism now teaches us that we are unable to keep any of them without the assistance of God's grace, and even then we cannot obey them perfectly in this life, *i.e.*, we cannot consistently and without interruption love and obey God with all our heart, soul, strength and mind (Matt. 22:37, 39), because we disobey daily in thought, word and deed.

The Shorter Catechism's answer to this question is not only more concise than that of the Larger Catechism, it is more precise: *No mere man, since the fall is able in this life perfectly to keep the commandments of God, but doth daily break them, in thought, word and deed.* (SC, Q. 82). The precision of this answer caused Dr. Ashbel Green to write: "That admirable discrimination, united with conciseness and perspicuity, which characterizes the whole of our Shorter Catechism, is strikingly visible in the Answer before us."[1] Between both answers, LCQ 149 and SCQ 82 we obtain a full and clear answer to the question: *Is any man able perfectly to keep the commandments of God?*

First, *no mere man* is able to keep God's Law perfectly. Jesus, who did obey God perfectly while on earth, is not a *mere* man. He is

---

1. Alexander Whyte, *A Commentary on the Shorter Catechism* (Edinburgh: T & T Clark, 1961), 154–55.

the virgin-born God-man. Regarding all other *mere* human beings: "all have sinned and come short of the glory of God" (Rom. 3:23). "For we all stumble in many ways" (James 3:2).

Second, no one *since the fall*, is able to keep the Law perfectly, but before the fall of man into sin, Adam and Eve were able to obey God perfectly being created upright in a state of innocence: "God made men upright, but they have sought out many devices" (Eccl. 7:29).

Third, no one is able to keep God's Law perfectly *in this life*, but after we are perfected in holiness at death Christians will obey God perfectly in His blissful presence forever. Indeed, there is not a righteous man on earth who continually does good and who never sins (Eccl. 7:20).

Fourth, no one is able to obey God's Law *perfectly* in this life, but with the assistance of God's grace, believers in Jesus can and do obey God's Law from the heart (Eph.2:10). For those in Christ, condemnation for sin has been removed from them because of the sacrifice of Christ and the work of the Holy Spirit liberating them from the power of sin "in order that the requirement of the Law might be fulfilled in us who do not walk according to the flesh, but according to the Spirit" (Rom. 8:4). Jesus said that as we abide in Him, we will "bear fruit... more fruit... much fruit" (John 15:1–5).

Fifth, no one can obey God's Law *of himself*, for sinful man is "helpless" (Rom. 5:6), in and of himself, and as Jesus said, "apart from Me you can do nothing" (John 15:5). "The mind set on the flesh is hostile toward God; for it does not subject itself to the Law of God, for it is not even able to do so" (Rom. 8:7).

Sixth, not even believers assisted *by any grace received*, can keep the Law of God perfectly in this life. God's grace does enable a believer to love and obey God from the heart and with increasing consistency, but God has made no promise to the believer that He will free him from all the sin that remains within him before he dies and goes to heaven. "God is pleased to deny his people that perfection of holiness here which they shall attain to hereafter, that he may give them daily occasion to exercise the duties of self-denial, mortification of sin, faith and repentance, which redound to his own glory and their spiritual advantage."[2] Attaining perfection in this life would be inconsistent "with the nature of spiritual growth in grace, which is gradual; for the saints do not attain the full stature of perfect men in Christ Jesus until they arrive at glory."[3] As the apostle John said of all believers: "If we say that we have no sin, we are deceiving ourselves and the truth is not in us" (1 John 1:8). Paul confessed the reality of an inner struggle within himself as a believer between his new self in Christ and the sin that remained within him in Romans 7:18–19.

At this juncture three texts that seem on the surface to contradict this Catechism answer should be explained. The first is Genesis 6:9 which says in the KJV: "Noah was a just man and perfect in his generations, and Noah walked with God." The second is 1 Corinthians 2:6 in the KJV which says: "Howbeit we speak wisdom among them that are perfect." And the third is 1 John 3:6, 9 in the KJV: "Whosoever abideth in Him sinneth not: whosoever sinneth hath not seen Him, neither known Him.... Whosoever is born of God doth not commit sin; for his seed remaineth in him: and he cannot sin, because he is born of God." How are these verses to be properly interpreted?

Concerning Noah's "perfection" as recorded in Genesis 6:9: Noah was a righteous man, who manifested a consistency of character and general conformity to God's standard of righteousness. Alone in his generation and among his contemporaries, he was "perfect," *i.e.*, blameless, whole-hearted, complete, a well-rounded believer, who walked with God in fellowship with Him. His conduct was above reproach among the people of his time. His irreproachable life of righteousness was an exception among his contemporaries. And yet despite his "perfection," his "blamelessness," although more holy and circumspect than anyone around him, he was a sinner, as the sad incident of his drunkenness shows (Gen. 9:21).

Concerning the "perfect" ones among whom Paul preached in 1 Corinthians 2:6: Paul is informing the Corinthian Church that al-

2. Thomas Ridgeley, *Commentary on the Larger Catechism*, 2 vols. (Edmonton, Canada: Still Waters Revival Books, [1855] 1993), 2:424.

3. Alexander S. Paterson, *A Concise System of Theology on the Basis of the Shorter Catechism* (New York: Obert Carter and Brothers, 1856), 255.

though he does not teach human wisdom to them, he does teach them revealed wisdom from God, for they are not those who consider it foolishness, but those who consider his preaching the power of God unto salvation. They receive his preaching as the word of God because they are "perfect," *i.e.*, mature, full-grown, complete in Christ (1 Cor. 1:4–8), competent to understand having the mind of Christ (1 Cor. 2:16). The "perfect" then, are not the sinlessly perfect, but the believers as opposed to unbelievers, those taught by the Spirit of God and enabled by Him to understand and believe the Word of God as opposed to those whose minds have not yet been renewed by the Spirit (1 Cor. 2:14).

Now we come to 1 John 3:6, 9: "Whosoever abideth in Him sinneth not: whosoever sinneth hath not seen Him, neither knows Him.... Whoever is born of God doth not commit sin; for his seed remaineth in him: and he cannot sin, because he is born of God." If these verses in the King James Version mean what they appear to mean then anybody who ever sins in the slightest way is not a true Christian, for true Christians would then be unable to sin. But is that in fact what this text means? To understand it correctly we must remember two principles of interpretation: (1) A text must be interpreted in the light of its context; and (2) In Greek the present tense in verbs denotes continuous or habitual action and not just present action as in English. For example, in Greek the sentence, "I am painting my wagon," denotes "I keep on painting my wagon continuously."

Our text is a strong statement, but it must be read in the light of the fact that the apostle John has already stated in his epistle that the children of God do in fact commit sins and remain children of God because they have an advocate in Jesus Christ: "My little children, I am writing these things to you that you may not sin. *And if anyone* [*i.e.*, the believers to whom this epistle is written] sins, we have an Advocate with the Father, Jesus Christ the righteous" (1 John 2:1. Emphasis added). In fact, in chapter one, John makes clear that any believer that says he does not sin is a liar (1:8). He then reveals God's provision for continual forgiveness and continual cleansing in the believer's life: continual confession of sin (1:9). So then, believers can and do sin. Whatever is the point of 3:6 and 9, they cannot contradict or say more than is said in 1:8–2:1.

Careful notice should also be made of the present tense of the verbs in 1 John 3:6, 9. Therefore the point John is making is this: Every true believer, having been born of God and in a regenerate condition, who is continuously abiding in Him, does not keep on sinning habitually and continuously as the dominant activity of his life. Such a person who does sin habitually and continuously is not a Christian at all, "'But there is a world of difference between one sin in a struggle against sin (2:1) and the habit of sin (3:6, 9) which is what John is seeking to prevent' [Robertson]. Sin is not in the believer the ruling principle, as it is in the case of the defiant, persistent sinner."[4] The reason the believer in Christ is no longer a slave to sin—although he does continue to sin and finds a remedy for his sin in Christ—is that he has been "born of God, because His seed abides in him; and he cannot sin, because he is born of God." The "seed" of new life in Christ implanted in the heart of the child of God is certain to grow so that the person who has experienced regeneration cannot fall back into his unregenerate life that was dominated by sinful thoughts and behavior, although lapses into sin may occur.

The Constancy of Disobedience

The second point of Question 149 is this: not only is it impossible for mere man to obey God's Laws perfectly in this life, but he *doth daily break them in thought, word, and deed.* This is to say that a day does not pass when we do not sin continually *in thought, word and deed.* It is clear that the believer is continually sinning from the fact that he is commanded to continue to confess his sins to Him who is "faithful and just to forgive" (1 John 1:9). Of course, the poor unbeliever does nothing but sin daily, since "those who are in the flesh cannot please God" (Rom. 8:8); therefore "there is none righteous, not even one" (Rom. 3:10).

We break God's commandments in our *thoughts* everyday when we entertain unworthy and unbelieving ideas and conceptions of God that dishonor His perfections and providence or that are in-

4. Alexander Ross, *The New International Commentary on the New Testament: The Epistles of James and John* (Grand Rapids, MI: William B. Eerdmans Publishing Co., [1954] 1967), 183.

consistent with His self-revelation in the Bible and in Christ. As the Lord said to Israel in Psalm 50:21: "You thought that I was just like you; I will reprove you, and state the case in order before your eyes." God rebukes the wicked here because they inferred from God's patience with them, not destroying them for their sin, that He is weak and irresolute in punishing sin. In Psalm 94:7, the wicked are quoted as saying, "The LORD does not see, nor does the God of Jacob pay heed." Here again they sin in their thoughts by thinking that God is less than He is, and that He is blind and indifferent to their sins. In Zephaniah 1:12, the Lord warns the wicked of His judgment: "And it will come about at that time that I will search Jerusalem with lamps, and I will punish the men who are stagnant in spirit, who say in their hearts, 'The LORD will not do good or evil!'" The punishment God will bring upon the wicked in this instance is because of the sinful thoughts about God in their hearts. They deluded themselves into thinking that God will not keep His threats or His promises. He is all bluff, just like all the other self-made gods of the heathen.

We also break God's commandments in our thoughts when we entertain sinful thoughts with reference to ourselves and our life in this world: when our thoughts are consumed with self-gratification, self-applause, and self-love. As Paul said in Romans 12:3, "For through the grace given to me I say to every man among you not to think more highly of himself than he ought to think; but to think so as to have sound judgment." Every person is open to be deceived by the arrogance of his heart (Ob. 3). Furthermore we sin in our minds with reference to other people when we meditate and indulge ourselves in envy, jealousy, sexual lust, ungodly hatred, revenge and bitterness. Esau sinned against Jacob by bearing a grudge in his heart because of the blessing Jacob received from their father (Gen. 27:41), which filled him with murderous thoughts.

What makes sinful thoughts so evil and so dangerous is that they are the source from which sinful words and actions flow. We live like we live because we think like we think, or to use the words of Proverbs, "as a man thinks in his heart, so is he." Jesus said that "the mouth speaks out of that which fills the heart" (Matt. 12:34). Therefore we must take the proper remedy and preventive against sinful thoughts, which is "the Spirit's taking the things of Christ and showing them unto us, John xvi:14, by which they will become the subject matter of our meditation and highest esteem; for where the treasure is, there will be the heart also, Matt. vi:21."[5] Depending upon the Spirit of Christ to give us the strength (Philippians 4:13), we must discipline ourselves to obey Philippians 4:8: "whatever is true, whatever is honorable, whatever is right, whatever is pure, whatever is lovely, whatever is of good repute, if there is any excellence and if anything worthy of praise, let your mind dwell on these things."

How do we break the commandments of God with our *words*, *i.e.*, our verbal expressions and conversations? The Epistle of James speaks of the tongue as untamable and as "a restless evil and full of deadly poison" (3:8). The book of Proverbs has much to say about sinning with words: "The one who guards his mouth preserves his life; the one who opens wide his lips comes to ruin" (13:3). "Death and life are in the power of the tongue, and those who love it will eat its fruit" (18:21). "He who restrains his words has knowledge" (17:27). "He who guards his mouth and his tongue guards his soul from troubles" (21:23). In Psalm 34:13, the Lord warns us: "Keep your tongue from evil, and your lips from speaking deceit"; and in Psalm 39:1 David says, "I will guard my ways, that I may not sin with my tongue; I will guard my mouth as with a muzzle, while the wicked are in my presence." John Calvin once wrote that "there is nothing more slippery or loose than the tongue."

So then, how do we sin with our tongues?

(1) We sin when we use "careless and useless words." Jesus said, "every careless word that man shall speak, they shall render account for it in the day of judgment. For by your words you shall be justified, and by your words you shall be condemned" (Matt. 12:36–37). Human beings are accountable to God for every word they speak. On Judgment Day they shall be called upon to account for every careless and useless word they have ever spoken, *i.e.*, language that is not carefully considered be-

5. James Fisher, *Fisher's Catechism*, (Presbyterian Board of Publishing and Sabbath School Work, 1911), 140.

fore spoken, that is empty of purpose and meaning and therefore unprofitable to anyone.

> There are few of our Lord's sayings which are so heart-searching as this. There is nothing, perhaps, to which most men pay less attention than their words. They go through their daily work, speaking and talking without thought or reflection, and seem to fancy that if they do what is right, it matters but little what they say. But is it so? Are our words so utterly trifling and unimportant? We dare not say so, with such a passage of Scripture as this before our eyes. Our words are the evidence of the state of our hearts, as surely as the taste of water is an evidence of the state of the spring.[6]

(2) We sin when we speak in a way that dishonors God by the kind of language we use or by the content of our conversations. Concerning the wicked, the psalmist declares: "they have set their mouth against the heavens, and their tongue parades through the earth.... And they say, 'How does God know? And is there knowledge with the Most High?'" (Ps. 73:9, 11). The wicked who prosper speak audaciously and "profanely against God's name, word, worship, providence, gospel and people; they pour contempt on all serious piety, they make light of eternal things. They blaspheme."[7] The wicked speak derogatorily of God.

(3) We sin with our words when we injure or slander other people or ourselves. David prays that the Lord would deliver him from wicked and violent men who devise evil against him in their hearts and who "continually stir up wars against him and sharpen their tongues as a serpent; poison of a viper is under their lips" (Ps. 140:3).

---

6. J.C. Ryle, *Expository Thoughts on the Gospels,* 7 vols. (NY: Baker & Taylor Co., n.d.), 1:132–33.

7. William S. Plumer, *Psalms: A Critical And Expository Commentary With Doctrinal & Practical Remarks* (Edinburgh: The Banner of Truth Trust, 1975), 711.

> The arts of falsehood, slander and abuse are as old as sin in the world.... "All persecutors of the church in every age have been thus distinguished—they have first traduced (slandered) the objects of their hate, and then thirsted for their blood" [Morison] "Slander and calumny (false statements maliciously intended to hurt someone) always precede and accompany persecution, because malice itself cannot excite people against a good man, as such; to do this, he must first be represented as a bad man. Thus David was hunted as a rebel, Christ was crucified as a blasphemer, and the primitive Christians were tortured as guilty of incest and murder" [Horne].[8]

We also obviously break God's commandments by our *deeds,* by committing those sins in our outward behavior that we have thought in our minds and desired in our hearts, which sinful actions are inconceivably more than can be listed in a book. It is for this reason that David prayed Psalm 40:11–12:

> Thou, O LORD, wilt not withhold Thy compassion from me;
> Thy lovingkindness and Thy truth
> Will continually preserve me,
> For evils beyond number have surrounded me;
> My iniquities have overtaken me, so that I am not able to see;
> They are more numerous than the hairs of my head;
> And my heart has failed me.

> Though our views of sin may through life be inadequate, yet we have no reason for believing that our sanctification will progress rapidly, or ever be perfected without our experiencing a deep sense of personal vileness and ill-desert.... A perfect view of his iniquities would sink any man in despair, unless he had far clearer apprehensions of God's mercy in Christ than are attained by the majority of converted men. Let us ask for such a sense of our sins, as we can bear, and as will make the cross of Christ most dear to us. "Nothing can

8. Plumer, *Psalms,* 1169.

so empty a man, and lay him low, and fill him with confusion of face, as his sin pursuing him" [Dickson]. Whatever thus abases him is useful to him.[9]

The Lesson of This Answer

What may we learn from man's inability to keep the commandments perfectly in this life? A. That we must be wholly indebted to the free grace of God, for salvation and eternal life, Tit. iii:5, and not to anything in ourselves, who are, at best, but unprofitable servants, Luke xvii:10.[10]

The Degrees & Aggravations of Sin

Q. 150: Are all transgressions of the law of God equally heinous in themselves, and in the sight of God?

A.: All transgressions of the law of God are not equally heinous; but some sins in themselves, and by reason of several aggravations, are more heinous in the sight of God than others.

The Degrees of Sin

Although *every sin deserveth God's wrath and curse, both in this life, and that which is to come* (SC, Q. 84), some *sins... are more heinous in the sight of God than others* (SC, Q. 83). Some sins are more abominable, hateful, offensive, odious and atrocious to God than others, although He hates all sin. The Old Testament makes this distinction in Ezekiel 8:6, where God said, "Son of man, do you see what they are doing, the great abominations which the house of Israel are committing here, that I should be far from My sanctuary?

9. Plumer, *Psalms,* 485.
10. Fisher, *Fisher's Catechism,* 140.

But yet you will see still greater abominations." Some abominations are "great" and other abominations are "greater."

Jesus made this point time and again. In His Sermon on the Mount Jesus made a distinction between sins, calling some "specks" and others "logs":

> And why do you look at the speck in your brother's eye, but do not notice the log that is in your own eye? Or how can you say to your brother, "Let me take the speck out of your eye," and behold, the log is in your own eye? You hypocrite, first take the log out of your own eye; and then you will see clearly to take the speck out of your brother's eye (Matt. 7:3–5).

However heinous another person's sin is, a would-be critic, who refuses to deal with his self-righteousness and hypocrisy is the worse sinner. His sin is not merely a "speck", it is a "log" in God's sight. In Matthew 23:11, Jesus denounced the Pharisees as hypocrites, because "they are the ones who devour widows' houses, and for appearance's sake offer long prayers; these will receive greater condemnation" (Mark 12:40). Here we see that some sins are more wicked than others because some sins deserve "greater condemnation" than others. In denouncing Chorazin and Bethsaida for their impenitency, Jesus says to these cities: "If the miracles had occurred in Tyre and Sidon which occurred in you, they would have repented long ago in sackcloth and ashes. Nevertheless I say to you, it shall be more tolerable for Tyre and Sidon in the day of judgment, than for you" (Matt. 11:21–22). In other words the sins of Chorazin and Bethsaida are more henious than the sins of Tyre and Sidon, therefore deserving greater punishment. And in John 19:11, Jesus, on trial before Pontius Pilate, rebukes Pilate, saying, "You would have no authority over Me, unless it had been given you from above; for this reason he who delivered Me up to you has the greater sin." As evil as Pilate's treatment of Jesus was, Caiaphas, the high priest, who handed Jesus over to Pilate, was guilty of "the greater sin," which means that Pilate's sin was "the lesser sin."

What makes some sins more heinous and offensive to God than others? Our Catechism Q. 150 answers: *some sins in themselves, and by reason of several aggravations, are more heinous in the sight of God than others.* In other words, some sins are more heinous because of their very nature, and others are more heinous because of the aggravating circumstances that accompany them.

What is it about the nature of some sins that makes them more heinous than others?

> Sins committed more immediately [directly, defiantly and audaciously] against God, or the first table of his law, are more heinous in their own nature, than sins committed more immediately against man, or any precept of the second table. Likewise, some sins against the second table are more heinous in themselves, than other sins against the said table.... [For example,] Blasphemy against God is more heinous in its own nature, than defaming, or speaking evil of our neighbour, 1 Sam. ii:25; and adultery is more heinous than theft, Proverbs vi:33 to the end of the chapter.[11]

1 Samuel 2:25 says that "if one man sins against another, God [represented through judges] will mediate for him; but if a man sins against the LORD, who can intercede for him?" The point is that, although a person may mediate between human beings when they sin against each other, some sins are so heinous in their very nature, such as those of Hophni and Phineas, that the mediator between the offenders and God must be far more than a mere human judge. And Proverbs 6:29–35 shows us that adultery is more heinous than other sins committed against other human beings, such as theft, because of its consequences:

> So is the one who goes in to his neighbor's wife; whoever touches her will not go unpunished. Men do not despise a thief if he steals to satisfy himself when he is hungry; but when he is found, he must repay seven fold; he must give all the substance of his house. The one who commits adultery with a woman is lacking sense; he who would destroy himself does it.

---

11. Fisher, *Fisher's Catechism*, 141.

Theft is so wicked that if a man commits this sin "he must give all the substance of his house," but adultery is so much more wicked that if a man commits it he "would destroy himself."

> Some few of the least considerate Christians have pretended that all sins are equal. Their reasons for it are not worth the mentioning; for the conceit is so groundless, and so repugnant to the common sense of mankind, that barely to speak of it is to expose it, and it carries its own confutation with it. For a man must be very weak to imagine that *theft*, suppose, is as great a sin as murder; or *telling a lie* as wicked a thing as *robbing a house*, or *plundering a church*, or *firing a town*. Everybody is sensible of a difference between high crimes and trivial trespasses; between sins of the first magnitude and slight offences; our Lord therefore compares some to *gnats*, while He compares other to *camels*; some to *motes* in the eye, others to *beams*.[12]

The Aggravations That Make Some Sins Worse Than Others

Q. 151: What are those aggravations that make some sins more heinous than others?

A.: Sins receive their aggravations,

1. From the persons offending; if they be of riper age, greater experience or grace, eminent for profession, gifts, place, office, guides to others, and whose example is likely to be followed by others.
2. From the parties offended: if immediately against God, his attributes, and worship; against Christ, and his grace; the Holy Spirit,

12. Waterland, quoted in Whyte, *A Commentary on the Shorter Catechism*, 157.

his witness, and workings; against superiors, men of eminency, and such as we stand especially related and engaged unto; against any of the saints, particularly weak brethren, the souls of them, or any other, and the common good of all or many.

3. From the nature and quality of the offence: if it be against the express letter of the law, break many commandments, contain in it many sins: if not only conceived in the heart, but breaks forth in words and actions, scandalize others, and admit of no reparation: if against means, mercies, judgments, light of nature, conviction of conscience, publick or private admonition, censures of the church, civil punishments; and our prayers, purposes, promises, vows, covenants, and engagements to God or men: if done deliberately, wilfully, presumptuously, impudently, boastingly, maliciously, frequently, obstinately, with delight, continuance, or relapsing after repentance.
4. From circumstances of time and place: if on the Lord's day, or other times of divine worship; or immediately before or after these, or other helps to prevent or remedy such miscarriages: if in public, or in the presence of others, who are thereby likely to be provoked or defiled.

From the Person Offending

> The priests did not say, "Where is the LORD?" And those who handle the law did not know Me; the rulers also transgressed against Me, and the prophets prophesied by Baal and walked after things that did not profit (Jer. 2:8).

It is bad enough when the masses sin against God, but when "priests... those who handle the Law... the rulers... and the prophets" sin against God, their transgression is far more heinous, for they not only abuse their office, position, authority, eminence and gifts, they also by their sinful example encourage the masses to sin all the more.

If They Be of Riper Age

> A poor, yet wise lad is better than an old and foolish king who no longer knows how to receive instruction (Eccl. 4:13).

If people are older and more mature, who have experienced much in this life, their sins are more aggravated and more offensive to God than those sins committed by the young and inexperienced. Those advanced in years should know better.

Rather than becoming wiser and more godly as their years advance, some people become more arrogant, self-righteous, and self-sufficient, unable to receive criticism or instruction, as Ecclesiastes 4:13 points out. Such an attitude in older people is more offensive than a similar one in young people. It shows that such a person may have outlived his usefulness, "and a wise youth, even though he is poor, is certainly to be preferred."[13]

If They Be of Greater Experience or Grace

> For it came about when Solomon was old, his wives turned his heart away after other gods; and his heart was not wholly devoted to the LORD his God, as the heart of David his father had been. For Solomon went after Ashtoreth the god-

---

13. H. C. Leupold, *An Exposition of Ecclesiastes* (Grand Rapids, MI: Baker Book House, [1952] 1968), 113.

> dess of the Sidonians and after Milcom the detestable idol of the Ammonites. And Solomon did what was evil in the sight of the LORD, and did not follow the LORD fully, as David his father had done.... Now the LORD was angry with Solomon because his heart was turned away from the LORD, the God of Israel, who had appeared to him twice (1 Kings 11:4–6, 9).

The longer someone has walked with God as a faithful Christian, who has experienced the freeness, cleansing and saving power of God's grace in Jesus Christ, the more wicked his sins are. For after having known the riches of God's grace, enabling him to put to death sin and to cultivate the fruit of the Spirit, he has less excuse for his sins than the young believer just starting out in his Christian life.

This is why Solomon's sins as an old man were so grievous. How perverted it is that Solomon, the world's wisest man, in his old age, should be ensnared in sexual lusts and the allurements of idolatry. When a man as wise as Solomon, so good a man, so zealous for the pure worship of God, who had warned so many of the dangers of evil, abandons all he knows to be true and right to do wrong—this most surely is a far more wicked sin and far more offensive to God, than if a lesser man had done such a thing.

> Never was gallant ship so wrecked; never was crown so profaned.... Let him that thinks he stands take heed lest he fall. We see how weak we are of ourselves, without the grace of God; let us therefore live in a constant dependence on that grace.... So what need those have to stand upon their guard who have made a great profession of religion, and shown themselves forward and zealous in devotion, because the devil will set upon them most violently, and, if they misbehave, the reproach is the greater. It is the evening that commends the day; let us therefore fear, lest, having run well, we seem to come short.[14]

---

14. Matthew Henry, *Matthew Henry's Commentary on the Whole Bible*, 6 vols. (Peabody, MA: Hendrickson Publishers, [1991] 1992), 2:493.

If They Be Eminent for Profession

> However, because by this deed you have given occasion to the enemies of the LORD to blaspheme, the child also that is born to you shall surely die (2 Sam. 12:14).

King David was well-known for his devotion to the Lord God. He professed not only that he trusted in God as a nursing infant, but that he enjoyed fellowship with God in his mother's womb (Ps. 22:9–10). Throughout his life he did not hesitate to speak in the Lord's behalf and to perform many courageous acts in His name, the most famous of which was his testimony before Goliath (1 Sam. 17:44–47). This made his adultery with Bathsheba and his conspiracy to murder her husband all the more heinous, because, as God's prophet said to him, "by this deed you have given occasion to the enemies of the LORD to blaspheme." Such sinful acts were so offensive to God that, although he forgave David when David confessed his sin (Ps. 51; 2 Sam. 12:13), certain consequences flowed from his sin—the death of his and Bathsheba's child. Because God's enemies were given the occasion to blaspheme Him because of David's sin, David's son would have to die. "To put it another way, we may say that God took the child to Himself 'in order to vindicate His reputation for righteousness among the nations' [Laney]."[15]

If They Be Eminent for Gifts

> And that slave who knew his master's will and did not get ready or act in accord with his will, shall receive many lashes, but the one who did not know it, and committed deeds worthy of a flogging, will receive but few. And from everyone who has been given much shall much be required; and to whom they entrusted much, of him they will ask all the more (Luke 12:47–48).

---

15. Gordon Keddie, *Triumph of the King: The Message of II Samuel* (England: Evangelical Press, 1990), 113.

This story of Jesus makes clear that in hell all will be punished for their sins, but some will receive "many lashes" while others will receive "but few." These degrees or levels of punishment are determined by whether a person sinned, knowing God's will, or whether he sinned in ignorance of His will. "Those who are eternally lost will undergo different grades of punishment, justly apportioned by Him who knows precisely how great the privileges [and gifts] were and thus also how great each one's responsibility was."[16]

The principle revealed here is: *to whom much is given much is required.*

> The point is that the person receives a free and generous gift; he is highly favored in being so blessed. The result is that he is to act accordingly. To the degree that he has been blessed, to that degree he ought to be grateful, use what has been given him according to the nature of the gift and according to the giver's gracious will. For him to be ungrateful, act as if this was not a gracious gift, abuse it, etc., is abominable and contrary to every proper human expectation.[17]

If They Be Eminent for Place

> Then I said, "They are only the poor,
> They are foolish;
> For they do not know the way of the LORD
> Or the ordinance of their God.
> I will go to the great
> And will speak to them,
> For they know the way of the LORD,
> And the ordinance of their God."
> But they too, with one accord, have broken the yoke
> And burst the bonds (Jer. 5:4–5).

16. Norval Geldenhuys, *New International Commentary on the New Testament: Commentary on the Gospel of Luke* (Grand Rapids, MI: Wm. B. Eerdmans, [1951] 1966), 365.

17. R. C. H. Lenski, *The Interpretation of St. Luke's Gospel* (Minneapolis, MN: Augsburg Publishing House, [1946] 1961), 711.

The moral corruption found among the obscure and poor masses was also found among the leaders and eminent people in Israelite culture. Their sin was worse and even more inexcusable, for unlike the masses who had little schooling in the way of the Lord, these eminent citizens were well educated in "the way of the LORD and the ordinance of their God." They should have excelled in righteousness, but instead they rebelled with the rest, therefore they experienced divine judgment for breaking their covenant vows and responsibilities to God and to the people. If anyone thinks that these eminent citizens were better than the common people, he is sadly mistaken. They should have been, but they were worse, because they knew better and were abusing their high places in society.

If They Be Eminent for Office

> Nathan then said to David, "You are the man! Thus says the LORD God of Israel, 'It is I who anointed you king over Israel and it is I who delivered you from the hand of Saul. I also gave you your master's house and your master's wives into your care, and I gave you the house of Israel and Judah; and if that had been too little, I would have added to you many more things like these! Why have you despised the word of the LORD by doing evil in His sight?' … Now therefore the sword shall never depart from your house" (2 Sam. 12:7–10).

King David was not only known far and wide for his devotion to God and his courage in serving him, he also held the highest office in the nation of Israel—that of king. For someone so eminent in this kingly office to commit adultery and conspire to commit murder is to sin against God far more grievously than if a common man had done these things, evil as he would be. Through His prophet, Nathan, God rebukes David, bringing him to conviction of sin and repentance. He reminds him that God himself put him in office, that He personally has given David great responsibilities and privileges. He then cuts David's conscience to the quick saying that in committing these sins he showed that "he despised the word of the LORD by doing evil in His sight." Therefore, because his sin was so evil and so aggravated in God's sight, because of the high office David held, God said to David that the consequences of his action would be that "the sword shall never depart from your house," *i.e.*, your newborn baby of Bethsheba must die that God's name may be vindicated.

If They Be Eminent Guides to Others

> But if you bear the name Jew, and rely upon the Law, and boast in God, and know His will, and approve the things that are essential, being instructed out of the Law, and are confident that you yourself are a guide to the blind, a light to those who are in darkness, a corrector of the foolish, a teacher of the immature, having in the Law the embodiment of knowledge and of the truth; you therefore who teach another, do you not teach yourself? You who preach that one should not steal, do you steal? You who say that one should not commit adultery, do you commit adultery? You who abhor idols, do you rob temples? You who boast in the Law, through your breaking the Law, do you dishonor God? For "the name of God is blasphemed among the Gentiles because of you," just as it is written (Rom. 2:17–24).

The Apostle Paul has just established the principle that "not the hearers of the Law are just before God, but the doers of the Law will be justified" (2:13). Now he applies this principle to anyone who calls himself a Jew

> directly and pointedly and shows him that all the privileges and prerogatives he enjoyed only aggravated his condemnation if he failed to carry into effect the teaching which he inculcated. This is clearly the challenge of verses 21–23. In verses 17–20 we have an enumeration of the privileges and prerogatives on which the Jew prided himself.... The more enhanced the privilege the more heinous become the sins exposed.[18]

---

18. John Murray, *The New International Commentary on the New Testament: The Epistle to the Romans,* 2 vols. (Grand Rapids, MI: William B. Eerdmans Publishing Co., 1959), 1:81.

If They Be Those Whose Example is Likely to be Followed by Others

> But when Cephas came to Antioch, I opposed him to his face, because he stood condemned. For prior to the coming of certain men from James, he used to eat with the Gentiles; but when they came, he began to withdraw and hold himself aloof, fearing the party of the circumcision. And the rest of the Jews joined him in hypocrisy, with the result that even Barnabas was carried away by their hypocrisy. But when I saw that they were not straightforward about the truth of the gospel, I said to Cephas in the presence of all, "If you, being Jew, live like the Gentiles and not like the Jews, how is it that you compel the Gentiles to live like Jews?" (Gal. 2:11–14).

Peter's conduct was a contradiction of the truth of the gospel both he and Paul believed. Out of fear of the Judaizers he segregated himself from non-Jews in table fellowship. This was leaving the impression with many that a breach existed in the apostolate and that Peter was agreeing with the Judaizers that justification was not by faith in Christ alone, but by faith and meritorious obedience to the ceremonial laws of the Old Testament. This was a particularly heinous sin for Peter, so heinous in fact that he had to be publicly rebuked in the epistle to the Galatians by Paul himself. The reason it was so heinous for the apostle Peter to take such a course was because Peter was leaving an example that would likely be followed by others. "If Paul had not taken his stand against Peter that day, either the whole Christian church would have drifted into a Jewish backwater and stagnated, or there would have been a permanent rift between Gentile and Jewish Christendom."[19]

From the Parties Offended

> But when the vine-growers saw the son, they said among themselves, "This is the heir; come, let us kill him, and seize

19. John R. W. Stott, *The Message of Galatians*, (London: Inter-Varsity Press, 1968), 52.

> his inheritance." And they took him and cast him out of the vineyard, and killed him. Therefore when the owner of the vineyard comes, what will he do to those vine-growers? They said to Him, "He will bring those wretches to a wretched end" (Matt. 21:38–41).

Not only does the character and position of the person sinning aggravate his or her sin, but the position, character and relation of the person or persons sinned against aggravate the heinousness of sin. What caused these vine-growers to experience such a terrible judgment—wretches being brought to a wretched end—was that they offended and enraged their employer, the owner of the vineyard, by killing his son when he came to collect the profit of the grapes rightly due his father. It is bad enough to offend any, but for employees (inferiors) to offend employers (superiors) upon whom they are dependent for a livelihood is even more wicked, as well as stupid.

If Immediately Against God

> But Peter said, "Ananias, why has Satan filled your heart to lie to the Holy Spirit, and to keep back some of the price of the land? While it remained unsold, did it not remain your own? And after it was sold, was it not under your control? Why is it that you have conceived this deed in your heart? You have not lied to men, but to God." And as he heard these words, Ananias fell down and breathed his last; and great fear came upon all who heard it (Acts 5:3–5).

All sin is against God, and some sins are directly, knowingly and deliberately against God. All sin is heinous because it is against God, sins committed directly and knowingly against God are far more heinous, deserving the greater condemnation.

It is bad enough to lie to your brothers and sisters in Christ, it is far worse to lie directly against God, who knows our hearts through and through. It was for this reason that God killed Ananias and Sapphira his wife so suddenly and so swiftly. They not only lied to the church about the amount of funds they were giving to God, they lied to God Himself before whose face they spoke their lie.

> Against Thee, Thee only, I have sinned, and done what is evil in Thy sight, so that Thou art justified when Thou dost speak, and blameless when Thou dost judge (Ps. 51:4).

King David was broken because of his sin with Bathsheba and against her husband, Uriah; but what brought him the most grief was not that he had sinned against them, which he had, or that he had sinned against Israel, which he had, but because he had deliberately and against better knowledge and conscience sinned directly against God his Lord and Savior. Nothing else he could have done or ever do was worse than this: "Against Thee, Thee only, I have sinned, and done what is evil in Thy sight." This moved him to confess that God would be just and blameless in whatever He chose to bring against him in judgment.

If Immediately Against God's Attributes

> Or do you think lightly of the riches of His kindness and forbearance and patience, not knowing that the kindness of God leads you to repentance? (Rom. 2:4).

The magnitude of God's goodness and kindness to us is infinite. He is super-abundantly generous to us, who are undeserving of anything from God but His wrath. Everyday we should praise God for His forbearance, long-suffering and patience with us. The great purpose of God's goodness to us is to lead us to repentance of sin and faithfulness to Him out of gratitude for such a display of His glorious perfections in our lives. Hence to despise, think lightly, underestimate or to fail to give God's perfections the esteem they are due is tantamount to scorning and treating with contempt those very perfections. It is a most heinous sin to disregard or be ungrateful for the bestowal of God's riches in our lives, not allowing their bestowal to lead us to repentance and renewed obedience.

If Immediately Against God's Worship

> "But when you present the blind for sacrifice, is it not evil? And when you present lame and sick, is it not evil? Why not offer it to your governor? Would he be pleased with you? Or would he receive you kindly?" says the LORD of hosts.... "But cursed be the swindler who has a male in his flock, and vows it, but sacrifices a blemished animal to the Lord, for I am a great King," says the LORD of hosts, "and My name is feared among the nations" (Mal. 1:8, 14).

Deliberate and conscious corruption of the worship of God is a sin whose wickedness is of the highest magnitude. During Malachi's day the people were corrupting God's worship by presenting blind and lame and sick animals to be sacrificed rather than perfect and unblemished animals as required; and by offering unsuitable and coarse and moldy bread on the table of showbread in the Temple. They were trying to secure God's favor by a general correctness in the externals of worship, but for them it was not worth the effort to be carefully and painstakingly obedient to God's ordinances from the heart, and so God considers their negligence in worship as despising Him. Such actions are a great affront to God and a great wrong to our own souls.

Why is God not satisfied with partial and hypocritical worship that may be generally correct in externals? Why is God so greatly offended when we sin immediately against God's worship? Nothing is as precious to God as His worship. He has instituted in His Law how He desires His people to worship Him. In "playing fast and loose" with the details of that Law and its ordinances of worship, our unfaithfulness to and contempt for God is sufficiently evident.

We should always carefully consider the holy character and glorious perfections of the God with whom we have to do whenever we engage ourselves in worship.

> If then we have a desire to worship God aright, we must remember how great he is; for his majesty will raise us up above the whole world, and cease will that audacity which possesses almost all mankind; for they think that their own will is a

> law, when they presumptuously obtrude anything on God. The greatness of God then ought to humble us, that we may not worship him according to the perceptions of our flesh, but offer him only what is worthy of his celestial glory.[20]

If Immediately Against Christ and His Grace

> For this reason we must pay much closer attention to what we have heard, lest we drift away from it. For if the word spoken through angels proved unalterable, and every transgression and disobedience received a just recompense, how shall we escape if we neglect so great a salvation? (Heb. 2:1–3).

> See to it that you do not refuse him who is speaking. For if those did not escape when they refused him who warned them on earth, much less shall we escape who turn away from Him who warns from heaven (Heb. 12:25).

To sin directly and knowingly against Christ and His gospel of grace is a sin of aggravated wickedness because it is slighting and treating with contempt the only remedy which God's wisdom has provided for our sin and guilt: "there is salvation in no one else; for there is no other name under heaven that has been given among men, by which we must be saved" (Acts 4:12). Therefore there can be no escape from eternal punishment for someone who neglects "so great a salvation."

These two passages, Hebrews 2:1–3 and Hebrews 12:25, are both applications of the Biblical principle: to whom much is given much is required. Contrary to the popular idea that Christians today are less accountable to be strictly obedient to the Word of Christ than were the Old Testament believers to the Law of Moses; however, such a view could not be farther from the truth. Because we have a more complete knowledge of the gospel and covenant of God than the Old Testament believers, due to the completion of the gos-

---

20. John Calvin, *Commentaries on the Twelve Minor Prophets*, trans. by Rev. John Owen, 5 vols. (Edinburgh: Calvin Translation Society, 1843; reprint Grand Rapids, MI: Baker Book House, 1979), 5:512.

pel and of the Biblical revelation, we are more accountable to be strictly faithful to God than were the Old Testament believers. Therefore "we must pay much closer attention" to the Word of Christ, for if disobedience to the "unalterable" revelation of the Old Testament received its "just recompense," how can we today expect to escape even greater judgment if we neglect the salvation Christ brings in the gospel, to which God Himself bore witness through the Spirit-wrought miraculous works of Christ's apostles? As Hebrews 12:25 teaches us, if the Old Testament believers who refused the word of the prophets did not escape God's judgment, "much less shall we escape" who refuse the word of Christ and His grace offered to us in the preached word.

If Immediately Against the Holy Spirit

> Therefore I say to you, any sin and blasphemy shall be forgiven men; but blasphemy against the Spirit shall not be forgiven. And whoever shall speak a word against the Son of Man, it shall be forgiven him; but whoever shall speak against the Holy Spirit, it shall not be forgiven him, either in this age, or in the age to come (Matt. 12:31–32).

Gary Crampton has carefully defined the blasphemy of the Holy Spirit spoken of here:

> The blasphemy of the Holy Spirit consists of the willful rejection and slandering of the witness of the Holy Spirit with regard to the grace of God in Christ. It also includes attributing it to Satan, after having been convicted of its truth. It presupposes an honest revelation of this grace, via the Word of God by the Holy Spirit, which cannot honestly be denied. The convicted sinner rejects the truth even though it contradicts the illumination of his mind and conscience and the verdict of his heart. In so doing he attributes what he knows to be the work of God's Spirit to the devil. The sinner thereby blasphemes God and His Word (Num. 15:30, 31), tramples the Son of God underfoot, and insults the Holy Spirit (Heb. 10:29). Thus the whole of the Trinity is blasphemed when the

> Holy Spirit is blasphemed.... The sin is unpardonable because God has so decreed it, not because it is beyond the merits of Christ's sacrifice.[21]

As William Lane has written in his commentary on Mark 3:28–30, which is a parallel passage to Matthew 12:31–32:

> Jesus affirms that all the sins of men are open to forgiveness, with one fearful exception. Blasphemy against the Holy Spirit forever removes a man beyond the sphere where forgiveness is possible. This solemn warning must be interpreted in the light of the specific situation in which it was uttered. Blasphemy is an expression of defiant hostility toward God.... This is the danger to which the scribes exposed themselves when they attributed to the agency of Satan the redemption brought by Jesus. The expulsion of demons was a sign of the intrusion of the Kingdom of God. Yet the scribal accusations against Jesus amount to a denial of the power and greatness of the Spirit of God. By assigning the action of God to a demonic origin the scribes betray a perversion of spirit which, in defiance of the truth, chooses to call light darkness. In this historical context, blasphemy against the Holy Spirit denotes the conscious and deliberate rejection of the saving power and grace of God released through Jesus' word and act. Jesus' action in releasing men from demonic possession was a revelation of the Kingdom of God which called for decision. Yet his true dignity remained veiled, and the failure of the scribes to recognize him as the Bearer of the Spirit and the Conqueror of Satan could be forgiven. The considered judgment that His power was demonic, however, betrayed a defiant resistance to the Holy Spirit. This severe warning was not addressed to laymen but to carefully trained legal specialists whose task was to interpret the biblical Law to the people. It was their responsibility to be aware of God's redemptive action.

---

21. Gary Crampton, *The Blasphemy of the Holy Spirit* (Lakeland, FL: Whitefield Press, 1987), 12.

> Their insensitivity to the Spirit through whom Jesus was qualified for his mission exposed them to grave peril.... The use of the imperfect tense of the verb in the explanatory note, "because *they were saying* that he is possessed," implies repetition and a fixed attitude of mind, the tokens of callousness which brought the scribes to the brink of unforgivable blasphemy.[22]

If Immediately Against the Spirit's Witness

> And do not grieve the Holy Spirit of God, by whom you were sealed for the day of redemption (Eph. 4:30).

All malicious, offensive, unwholesome and impure language in Christians is not only harmful to others, but it also grieves the Holy Spirit of God (Eph. 4:29–30). The church is the temple of the Holy Spirit, therefore we should treat every member of the Christian temple with dignity and reverence, lest we defile God's holy temple; for anyone who defiles it God will destroy because such acts are so offensive to Him (1 Cor. 3:16, 17). To pollute the minds of other Christians or to injure them by words is a profanation of the temple of God and an offense to the Holy Spirit.

> Reverence, therefore, for the Holy Spirit who dwells in others, and for that same Spirit as dwelling in ourselves, should prevent our ever giving utterance to a corrupting thought. The Spirit, says the apostle, is *grieved*. Not only is his holiness offended, but his love is wounded. If any thing can add to the guilt of such conduct, it is its ingratitude, for it is by Him, as the apostle adds, *We are sealed unto the day of redemption.* His indwelling certifies that we are the children of God, and secures our final salvation.... To grieve him, therefore, is to wound him on whom our salvation depends. Though he will not finally withdraw from those in whom

---

22. William Lane, *The New International Commentary on the New Testament: The Gospel According to Mark* (Grand Rapids, MI: William B. Eerdmans Publishing Co., 1974), 144–56.

> he dwells, yet when grieved he withholds the manifestations of his presence. And a disregard for those manifestations is proof that we have not the Spirit of Christ and are none of his.[23]

If Immediately Against the Spirit's Workings

> For in the case of those who have once been enlightened and have tasted of the heavenly gift and have been made partakers of the Holy Spirit, and have tasted the good word of God and the powers of the age to come, and then have fallen away, it is impossible to renew them again to repentance, since they again crucify to themselves the Son of God, and put Him to open shame (Heb. 6:4–6).

Only the Holy Spirit can convict a person of his sin, enlighten him regarding the truth of the gospel of Christ, persuade a person of the authority of God's Word, renew his heart and bring him to faith in Christ. If someone sits under the preaching of the Word of God in a faithful church, and experiences something of the power of the Spirit in that Word and in interrelationships of the body of Christ, and persistently refuses to submit Himself to Christ in faith and obedience, he may come to the point that he so hardens his heart that he completely apostatizes, and the Holy Spirit leaves him to himself and to his resistance to Him. Even the beginnings of such an attitude and response to the Spirit's working is a heinous and dangerous sin.

If Against Superiors, Men of Eminency

> Not so with My servant Moses, he is faithful in all My household; with him I speak mouth to mouth, even openly, and not in dark sayings, and he beholds the form of the LORD. Why then were you not afraid to speak against My servant, against Moses? So the anger of the LORD burned against them and He departed (Num. 12:7–9).

---

23. Charles Hodge, *A Commentary on Ephesians* (Grand Rapids, MI: William B. Eerdmans Publishing Co., n.d.), 274–75.

When Miriam and Aaron complained against Moses, their brother, unjustly and audaciously, because of his marriage to a woman of another race, "the anger of the LORD burned against them" (Num. 12:9), because they dared to sin against their covenantal superior, God's servant and mouthpiece and representative. Unjust criticism of Moses as their brother was bad enough, but unjust criticism of their superior was an aggravated sin in God's sight.

> And the people will be oppressed,
> Each one by another, and each one by his neighbor;
> The youth will storm against the elder,
> And the inferior against the honorable (Isa. 3:5).

Isaiah 3 is a description of God's judgment upon an apostate culture. It impresses us with the folly of relying on man instead of God. The removal of effective leadership from a culture leads to anarchy and lawlessness. And one of the signs of the moral degeneration of a society under divine judgment is that those who belong to the lowest ranks of society will despise those in the more honorable and productive ranks of society. Such defiance and disrespect are aggravated sins.

> Disrespect for age and for those deserving respect is a sign of pure barbarism. In such times, when the government itself is no longer responsible, the lowest classes gain the upper hand. It is a time when neither life nor property is safe, and when the decencies of life are constantly violated. Good government is one of God's best gifts to a sinful race. How great then is the sin of those who refuse to concern themselves with their responsibilities as citizens of the state![24]

24. Edward J. Young, *The New International Commentary on the Old Testament: The Book of Isaiah*, 3 vols. (Grand Rapids, MI: William B. Eerdmans Publishing Co., 1965), 1:145.

If Against Such as We Stand Especially Related and Engaged Unto

The eye that mocks a father
And scorns a mother,
The ravens of the valley will pick it out,
And the young eagles will eat it (Prov. 30:17).

God takes careful note of the way children treat their parents, because of the intimate relationship children have to their parents. God will judge children for their bad looks and gestures to them as surely as He will judge their bad language to them. There is no escaping God's eye. God also will severely punish those children who think it is beneath them to submit to their parents' authority and who refuse to obey their parents cheerfully (2 Sam. 18:17). "Those that dishonour their parents shall be set up as monuments of God's vengeance; they shall be hanged in chains, as it were, for the birds of prey to pick out their eyes, those eyes with which they looked so scornfully on their good parents."[25]

For it is not an enemy who reproaches me,
Then I could bear it;
Nor is it one who hates me
who has exalted himself against me,
Then I could hide myself from him.
But it is you, a man my equal,
My companion and my familiar friend.
We who had sweet fellowship together,
Walked in the house of God in the throng (Ps. 55:12–14).

David was deeply grieved over the atrocious hypocrisy and treachery of some unnamed person against him. What grieves him the most is that this one who betrayed him was not an avowed enemy but a dear and close friend, with whom David had shared his most secret thoughts, and had often walked to the House of God together talking as two old friends. "Were friendships sacred and

25. Henry, *Matthew Henry's Commentary on the Whole Bible*, 3:797.

never disgraced by treachery, some might doubt the depravity of man. But as things are, there is no room for incredulity."[26]

If Against Any of the Saints

> I have heard the taunting of Moab
> And the revilings of the sons of Ammon,
> With which they have taunted My people
> And become arrogant against their territory....
>
> This they will have in return for their pride, because they have taunted and become arrogant against the people of the LORD of hosts. The LORD will be terrifying to them, for He will starve all the gods of the earth; and all the coastlands of the nations will bow down to Him,
> every one from his own place (Zeph. 2:8, 10–11).

The nations of Moab and Ammon were known for their arrogance, inhumane cruelty and hostility toward Israel, the covenant people of God. They tried to dominate God's people and use any means to steal their land. They rebelled against the Lord by harassing, taunting and attacking His chosen people. Therefore, although their cruelty to others was wicked, their hostility toward Israel, the chosen people of God who were dear to His heart, was of aggravated guilt and hence the Lord punished them severely as our text reveals.

> And whoever receives one such child in My name receives Me; but whoever causes one of these little ones who believe in Me to stumble, it is better for him that a heavy millstone be hung around his neck, and that he be drowned in the depth of the sea (Matt. 18:5–6).

The children of believers are particularly special in the eyes of the Lord. He has determined to be the God of His people and their descendants down through their generations (Gen. 17:7). These children who were brought to Jesus were brought by believing parents who looked to Christ to bless them. He counts

26. Plumer, *Psalms*, 581.

them as His own, as citizens of His kingdom, and in fellowship with Him. Therefore any attempt on the part of anyone to draw them away from Him and lead them into a life of sin will be punished severely. Misleading children is bad enough, but misleading children of the covenant, because of their close relation to Jesus, is so wicked that "'Whoever causes one of these little ones who believe in Me to stumble, it is better for him that a heavy millstone be hung around his neck, and that he be drowned in the depth of the sea' said Jesus."

If Against Particularly Weak Brethren

> But take care lest this liberty of yours somehow become a stumbling block to the weak. For if someone sees you who have knowledge dining in an idol's temple, will not his conscience, if he is weak, be strengthened to eat things sacrificed to idols? For through your knowledge he who is weak is ruined, the brother for whose sake Christ died. And thus, by sinning against the brethren and wounding their conscience when it is weak, you sin against Christ. Therefore, if food causes my brother to stumble, I will never eat meat again, that I might not cause my brother to stumble (1 Cor. 8:9–13).

> Therefore let us not judge one another any more, but rather determine this—not to put an obstacle or a stumbling block in a brother's way.... For if because of food your brother is hurt, you are no longer walking according to love. Do not destroy with your food him for whom Christ died. It is good not to eat meat or to drink wine, or to do anything by which your brother stumbles (Rom. 14:13, 15, 21).

Leading weaker, less knowledgeable and less mature brothers and sisters into sin by our careless enjoyment of the liberty we have in Christ is a heinous sin because it is so destructive to our weaker brothers and sisters. A mature Christian, who appreciates his liberty in Christ, is so concerned with edifying his brothers and sisters in Christ that he is willing to forego the enjoyment of some of his liberties, if his enjoyment of them encourages others to sin against God. He does not want to be "a stumbling block to the weak." It grieves him to think that through unwise actions on his part he ruins his brother. He will enjoy his Christian liberties wisely, because he does not want his weaker brother to "stumble," *i.e.*, to sin (James 3:2). Far be it from him to "put an obstacle or a stumbling block in a brother's way" that would have the effect of hurting or destroying his brother physically, morally, emotionally or spiritually. What makes such sin so heinous is: (1) It is a sin against love. If we are careless about our brother's spiritual welfare we "are no longer walking according to love;" (2) We are destroying our brother "for whom Christ died" and "wounding their conscience when it is weak;" and (3) We "sin against Christ" Himself.

If Against the Souls of Them, or Any Other

> Woe to you, scribes and Pharisees, hypocrites, because you travel about on sea and land to make one proselyte; and when he becomes one, you make him twice as much a son of hell as yourselves (Matt. 23:15).

In this verse Jesus is denouncing the Jews of His day because of what they were doing to the *souls* of their "converts," who were called "proselytes." In the first century the Jews were actively involved in missionary activity, they were willing to "travel about on sea and land to make one proselyte." They were not content to make a Gentile a Jew, rather the "proselyte" was lead to

> become a full-fledged, legalistic, ritualistic, hair-splitting Pharisee, one filled with fanatical zeal for his new salvation-by-works religion. As Jesus implies, soon this new convert would even out-Pharisee the Pharisees in bigotry, for it is a fact that new converts frequently outdo themselves in becoming fanatically devoted to their new faith.[27]

---

27. William Hendriksen, *New Testament Commentary: Exposition of the Gospel According to Matthew* (Grand Rapids, MI: Baker Book House, [1973] 1975), 829.

In so doing the Pharisees were making their converts "twice as much [sons] of hell" as themselves. Hence, Jesus pronounces His *woe* against them, denouncing them and calling down God's judgment upon them for "trafficking" in the souls of men, careless of their eternal destiny.

If Against the Common Good of All or Many

> Did not Achan the son of Zerah act unfaithfully in the things under the ban, and wrath fall on all the congregation of Israel? And that man did not perish alone in his iniquity (Josh. 22:20).

It is bad enough when a person commits a sinful act that injures another person, but when that person knows that such an act will injure many people and whole communities, and he commits that act anyway, his crime is far more wicked. Such was the case of "Achan the son of Zerah."

After a glorious victory at Jericho, the Israelite armies faced defeat in their first assault on Ai. Joshua could not understand why. So the Lord told him that someone had disobeyed His direct command and had stolen some of the spoils of Jericho, which God had expressly forbidden since He had placed the city and everything in it under the "ban" (*Herem*).

The culprit was discovered. It was Achan, who "saw among the spoil a beautiful mantle from Shinar and two hundred shekels of silver and a bar of gold fifty shekels in weight... [and] took them," hiding them under the floor of his tent (Josh. 7:21). Therefore, because of his heinous sin of placing the enjoyment of his own pleasures above the welfare and *common good* of the whole nation, Achan, his family and all his possessions were stoned with stones; and they burned them with fire after they had stoned them with stones (Josh. 7:25).

From the Nature and Quality of the Offense

> Men do not despise a thief if he steals to satisfy himself when he is hungry; but when he is found, he must repay sevenfold;

> he must give all the substance of his house. The one who commits adultery with a woman is lacking sense; he who would destroy himself does it. Wounds and disgrace he will find, and his reproach will not be blotted out (Prov. 6:30–33).

Although this proverb does not offer an excuse or impunity to a thief, for even theft because of hunger is justly punished with a "sevenfold" restitution, yet such a thief who steals not out of greed but because of hunger is not despised; rather he is pitied although not excused. On the other hand, someone who commits adultery is not lacking bread, he is lacking understanding—willing to satisfy his senses even if such acts are self-destruction. He deserves and receives no sympathy. The thief may have felt forced into stealing or starving, but the adulterer chose his course gladly. This is the greater sin. In other words, the nature of the offense often aggravates the guilt of the sin, thereby increasing the degree of judgment deserved. What follows are descriptions of the nature and quality of a sinful act that aggravate the guilt of that sin.

If It Be Against the Express Letter of the Law

> And now, our God, what shall we say after this? For we have forsaken Thy commandments, which Thou has commanded by Thy servants the prophets, saying, "The land which you are entering to take possession of it is an unclean land with the uncleanness of the peoples of the lands, with their abominations which have filled it from end to end and with their impurity. So now do not give your daughters to their sons nor take their daughters to your sons, and never seek their peace or their prosperity, that you may be strong and eat the good things of the land and leave it as an inheritance to your sons forever" (Ezra 9:12).

Sin committed in ignorance is still sin. A person who sins, being caught off guard, at a particularly vulnerable moment, is still accountable for his actions (Gal. 6:1). But when someone has a clear understanding of what God commands or forbids him, when he knows *the express letter of the Law,* and still transgresses that Law anyway in order to satisfy the desires and appetites of his inner life, in spite of the fact that it displeases the Lord, that person's guilt is far greater and he is deserving of far heavier judgment. This was the case in Ezra's day as is evident in his confession of his nation's sins (9:10–12). The people were letting their children intermarry with pagans, which they knew was expressly forbidden by the Lord. They were without excuse.

> Now the LORD was angry with Solomon because his heart was turned away from the LORD, the God of Israel, who had appeared to him twice, and had commanded him concerning this thing, that he should not go after other gods; but he did not observe what the LORD had commanded (1 Kgs. 11:9–10).

The same was true of King Solomon. The Lord came to him twice and personally told him not to "go after other gods; but he did not observe what the LORD had commanded." When a person sins knowingly and deliberately in the face of the express verbal command of God, it can be only for one reason: "his heart was turned away from the LORD!" Ingratitude and conscious rebellion of the most wicked sort!

If It Break Many Commandments, Contain In It Many Sins

> Therefore consider the members of your earthly body as dead to immorality, impurity, passion, evil desire, and greed, which amounts to idolatry (Col. 3:5).

Sins of aggravated guilt are those that, in the committing of them, include the committing of many other sins. According to the Apostle Paul "immorality" includes the sins of "impurity, passion, evil and greed," which is itself "idolatry." One thing leads to another! Greed and covetousness are linked with immorality because they seek satisfaction in what is not lawful, not being satisfied with what is lawful. Immorality is also theft because it is "a defrauding of one's neighbour by possessing that which is especially his."[28] Im-

---

28. Herbert Carson, *The Epistles of Paul to the Colossians and Philemon: An*

morality, along with all these other sins connected with it, is also idolatry, because "it concentrates the whole being upon something other than God."[29]

> For the love of money is a root of all sorts of evil, and some by longing for it have wandered away from the faith, and pierced themselves with many a pang (1 Tim. 6:10).

"The love of money" is especially wicked because it is the root of countless other evils—there is no evil that it is not capable of producing: fraud, lying, perjury, cheating, theft, cruelty, corruption, quarreling, hatred, envy, murder, immorality—in short, every kind of sin imaginable. The most aggravated sin growing from the love of money is apostasy, rebellion against the true faith of the Bible, "for they who are diseased with this disease are found to degenerate gradually, till they entirely renounce the faith."[30]

If [It Is] Not Only Conceived in the Heart, But Breaks Forth in Words and Actions

> Woe to those who scheme iniquity,
> Who work out evil on their beds!
> When morning comes, they do it,
> For it is in the power of their hands (Mic. 2:1).

It is bad enough to sin thoughtlessly because of a sudden impulse. It is far worse to commit a sin deliberately and purposely after much thought and planning of the particular sin. It is evil to commit a sin against another person after deliberate planning, simply because one has the power to do so, not caring at all that what he does is wrong.

Introduction and Commentary (Grand Rapids, MI: William B. Eerdmans Publishing Co., [1960] 1972), 82.

29. Carson, *The Epistles of Paul to the Colossians and Philemon: An Introduction and Commentary*, 82.

30. John Calvin, *Commentaries on the First Epistle to Timothy*, trans. Rev. William Pringle (Edinburgh: Calvin Translation Society, 1843; reprint Grand Rapids, MI: Baker Book House, 1979), 160.

This was the case in Micah's day. Evil people, motivated by covetousness and greed, schemed how to take control of the wealth of the weak, and they carried out their schemes with all their might, not caring that they were sinning against God, or that what they were doing was public. Such evil scheming that erupts in public evil acts and words is especially wicked in God's sight.

If [it] Scandalize Others

> Woe to the world because of its stumbling blocks! For it is inevitable that stumbling blocks come; but woe to that man through whom the stumbling block comes! (Matt. 18:7).

Sin that encourages sin in others is particularly wicked. To *scandalize others* is to place stumbling blocks in their lives that cause them to fall into sin. Anyone who places stumbling blocks in the path of those trying to do right belong to the "world," mankind in rebellion against and alienated from God. The seriousness of this sin in Jesus' estimation is seen in the fact that He denounces and judges the whole world for tempting people to do evil. Furthermore, He pronounces divine denunciation upon any one "through whom the stumbling block comes." "Neither God's eternal decrees nor the facts of history offer any excuse for the terrible sin of enticing others to do wrong."[31]

> You who boast in the Law, through your breaking the Law, do you dishonor God? For "the name of God is blasphemed among the Gentiles because of you," just as it is written (Rom. 2:23–24).

With a series of pungent and rebuking questions in Romans 2:21–23, Paul exposes and condemns the flagrant inconsistency between profession and practice in the Jews of his day. In verses 23–24, he reminds them that

> transgression of the law is a dishonouring of God; it deprives him of the honor due to his name and offers insult to the

31. Hendriksen, *Exposition of the Gospel According to Matthew*, 691.

majesty of which the law is the expression.... The thought in the apostle's application of the text [Isa. 52:5 which is quoted in Rom. 2:24] is that the vices of Jews give occasion to the Gentiles to blaspheme the name of God. The reasoning of the Gentiles is to the effect that a people are like their God and if the people can perpetrate such crimes their God must be of the same character and is to be execrated accordingly. The tragic is apparent. The Jews who claimed to be the leaders of the nations for the worship of the true God had become the instruments of provoking the nations to blasphemy. With this the indictment has reached its climax.[32]

If [It] Admit of No Reparation

> The one who commits adultery with a woman is lacking sense; he who would destroy himself does it. Wounds and disgrace he will find, and his reproach will not be blotted out. For jealousy enrages a man, and he will not spare in the day of vengeance. He will not accept any ransom, nor will he be content though you give many gifts (Prov. 6:32–35).

If a sinful act so injures a relationship beyond repair, making restoration to good condition impossible, that act is particularly evil and deserving of severe punishment. For example, adultery can destroy at least one marriage, and at least one individual life. The wounds caused by adultery, along with the disgrace that goes with it, can be so deep that they cannot be healed. Disgrace, jealousy, desire for revenge and alienation can be so intense and deep-seated that the adultery is never forgiven, reconciliation is never made, trust and affection are never restored and happiness is never resumed.

> If a man is found lying with a married woman, then both of them shall die, the man who lay with the woman, and the woman; thus you shall purge the evil from Israel (Deut. 22:22). (Compare with Deut. 22:28–29.)

---

32. Murray, *The Epistle to the Romans*, 1:85.

Adultery is so evil that the only just response a society can give it is death. In other words, adultery is such an aggravated sin that God considers it a capital crime. Because it is an assault on the home and family, the basic building block of a just and free culture, both the convicted adulterer and adulteress are to be executed by the state after a fair trial.

If [It Is] Against Means

> Then He began to reproach the cities in which most of His miracles were done, because they did not repent. "Woe to you, Chorazin! Woe to you, Bethsaida! For if the miracles had occurred in Tyre and Sidon which occurred in you, they would have repented long ago in sackcloth and ashes. Nevertheless I say to you, it shall be more tolerable for Tyre and Sidon in the day of judgment, than for you. And you, Capernaum, will not be exalted to heaven, will you? You shall descend to Hades; for if the miracles had occurred in Sodom which occurred in you, it would have remained to this day. Nevertheless I say to you that it shall be more tolerable for the land of Sodom in the day of judgment, than for you" (Matt. 11:20–24).

Sins against the divinely instituted means of saving grace, viz., the inward means of faith and repentance, and the outward means of the preached Word, prayer, and the sacraments of baptism and the Lord's Supper—by neglect, misuse or contempt—are most heinous, because to sin against the means of saving grace, is to sin against saving grace and to sin against the Savior. To neglect, misuse or treat contemptuously the means of grace is to cut oneself off from God's requirements for escaping His wrath and curse due us for our sin.

Chorazin, Bethsaida and Capernaum, on the northern shore of the Sea of Galilee, had the unique privilege of having Jesus Himself visit them, preach to them and perform miracles in their midst, and yet they refused to repent of their sins and believe in Him. Therefore, because this is such an evil and ungrateful and inexcusable thing in Jesus' eyes, He said to those cities that it will be more tolerable for the pagan cities of Tyre, Sidon, and Sodom than for these Jewish cities in the Day of Judgment.

If [It Is] Against Mercies

> Listen, O heavens, and hear, O earth;
> For the LORD speaks,
> "Sons I have reared and brought up,
> But they have revolted against Me.
> An ox knows its owner, and a donkey its master's manger,
> But Israel does not know,
> My people do not understand" (Isa. 1:2–3).

God graciously and mercifully adopted His people as His own sons and throughout their history in the Old Testament raised them and cared for them as sons, and yet in total ingratitude for those *mercies* Israel revolted against her Lord and Father. Even oxen and donkeys act better than that. This contrast between God's free grace in adopting and caring for His people and their rebellion against Him causes their sin to appear all the more heinous. Israel's apostasy, rebellion and idolatry are not only inexcusable sins, they are grossly wicked and of aggravated guilt.

If [it is] Against Judgments

> O LORD, do not Thine eyes look for truth?
> Thou hast smitten them,
> But they did not weaken;
> Thou hast consumed them,
> But they refused to take correction.
> They have made their faces harder than rock;
> They have refused to repent (Jer. 5:3).

> "So two or three cities would stagger
> to another city to drink water,
> But would not be satisfied;
> Yet you have not returned to Me," declares the LORD.
> "I smote you with scorching wind and mildew;
> And the caterpillar was devouring

Your many gardens and vineyards, fig trees and olive trees;
Yet you have not returned to Me," declares the LORD.
"I sent a plague among you after the manner of Egypt;
I slew your young men by the sword
along with your captured horses,
And I made the stench of your camp rise up in your nostrils;
Yet you have not returned to Me," declares the LORD.
"I overthrew you as God overthrew Sodom and Gomorrah,
And you were like a firebrand snatched from a blaze,
Yet you have not returned to Me," declares the LORD...
"Prepare to meet your God, O Israel" (Amos 4:8–12).

In these two texts we see examples of Israel's aggravated sins *against judgments, i.e.*, audacious and blatant rebellion against God immediately in the face of God's recent and devastating judgments on her for her impenitence. God beats her down for her sin, but she gets up and continues to blaspheme Him right in His face, with His hand already poised to come down upon her again.

Jeremiah brings out the hardness of Israel's heart: "Thou hast smitten them but they did not weaken; Thou hast consumed them, but they refused to take correction. They have made their faces harder than rock; they have refused to repent." God's severe judgment was to encourage Israel to correct her ways by repentance; but instead of repenting, she hardened her heart, clenched her teeth, and continued her rebellion against the God who had the power to destroy her completely.

> They had *hardened their faces,* that is, that they were wholly without shame; for they had cast away everything like reason, and made no difference between right and wrong...they *refused to turn*...they sinned and went astray, not through mistake or [lack] of knowledge, but...they disregarded their own safety through wilful and deliberate wickedness, and... they knowingly and avowedly rejected God.[33]

33. John Calvin, *Commentaries on the Book of the Prophet Jeremiah*, trans. by Rev. John Owen, 2 vols. (Edinburgh, Calvin Translation Society, 1843; reprint Grand Rapids, MI: Baker Book House, 1979), 1:260–61.

Therefore, God brought upon them His extreme vengeance. Amos makes the same point.

If [It Is] Against [The] Light of Nature

> For this reason God gave them over to degrading passions; for their women exchanged their natural function for that which is unnatural, and in the same way also the men abandoned the natural function of the woman and burned in their desire toward one another, men with men committing indecent acts and receiving in their own persons the due penalty of their error (Rom. 1:26–27).

All sin is a perversion of God's moral order. Homosexuality is a particularly gross and wicked sexual perversion. In lesbianism, women pervert "their natural function for that which is unnatural;" and in male homosexuality men pervert "the natural function of the woman," and commit "indecent acts" with each other, "receiving in their own persons the due penalty of their error." And when they commit these unnatural acts, these acts that are perversions of God's moral and social order for human beings established at creation, they know better. They sin against better knowledge. Not only does the written Law of God condemn them, their own consciences as human beings that have the work of the Law written on them, their own physical constitution and the whole created order speak against their perversion. Therefore they bring upon themselves the consequences and punishments they deserve for their most heinous sin, consisting in "the gnawing unsatisfied lust itself, together with the dreadful physical and moral consequences of debauchery."[34]

If [It Is] Against Conviction of Conscience

> And, although they know the ordinance of God, that those who practice such things are worthy of death, they not only do the same, but also give hearty approval to those who practice them (Rom. 1:32).

---

34. W. G. T. Shedd, quoted in Murray, *The Epistle to the Romans*, 1:48.

Every human being knows that sin against God deserves to be punished because every human being has a conscience and is created in the image of God, although he is now fallen, suppressing the truth in unrighteousness. "Knowledge of God's penal judgment as it issues in the torments of life to come is recognized... by the apostle as belonging to these with whom he is now concerned."[35] Nevertheless unregenerate mankind continues to sin against God and to encourage and give hearty approval to other people to sin against God, knowing their sin to be deserving of certain divine punishment. Unregenerate man is not only determined to damn himself, he also congratulates others for doing those things that he knows will damn them. Sinning in defiance of a conscience that convicts of sin is particularly heinous to God.

> Yet you, his son, Belshazzar, have not humbled your heart, even though you knew all this, but you have exalted yourself against the Lord of heaven (Dan. 5:22–23).

Belshazzar is an example of a man who sinned against the *conviction of conscience.* In spite of the fact that Belshazzar "knew" how God had punished Nebuchadnezzar for not recognizing that "the Most High God is ruler over the realm of mankind, and that He sets over it whomever He wishes" (5:21), in spite of the fact that he "knew" that such arrogance and idolatry angered the God of Heaven, nevertheless he did not humble his heart before God, but instead exalted himself against the Lord of heaven: "But the God in whose hand are your life-breath and your ways, you have not glorified" (5:23). Therefore, for his aggravated sin God brought him and his empire to an end at the hands of the Medes and Persians (5:28).

> Reject a factious man after a first and second warning, knowing that such a man is perverted and is sinning, being self-condemned (Tit. 3:10–11).

A church member who is persistently divisive in a church, because of his wicked behavior or false doctrine, after repeated warnings, is to be officially excluded from the fellowship of the church,

---

35. Murray, *The Epistle to the Romans,* 1:51.

that is, he is to be excommunicated, because such a person is impenitently "perverted," *i.e.*, morally twisted. What makes his sinning so bad is the fact that he knows he is sinning, he knows he should not be doing what he is doing, he is "self-condemned." His conscience condemns him, and his church has repeatedly warned him, but he persists to cause trouble in the church of God.

If [It Is] Against Public or Private Admonition

> A man who hardens his neck after much reproof
> Will suddenly be broken beyond remedy (Prov. 29:1).

A person who persistently and stubbornly hardens himself against Biblical admonition and counseling will suddenly find himself hopelessly abandoned by God. This is illustrated in such passages as Jer. 19:10, 11; Prov. 1:24–33; 10:17; 5:12; 12:1, 2; Ex. 32:9; 2 Chron. 36:13–14; Neh. 9:29; Isa. 48:8; Jer. 26:23; Zech. 7:11, 12; and Acts 7:51. "Those that will not be reformed must expect to be ruined."[36]

> No remedy—not even the Gospel—can remedy this case. As they lived, so they die, so they stand before God—*without remedy*. No blood—no advocate, pleads for them. As they sink into the burning lake, every billow of fire, as it rolls over them, seems to sound—*without remedy*.[37]

Not giving heed to *public or private admonition* from the Word of God is a most grievous sin.

If [It Is] Against Censures of the Church

> Reject a factious man after a first and second warning (Tit. 3:10).

As we saw above, this "factious man" is a divisive, schismatic influence in the church, destructive of the church's unity and purity because of his evil behavior and/or false doctrine. Such a person is

---

36. Henry, *Matthew Henry's Commentary on the Whole Bible*, 3:788.

37. Charles Bridge, *An Exposition of Proverbs* (Marshallton, DE: The National Foundation for Christian Education, n.d.), 556.

not to be tolerated. He is to be lovingly and firmly disciplined by being called to account for his sin and officially reprimanded, warned and admonished by the church. If he defiantly and impenitently rejects the *censures* of the church, *i.e.*, church discipline, he is to be officially "reject"(ed) by the church, *i.e.*, excommunicated. Church discipline is a mark of a true church, along with the preaching of the Word of God and the administration of the sacraments of baptism and the Lord's Supper. It was instituted by Christ, when he gave the church "the keys of the kingdom" (Matthew 16 and 18) and is therefore a means of grace for the church, strengthening her purity and unity and holiness. To sin against the *censures of the church* is to sin against Christ, the Head of the Church.

If [It Is] Against Civil Punishments

> Though you pound a fool in a mortar with a pestle
> along with crushed grain,
> Yet his folly will not depart from him (Prov. 27:22).
>
> They struck me, but I did not become ill;
> They beat me, but I did not know it.
> When shall I awake?
> I will seek another drink (Prov. 23:35).

These two proverbs teach us that sins *against civil punishments* are of aggravated guilt deserving of increased punishment.

> Let every person be in subjection to the governing authorities. For there is no authority except from God, and those which exist are established by God. Therefore he who resists authority has opposed the ordinance of God; and they who have opposed will receive condemnation upon themselves" (Rom. 13:1–2).

Therefore to sin against the civil authorities when they are being faithful to their God-given responsibility of obeying and enforcing Biblical Law, is to sin against the source of that Law and of that civil institution—God Himself. When the civil magistrate governs in accordance with the revealed will of God, he is backed by God's own authority. Therefore he who resists lawful authority resists God, making him a rebel in God's universe under God's condemnation.

Proverbs 27:22 applies to civil punishments, but not exclusively; its application is more sweeping. It is easier to pound the husk off the grain than it is to remove folly from a fool, *i.e.*, to remove hostility to God's Word from one who despises the direction of God's Word. Ultimately only God can separate folly from a fool, and make him a wise man. But when a fool spurns the efforts of the wise to expel folly from him—parents, ministers, civil magistrates—he is spurning those who stand in the authority of God.

The same could be said of Proverbs 23:35. It applies to civil punishments and more. Verses 29–35 warn of the dangers of drunkenness; thereby encouraging us to govern our appetites and desires, not by sense or reason, but by the Word of God. It is almost as difficult to separate alcohol from one given to drunkenness as it is to separate folly from a fool. When a drunk is admonished by friends and family, disciplined by the church, and punished by the state, rather than repenting, he hardens himself against their efforts, and seeks only another drink. He has lost a sense of shame. He has calloused his conscience. He has no regard for the injuries he is causing others and himself. He has surrendered his reason to his appetites and cravings, "that he longs to be bound again, and only seeks relief from his temporary *awakening* to a sense of his misery, by yielding himself up again to his ruinous sin (Jer. ii:25)."[38] Such a pathetic person is to be pitied, but he is also to be soundly condemned for his aggravated sin.

If It Is Against our Prayers, Purposes and Promises

> When He killed them, then they sought Him,
> And returned and searched diligently for God;
> And they remembered that God was their rock,
> And the Most High God their redeemer.
> But they deceived Him with their mouth,
> And lied to Him with their tongue.

---

38. Bridges, *An Exposition of Proverbs*, 443.

For their heart was not steadfast toward Him,
Nor were they faithful in His covenant (Ps. 78:34–37).

Here is a clear instance of aggravated guilt seen in "playing games" with God, when we know better and when we know He knows better. The death of some of their friends produced some effect in the people of Israel. It frightened them into praying intensely for God's protection and into strong promises of rededication to God to live diligently for Him, because they did not want to experience the suffering and death their friends had suffered at the display of God's omnipotence in their deaths. For a brief time they promised to live more faithfully, but when the fear dissipated and things returned to normal, their promises and prayers evaporated, proving to God that all their promises and confessions were deceitful lies to Him, "for their heart was not steadfast toward Him, nor were they faithful in His covenant." Unfaithfulness to God is bad enough, but unfaithfulness in the face of knowledge of the truth, earnest prayers, confessions of sins, and promises to do better, is even more heinous to God.

> When under a conviction of their wickedness they acknowledged that they were justly punished, and yet did not with sincerity of heart humble themselves before God, but rather mocked him, intending to put him off with false pretences, their impiety was the less excusable.... The language implies that they were not carried away inadvertently, or deceived through ignorance, but that they had provoked the wrath of God, by dealing treacherously, as it were with deliberate purpose.... It is, therefore, not enough to yield an assent to the divine word, unless that assent is accompanied with true and pure affection, so that our hearts may not be double or divided.[39]

For long ago I broke your yoke
And tore off your bonds;
But you said, "I will not serve!" [KJV—"I will not transgress"]

39. John Calvin, *Commentaries on the Book of Psalms*, 5 vols. (Edinburgh: Calvin Translation Society, 1843; reprint Grand Rapids, MI: Baker Book House, 1979), 3:53.

> For on every high hill and under every green tree
> You have lain down as a harlot (Jer. 2:20).

This text presents us with another example of a sin *against prayers, purposes and promises,* and therefore of aggravated guilt. God graciously and repetitively came to Israel's deliverance from those who would enslave her. In a hypocritic attempt to insure God's favor on them, Israel would promise God, "I will not transgress your Law by serving other gods." And yet, it was all a sham, for in her heart, Israel had no intention of ceasing her idolatry. No sooner had she made the promise than "on every high hill and under every green tree [she would lay] down as a harlot."

> Then they said to Jeremiah, "May the LORD be a true and faithful witness against us, if we do not act in accordance with the whole message with which the LORD your God will send you to us. Whether it is pleasant or unpleasant, we will listen to the voice of the LORD our God to whom we are sending you, in order that it may go well with us when we listen to the voice of the LORD our God.... The LORD has spoken to you, O remnant of Judah, "Do not go into Egypt!" You should clearly understand that today I have testified against you. For you have only deceived yourselves; for it is you who sent me to the LORD your God, saying, "Pray for us to the LORD our God; and whatever the LORD our God says, tell us so, and we will do it." So, I have told you today, but you have not obeyed the LORD your God, even in whatever He has sent me to tell you. Therefore you should now clearly understand that you will die by the sword, by famine, and by pestilence, in the place where you wish to go to reside (Jer. 42:5–6, 19–22).

Jeremiah 42 is a record of the final phase of Jeremiah's ministry, which would end in Egypt. The leaders and the people, feeling very religious and very afraid, requested Jeremiah to get a message from God for them concerning their decision to leave Judah and migrate to Egypt. Jeremiah loved his people to the last and was more than willing to answer their request. But, although their promise to God and confession of faith was beautiful and seemed sincere on the surface, the people had no intention of fulfilling their promise, and they paid no more attention to Jeremiah than they ever did.

In ten days the LORD's answer came. The delay increased their fear of Babylon's retaliation. The LORD's answer to Israel through Jeremiah was emphatic, clear and strong: "If you stay in Judah, Jehovah will build you up. He will remove the calamitous effects and intimidation of Babylon. He will dwell in Judah to save, deliver, heal, restore, show compassion and guide. Covenant life and covenant blessing will be restored with obedience to the word of Jehovah. But if you set your mind to go to Egypt, Jehovah will see to it that you will die by the sword, famine and pestilence, and there will be no survivors." But the mind of the people was made up, regardless of what Jehovah said. Their fears would not be removed by the Lord's promises. They were going to Egypt regardless of what God said, or regardless of what they promised God. What a pathetic sight! How deserving they were of severe judgment because they made a beautiful promise to God with no intention to fulfill it!

If It Is Against Our Vows

> When you make a vow to God, do not be late in paying it, for He takes no delight in fools. Pay what you vow! It is better that you should not vow than that you should vow and not pay. Do not let your speech cause you to sin and do not say in the presence of the messenger of God that it was a mistake. Why should God be angry on account of your voice and destroy the work of your hands? (Eccl. 5:4–6).

We should never attempt to bribe God with vows. How frivolous and unbecoming can mere mortals act? "God is in heaven and [we] are on earth," Solomon reminds us. Therefore our words should be few. And thereby we are rebuked for all pretense, hypocrisy, and superficial religiosity that hopes to be heard for its "much speaking." But when vows are made to God, they must be carried out. Ananias and Sapphira sinned against their vow to God and experienced His deadly judgment (Acts 5:1–11).

A vow *is not to be made to any creature, but to God alone: and that it may be accepted, it is to be made voluntarily, out of faith, and conscience of duty, in way of thankfulness for mercy received, or for the obtaining of what we [need]; whereby we more strictly bind ourselves to necessary duties, or to other things, so far and so long as they may fitly conduce thereunto* (WCF, XXII, vi). Therefore making vows and not keeping them honestly and diligently is an insult to God. Disregarding our vows is also blatant hypocrisy, because the intent of a vow is to bind us more strictly to our duties commanded by God. In His Law God binds us by His command; and in our vows, we bind ourselves by our own voluntary engagement to be faithful and diligent in our duties. Therefore to take a vow with no intention to perform it, or with no perseverance in the performing of it is a sin of aggravated guilt.

> It is a snare for a man to say rashly, "It is holy!"
> And after the vows to make inquiry (Prov. 20:25).

Rash vows and rash decisions concerning the sanctity of an issue are warned against in this proverb. To pronounce something holy is to dedicate it to God. This is a verbal picture of an impulsive person committing himself for more than he seriously intends to perform. Such covenant breaking and disregarding of vows made to God are forbidden because they are insulting to God.

If It Is Against Our Covenants

> I will also bring upon you a sword which will execute vengeance for the covenant; and when you gather together into your cities, I will send pestilence among you, so that you shall be delivered into enemy hands (Lev. 26:25).

Life in the bond of God's covenant is a sphere of special blessings and special curses. If we are faithful to that bond in obedience to God's word, we will experience special blessings; but if we are defiantly unfaithful to that bond we deserve special curses from God. Those blessings and those curses are spelled out in Leviticus 26 and Deuteronomy 28. One of those curses is Leviticus 26:25, where God promises to execute His vengeance on defiant covenant-breakers by sending the sword and pestilence upon them until they are so weakened that they are "delivered into enemy hands." The reason God responds so severely to defiant unfaithfulness to His covenant is that He highly values it as a gift of His unmerited grace and love for His people.

If It Is Against Our Engagements to God or Men

> "Now he despised the oath by breaking the covenant, and behold, he pledged his allegiance, yet did all these things; he shall not escape." Therefore, thus says the Lord God, "As I live, surely My oath which he despised and My covenant which he broke, I will inflict on his head" (Ezek. 17:18–19).

God takes oaths seriously that are made in His name. When we swear to engage ourselves to a certain service, commitment or course, we call God to witness our oath of engagement and to judge us if we break that oath. In Ezekiel 17:11–21, we read that Zedekiah took an oath to Nebuchadnezzar to remain in a position of subservient leadership under him in Judah. He broke this oath and sought an alliance with Egypt to escape Nebuchadnezzar's authority over him. In God's eyes, this was the same as breaking an oath made with Him (2 Chron. 36:13). Therefore, God used Nebuchadnezzar and the Babylonians to subdue the oath-breaking Zedekiah. "Scripture teaches that an oath must be honored, even if entered into unwisely, as the incident of the Gibeonites reveals (Josh. 9:19–20; 2 Sam. 21:1–3)."[40] From this incident we learn that breaking our engagements to men or to God is an aggravated sin in God's sight.

If It Is Done Deliberately

> He plans wickedness upon his bed;
> He sets himself on a path that is not good;
> He does not despise evil (Ps. 36:4).

40. *Liberty Bible Commentary*, ed. Jerry Falwell, 2 vols. (Lynchburg, VA: The Old-Time Gospel Hour, 1982), 1:1565.

Allowing ourselves to be "caught in a trespass" (Gal. 6:1), is bad enough, but deliberately planning to sin and then carrying through with it is even more wicked. For this reason the psalmist prays, not only that God will forgive him of "hidden faults", but also that God would "keep back Thy servant from presumptuous sins" (Ps. 19:12–13). To deliberately set yourself on a course of action that is not good is not to hate evil and love good. It is to be anti-godly since God hates evil and loves good. "Diligence in doing evil is a mark of deep depravity."[41]

If It Is Done Wilfully

> Thus says the LORD,
> "Stand by the ways and see and ask for the ancient paths,
> Where the good way is, and walk in it;
> And you shall find rest for your souls.
> But they said, 'We will not walk in it.'
> And I set watchmen over you, saying,
> 'Listen to the sound of the trumpet!'
> But they said, 'We will not listen.'
> Therefore hear, O nations,
> And know, O congregation, what is among them.
> Hear, O earth, behold,
> I am bringing disaster on this people..." (Jer. 6:16–19a).

Deliberately, self-consciously and defiantly sinning against God is a far more heinous crime than being overcome by a sin in the heat of temptation. Both are sinful, heinous and inexcusable in the sight of God. But willful, determined sin often brings disaster from the throne of God, as in the case described in this text. When disaster came upon them, they could not complain against God's justice. God had clearly revealed to them the way in which God wanted them to walk. He had trumpets blasted in their ears. But they refused to obey. "The Prophet teaches us here that the fault of the people could not be extenuated as though they had sinned through

41. Plumer, *Psalms*, 444.

ignorance; for they had been warned more than necessary by God."[42] Their disaster was caused not by the stupidity of the people, but because of their perversity revealed in their willful sin.

If It Is Done Presumptuously

> He who strikes a man so that he dies shall surely be put to death. But if he did not lie in wait for him, but God let him fall into his hand, then I will appoint you a place to which he may flee. If, however, a man acts presumptuously toward his neighbor, so as to kill him craftily, you are to take him even from My altar, that he may die (Ex. 21:12–14).

Accidental manslaughter in the Old Testament was punished by confinement in a city of refuge for a time; premeditated murder was punished by excommunication and death: "you must take him even from My altar that he may die." To plan the murder of another person is to act "presumptuously toward his neighbor." The Hebrew word translated "presumptuously" signifies to act proudly and in a high-handed manner. The person who sins "presumptuously" sins, "not ignorantly or inadvertently, but willfully, knowingly, of set purpose, inasmuch as such an offender is considered as disobeying the known law of God through the *pride*, *self-sufficiency* and *presumptuous elation* of his spirit."[43] (See also Deut. 17:12; 18:22; 2 Sam. 2:19–23; 3:26, 27; 1 Kgs. 2:28–32.)

Therefore the psalmist prays: "Keep back thy servant from presumptuous sins; let them not rule over me" (Ps. 19:13). By "presumptuous sins" he means sinning with "proud contempt and obstinacy." By "keep back" "he intimates that such is the natural propensity of the flesh to sin, that even the saints themselves would immediately break forth, or rush headlong into it, did not God, by His own guardianship and protection, keep them back." It should also be noted that he refers to himself as "Thy servant." That is the motive behind and the argument for his petition.

---

42. Calvin, *Commentaries on the Book of the Prophet Jeremiah*, 1:340.

43. George Bush, *Notes on Exodus* (NY: Newman and Ivison, 1852; reprint MN: James Family Christian Publishers, 1979), 15.

> It is to be observed, that while he calls himself *the servant of God,* he nevertheless acknowledges that he had need of the bridle, lest he should arrogantly and rebelliously break forth in transgressing the law of God. Being regenerated by the Spirit of God, he groaned, it is true, under the burden of his sins; but he knew, on the other hand, how great is the rebellion of the flesh and how much we are inclined to forgetfulness of God, from which proceed contempt of His majesty and all impiety.... Let us learn, then, even although the unruliness of our wayward flesh, has been already subdued by the denial of ourselves, to walk in fear and trembling; for unless God restrain us, our hearts will violently boil with a proud and insolent contempt of God.... By these words ["let them not rule over me"] he expressly declares that unless God assist him, he will not only be unable to resist, but will be wholly brought under the dominion of the worst vices.[44]

> But the person who does anything defiantly, whether he is native or an alien, that one is blaspheming the LORD; and that person shall be cut off from among his people. Because he has despised the word of the LORD and has broken His commandment, that person shall be completely cut off; his guilt shall be on him (Num. 15:30–31).

In Numbers 15:22–31, provisions are made for "sinning unintentionally" (15:22–29), and for "sinning defiantly" (15:30–31). It is obvious from the requirements set forth here for dealing with each case, that sinning defiantly is a far more aggravated sin that sinning unintentionally. If anybody in Israel—"native or alien"—blasphemes God by sinning defiantly, he is to be "cut off from" the covenant people, "completely cut off," because his defiance shows that at heart he despises the word of the Lord whom he professes to believe.

John Calvin applies this text to defiant sinning in worship. To do something defiantly or with a high hand, he wrote,

44. Calvin, *Commentaries on the Book of Psalms,* 1:330–31.

> is nothing more than to attempt, or undertake proudly, what is not lawful; for our hands ought to be guided, and, as it were, restrained by God's word, lest they should lift themselves up. But although men's hands are used in various acts of audacity and wantonness, yet here there is especial mention of the profanation of God's true and legitimate worship, when anything is invented inconsistent with its purity; for the punishment is not decreed against thefts, or murders, or other similar crimes, but against the perverse imaginations, which tend to the corruption of religion.... For it is no light offence to transgress the bounds which God hath placed. Now, it is certain that all self-invented services betray an impious contempt of God, as if men designedly despised Him, and spurned at His commands. Whence we infer, that nothing is more opposed to perfect and sincere religion than that temerity [rashness and extreme boldness] which induces men to follow whatever course they please.[45]

If It Is Done Impudently

> So she seizes him and kisses him,
> And with a brazen face she says to him:
> "I was due to offer peace offerings;
> Today I have paid my vows.
> Therefore I have come out to meet you,
> To seek your presence earnestly,
> And I have found you.
> I have spread my couch with coverings..." (Prov. 7:13–16a).

In this picture portrayed in Proverbs we see a shocking example of sinning *impudently* or shamelessly, with no regard for moral propriety or the heinousness of such acts. "With a brazen face," *i.e.*, without any sense of shame, this immoral woman seduces the naïve young man by impressing him with her religiosity and with her be-

---

45. John Calvin, *Commentary on the Four Last Books of Moses*, trans. by Rev. Charles William Bingham, 4 vols. (Edinburgh: Calvin Translation Society, 1843; reprint Grand Rapids, MI: Baker Book House, 1979), 2:91–92.

lief that God brought him into her life as answered prayer. She tells him she is seducing him because it is the will of God for both of them. How shameless!

> Therefore the showers have been withheld,
> And there has been no spring rain.
> Yet you had a harlot's forehead;
> You refused to be ashamed (Jer. 3:3).

God's disciplinary judgments on His covenant people did not move them to repentance, they were determined to carry on their unfaithfulness as shamelessly as a prostitute goes to her client. "God had from heaven given to the Jews manifest tokens of his displeasure, and yet without any benefit; for they had the [determination] of a harlot, and felt no shame; that is, they were moved by no judgments of God, and could not bear to be corrected."[46]

If It Is Done Boastingly

> Why do you boast in evil, O mighty man?
> The lovingkindness of God endures all day long (Ps. 52:1).

> After his horrid butchery, Doeg spoke and acted as though he had done a brave thing [1 Sam. 21:1–9; 22:6–23]. No other man in Saul's camp dared to perpetrate the atrocity.... One of the most decisive evidences of reprobacy is to glory in our shame... Slade: "It is bad enough to imagine and to do mischief; but far worse to boast of it."[47]

However in the most treacherous times for God's people, God's lovingkindness toward them is unfailing.

If It Is Done Maliciously

> I wrote something to the church; but Diotrephes, who loves to be first among them, does not accept what we say. For this reason, if I come, I will call attention to his deeds which he

---

46. Calvin, *Commentaries on the Book of the Prophet Jeremiah*, 1:159.
47. Plumer, *Psalms*, 566, 568–69.

> does, unjustly accusing us with wicked [malicious] words; and not satisfied with this, neither does he himself receive the brethren, and he forbids those who desire to do so, and puts them out of the church (3 John 9–10).

John cannot overlook Diotrephes' contumacy, (*i.e.*, unyielding obstinacy and stubborn refusal to submit to the legitimate authority of apostles), thus he must take disciplinary action. The seriousness of Diotrephes' conduct is exposed in three phrases: (1) He was "unjustly accusing us with wicked words," maliciously making baseless and empty charges and accusations against John; (2) He also would not "receive the brethren," *i.e.*, probably missionaries; and (3) He forbade his church to receive the missionaries with respect and hospitality, and any who dare do so, he "puts them out of the church."

Because Diotrephes "loves to be first among them," *i.e.*, the preachers, he refused to submit to the authority of the apostle John, *i.e.*, he "does not accept what we say." He was "glory-hungry," craving the authority and preeminence of the apostle John, and the church's love for John and the preachers. His sin of contumacy was aggravated by his malicious slander of John and his unjust treatment of faithful believers. "Diotrephes slandered John, cold-shouldered the missionaries and excommunicated the loyal believers because he loved himself and wanted to have the pre-eminence."[48]

If It Is Done Frequently

> Surely all the men who have seen My glory and My signs, which I performed in Egypt and in the wilderness, yet have put Me to the test these ten times and have not listened to My voice, shall by no means see the land which I swore to their fathers, nor shall any of those who spurned Me see it (Num. 14:22–23).

Sinning once is bad enough; but committing the same sin repetitively is worse, especially since we have no excuse to sin at all, because of God's all-sufficient grace. That was true of Israel in the wilderness.

---

48. John R. W. Stott, *The Epistles of John: An Introduction and Commentary* (Grand Rapids, MI: William B. Eerdmans Publishing Co., 1964), 228.

They had witnessed the display of the Lord's glory in many miraculous ways in both Egypt and the wilderness, but time after time—"ten times"—they kept complaining of God's providence, resisting God's authority, and refused to "listen to My voice." This frequent and repetitive transgression of God's Law so aggravated the heinousness of their actions that God punished them severely by refusing to allow those who "spurned" God to see the Land of Promise.

If It Is Done Obstinately

> But they refused to pay attention, and turned a stubborn shoulder and stopped their ears from hearing. And they made their hearts like flint so that they could not hear the law and the words which the LORD of hosts had sent by His Spirit through the former prophets; therefore great wrath came from the LORD of hosts. (Zech. 7:11–12)

It is difficult to imagine anyone sinning more *obstinately* than Israel, at this point in time, who did everything they could to keep from hearing the prophets of the Lord preaching His word. Therefore, not only did wrath come upon them, but because of the aggravated sin "great wrath came from the LORD of hosts." Because they obstinately refused

> to wear the yoke of obedience, God laid upon them the yoke of oppression; and as they hardened their hearts like the diamond against God's word, God broke these hard hearts by his judgments. When these judgments came down on them, they cried to God, but as they had refused to hear him, he then refused to hear them.[49]

If It Is Done With Delight

> Discretion will guard you,
> Understanding will watch over you,

49. Thomas V. Moore, *A Commentary on Haggai, Zechariah and Malachi* (NY: Robert Carter, 1856; reprint Edinburgh: The Banner of Truth Trust, [1961] 1974), 109.

> To deliver you from the way of evil,
> From the man who speaks perverse things;
> From those who leave the paths of uprightness,
> To walk in the ways of darkness;
> Who delight in doing evil,
> And rejoice in the perversity of evil (Prov. 2:11–14).

Submission to the Word of God for Jesus' sake brings with it wisdom, understanding and discretion that delivers us, not only from those apostates who speak perversities, but also from those "who delight in doing evil, and rejoice in the perversity of evil." What makes the apostate so wicked is that he tries to seduce others into apostasy, he deliberately and defiantly rejects "the paths of righteousness" in which he had professed to walk, choosing rather to "walk in the ways of darkness." But, worst of all, "he delights in doing evil and rejoices in the perversity of evil." Because of this *delight* and joy in sinning, he will be "cut off from the land, and... uprooted from it" (v. 22), and driven away into everlasting ruin.

If It Is Done With Continuance

> Because of the iniquity of his unjust gain [covetousness]
> I was angry and struck him;
> I hid My face and was angry,
> And he went on turning away, in the way of his heart
> (Isa. 57:17).

Refusing to repent of a sin and stop doing it, but continuing in it is particularly heinous to God. God punished Israel for "the covetous iniquity", by "striking" him, hiding His face from him, and pouring out His anger on him, and yet "he went on turning away," continuing his iniquity inexcusably, following "the way of his heart," which was totally depraved.

If It Is A Relapsing After Repentance

> The word which came to Jeremiah from the LORD, after King Zedekiah had made a covenant with all the people who

were in Jerusalem to proclaim release to them, that each man should set free his male servant and each man his female servant, a Hebrew man or a Hebrew woman; so that no one should keep them, a Jew his brother, in bondage. And all the officials and all the people obeyed, who had entered into the covenant that each man should set free his male servant and each man his female servant, so that no one should keep them any longer in bondage; they obeyed, and set them free. But afterward they turned around and took back the male servants and the female servants, whom they had set free, and brought them into subjection for male servants and for female servants (Jer. 34:8–11).

For if after they have escaped the defilements of the world by the knowledge of the Lord and Savior Jesus Christ, they are again entangled in them and are overcome, the last state has become worse for them than the first. For it would be better for them not to have known the way of righteousness, than having known it, to turn away from the holy commandment delivered to them. It has happened to them according to the true proverb, "A dog returns to its own vomit," and "a sow, after washing, returns to wallowing in the mire" (2 Pet. 2:20–22).

From Circumstances of Time and Place

"Will you steal, murder, and commit adultery, and swear falsely, and offer sacrifices to Baal, and walk after other gods that you have not known, then come and stand before Me in this house, which is called by My name and say, "We are delivered!"—that you may do all these abominations? Has this house, which is called by My name, become a den of robbers in your sight? Behold, I, even I have seen it," declares the LORD (Jer. 7:9–11).

Judah had rejected the demands of God's covenant in her daily life. In spite of such apostasy, they "come and stand before Me in this house, which is called by My name." The words, "stand before," imply submission and surrender for service.

> The secular parallel is of a vassal standing before his overlord in acknowledgement of the overlord's sovereignty and in submission to his overlord for whatever the overlord lays upon him. The very presence of the vassal in the palace of the suzerain was filled with deep significance. It was unthinkable that a rebel vassal should go through such a form in the absence of complete allegiance.... The hypocrisy of the people of Judah was that, despite having breached the covenant stipulations, they appeared in the presence of Yahweh their sovereign Lord and asserted their own inviolability—*We are safe!* (v. 10). They deluded themselves into thinking they were safe to continue breaking the covenant.[50]

How dare Judah go to congregational worship on the Sabbath and praise God for their deliverance from their enemies, and live in moral rebellion against Him throughout the week! How dare they think that by worshipping God one day a week, they could persuade God to let them "do all these abominations"! What makes them think they can play the hypocrite in public worship in "this house, which is called by My name," and make it a "den" of wicked people playing worship to manipulate God, and get away with it? To such people the Lord declares, "Behold, I, even I have seen it!" Regardless of what they think, there is no security in congregational worship from the eyes of the Searcher of all hearts.

If It Is Done on The Lord's Day

> Moreover, the LORD said to me, "Son of man, will you judge Oholah and Oholibah? Then declare to them their abominations. For they have committed adultery, and blood is on their hands. Thus they have committed adultery with their idols and even caused their sons, whom they bore to Me, to

50. J. A. Thompson, *The New International Commentary on the Old Testament: Jeremiah*, ed. by R.K. Harrison (Grand Rapids, MI: William B. Eerdmans Publishing Co., 1980), 280–81.

> pass through the fire to them as food. Again, they have done this to Me: they have defiled My sanctuary on the same day and have profaned My sabbaths. For when they had slaughtered their children for their idols, they entered My sanctuary on the same day to profane it; and lo, thus they did within My house (Ezek. 23:36–39).

Oholah and Oholibah were abominable in the sight of God for committing adultery with their idols and for sacrificing their little children in a fire in idolatrous worship to their false gods. That was hideous enough. But what aggravated their bloodthirsty sin was: (1) These little children were those whom these two women "bore to ME," *i.e.*, they were covenant children, who bore the sign of the covenant, and whom the Lord had claimed for Himself; and (2) They slaughtered their children "on the same day" that they entered God's sanctuary—the Sabbath. Their very presence defiled the sanctuary and profaned the Sabbath.

> It was unnatural and barbarous for them to slay their children, impious to offer them to idols, to devils; and to do those things upon the sabbath days, wherein they were to rest from ordinary works, how extremely wicked and abominable was it! and then after such evils to come into the temple, and appear before God, as if they had done no wickedness."[51]

Since Jesus Christ and His Spirit-inspired apostles changed the Sabbath day from Saturday to Sunday, the first day of the week, the Lord's Day, is the Christian Sabbath (Heb. 4). Therefore we can properly apply this incident in Ezekiel 23:36–39 to the Lord's Day and say that, whereas sin is heinous whenever it is committed, it is particularly heinous when committed upon the Lord's holy Day.

If It Is Done on Other Times of Divine Worship

> "Why have we fasted and Thou dost not see? Why have we humbled ourselves and Thou dost not notice?" Behold, on the day of your fast you find your desire, and drive hard all

51. William Greenhill, *An Exposition of Ezekiel* (Edinburgh: The Banner of Truth Trust, [1863] 1994), 567.

> your workers. Behold, you fast for contention and strife and to strike with a wicked fist. You do not fast like you do today to make your voice heard on high. Is it a fast like this which I choose, a day for a man to humble himself? Is it for bowing one's head like a reed, and for spreading out sackcloth and ashes as a bed? Will you call this a fast, even an acceptable day to the LORD? (Isa. 58:3–5).

> While Israel remained at Shittim, the people began to play the harlot with the daughters of Moab. For they invited the people to the sacrifices of their gods, and the people ate and bowed down to their gods. So Israel joined themselves to Baal of Peor, and the LORD was angry against Israel.... Then behold, one of the sons of Israel [Zimri] came and brought to his relatives a Midianite woman, in the sight of Moses and in the sight of all the congregation of the sons of Israel, while they were weeping at the doorway of the tent of meeting. When Phinehas the son of Eleazar, the son of Aaron the priest, saw it, he arose from the midst of the congregation, and took a spear in his hand; and he went after the man of Israel into the tent, and pierced both of them through, the man of Israel and the woman, through the body. So the plague on the sons of Israel was checked (Num. 25:1–3, 6-8).

This startling incident makes unmistakably clear: sin during times of worship is particularly wicked and more heinous than sins committed in other circumstances in the sight of the Lord.

Never Was Sin More Daring Than in Zimri...

Zimri was openly immoral with Cozbi, the Midianite woman. In unparalleled daring, with idolatrous defiance before God in his heart, he paraded his "harlot" before his friends and family who were "weeping at the doorway of the tent of meeting," *i.e.*, the Tabernacle, who were assumedly mourning over their sin and praying that God would turn away His anger from His people. What's more, Zimri was a civil magistrate who was to enforce God's Law and execute capital criminals, *e.g.*, convicted adulterers. He thought himself to be above the law. He feared neither the law, nor those who enforced it, nor the Lawgiver Himself. His sin was an affront to God's justice, God's covenant, and God's house of worship.

Never Was Faithfulness More Daring Than in Phinehas

Phinehas was the grandson of Aaron. Out of zeal for Jehovah and jealousy for His name, when he saw Zimri's affront to God, Phinehas took a spear and impaled both Zimri and Cozbi, thereby bringing God's avenging judgment on them.[52] He did not do this in a rage or for some sinful motive, but because "he was jealous for his God" (v. 13). God Himself recognized Phinehas' true motive, when he said that Phinehas "was zealous for My sake" (v. 11). And God richly blessed him for executing this adulterous and blasphemous couple. God gave him His "covenant of peace," promising to give him and his posterity all He had promised in His covenant (v. 12); and He gave to his descendants His "covenant of perpetual priesthood" (v. 12–13).

If It Is Done Immediately Before or After Divine Worship

> Therefore when you meet together, it is not to eat the Lord's Supper, for in your eating each one takes his own supper first; and one is hungry and another is drunk (1 Cor. 11:20–21).

Some people in the church in Corinth were not acting like Christians when they came to church to celebrate the Lord's Sup-

---

52. Phinehas was not taking the law in his own hands. He was not acting as a vigilante. It is wrong for private citizens to execute people for their crimes, even if the civil government will not do so. Phinehas was not acting as a private citizen. Matthew Henry points out the rightness of his action: "It is not at all difficult to justify Phinehas in what he did; for, being now heir-apparent to the high-priesthood, no doubt he was one of those judges of Israel whom Moses had ordered, by the divine appointment, to slay all those whom they knew to have joined themselves to Baal-peor [25:3–4], so that this gives no countenance at all to private persons, under pretense of zeal against sin, to put offenders to death, who ought to be prosecuted by due course of law. The civil magistrate is the avenger, to *execute* [God's] *wrath upon him that doeth evil,* and no private person may take his work out of his hand" (Henry, *Matthew Henry's Commentary on the Whole Bible,* 1:538).

per. At family suppers they greedily satisfied their own appetites with their gourmet food with no regard for the poor members of the church who had little to eat.

> So when He had dipped the morsel, He took and gave it to Judas, the son of Simon Iscariot. And after the morsel, Satan then entered into him. Jesus therefore said to him, "What you do, do quickly." ... And so after receiving the morsel he went out immediately; and it was night (John 13:26b–27, 30).

Judas' betrayal of Jesus was the most wicked crime ever committed, but its heinousness was aggravated even more, because he had just had the Lord's Supper with Jesus: "And so after receiving the morsel he went out immediately; and it was night." When we sin immediately after spending time in the worship of God, our sin is all the more wicked in God's sight.

If It Is Done in the Face of Other Helps to Prevent or Remedy Such Miscarriages

> And after all that has come upon us for our evil deeds and our great guilt, since Thou our God has requited us less than our iniquities deserve, and has given us an escaped remnant as this, shall we again break Thy commandments and intermarry with the peoples who commit these abominations? Wouldst Thou not be angry with us to the point of destruction, until there is no remnant nor any who escape? (Ezra 9:13–14).

If It Is Done in Public, or In the Presence of Others, Who Are Thereby Likely to Be Provoked or Defiled

> Now Eli was very old; and he heard all that his sons were doing to all Israel, and how they lay with the women who served at the doorway of the tent of meeting. And he said to them, "Why do you do such things, the evil things that I hear from all these people? No, my sons; for the report is not good which I hear the LORD's people circulating (1 Sam. 2:22–24).

So they pitched a tent for Absalom on the roof, and Absalom went in to his father's concubines in the sight of all Israel (2 Sam. 16:22).

The Lessons of This Answer

We must be "more humbled and abased before the Lord, under a sense of our sins thus aggravated, Ezra ix:6; and likewise so much the more...admire the riches of pardoning mercy, as extended to the very chief of sinners, 1 Tim. i:13,15."[53] Ezra 9:6 records Ezra's prayer: "O my God, I am ashamed and embarrassed to lift up my face to Thee, my God, for our iniquities have risen above our heads, and our guilt has grown even to the heavens."

The Desert of Every Sin

Q. 152: *What doth every sin deserve at the hands of God?*

A.: Every sin, even the least, being against the sovereignty, goodness, and holiness of God, and against his righteous law, deserveth his wrath and curse, both in this life, and that which is to come; and cannot be expiated but by the blood of Christ.

The Desert of Every Sin Even The Least

Every sin, even the smallest and seemingly least significant, because of its nature, deserves severe and eternal punishment from God. Why? All sin is *against the sovereignty, goodness, and holiness of God, and against His righteous law.* Everything sin is, is contrary to everything God is. Sin is transgression against the Law of the infinitely holy God making sin infinitely heinous deserving of infinite punishment, because the heinousness of any sin determines the severity of punishment of that sin, and the more valuable the life

53. Fisher, *Fisher's Catechism*, 144.

of the one sinned against, the greater the punishment (Deut. 19:21). Every sin is a violation of God's law, rebellion against His sovereignty, ingratitude for and abuse of His goodness, an offense to His justice and an insult to His holiness; therefore any and every sin renders the sinner guilty before God, deserving of *His wrath and curse, both in this life, and that which is to come.* For the nature of the punishments sin deserves in this life and in the next, see Larger Catechism Questions 28–29.

The Scriptural support of the statements in the previous paragraph are as follows:

- Every sin, even the smallest, is a violation of God's Biblical Law: "Everyone who practices sin also practices lawlessness; and sin is lawlessness" (1 John 3:4).
- Every sin is rebellion against God's sovereignty:

> If, however, you are fulfilling the Law of our King, according to the Scripture, "You shall love your neighbor as yourself," you are doing well. But if you show partiality, you are committing sin and are convicted by the Law as transgressors. For whoever keeps the whole Law and yet stumbles in one point, he has become guilty of all. For He who said, "Do not commit adultery," also said, "Do not commit murder." Now if you do not commit adultery, but do commit murder, you have become a transgressor of the Law (James 2:8–11).

Disobedience to our sovereign God at any point places us outside the circle of Law at that point, and therefore in the position of rebels, because His Law is the expression of His sovereignty.

- Every sin is ingratitude for and abuse of His goodness. The God against whom we sin is the God of infinite and abundant generosity, a God of grace, mercy, love and patience. He is our good Creator and our loving Redeemer. Remember that the Ten Commandments begin with these words: "I am the LORD your God, who brought you out of the land of Egypt, out of the house of slavery" (Ex. 20:2). And the apostle Paul reminds us that to sin is to "think lightly of the riches of His kindness and forbearance and patience, not knowing that the kindness of God leads you to repentance" (Rom. 2:4). Therefore all sin deserves God's "wrath and indignation" (2:8); and unless we repent of our sins and believe in Christ, we "are storing up wrath [for ourselves] in the day of wrath and revelation of the righteous judgment of God" (2:5).

- Every sin is offensive to God's justice:

> Thou dost sit on the throne judging righteously. Thou hast rebuked the nations, Thou hast destroyed the wicked; Thou hast blotted out their name forever and ever. The enemy has come to an end in perpetual ruins...But the LORD abides forever; He has established His throne for judgment, and He will judge the world in righteousness (Ps. 9:4b–8a).

- Every sin is an insult to God's holiness. After sending fire to destroy Nadab and Abihu for trying to worship God in a way not commanded by Him, He explains why their sin deserved such severe punishment: "By those who come near Me I will be treated as holy, and before all the people I will be honored" (Lev. 10:3). Therefore the Lord commands His people: "For I am the LORD your God. Consecrate yourselves therefore, and be holy; for I am holy" (Lev. 11:44a).
- Therefore every sin, even the least, deserves God's *wrath and curse*. "The sons of disobedience are by nature children of wrath" (Eph. 2:2), who are under God's curse, for God's Word says: "Cursed is every one who does not abide by all things written in the book of the Law, to perform them" (Gal. 3:10 quoting Deut. 27:26).
- Sin deserves the infliction of God's wrath in this life. In fact "God is angry with the wicked everyday" (Ps. 7:11, KJV). "He who believes in the Son has eternal life; but he who does not obey the Son shall not see life, but the wrath of God abides on him" (John 3:36). Leviticus 26 and Deuteronomy 28 define some of the ways God's anger and curse are manifested in the life of the impenitent in this life.

- Sin also deserves God's eternal wrath and curse in the life to come after death in eternity. On Judgment Day Jesus will say to the condemned reprobate: "Depart from Me, accursed ones, into the eternal fire which has been prepared for the devil and his angels" (Matt. 25:41). Then, with this pronouncement, the wicked "will go away into eternal punishment" (25:46).

Since every sin deserves eternal punishment because the nature of all sin is the same in God's sight, the Roman Catholic distinction between mortal and venial has no basis in Scripture, and is in fact a contradiction of Scripture. What is this distinction? Mortal sins, they say, deserve eternal punishment, but venial sins may be atoned for by human satisfactions and penances, because, in their nature, they are so small that they do not deserve eternal punishment. "This is an opinion highly derogatory to the glory of God, and opens a door to licentiousness."[54] Not even the least sin can be expiated but by the blood of Christ (Heb. 9:22; 1 Pet. 1:18, 19).

The Only Expiation For Sin: By the Blood of Jesus

Since every sin of every human being deserves God's *wrath and curse, both in this life, and that which is to come,* does that mean that every human being will suffer that eternal punishment? Two explanations must be given in answer to that question. First, since the nature of sin never changes and since what it deserves never changes, therefore, if sinners are to be reconciled with God, their sins must be "expiated," that is, their sins must be forgiven and the curse of the Law removed; but, second, no expiation is possible without a propitiation, for "without the shedding of blood there is no forgiveness" (Heb. 9:22). God's anger must be turned away by a substitutionary sacrifice and God's justice must be satisfied by that sacrifice before forgiveness of sin is possible with God. And sin *cannot be expiated but by the blood of Christ.* Christ's sacrificial death is that one and only propitiation provided by God: "He [Christ] had to be made like His brethren in all things, that He might become a

54. Ridgeley, *Commentary on the Larger Catechism*, 2: 431.

merciful and faithful high priest in things pertaining to God, to make propitiation for the sins of the people" (Heb. 2:17).

> It is one thing for a sin to deserve the wrath and curse of God, and another thing for the sinner to be liable and exposed to it. The former arises from the heinous nature of sin, and is inseparable from it; the latter is inconsistent with a justified state. Nothing can take away the guilt of sin, but the atonement made by Christ, and that forgiveness or freedom from condemnation which God is pleased to bestow as the consequence of the atonement. It is this which discharges a believer from a liability to the wrath and curse of God.[55]

The Lesson of This Answer

What may we learn from this consideration of the deserts of sin? "The amazing love of God, in transferring the guilt and punishment of sin to the glorious Surety, making 'him to be sin for us, who knew no sin, that we might be made the righteousness of God in him.'"[56]

Q. 153 What doth God require of us, that we may escape his wrath and curse due to us by reason of the transgression of the law?

A.: That we may escape the wrath and curse of God due to us by reason of the transgression of the law, he requireth of us repentance toward God, and faith toward our Lord Jesus Christ, and the diligent use of the outward means whereby Christ communicates to us the benefits of his mediation.

---

55. Ridgeley, *Commentary on the Larger Catechism*, 2:431.
56. Fisher, *Fisher's Catechism*, 145.

> To escape the wrath and curse of God due to us for sin, God requireth of us faith in Jesus Christ, repentance unto life, with the diligent use of all the outward means whereby Christ communicateth to us the benefits of redemption. (SC, Q. 85)

The answer to Question 153 is a most important answer in the Larger Catechism. If we do not escape the wrath and curse of God due our sins, all is lost forever! If we are unclear, uncertain or mistaken in our answer to Question 153, we place our lives at risk eternally!

The Required Means of Salvation as Gifts of God

Having set forth the truth that the only basis for the removal of the sinner's guilt and the satisfaction of God's justice is *the blood of Christ*, the Catechism now explains the divinely ordained (instrumental) means by which this salvation in Christ is received and experienced by an individual. However it must be made absolutely clear at this point that the means God requires of us to receive salvation are not meritorious, nor are they the procuring cause of our salvation, nor are they the means by which our sin is expiated, nor do they in any way complete the finished redemptive work of Christ (Heb. 9:12). These means which God requires of us are also gifts of God, who enables us to do what He demands of us (Eph. 2:8–10). Although we are commanded to "work out our salvation with fear and trembling," at the same time, "it is God who works within us to will and to do, of His good pleasure" (Phil. 2:12, 13). In the promise of the new birth and change of heart, in Ezekiel 36, God also promises that because of the regeneration of the otherwise weak, helpless and spiritual sinner: "I will... cause you to walk in My statutes, and you shall keep My judgments and do them" (36:27). Faith in Christ is "a gift of God" (Eph. 2:8–9). God must graciously "grant" repentance, as forgiveness of sins, before either can be experienced (Acts 5:31). And the diligent use of the means of grace, such as Bible reading, prayer, worship, and the sacraments of baptism and the Lord's Supper is also the product of God's work within the believer (Ezek. 36:27).

The Impossibility of Any Means of Salvation in Man

It must also be pointed out that no other way to escape God's wrath and curse is possible in anything we do in and of ourselves. "All our righteousnesses are as filthy rags" (Isa. 64:6), and "by the works of the Law shall no flesh be justified" (Gal. 2:16). In fact the epistle to the Galatians was written to expose the futility and absurdity of self-justification by working to merit God's favor and to declare that the only way to acceptance with God is justification by faith in Christ alone. The Law of God, which cannot justify, closes off all other avenues of escape and drives us to Christ as our only hope (Gal. 3:22–24). Because of unregenerate man's total depravity and total inability to please God (Rom. 8:6–8) salvation by any other means than those required by God is an absolute and total impossibility, for "without faith it is impossible to please Him" (Heb. 11:6).

The Prerogative of God to Determine Means of Salvation

Whosoever will may come to God for salvation from sin, but everybody who comes to God must come God's required way, or else his coming is in vain. Only God has the prerogative to set the terms of peace between Himself and sinners. Only God has the prerogative to determine how He will be approached, worshipped and served by sinners. Some who desire rest from sin and rest with God have not been given that rest, because "the Word they heard did not profit them, because it was not united by faith in those who heard" (Heb. 4:2). Esau, "when he desired to inherit the blessing... was rejected, for he found no place for repentance, though he sought for it with tears" (Heb. 12:17). And as Hebrews 4:6 and 11 teach us: "those who formerly had good news preached to them failed to enter because of disobedience.... Let us therefore be diligent to enter that rest, lest anyone fall through following the same example of disobedience."

The Means of Salvation As The Requirements of God

God does not issue a powerless invitation to sinners to escape His wrath due them for their sin through faith, repentance and diligent use of the means of grace, He commands sinners to believe in Jesus, repent of their sin and use the outward means of grace. All human beings have the DUTY to do these things, (the ability for the doing of them comes from the Spirit of God). Therefore, not to believe in Christ, repent of sin and take up the means of grace is to live in defiant disobedience to the living God, making that one deserving of eternal condemnation. As Jesus said to the Pharisee, Nicodemus: "He who believes in Him is not judged; he who does not believe has been judged already, because he has not believed in the name of the only begotten Son of God" (John 3:18).

> And this is His commandment, that we believe in the name of His Son Jesus Christ, and love one another, just as He commanded us. And the one who keeps His commandments abides in Him, and He in him (1 John 3:23–24a).

The fact that God commands faith in Christ makes it everyone's duty to believe in Christ; but, more than that, God's command to believe is everyone's warrant to believe and by believing to receive salvation. It is every one's guarantee that if he believes in Christ he will be saved from sin.

> Is there not here a word in season for you, O sinner, whoever you are, however guilty and however helpless, poor and needy, lost and undone? You, as it might seem, are in no condition to keep God's commandments so as to please Him; and you cannot venture to ask anything, or to hope that you will receive anything, at His hands. Nay; but here is something you may do, and that will be very pleasing to Him. "*Believe on the name of His Son Jesus Christ.*" It is true that He will not be pleased with your keeping any other commandment; but He will be pleased with your keeping that one. You may not be in circumstances to do anything else that will be pleasing in His sight; but you are in the very circumstances to do that which will please Him best. He asks you if you will not do Him this pleasure, "*to believe on the name of His Son Jesus Christ.*" Be it that you cannot receive anything you ask otherwise than on the footing of your keeping His com-

mandments and doing those things that are pleasing in His sight. Here is the commandment for you, here and now, to keep. Here is the thing pleasing in His sight for you here and now to do. Without faith it is impossible to please God; but faith pleases Him; it pleases Him well. Then believe now.

And take a right view of the duty of believing. It is not using a great liberty to believe on the name of Jesus; it is simply "*keeping the commandment of God.*" The liberty is all the other way. You use a great liberty when you refuse to believe. Be not disobedient; displease not God by unbelief; rather please Him by believing. And believing, ask what you will, and it shall be given you.

Keep on believing. Continue to believe more and more, simply because you see and feel it more and more to be "*His commandment that you should believe on the name of His Son Jesus Christ.*" Unbelief, in you who have believed, is aggravated disobedience. And, as such, it is and must be especially displeasing to God.... You cannot displease the Father more than by dishonoring the Son; refusing to receive Him, and rest upon Him, and embrace Him, and hold Him fast, and place full reliance upon Him as redeemer, brother, friend. Do not deceive yourselves by imagining that there may be something rather gracious in your doubts and fears; your unsettled and unassured frame of mind; as if it betokened humility, and a low esteem of yourselves. Beware lest God see in it only a low esteem of His Son Jesus Christ.[57]

57. Robert Candlish, *Exposition of 1 John* (Grand Rapids, MI: Associated Publishers, n.d.), 149–50.

The Required Means of Escape From the Wrath and Curse of God Due our Sins

The Bible is clear and unequivocal regarding this question: "How may we escape the wrath and curse of God due to us for our sins?" Both Testaments agree completely on the answer.

The Three Required Means of Escape From God's Wrath

The Teaching of the Old Testament

The Old Testament declares: "Come, eat of my food, and drink of the wine I have mixed. Forsake your folly and live, and proceed in the way of understanding" (Prov. 9:5–6). Proverbs 9 draws a contrast between the banquet of salvation in the house of wisdom (vss. 1–6), and the banquet of evil in the house of folly (vss. 13–18). This chapter, as chapter 8, also personifies "Wisdom." In Proverbs 8:22–31, Wisdom is personified as the One equal with God, but distinct from God, *i.e.*, the Second Person of the Trinity, the Son of God (Col. 1:16–18; 2:9). In Proverbs 8:18, Wisdom declares that "riches and honor are with Me". And in Colossians 2:3, we learn that in Christ "are hidden all the treasures [or "riches"] of wisdom and knowledge." Therefore, in Proverbs 9, "Wisdom" is Christ, the Son of God, and the sumptuous banquet He has in His glorious House, to which He invites everybody, is nothing less than the banquet of salvation, to which He refers in His parable of the Great Banquet to which His servants are to invite everybody in the "highways and byways" to come in and dine.

Therefore, the terms of entrance to Wisdom's banquet are identical with Christ's offer of salvation, as would be expected since Christ is the Divine Wisdom incarnate. Just as Jesus in the New Testament calls upon people to follow Him and enjoy the blessings of the kingdom of God in Him (Mark 1:15) so in Proverbs 9, Wisdom invites people: "Come, eat of My food, and drink of the wine I have mixed" (9:5). In other words, "Come to Me in faith, believe in Me, receive Me and the salvation I offer." And just as Jesus calls upon people to repent of their sins as they come to

Him in faith (Mark 1:15) so Wisdom invites people: "Forsake your folly and live" (9:6). Just as Jesus said that we are His friends if we obey His commands (John 15:14), so Wisdom demands that those who come to His banquet in His House must "proceed in the way of understanding" (9:6), *i.e.*, they must live day by day in "the way of understanding" set forth in His Word, in obedience and submission to that revealed way of life, because "faith without works is dead" (James 2:26).

The Teaching of the New Testament

In the Sermon on the Mount, Jesus declares: "Enter by the narrow gate.... For the gate is small, and the way is narrow that leads to life" (Matt. 7:13–14). In this powerful figure, Jesus tells us clearly the way to eternal life: going through the small "gate" and walking down the narrow "way." We enter the Christian life, life in the Kingdom of God, through the gate of penitent faith, and, having entered that "gate," we proceed down the narrow "way" of Christian discipleship, *i.e.*, submission and obedience to the King of the kingdom of God, which leads to "life." Now notice the emphases: (1) We must enter the gate to get on the way that leads to life. (2) Walking down the way is evidence that we have gone through the gate. (3) It is entering the gate by penitent faith (Mark 1:15) and walking down the way of obedience to the Word of Christ the King that leads to eternal life. Jesus said: "My sheep hear My voice, and I know them, and they follow Me; and I give eternal life to them" (John 10:27).

The Apostle Paul makes this same emphasis: "But now having been freed from sin and enslaved to God, you derive your benefit, resulting in sanctification, and the outcome, eternal life" (NASB, Rom. 6:22).[58] Having been justified by faith in Christ alone and brought into union and communion with God, ("freed from sin and enslaved to God"), the effect of this new relationship is the power to manifest holiness of attitude, character and behavior ("sanctifica-

58. The New International Version translates Romans 6:22 in this manner: "But now that you have been set free from sin and have become slaves to God, the benefit you reap leads to holiness, and the result is eternal life." The Amplified Bible has it: "But now since you have been set free from sin and have become slaves of God, you have your present reward in holiness and its end is eternal life."

tion") in our everyday living, and the "outcome" or end of the entire salvation process is "eternal life" with God in Christ (Rom. 6:23). Notice the inseparable connection between justification, sanctification and glorification: (1) All whom God justifies He sanctifies. (2) Sanctification is proof of justification. (3) Sanctification, *i.e.*, a life of obedience to God empowered by the Holy Spirit, is as necessary to enjoying eternal life as is justification by faith, *i.e.*, the divine declaration that we who believe in Jesus are forgiven of our sins and credited with the righteousness of Christ, thereby adopted into the family of God, on the basis of the finished work of Christ.

Therefore, our Catechisms do not overstate themselves in the answer to Question 153 in the Larger Catechism and to Question 85 in the Shorter Catechism. Faith in Christ is commanded of us, if we are to be saved from sin: "Believe in the Lord Jesus, and you shall be saved, you and your household" (Acts 16:31). "Without faith it is impossible to please Him [God]" (Heb. 11:6). This faith is always accompanied with repentance and is inseparable from it: "Jesus came...preaching the gospel of God, and saying, 'The time is fulfilled, and the kingdom of God is at hand; repent and believe the gospel'" (Mark 1:14, 15). As Paul wrote concerning the Thessalonian Christians: "For they themselves report about us what kind of a reception we had with you, and how you turned from idols to serve a living and true God, and to wait for His Son from heaven, whom He raised from the dead, that is Jesus, who delivers us from the wrath to come" (1 Thess. 1:9, 10). And this penitent faith, if it is genuine, Spirit-produced faith, will always be accompanied with a life of obedience to the Word of God. After warning about apostasy in Hebrews 6:1–8, Paul tells his readers that he is "convinced of better things concerning you, and things that accompany [or "belong to"] salvation" (6:9). And what are those virtues that "accompany salvation" and true saving faith? "Work" for God (vs. 10a) "love" for the Lord's "name" (vs. 10b), "ministering to the saints" (vs. 10c), and "diligence" (vs. 11). Since the Word of God commands us to take advantage of those instruments or means which He has instituted for us and by which He *communicates to us the benefits of redemption*, we will be diligent at putting those means to good use regularly. Therefore, if we do not diligently use these means of grace, we should not expect to be saved, because it is by these means that *Christ communicates to us the benefits of His mediation*, without which we are most definitely and eternally lost. To separate ourselves, then, from the means of grace is to separate ourselves from Christ! "A neglect or contempt of the means of divine appointment, for communicating the benefits of redemption, is, in the sight of God, the same thing as a neglect or contempt of these inestimable benefits themselves."[59] For example, the preached Word of God is a means of grace; and to the preachers of the Word sent out by Him, Christ said: "He who despises you, despises Me; and he who despises Me, despises Him who sent Me" (Luke 10:16).

Faith in Jesus Christ

> Justifying faith is a saving grace, wrought in the heart of a sinner by the Spirit and word of God, whereby he, being convinced of his sin and misery, and of the disability in himself and all other creatures to recover him out of his lost condition, not only assenteth to the truth of the promise of the gospel, but receiveth and resteth upon Christ and his righteousness, therein held forth, for pardon of sin, and for the accepting and accounting of his person righteous in the sight of God for salvation. (WLC, Q. 72)

> Faith in Jesus Christ is a saving grace, whereby we receive and rest upon him alone for salvation, as he is offered to us in the gospel. (SC, Q. 86)

Faith is the open, empty hand that receives Christ in all His offices as prophet, priest and king, His righteousness, and the totality of His salvation. (For an extensive explanation of the nature of true faith and its connection with salvation see my comments on Larger Catechism Q. 72, "The Nature of True Faith.")

---

59. Fisher, *Fisher's Catechism*, 147.

Repentance of Sin

I. Repentance unto life is an evangelical grace, the doctrine whereof is to be preached by every minister of the gospel, as well as that of faith in Christ.

II. By it a sinner, out of the sight and sense, not only of the danger, but also of the filthiness and odiousness of his sins, as contrary to the holy nature and righteous law of God, and upon the apprehension of his mercy in Christ to such as are penitent, so grieves for and hates his sins, as to turn from them all unto God, purposing and endeavouring to walk with him in all the ways of his commandments.

III. Although repentance be not to be rested in, as any satisfaction for sin, or any cause of the pardon thereof, which is the act of God's free grace in Christ; yet is it of such necessity to all sinners, that none may expect pardon without it.

IV. As there is no sin so small but it deserves damnation; so there is no sin so great, that it can bring damnation upon those who truly repent.

V. Men ought not to content themselves with a general repentance, but it is every man's duty to endeavour to repent of his particular sins particularly.

VI. As every man is bound to make private confession of his sins to God, praying for the pardon thereof; upon which, and the forsaking of them, he shall find mercy; so he that scandalizeth his brother, or the church of Christ, ought to be willing, by a private or publick confession and sorrow for his sin, to declare his repentance to those that are offended; who are thereupon to be reconciled to him, and in love to receive him. (WCF, XV).

> Repentance unto life is a saving grace, wrought in the heart of a sinner by the Spirit and word of God, whereby, out of the sight and sense, not only of the danger, but also of the filthiness and odiousness of his sins, and upon the apprehension of God's mercy in Christ to such as are penitent, he so grieves for and hates his sins, as that he turns from them all to God, purposing and endeavouring constantly to walk with him in all the ways of new obedience. (WLC, Q. 76)

> Repentance unto life is a saving grace, whereby a sinner, out of a true sense of his sin, and apprehension of the mercy of God in Christ, doth, with grief and hatred of his sin, turn from it unto God, with full purpose of, and endeavour after, new obedience. (SC, Q. 87)

(For an extended explanation of true repentance of sin see my comments on Larger Catechism Q. 76, "Turn or Burn! The Meaning of Repentance.")

Why does the Larger Catechism Q. 153, in telling us what God requires of us that we might escape His wrath, say, *He requireth of us repentance toward God, and faith toward our Lord Jesus Christ,* while the Shorter Catechism Q. 85 says that *God requireth of us faith in Jesus Christ, repentance unto life?* The point is that in the Larger Catechism repentance is placed before faith; and in the Shorter Catechism faith is placed before repentance. What is the point being made here? It is not that repentance precedes faith or that faith precedes repentance, but that repentance is an essential component of faith and faith is an essential component of repentance. The Westminster Confession of Faith (XV, ii) makes clear that repentance is not true repentance without the *apprehension of God's mercy in Christ.* Zechariah 12:10 says that "they will *look on Me* whom they have pierced; and they will *mourn for Him*" (emphasis added), showing us the unity of faith in Christ and repentance of sin. In Acts 20:18,20,21, Paul tells the Ephesian elders: "You yourselves know... how I did not shrink from declaring to you anything that was profitable, and teaching you publicly and from house to house, solemnly testifying to both Jews and Greeks *of repentance toward God and faith in our Lord Jesus Christ*" (emphasis added). "These two together constitute the whole of practical religion, and comprise all the lawful and obligatory themes of evangelical instruction."[60]

Repentance unto life and faith in Christ are twin gifts of God, both contained in the gift of the new heart in regeneration. They cannot exist apart from each other; one does not precede the other in the regenerate person. They may stimulate each other, but as soon as a person begins to believe in Jesus, he also begins to repent of his sins. The very first actions of faith imply repentance.

> Repentance is the right sense and volition which the renewed heart has of its sin; faith is the turning of that heart from its sin to Christ. Repentance feels the disease, faith embraces the remedy.[61]

Why is this point such an important one? First, to say that faith can exist without repentance "gives a degrading... character to repentance; as though the sinner selfishly conditioned his willingness to feel aright concerning his sin, on the previous assurance of impunity."[62] Second, "Godly sorrow for sin must be presupposed or implied in the first actings of faith, because faith embraces Christ as a Savior from sin.... Surely the Scriptures do not present Christ to our faith only, or even mainly, as a way of impunity,"[63] *i.e.*, merely as a way to escape punishment with no desire to escape sinning. "There can be no embracing of Christ with the heart, as a whole present Saviour, unless sin be felt to be in itself a present evil; and there be a genuine desire to avoid it as well as its penalty."[64] Third, some Bible passages indicate that faith and repentance are inseparable twin gifts of God given and exercised at the same time (Mark

60. J.A. Alexander, *Commentary on the Acts of the Apostles* (London: The Banner of Truth Trust, [1857] 1991), 244.

61. Robert L. Dabney, *Lectures in Systematic Theology* (Grand Rapids, MI: Zondervan Publishing House, [1878] 1975), 658.

62. Dabney, *Lectures in Systematic Theology*, 657.

63. Dabney, *Lectures in Systematic Theology*, 657–58.

64. Dabney, *Lectures in Systematic Theology*, 658.

1:15; Acts 2:38; 5:31; 20:21; 2 Tim. 2:25). Saving faith, therefore, is penitent faith and repentance unto life is believing repentance.

> The interdependence of faith and repentance can be readily seen when we remember that faith is faith in Christ for salvation from sin. But if faith is directed to salvation from sin, there must be hatred of sin and the desire to be saved from it. Such hatred of sin involves repentance which essentially consists in turning from sin unto God. Again, if we remember that repentance is turning from sin unto God, the turning to God implies faith in the mercy of God as revealed in Christ. It is impossible to disentangle faith and repentance. Saving faith is permeated with repentance and repentance is permeated with faith.[65]

Diligence in the Use of the Outward Means of Grace

Along with *repentance toward God and faith toward our Lord Jesus Christ*, God also requires *the diligent use of the outward means whereby Christ communicates to us the benefits of His mediation*, if we are to escape the wrath and curse of God due to us for our sins. (1) What is meant by *outward means*? (2) What is meant by *whereby Christ communicates to us the benefits of His mediation*? (3) What is meant by *the diligent use of the outward means*? and (4) Why is the diligent use of the outward means a divine requirement in order to escape God's wrath and curse on sin?

What is Meant By Outward Means?

The *means* or instruments which God has provided for us and through which He brings the benefits of salvation into our lives have been designated as internal or inward means of grace and external or outward means of grace. The former include faith and repentance, which are both rooted in the heart and are so inseparably connected with salvation that no one who believes in Jesus and repents of his sins can possibly perish. "The graces [gifts] of faith and

65. John Murray, *Redemption Accomplished and Applied* (Grand Rapids, MI: William B. Eerdmans Publishing Co., 1955), 113.

repentance, together with all others which accompany or flow from them, are the fruits and effects of Christ's mediation [*i.e.*, His saving work as our Mediator]; and hence are sometimes called saving graces."[66] Faith and repentance are wrought in the heart by the power of the Holy Spirit, and are, therefore, properly called internal or inward means of grace and salvation. External or *outward means* are ordinances instituted by God which He commands us to use diligently with the confident hope of continuing to receive God's saving grace and the benefits of salvation from God. As we use these means of grace, such as the reading of the Bible, listening to the preached Word, prayer, worship, and the right use of the sacraments of baptism and the Lord's Supper, we are to pray earnestly that God would work His grace in our hearts through them. Their power to bring God's grace to us is not in the means, but in the sovereign pleasure of the God of all grace.

What is Meant By "Whereby Christ Communicates to Us the Benefits of His Mediation"?

Means of grace are not only Christian *duties* performed in obedience to God, who instituted them as the way He desires to be worshipped by His creatures, they are also *promises* from God by which He assures His people of His presence and His blessing: "where I cause My name to be remembered, I will come to you and bless you" (Ex. 20:24). By them, He encourages His people to observe them diligently in the hope and faith that through them God will bring His presence and blessings into their lives. As God works grace through them, they are called "means of grace;" and

> as he seldom works grace without first inclining persons to attend on him in them, and wait for his salvation, they are called the ordinary means of grace; and as they have not in themselves a tendency to work grace, without the inward and powerful influences of the Holy Spirit accompanying them,

66. Ridgeley, *Commentary on the Larger Catechism*, 2:432.

> they are distinguished from it, and accordingly styled the outward means of grace.[67]

Through these outward means of grace, such as the Word, sacraments and prayer, God works the benefits of salvation by grace into the heart of the believer. He makes them *effectual...for their salvation* (WLC, Q. 154). This is what Peter was getting at when He wrote: "And corresponding to that, baptism now saves [present continuous tense] you—not the removal of dirt from the flesh, but an appeal to God for a good conscience—through the resurrection of Jesus Christ" (1 Pet. 3:21). He is not attributing saving power to the water of baptism, nor is he saying that water-baptism is an absolute prerequisite to salvation. Rather he is saying that by the sacrament of baptism, the resurrected Christ continues to administer and convey the blessings of salvation into the lives of His people, which blessings are theirs by grace through faith in Christ alone signified and sealed in baptism.

The Apostle Paul informs us that Christ loved His bride, the church, and gave Himself on the cross for her "that He might sanctify her, having cleansed her by the washing of water with the word" (Eph. 5:26). Here we read of Christ making effectual His Word and baptism in His Church unto her eternal salvation. How does the Word and baptism sanctify and cleanse the church?

> God is pleased to connect the benefits of redemption with the believing reception of the truth. And he is pleased to connect these same benefits with the believing reception of baptism. That is, as the Spirit works with and by the truth, so he works with and by baptism, in communicating the blessings of the covenant of grace. Therefore, as we are said to be saved by the word, with equal propriety we are said to be saved by baptism; though baptism without faith is as of little effect as is the word of God to unbelievers.... Besides, the benefits of redemption... are not conveyed to the soul once for all. They are reconveyed and appropriated on every new

67. Ridgeley, *Commentary on the Larger Catechism*, 2:433.

> act of faith, and on every new believing reception of the sacraments [and of the Word].[68]

Or as Paul said in 1 Corinthians 1:18: "For the preaching of the cross is to those who are perishing foolishness, but to us who are being saved it is the power of God."

Both Catechisms emphasize the point that by the outward means of grace *Christ communicates to His church the benefits of His mediation* or *the benefits of redemption.* The crucified, risen and exalted Christ by His Holy Spirit confers and imparts personally to His people all the benefits of redemption which He accomplished for them once-for-all in His life, death and resurrection as the Mediator of the New Covenant. This bestowal of the blessings of salvation brings them into intimate, vital union and communion with Himself and with each other by grace through faith. Paul asks: "Is not the cup of blessing which we bless a sharing in the blood of Christ? Is not the bread which we break a sharing in the body of Christ? Since there is one bread, we who are many are one body; for we all partake of the one bread" (1 Cor. 10:16, 17). "Sharing" is the Greek word, *koinonia,* meaning a sharing, participation, fellowship, a communion. Therefore, when we participate worthily in the Lord's Supper, as an outward means of grace, we commune, participate, fellowship, share in the benefits of the shed blood and broken body of Christ; and in sharing in those benefits, we enjoy communion with Christ Himself and with all other believers in the body of Christ.

What is Meant By "the Diligent Use of the Outward Means"?

To neglect the outward means of the saving grace of Christ is to reject Christ, despise our own souls and deprive ourselves of the inestimable advantage of God's instituted means of grace. Therefore we must take advantage of all opportunities to use those precious means.

---

68. Charles Hodge, *Commentary on the Epistle to the Ephesians* (Grand Rapids, MI: William B. Eerdmans Publishing Co., n.d.), 322–23.

Question 153 emphasizes that this required use of the means of grace must be *diligent,* if it is to conform to what God requires of us to escape the wrath of God. We must not use the outward means of grace in a careless, haphazard or indifferent manner, as though we neither expected nor desired to receive anything from God through them. Diligence implies not only taking advantage of every opportunity to use the means of grace, but also earnestly desiring and expecting God's grace through these means.

> God commands the use of the sacraments. He would command nothing that was superfluous or vain. Therefore the sacraments are necessary. God has promised His grace along with the use of the sacraments. No man dare neglect the offered grace of God without condemnation. Therefore, the diligent use of the sacraments is necessary.... "It is true that, by neglecting Baptism, we are excluded from salvation; and in this sense I acknowledge that it is necessary; but it is absurd to speak of salvation as being confined to the sign" [Calvin].... To reject the sacraments is therefore to reject the Word.[69]

> By our attendance on his ordinances, we testify our approbation [approval and satisfaction] of that method which he has ordained for the application of redemption; and by our perseverance in it, determining not to leave off waiting till we have obtained the blessing expected, we proclaim the valuableness of that method, and subscribe to the sovereignty of God in dispensing those blessings to his people which they stand in need of, as well as pray and hope for them in his own time and way. Thus we are to wait on [diligently use] the means of grace.[70]

---

69. Ronald Wallace, *Calvin's Doctrine of the Word and Sacrament* (London/ Edinburgh: Oliver & Boyd, 1953), 239–40.

70. Ridgeley, *Commentary on the Larger Catechism*, 2:433.

Why is The Diligent Use of the Outward Means A Divine Requirement in Order to Escape God's Wrath and Curse on Sin?

> The use of them is most necessary, because we are commanded by God to make use of them. Every thing which he hath commanded is most necessary, both with respect to himself and with respect to us;—with respect to himself, to show his authority and his love; and with respect to us, to show our love to him, and our regard for his word and authority.[71]

Appendix:

How Does Larger Catechism Q. 70 Relate to Larger Catechism Q. 153?

> Justification is an act of God's free grace unto sinners, in which he pardoneth all their sins, accepteth and accounteth their persons righteous in his sight; not for anything wrought in them, or done by them, but only for the perfect obedience and full satisfaction of Christ, by God imputed to them, and *received by faith alone.* (Q. 70. Emphasis added)

> That we may escape the wrath and curse of God due to us by reason of the transgression of the law, he requireth of us repentance toward God, and faith toward our Lord Jesus Christ, and the diligent use of the outward means whereby Christ communicates to us the benefits of his mediation. (Q. 153)

Some would try to play these two answers against each other as if they contradicted each other. LCQ. 70 teaches us that our sins are pardoned and we are accepted with God *by faith alone.* LCQ. 153 states that to escape the wrath and curse of God due to us because of our sinfulness, God not only requires of us faith in Christ, but He also *requires of us repentance... and the diligent use of the outward*

---

71. Paterson, *A Concise System of Theology on the Basis of the Shorter Catechism*, 264.

means. Do these two answers contradict each other or supplement one another? The context of LCQ. 70 is LCQ. 153. LCQ. 153 is the "big picture" and LCQ. 70 is a "frame" in that picture. LCQ. 70 is concerned with one aspect of the order of salvation, *i.e.*, justification. LCQ. 153 is concerned with the entirety of the application of salvation to us, *i.e.*, regeneration, effectual calling, justification, adoption, sanctification and glorification.

The faith by which we are justified is not dead faith. It is a living faith that manifests itself in repentance, obedience to God and an earnest desire to benefit from all the means of grace appointed by God for our spiritual growth. This repentance, diligent obedience, and spiritual desire are the *means* by which God applies His salvation to our lives and the *evidences,* not only that our faith is true, but that we do in fact possess salvation. Moreover, they are not only internal means of saving grace, they are a part of the salvation that is ours by grace.

> For by grace you have been saved through faith; and that not of yourselves, it is the gift of God (Eph. 2:8).
>
> He is the one whom God exalted to His right hand as a Prince and a Savior, to grant repentance to Israel, and forgiveness of sins (Acts 5:31).
>
> And we are witnesses of these things; and so is the Holy Spirit, whom God has given to those who obey Him (Acts 5:32).

James Fisher and Ebenezer Erskine, in their "catechism" on the Westminster Shorter Catechism, give us these helpful remarks on the issue we are considering.

> *Q. Can we [escape the wrath and curse of God, due to us for sin] by anything we can do of ourselves?* A. No, surely; for "all our righteousnesses are as filthy rags," Isa. lxiv:6; and, "by the works of the Law, shall no flesh be justified," Gal. ii:16.
>
> *Q. Why then does the answer say, that to escape the wrath and curse of God, due to us for sin, [God requires of us, faith in Jesus Christ, repentance unto life, and a diligent use of all*

the outward means]? A. Because, though these duties, as performed by us, can neither give a title to, nor possession of eternal life; yet God appoints and requires them, both as they are *means* of conveying and improving the salvation purchased, 1 Cor. 1:21, and likewise, as they are *evidences* of our interest in it, when conveyed, John vi:47.

Q. Why does God require [faith in Jesus Christ] as the sovereign means of escaping His wrath and curse? A. Because there is salvation in no other; there being "no other name under heaven, given among men, whereby we must be saved," Acts iv:12.

Q. Why is [repentance unto life] required? A. Because it is the inseparable fruit and effect of faith or believing, Zech. xii:10....

Q. Why does God require of us [the diligent use of all the outward means whereby Christ communicates to us the benefits of redemption]? A. Because a neglect or contempt of the means of divine appointment for communicating the benefits of redemption, is, in the sight of God, the same thing as a neglect or contempt of these inestimable benefits themselves, Luke x:16.

Q. Can our believing, repenting and diligent use of means, as they are acts of ours, be the procuring cause of our escaping wrath, or found [be the basis for] our title to life and salvation? A. No; for "by the deeds of the law, there shall no flesh be justified in His sight," Rom. iii:20. Our security from wrath and our title to heaven, are founded on the imputation of the surety righteousness [of Christ] alone, Isa. xlv:25.

Q. What would be the consequence of making our faith, repentance, and good works, the procuring cause of our escaping the wrath and curse of God due to us for sin? A. This would be setting aside the satisfaction of Christ, and making a saviour of our duties, than which nothing could nail us more effectually down under the curse, Gal. iii:10.

Q. Is our escaping the wrath and curse of God suspended on the condition of our faith, repentance, and diligent use of the outward means? A. No; for, if any promised blessing were suspended upon the condition of our personal obedience, it would be the very form of the covenant of works, Rom. x:5.

Q. What connexion does faith, repentance, and the use of outward means, have with salvation? A. They have the connection of appointed means prescribed by God himself, which, by his blessing, are subservient for such a valuable end; being themselves a part of salvation, and evidences of it, 2 Thess. ii:13.

Q. How is faith in Jesus Christ connected with salvation? A. As it is the hand that receives Christ and His righteousness, as the all of our salvation, Ps. lxviii:31; John i:12.

Q. How is repentance unto life connected with salvation? A. As it consists in that godly sorrow for sin, flowing from faith, which is both the exercise and ornament (in some measure) of all the travelers Zion-ward, while in this world, Jer. l:4; 2 Cor. vii:11.

Q. How is the diligent use of outward means connected with salvation? A. As it is by them that [Christ communicates to us the benefits of redemption], Prov. ii:1–16.[72]

72. Fisher, *Fisher's Catechism*, 146–48.

CHAPTER THIRTY-FIVE

The Saving Power of the Reading and Preaching of the Word of God

"To neglect either of these [reading and preaching of the Word] is to despise our own souls, and deprive ourselves of the advantage of God's instituted means of grace."

~Thomas Ridgeley

FOR WHATEVER WAS WRITTEN IN EARLIER TIMES WAS WRITTEN FOR OUR INSTRUCTION, SO THAT THROUGH PERSEVERANCE AND THE ENCOURAGEMENT OF THE SCRIPTURES WE MIGHT HAVE HOPE.

ROMANS 15:4

The Saving Power of the Reading and Preaching of the Word of God

---

Q. 154: What are the outward means whereby Christ communicates to us the benefits of his mediation?

A.: The outward and ordinary means whereby Christ communicates to his church the benefits of his mediation, are all his ordinances; especially the word, sacraments, and prayer; all which are made effectual to the elect for their salvation.

Q. 155: How is the word made effectual to salvation?

A.: The Spirit of God maketh the reading, but especially the preaching of the word, an effectual means of enlightening, convincing, and humbling sinners; of driving them out of themselves, and drawing them unto Christ; of conforming them to his image, and subduing them to his will; of strengthening them against temptations and corruptions; of building them up in grace, and establishing their hearts in holiness and comfort through faith unto salvation.

Q. 156: Is the word of God to be read by all?

A.: Although all are not to be permitted to read the word publickly to the congregation, yet all sorts of people are bound to read it apart by themselves, and with their families: to which end, the holy scriptures are to be translated out of the original into vulgar languages.

Q. 157: How is the word of God to be read?

A.: The holy scriptures are to be read with an high and reverent esteem of them; with a firm persuasion that they are the very word of God, and that he only can enable us to understand them; with desire to know, believe, and obey the will of God revealed in them; with diligence, and attention to the matter and scope of them; with meditation, application, self-denial, and prayer.

Q. 158: By whom is the word of God to be preached?

A.: The word of God is to be preached only by such as are sufficiently gifted, and also duly approved and called to that office.

Q. 159: How is the word of God to be preached by those that are called thereunto?

A.: They that are called to labour in the ministry of the word, are to preach sound doctrine, diligently, in season and out of season; plainly, not in the enticing words of man's wisdom, but in demonstration of the Spirit, and of power; faithfully, making known the whole counsel of God: wisely, applying themselves to the necessities and capacities of the hearers; zealously, with fervent love to God and the souls of his people; sincerely, aiming at his glory, and their conversion, edification, and salvation.

Q. 160: What is required of those that hear the word preached?

A.: It is required of those that hear the word preached, that they attend upon it with diligence, preparation, and prayer; examine what they hear by the scriptures; receive the truth with faith, love, meekness, and readiness of mind, as the word of God; meditate, and confer of it; hide it in their hearts, and bring forth the fruit of it in their lives.

The Vital Importance of the Reading and Preaching of the Bible

> To neglect either of these is to despise our own souls, and deprive ourselves of the advantage of God's instituted means of grace. Hence, we are not to content ourselves with merely the reading of the word of God in our closet or families, but we must embrace all opportunities for hearing it preached in a public manner, the one being no less an ordinance of God than the other.[1]

Understanding Sin and Salvation is Vital to Appreciating the Reading and Preaching of the Bible

> Every sin, even the least, being against the sovereignty, goodness, and holiness of God, and against his righteous law, deserveth his wrath and curse, both in this life, and that which is to come; and cannot be expiated but by the blood of Christ. (WLC, Q. 152)

---

1. Thomas Ridgeley, *Commentary on the Larger Catechism*, 2 vols. (Edmonton, Canada: Still Waters Revival Books, [1855] 1993), 2:444.

A high and proper appreciation of Bible reading and preaching is impossible without a true understanding of the consequences of sin and the salvation from sin we have in Jesus Christ.[2] Sin, *i.e.*, any lack of conformity to or transgression of the Law of God, is so heinous in the sight of God that even the smallest of sins is not only a violation of the Law of God, but it is so offensive to His holiness that His anger burns against it: "For the wrath of God is revealed from heaven against all ungodliness and unrighteousness of men" (Rom. 1:18). Anybody who commits any sin whatever stands guilty before God and deserving of His just punishment (Rom. 3:23; 6:23).

Because sin is an offense to the character and perfections of God, and a violation of His revealed Law, all sin deserves His anger, curse, condemnation and punishment in this life and after death. Furthermore, man can do nothing to save himself from the punishment his sins deserve, from sin itself, or from its consequences. The good news of the gospel of the Bible is that "nothing can take away the guilt of sin, but the atonement made by Christ.... This punishment cannot be expiated any otherwise than by the blood of Christ."[3] The substitutionary, propitiatory, sacrificial death of Jesus Christ satisfied God's justice which demanded punishment for broken law and turned away God's anger from those for whom Christ died thus redeeming God's people from their sins and reconciling them to God: "and not through the blood of goats and calves, but through His own blood, He entered the holy place, once-for-all, having obtained eternal redemption" (Heb. 9:12).

The Way to Escape the Curse of God Due to Us for Our Sin

> That we may escape the wrath and curse of God due to us by reason of the transgression of the law, he requireth of us repentance toward God, and faith toward our Lord Jesus Christ, and the diligent use of the outward means whereby

2. This topic is discussed at length in the commentary on WLC, Q. 152-153, but is revisited here as it specifically pertains to the means of grace, especially the *word*.

3. Ridgeley, *Commentary on the Larger Catechism*, 2:431.

Christ communicates to us the benefits of his mediation. (WLC, Q. 153)

Having set forth the truth that the only basis for the removal of the sinner's guilt and the satisfaction of God's justice is *the blood of Christ,* (Question 152), the Catechism now explains the divinely ordained way by which a person may escape the wrath of God due him for his sins.

If Jesus Christ fully and perfectly turned away God's anger from all His people, reconciling them to God, once-and-for-all saving them from sin and all its consequences, how can it be said that by means of faith,[4] repentance[5] and the diligent use of the means of grace, we may escape the wrath and curse of God?

God commands repentance, faith, and the diligent use of the means of grace, not to complete Christ's expiation of sin, nor to merit salvation in some manner, but as the way to salvation from sin. Faith, repentance and diligence are gifts of God's grace and the effects of the regenerating, sanctifying work of the Holy Spirit—God gives the salvation and the means he has commanded of us to receive salvation. "The graces of faith and repentance [and diligence] are necessary to evidence our interest in what He has done and suffered for us and are inseparably connected with salvation; though they do not give us a right and title to eternal life, as Christ's righteousness does."[6]

The Diligent Use of the Means of Grace

Q. 154: What are the outward means whereby Christ communicates to us the benefits of his mediation?

4. Faith in Jesus Christ is a saving grace, whereby we receive and rest upon him alone for salvation, as he is offered to us in the gospel (WSC, Q. 86).

5. Repentance unto life is a saving grace, whereby a sinner, out of a true sense of his sin, and apprehension of the mercy of God in Christ, doth, with grief and hatred of his sin, turn from it unto God, will full purpose of, and endeavour after, new obedience (WSC, Q. 87).

6. Ridgeley, *Commentary on the Larger Catechism*, 2:432.

A.: The outward and ordinary means whereby Christ communicates to his church the benefits of his mediation, are all his ordinances; especially the word, sacraments, and prayer; all which are made effectual to the elect for their salvation.

The diligent use of the external means of grace is also required of us if we are to escape the wrath of God. These means of grace include *all His ordinances, i.e.,* whatever He has commanded of us in the Bible (Matt. 28:20), but *especially* those means of grace include *the word, sacraments, and prayer* (Matt. 28:19–20; Acts 2:42, 46, 47). And it should be noted that it is the *diligent* use of God's means of saving grace that is emphasized in the answer to Question 153. We must not use them in a careless, haphazard or indifferent manner, as though we neither expected nor desired to receive anything from God through them. Diligence implies taking advantage of every opportunity to use these means of grace, and earnestly desiring and expecting God's grace through these means.

Why are we to be *diligent* in our use of *the word, sacraments and prayer*? Because these are the means *whereby Christ communicates to us the benefits of His mediation.* Means of grace are not only Christian *duties* performed in obedience to God, who instituted them as the way He desires to be worshipped and served by His creatures, they are also *promises* from God by which He assures His people of His presence and His blessing: "where I cause My name to be remembered, I will come to you and bless you" (Ex. 20:24). He encourages His people to observe them diligently in the hope and faith that through them God will bring His presence and blessings into their lives. As God works grace through them, they are called "means of grace;" and

> as he seldom works grace without first inclining persons to attend on Him in them, and wait for his salvation, they are called the "ordinary" means of grace; and as they have not in themselves a tendency to work grace, without the inward and powerful influences of the Holy Spirit accompanying them,

> they are distinguished from it, and accordingly styled the outward means of grace.[7]
>
> The use of them [the outward means of grace] is most necessary, because we are commanded by God to make use of them. Every thing which he hath commanded is most necessary, both with respect to himself and with respect to us;—with respect to himself, to show his authority and his love; and with respect to us, to show our love to him, and our regard for his word and authority.[8]

The Saving Effects of the Reading and Preaching of the Bible

Q. 155: How is the word made effectual to salvation?

A.: The Spirit of God maketh the reading, but especially the preaching of the word, an effectual means of enlightening, convincing, and humbling sinners; of driving them out of themselves, and drawing them unto Christ; of conforming them to his image, and subduing them to his will; of strengthening them against temptations and corruptions; of building them up in grace, and establishing their hearts in holiness and comfort through faith unto salvation.

One of the fundamental emphases of Biblical and Reformed Christianity is the unity of the Holy Spirit and the Word of God. The Holy Spirit works in us with the Word of God; and the Word of God

7. Ridgeley, *Commentary on the Larger Catechism*, 2:433.

8. Alexander S. Paterson, *A Concise System of Theology on the Basis of the Shorter Catechism* (New York: Obert Carter and Brothers, 1856), 264.

is powerless in us without the Holy Spirit. Hence the Bible is called "the sword of the Spirit, which is the Word of God" (Eph. 6:17).

Since saving grace is a gift of the Spirit, since God's Spiritual gifts are also gifts of His grace, and since the Spirit works in unity with the Word, therefore, the Holy Spirit makes the reading and preaching of the Word effective as a means of saving grace in His people, *enlightening, convincing, and humbling...driving them out of themselves...drawing them to Christ...conforming them in his image...subduing them to his will...strengthening them...building them up in grace...establishing their hearts.*

How does the Holy Spirit make the reading and preaching of the Word of God an effective means of saving grace to us and in us from Christ?

The Enlightening of the Inner Life

> The commandment of the LORD is pure,
> Enlightening the eyes (Ps. 19:8).

By these words, the psalmist is teaching us that it is only by the Biblical revelation that

> we find the difference between good and evil laid down, and that it is in vain to seek it elsewhere, since whatever men devise of themselves is mere filth and refuse, corrupting the purity of the life. He farther intimates that men, with all their acuteness, are blind, and always wander in darkness, until they turn their eyes to the light of heavenly doctrine. Whence it follows, that none are truly wise but those who take God for their conductor and guide, following the path which he points out to them, and who are diligently seeking after the peace which he offers and presents by his Word.[9]

The resurrected Christ called Paul to be an apostle and minister of the Word of God to the Gentiles, by his witnessing, preaching

---

9. John Calvin, *Commentaries on the Book of Psalms*, 5 vols. (Edinburgh: Calvin Translation Society, 1843; reprint Grand Rapids, MI: Baker Book House, 1979), 1:321.

and teaching of that Word "to open their eyes so that they may turn from darkness to light and from the dominion of Satan to God" (Acts 26:18). Only the Spirit of God can open the eyes of the spiritually blind and turn them from darkness to light. But here the apostle and minister Paul is said to open eyes and to turn men from darkness to light and from the tyranny of Satan to God. Such expressions are not unusual in the Bible, for

> God doth translates unto his ministers that honour which is due to himself alone, not that he may take anything from himself, but that he may commend that mighty working of his Spirit which he does show forth in them. For he doth not send them to work, that they may be dead instruments, or, as it were, stage-players; but that He may work mightily by their hand. But it dependeth upon the secret power of his Spirit that their preaching is effective, who worketh all things in all men, and which only giveth the increase. Therefore, teachers are sent, not to utter their words in vain in the air, or to beat the ears only with a vain sound, but to bring lively light to the blind, to fashion again men's hearts unto the righteousness of God, and to ratify the grace of salvation which is gotten by the death of Christ. But they do none of all these, save only inasmuch as God works by them, that their labour may not be in vain, that all the praise may be his, as the effect comes from Him.[10]

> By the Word the mind is *enlightened* and furnished with the knowledge of divine truths, which is a very great privilege [Neh. 8:8; Acts 26:18. "The commandment of the LORD is pure, enlightening the eyes" (Ps. 19:8)]. As faith is inseparably connected with salvation, so the knowledge of the doctrines of the gospel is necessary to faith, and this is said to "come by hearing" [Rom. 10:17]. We must not content ourselves, however, with a mere assent to what is revealed in the

10. John Calvin, *Commentary upon the Acts of the Apostles*, trans. by Christopher Fetherstone, ed. by Henry Beveridge, 2 vols. (Edinburgh: Calvin Translation Society, 1843; reprint Grand Rapids, MI: Baker Book House, 1979), 2:380–81.

> word of God; but must duly weigh the tendency of it to our sanctification and consolation, and admire the beauty, excellency, and glory that there is in the great doctrines of the gospel, as the divine perfections shine forth in them to the utmost.—And when we find our hearts filled with love to Jesus Christ, in proportion to those greater measures of light which He is pleased to impart to us, so that we grow in grace as well as in the knowledge of our Lord and Savior Jesus Christ, then the word may be said to be made effectual to our salvation, as our minds are very much enlightened and improved in the knowledge of those things which lead to it.[11]

The Conviction of Sin

> But if all prophesy, and an unbeliever or an ungifted man enters, he is convicted by all, he is called to account by all; the secrets of his heart are disclosed; and so he will fall on his face and worship God, declaring that God is certainly among you (1 Cor. 14:24–25).

Although 1 Corinthians 14 is a difficult chapter to understand, since it deals with miraculous gifts of the Spirit that ceased with the Apostolic Age, almost two thousand years ago,[12] the main point made in these verses is a clear and an important one: when an unbeliever hears the prophetic word, *i.e.*, the preaching of the verbal and inerrant revelation from God, under the convicting work of the Holy Spirit, what he hears comes with conviction to his heart and mind. The Spirit convinces him of the truth of what he has heard, convicts him of his sin, and of his need of Christ's righteousness and of God's judgment on sin, and convinces him that Jesus Christ is the Son of the living God:

> And He, [the Holy Spirit sent by Christ], when He comes, will convict the world concerning sin, and righteousness and

11. Ridgeley, *Commentary on the Larger Catechism*, 2:444–45.

12. For a helpful exposition of 1 Corinthians 12–14, see Charles Hodge's *A Commentary on The First Epistle to the Corinthians* in the Geneva Commentary Series published by The Banner of Truth Trust.

> judgment: concerning sin, because they do not believe in Me [Jesus]; and concerning righteousness, because I go to the Father... and concerning judgment, because the ruler of this world [Satan] has been judged (John 16:8–11).

That convicted hearer is searched and tried by the Word of God, which discerns the thoughts and intentions of the heart (Heb. 4:12).

> The result of this searching examination is, *that the secrets of his heart are made manifest*; that is, they are revealed to himself. His real character and moral state, with regard to which he was before ignorant, are made known to him. The effect of this is humility, contrition, self-condemnation, and turning unto God.[13]

"And so he will fall on his face and worship God, declaring that God is certainly among you" (1 Cor.14:25).

> The first step in religion is entire self-abasement; such a conviction of sin, *i.e.*, of guilt and pollution, as shall lead to self-condemnation and self-abhorrence, and to a complete renunciation of all dependence on our own righteousness and strength. When the soul is thus humbled God reveals himself sooner or later, in mercy, manifesting himself as reconciled in Jesus Christ; and then we *worship him*. This expresses reverence, love and confidence. It is the return of the soul to the favour and fellowship of God. One who has had such an experience cannot keep it to himself. The apostle therefore describes the convert as *declaring, i.e., proclaiming aloud that God is in you of a truth.*[14]

As Leon Morris has instructed us,

> The effect of the prophetic word is to reveal to the man his state. His whole inner being is searched out. Those things he

13. Charles Hodge, *A Commentary on the First Epistle to the Corinthians* (London: The Banner of Truth Trust, [1958] 1964), 298.

14. Hodge, *A Commentary on the First Epistle to the Corinthians*, 298–99.

fondly imagined to be locked within *his heart* he finds reproved and judged, and he can only ascribe this to the activity of God. The exercise of prophesy results thus in the man coming to *worship God,* and to recognize the presence of God in His Church.[15]

The Humbling of the Sinner

> Now in the eighteenth year of his [King Josiah's] reign, when he had purged the land and the House, he sent Shaphan the son of Azaliah...to repair the House of the LORD his God.... When they were bringing out the money which had been brought into the House of the LORD, Hilkiah the priest found the Book of the Law of the LORD given by Moses.... Moreover, Shaphan the scribe told the king saying, "Hilkiah the priest gave me a book." And Shaphan read from it in the presence of the king. And it came about when the king heard the words of the Law that he tore his clothes. Then the king commanded Hilkiah... saying, "Go, inquire of the LORD for me and for those who are left in Israel and in Judah, concerning the words of the Book which has been found; for great is the wrath of the LORD which is poured out on us because our fathers have not observed the Word of the LORD, to do according to all that is written in this Book." So Hilkiah and those whom the king had told went to Huldah the prophetess... [and she said with reference to king Josiah] "Because your heart was tender and you humbled yourself before God, when you heard His words against this place and against its inhabitants, and because you humbled yourself before Me, and wept before Me, I truly have heard you," declares the LORD (2 Chron. 34:8–27).

Godly King Josiah of Judah was convicted and humbled by the reading of the Word of God, which was probably the book of Deuteronomy, which had been lost in the Temple until Josiah had begun

15. Leon Morris, *The First Epistle of Paul to the Corinthians: An Introduction and Commentary* (London: The Tyndale Press, [1958] 1966), 198.

its renovation. Thus the written Word of God is made effective by the Spirit in the applying of saving grace to God's people

> when what is contained in it tends to HUMBLE us and lay us low at the foot of God;when we acknowledge that all His judgments are right, or whatever punishments have been inflicted in execution of the threatenings which He has denounced have been less than our iniquities deserve; and when we receive reproofs for sins committed, with a particular application of them to ourselves, and are sensible of the guilt we have contracted.[16]

> We may hence learn, whenever we read or hear the word of God, to affect our hearts with it, and to get them possessed with a holy fear of that wrath of God which is there revealed against all ungodliness and unrighteousness of men, as Josiah's tender heart was. When he heard the words of the Law he "rent his clothes" (v. 19), and God was well pleased with his doing (v. 27). Were the things contained in the Scripture new to us, as they were here to Josiah, surely they would make deeper impressions upon us than commonly they do; but they are not the less weighty, and therefore should not be the less considered by us, for their being well know. Rend the heart therefore, not the garments.[17]

The Driving of Sinners Out of Themselves and Drawing Them to Jesus Christ

> "Therefore let all the house of Israel know for certain that God has made Him both Lord and Christ—this Jesus whom you crucified." Now when they heard this, they were pierced to the heart, and said to Peter and the rest of the apostles, "Brethren, what shall we do?"... Then they that gladly received his Word were baptized (Acts 2:36, 37, 41).

16. Ridgeley, *Commentary on the Larger Catechism*, 2:445.

17. Matthew Henry, *Matthew Henry's Commentary on the Whole Bible*, 6 vols. (Peabody, MA: Hendrickson Publishers, [1991] 1992), 2:786.

> But an angel of the Lord spoke to Philip saying, "Arise and go south to the road that descends from Jerusalem to Gaza. (This is a desert road.) And he arose and went; and behold, there was an Ethiopian eunuch, a court official of Candace, queen of the Ethiopians, who was in charge of all her treasure; and he had come to Jerusalem to worship. And he was returning and sitting in his chariot and was reading the prophet Isaiah. And the Spirit said to Philip, "Go up and join this chariot." And when Philip had run up, he heard him reading Isaiah the prophet, and said, "Do you understand what you are reading?" And he said, "Well, how could I, unless someone guides me?" And he invited Philip to come up and sit with him.... And Philip opened his mouth, and beginning from this Scripture he preached Jesus to him.... And he answered and said, "I believe that Jesus Christ is the Son of God." And he ordered the chariot to stop; and they both went down into the water, Philip as well as the eunuch; and he baptized him (Acts 8:26–38).

What we observe in both of these New Testament texts is how the Word of God is made effective in applying saving grace in that it has the Spirit-wrought power to *drive sinners out of themselves* and to *draw them to Jesus Christ* for salvation from sin. The Word of God does this, on the one hand, by showing them the utter impossibility of saving themselves by doing anything which might merit for them justification with God; and, on the other hand, by drawing and leading them to Christ, whom they are enabled by the Spirit to receive by faith as their Lord and Savior, as He is revealed in the gospel. "Thus Christ is set forth in the gospel; and when the word is made effectual to salvation, the soul is induced, or, as it were, constrained to love him, and to yield the obedience of faith to him in all things."[18]

---

18. Ridgeley, *Commentary on the Larger Catechism*, 2:447.

The Conforming of the Soul to the Image of God

> But to this day whenever Moses is read, a veil lies over their heart; "but whenever a man turns to the Lord, the veil is taken away." Now the Lord is the Spirit; and where the Spirit of the Lord is, there is liberty. But we all, with unveiled face beholding as in a mirror the glory of the Lord, are being transformed into the same image from glory to glory, just as from the Lord, the Spirit (2 Cor. 3:15–18).

Sin has defaced the image of God in us so that mankind is now hostile to God and in rebellion against Him. Sin has made man abominable and filthy in God's sight. As long as a person remains under the curse of sin, all communion with God is impossible.

> Now, when the Spirit of God communicates special grace to sinners, he stamps this image afresh upon the soul, which he renews in knowledge, righteousness and holiness; he sanctifies all its powers and faculties, and subdues the will, so that it yields a cheerful obedience to the will of God.[19]

The passage quoted above from 2 Corinthians 3 makes this point powerfully. When the Biblical revelation is read and the Spirit removes the "veil" of unbelief from the hearers, it effectively reveals "the glory of the Lord" to the believer's heart, which has the effect of causing him progressively to be "transformed into the same image from glory to glory" in the power of the Spirit of the Lord.

The Subduing of the Soul to the Will of God

> But thanks be to God that though you were slaves of sin, you became obedient from the heart to that form of teaching to which you were committed, and having been freed from sin, you became slaves of righteousness (Rom. 6:17–18).

The believer in Jesus had undergone the most extensive and amazing transformation possible for a human being to experience

---

19. Ridgeley, *Commentary on the Larger Catechism*, 2:447.

in this life. He has undergone a change of character and of his entire inner life. He has experienced a change of "heart," and not merely of emotions or of intellect. What he was, he is no more. He was a slave to sin, now he is freed from the tyranny and has been liberated to live in obedience to God as a willing and glad slave of righteousness.

This change is accomplished by God Himself using His Word, *i.e.*, His "form of teaching." This "form of teaching" is the full doctrine Paul has been elaborating in Romans and nothing less (2 Tim. 1:13; 6:20). God pours us into the "mould" ("form") of the Word of God and then causes its promises, laws, truths and threats to work on us in the power of the Holy Spirit, shaping us more and more, from the inside out, into the image of Christ (Rom. 8:29).

The evidence that this change in slaveries has taken place in us is our "becoming obedient from the heart to that form of teaching" "into which we were poured," so that we are not "slaves of righteousness." *Now our hearts have been subdued to the will of God.* Now we yield to God out of gratitude for Christ cheerful obedience to His revealed will, and we delight in His Law. Our heart's prayer is, "Speak, Lord, for Thy servant heareth."

Using the imagery of warfare, the apostle Paul teaches us that the Word of God is a "divinely powerful weapon" (2 Cor. 10:4). It is in fact "the Sword of the Spirit" (Eph. 6:17). By the proper use of that weapon of the Word of God, we, as believers are "destroying speculations and every lofty thing raised up against the knowledge of God, *and we are taking every thought captive to the obedience of Christ,* and we are ready to punish all disobedience, whenever your obedience is complete" (2 Cor. 10:5–6; emphasis added).

The Strengthening of the Heart Against Temptation

> Moreover, by them [the revealed words of God]
> Thy servant is warned;
> In keeping them there is great reward (Ps. 19:11).

> In addition to all, taking up the shield of faith with which you will be able to extinguish all the flaming missiles of the evil

> one. And take the helmet of salvation, and the sword of the Spirit, which is the word of God (Eph. 6:16–17).

The Word of God has the power to strengthen and fortify the believer's heart against temptation and the corruption of sin. By it God's servants are "warned." In Psalm 19:11, David is describing the practical influence of God's Word on his life: it has warned him of evil and thereby protected him from evil. By his own example he sets forth this principle:

> If persons wish to have a proper method for governing the life well, the law of God alone is perfectly sufficient for this purpose; but that, on the contrary, as soon as persons depart from it, they are liable to fall into numerous errors and sins... he who yields himself to God to be governed by him is made circumspect and cautious."[20]

Furthermore, although Satan hurls temptations to sin at us with the force of "flaming missiles," nevertheless believers can deflect and "extinguish" them by "the shield of faith" in the Word of God, by "the helmet of salvation," *i.e.*, grateful meditation on the salvation revealed in "the Sword of the Spirit, which is the Word of God." The Sword which the Spirit gives the believer is what God has spoken, *i.e.*, the entire written Word of God.

> This is sharper than any two-edged sword. It is the wisdom of God and the power of God. It has a self-evidencing light. It commends itself to the reason and conscience. It has the power not only of truth, but of divine truth. Our Lord promised to give to His disciples a word and wisdom which all their adversaries should not be able to gainsay or resist. In opposition to all error, to all false philosophy, to all false principles of morals, to all sophistries of vice, to all the suggestions of the devil, the sole, simple and sufficient answer is the word of God. This puts to flight all the powers of darkness. The Christians finds this to be true in his individual experience. It dissipates his doubts; it drives away his fears; it

20. Calvin, *Commentaries on the Book of Psalms*, 1:325.

> delivers him from the power of Satan. It is also the experience of the church collective. All her triumphs over sin and error have been effected by the word of God. So long as she uses this and relies on it alone, she goes on conquering; but when any thing else, be it reason, science, tradition, or the commandments of men, is allowed to take its place or to share its office, then the church, or the Christian, is at the mercy of the adversary.[21]

This was the method of Jesus Himself in resisting the temptations of Satan in the Wilderness. With each Satanic temptation, Jesus resisted temptation and repelled the tempter simply by believing and quoting the Word of God (Matt. 4:1–11). When tempted to satisfy his hunger and turn the rocks into bread, Jesus said, "It is written, 'Man shall not live on bread alone, but on every word that proceeds out of the mouth of God.'" When tempted to throw Himself off the pinnacle of the Temple to prove His power, Jesus answered, "It is written, 'You shall not tempt the Lord your God.'" And when tempted to submit to Satan in order to receive universal sovereignty over the nations without facing the cross, Jesus said, "Begone, Satan! For it is written, 'You shall worship the Lord your God, and serve Him only.'" And Satan's response to Christ's resistance of Him with the Word of God is described in verse 11: "Then the devil left Him." Jesus could quote the Word of God so specifically and pointedly, because He devotedly read and studied the Word of God, and hence it strengthened His human heart against temptations and the corruptions of sin and Satan.

Anything that has a tendency to alienate us and our affections from God is a temptation. Temptations corrupt us when we embrace them and give in to them. The Holy Spirit uses the Word of God to strengthen us against temptation and corruption by helping us detect the fallacies of temptations, the treacherous schemes of Satan, and the dangerous tendencies in them. He then fortifies us against them,

---

21. Charles Hodge, *A Commentary on Ephesians* (Grand Rapids, MI: William B. Eerdmans Publishing Co., n.d.), 389.

> by presenting other and better objects to engage our affections, and leading us to the knowledge of those glorious truths which may prevent a sinful compliance with the solicitations of the devil. According to the nature of the temptation which may occur, we are directed to the precepts or promises contained in the Word of God, which, being duly improved by us [*i.e.*, put into practice by us], have a tendency to keep the heart steady and fixed in the ways of God.[22]

The Building Up of the Soul in Grace

> And now I commend you to God and to the word of His grace[23], which is able to build[24] you up and to give you the inheritance[25] among all those who are sanctified[26] (Acts 20:32).

Paul is bidding farewell to the church in Ephesus. Paul will no longer be there in person for pastoral guidance and wise counsel.

> But, though Paul might go, God was ever with them, and so was God's word which they had received—the word that proclaimed His grace in redeeming them and His grace in sanctifying them. To God, then, and to this word of His, Paul solemnly committed them. By that word, as they accepted and obeyed it, they would be built up in faith and love together with their fellow-Christians; by that word, too, they were as-

22. Ridgeley, *Commentary on the Larger Catechism*, 2:447.

23. "The word of God's grace" means that the written Word of God is the instrument of God by which He accomplishes what is ascribed to it: the salvation of sinners by grace.

24. "Build up," or "edify," is one of Paul's favorite expressions to signify the progress of sanctification and maturation in the believer's heart and life toward the planned goal God has for him. See 1 Cor. 3:10; 12:14; Eph. 2:20; Col. 2:7; Jude 20.

25. "Inheritance" denotes the possession of the believer of all the rights and privileges of sons of God.

26. The "sanctified" has reference to those who have by God's gracious calling been separated from the world to God, who have been called out of darkness into life, and who are being made holy by the sanctifying Spirit, as the very goal of their salvation.

> sured of their inheritance among all the people of God, sanctified by His grace. In due course Paul and all the apostles passed from earthly life; but the apostolic teaching which they left behind as a sacred deposit to be guarded by their successors, preserved not merely in the memory of their hearers but in the Scriptures of the NT canon, remains with us to this day as the word of God's grace. And those are most truly in apostolic succession who receive this apostolic teaching, along with the rest of Holy Writ, as their rule of faith and practice.[27]

> Grow in the grace and knowledge of our Lord and Savior Jesus Christ. To Him be the glory, both now and to the day of eternity. Amen (2 Pet. 3:18).

The Christian life is a process of growth that is gradual and progressive, and which begins with regeneration. It is a growth in "the grace and knowledge of our Lord and Savior Jesus Christ." This means that, now, we, as believers in Jesus, are in the realm where grace reigns (Rom. 3:21–26). In that realm of God's unmerited favor, we

> grow in the life into which [we] have been brought by the death of Christ and His resurrection, and as a result of His grace develop and expand and increase and go forward... to be a Christian means that I am the special object of God's favour and kindness.... The more I live the Christian life, the more obedient I am, the more will I experience the favour of God. That is growing in the grace of the Lord Jesus Christ.... But I am also to grow in "the knowledge of the Lord Jesus Christ." What does it mean? That is Peter's way of saying that I am to grow in my understanding of the truth.... It means that I should increase and grow in my knowledge concerning Him, in my knowledge of what He has done and of what He has brought to this world.... But I think that, in addition, it

27. F. F. Bruce, *The New International Commentary on the New Testament: Commentary on the Book of the Acts* (Grand Rapids, MI: William B. Eerdmans Publishing Co., [1954] 1964), 417–18.

means this: not only the knowledge concerning Him, but a knowledge of Him. I must grow in my knowledge of the Lord Jesus Christ, by which is meant my communion with Him; my sense of a personal relationship to Him must increase.... Why is it thus important for us to grow in both these main respects? The answer is, of course, that it is the only way to stand firm and solid, and it is the only way to meet the contradictions of this life and of this world. The more I know the favour of Christ the more I shall be able to smile in the face of adversity.[28]

The Establishing of the Heart in Holiness and Comfort Through Faith Unto Salvation

Now to Him who is able to *establish*[29] you according to my gospel and the preaching of Jesus Christ (Rom. 16:25; emphasis added).

And we sent Timothy, our brother and God's fellow-worker in the gospel of Christ, to *strengthen and encourage*[30] you as to your faith...as we night and day keep praying most earnestly that we may see your face, and may *complete what is lacking*[31] in your faith. Now may our God and Father Himself

28. Martyn Lloyd-Jones, *Expository Sermons on 2 Peter* (Edinburgh: The Banner of Truth Trust, 1983), 226–27.

29. "Establish" here refers to the stabilizing, fortifying, and confirming of believers by the apostolic word of the gospel so that they will not be victims of Satan's schemes, and be seduced away from the gospel by deceivers and false teachers.

30. "Strengthen and encourage" have reference to the effect of Paul's preaching on the Thessalonian church. "To strengthen" has the idea of establishing or putting in a buttress or support or firm foundation. "To encourage" means "to call to the side of" a person to help or strengthen. So then, Timothy's visit and preaching was "for the purpose of buttressing their faith. He came to encourage them with a view to the strengthening of their faith" (Leon Morris, *The New International Commentary on the New Testament: The First and Second Epistles to the Thessalonians* [Grand Rapids, MI: William B. Eerdmans Publishing Co., (1959) 1964], 100–101).

31. Paul's preaching would "complete what is lacking in your faith," *i.e.*, in the faith of the Thessalonian Christians. In Paul's joy at the faith of his new converts, "he was not oblivious to the sterner realities of the situation. His desire to be with

> and Jesus our Lord direct our way to you; and may the Lord cause you to increase and abound in love for one another, and for all men, just as we also do for you; so that He may *establish your hearts unblameable in holiness*[32] before our God and Father at the coming of our Lord Jesus with all His saints (1 Thess. 3:2, 10–13; emphasis added).

> For whatever was written in earlier times was written for our instruction, that through perseverance and the *encouragement of the Scriptures we might have hope* (Rom. 15:4; emphasis added).

All of these NT texts speak of the effectiveness of the written and preached Word of God to "establish" us, to "strengthen and encourage" us in the faith, to "complete what is lacking" in our faith, to "establish [our] hearts unblameable in holiness," in order that "through perseverance and the encouragement of the Scriptures we might have hope." To summarize with the words of our Catechism: *The Spirit of God makes the reading, but especially the preaching of the Word, an effectual means of...establishing their hearts in holiness and comfort through faith unto salvation.*

The work of grace in the soul is not immediately brought to perfection in this life, but is, in a progressive way, making advances in us toward perfection. We are first made holy by the renovation of our hearts and lives in regeneration, and made partakers of those spiritual encouragements which accompany and flow from the

---

them was accompanied by the desire to be useful by remedying [by his teaching] the defects there were in that faith.... As a true pastor he knew that there was much that had to be done for them. It was his aim to play some part in seeing that they were set forward on the right road" (Morris, *The First and Second Epistles to the Thessalonians*, 109–110).

32. "Establish your hearts unblameable in holiness" also describes the effect of Paul's preaching. "It is easy enough for men to become a prey to fears and alarms, to take up every new doctrine, to accept the unreasoning hope that leads inevitably to irresolution, disillusionment and disaster. Paul longs to see his converts delivered from all such instability. He prays that they may have such a sure basis in love that they will be delivered from all this sort of thing. If God gives them this good gift He will establish their whole personality" (Morris, *The First and Second Epistles to the Thessalonians*, 113).

work of sanctification within us; and then we are built up in holiness and encouragement, and so go to greater and greater moral strength and fortitude and consistent living in the ways of God for us. Now this work is produced in us by the preached Word empowered by the Spirit, as each of the above texts show, so that every step we take in our way to heaven, from the time that our faces are first turned toward God, we are enabled by the Word and Spirit to go on safely and assuredly, until the work of grace is perfected in glory in death and resurrection.

Romans 15:4 makes the point that the Bible was written for "our instruction, that through perseverance and the encouragement of the Scriptures we might have hope."

> The instruction which the Scriptures impart is directed to patience and comfort. Patience is endurance and stedfastness. Both the stedfastness and the comfort [encouragement] are derived from the Scriptures and are, therefore, dependent upon these Scriptures and draw their character and value from them. These are generated by Scripture and their quality is determined by Scripture. However, the stedfastness and consolation are said to be the means of something more ultimate, namely, hope. Hope in this case is to be understood of that which the believer entertains, the state of mind. There cannot be the exercise of hope except as it is directed to an object, that hoped for. But to "have hope" is to exercise hope.... In this text the instruction, stedfastness, and consolation derived from Scripture are all represented as contributing to this exercise of hope and thereby is demonstrated the significance for the believer and for the fellowship of the saints of the prospective outreach which hope implies (*cf.* 8:23–25 and vs. 13).[33]

One final word on the Catechism's expression that the Word of God is effective in *establishing their hearts in holiness and comfort*

33. John Murray, *The New International Commentary on the New Testament: The Epistle to the Romans*, 2 vols. (Grand Rapids, MI: William B. Eerdmans Publishing Co., 1959), 2:199–200.

through faith unto salvation. The effect of the Word of God is received *through faith unto salvation.* The Word demands a response on our part. There can be no passive or fatalistic understanding of the effect of the Word of God on us. These benefits of salvation that Christ communicates to us through the written Word, read and preached, as a means of grace, to be received, must be received by faith alone, which faith is a gift of God. "Without faith it is impossible to please God." And so, Paul begins his great epistle on justification, the book of Romans, with this emphasis: "For I am not ashamed of the gospel, for it is the power of God for salvation *to everyone who believes,* to the Jew first and also to the Greek" (Rom. 1:16).

> The gospel is the omnipotence of God operative unto salvation.... [But] the power of God unto salvation of which the gospel is the embodiment is not unconditionally and universally operative unto salvation. It is of this we are advised in the words "to everyone who believeth." This informs us that salvation is not accomplished irrespective of faith.[34] Hence the salvation with which Paul is going to deal in this epistle has no reality, validity, or meaning apart from faith."[35]

The Reading of the Bible

The Command to Read the Bible

> Seek from the Book of the LORD, and read (Isa. 34:16).

> I adjure you by the Lord to have this letter read to all the brethren (1 Thess. 5:27).

34. "The priority of effectual calling and of regeneration in the *ordo salutis* [order of salvation] should not be allowed to prejudice this truth either in our thinking or in the preaching of the gospel. It is true that regeneration is causally prior to faith. But it is only *causally* prior and the adult person who is regenerated always exercises faith. Hence the salvation which is of the gospel is never ours apart from faith. This is true even in the case of infants, for in regeneration the germ of faith is implanted" (Murray, *The Epistle to the Romans,* 1:27, ftnt).

35. Murray, *The Epistle to the Romans,* 1:27.

> And when this letter is read among you, have it also read in the church of the Laodiceans; and you, for your part read my letter that is coming from Laodicea (Col. 4:16).

In the Bible, God has not only commanded that the Bible be read in worship, but also how, when, where and by whom it is to be read (Deut. 17:18–20; 31:11–13; Isa. 34:1, 16; Jer. 22:29; John 5:39; Col. 4:16; 1 Thess. 5:27; E. 24:7; Josh. 8:34–35; 2 Kgs. 21:12–14; 22:8–13; 23:1–3; Jer. 36:2–3; 36:4–7)

The Importance of Bible Reading in Public Worship

> The strength of the Christian faith is the strength of the word of God. Christianity is a revealed religion, a divinely revealed religion, and the revelation that establishes it is a written one, the Holy Scriptures.... More than anything else it was the publication of the Greek New Testament and the translation of the Scriptures into the common languages of the peoples of Europe that brought about the great Protestant Reformation.... The importance of the Scriptures to the Christian faith cannot be overstated or overemphasized, and their being publicly read as the very word of God, as a separate and distinct act of worship to that God, is a quintessential part of the Christian faith.[36]

> Reformed churches have a sound and Biblical tradition of giving adequate attention to the reading of the Word of God to the people.... If the word of God does not have an honored place in our services then we are neither Biblical nor Reformed.... Without the proper reading of the Scripture there can be little blessing and fruit in the ministry and life of the church.[37]

36. Louis DeBoer, "The Reading of the Scriptures," *Worship in the Presence of God*, ed. by David Lachman and Frank Smith (Greenville, SC: Greenville Presbyterian Theological Seminary Press, 1992), 137–38.

37. DeBoer, "The Reading of the Scriptures," 142–43.

The Example of King Hezekiah in 2 Kings 21:12–14

During the administration of King Ahaz of Judah, apostasy had brought Judah to near ruin.

> God in judgment had precipitated a destructive fratricidal war with Israel, and Ahaz in desperation sought Assyrian assistance in his troubles, bringing that imperialistic power into the politics of Palestine. Judah was spared, and survived an Assyrian invasion under Sennacherib because Ahaz's heir, Hezekiah, reformed the land according to all the commandments of the word of the Lord. Such reformation is impossible without extensive reading and application of the Word of God. It literally means a reforming of all things to bring them into conformity with that word. It was just such a submissive and reverent reading of God's word by Judah's king, and ultimately by the priests, the Levites, and the people that led to Judah's deliverance from the abyss into which Ahaz's apostasy had almost precipitated it.[38]

The Example of King Josiah in 2 Kings 22:8–13; 23:1–3

Judah was invaded by the Babylonians, her king, Mannaseh was taken captive, and his heir, Amon, was assassinated.

> At this critical juncture the nation was again spared, and drawn back from the abyss of final destruction by a reformation that was led by Josiah, their king, reformation that was precipitated by the discovery and the reading of a scroll of the word of the Lord.... Not only does the reading of the word of God provide the very foundation for the existence of the nation but the contrary is also true. The refusal to read the word of the Lord can be the specific cause of national destruction.[39]

---

38. DeBoer, "The Reading of the Scriptures," 144.
39. DeBoer, "The Reading of the Scriptures," 145–46.

The Power of Bible Reading in Worship

Every time in His providence God causes His Word to be read, He accomplishes His eternal purposes: "So shall My word be which goes forth from My mouth; it shall not return to Me empty, without accomplishing what I desire, and without succeeding in the matter for which I sent it" (Isa. 55:11).

> Such is the power of the Word of God. It should be publicly read with the recognition that it has such power. We ought never to be timid and apologetic in our public readings, as if our ministry were weak and ineffectual. We are handling a word that is sharper than a two edge sword and each swing will have eternal consequences.[40]

The Persons Who Should Read the Bible

Q. 156: Is the word of God to be read by all?

A.: Although all are not to be permitted to read the word publickly to the congregation, yet all sorts of people are bound to read it apart by themselves, and with their families: to which end, the holy scriptures are to be translated out of the original into vulgar [common] languages.

Everybody Should Read the Bible for Themselves and With Their Families.

> And these words, which I am commanding you today, shall be on your heart; and you shall teach them diligently to your sons and shall talk of them when you sit in your house and when you walk by the way and when you lie down and when you rise up (Deut. 6:6–7).

40. DeBoer, "The Reading of the Scriptures," 155.

Everybody who wants to be saved from sin and accepted with God should be well acquainted with the Bible. Everybody who loves his family should read the Bible to his family, as well as in private. Thus, Bible reading is one of the great duties and privileges of life. We are only hurting ourselves and our families when we neglect the reading of it. If we do not read it, since it is a "lamp to our feet," we live in darkness. Since it is a "sword," we are vulnerable to all who would harm us; and since it is "nourishing food," we starve without it.

Not Everybody is Allowed to Read the Word in Public Worship.

God has regulated all the details of His worship in His all-sufficient Word, to which nothing is ever to be added or subtracted (Deut. 4:2; 12:32). God alone has the prerogative to determine what may and may not be done in His worship. In the governing of our worship of God, man's desires are nothing. God's desires are everything, and He has expressed His desires as to how He wants us to worship Him in His Word.

The Bible teaches that not everybody has the authority to lead the congregation in reading the Bible in public worship. No Christian may assume that it is his right to read the Bible in public worship simply because he is a Christian. Christ Himself did not assume the authority and duties of a high priest, until God bestowed that authority and office on Him (Heb. 5:4–6).

So then, to whom has God given the authority and office to read the Bible in public worship, according to the teaching and examples in the Bible?

> From Moses, who delegated the public reading of the Scriptures to the sons of Levi, to Christ, who by example publicly read the sacred scroll in the synagogue of Nazareth, we see that by both precept and example the Scriptures teach that only those ordained and set apart to that office may publicly read the word of God.[41]

41. DeBoer, "The Reading of the Scriptures," 156.

> Nor ought any to be appointed to read, but such as are grave, pious, and able to read distinctly, for the edification of others. And who is so fit for this work, as the minister whose office is, not only to read the scripture, but to explain it in the ordinary course of his ministry?[42]

Everybody Should Be Able to Read the Bible in His Own Language.

The Bible is to be read with understanding if it is to benefit us; therefore, this makes absolutely necessary two things: (1) That the Bible be translated into the languages people understand; and (2) That people learn to read well.... *Every person that can read, is to be exhorted to read the Scriptures privately, (and all others that cannot read, if not disabled by age, or otherwise, are likewise to be exhorted to learn to read), and to have a Bible* (Westminster Directory for the Publick Worship of God, 376).

> But because these original tongues, [the languages in which the Bible was originally written—Hebrew and Greek], are not known to all the people of God, who have right unto and interest in the scriptures, and are commanded, in the fear of God, to read and search them [John 5:39], therefore they are to be translated into the vulgar [common or vernacular] language of every nation unto which they come [1 Cor. 14:6f], that the word of God dwelling plentifully in all, they may worship him in an acceptable manner [Col. 3:16], and, through patience and comfort of the scriptures, may have hope [Rom. 15:4]. (WCF, I, viii)

We must make sure that the version we use in Bible reading is an accurate and readable translation and not a paraphrase. In a translation, the translator puts into English what the original writers wrote (in Hebrew and Greek); and in a paraphrase, the author puts into English what he thinks the original writers meant by what

42. Ridgeley, *Commentary on the Larger Catechism*, 2:448–49.

they wrote. Paraphrases have their place, but good translations are what we need to read and study the written Word of God.

The Manner in Which the Bible Should Be Read

Q. 157: How is the word of God to be read?

A.: The holy scriptures are to be read with an high and reverent esteem of them; with a firm persuasion that they are the very word of God, and that he only can enable us to understand them; with desire to know, believe, and obey the will of God revealed in them; with diligence, and attention to the matter and scope of them; with meditation, application, self-denial, and prayer.

And all the people gathered as one man at the square which was in front of the Water Gate, and they asked Ezra the scribe to bring the book of the law of Moses which the LORD had given to Israel. Then Ezra the priest brought the law before the assembly of men, women, and all who could listen with understanding, on the first day of the seventh month. And he read from it before the square which was in front of the Water Gate from early morning until midday, in the presence of men and women, those who could understand; and all the people were attentive to the book of the law. And Ezra the scribe stood at a wooden podium which they had made for this purpose. And beside him stood Mattithiah, Shema, Anaiah, Uriah, Hilkiah, and Maaseiah on his right hand; and Pedaiah, Mishael, Malchijah, Hashum, Hashbaddanah, Zechariah and Meshullam on his left hand.

And Ezra opened the book in the sight of all the people for he was standing above the people; and when he opened it, all the people stood up. Then Ezra blessed the LORD the great

> God. And all the people answered, "Amen, Amen!" while lifting up their hands; then they bowed low and worshipped the Lord with their faces to the ground. Also Jeshua, Bani, Sherebiah...and the Levites, explained the law to the people while the people remained in their place. And they read from the book, from the law of God, translating [explaining] to give the sense so that they understood the reading (Neh. 8:1–8).

Several important points should be made about this text. First, the written Word of God was read with authority. It was read in "the square which was in front of the Water Gate," *i.e.*, the public center. And it was read by one who himself possessed authority, flanked by others in authority, standing over and above the congregation behind a "wooden podium." It was "an imposing sight and an authoritative setting."[43] Second, the reading of the written Word of God inspired deep reverence in the congregation for God and His Word, as they stood to hear the reading. Third, the written Word was carefully read and explained to the congregation "to give the sense so that they understood the reading."

Therefore, the Bible must not only be read, it must be read properly. The Larger Catechism explains how the Bible is to be read in Q. 157: First, the Holy Scriptures must be read with *an high and reverent esteem* of them. "They are more desirable than gold, yes, than much fine gold; sweeter also than honey and the drippings of the honeycomb" (Ps. 19:10). When Ezra had read the Word of God publicly, "from morning to midday," the people stood to hear it and "the ears of all the people were attentive to the book of the Law... And Ezra blessed the Lord, the great God; and all the people answered, "Amen, Amen!" with lifting up their hands; and they bowed their heads, and worshipped the Lord" (Neh. 8:3–6). When Moses "took the Book of the Covenant and read it in the hearing of the people" the people said, "All that the LORD has spoken we will do, and we will be obedient" (Ex. 24:7). God blessed Josiah because of the reverent way he read the Word of God:

43. DeBoer, "The Reading of the Scripture," 150.

"'Because your heart was tender and you humbled yourself before God, when you heard His words against this place and against its inhabitants, and because you humbled yourself before Me, tore your clothes, and wept before Me, I truly have heard you,' declares the LORD" (2 Chron. 34:27).

Second, the Scriptures must be read with a *firm persuasion that they are the very word of God.* As Peter said in his second epistle:

And so we have the prophetic word made more sure, to which you do well to pay attention as to a lamp shining in a dark place, until the day dawns and the morning star arises in your hearts. But know this first of all, that no prophecy of Scripture is a matter of one's own interpretation, for no prophecy was ever made by an act of human will, but men moved by the Holy Spirit spoke from God (2 Pet. 1:19–21).

Reading the Scriptures with a *firm persuasion that they are the very word of God* implies several things. (1) It means that we must read the Bible accurately.

The Bible is an inspired book. It is a work of God. It is the work of the Holy Spirit of Truth. As such it is perfect, and any deviation from perfection must mar that perfection and introduce potential error. Therefore the reading must be precise and as perfect as fallible men are capable of. The Word of God must be handled as just that, the Word of God. A word whose every jot and tittle shall come to pass; a word that shall never change.... Now if major doctrines can be hung on the authority of singular points of Scripture then we can see the perfection and authority of the word that God has given. Then we can see that all paraphrases and loose renderings are anathema. Then we can see the absolute importance of reading the Scriptures with power, authority and precision.[44]

(2) "Whatever is revealed in it [the Bible] is to be admired and depended on for its unerring wisdom and infallible verity; so that it

44. DeBoer, "The Reading of the Scriptures," 150–52.

is impossible for those who understand and improve [apply] it, to be turned aside by it from the way of truth."[45] (3) We should give the Bible the same reverence we give to the Living God since it is His Word. (4) We must understand that

> there is only one who can prove that God is the author of Scripture, and that is God himself: "I reply that the witness of the Spirit transcends all reasoning. For even as God alone is sufficient witness to himself in his Word, so also that Word will not find belief in the hearts of men before it is sealed by the inward witness of the Spirit. It is therefore necessary that the same Spirit who spoke by the mouth of the Prophets shall penetrate into our hearts to convince us that what had been divinely commanded had been faithfully declared"[Calvin].[46]

Third, when we read the Bible, we must be *conscious that only God can enable us to understand it* properly, truly and savingly (2 Cor. 3:13–16). "For the LORD gives wisdom; from His mouth come knowledge and understanding" (Prov. 2:6). The disciples on the road to Emmaeus did not understand the words of the risen Christ until "He opened their minds to understand the Scriptures" (Luke 24:45).

Fourth, we must read the Bible with a *desire to know, believe and obey His will* revealed in it. We are to read the Bible as heads of state and judges are required by God to read the Bible:

> you shall be careful to observe according to all that they teach you.... And it shall be with him, and he shall read it all the days of his life, that he may learn to fear the LORD his God, by carefully observing all the words of this law and these statutes, that his heart may not be lifted up above his countrymen and that he may not turn aside from the commandment, to the right or the left (Deut. 17:10, 18–20).

> We must also read the word of God with a desire to have our faith established by it, that our feet may be set upon a rock, and we may be delivered from all manner of doubts and hes-

45. Ridgeley, *Commentary on the Larger Catechism*, 2:452.

46. T.H.L. Parker, *Calvin's Preaching* (Edinburgh: T&T Clark; reprint Louisville, KY: Westminster/ John Knox Press, 1992), 4.

> itations.... And we ought to desire, not only to believe, but to yield a constant and cheerful obedience to everything which God therein requires of us.[47]

True faith *believeth to be true whatsoever is revealed in the word, for the authority of God himself speaking therein; and acteth differently upon that which each particular passage thereof containeth; yielding obedience to the commands, trembling at the threatenings, and embracing the promises of God for this life and that which is to come. But the principal acts of saving faith are, accepting, receiving, and resting upon Christ alone for justification, sanctification, and eternal life, by virtue of the covenant of grace.* (WCF, XIV,ii)

Fifth, we must read the Bible *diligently.* "Now these were more noble-minded than those in Thessalonica, for they received the word with great eagerness, examining the Scriptures daily, to see whether these things were so" (Acts 17:11).

Sixth, we must read the Bible with *full attention to its message, context, scope, framework and purpose.*

> And when Philip had run up, he heard him reading Isaiah the prophet, and said, "Do you understand what you are reading?" And he said, "Well, how could I, unless someone guides me?" And he invited Philip to come up and sit with him.... And the eunuch answered Philip and said, "Please tell me, of whom does the prophet say this? Of himself, or of someone else?" And Philip opened his mouth, and beginning from the Scripture he preached Jesus to him (Acts 8:30–35).

The central message of the Bible is Christ. The context of the Bible is the history of Israel from Creation to the Apostolic Church. The scope (range of concern) of the Bible is as wide as life. The framework of the history and theology of the Bible is the Covenant of God. And the purpose of the Bible is the glory of God in the consummation of salvation in Christ. All this means that the Bible must be read contextually, *i.e.,* in context.

---

47. Ridgeley, *Commentary on the Larger Catechism,* 453.

> This includes both the context in which it [a text] is placed in the Scriptures and the context of the circumstances in which it is read. A prime example of this is the public reading of the Scriptures by our Lord Jesus Christ in the synagogue of Nazareth...Luke 4:16–21.... We must faithfully read the Word in its Scriptural and in its historical context.[48]

Each text has a fourfold context: (1) The entire Bible; (2) The Testament, Old or New; (3) The Book in which it is located; (4) Its immediate context, historically and with reference to the paragraphs that precede and follow it.

Seventh, our reading of the Bible must be accompanied with *meditation* on it. The person blessed by God is described as one whose "delight is in the law of the LORD; and in His law does he meditate day and night" (Ps. 1:2). David sings: "O how I love Thy law! It is my meditation all the day" (Ps. 119:97).

Eighth, it must also be accompanied with an *honest application* of what we read to our lives and daily circumstances.

> Go, inquire of the LORD for me, and for them that are left in Israel and in Judah, concerning the words of the book that is found; for great is the wrath of the LORD that is poured out upon us, because our fathers have not kept the word of the LORD, to do after all that is written in this book (2 Chron. 34:21).

Ninth, we are to read and apply the Bible with an attitude of *self-denial.* As Proverbs 3:5 commands us: "Trust in the LORD with all your heart; and do not lean on your own understanding."

> Our thoughts should be wholly and intensely taken up with the subject of it as persons who are studiously, and with the greatest earnestness pressing after the knowledge of those doctrines which are of the highest importance, that our profiting in the study of it may appear to ourselves and others. As to the exercise of self-denial, all those perverse reasonings which our carnal minds are prone to suggest against the

48. DeBoer, "The Reading of the Scriptures," 152–53.

> matter of divine revelation, are to be laid aside.... Our reason is not to be considered as useless; but we must desire that it may be sanctified, and inclined to receive whatever God is pleased to impart. We are to exercise the grace of self denial also with respect to that obstinacy of our wills whereby they are naturally disinclined or acquiesce in, approve of, and yield obedience to, the will of God; so that we may be entirely satisfied that every thing which He commands in His word, is holy, just and good.[49]

Tenth, the Bible must be read with *fervent prayer.*

> My son, if you will receive my saying,
> And treasure my commandments within you,
> Make your ear attentive to wisdom,
> Incline your heart to understanding;
> For if you cry for discernment,
> Lift your voice for understanding;
> If you seek her as silver,
> And search for her as for hidden treasures,
> Then you will discern the fear of the LORD,
> And discover the knowledge of God (Prov. 2:1-5).

"But if any of you lacks wisdom, let him ask of God, who gives to all men generously and without reproach, and it will be given to him" (James 1:5). Since any benefit we receive from reading the Bible is a gift of God, we must humbly supplicate Him to give such benefits to us as we read His Word. Our prayer should be, "Open my eyes, that I may behold wonderful things from Thy Law" (Ps. 119:18).

The Reading of the Bible in Public Worship According to the Westminster Directory for the Public Worship of God, "Of Publick Reading of the Holy Scriptures"

> Reading of the word in the congregation, being part of the publick worship of God, (wherein we acknowledge our dependence upon him, and subjection to him), and one means

49. Ridgeley, *Commentary on the Larger Catechism*, 2:453.

sanctified by him for the edifying of his people, is to be performed by the pastors and teachers.

Howbeit, such as intend the ministry, may occasionally both read the word, and exercise their gift in preaching in the congregation, if allowed by the presbytery thereunto.

All the canonical books of the Old and New Testament, (but none of those which are commonly called *Apocrypha*), shall be publickly read in the vulgar tongue [vernacular language], out of the best allowed translation, distinctly, that all may hear and understand.

How large a portion shall be read at once, is left to the wisdom of the minister; but it is convenient, that ordinarily one chapter of each Testament be read at every meeting; and sometimes more, where the chapters be short, or the coherence of the matter requireth it.

It is requisite that all the canonical books be read over in order, that the people may be better acquainted with the whole body of the scriptures; and ordinarily, where the reading in either Testament endeth on one Lord's day, it is to begin the next.

We commend also the more frequent reading of such scriptures as he that readeth shall think best for edification of his hearers, as the book of Psalms, and such like.

When the minister who readeth shall judge it necessary to expound any part of what is read, let it not be done until the whole chapter or psalm be ended; and regard is always to be had unto the time, that neither preaching, nor other ordinances be straitened, or rendered tedious. Which rule is to be observed in all other publick performances.

Beside publick reading of the holy scriptures, every person that can read, is to be exhorted to read the scriptures privately, (and all others that cannot read, if not disabled by age, or otherwise, are likewise to be exhorted to learn to read), and to have a Bible.

The Preaching of the Bible

If worship can be defined as the activity of ascribing the proper worth to God and, then, of extolling that worth, the preaching of the Word is foundational for it. The Bible, after all, is essentially the story of God, His person, His perfections, His plan, His purposes, His works and His words. And preaching is the first and foremost means to make this story known in its totality and in its details. So Scripture is indispensable for a full view or a glimpse, for that matter, of the worth of God. And preaching is of the highest significance if one is to enjoy that view or catch that glimpse. In a nutshell, in the Word of God the worth of God is on display and through the preaching of the Word that worth is grasped in its full-orbed totality and in its many facets.[50]

The Preachers of the Bible

Q. 158: By whom is the word of God to be preached?

A.: The word of God is to be preached only by such as are sufficiently gifted [1 Tim. 3:2f; Eph. 4:8–11; Hos. 4:6; Mal. 2:7], and also duly approved and called to that office [Jer. 14:15; Rom. 10:15; Heb. 5:4; 1 Cor. 12:28,29; 1 Tim. 3:10; 1 Tim. 4:14; 5:22].

The Bible clearly identifies those whom God wants to preach the Bible to His people as those whom He has personally called to the office of minister of the gospel (preaching elder), whom He has equipped with Spiritual gifts qualifying and enabling them to carry out that calling as preachers of the Word of God (2 Cor. 3:5, 6). "God

50. Henry Krabbendam, "Worship and Preaching," *Worship in the Presence of God*, ed. by David Lachman and Frank Smith (Greenville, SC: Greenville Presbyterian Theological Seminary Press, 1992), 157.

must have called and commissioned him (Heb. 5:4), and Christ must have presented him to the Church as His personal gift (Eph. 4:11)."[51] As the Larger Catechism Q. 159 teaches us: those who have the divine authority to preach the Word of God are those *that are called to labour in the ministry of the word.*

The great 17th Century Scottish Presbyterian, George Gillespie, who was a commissioner to the Westminster Assembly, set forth the Biblical basis for this answer in our Catechism in his book, *The Works of George Gillespie,* Vol. 2. His arguments have never been refuted.

His first argument is:

> God hath appointed the ministers of the word, lawfully called and ordained, and no other, to be the stewards and dispensers of the mysteries of Christ, 1 Cor. iv:1—'Let a man so account of us, as of the ministers of Christ, and stewards of the mysteries of God. Moreover it is required of stewards that a man be found faithful;'—which the Apostle doth not only apply to himself and Apollos, ver. 6, (where, by the way, it may be remembered that Apollos was neither an apostle, nor evangelist, but a powerful minister of the gospel,) and to Sosthenes (as appeareth by comparing the text now cited with 1 Cor. i:1), but he also applieth the same to every lawful bishop, or ordinary minister, Tit. i:7, for a bishop must be blameless as the steward of God, and this steward is ordained, ver. 5. So Luke xii:42—'Who then is that faithful and wise steward, whom his Lord shall make ruler over his household, to give them their portion of meat in due season?' It is not Christ's will that any one of the household who is faithful, wise and discreet, may take upon him the steward's office, to dispense meat to the rest; but there is a steward constituted and appointed for that purpose; there are stewards appointed in the church, which is the house of the living God, and those to continue till the coming of Christ... ver. 43, 46.[52]

51. Krabbendam, "Worship and Preaching," 165.

52. George Gillespie, "A Treatise of Miscellany Questions," *The Works of George Gillespie,* 2 vols. (Edinburgh: Robert Ogle and Oliver & Boyd, 1846; reprint Canada: Still Waters Revival Books, 1991), 2:37.

His second argument is: "Ministers lawfully called and ordained, and none other, hath Christ appointed to be pastors and shepherds, to feed the flock of God, Jer. iii:15; Eph. iv:11; Acts xx:28; 1 Pet. v:2."[53]

His third argument is:

> Ezekiel's vision concerning the new temple is generally acknowledged to be an evangelical prophecy.... Now, among other things, it is there prophesied concerning the ministers of the gospel, Ezek. xliv:16, 'They shall enter into my sanctuary, and they shall come near unto my table to minister unto me; and they shall keep my charge,' whereof we can make no gospel sense, except it belong to the charge of ministers, lawfully called and entered into that work, [to preach and] to administer the sacraments, and namely, that of the Lord's supper at His table. These ministers are also in that chapter plainly distinguished from the people, or children of Israel, ver. 15, 19, 22, 23, 28.[54]

His fourth argument is:

> Christ gives a commission to the apostles to teach, and baptize, and extends the same commission to all teaching ministers to the end of the world, Matt. xxviii:19, 20, from which place it is plain, 1. That Jesus Christ would have the distinction of teachers and taught, baptisers and baptised, to have place in the church alway, even unto the end. 2. That the commission to teach and baptise was not given to all who believe in Jesus Christ, but to some only. 3. That these some who received this commission are not only the apostles but ordinary ministers, as is manifested by the explaining of the commission, and promise to the end of the world.[55]

His next argument is:

53. Gillespie, *The Works of George Gillespie*, 2:37.
54. Gillespie, *The Works of George Gillespie*, 2:37.
55. Gillespie, *The Works of George Gillespie*, 2:38.

> We have clear and convincing examples in the New Testament, that [preaching and] the sacraments were administered by public ministers, called and appointed thereunto, as baptism by John (John i:33, 'He hath sent me to baptise'), and frequently by the apostles, in the story of the Acts. The Lord's supper, administered by Christ himself... and by the Apostle Paul, Acts xx:7, 11. So 'the breaking of bread' is joined with 'the apostles' doctrine and fellowship,' Acts ii:42; ministers being also called the stewards and dispensers of the mysteries of God.... So that a lawful minister may in faith administer, and the receivers receive from him in faith, [preaching and] the sacraments, having Scripture warrants for so doing; but there is neither any commission from Christ to such as are no church officers to administer the sacraments [or to preach], nor can there any clear example be found in the New Testament, of administering either the one sacrament or the other [or preaching] by any person who can be proved not to have been a minister lawfully called and ordained. Therefore such persons cannot in faith administer, nor others in faith receive from them, either baptism or the Lord's supper, [or the preaching of the word].[56]

Finally,

> that one text, Eph. iv:11–13, is enough to put to silence the gainsayers, 'And He gave some apostles, and some prophets, and some evangelists, and some pastors and teachers, for the perfecting of the saints.'... Is not the administration of the sacraments [and preaching] a perfecting of the saints...? Are we not told that this shall continue till the whole number of the elect be fulfilled? And whom hath Christ given to his church for this work? Hath he given any other but pastors and teachers (setting aside the extraordinary offices), and who are the pastors and teachers appointed hereunto? All, or whosoever will? Nay, not all, but some, saith the text.[57]

56. Gillespie, *The Works of George Gillespie,* 2:38.
57. Gillespie, *The Works of George Gillespie,* 2:38.

The Manner in Which The Bible is to Be Preached

Q. 159: How is the word of God to be preached by those that are called thereunto?

A.: They that are called to labour in the ministry of the word, are to preach sound doctrine, diligently, in season and out of season; plainly, not in the enticing words of man's wisdom, but in demonstration of the Spirit, and of power; faithfully, making known the whole counsel of God: wisely, applying themselves to the necessities and capacities of the hearers; zealously, with fervent love to God and the souls of his people; sincerely, aiming at his glory, and their conversion, edification, and salvation.

The great Seventeenth Century English Presbyterian, Richard Baxter, gives this solemn counsel to preachers:

> Take heed to yourselves, therefore, lest you should be void of that saving grace of God which you offer to others, and be strangers to the effectual workings of that gospel which you preach.... Many a preacher is now in hell, that hath a hundred times called upon his hearers to use the utmost care and diligence to escape it.... Believe, it, brethren, God never saved any man for being a preacher, nor because he was an able preacher; but because he was a justified, sanctified man, and consequently faithful in his Master's work. Take heed therefore, to yourselves first, that you be that which you persuade your hearers to *be.*[58]

58. Richard Baxter, *Gildas Salvianus: The Reformed Pastor*, ed. by John T. Wilkinson (London: The Epworth Press, [1939] 1950), 158.

How, then, is the word of God to be preached by those whom God has called and equipped to preach it?

First, what preachers preach must be *sound doctrine.* Paul exhorted Titus: "But speak the things that become sound doctrine" (Titus 2:1).

Second, preachers must preach *diligently.* Speaking of Apollos, Luke writes: "This man was instructed in the way of the Lord; and, being fervent in the spirit, he spoke and taught diligently the things of the Lord" (Acts 18:25).

Third, preachers must preach *in season and out of season, i.e.,* when it is popular and convenient to do so and when it is not. Paul exhorted Timothy: "Preach the word, be instant in season and out of season" (2 Tim. 4:2).

Fourth, preachers must preach *plainly.* Paul testified: "Yet in the church I had rather speak five words with my understanding, that by my voice I might teach others also, than ten thousand words in an unknown tongue" (1 Cor. 14:19). "We use great plainness of speech" (2 Cor. 3:12).

Fifth, preachers must *not* preach *in the enticing words of man's wisdom, but in demonstration of the Spirit, and of power.* Paul said of his own preaching:

> And I was with you in weakness and in fear and in much trembling. And my message and my preaching were not in persuasive words of wisdom, but in demonstration of the Spirit and of power, that your faith should not rest on the wisdom of men, but on the power of God (1 Cor. 2:3–5).

Sixth, preachers must preach *faithfully.* God said: "The prophet who has a dream may relate his dream, but let him who has My word speak My word in truth [faithfulness]. What does straw have in common with grain?" declares the LORD (Jer. 23:28). "Let a man regard us in this manner, as servants of Christ, and stewards of the mysteries of God. In this case, moreover, it is required of stewards that one be found trustworthy" (1 Cor. 4:1, 2).

Seventh, preachers must *make known the whole counsel of God.* As Paul said: "For I did not shrink from declaring to you the whole purpose [counsel] of God" (Acts 20:27). In other words, the preacher is to preach *only* the Bible and *all* of the Bible.

Eighth, preachers must preach *wisely.* In proclaiming Christ, preachers are to encourage "every man and teaching every man with all wisdom, that we may present every man complete in Christ" (Col. 1:28). Paul exhorts Timothy: "Be diligent to present yourself approved to God as a workman who does not need to be ashamed, handling accurately the word of truth" (2 Tim. 2:15).

Ninth, preachers must *apply themselves to the necessities and capacities of their hearers.* Because of the condition of the Corinthian Christians at one point, Paul said: "I gave you milk to drink, not solid food; for you were not yet able to receive it. Indeed, even now you are not yet able, for you are still fleshly. For since there is jealousy and strife among you, are you not fleshly, and are you not walking like mere men?" (1 Cor. 3:1–3). The author of Hebrews makes a similar point in Hebrews 5:12–15. Furthermore, Jesus asked, "Who then is the faithful and sensible steward, whom his master will put in charge of his servants, to give them their rations at the proper time?" (Luke 12:42)

Tenth, preachers must preach *zealously.* Again, it was said of Apollos, that he was "fervent in spirit" in his bold and powerful preaching and teaching (Acts 18:25).

Eleventh, preachers must preach *with fervent love of God.* As Paul testified: "for if we are beside ourselves, it is for God; if we are of sound mind, it is for you. For the love of Christ controls us" (2 Cor. 5:13–14). "Some, to be sure, are preaching Christ even from envy and strife, but some also from good will; the latter do it out of love, knowing that I am appointed for the defense of the gospel" (Phil. 1:15–16).

Twelfth, preachers must preach *with a fervent love for the souls of their people.* A prime example of this love was Epaphras: "Epaphras, who is one of your number, a bondslave of Jesus Christ, sends you his greetings, always laboring earnestly for you in his prayers, that you may stand perfect and fully assured in all the will of God" (Col. 4:12). The apostle Paul is another example: "And I will most gladly spend and be expended for your souls. If I love you the more, am I to be loved the less?" (2 Cor. 12:15)

Thirteenth, preachers must preach *sincerely,* "for we are not like many, peddling the word of God, but as from sincerity, but as from God, we speak in Christ in the sight of God" (2 Cor. 2:17). Furthermore, "we have renounced the things hidden because of shame, not walking in craftiness or adulterating the word of God, but by the manifestation of truth commending ourselves to every man's conscience in the sight of God" (2 Cor. 4:2).

Fourteenth, preachers must *aim for the glory of God in their preaching.*

> For our exhortation does not come from error or impurity or by way of deceit; but just as we have been approved by God to be entrusted with the gospel, so we speak, not as pleasing men but God, who examines our hearts. For we never came with flattering speech, as you know, nor with a pretext for greed—God is witness—nor did we seek glory from men, either from you or from others, even though as apostles of Christ we might have asserted our authority" (1 Thess. 2:3–6).

As Jesus said regarding Himself: "He who speaks from himself seeks his own glory; but He who is seeking the glory of the One who sent Him, He is true, and there is no unrighteousness in Him" (John 7:18).

Fifteenth, preachers must *aim for the conversion of their hearers.* We see this in Paul's preaching especially:

> For though I am free from all men, I have made myself a slave to all, that I might win the more. And to the Jews I became a Jew, that I might win Jews; to those who are under the Law, as under the Law, though not being myself under the Law, that I might win those who are under the Law; to those who are without law, as without law, thought not being with the law of God but under the law of Christ, that I might win those who are without law. To the weak I became weak, that I might win the weak; I have become all things to all men, that I may by all means save some. And I do all things for the sake of the gospel, that I may become a fellow partaker of it (1 Cor. 9:19–23).

Sixteenth, preachers must *aim for the edification of their hearers.* As Paul said: "it is in the sight of God that we have been speaking in Christ; and all for your upbuilding, beloved" (2 Cor. 12:19). "Let all things be done for edification" (1 Cor. 14:26).

Seventeenth, preachers must *aim for the salvation of their hearers, i.e.,* deliverance from sin's punishment, power and presence, including victory over sin in our daily struggles. Paul's instruction to ministers is this: "Pay close attention to yourself and to your teaching; persevere in these things; for as you do this you will insure salvation both for yourself and for those who hear you" (1 Tim. 4:16). God sends forth ministers and witnesses "to open their eyes, and to turn them from darkness to light, and from the power of Satan unto God, that they may receive forgiveness of sins, and inheritance among them which are sanctified by faith that is in me" (Acts 26:18).

The Hearing of the Bible Preached

Q. 160: What is required of those that hear the word preached?

A.: It is required of those that hear the word preached, that they attend upon it with diligence, preparation, and prayer; examine what they hear by the scriptures; receive the truth with faith, love, meekness, and readiness of mind, as the word of God; meditate, and confer of it; hide it in their hearts, and bring forth the fruit of it in their lives.

In His parables on the Kingdom, Jesus taught His disciples that His Kingdom would manifest its saving power in people's lives and societies through the faithful preaching of the gospel of that Kingdom: "And He was saying to them, 'A lamp is not brought to be put under a peck-measure, is it, or under a bed? Is it not brought to be put on the lampstand? For nothing is hidden, except to be revealed;

nor has anything been secret, but that it should come to light. If any man has ears to hear, let him hear.'" (Mark 4:21–23). He went on to tell them that, since the kingdom advances through the preaching of the gospel, we must give the preaching of the gospel the best attention we are capable of giving it: "Take care WHAT[59] you listen to. By your standard of measure it shall be measured to you; and more shall be given you besides. For whoever has, to him shall more be given; and whoever does not have, even what he has shall be taken away from him" (Mark 4:24–25).

So then, *how* are we to hear preaching in a way that pleases God and benefits ourselves?

First, we must listen to preaching with *diligence.* Wisdom incarnate says: "Blessed is the man who hears Me, watching daily at My gates, waiting at the posts of My doors" (Prov. 8:34). Because believers crave the spiritual nourishment and stimulation of the Word of God, they cannot get enough of the preached Word. They order their lives and discipline themselves to make sure they are present when the Word is preached, unless they are providentially hindered.

Second, before we hear the preaching of the Word, we must endeavor to *prepare* ourselves for hearing it properly. "Therefore, putting aside all malice and all guile and hypocrisy and envy and all slander, like newborn babes, long for the pure milk of the word, that by it you may grow in respect to salvation, if you have tasted the kindness of the Lord" (1 Pet. 2:1–3). We should consider how much we need the instruction it provides and the truths in it brought to our memory. We should consider that God has instituted preaching for His glory and our benefit, that it is "the power of God unto salvation." "As it is stamped with his authority, so we may depend on it that his eye will be upon us, to observe our frame of spirit under the Word. We ought likewise to have an awful sense of His perfections, to excite in us an holy reverence."[60]

Third, we are to hear preaching *prayerfully:* "Open my eyes, that I may behold wonderful things from Thy Law" (Ps. 119:18).

59. Luke 8:18 has: "Therefore take care HOW you listen."

60. Ridgeley, *Commentary on the Larger Catechism*, 2:480.

> Praying always with all prayer and supplication in the Spirit, and watching thereunto with all perseverance and supplication for all saints; and for me, that utterance may be given to me, that I may open my mouth boldly, to make known the mystery of the gospel (Eph. 6:18, 19).

Since God in Christ by the Spirit promises to give Himself and His blessing to His children through the preaching of the Word, those children will earnestly beseech God to give what He has promised, and will not "let Him go" until He has so blessed them.

Fourth, while we are listening to the preaching of the Word, we should sit under a preacher whose faithfulness to the Word we trust; and even then, to *examine* carefully what is preached to ensure that it is in accordance with the written Word so that we will be followers of God and not of men, believers of the truth not believers in error. As the Bible says of the Christians at Berea: "Now these were more noble-minded than those in Thessalonica, for they received the word with great eagerness, examining the Scriptures daily, to see whether these things were so" (Acts 17:11). The attitude described in this verse is not an attitude of superiority and suspicion, which always tries to catch the preacher in a wrong statement; but one of genuine submission to the written Word, which is the standard and source of the preached Word. Moreover, the humble believer submits to the Living Word speaking His written Word in the preached Word.

Fifth, we must *receive the truth* in preaching with *faith.* "For indeed we have had good news preached to us, just as they also; but the word they heard did not profit them, because it was not united with faith in those who heard" (Heb. 4:2). Without faith, it is impossible to please God, because faith is the open, empty, outstretched hand that receives Christ and His blessings of salvation offered in the preached Word. Faith comes to Christ, clings to Christ, and feeds upon Christ in the preached Word.

Sixth, we must hear preaching with *love.* God will punish His hardened enemies "because they did not receive the love of the truth so as to be saved" (2 Thess. 2:10). True believers love intensely the divine truth they hear in the preached Word, because God's revealed truth is the avenue by which their beloved Savior comes to them and loves them and communes with them. Because they love the Living Word, they love the written Word and the preached Word, for both bring them closer to Him Whom they love with all their hearts and souls.

Seventh, we must hear preaching with *meekness and readiness of mind.* "Therefore putting aside all filthiness and all that remains of wickedness in humility [*i.e.*, in meekness] receive the word implanted, which is able to save your souls" (James 1:21). The Berean Christians were more noble that those in Thessalonica because "they received the word with great eagerness [*i.e.*, all readiness of mind]" (Acts 17:11). *Meekness* and *readiness of mind* have reference to teachableness. If we are going to benefit from the preached Word, we must be open, teachable and eager to hear it and to benefit from it. With John Calvin, we must pray that God would subdue our hearts to teachableness.

Eighth, we must give the preached Word the *same attention* we give *the word of God* written and the Living Word who preaches to us in and through both. "And for this reason we also constantly thank God that when you received from us the word of God's message, you accepted it not as the word of men, but for what it really is, the word of God, which also performs its work in you who believe" (1 Thess. 2:13). If a person loves Christ, he loves the Bible, and he hungers for the preaching of the Bible. If a person does not love to hear the Bible preached, and submit to Christ in it, He cannot be said to love Christ. To believe in Christ is to believe Christ. We must revere the Word of God as we revere God the Word.

Ninth, we must *meditate* on the preached Word. As Jesus said: "Let these words sink into your ears; for the Son of Man is going to be delivered into the hands of men" (Luke 9:44). And the author of Hebrews exhorts us: "For this reason we must pay much closer attention to what we have heard, lest we drift away from it. For if the word spoken through angels proved unalterable, and every transgression and disobedience received a just recompense, how shall we escape if we neglect so great a salvation?" (Heb. 2:1–3). To meditate on the preached Word is to talk to yourself about that Word. Rehearse to yourself what exactly was preached. Ask yourself how it applies to your life and situation. Repent of anything in your life that contradicts it. Bring your mind and life into conformity to it. Thank God for it.

Tenth, we must have *conversations* about the preached Word with our family and friends, as Christ's disciples on the road to Emmaus, when Christ came to them:

> And they were conversing with each other about all these things which had taken place. And it came about that while they were conversing and discussing, Jesus Himself approached, and began traveling with them.... And their eyes were opened and they recognized Him; and he vanished from their sight. And they said to one another, "Were not our hearts burning within us while He was speaking to us on the road, while He was explaining the Scriptures to us?" And they arose that very hour and returned to Jerusalem, and found gathered together the eleven and those who were with them, saying, "The Lord has really risen, and has appeared to Simon." And they began to relate their experiences on the road and how He was recognized by them in the breaking of the bread. And while they were telling these things, He Himself stood in their midst" (Luke 24:14–15, 31–36).

Furthermore, we should especially converse about the preached Word with our family: "And these words, which I command you this day, shall be in your heart; and you shall teach them diligently to your children, and shall talk of them when you sit in your house, and when you walk by the way and when you lie down, and when you rise up" (Deut. 6:6, 7). Talking to each other about the preached Word in our families and with our friends, not only deepens our love for each other, but it also has a sanctifying effect on the lives of every believer involved in the conversation. As we share our thoughts about a sermon, the sermon still preaches to us, and becomes bigger and bigger in its message and impact, as we learn and benefit from the insights of each other into the sermon preached.

Eleventh, we must *hide in our hearts* the preached Word.

My son, if you will receive my sayings,
And treasure my commandments within you,
Make your ear attentive to wisdom,
Incline your heart to understanding;
If you seek her as silver,
And search for her as for hidden treasures;
Then you will discern the fear of the LORD,
And discover the knowledge of God (Prov. 2:1–5).

As David sang: "Thy word I have treasured [hid] in my heart, that I may not sin against Thee" (Ps. 119:11). "If God's word is carved in our hearts, we will be more able to resist the assaults of Satan; and therefore the prophet desires God to instruct him daily more and more in it" (1599 Geneva Bible). Hiding the Word in our hearts involves concentrated listening to it as it is read and preached, applying it to our hearts and lives as it is being preached and afterwards, thinking about it, memorizing it, and sharing it with others.

Twelfth, we must *bring forth the fruit,* effects and benefits of the preached Word *in our lives.* "And the seed in the good ground, these are the ones who have heard the word in an honest and good heart, and hold it fast, and bear fruit with perseverance" (Luke 8:15). "But prove yourselves doers of the word, and not merely hearers who delude themselves.... But one who looks intently at the perfect law, the law of liberty and abides by it, not having become a forgetful hearer but an effectual doer, this man shall be blessed in what he does" (James 1:22, 25). A Christian is not simply a hearer of the preached Word, he is a doer of the preached Word. He manifests the power of that Word in his everyday behavior. People can see how the preached Word has benefited and changed him. Holding fast to it in our hearts and minds bears fruit in our behavior. This is proof of Spiritual life. *Fruit* comes in no other way. "Mushrooms spring up overnight, but they are usually poisonous. The best fruits require time, cultivation, patience."[61]

61. A.T. Robertson, *Robertson's Word Studies* http://www.godrules.net/library/robert/robertluk8.htm

The Power of Preaching

The Greatness of This Power

> For as the rain and the snow come down from heaven, and do not return there without watering the earth, and making it bear and sprout, and furnishing seed to the sower and bread to the eater; so shall My word be which goes forth from My mouth; it shall not return to Me empty, without accomplishing what I desire, and without succeeding in the matter for which I sent it. For you will go out with joy, and be led forth with peace; the mountains and the hills will break forth into shouts of joy before you, and all the trees of the field will clap their hands (Isa. 55:10–12).

> The Word is like the sun in the firmament. Thereunto it is compared at large Ps 19. It hath virtually in it all spiritual light and heat. But the preaching of the word is as the motion and beams of the sun, which actually and effectually communicate that light and heat unto all creatures, which are virtually [essentially and energetically] in the sun itself.[62]

> It is the meaning of the Word which is the Word indeed; it is the sense of it which is its soul...preaching in a more especial manner reveals God's Word.[63] When an ointment box is once opened, then it casts its savor about; and when the juice

62. John Owen, quoted in Peter Lewis, *The Genius of Puritanism* (Sussex: Carey Publications Limited, n.d.), 42.

63. "This is not to elevate preaching to an equality with Scripture. Scripture is definitive and sovereign; preaching must be derivative and subordinate. Obviously Scripture does not have to conform to preaching; preaching must conform to Scripture. It is the humble position of preaching as derivative and subordinate that is precisely its glory. According to Calvin, then, preaching so to say 'borrows' its status of 'Word of God' from Scripture. It is the Word of God inasmuch as it delivers the Biblical message, which is God's message or Word. But 'God's Word' means, for Calvin, that which is spoken by God; not simply in its first giving but in its every repetition. It does not somehow become weakened by repetition so as to become less and less God's Word" (Parker, *Calvin's Preaching*, 23–24).

of the medicinal herb is once strained out and applied, then it heals.[64]

The Accomplishments of This Power

What does the power of the preached Word accomplish in the hearts and lives of God's people?

> Many are the singular benefits that come to men thereby. First, the Holy Ghost is here given, Acts 10:44. Secondly, men's hearts are here opened, Acts 16:14. Thirdly, the fear of God doth here fall upon men, Acts 13:16. Fourthly, the proud and stony heart of men is here tamed, melted and made to tremble, Is. 66:2. Fifthly, the faith of God's elect is here begotten, Rom. 10:14. Sixthly, men are here sealed by the Holy Spirit of promise, Eph. 1:3. Seventhly, here the Spirit speaketh to the churches, Eph. 1:13. Eighthly, Christ here comes to sup with men, Rev. 3:20, let men tell of their experience, whether ever their hearts tasted of the refreshing of Christ till they devoted themselves to the hearing of the Word. Ninthly, the painful distress of the afflicted conscience is here or nowhere cured by hearing, the bones that God has broken receive joy and gladness, Ps. 51:8. Tenthly, what shall I say, but as the Evangelical Prophet saith? If you can do nothing else, yet 'hear and your soul shall live' Is. 55:3. Live, I say, the life of grace, yea, and the life of glory: for salvation is brought to us by hearing, Acts 28:28.[65]

The Reason for This Power

What makes the preached Word so powerful that it accomplishes things only God can accomplish? The answer is not to be found in the eloquence or skill of the preacher, nor is it found in the appeal of the human voice. It is to be found in the connecting of the preaching of Christ, the Living Word, with the preaching of man as that man faithfully expounds the written Word, having been sent

64. Thomas Goodwin, quoted in Lewis, *The Genius of Puritanism*, 42.
65. Nicholas Byfield, quoted in Lewis, *The Genius of Puritanism*, 42–43.

by Christ Himself to preach His Word (Rom. 10:15). By His Spirit and Word, the risen, exalted and reigning Christ continues to preach the gospel through the faithful preaching of ministers of the gospel and the faithful witness of the Church. This is the teaching of both the Old Testament and the New Testament.

The Teaching of the Old Testament on the Power of Preaching

The book of Amos is about preaching and its power. In Amos 1:2, preaching is described as THE ROARING OF THE LORD: "The LORD roars from Zion, and from Jerusalem He utters His voice." Amos alludes to this verse when, in 3:8, with reference to his own prophesying of the secret counsels of the Lord, he says: "A lion has roared! Who will not fear? The LORD God has spoken! Who can but prophesy?"

A lion roars when he is about to make his last leap, which is so fatal to its victim (Amos 3:4; Isa. 5:29). His roaring indicates his hunger and his eagerness to satisfy it (Ps. 22:13; 1 Pet. 5:8), his joyful assurance of victory (Isa. 5:29), his defiance of any intruder (Jdgs. 14:5). His roaring, heard far and wide, threatening immediate danger (Jer. 25:30, 31), strikes terror into the hart of man and beast (Amos 3:8).

The name, "LORD," in Amos 1:2, is the English translation of "JEHOVAH." Jehovah, the God of the whole earth and the covenant Lord and Savior of Israel, roars! He is the Creator of the universe, the Lord of history, the Judge of the reprobate and apostate, and the Savior of the people of God. "He is working out his purposes of redemption in all history, which is His Story, a narrative of the triumph of redeeming love."[66]

The roar of Jehovah comes "from Zion" and "from Jerusalem." In Jerusalem on Mount Zion stood the Temple, the Dwelling Place and Sanctuary of Jehovah, the Palace of Jehovah, the Divine King of Israel, the Supreme Place of Jehovah's Revelation to His People (Ex. 25:21, 22; 29:42, 43; 40:33–38; Num. 7:89; Lev. 1:1; 1 Kgs 8:10,11). In

66. Ray Beeley, *Amos: An Introduction and Commentary* (London: The Banner of Truth Trust, [1969] 1970), 28.

the New Testament, the Church of Jesus Christ is the Temple, Dwelling Place, Sanctuary, and Palace of God, wherein He reveals Himself and His will to His people by His Word and Spirit (Ephesians 2:18–22).

The roar of the Lord is to be heard in the preaching of His servants. In Amos 1:1, His roar goes forth from "Zion" and "Jerusalem," which were symbolic of the Church (Heb. 12:22–24). Also in verse 1 we have two parallel phrases, "the LORD roars from Zion and from Jerusalem He utters His voice." Beginning with verse 3, and appearing about sixty times throughout the book of Amos, are phrases like "thus says the LORD" indicating that Amos is identifying his written sermon with the very words of God. And in Amos 3:8, he says that prophesying is the faithful preaching of what "the LORD God has spoken." So then, when God's prophet preaches, it can be said of him, or better, of God's preaching through him: "A lion roared! Who will not fear?" What Amos preached happened, because it was the Word of the Lord. No man or nation can silence or overcome the roaring of the Lord in the preaching of men!

The Teaching of the New Testament on The Power of Preaching

> "Whoever will call upon the name of the Lord will be saved." How then shall they call upon Him in whom they have not believed? And how shall they believe in Him Whom they have not heard? AND HOW SHALL THEY HEAR WITHOUT A PREACHER? And how shall they preach unless they are sent? Just as it is written, "How beautiful are the feet of those who bring glad tidings of good things!" (Rom. 10:13–15).

This passage presents us with the normal way God captures a person's heart by the gospel. The linkage and progression of 10:13–15 should be carefully noted. A person cannot call upon the name of the Lord, *i.e.*, worship Jesus as Lord, unless he believes in Jesus as His own Lord and Savior (10:14a). A person cannot believer in Christ until he has heard Christ speak to his heart (10:14b; John 10:27). A person cannot hear the voice of Christ except through the preached Word of an ordained "herald" (κηρυξ, κηρυσσω),[67] or minister (10:14c). And a person cannot preach, *i.e.*, authoritatively herald or proclaim the gospel, unless Christ has sent him to preach through the ordination of Christ's Church (10:15).

The focal point of this passage is the sentence in 10:14: "And how shall they believe in Him Whom they have not heard?" You cannot believe in Jesus Christ as your Lord and Savior until He personally and powerfully speaks His Word to your heart. The point of this statement is not that we must hear about Jesus to believe in Him, however true that surely is. The point is far more profound. No one will bow before Christ in worship and surrender, who does not believe in Him; and no one will believe in Him who has not been called personally by Christ

---

67. The verb, kerusso, κηρυσσω, means to herald, preach, or proclaim. From this verb comes the noun, kerux, κηρυξ, meaning herald or preacher. The verb occurs 33 times in the Septuagint and over 61 times in the Greek New Testament. This verb denotes the authoritative proclamation of the Word of God by Christ or by a preacher sent by Christ to proclaim that Word (Mark 3:14; 1 Cor. 15:1–4).

Romans 10:15 tells us that "without commissioning and sending [by Christ] there are no preachers, and without preachers there is no proclamation. True proclamation does not take place through Scripture alone, but through exposition, Lk 4:21. God does not send books to men; He sends messengers. By choosing individuals for this service, He institutes the office of proclamation. Not every Christian is called to preach.... Without the resurrection [of Jesus] there would be no preaching office. It exists only because the risen Lord has charged His disciples to declare the message [kerygma,κηρυγμα].... A preacher is not a reporter who recounts his own experience. He is the agent of someone higher whose will he loudly and clearly makes known to the public. Without calling and sending, preaching is a self-contradiction and even a deception. It holds out something which has no reality. If there is no sending, the preaching of Christ is propaganda, not mission." (*Theological Dictionary of the New Testament,* ed. Gerhard Kittel, trans. and ed. by Geoffrey W. Bromiley, 6 vols. [Grand Rapids, MI: William B. Eerdmans Publishing Co., (1965) 1968], 3:712–13.)

Kerux, meaning preacher, occurs in 1 Tim. 2:7; 2 Tim. 1:11 and 2 Pet. 2:5. *Kerygma,* meaning the message preached, occurs in Matt. 12:41; Luke 11:32; Rom. 16:25; 1 Cor. 1:21; 2:4; 15:14; 2 Tim. 4:17; Tit. 1:3. *Kerusso,* meaning preaching, occurs in Matt. 3:11; 4:17, 23; 9:35; 10:7, 27; 11:1; 24:14; 26:13; Mark 1:4,7,14,38,39,45; 3:14; 5:20; 6:12; 7:36; 13:10; 14:9; 16:15,20; Luke 3:3; 4:18,19,44; 8:1,39; 9:2; 12:3; 24:47; Acts 8:5; 9:20; 10:37,42; 15:21; 19:13; 20:15; 28:31; Rom. 2:21; 10:8,14,15; 1 Cor. 1:23; 9:27; 15:11,12; 2 Cor. 1:19; 4:5; 11:4; Gal. 2:2; 5:11; Phil. 1:15; Col. 1:23; 1 Thess. 2:9; 1 Tim. 3:16; 2 Tim. 4:2; 1 Pet. 3:19; Rev. 5:2. It is obvious from a look at these references that *the emphasis in the NT is not on the preacher, but on the preaching of the Word of God.*

to follow Him, out of darkness into light (1 Pet. 2:9). As Jesus Himself said, "My sheep hear My voice, and I know them, and they follow Me, and I give them eternal life" (John 10:27, 28).

In John's Gospel, Jesus said, "Truly, truly, I say to you, he who hears My word and believes Him who sent Me, has eternal life.... Truly, truly, I say to you, an hour is coming, and now is, when the dead shall hear the voice of the Son of God; and those who hear shall live" (John 5:24–25). In order to be awakened out of spiritual death into newness of life and be enabled to embrace Christ in faith as Lord and Savior, Christ must reveal the glory and knowledge of God Himself directly to our hearts (2 Cor. 4:4–6a). He must speak life to us, not in an audible voice, but powerfully and inwardly and irresistibility by His Spirit in the heart.

According to Romans 10:14, where can we expect to hear the powerful Word of Christ unto the saving and sanctifying of our lives? Answer: In the preached Word! Romans 10:14 and 15 link the voice of Christ with the heralding of Christ's written Word by those sent by Christ to preach. Christ is not limited to human preachers, but He certainly has tied us to them as instruments in His hands, as pipes through whom His voice comes. The instruments are nothing. The Master Carpenter is everything. Man's voice is weak. Christ's voice is life. Listen for His voice in the preaching of men, because His voice raises the dead, giving, sustaining and enriching life.

Several texts in the New Testament speak of this relation between Christ's preaching and man's preaching (Luke 10:1–20; 1 Thess. 2:13; 2 Tim. 4:17; 1 Pet. 4:11; Rom. 15:8–9, 15–19; Rom. 16:25–27 and Eph. 2:17). They all confirm the observation of John Calvin:

> It is certain that if we come to church we shall not hear only a mortal man speaking but we shall feel (even by his secret power) that God is speaking to our souls, that he is the teacher... He so touches us that the human voice enters into us and so profits us that we are refreshed and nourished by it. Just as Christ is present at the Supper spiritually, that is, by the working of the Spirit, so he is present in the preaching spiritually—by the working of the Spirit.... [That] is why Calvin calls the pulpit the throne of God: "*voilá* the pulpit, which is

> the throne...of God, from which He wills to govern our souls." Calvin even goes so far as to say that the pulpit is God's "seat of justice," *i.e.*, the judgment seat or tribunal of God, where the Church confesses its guilt and runs to the mercy of God as its only refuge.[68, 69]

When Christ preaches in our preaching, confirming the Word we proclaim (Isa. 44:26), "the power of this preached word is the very power of God (1 Cor. 1:18), for it accomplishes the works which the Godhead alone is able to perform in the hearts of lost men; its effectiveness is divine. It produces the very fruits of God (Col. 1:6)."[70]

The preached Word—the preached Christ—is a recreative, restorative force because in it Jesus Christ gives what He preaches. He brings what He declares. He causes to happen what He preaches to our hearts. When the preacher preaches Christ's Word, Christ causes that Word to happen. In preaching, Christ actually "confirms the promises to the patriarchs" in His Church, as the living Administrator of God's Covenant (Rom. 15:8).

In Mark 1:14–15, it is said that Christ preaches the Kingdom of God. In that same verse, it also says that His presence and activity bring the Kingdom of God in all its saving power to bear upon the sinfulness of men's hearts and societies until those hearts and societies are fully permeated with the leavening influence of the gospel (Matt. 13:33). Through the preaching of the Kingdom of the reigning Christ, that same Christ puts down all opposition to Him in all areas, for "He must reign until He puts all His enemies under His feet" (1 Cor. 15:24–25).

---

68. "To ascribe such absolute authority to preaching is clearly extremely dangerous. The opportunities for mischievous and arrogant misuses are endless" (Parker, *Calvin's Preaching*, 43). However there are "two major counterweights" which put the preacher "firmly in his place as a mere messenger. The one is that he is to put forward nothing but what God has declared in Holy Scripture; the other that he is an envoy and not the sovereign. So we find that the absolute authority is always ascribed to the message. The bearer of the message is himself humbled by its authority" (Parker, *Calvin's Preaching*, 43).

69. Parker, *Calvin's Preaching*, 42–43.

70. Pierre Marcel, *The Relevance of Preaching*, trans. by Rob Roy McGregor (Grand Rapid, MI: Baker Book House, 1963), 14.

In Mark 1:15, it is also said that Christ preaches repentance. And in Acts 5:31, we see that Christ was exalted to the position of Prince and Savior "to grant repentance" to Jews and Gentiles (Acts 11:18). Therefore, as we preach repentance, and as Christ preaches through us, we can be sure that men, women and children from all walks of life will repent of their sins and receive Christ as their Lord and Savior (Acts 17:30).

In Ephesians 2:17, it is said that Christ preaches "peace." And in John 16:33, we read that Christ brings and bestows peace. Peace means reconciliation with God through Christ's atonement, the restoration of God's order on earth, the healing of broken relationships, and the inner calmness of soul and blessed assurance that comes with the believing reception of Christ as Lord and Savior. Through our preaching, the Lord Jesus Christ will accomplish these things in our world and in our hearts.

Praise God for a preached Christ and a preaching Christ!

Conclusions

> The glory of God so shines in His Word, that we ought to be so much affected by it, whenever He speaks by His servants, as though He were nigh to us, face to face."[71]

The Task of the Preacher

> The task of the preacher of the Word is to expound the scripture in the midst of the worshipping Church, preaching in the expectancy that God will do, through his frail human word, what He did through the Word of His prophets of old, that God by His grace will cause the word that goes out of the mouth of man to become also a Word that proceeds from God Himself, with all the power and efficacy of the Word of the Creator and Redeemer.... The task of preaching must therefore be undertaken, and the word of the preacher should be heard, in the expectancy that Christ the Mediator will come

71. John Calvin, quoted in Ronald S. Wallace, *Calvin's Doctrine of the Word and Sacrament* (London/ Edinburgh: Oliver and Boyd, 1953), 82.

> and give His presence where the Gospel is preached, and cause men to hear His voice through the voice of the minister.[72]

The Token of the Presence of God

Through the preaching of the Word of God, God Himself draws near to His people and makes His presence known in and among them. Preaching is the token of the presence of God, and the means by which He comes to us (Mark 1:15).

The Instrument of Christ's Rule Over Us

The preached Word is the means whereby "Christ establishes His rule in the hearts of His people." John Calvin makes the claim that

> preaching is such a mighty instrument in the hand of the Lord that through its means not only does Christ create and uphold and rule His Church, but also in a hidden way directs the whole course of history and creates the disturbance amongst the nations that is to bring about the consummation of His eternal purpose. Preaching is the *banner which shall stand for an ensign to the peoples* [Isa. 11:10]. "We know that this was fulfilled by the preaching of the gospel, and indeed was more illustrious than if Christ had soared above the clouds." Preaching establishes the Kingdom of God far and wide wherever the disciples of Jesus go and proclaim His Word.... The Kingdom consists in the preaching of the Gospel.... They [His disciples in Acts 1:8] heard that Christ reigns whenever He subdues the world to Himself by the preaching of the gospel.[73]
>
> Preaching is not only the sceptre by which Christ rules within His Church but also the sword in the hand of the Church by which secretly and unknown even to itself the Church rules or brings judgment amongst the nations [Eph. 6:7]....

72. John Calvin, quoted in Wallace, *Calvin's Doctrine of the Word and Sacrament,* 83.

73. John Calvin, quoted in Wallace, *Calvin's Doctrine of the Word and Sacrament,* 86.

> *He shall smite the wicked with the Word of His mouth and shall slay them with the breath of His lips* (Isa. 11:41).[74]

The Effective Accomplishing of the Word's Commands and Promises

The Word of God is

> always mighty in power to effect what God promises and commands, even though that Word may be uttered through the frail human words of the preacher. God's Word cannot be divorced from His action.... Thus when God speaks through the mouth of the preacher offering forgiveness, those who hear the Word in faith are there and then really absolved from their sins, for the Word effects what it declares.[75]

As Jehovah said: "My word... shall not return to Me empty, without accomplishing what I desire, and without succeeding in the matter for which I sent it" (Isa. 55:11).

The Preached Word and the Power of the Holy Spirit

The preacher of the Word has no control over the Word. "The word of the preacher can only become the Word of God through a sovereign and free act of the Holy Spirit, by whose power alone preaching can be effective."[76]

Preaching may thus fail to be the Word of God. The act may remain on a merely human level throughout, in which case the preacher with all his eloquence and skill and fervour will accomplish nothing. When Paul calls himself a *minister of the Spirit,* "he does not mean by this that the grace of the Holy Spirit and His influence were tied to his preaching so that he could whenever he pleased breathe forth the Spirit along with the utterance of the voice.... It is one thing for Christ to connect His influence with a man's doctrine..., and quite another for the man's doctrine to have such efficacy of itself. We are

74. Wallace, *Calvin's Doctrine of the Word and Sacrament,* 86.
75. Wallace, *Calvin's Doctrine of the Word and Sacrament,* 88.
76. Wallace, *Calvin's Doctrine of the Word and Sacrament,* 89.

then, *ministers of the Spirit,* not as if we held Him enclosed... within us, or as it were captive...not as if we could at our pleasure confer His grace upon all." "God sometimes connects Himself with His servants and sometimes separates Himself from them:... He never resigns to them His own office." "When God separates Himself from His ministers, nothing remains in them."[77]

The Preached Word Condemns When Not Received in Faith

"When the Word of God comes through preaching its effectiveness does not depend on the receptiveness of the hearer (though the nature of its effect may be so determined)."[78] Although preaching proceeds from frail men, nevertheless, when the preached Word is accompanied with the power of the Spirit, it will accomplish God's purposes in the hearts of all the hearers, saving some and hardening others, because "there is... nothing to hinder the Spirit from putting forth His power in the word preached."[79]

> 'If anyone thinks that the air is beaten by an empty sound when the Word of God is preached, he is greatly mistaken, for it is a living thing and full of hidden power, *which leaves nothing in man untouched*' [Calvin]. Thus the true preaching of the Word of God, if it does not find a willing response through faith in the hearer, can, instead of bringing blessing and salvation, rouse within men the opposite effect and harden the heart instead of blessing it.[80]

(See 2 Cor. 2:14–17 and Heb. 4:12.)

The Two-Fold Effect of the Preached Word

Preaching has a two-fold effect: it either softens or hardens the heart (2 Cor. 2:14–17; Matt.13:10–17). It either saves or condemns

77. John Calvin, quoted in Wallace, *Calvin's Doctrine of the Word and Sacrament,* 90.

78. Wallace, *Calvin's Doctrine of the Word and Sacrament,* 91.

79. Wallace, *Calvin's Doctrine of the Word and Sacrament,* 92.

80. Wallace, *Calvin's Doctrine of the Word and Sacrament,* 92.

the hearer. As Calvin said, "The gospel is never preached in vain, but has invariably an effect, either for life or death."[81] The sword of the preached Word is sharp and two-sided (Heb. 4:11–12). In preaching, the minister uses the keys of the kingdom which Christ gave His Church to "bind and loose" (Matt. 16:19).

> Thus it is that it is a fearful thing for men to be confronted with the grace of God offered through the preaching of the Word. Grace can so easily be made by man's decision to show its other side, which is judgment, and can indeed be turned into its very opposite. Through the preaching of the Word the judgment of the world is continually proceeding.... Since the Word is the scepter of Christ's Kingdom 'it cannot be rejected without treating Him with open contempt.... No crime is more offensive to God than contempt for His Word.'... 'The pastor ought to have two voices: one for gathering the sheep; and another for warding off and driving away wolves and thieves. The Scripture supplies him with the means of doing both' [Calvin].[82]

81. Wallace, *Calvin's Doctrine of the Word and Sacrament,* 93.
82. Wallace, *Calvin's Doctrine of the Word and Sacrament,* 94–95.

Appendix:
The Preaching of the Word of God According to the Westminster Directory for the Publick Worship of God

Preaching of the word, being the power of God unto salvation, and one of the greatest and most excellent works belonging to the ministry of the gospel, should be so performed, that the workman need not be ashamed, but may save himself, and those that hear him.

It is presupposed, (according to the rules for ordination), that the minister of Christ is in some good measure gifted for so weighty a service, by his skill in the original languages, and in such arts and sciences as are handmaids unto divinity; by his knowledge in the whole body of theology, but most of all in the holy scriptures, having his senses and heart exercised in them above the common sort of believers; and by the illumination of God's Spirit, and other gifts of edification, which (together with reading and studying of the word) he ought still to seek by prayer, and an humble heart, resolving to admit and receive any truth not yet attained, whenever God shall make it known unto him. All which he is to make use of, and improve, in his private preparations, before he deliver in public what he hath provided.

Ordinarily, the subject of his sermon is to be some text of scripture, holding forth some principle or head of religion, or suitable to some special occasion emergent; or he may go on in some chapter, psalm, or book of the holy scripture, as he shall see fit.

Let the introduction to his text be brief and perspicuous, drawn from the text itself, or context, or some parallel place, or general sentence of scripture.

If the text be long, (as in histories or parables it sometimes must be), let him give a brief sum of it; if short, a paraphrase thereof, if need be: in both, looking diligently to the scope of the text, and pointing at the chief heads and grounds of doctrine which he is to raise from it.

In analyzing and dividing his text, he is to regard more the order of matter than of words; and neither to burden the memory of the hearers in the beginning with too many members of division, nor to trouble their minds with obscure terms of art.

In raising doctrines from the text, his care ought to be, *First,* That the matter be the truth of God. *Secondly,* That it be a truth contained in or grounded in that text, that the hearers may discern how God teacheth it from thence. *Thirdly,* That he chiefly insist upon those doctrines which are principally intended, and make most for the edification of the hearers.

The doctrine is to be expressed in plain terms; or, if anything in it need explication, it is to be opened, and the consequence also from the text cleared. The parallel places of scripture, confirming the doctrine, are rather to be plain and pertinent, than many, and (if need be) somewhat insisted upon, and applied to the purpose in hand.

The arguments or reasons are to be solid, and, as much as may be, convincing. The illustrations, of what kind soever, ought to be full of light, and such as may convey the truth into the hearer's heart with spiritual delight.

If any doubt obvious from scripture, reason, or prejudice of the hearers, seem to arise, it is very requisite to remove it, by reconciling the seeming differences, answering the reasons, and discovering and taking away the causes of prejudice and mistake. Otherwise it is not fit to detain the hearers with propounding or answering vain or wicked cavils, which, as they are endless, so the propounding and answering of them doth more hinder than promote edification.

He is not to rest in general doctrine, although never so much cleared and confirmed, but to bring it home to special use, by application to his hearers: which albeit it prove a work of great difficulty to himself, requiring much prudence, zeal and meditation, and to the natural and corrupt man will be very unpleasant; yet he is to endeavour to perform it in such a manner, that his auditors may feel the word of God to be quick and powerful, and a discerner of the thoughts and intents of the heart; and that, if any unbeliever or ignorant person be present, he may have the secrets of his heart made manifest, and give glory to God.

In the use of instruction or information in the knowledge of some truth, which is a consequence from his doctrine, he may (when convenient) confirm it by a few firm arguments from the text in hand, and other places of scripture, or from the nature of that common-place in divinity, whereof that truth is a branch.

In confutation of false doctrines, he is neither to raise an old heresy from the grave, nor to mention a blasphemous opinion unnecessarily: but, if the people be in danger of an error, he is to confute it soundly, and endeavour to satisfy their judgments and consciences against all objections.

In exhorting to duties, he is, as he seeth cause, to teach also the means that help to the performance of them.

In dehortation, reprehension and publick admonition, (which require special wisdom), let him, as there shall be cause, not only discover the nature and greatness of the sin, with the misery attending it, but also shew the danger his hearers are in to be overtaken and surprised by it, together with the remedies and best way to avoid it.

In applying comfort, whether general against all temptations, or particular against some special troubles or terrors, he is carefully to answer such objections as a troubled heart and afflicted spirit may suggest to the contrary.

It is also sometimes requisite to give some notes of trial, (which is very profitable, especially when performed by able and experienced ministers, with circumspection and prudence, and the signs clearly grounded on the holy scripture), whereby the hearers may be able to examine themselves whether they have attained those graces, and performed those duties, to which he exhorteth, or be guilty of the sin reprehended, and in danger of the judgments threatened, or are such to whom the consolations propounded do belong; that accordingly they may be quickened and excited to duty, humbled for their wants and sins, affected with their danger, and strengthened with comfort, as their condition, upon examination, shall require.

And, as he needeth not always to prosecute every doctrine which lies in his text, so is he wisely to make choice of such uses, as, by his residence and conversing with his flock, he findeth most needful and seasonable; and, amongst these, such as may most draw their souls to Christ, the fountain of light, holiness, and comfort.

This method is not prescribed as necessary for every man, or upon every text; but only recommended, as being found by experience to be very much blessed of God, and very helpful for the people's understandings and memories.

But the servant of Christ, whatever his method be, is to perform his whole ministry:

1. Painfully [*i.e.*, painstakingly], not doing the work of the Lord negligently.

2. Plainly, that the meanest may understand; delivering the truth not in the enticing words of man's wisdom, but in demonstration of the Spirit and of power, lest the cross of Christ should be made of none effect; abstaining also from an unprofitable use of unknown tongues, strange phrases, and cadences of sounds and words; sparingly citing sentences of

ecclesiastical or other human writers, ancient or modern, be they never so elegant.

3. Faithfully, looking at the honour of Christ, the conversion, edification, and salvation of the people, not at his own gain or glory; keeping nothing back which may promote those holy ends, giving to every one his own portion, and bearing indifferent respect unto all, without neglecting the meanest, or sparing the greatest, in their sins.

4. Wisely, framing all his doctrines, exhortations, and especially his reproofs, in such a manner as may be most likely to prevail; shewing all due respect to each man's person and place, and not mixing his own passion or bitterness.

5. Gravely, as becometh the word of God; shunning all such gesture, voice, and expressions, as may occasion the corruptions of men to despise him and his ministry.

6. With loving affection, that the people may see all coming from his godly zeal, and hearty desire to do them good. And,

7. As taught of God, and persuaded in his own heart, that all that he teacheth is the truth of Christ; and walking before his flock, as an example to them in it; earnestly, both in private and publick, recommending his labours to the blessing of God, and watchfully looking to himself, and the flock whereof the Lord hath made him overseer: so shall the doctrine of truth be preserved uncorrupt, many souls converted and built up, and himself receive manifold comforts of his labours even in this life, and afterward the crown of glory laid up for him in the world to come.

Where there are more ministers in a congregation than one, and they of different gifts, each may more especially apply himself to doctrine or exhortation, according to the gift wherein he most excelleth, and as they shall agree between themselves.

Chapter Thirty-Six

The Sacraments in the Worship of God

"God commands the use of the sacraments. He would command nothing that was superfluous or vain. Therefore the sacraments are necessary. God has promised His grace along with the use of the sacraments. No man dare neglect the offered grace of God without condemnation."

~ *Ronald Wallace*

Is not the cup of blessing which we bless a sharing in the blood of Christ? Is not the bread which we break a sharing in the body of Christ? Since there is one bread, we who are many are one body; for we all partake of the one bread.

1 Corinthians 10:16–18

The Sacraments in the Worship of God

Q. 161: How do the sacraments become effectual means of salvation?

A.: The sacraments become effectual means of salvation, not by any power in themselves, or any virtue derived from the piety or intention of him by whom they are administered, but only by the working of the Holy Ghost, and the blessing of Christ, by whom they are instituted.

Q. 162: What is a sacrament?

A.: A sacrament is an holy ordinance instituted by Christ in his church, to signify, seal, and exhibit unto those that are within the covenant of grace, the benefits of his mediation; to strengthen and increase their faith, and all other graces; to oblige them to obedience; to testify and cherish their love and communion one with another; and to distinguish them from those that are without.

Q. 163: What are the parts of a sacrament?

A.: The parts of a sacrament are two; the one an outward and sensible sign, used according to Christ's own appointment; the other an inward and spiritual grace thereby signified.

Q. 164: How many sacraments hath Christ instituted in his church under the New Testament?

A.: Under the New Testament Christ hath instituted in his church only two sacraments, baptism and the Lord's Supper.

Q. 165: What is Baptism?

A.: Baptism is a sacrament of the New Testament, wherein Christ hath ordained the washing with water in the name of the Father, and of the Son, and of the Holy Ghost, to be a sign and seal of ingrafting into himself, of remission of sins by his blood, and regeneration by his Spirit; of adoption, and resurrection unto everlasting life; and whereby the parties baptized are solemnly admitted into the visible church, and enter into an open and professed engagement to be wholly and only the Lord's.

Q. 166: Unto whom is baptism to be administered?

A.: Baptism is not to be administered to any that are out of the visible church, and so strangers from the covenant of promise, till they profess their faith in Christ, and obedience to him, but infants descending from parents, either both, or but one of them, professing faith in Christ, and obedience to him, are in that respect within the covenant, and to be baptized.

Q. 167: How is our baptism to be improved by us?

A.: The needful but much neglected duty of improving our baptism, is to be performed by us all our life long, especially in the time of temptation, and when we are present at the administration of it to others; by serious and thankful consideration of the nature of it, and of the ends for which Christ instituted it, the privileges and benefits conferred and sealed thereby, and our solemn vow made therein; by being humbled for our sinful defilement, our falling short of, and walking contrary to, the grace of baptism, and our engagements; by growing up to assurance of pardon of sin, and of all other blessings sealed to us in that sacrament; by drawing strength from the death and resurrection of Christ, into whom we are baptized, for the mortifying of sin, and quickening of grace; and by endeavouring to live by faith, to have our conversation in holiness and righteousness, as those that have therein given up their names to Christ; and to walk in brotherly love, as being baptized by the same Spirit into one body.

Q. 168: What is the Lord's supper?

A.: The Lord's supper is a sacrament of the New Testament, wherein, by giving and receiving bread and wine according to the appointment of Jesus Christ, his death is shewed forth; and they that worthily communicate feed upon his body and blood, to their spiritual nourishment and growth in grace; have their union and communion with him confirmed; testify and renew their thankfulness, and engagement to God, and their mutual love and fellowship each with other, as members of the same mystical body.

Q. 169: How hath Christ appointed bread and wine to be given and received in the sacrament of the Lord's supper?

A.: Christ hath appointed the ministers of his word, in the administration of this sacrament of the Lord's supper, to set apart the bread and wine from common use, by the word of institution, thanksgiving, and prayer; to take and break the bread, and to give both the bread and the wine to the communicants; who are, by the same appointment, to take and eat the bread, and to drink the wine, in thankful remembrance that the body of Christ was broken and given, and his blood shed, for them.

Q. 170: How do they that worthily communicate in the Lord's supper feed upon the body and blood of Christ therein?

A.: As the body and blood of Christ are not corporally or carnally present in, with, or under the bread and wine in the Lord's supper, and yet are spiritually present to the faith of the receiver, no less truly and really than the elements themselves are to their outward senses; so they that worthily communicate in the sacrament of the Lord's supper, do therein feed upon the body and blood of Christ, not after a corporal and carnal, but in a spiritual manner; yet truly and really, while by faith they receive and apply unto themselves Christ crucified, and all the benefits of his death.

Q. 171: How are they that receive the sacraments of the Lord's supper to prepare themselves before they come unto it?

A.: They that receive the sacrament of the Lord's supper are, before they come, to prepare themselves thereunto, by examining themselves of their being in Christ, of their sins and wants; of the truth and measure of their knowledge, faith, repentance; love to God and the brethren, charity to all men, forgiving those that have done them wrong; of their desires after Christ, and of their new obedience; and by renewing the exercise of these graces, by serious meditation, and fervent prayer.

Q. 172: May one who doubteth of his being in Christ, or of his due preparation, come to the Lord's supper?

A.: One who doubteth of his being in Christ, or of his due preparation to the sacrament of the Lord's supper, may have true interest in Christ, though he be not yet assured thereof; and in God's account hath it, if he be duly affected with the apprehension of the want of it, and unfeignedly desires to be found in Christ, and to depart from iniquity: in which case (because promises are made, and this sacrament is appointed, for the relief even of weak and doubting Christians) he is to bewail his unbelief, and labour to have his doubts resolved; and, so doing, he may and ought to come to the Lord's supper, that he may be further strengthened.

Q. 173: May any who profess the faith, and desire to come to the Lord's supper, be kept from it?

A.: Such as are found to be ignorant or scandalous, notwithstanding their profession of faith, and desire to come to the Lord's Supper, may and ought to be kept from that sacrament, by the power which Christ hath left in His church, until they receive instruction, and manifest their reformation.

Q. 174: What is required of them that receive the sacrament of the Lord's supper in the time of the administration of it?

A.: It is required of them that receive the sacrament of the Lord's supper, that, during the time of the administration of it, with all holy reverence and attention they wait upon God in that ordinance, diligently observe the sacramental elements and actions, heedfully discern the Lord's body, and affectionately meditate on his death and sufferings, and thereby stir up themselves to a vigorous exercise of their graces; in judging themselves, and sorrowing for sin; in earnest hungering and thirsting after Christ, feeding on him by faith, receiving of his fulness, trusting in his merits, rejoicing in his love, giving thanks for his grace; in renewing of their covenant with God, and love to all the saints.

Q. 175: What is the duty of Christians, after they have received the sacrament of the Lord's supper?

A.: The duty of Christians, after they have received the sacrament of the Lord's supper, is seriously to consider how they have behaved themselves therein, and with what success; if they find quickening and comfort, to bless God for it, beg the continuance of it, watch against relapses, fulfil their vows, and encourage themselves to a frequent attendance on that ordinance: but if they find no present benefit, more exactly to review their preparation to, and carriage at, the sacrament; in both which, if they can approve themselves to God and their own consciences, they are to wait for the fruit of it in due time: but, if they see they have failed in either, they are to be humbled, and to attend upon it afterwards with more care and diligence.

Q. 176: Wherein do the sacraments of baptism and the Lord's supper agree?

A.: The sacraments of baptism and the Lord's supper agree, in that the author of both is God; the spiritual part of both is Christ and his benefits; both are seals of the same covenant, are to be dispensed by ministers of the gospel, and by none other; and to be continued in the church of Christ until his second coming.

Q. 177: Wherein do the sacraments of baptism and the Lord's supper differ?

A.: The sacraments of baptism and the Lord's Supper differ, in that baptism is to be administered but once, with water, to be a sign and seal of our regeneration and ingrafting into Christ, and that even to infants; whereas the Lord's Supper is to be administered often, in the elements of bread and wine, to represent and exhibit Christ as spiritual nourishment to the soul, and to confirm our continuance and growth in Him, and that only to such as are of years and ability to examine themselves.

The Effectiveness of the Sacraments As Means of Grace and Salvation

---

Q. 161: How do the sacraments become effectual means of salvation?

A.: The sacraments become effectual means of salvation, not by any power in themselves, or any virtue derived from the piety or intention of him by whom they are administered, but only by the working of the Holy Ghost, and the blessing of Christ, by whom they are instituted.

There is a sense in which the neglect of the sacraments would destroy the soul. To observe them is God's command. He who willingly disobeys this command, and perseveres, will thereby destroy his soul, just for the same reason that any wilful disobedience will. But then, it is not the lack of the sacraments, but the impenitent state of the soul, which is the true cause of ruin.[1]

The Definition of the Word "Sacrament"

The Greek word for sacrament is *mysterion*, from which we get the word "mystery." In the Bible, a "mystery" is something unknown until divinely revealed. "Every Sacrament is a mystery. There is no Sacrament but contains a high and divine mystery."[1] To the Romans, the Latin word for sacrament, sacramentum, signified the oath that a soldier took pledging his allegiance to his commander when he entered the military. In this light "the Christian is a soldier enlisted and sworn, in the Lord's Supper, to die for Jesus."[2]

The Meaning of "Effectual Means of Salvation"

The Effective Means of Grace

God-ordained aids to faith are called "the effectual, or effective, means of salvation." These "external" means of the saving grace of God, (*i.e.*, the sacraments, Bible reading, Bible preaching and prayer), are the instruments which God has provided for us to use diligently, through which He brings the benefits of salvation into our lives. As we use these means of grace, we are to pray earnestly that God would use them to work His grace in our hearts. "Every duty which is to be performed by God's express command, and which he has designed to be a pledge of his presence" is a means of grace.[3]

The Biblical Basis for This Viewpoint

Peter makes the point that the sacraments are "effectual means of salvation," when he writes: And "corresponding to that, baptism now saves you—not the removal of dirt from the flesh, but an appeal to God for a good conscience—through the resurrection of Christ"

---

1. Robert Bruce, *The Mystery of the Lord's Supper*, trans. and ed. by Thomas Torrance (London: James Clark & Co., 1958), 52.

2. Dabney, *Lectures in Systematic Theology*, 728.

3. Thomas Ridgeley, *Commentary on the Larger Catechism*, 2 vols. (Edmonton, Canada: Still Waters Revival Books, [1855] 1993), 2:484.

(1 Pet. 3:21). He is not attributing saving power to the water of baptism, nor is he saying that water-baptism is an absolute prerequisite to salvation. Rather he is saying that by the sacrament of baptism, the resurrected Christ continues to administer and convey the blessings of salvation into the lives of His people, which are theirs by grace through faith in Christ alone.

The Giver and the Sacramental Gifts

These holy signs are not merely jogs for the memory, whose only effect is psychological. No, the sacrament may not for a moment be detached from the Giver of the sacraments. The signs, instituted by divine sovereignty and therefore filled with the power of his hand, are of great significance for faith.[4]

The Necessity for the Diligent Use of the Sacraments

"That we may escape the wrath and curse of God due to us by reason of the transgression of the law, he requireth of us repentance toward God, and faith toward our Lord Jesus Christ, and THE DILIGENT USE OF THE OUTWARD MEANS whereby Christ communicates to us the benefits of his mediation" (WLC, Q. 153; emphasis added). We must not use the means of grace in a careless, haphazard or indifferent manner, as though we neither expected nor desired to receive anything from God through them. Diligence implies taking advantage of every opportunity to use these means of grace, and earnestly desiring and expecting God's grace through these means.

> God commands the use of the sacraments. He would command nothing that was superfluous or vain. Therefore the sacraments are necessary. God has promised His grace along with the use of the sacraments. No man dare neglect the offered grace of God without condemnation. Therefore, the diligent use of the sacraments is necessary.... "It is true that, by neglecting baptism, we are excluded from salva-

4. G. C. Berkouwer, *Studies in Dogmatics: The Sacraments* (Grand Rapids, MI: William B. Eerdmans Publishing Co., 1969), 81.

tion; and in this sense I acknowledge that it is necessary; but it is absurd to speak of salvation as being confined to the sign" [Calvin].... To reject the sacraments is therefore to reject the Word.[5]

The Source of the Sacraments' Power

The Spirit of Christ

The Power of the Spirit

How do the sacraments become such powerful means of God's saving grace? From what source do they derive their effectiveness? Not by any power in themselves, as if by magic or superstition, as if a mere correct and physical participation in the sacraments itself was sufficient to be blessed by them, whether or not there is faith in the heart. Nor does their power reside in the minister who gives the sacraments. Neither his piety, nor lack thereof, nor any intention or desire within himself, adds to or detracts from the power of the sacraments. Although ministers are called in the New Testament "stewards of the mysteries of God," *i.e.*, the officers to whom God has given the duty of the administration of the Word and sacraments, nevertheless, they do not have any power in the least to confer that saving grace which is Christ's gift. Only Christ by His Holy Spirit makes the sacraments effective in the lives of those for whom they were intended. Their power comes from Him. The Apostle Paul wrote in 1 Corinthians 3:6–7, "I have planted, Apollos watered; but God gave the increase. So then neither is he that planteth anything, neither he that watereth; but God that giveth the increase." And in 1 Corinthians 12:13 he wrote, "By one Spirit are we all baptized into one body."

---

5. Ronald Wallace, *Calvin's Doctrine of the Word and Sacraments* (Edinburgh: Oliver & Boyd, 1953), 239–40.

The Work of the Spirit

Although Christ's physical body is distant from our physical bodies, Christ is not distant from us, for He is brought near by the Holy Spirit in the word and sacraments: "He (the Spirit) shall glorify Me; for He shall take of Mine, and shall disclose it to you" (John 16:14). Nothing in the sacraments will do us any good, except the Holy Spirit enlightens our minds and fills our hearts with the presence of Christ.

> What does this Spirit do as soon as He comes into us? He chases away darkness out of our understanding. Whereas before I knew not God, now I see Him, not only with a general knowledge that He is God, but I know that He is God in Christ. What else does the Holy Spirit do? He opens the heart as well as the mind. Those things on which I bestowed the affection of my heart, and employed the love of my soul, are now, by the working of the Holy Spirit, made gall to me. He makes me hate them as much as poison. He produces such an inward disposition in my soul that He makes me turn and flee from the very thing on which I poured out my love before, and instead to pour it out upon God. This is a great perfection, but nevertheless, in some measure He makes me love God better than anything else. He changes the affections of my soul.[6]

The Absence of the Spirit

If the Holy Spirit is absent, the sacraments accomplish

> nothing more in our minds than the splendor of the sun shining upon blind eyes, or a voice sounding in deaf ears. Therefore, I make such a division between Spirit and sacraments that the power to act rests with the former, and the ministry alone is left to the latter—a ministry empty and trifling, apart from the action of the Spirit, but charged with

6. Bruce, *The Mystery of the Lord's Supper*, 95.

great effect when the Spirit works within and manifests his power.... That the Word may not beat your ears in vain, and that the sacraments may not strike your eyes in vain, the Spirit shows us that in them it is God speaking to us, softening the stubbornness of our heart, and composing it to that obedience which it owes the Word of the Lord. Finally, the Spirit transmits those outward words and sacraments from our ears to our soul.[7]

The Spirit's Delivery of Christ to Us

No one has power to deliver Christ Jesus to us, but God Himself, and His Holy Spirit. And therefore, properly speaking, no one can deliver Christ except God Himself by His own Spirit. He is delivered by the ministry of the Holy Spirit. It is the Holy Spirit who seals Him up in our hearts, and confirms us more and more in Him (2 Cor. 1:22).[8] [See John 16:13–15.]

The Emptiness of the Sacraments without Christ's Spirit

As, "without Christ we can do nothing" [Jn. 15:5], so without his blessing we can receive nothing. Ordinances are only the channel through which grace is conveyed. But Christ is the author and finisher of faith; and he conveys his grace by his Spirit, when he brings the heart into a good frame, and excites suitable acts of faith and love in those who are engaged in the ordinances, and maintains the lively impressions of them, which have a tendency to promote the work of grace in the whole conduct of their lives.[9]

---

7. John Calvin, *Institutes of the Christian Religion*, ed. by John T. McNeill, trans. by Ford Lewis Battles, 2 vols. (Philadelphia: Westminster Press, 1960), 2:1284–86.

8. Bruce, *The Mystery of the Lord's Supper*, 45.

9. Ridgeley, *Commentary on the Larger Catechism*, 2:488.

The Larger Catechism and Roman Catholicism

The Larger Catechism's answer to Question 161 is a refutation of two doctrines of Roman Catholicism: (1) that the sacraments, when correctly administered, are in themselves effective to confer grace; and (2) that the intention of the priest is essential to the sacrament, "so that if a priest goes through all the forms of administering baptism or the Lord's supper, and does not in his own mind *intend* to administer it, it is in fact no sacrament."[10] The problem with each of these doctrines of Rome should be obvious. If point one is correct, then they would effectively confer saving grace upon all who received them: in the mere operation of the visible sacraments, they would be operative in giving grace.[11] However, the Bible speaks of some who received the sacraments, but who were not partakers of the saving grace of God, such as Simon Magus (Acts 8:13, 23). If point two is correct then one administering the sacrament would be placed in God's position. Furthermore, if point two is true, then no one could ever be certain that he had received the sacrament, because he could not see the intentions of the priest's heart, to discover his intention.

The Word of God

The Indispensability of the Word of God to the Sacraments

"The grace which is exhibited in or by the sacraments, rightly used, is not conferred by any power in them; neither doth the efficacy of a sacrament depend upon the piety or intention of him that does administer it:, but upon the work of the Spirit, AND THE WORD of institution; which contains, together with a precept au-

10. Robert Shaw, *The Reformed Faith* (Inverness, Scotland: Christian Focus Publications, [1845] 1974), 281.

11. "...*opus operatum* is not only false but contradicts the nature of the sacraments, which God so instituted that believers, poor and deprived of all goods, should bring nothing to it but begging." (Calvin, *Institutes of Christian Religion,* 2:1303.)

thorizing the use thereof, a promise of benefit to worthy receivers" (WCF, XXVII,iii; emphasis added).

> The right administering of the sacrament cannot stand apart from the Word. For whatever benefit may come to us from the Supper requires the Word: whether we are to be confirmed in faith, or exercised in confession, or aroused to duty there is need of preaching.... Living preaching which edifies its hearers, penetrates into their very minds, impresses itself upon their hearts and settles there, and reveals its effectiveness in the fulfillment of what it promises.[12]

"For the preaching of the cross is to those who are perishing foolishness, but to us who are being saved it is the power of God.... God was well pleased through the foolishness of preaching to save those who believe" (1 Cor. 1:18, 21).

The Unity of the Word of God and the Spirit of God

The unity of the Spirit of God and the Word of God is a fundamental teaching of the Bible: "the sword of the Spirit, which is the word of God" (Eph. 6:17). The Spirit works with the Word; and the Word is powerless without the Spirit. This is especially true with reference to the sacraments. It is only the Word of God that makes the visible elements a sacrament and means of grace.

The sacraments are meaningless signs without the written and preached Word, for, as Calvin says, "the sacrament requires preaching to beget faith.... Accordingly, when we hear the sacramental word mentioned, let us understand the promise, proclaimed in a clear voice by the minister, to lead the people by the hand wherever the sign tends and directs us."[13] The preached Word makes us understand what the visible sign means; and the sign conveys to believers what the Word promises. "Hence, any man is deceived who thinks anything more is conferred upon him through the sacra-

12. Calvin, *Institutes of the Christian Religion*, 2:1416.
13. Calvin, *Institutes of the Christian Religion*, 2:1279–80.

ments than what is offered by God's Word and received by him in true faith."[14]

The Sacrament and the Revealed Promise

> A sacrament is never without a preceding promise but is joined to it as a sort of appendix, with the purpose of confirming and sealing the promise itself, and of making it more evident to us.... By this means God provides first for our ignorance and dullness, then for our weakness. Yet, properly speaking, it is not so much needed to confirm His Sacred Word as to establish us in faith in it. For God's truth is of itself firm and sure enough, and it cannot receive better confirmation from any other source than from itself. But as our faith is slight and feeble unless it be propped on all sides and sustained by every means, it trembles, wavers, totters, and at last gives way.[15]

Hence, "a sacrament consists of the Word and the outward sign."[16]

The Relation of the Word and the Signs

> The sacraments are more than mere seals added to the Word to confirm it. They are also true visible representations of the invisible spiritual things to which the Word directs us.... The sacraments are so designed that the man who is pointed to them by the Word is able to see in the form of the action and in the use of the elements the very promises of the Word set forth patently and visibly.... Thus the sacraments in confirming the promises of the Word also clarify them, and, as Calvin points out, it is precisely because they clarify them that they are most effective in confirming them.[17]

14. Calvin, *Institutes of the Christian Religion*, 2:1290.
15. Calvin, *Institutes of the Christian Religion*, 2:1278.
16. Calvin, *Institutes of the Christian Religion*, 2:1279.
17. Wallace, *Calvin's Doctrine of the Word and Sacrament*, 139–41.

The Definition and Purpose of A Sacrament

Q. 162: What is a sacrament?

A.: A sacrament is an holy ordinance instituted by Christ in his church, to signify, seal, and exhibit unto those that are within the covenant of grace, the benefits of his mediation; to strengthen and increase their faith, and all other graces; to oblige them to obedience; to testify and cherish their love and communion one with another; and to distinguish them from those that are without.

The Definition of a Sacrament

A sacrament can be defined from several perspectives. It is an visible sign of a spiritual blessing of salvation. A sacrament is a sign and seal of the covenant of grace (Gen. 17:10–11; Rom. 4:11). It is an "aid to our faith related to the preaching of the gospel."[18] Sacraments are "*testimonies* of grace and salvation from the Lord," and "*marks* of profession by which we openly swear allegiance to God."[19]

> I take the word *Sacrament* as it is taken and used today in the Church of God, for a holy sign and seal that is annexed to the preached Word of God to seal up and confirm the truth contained in the same Word, but in such a way that I do not call the Seal separated from the Word, the Sacrament.... Well has Augustine said, "Let the Word come to the element and you shall have a Sacrament."... Thus I call a Sacrament the Word and Seal conjointly.[20]

Four things concur to constitute a sacrament: (1) a visible element and action; (2) a covenanted blessing symbolized in and rep-

18. Calvin, *Institutes of the Christian Religion*, 2:1276.
19. Calvin, *Institutes of the Christian Religion*, 2:1296.
20. Bruce, *The Mystery of the Lord's Supper*, 41–42.

resented to the senses by the element; (3) a mutual pledge and seal of this covenant between God and man; and (4) an express institution of the sacrament by God in the Bible.

The Persons To Whom the Sacraments are Given

The sacraments are to be given to those who are within God's visible covenant community, the visible church (Gen. 17; 1 Cor. 10–11). Circumcision was the sign or mark of the covenant in the Old Testament, marking one's public initiation into the visible covenant community, presupposing membership in that community (Gen. 17:7); and Passover was the celebration of the basis of the covenant community's standing before God—the sacrificial death of Jesus Christ (Lev. 16). These two Old Testament sacraments of circumcision and Passover were sacraments of the Old Testament Church, the visible congregation of the Lord (Acts 13:48; Ex. 12). Only those in the Church had a right to them and could enjoy their benefits. Circumcision was administered to new male believers upon profession of their faith and public entrance into the covenant community. Only those who were circumcised, and therefore members of the covenant community, could partake of the Passover feast (Ex. 12:48).

In the New Testament, baptism, which is the fulfillment of circumcision (Col. 2:11, 12), is our public initiation into the visible church, presupposing membership in the church by faith. It was administered to converts upon their profession of faith in Christ, and to the household of those who made such a profession (Acts 2:38; Acts 16:31–34; etc.) The point is that baptism is inseparable from the visible church, being the initiatory sacrament of the visible church, which is comprised of all those who profess faith in Christ, along with their children (Acts 16:31).

The Lord's Supper, which is the fulfillment of Passover (Matt. 26:19–30; 1 Cor. 5:7, 8; 10:16–18, 11:23–30), points us to the spiritual food by which we mature as members of Christ's church (1 Cor. 10:1–4). Just as Passover was only for those who were circumcised (Ex. 12:48), so the Lord's Supper is only for those who are baptized, and hence, members in good standing, *i.e.*, not under church discipline (1 Cor. 5:1–8), of the visible church of Christ. *Therefore, bap-*

tism and the Lord's Supper are sacraments of the visible church, so that, only those in the visible church may partake of them and enjoy their benefits; and only ordained ministers of the church may administer them, as we shall see later.

In 1 Cor. 11:20–22, Paul admonishes the visible, organized church in Corinth by saying, "when you meet together, it is not to eat the Lord's Supper." He then instructs them on the proper administration and reception of the Lord's Supper (vss. 23–30). The question is: when did the Corinthians meet together to receive the Lord's Supper? Did it take place at informal gatherings of Christians in each other's homes? Did it take place in each family, administered by the father? Or did it take place in the congregational worship of the church? Furthermore, who was allowed to partake? Anybody present at the time? Or, actual members of the visible church at Corinth?

1 Corinthians 11:20–22 answers these questions. In 11:20 Paul says, "when YOU meet together." To whom was he speaking? "You" in verse 20 refers to the recipients of the First Epistle to the Corinthians, identified in 1:2 as "the church of God which is at Corinth..., with all who in every place call upon the name of our Lord Jesus Christ." This obviously refers to the local, visible, organized church in Corinth, along with the visible and organized church of God throughout the world,[21] which church comprises all those who have made a public and credible profession of faith in Jesus Christ before the elders of the church, who as shepherds of the flock under Christ are to act as guardians of the membership of the church (Acts 20:28), and who are to receive into and exclude from membership in the church accord-

---

21. "With all who in every place call upon the name of our Lord Jesus Christ." (1) To call upon the name of the Lord Jesus is to invoke His aid, as our almighty and sovereign God incarnate (Acts 9:14, 21; 22:16; Rom. 10:13; 2 Tim. 2:22). To call upon the name of Jesus as Lord is to worship Him as the Lord. All Christians everywhere are worshipers of Christ. (2) "In every place" implies "in every meeting-place" or "in every gathering-place." "Thus the Corinthians are reminded that they are not alone; rather there are those all over the world who call on the name of the Lord when they meet together.... The one whom the Corinthians call "Lord" is also Lord of the whole church, and as such is finally to have His way among them as he does in the other churches" (Gordon Fee, *The New International Commentary on the New Testament: The First Epistle to the Corinthians* [Grand Rapids, MI: William B. Eerdmans Publishing Co., 1987], 34).

ing to the Word of God (Matt. 16:19; 18:15–20). The households of believers in Christ are also counted as members of the visible church (Gen. 17:7–14; Acts 16:31). So then, we learn that the sacraments are for members of the visible, organized church.[22]

Furthermore, they must be members of not just any church, but of a church that bears the marks of a true church, according to the Bible, which marks are: (1) The faithful preaching of the Word of God (Acts 20:27–32); (2) The administration of the Sacraments of Baptism and the Lord's Supper (Matt. 28:19; 1 Cor. 11:23–26); and (3) The faithful practice of church discipline (1 Cor. 5; Matt. 18:15–20). Any organization or gathering, which calls itself a church, is not a true church, if it does not bear the marks of a true church. True Christians want to be members of true churches.[23]

The next question 1 Corinthians 11 answers is: When are the members of the church supposed to receive the sacrament? Anytime, anywhere? Or, at a specific time, and a specific place? Informally, whenever they get together for any reason? Or, in congregational worship? The answer is to be found in 11:18, where Paul is telling them, "when you come together as a church," or literally "in church," you should take the Lord's Supper. In this phrase, the word "church" is without an article ("the") and therefore is an expression like our "in church," *i.e.*, in the assembly gathered for public worship. The word for church in this verse (*ekklesia*), in the New Testa-

---

22. We know Paul is addressing an organized church in Corinth, and not simply an informal gathering of Christians, by several things in this epistle. (1) Paul reminds the Corinthian church of the implications of their baptism, by which they were publicly initiated into the visible church, 1:13. (2) Paul refers to the role of other preachers in the life of this church (3:4–15). (3) He speaks of them collectively as "the Temple of God" (3:16), where, as in the Old Testament covenant community, God's Spirit lives. (4) In 1 Corinthians 5, he assists the church in the administering of church discipline and excommunication. (5) In 6:1–8, he urges Christians to take complaints against each other to the church courts, rather than to the civil courts, if possible. (6) In 9:1–14, Paul explains the church's duty to financially support the preacher for his preaching. (7) Paul corrects and clarifies some of the worship practices of the church (1 Cor. 11, 12, 14). (8) Paul directs the Corinthian church to receive offerings for needy saints, just as he directs other "churches" (16:1–4). (9) In 16:16, Paul calls upon the Corinthian church to "be in subjection" to its ordained ministers who preach the word.

23. Only churches can plant churches.

ment never means a building. The phrase, then, means, "when you, the local congregation of those who profess Christ, and your children, under the spiritual oversight of elders, formally assemble for public worship." So then, again, Paul answers our questions: the Lord's Supper is to be received by members in good standing, *i.e.*, not under church discipline, in a church bearing the marks of a true church administered by a minister of the gospel, in a public worship service. (We will show that only ministers of the gospel should administer the sacraments later in this chapter.)

The Purpose of a Sacrament

The Representation of Christ in the Sacraments (WCF, XXVII, i)

The sacraments are signs or pictures of the truths they represent and convey to us. They present to our eyes the revealed truth about Christ and His blessings in a comparable manner to that in which they are presented to our ears in the preaching of the Word of God. "The Word leads us to Christ by the ear; the Sacraments lead us to Christ by the eye."[24] "Christ is the matter or (if you prefer) the substance of all the sacraments; for in him they have all their firmness, and they do not promise anything apart from him."[25]

The Giving of the Whole Christ in the Sacraments

The Same Work of the Word and the Sacraments

The sacraments NOT ONLY REPRESENT Christ and His benefits, they ALSO GIVE Christ and His benefits to believers (1 Cor. 1:30). That which is offered to believers in the Word and sacraments is Christ Himself, and neither promises anything apart from Him (2 Cor. 1:18–22). The sacraments do the same work as the Word of God: they "offer and set forth Christ to us, and in him the treasures

24. Bruce, *The Mystery of the Lord's Supper*, 39.
25. Calvin, *Institutes of the Christian Religion*, 2:1291.

of heavenly grace. But they avail and profit nothing unless received by faith."[26]

The Biblical Basis for This Viewpoint

The Communion in the Body and Blood of Jesus

In 1 Corinthians 10:16–18 we read, "Is not the cup of blessing which we bless a sharing in the blood of Christ? Is not the bread which we break a sharing in the body of Christ? Since there is one bread, we who are many are one body; for we all partake of the one bread. Look at the nation Israel; are not those who eat the sacrifices sharers in the altar?" Notice three points in this text: (1) In taking the Lord's Supper we actually share, participate, fellowship, and commune, (*koinonia*), in the body and blood of Jesus Christ, and in what the sacrifice of His body and the shedding of His blood accomplished for us. (2) Those who take the Lord's Supper are one body in Christ. (3) In Old Testament Israel, the faithful offerers of sacrifices shared in and had communicated to them the spiritual redemption signified by the altar and its sacrifice, so it could be said of them that in eating the sacrificial meal they were "sharers in the altar." These verses, obviously, speak of a spiritual communion not a literal, physical mixing.[27] Nor do they imply that the sacraments convey grace merely in the taking of them, with no reference to faith in the heart.

This communion, participation and fellowship (*koinonia* in Greek), is the heart of the Lord's Supper. The bread and wine are our life, strength and joy because that which is received in the bread and wine is Christ and the beneficial results of His sacrificed body and blood. The Lord's Supper is the means by which the benefits of Christ's sacrifice are brought more fully into our hearts (1 Cor. 1:30–31). In fact, when we come to the Lord's Table in faith, we

26. Calvin, *Institutes of the Christian Religion*, 2:1292.

27. "I frankly confess that I reject their teaching of the mixture, or transfusion, of Christ's flesh with our soul. For it is enough for us that, from the substance of his flesh Christ breathes life into our souls—indeed, pours forth his very life into us—even though Christ's flesh itself does not enter into us" (Calvin, *Institutes of the Christian Religion*, 2:1404).

commune with Jesus Christ in person, we receive Christ Himself. AS SOON AND AS TRULY as our mouths take in the bread and wine, our hearts receive Christ by faith. We eat and nourish ourselves upon Christ with our hearts, as our mouths eat the elements of bread and wine. This is not a physical eating of Christ or a physical communion. Neither Christ nor the benefits of His redemptive work are received by the physical mouth, but by faith alone (John 3:16). However, in the sacraments we do, by faith and in fact, commune with the Living Christ. This is beyond our comprehension: the presence of Christ, who is sitting at God's right hand, infinitely transcendent over us, is brought infinitely near us by His Spirit through the means of grace. What an awesome mystery!

The Westminster Confession of Faith teaches us that true believers do, really and spiritually, but not physically, receive and feed upon the crucified and exalted Christ, and receive by faith all the benefits of His death and resurrection (Chapter 29). Robert Shaw in *The Reformed Faith* says that "while the worthy receivers outwardly partake of the visible elements in this sacrament, they inwardly, by faith, receive and feed upon Christ crucified."[28] And Charles Hodge of Princeton Seminary says that "every time...the consecrated wine touches the believer's lips, he receives anew the application of the blood of Christ for the remission of his sins and his reconciliation with God."[29]

The Spiritual Food, Spiritual Drink and Spiritual Baptism

Because the sacraments really signify, seal and give Christ and the benefits of salvation to believing recipients, they can be said to be "Spiritual food" and "Spiritual drink" (1 Cor. 10:3–4). They can be considered such, not only because the Spiritual blessings of which they are signs and seals are from Heaven, but because the blessings of the sacrament are Spirit-produced, and therefore, cause us to live everyday in total and conscious dependence on the re-

28. Shaw, *The Reformed Faith*, 303.

29. Charles Hodge, *A Commentary on The First Epistle to the Corinthians* (London: The Banner of Truth Trust, [1958] 1964), 228.

sources of Christ's self-surrender on the Cross for us, which resources are the gift of the Holy Spirit, who is continually poured out on us (Acts 1:8). In the Lord's Supper, we are "all made to drink of one Spirit" (1 Cor.12:13b). And by the sign and seal of water-baptism, "by one Spirit we were all baptized into one body" (1 Cor. 12:13a). Therefore, the Lord's Supper is "Spiritual food" and "Spiritual drink," and baptism is baptism by the Spirit, because the sacraments convey those blessings to believers which were purchased by the death of Christ, one of which was the gift of the Holy Spirit of God in all His gifts and influences.

The Communication of the Whole Christ in the Sacraments

That which is signified and given in the Sacraments is

> *the whole Christ with His whole gifts, benefits and graces, applied and given to my soul.* I do not call the thing signified by the signs of bread and wine the benefits of Christ, the graces of Christ, or the virtue that flows out of Christ only, but I call the thing signified together with the benefits and virtues flowing from Him, the very substance of Christ Himself, from which this virtue flows. The substance with the virtues, gifts and graces that flow from the substance, is the thing signified here. As for the virtue and graces, that flow from Christ, it is not possible for you to partake of the virtue that flows from His substance, without first partaking of the substance itself.... Thus it is impossible for me to get the juice and virtue that flow out of Christ without first getting the substance, that is, Christ Himself.... It is the whole Christ, God and man, without separation of His natures, without distinction of His substance from His graces, that I call the thing signified by the signs in the Sacrament.... Therefore, in order that the Sacrament may nourish you to life everlasting, you must get in it your whole Savior, the whole Christ, God and man, with all His graces and benefits, without separation of His substance from His graces, or of the one nature

> from the other. And how do I get Him? Not by my mouth. It is vain to think that we will get God by our mouth, but we get Him by faith.... So, if ever you are to get good out of the Sacrament, you must get the whole Christ. Moreover, there is no instrument with which you may lay hold of Him, but faith.[30]

"As you therefore received Christ Jesus the Lord, so walk in Him" (Col. 2:6). "He who HAS THE SON has life" (1 John 5:12). "... all things belong to you, and you belong to Christ" (1 Cor. 3:22–23).

The Believer's Mystical Union with Christ

The Centrality of Our Union with Christ

> "Let us mark well what this word *Christianity* meaneth: its meaning is to be members of the Son of God." "When the apostle defines the Gospel, and the use of it, he says that we are called to be partakers of our Lord Jesus Christ, and to be made one with Him, and to dwell in Him, and He in us; and that we be joined together in an inseparable bond" [Calvin].[31]

"Abide in Me and I in you. As the branch cannot bear fruit of itself, unless it abides in the vine, so neither can you, unless you abide in Me" (John 15:4). "I do not ask in behalf of these alone, but for those also who believe in Me through their word; that they may all be one; even as Thou, Father, are in Me, and I in Thee, that they also may be in Us... I in them, and Thou in Me, that they may be perfected in unity" (John 17:20–23). "So we, who are many, are one body in Christ" (Rom. 12:5). "Christ in you, the hope of glory.... And in Him you have been made complete" (Col. 1:27; 2:10.)

> The nature of this union with Christ is, however, such a spiritual mystery in itself that it is incomprehensible to the natural mind. It is extremely difficult even for believers to grasp its meaning and reality. Therefore God appoints the two sacraments chiefly in order to depict visibly this particular mys-

---

30. Bruce, *The Mystery of the Lord's Supper*, 45–47.
31. Wallace, *Calvin's Doctrine of the Word and Sacrament*, 143.

tery, so that by their use we may come to know and understand better the nature of our union with Christ.[32]

The Necessity and Nature of Our Union with Christ

Since Christ has thus worked out our salvation in and through His human body and human nature, it follows that the benefits of His work are not available for us, unless we ourselves are brought into some kind of communion with the human nature, and indeed with the body, in which all the work of our salvation was performed, ["communion in the blood of Christ...communion in the body of Christ" (1 Cor. 10:16)]. Participation in the blessings which Christ died and rose to win for us is inseparable from communion with His person... ["Do not work for the food that perishes, but for the food which endures to eternal life, which the Son of Man shall give to you.... This is the work of God, that you BELIEVE IN HIM whom He has sent" (John 6:27, 29).] "The flesh of Christ gives life, not only because we once obtained salvation by it, but because now, while we are made one with Christ by a sacred union, the same flesh breathes life into us, or to express it more briefly, because ingrafted into the body of Christ by the secret agency of the Spirit we have life in common with Him. For from the hidden fountain of the Godhead life was miraculously infused into the body of Christ, that it might flow from thence to us." ... ["The Son also gives life to whom He wishes.... For just as the Father has life in Himself, even so He gave to the Son also to have life in Himself" (John 5:21, 26).]

Even though this "power"...communicated through the human nature of Christ to those united to Him comes from another source than that flesh itself (*i.e.*, from the divine nature), nevertheless "His flesh as a channel, conveys to us that life which dwells intrinsically... in His divinity." ... ["For in Him all the fulness of Deity dwells in bodily form, and in Him you have been made complete" (Col. 2:9, 10).]

32. Wallace, *Calvin's Doctrine of the Word and Sacrament*, 143–44.

> In this union there takes place what Calvin calls a "wondrous exchange" made by the boundless goodness of God, whereby Christ takes upon Himself what is ours, and transfers to us what is His own.... "Having received our mortality, He has bestowed on us His immortality. Having undertaken our weakness, He has made us strong in His strength. Having submitted to our poverty, He has transferred to us His riches. Having taken upon Himself the burden of our unrighteousness with which we were oppressed, He has clothed us with His righteousness."
>
> His whole strength, power and majesty, is here made to consist in gifts of the Spirit. Although Christ was not deficient in gifts of this kind, yet as He took upon Him our flesh, it was necessary that He should be enriched with them, that we might afterwards be made partakers of all the blessings of which otherwise we are destitute; for *out of* His fulness, as John says, we *must draw as from a fountain,* (John 1:16 and 7:37–8).... This refers to Christ's human nature; because He could not be enriched with a gift...except in so far as He became man. Besides, as He came down to us, so He received the gifts of the Spirit, that He might bestow them upon us" [Calvin].[33]

The Believer's Union with Christ Sealed by the Sacraments

Both sacraments have the same goal and purpose: to testify of Christ, to confirm our relation to Christ, to assist in effecting our union with Christ. Baptism bears witness to our initiation into this union (1 Cor. 12:13), and the Lord's Supper is a sign of our continuation in this union (1 Cor. 10:16).

33. Wallace, *Calvin's Doctrine of the Word and Sacrament*, 145–49.

The Believer's Union with Christ Effected by the Holy Spirit

Our mystical union with Christ is created and sustained by the work of the Holy Spirit (1 Cor. 12:13; 2 Cor. 1:21–22; Eph. 1:13; Eph. 4:4). It is the Holy Spirit "who enlightens our minds by faith [Eph. 1:18], who seals the adoption of God on our hearts [Gal. 4:4–6], who regenerates us into newness of life [John 3:3–8], who grafts us into the body of Christ [1 Cor. 12:13], that He may live in us and we in Him [Col. 1:27] [Calvin]."[34]

The Believer's Union with Christ the Basis of the Church

The Bible presents us with a close relationship between Christ and His Church. John Calvin's language reflects this close relationship.

> There are many passages in Calvin's writings where he uses the phrase about our being "ingrafted into the body of Christ" to refer simply to our admission into the Church and our union with the life of the Church. And there are passages where it is difficult to decide whether Calvin, when he speaks of the body of Christ, means the actual glorified body now in heaven or the Church. "God hath saved us by His mercy, the symbol and pledge of which He gave us in Baptism, by admitting us into His Church and ingrafting us into the body of His Son," Calvin can thus speak of admission into the Church and ingrafting into the body of Christ as the same thing.[35]

The Believer's Union with Christ A Pledge of Eternal Redemption

The sacraments are "eschatological signs," because

> they bear witness to a union that is begun, and more and more moving on to completion, but which can only be completed in heaven [Phil. 1:6].

34. Wallace, *Calvin's Doctrine of the Word and Sacrament*, 152.
35. Wallace, *Calvin's Doctrine of the Word and Sacrament*, 154–55.

> The true goal of all human life is union with God.... "The chief good of man is to be united to God, with whom is the fountain of life and all blessing." But this perfect union of man with God is now accomplished only in the person of Christ, who has entered the kingdom of heaven in our flesh and in whom there is set up a perfect and complete union between God and a human nature. Christ has, moreover, entered the kingdom of heaven not only in our flesh, "but as it were in our name," says Calvin, and it follows that "we are in a manner now seated in heavenly places, not entertaining a mere hope of heaven, but possessing it in our head."... This union between ourselves and the body of Christ is therefore eschatologically completed, the sacraments being a pledge of its present yet hidden fullness.
>
> Moreover, Calvin bids us note the fact that this union is a pledge not only of the redemption of our souls but also of our bodies, which through the sacraments have the sign engraven on them that they also, as well as our souls, are united to the body of Christ. "Observe that the spiritual connection which we have with Christ belongs not merely to the soul, but also to the body, so that we are *flesh of His flesh*, (Eph. 5:30).... "Our flesh is vivified by His immortal flesh, and shares in some manner in its immortality."[36]

To Signify to Covenant Members the Benefits of Christ's Redemptive Work

Sacraments are signs. They are tokens of God's covenant promises to us, which are ours because of the finished redemptive work of Jesus Christ. Augustine called a sacrament "a visible word," because "it represents God's promises as painted in a picture and sets them before our sight, portrayed graphically and in the manner of images."[37]

36. Wallace, *Calvin's Doctrine of the Word and Sacrament*, 156–57.
37. Calvin, *Institutes of the Christian Religion*, 2:1281.

> The sacraments, therefore, are exercises which make us more certain of the trustworthiness of God's Word.... Thus we might call them "the pillars of our faith." For as a building stands and rests upon its own foundation but is more surely established by columns placed underneath, so faith rests upon the Word of God as a foundation; but when the sacraments are added, it rests more firmly upon them as upon columns.[38]

> The words "seal and sign" refer, then, to an act of God; he signifies and seals by his promise.[39]

> The Sacrament is appointed that we may get a better hold of Christ than we got in the simple Word, that we may possess Christ in our hearts and minds more fully and largely than we did before, by the simple Word. That Christ may have more room in which to reside in our narrow hearts than He could have by the hearing of the simple Word, and that we may possess Him more fully, is a better thing. Even though Christ is the same in Himself, yet the better hold you have of Him, the surer you are of His Promise. The Sacraments are appointed that I may have Him more fully in my soul, that I may have the bounds of it enlarged, and that He may make the better residence in me.[40]

We call the sacraments "signs," because the Bible teaches us to call them "signs." Circumcision, which is fulfilled in baptism, is called "the sign of the covenant between Me and you" in Gen. 17:7, 10–11, and is referred to as "the sign of circumcision" in Romans 4:11. The Old Testament Passover, which is fulfilled in Christ (1 Cor. 5:7), and the Lord's Supper (Matt. 26:26–29), is referred to as a sign of God's covenant in Exodus 12:13, 23. Therefore, since the Old Testament sacraments are fulfilled in the New Testament sacraments, and since the Old Testament sacraments were signs of the

38. Calvin, *Institutes of the Christian Religion*, 2:1281.
39. Berkouwer, *Studies in Dogmatics: The Sacraments*, 136.
40. Bruce, *The Mystery of the Lord's Supper*, 64.

covenant, therefore, we should consider the New Testament sacraments of baptism and the Lord's Supper as signs of God's covenant, which is itself one in both testaments.

To *Seal* to Covenant Members the Benefits of Christ's Redemptive Work

The Seals in the Place of Miracles

Sacraments are seals (Rom. 4:11). They seal the promises of God's Word to our hearts. They seal and confirm to us the redemptive blessings they signify, *i.e.*, all the promises and blessings of the new covenant (1 Cor. 10:16). They are given as God's seals to confirm our faith, that He is our covenant God.

> Though the sacraments are ineffective without the Word, nevertheless the bare word cannot have its full effect without the sacraments. *The New Testament sacraments take the important place which miracles and visions and dreams and all the visible phenomena by means of which God revealed Himself had in the Old Testament times.* Though the Word preached appeals to us through the ear and thus begets faith in our hearts, nevertheless, through the sacraments God reinforces the appeal and power of the spoken Word.... Thus the sacraments confirm the word by making it more visible and concrete to the senses.... The sacraments "attest and ratify the benevolence of the Lord toward us." Calvin often draws a parallel between the function which miracles have in the Old Testament, and in the history of the early Church, and the part which the sacraments are meant to play in these days when they form the only visible element in God's ordinary revealing activity. *Miracles in their day acted as seals to confirm the word of God.*[41]

> The Lord offers us mercy and the pledge of his grace both in his Sacred Word and in his sacraments.... Sacraments are

41. Wallace, *Calvin's Doctrine of the Word and Sacrament*, 137–39.

> truly named the testimonies of God's grace and are like seals of the good will that He feels toward us, which by attesting that good will to us, sustain, nourish, confirm, and increase our faith.[42]

The Meaning of the Figure of a "Seal"

> Seals are distinct from signs in that they not only remind us of invisible things, but also authenticate these things to our religious consciousness by making them more certain and sure to us. During our daily practical life we constantly make use of seals, tokens for combating fraud, falsehood, and counterfeits. It is, in fact, necessary to distinguish the true from the false, what is authentic from what is not, the original from the counterfeit. A trade mark serves to authenticate and guarantee the source and quality of a product. Hallmarks declare the standard of alloy, the exact value, and the nationality of gold or silver articles. On weights and measures they testify to the accuracy of the inscription by reference to the scientifically determined original which they represent. Stamps, seals, and signatures guarantee the perfect authenticity of an important document.... Scripture attests the usage of seals when there is concern to prove that something is really authentic and when it is of importance to guarantee it against all falsification.[43]

As Greg Bahnsen has said in his tapes on Calvin's *Institutes*: in the Word, God makes promises to His people in Christ, and in the sacraments, He says to us, "And I really mean it." Sacraments can be said to be *God's oaths* to us confirming and guaranteeing to us the rich promises of His word:

> For when God made the promise to Abraham, since He could swear by no one greater, He swore by Himself, saying, "I will

---

42. Calvin, *Institutes of the Christian Religion*, 2:1282.

43. Pierre Marcel, *The Biblical Doctrine of Infant Baptism: Sacrament of the Covenant of Grace*, trans. by Philip E. Hughes (London: James Clarke and Co., [1953] 1959), 30.

> surely bless you, and I will surely multiply you." And thus, having patiently waited, he obtained the promise. For men swear by one greater than themselves, and with them an oath given as confirmation is an end of every dispute. In the same way God, desiring even more to show to the heirs of the promise the unchangeableness of His purpose, interposed with an oath, in order than by two unchangeable things, in which it is impossible for God to lie, we may have strong encouragement, we who have fled for refuge in laying hold of the hope set before us. This hope we have as an anchor of the soul (Hebrews 6:13–19).

And remember, God instituted sacramental seals, not because the Word needs them, but because we need them.

The Meaning of "Seal" (Sphragis) in the New Testament

In 1 Corinthians 9:2, Paul informs the Corinthian church that "you are the seal of my apostleship in the Lord." Their conversion, existence as a church, and recognition of his apostolic authority *confirm* the *trustworthiness* and *authenticity* of his apostleship. In Romans 4:11, circumcision is "a seal of the righteousness of the faith which he had while he was in uncircumcision." The seal *guarantees* righteousness to the believer. In receiving the seal of circumcision Abraham received "THE MEANS OF CONFIRMATION AND OF VERIFICATION."[44] In John 6:27, Jesus tells us not to "work for the food which perishes, but for the food which endures to eternal life, which the Son of Man shall give to you, for on Him the Father, even God, has set His seal." This refers to God's own witness regarding the identity of Jesus Christ (John 5:37), upon which divine witness our faith rests. This "sealing" witness of God *verifies* and *attests* to the truthfulness of Christ's claims. "It is clear from the New Testament, then, why the Christian Church began very early to describe that element of trustworthiness and confirmation with the word 'seal.'"[45]

---

44. Berkouwer, *Studies in Dogmatics: The Sacraments*, 140.
45. Berkouwer, *Studies in Dogmatics: The Sacraments*, 141.

The Sealing Work of the Holy Spirit

In 2 Corinthians 1:21–22, we read that "He who establishes us with you in Christ and appointed us is God, who also sealed us and gave us the Spirit in our hearts as a pledge (down payment)." In Ephesians 1:13–14, we read that,

> in Him (Christ), you also, after listening to the message of truth, the gospel of your salvation—having also believed, you were sealed in Him with the Holy Spirit of promise, who is given as a pledge of our inheritance, with a view to the redemption of God's own possession, to the praise of His glory.

And in Ephesians 4:30, Paul exhorts us not to "grieve the Holy Spirit of God, by whom you were sealed for the day of redemption."

To understand the sealing work of the Holy Spirit, we must be clear about the meaning of the figure of a seal. It is used to attest to the authenticity of written documents, for confirming and giving assurance, as a verifying testimony. A seal was a certificate of trustworthiness, a guarantee, and a pledge of faithfulness. The sealing work of the Holy Spirit confirms and strengthens the hope of the believer regarding the certain completion of his salvation in Christ. The Spirit Himself is God's gift to His child as a pledge and down-payment of his eternal security in His love. But beyond this, the sealing work of the Spirit keeps our minds in the love of God,

> giving stability to all the mental exercises of the believer which has so important and powerful a bearing on the hope and peace of the saint in this present life.... The nature of this sealing, then, in its special significance, is plain enough: it is an act of the Spirit's influence, giving *stability* and *strength* to all the exercises of the renewed soul, and thus adding clearness to the evidences of regeneration, giving force and definiteness to the doctrines and precepts of the word, infusing vigor into hope, multiplying comfort, and bestowing firmness and endurance on the zeal of the soul, and on all the energies of conduct. It is an action of the Holy Spirit assuring and adding vigor to all his work in the heart, giv-

> ing more definite, stable, and abiding form to all the graces, the germ of which he has implanted in regeneration.[46]

The Holy Spirit, as "the Spirit of Promise" is particularly the SEALER OF GOD'S COVENANT PROMISES revealed in His Word to the heart and life of the believer, enabling his faith to stand firm and unwavering on the sheer word of the Lord, trusting Him and His promises.

The Holy Spirit does this great and continuous work in the heart of the regenerate, in whom He dwells, with the Word of God and by means of the sacraments, as "sealing ordinances," although He is not limited to or dependent upon the sacraments. But, in His sovereignty, wisdom, and condescending grace He has chosen to use the sacraments as *signs* and *seals*, making us dependent upon them. By the sacraments, the Holy Spirit acts as God's "pledge" to us that we are eternally secure in Him. And as the Spirit *confirms* that "pledge" to us in the "sealing ordinances," our faith and Christian character are strengthened, stabilized and advanced.

In Revelation 7:2–10, we read that John saw an

> angel ascending from the rising of the sun, having the seal of the living God.... And I heard the number of those who were sealed, one hundred and forty-four thousand[47] sealed from

---

46. Curtis R. Vaughan, *The Gifts of the Holy Spirit* (London: The Banner of Truth Trust, [1894] 1975), 261, 263–64.

47. "The 144,000 sealed from every tribe of the sons of Israel" is obviously symbolic and figurative. (1) The book of Revelation was written to encourage the Christian Church, not apostate Judaism. (2) Throughout the New Testament the Christian Church is given names and descriptions that originally applied to the Old Testament covenant people, simply because the Church of God is one in Old Testament and New Testament, as we have seen. (3) In 7:9, the "144,000" of verse 4 are described "as a great multitude, which no one could count, from every nation and all tribes and peoples and tongues." It is obvious as the chapter proceeds that these two designations are for one and the same multitude, seen from one perspective, as the one covenant community of the Lord, and from another, as a community that is now not limited to one people, but is international and multitudinous in scope. (4) The number "144,000" is rich in symbolism. This number is comprised of TWELVE, the number of the Covenant people of God in the Old Testament with its twelve tribes, and the New Testament, with its twelve apostles, squared, then multiplied by 1000, (10 and its multiples symbolize "many," Deut. 1:11; 7:9; Ps. 50:10; 68:17; 84:10; 90:4). 1000 is 10x10x10, which indicates a perfect

> every tribe of the sons of Israel.... And behold a great multitude, which no one could count, from every nation and all tribes and peoples and tongues, standing before the throne and before the Lamb, clothed in white robes.

Here in vivid imagery we see the Angel of the Lord, "the Sun of Righteousness with healing in His wings" (Mal. 4:2; Luke 1:78), sealing the entirety of the (New) Covenant People of God, so that those who bear His seal are protected from His judgment upon the rebellious world (9:4; 14:1; 22:4). Those who bear the seal of God stand in total contrast to those who bear the mark of the beast (Rev. 13:16–17; 14:11). The seal of the living God is God's gift of power, guarantee of protection and mark of ownership (Ezek. 9:1–7). A believer sealed by God is thus empowered and protected and assured by Him that He belongs to the Lord. Only those bearing the "seal of the living God" will escape His judgment; all others bear "the mark of the Beast" and will perish under that judgment. Those in whom the Holy Spirit is working His sealing ministry by the Word of God and the sacraments are saved from the wrath of God, are protected from the evil of the world, are empowered to be faithful in the face of persecution, and are firmly assured of their security in the Lord.

The Seals and the Word of God

> The sacraments also serve to seal up and confirm the truth that is in the Word. The office of the seal appended to the evidence is not to confirm any other truth, than that which is in the evidence. Although you believed the evidence before, yet by the seals, you believe it better. But even so, the Sacrament assures you of no other truth than that contained within the Word. Nevertheless, because it is a seal annexed to the Word it persuades you better of its truth, for the more the

---

cube, reduplicated completeness. Here John pictures for us the New Israel of God as she was meant to be in all her perfection, symmetry and completeness. This is entirely in harmony with the picture of the City of the New Jerusalem in Revelation 21, with its 12 gates and 12 foundations. On the 12 gates are written the names of the 12 tribes of Israel, and on the 12 foundations the names of the 12 apostles. We also read of the City's wall as being 144 cubits in height (Rev. 21:17).

> outward senses are awakened, the more is the inward heart and mind persuaded to believe.
>
> Now the Sacrament awakens all the outward senses, such as the eye, the hand, and all the rest. When the outward senses are moved, without doubt the Holy Spirit concurs, moving the heart all the more. The Sacraments are therefore annexed to the Word, to seal up the truth contained in the Word, and to confirm it more and more in your heart. The Word is appointed to work belief, and the Sacrament is appointed to confirm you in this belief.... Therefore the whole concern of Christians should be, when they see the Sacraments and hear the Word, to find and feel in their hearts and minds, that which they hear and see.... Therefore, unless you strive for continual sanctification, and sever yourselves from everything that severs you from Christ, it is not possible for Him to live or dwell in you.[48]

The Biblical Basis for Calling the Sacraments Seals

Why do we believe that the sacraments are "seals"? Because in Romans 4:11, the sacrament of circumcision is referred to as "a seal of the righteousness of the faith which he [Abraham] had while uncircumcised." "Baptism is the circumcision of the New Testament, the initial sign of the same covenant; and baptized believers are children of Abraham's promises by faith" [Acts 2:38, 39; Gal. 3:7, 9, 27–29]."[49] Furthermore, the Passover in the Old Testament, which is fulfilled in Christ and the Lord's Supper in the New Testament (1 Cor. 5:7; Matt. 26:26–29), is also identified as a pledge, or sign of the covenant (Ex. 12:13, 23), guaranteeing to God's faithful people protection from the curse of death that would fall on the firstborn of Egypt. Since baptism fulfills circumcision, which is called a seal of the covenant, then baptism is a seal as well. And since the Lord's Supper fulfills the Passover, which is also called a pledge, or seal of the covenant, then the Lord's Supper is a pledge and seal as well.

48. Bruce, *The Mystery of the Lord's Supper*, 64–65.
49. Dabney, *Lectures in Systematic Theology*, 728.

To Exhibit *to Covenant Members the Benefits of Christ's Redemptive Work*

The Sacraments as Conveying Christ and Salvation to Us

To the authors of the Larger Catechism the word "exhibit" meant "to give," "communicate," "convey," or "apply," not just "to show forth." Therefore, they understood the sacraments not only as signifying and sealing the benefits of redemptive and covenant promises of God, but also as applying and conveying those benefits to believers. The point was that Christ, by His Spirit gives the benefits of redemption to those who observe the sacrament in a proper manner (1 Cor. 10:20–31; 11:23–34). He applies to believers all the benefits of the new covenant. The Westminster Confession of Faith says that "by the right use of this ordinance, the grace promised is not only offered, but *really exhibited* [*i.e.*, conveyed and applied] and *conferred* by the Holy Ghost" (XXVIII, vi; emphasis added).

The Biblical Basis for This Viewpoint

We know that the sacraments really confer and "exhibit" the blessings they represent for these reasons:

(1) Because the sacrament of circumcision/baptism offers and gives the blessings of the covenant of grace, the Old Testament sacrament of circumcision is actually called, not only the sign of the covenant, but "the covenant" itself: "This is My covenant, which you shall keep, between Me and you and your descendants after you: every male among you shall be circumcized.... Thus shall My covenant be in your flesh for an everlasting covenant" (Gen. 17:10, 13). Notice that the verse does not simply say that the sign of the covenant will be in you, but that the covenant itself, which the sacrament conveys to God's people, will be in you. "He who received the sign, was thereby at once entitled to the enjoyment of certain privileges, the signs and means of saving graces."[50]

(2) In Exodus 12:11, and elsewhere, the sacrificial lamb is called the Passover, because salvation from death based on the atoning

50. Dabney, *Lectures in Systematic Theology*, 729.

sacrifice was conveyed to Israel the night God saved their firstborn from death.

(3) In 1 Corinthians 11:24, 25, the bread and wine of the Lord's Supper are called the body and blood of Christ, not because they are literally such, but because of the intimate sacramental union between the sign and that which it signifies, and because Christ and the benefits of His redemptive work are offered and conveyed with the bread and wine in the Lord's Supper to the believer (1 Cor. 10:16). Jesus said that the cup of the Lord's Supper is "My blood of the covenant, which is to be shed on behalf of many for forgiveness of sins" (Matt. 26:28).

The Relation of the Sacraments to Jesus Christ

The sacraments signify and seal Christ and His benefits to us, because they "exhibit" or convey and give Christ and His benefits to us. They are not signs simply because they signify something, but because through them Christ gives us what they signify.

> I call them signs because they have the Body and Blood of Christ conjoined with them. Indeed, so truly is the Body of Christ conjoined with the bread, and the Blood of Christ conjoined with the wine, that as soon as you receive the bread in your mouth (if you are a faithful man or woman) you receive the Body of Christ in your soul, and that by faith. And as soon as you receive the wine in your mouth, you receive the Blood of Christ in your soul, and that by faith. It is chiefly because of this function that they are instruments to deliver and exhibit the things that they signify, and not only because of their representation are they called signs. For if they did nothing but represent or signify a thing absent, then any picture or dead image would be a Sacrament, for with every picture, the thing signified comes into your mind.... If, therefore, the sign of the Sacrament did no more than that, all pictures would be Sacraments; but the Sacrament exhibits and delivers the thing that it signifies to the soul and heart, as soon as the sign is delivered to the mouth.... Thus it is chiefly because the Lord has appointed the Sacraments as

> hands to deliver and exhibit the things signified, that they are called signs. As the Word of the Gospel is a mighty and potent instrument for our everlasting salvation, so the Sacrament is a potent instrument appointed by God to deliver to us Christ Jesus for our everlasting salvation.[51]

The Representation & Presentation of Jesus Christ in the Sacraments

What God pictures for us in the sacraments He really gives to believers in the sacraments. "In the sacraments the reality is given to us along with the sign."[52]

> Were all this not so, the whole instituting of sacraments on the part of God would be mockery and a lie. 'Unless we would charge God with deceit, we will never presume to say that He holds forth an empty symbol.'... Thus the function of the sacraments is not merely to produce a healthy psychological effect by depicting to the eyes doctrines and facts that must not be forgotten, but to be the instruments of a gracious divine action whereby what is represented to us is also presented to us.... 'The bread is called the body since it not only represents but also presents it to us.'... 'We are not in vain baptized with water by men, because Christ, who commanded the same to be done, will fulfill His office, and baptize us with the Spirit.' The sacraments are... signs not merely of something that happened once in the past, but of a present activity of God which is taking place in the midst of, and alongside, the human action. The sacraments thus deserve to be ranked along with the Word as true means of grace, and along with the Word of the Gospel can be called the *power of God unto salvation.*[53]

---

51. Bruce, *The Mystery of the Lord's Supper,* 44.

52. John Calvin, *Commentary on the Book of the Prophet Isaiah,* trans by Rev. William Pringle, 4 vols. (Edinburgh: Calvin Translation Society, 1843; reprint Grand Rapids, MI: Baker Book House, 1979), 1:211.

53. Wallace, *Calvin's Doctrine of the Word and Sacrament,* 159–60.

To Strengthen *and* Increase *the Faith and Spiritual Gifts of Believers*

The Sanctifying Effects of the Sacraments

The representing, sealing and conveying of Christ, His covenant promises, and the benefits of the redemption He accomplished, to the believer always has a continuous, sanctifying and edifying effect on his heart and life (1 Pet. 3:21). Salvation applied always enhances his love for Christ, strengthens his resistance to sin and his desire to live for Christ, increases his faith in Christ and His Word, and cultivates and increases the influence of the Holy Spirit on his character and behavior, conforming him more and more in the image of Christ: "For all of you who were baptized into Christ have clothed yourselves with Christ" (Gal. 3:27). "As you therefore have received Christ Jesus the Lord, so walk in Him, having been firmly rooted and now being built up in Him and established in your faith, just as you were instructed, and overflowing with gratitude" (Col. 2:6–7).

The Relation of Faith and the Sacraments

The sacraments "strengthen" and "increase" faith, but they do not give faith; rather, they presuppose faith (Rom. 4:11). The sacraments offer Christ to us, and Christ must be received by faith alone: "For he who eats and drinks, eats and drinks judgment to himself, if he does not judge the body rightly" (1 Cor. 11:29). *If we are to receive Christ in the Lord's Supper, we must bring to the Table of the Lord two mouths:* the mouth of our physical body to receive the bread and wine, and the mouth of faith by which we receive Christ. Augustine said, "A person cannot carry away from this sacrament more than he can collect in the vessel of faith." The point is a fundamental one: *the blessings offered and given in the sacraments by the Holy Spirit are always and only received by faith in Christ* (Gal. 2:16, 20). If a person has faith, however small or weak, he gets some hold on Christ in the sacraments; but if he is without faith, however clear his understanding of the sacrament, it is impossible for him to get any hold of Christ. See John 6:51–58, where faith in Christ is pictured by the figure of eating and drinking Him. "The Flesh and Blood of Christ, or Christ Himself, cannot be perceived, except by the eye of faith, or be received, except by the mouth of faith; nor He be laid hold of, except by the hand of faith."[54]

To Oblige *Believers to Greater Obedience*

The sacraments are "mutual and reciprocal signs," in that in them there is a "mutual agreement" between God and the believer,

> by which God binds us to Himself, and we mutually pledge our faith.... The ends of the sacraments are to be *marks and badges of Christian profession* and fellowship or fraternity, to be incitements to gratitude, and exercises to faith and a godly life; in short to be contracts binding us to this. But among other ends, the principal one is, that God may by means of them attest, represent, and seal His grace in us.[55]

There are two things to be considered in a sacrament: a command from Christ—"Take, eat"—and a promise from Christ—"This is My body." As the command requires obedience, so the promise requires belief.

> Do not come to the Sacrament, therefore, unless you come both in faith and in obedience. If you do not come with a heart ready to obey Christ, at least more than you have been in the habit of doing, you come to your own judgment. And if you bring a heart void of faith, you come to your own judgment. Thus let everyone who comes to the Sacrament, bring with him a heart determined on doing better, that is, to obey and believe Christ better than in the past.[56]

---

54. Bruce, *The Mystery of the Lord's Supper*, 97.

55. John Calvin, quoted in Wallace, *Calvin's Doctrine of the Word and Sacrament*, 141–42.

56. Bruce, *The Mystery of the Lord's Supper*, 63.

To Testify *to and* Cherish *the Believers' Love and Communion with One Another*

> I, therefore, the prisoner of the Lord, entreat you to walk in a manner worthy of the calling with which you have been called, with all humility and gentleness, with patience, showing forbearance to one another in love, being diligent to preserve the unity of the Spirit in the bond of peace. There is one body and one Spirit, just as also you were called in one hope of your calling; one Lord, one faith, one baptism (Eph. 4:1–5).

> In Baptism the baptized individual, as a member of Christ, is uprooted and separated from every corrupt source of life and introduced into a new sphere of common life which the members of Christ share with their exalted Head. Indeed, for Calvin each individual Christian's Baptism is merely the sharing of one common Baptism, which the whole Church shares in common with Christ.[57]

"As often as we partake of the symbol of the Lord's body, as a token given and received, we reciprocally bind ourselves to all the duties of love in order that none of us may permit anything that can harm our brother, or overlook anything that can help him."[58]

"For by one Spirit are we all baptized into one body, whether we be Jews or Gentiles, whether we be bond or free; and have all been made to drink into one Spirit" (1 Cor. 12:13). The Holy Spirit creates the Church, which is the Body of Christ on earth. He places all to whom He applies salvation into one Body by His regenerative, sanctifying grace which He represents, seals and conveys to them by Baptism. He sustains, nourishes and advances that spiritual unity of the Church through the Lord's Supper, by which believers drink into their own lives the Spirit of Christ, therefore, it can be called "Spiritual food" and "Spiritual drink" (1 Cor. 10:l–4).

57. Wallace, *Calvin's Doctrine of the Word and Sacrament*, 175.
58. Calvin, *Institutes of the Christian Religion*, 2:1422.

To Distinguish Believers from the World in Rebellion

The sacraments are not only signs and seals, they are also marks and badges (Gen. 17:11), identifying Christians, and separating Christians from the evil world around us in rebellion against God and under His curse. By the sacrament of baptism, God "brands" us as His own personal property, setting His mark on us that we are His, and that we are to live for His pleasure. The sacraments are badges we wear, of our profession of faith in Jesus Christ as our Lord and Savior, thereby "putting a visible difference between those who belong to the Church and the rest of the world, giv[ing] visibility to the Church, and separat[ing] its members from the world."[59]

The Parts of a Sacrament

Q. 163: What are the parts of a sacrament?

A.: The parts of a sacrament are two; the one an outward and sensible sign, used according to Christ's own appointment; the other an inward and spiritual grace thereby signified.

The First Part of a Sacrament: The Outward and Visible Sign

In the sacraments, there is some visible element and action, which together signify some spiritual benefit. This visible element and action "should... not be merely an arbitrary, but a natural sign of the grace signified; that is, it should have some natural analogy to suggest the related grace.... But it must be added, that a mere natural analogy does not constitute a sacrament. The analogy must be selected, and consecrated by the express institution of God."[60] These visible elements and actions must agree with the

59. Archibald A. Hodge, *The Confession of Faith* (London: The Banner of Truth Trust, [1958] 1964), 332.

60. John Calvin points out that Adam regarded the tree of life as sacrament and Noah considered the rainbow a sacrament, "because they had a mark en-

preaching of the Word and correspond with the spiritual reality they signify. Baptism is with water, which is ordinarily used for cleansing of the body, that we might be pointed to the cleansing of our minds, hearts, consciences and souls from the guilt and corruption of sin by the power of the Holy Spirit (Eph. 5:26; Tit. 3:5). And just as the Holy Spirit comes down from above, or is poured out from above, so the water of baptism is poured out or sprinkled profusely upon the head of the one being baptized. Furthermore, in baptism the recipient of the sacrament remains still and unmoved, in no way assisting, because in the regenerative work of the Spirit, the sinner is passive and the Spirit is active. In the Lord's Supper, bread and wine are used as symbols. Just as bread nourishes and wine nourishes and gladdens the physical body, Jesus Christ nourishes and gladdens His people with Himself. The minister acting in Christ's name administers the bread and wine, because Christ administers Himself to His people by His Spirit. The bread is broken, as was His body on the cross; and the wine is poured, as His blood was shed on the cross. Each participant takes the sacrament to himself and chews, swallows, and digests it, for Christ is to be received by each of us by faith in Him alone. Spiritual nourishment, like physical nourishment, requires personal and intelligent action on our part, and not passivity.

The Second Part of a Sacrament: The Inward and Spiritual Grace Signified in the Visible Sign

In a sacrament, the visible sign and the spiritual reality it signifies must be clearly distinguished. Both the sign and the spiritual blessing are contained in a sacrament, but also the sign and the

---

graved upon them by God's word, so that they were proofs and seals of his covenants. And indeed the tree was previously a tree, the rainbow a rainbow. When they were inscribed by God's word a new form was put upon them, so that they began to be what previously they were not.... If he [God] had imprinted such reminders upon the sun, stars, earth, stones, they would all be sacraments for us. Why are crude and coined silver not of the same value, though they are absolutely the same metal? The one is merely in the natural state; stamped with an official mark, it becomes a coin and receives a new valuation. And cannot God mark with His Word the things He has created, that what were previously bare elements may become sacraments?" (Calvin, *Institutes of the Christian Religion*, 2:1294–95).

blessing it signifies are not so linked that they cannot be separated; "and that even in the union itself the matter must always be distinguished from the sign, that we may not transfer to the one what belongs to the other."[61] Augustine said that "in the elect alone the sacraments effect what they represent."[62] Although the sacraments are offered to all, the blessing they signify are given only to the elect who believe. By faith we receive Christ by the visible sign; but without faith the participant in the Lord's Supper receives the visible sign without Christ. Speaking of the Lord's Supper, Calvin writes, "For the Lord's morsel was poison to Judas, not because he received evil, but because an evil man evilly received a good thing.... 'He who attains to the power of the sacrament...[is] he who eats with the heart, not he who presses with the teeth' [Augustine]."[63] Moreover, the reception of the spiritual realities signified by the sacraments is not tied to the moment the sacrament is received.

The Third Part of a Sacrament: The Sacramental Union of the Visible Sign and the Spiritual Grace

The Supplementing of the Larger Catechism's Answer with the Westminster Confession of Faith

The Westminster Confession of Faith, XXVII, ii, completes the answer to Larger Catechism Question 163: "There is in every sacrament a spiritual relation, or sacramental union, between the sign and the thing signified; whence it comes to pass that the names and effects of the one are attributed to the other." Without this "sacramental union" there are no sacraments; so then, there are really three parts of a sacrament and not just two. The failure to understand this statement in the Confession has led to many perversions of the sacraments.

61. Calvin, *Institutes of the Christian Religion*, 2:1290.
62. Calvin, *Institutes of the Christian Religion*, 2:1290.
63. Calvin, *Institutes of the Christian Religion*, 2:1291.

The Sacramental Union and Sacramental Language

The visible sign is the part of the sacrament we see and touch. The spiritual grace signified is Christ, the promises of the New Covenant and the benefits of the redemption accomplished by Him. The sacramental union is the divinely ordained relation between the sign and the signified blessing. This sacramental union depends entirely upon the institution of Christ. Because of this union a "sacramental language" is possible, in which the names of the signs and the spiritual blessings they signify are used interchangeably, not to destroy the difference between the sign and the spiritual grace, nor to indicate that the grace is inseparable from the sign, but to teach us that in the sacrament Christ really offers the spiritual blessing along with the visible to sign to all who receive the sacrament with faith. A symbol is often thought of and spoken of as if it were identical with what it stands for, although we know the two are distinguished from each other.[64] For example, Christ calls the literal cup of "the Last Supper" the covenant in His blood: "This cup which is poured out for you is the new covenant in My blood" (Luke 22:20). The cup is the new covenant! Now, obviously, this is not a literal statement. It is a sacramental way of saying things, because of the nature of the sacramental union.[65]

64. "In the sacraments we have such a close connection between the symbol and the spiritual gift which it represents that we can 'easily pass from the one to the other' in our speech and refer to the bread as being indeed the body of Christ, and Baptism as being the 'laver of regeneration' (Tit. 3:5) and as an act that washes our sins away (1 Pet. 3:21)" (Wallace, *Calvin's Doctrine of the Word and Sacrament*, 161).

65. "Whenever the sacraments are treated of, it is usual to transfer the name of the thing signified by metonymy to the sign. [Metonymy is "a figure of speech in which an idea is evoked or named by means of a term designating some associated notion." *The American Heritage Dictionary*]. Examples occur too frequently in Scripture for any opponents, however keen, to venture to deny that this mode of speech must be regarded as the general rule. Hence as the manna of old was spiritual food, as the water was Christ, as the Holy Spirit was a dove, as baptism was the laver of regeneration, so the bread is called the body and the wine the blood of Christ" (John Calvin, *Tracts and Treatises On the Doctrine and Worship of the Church*, trans. by Henry Beveridge, 3 vols. [Edinburgh: Calvin Translation Society, 1849; reprint Grand Rapids, MI: William B. Eerdmans Publishing Co., 1958], 2:243).

The Examples of Sacramental Language with Reference to Christ and His Redemptive Work

We have several scriptural examples of this sacramental way of expression: Christ is said to be "our Passover" in 1 Corinthians 5:7. The bread and wine are said to be the body and blood of Christ (1 Cor. 11:24–28). Baptism is said to save us (1 Pet. 3:21). Christ is said to be the rock from which we draw our spiritual drink (1 Cor. 10:1–4). Forgiveness of sin is said to come with baptism (Acts 2:38). In the Lord's Supper, we fellowship in the body and blood of Christ (1 Cor. 10:16). Romans 6:4 says that "we have been buried with Him through baptism into death." Colossians 2:11 speaks of our baptism and the work of the Spirit it signifies as a "circumcision made without hands." None of these statements is literal; they all presuppose a sacramental union of the sign and what it signifies. The point they are making is that the sacraments, closely coupled to what they signify, by divine institution, represent, seal and convey what they signify to those who receive them in faith. Christ is not literally the Passover, nor is He literally a rock or something we drink with our mouths. The bread and wine are not literally Christ's physical flesh and blood; nor does the water of baptism have a literal saving and forgiving power in it. But the Bible uses this sacramental way of speaking because the sacraments really do represent, signify, seal and apply Christ and the benefits of redemption to all who receive them by faith. And in the sacraments Christ really does offer Himself and these blessings to all who believe.

The Common Mode of Expression Throughout the Bible

This mode of speaking is more common in the Bible than one might think. When Moses describes the Glory Cloud leading the children of Israel on their journey, he does not say simply, "the cloud went before them," but "the Lord went before them" (Exod. 13:21), because the Cloud was a visualization and pledge of the Lord's presence with His people. The Lord was not literally in the Cloud, but sacramentally speaking, it was a sign of His presence. Also, when the Glory Cloud descended upon the Tabernacle, Exodus 34:5 says that the Lord descended, "the sacred name being applied to the visible symbol."[66] Furthermore, when the ark of the covenant at the blast of the trumpets was taken up to the Temple, the writer says, "God is gone up with a shout" (Ps. 47:5). In John 1:32 the dove, representing the Holy Spirit is said to be the Spirit Himself descending from heaven. The church is not only the body of Christ, with Him as the head; but 1 Corinthians 12:12 speaks of the church as Christ. And in Galatians 3:27 we are told that whoever is baptized in Christ has clothed himself with Christ. "Thus 'the name of the thing signified is aptly transferred to the sign' [Calvin]."[67]

The Illustration of the Ark of the Covenant in the Old Testament

This sacramental union can be illustrated in the role of the ark of the covenant in Old Testament Israel, and its relation to the presence of Jehovah. The ark of the covenant was "a most sure pledge, through which [Israel] was made more sure of the presence and favor of God and of His present help as often as [Israel] invoked Him."[68] See 1 Sam. 4:1–11; 5:1–6; 7:1–14. This is the reason for its designation as "the ark of the testimony." It was the place of God's self-testimony, God's self-revelation (2 Sam. 6:2). It testified to God's sovereignty over Israel and the whole earth (1 Sam. 3:3; Jer. 3:16, 17; Ps. 132:7). It was the place of propitiation, (*i.e.*, the turning away of God's anger by the offering of a substitutionary sacrifice), which was the basis of the reconciliation and fellowship between Jehovah and His people (Heb. 9).

The Intimate Connection Between Jehovah and His Ark

An intimate connection existed between Jehovah and His ark. "By this you shall know that the living God is among you, and that He will assuredly dispossess from before you the Canaanite.... Behold, the ark of the covenant of the Lord of all the earth is crossing over ahead of you into the Jordan" (Josh. 3:10–11). The leadership of

66. Wallace, *Calvin's Doctrine of the Word and Sacrament*, 162.

67. Wallace, *Calvin's Doctrine of the Word and Sacrament*, 162.

68. John Calvin quoted by Marten H. Woudstra, *The Ark of the Covenant From Conquest to Kingship* (Philadelphia: Presbyterian and Reformed, 1965), 19-20.

the ark of the covenant of the Lord across the Jordan River into Canaan was A SURE AND TRUE pledge from God ASSURING His people that He lived in and with Israel, His covenant people, and that He personally would drive out their enemies from before them. The holiness and mysterious power of the ark were not present because of some impersonal force mysteriously hidden in the sacred box. This is evident not only in the light of the condemnation of superstition throughout the Bible, but also because the ark had to be carried by the priests of Jehovah. The ark was not God, but it was a sign and seal of His presence; so that, as we have seen, when the ark was taken up into the Temple, it could be said that "God is gone up with a shout" (Ps. 47:5). God's presence was not inseparably tied to the ark, but His presence was pledged to His people by it.

The Relation of Faith and the Ark of the Covenant

God's presence was pledge in the ark of the covenant to those who had placed their faith in Him, and to them only! The symbolism of the ark does not work automatically, magically or "*ex opere operato.*" It must be remembered that God gave victory to His covenant people at Jericho, but gave them defeat at Ai. The point is that "it is not the absence or presence of the ark which causes defeat. That defeat is brought on by the breach of solemn interdict which Yahweh had placed on all Israel with regard to the disposition of the spoil from Jericho."[69] In other words, at Jericho, Israel had the ark and faith in God; but at Ai, they had the ark, but no obedient faith in God.

The "Sacramental" Nature of the Ark of the Covenant

The ark represented Jehovah and it was His pledge of His presence with His people. Jehovah identified Himself with His ark so that for the ark to lead Israel was for Jehovah to lead the people, and to stand before the ark was to stand before the Lord Himself. However, it must not be forgotten that *Jehovah's "presence is made secure in a saving manner only when this presence is grasped believingly."*[70]

69. Woudstra, *The Ark of the Covenant From Conquest to Kingship*, 56.
70. Woudstra, *The Ark of the Covenant From Conquest to Kingship*, 46.

1 Samuel 4:1–7 makes clear that "when this is not the case, the very opposite takes place."[71] Therefore, the ark possessed a holiness superior to all other objects and furniture connected with the Tabernacle (2 Sam. 6:6–11; 1 Chron. 15:1–3).

The Sins Against the Ark of the Covenant

Israel often committed two sins against Jehovah's ark: (1) they sometimes placed in it a misplaced and superstitious trust, rather than placing their trust in the Lord Himself; and (2) they sometimes exhibited an irreverent disregard for the ark, taking lightly the presence and demands of Jehovah, of which it was a sign. To sin against the ark in either of these ways was to sin against the ark's God!

The Centrality of the Old Testament Ark to the Faith of Old Testament Believers

The ark was so central to Old Testament faith and worship that it was never depreciated as a religious symbol. It was

> temporarily rendered inactive when the necessary interaction of faith and symbol had deteriorated to a superstitious and mechanistic manipulation of the symbol.... But this abuse of the ark does in no way detract from its rightful use. Hence the ark stands out in all its holy majesty at the crossing of the Jordan. And even in the period during which the element of "interaction" has sunk to its lowest level the ark's honor is vindicated in the face of Israel's hereditary enemies. This shows that this element of interaction must not be viewed in dialectic fashion, as if the manifestation of the glory of Yahweh in and through the ark were in any way correlative to the faith of Yahweh's worshippers. *Faith puts its trust in the trustworthiness of divinely instituted symbols. But the divine symbols do not derive their efficacy from the faith which reposes in them.*[72]

---

71. Woudstra, *The Ark of the Covenant From Conquest to Kingship*, 46.
72. Woudstra, *The Ark of the Covenant From Conquest to Kingship*, 144.

They derive their effectiveness from the sovereign and gracious institution of the sacraments as signs, seals and conveyers of His holy presence to His believing and obedient people.

The Vital Importance of the Sacramental Union

It is this sacramental union that makes a sacrament a sacrament and means of grace. Remove this sacramental union and the sacraments are destroyed. If that divinely ordained relation is removed, completely mixing the sign and the things signified, then the water is literally the Holy Spirit and the bread and wine are literally Christ's body and blood. If this union is removed and the sign and the spiritual blessing are totally separated, the visible sacraments are empty, unnecessary and useless. A sacrament is a sign, and the sign is in the relationship, the sacramental union. Take away either the things signified or the relation of the sign to what it signifies, and we lose the sacrament. Remove the sacramental union and we destroy the sacrament. Mix the sign and that which it signifies, destroy the union between them, and we also lose the sacrament. Convert the one into the other and the sacrament is also lost, because the relation between them vanishes.

The distinction between the visible sacrament and the truth of the sacrament must be kept clear, while at the same time believing that the sacraments have been joined to that which they signify. "*Faith lives in the connection between sign and that which is signified*; but Judas [Matt. 26:20–30], and Simon the magician [Acts 8:18–24], who received the sacrament, did not receive Christ who is signified by it, for 'He is only administered to believers.'"[73]

The Nature of the Sacramental Union

The Nature in Which the Visible Sign and the Spiritual Grace Signified Are Not Conjoined

What is the nature of this relation between sign and spiritual blessing signified, this sacramental union? How are they conjoined

73. Berkouwer, *Studies in Dogmatics: The Sacraments*, 81.

or coupled together? It may be helpful, first of all, to describe how they are NOT coupled together. You can see clearly with your own eyes that the sign and the grace are *not locally joined.* That is, they are not in the same place. Water is in the bowl. Bread and wine are on the Table. Christ is neither in the bowl nor on the table, but in Heaven. You can also see that they are *not joined literally or physically.* The water does not literally touch the Holy Spirit and the bread and wine do not literally touch Christ. Neither are they *visibly joined,* for although the water, bread and wine are visible to the eye, Christ is not. If Christ and the signs were locally, physically and visibly joined together, why would I need the water, bread and wine?

The Mystery of the Sacramental Union

Therefore, we should be able to see that this sacramental union is a spiritual union and a great mystery. It is not possible to show to the eye how the two are joined together. To understand this secret, mystical, and spiritual union, our minds must be "enlightened with a heavenly sight.... Unless you have this heavenly illumination you can understand neither your own conjunction with Christ, nor the conjunction between the sign and the thing signified in the Sacrament."[74]

The Similarity of the Sacramental Union to the Relation of the Preached Word and the Spiritual Realities Signified in That Word

It may also be helpful to us in understanding how the sign and the grace are joined together, to compare this sacramental relation with the relation between the preached Word and the spiritual realities signified in that Word. The close connection between the Word of Christ you hear, and the Christ the Word brings to you during the preaching of it, is similar to the close connection between the sacramental sign and the Christ signified in the sacrament. When the preacher speaks of Christ in the gospel, although Christ is seated in Heaven and we are on earth, the preacher no sooner preaches Christ

74. Bruce, *The Mystery of the Lord's Supper,* 52–53.

to us and Christ comes to our minds, showing us that there is a close connection between the Word and that which is signified by that Word. The same is true of the sacrament, because

> the sacrament is nothing else but a visible Word. Why do I call it a visible Word? Because it conveys the signification of it by the eye to the mind. Just as in the audible word the signification of it is conveyed by the ear to the mind, so in the same Sacrament, as often as you see it, you will no sooner see the bread with your eye, than the Body of Christ will come into your mind; you will no sooner see the wine, than with preaching and exposition of the Sacrament the Blood of Christ will come into your mind.[75]

The Two Elements which Compose the Sacramental Union

So then, this sacramental union, (conjunction, joining together of sign and grace), consists of two things. FIRST, there must be a definite similarity and analogy between the sign and the grace signified, and this likeness must be easily perceived. "Think of how the bread is able to nourish your body for this earthly and temporal life; so the flesh of Christ, signified by the bread, is able to nourish both body and soul to life everlasting."[76] SECOND, there must be a continual and mutual concurrence of the sign and the grace signified, *i.e.*, a joint offering and a joint receiving. The sign and the grace signified are offered together and received together at the same time, the sign with the mouth and the grace with faith. But beware of conflating them, and of turning one into the other, "keep each of them in its own integrity, without confusion or mixture of the one with the other."[77]

75. Bruce, *The Mystery of the Lord's Supper,* 54.
76. Bruce, *The Mystery of the Lord's Supper,* 55.
77. Bruce, *The Mystery of the Lord's Supper,* 55.

The Freedom of God and The Sacraments

However, we must keep clearly in mind that, although a close, mystical and spiritual relation exists between sign and grace signified, this sacramental union "is nevertheless so transcendent and freely personal [on God's part] that even in the event of the sacrament becoming effectual we must always in our thinking hold the grace and action of God as being quite distinct from our human activity."[78]

The Main Lesson to be Learned Concerning the Sacramental Union

What is the main lesson we are to learn from all this? How important is all this for us to learn? How is it to be applied to our daily lives? In this:

> that this great and mystical conjunction between the God of glory and us may be increased. It is in this conjunction alone that our weal, felicity and happiness in this life and in the life to come, consist: that He is so careful to conjoin Himself with His Word and Sacraments that we, in His Word and Sacraments may be conjoined with Him.... There is no other lesson in Christianity than this; this is the first and the last lesson: to shake off your lust and affections more and more, and so more and more to renounce yourself that you may embrace Christ.[79]

The Manner in Which the Signs And the Spiritual Blessings They Signify are Conveyed and Received

Although the visible sign and the spiritual grace it signifies are inseparable, they are also distinguishable from each other. Therefore, the question arises: how is the visible sign delivered to us and how is the spiritual grace it signifies delivered to us and how are we to receive the sign and the grace? The answer to this question is to

---

78. Wallace, *Calvin's Doctrine of the Word and Sacrament*, 163.
79. Bruce, *The Mystery of the Lord's Supper*, 55–57.

be found in the following important distinctions we must always keep clear in our minds when we partake of the sacraments.

The Two Givers

The visible sign and the spiritual grace signified are not both given by the same person, but by two persons.

The water of baptism and the bread and wine of the Lord's Supper are given to us by the minister of the gospel. The spiritual blessing signified in the sign is given to us by our Mediator and Lord.

> Therefore, there are two givers in this Sacrament: the Minister gives the earthly thing, Christ Jesus, the Mediator, gives the heavenly thing in this Sacrament.... Do not think, therefore, that you will receive the Spirit from the hands of man; you will receive Him from the hands of Christ Himself alone.... Therefore you ought always to pray that the Lord may water your hearts by His Holy Spirit, as He waters your ears by the hearing of the Word.[80]

As John the Baptist drew the contrast between his person and part in baptism and Christ's person and part in baptism, "As for me, I baptize you with water; but He who is mightier than I is coming, and I am not fit to untie the thong of His sandals; He Himself will baptize you with the Holy Spirit and fire" (Luke 3:16).

The Two Gifts

The visible sign and the spiritual grace signified are not given in the same act, but in two actions.

As there are two persons who offer the sign and the grace it signifies, so these are offered and given in two distinct actions: "Christ, who is the heavenly thing, is offered and given to you by an inward, secret and spiritual action, which is not subject to the outward eye. The sign, again, is offered and given in an outward action in a corporal and visible way."[81]

---

80. Bruce, *The Mystery of the Lord's Supper*, 60–61.
81. Bruce, *The Mystery of the Lord's Supper*, 61.

The Two Receiving Instruments

The visible sign and the spiritual grace signified are not offered to one receiving instrument, but to two.

In the Lord's Supper, for example, the instrument that receives the sign is the mouth; but the grace signified, which is Christ, is never offered to the physical mouth. The Bible is emphatic from beginning and end that there is no other way of receiving Christ but by faith alone.

> There is no instrument, either hand or mouth, by which we may lay hold of Christ, but faith alone. As Christ, who is the thing signified, is grasped by the hand and mouth of faith, so the sign, which signifies Christ, is grasped by our own natural mouth and hand.... Thus the sign and the thing signified are offered and given, not to one instrument, but to two, the one to the mouth of the body, the other to the mouth of the soul.[82]

The Two Receivers

The visible sign and the spiritual grace signified are not given and received by the same action but by two actions.

We must "distinguish between the outward and the inward action" by which the sign and what it signifies are received by us.

> You may be quite sure that if you are faithful, Christ is as busy working inwardly in your soul, as the Minister is working outwardly in regard to your body. See how busy the Minister is in breaking the bread, in pouring out the wine, in giving the bread and wine to you. Christ is just as busy, in breaking His own Body unto you, and in giving you the juice of His own Body in a spiritual and invisible way. Preserve this distinction, then, and you may assure yourself that by faith Christ is as fully occupied with your soul in nourishing it, as

82. Bruce, *The Mystery of the Lord's Supper,* 61.

> the Minister is outwardly with your body. Keep this, and you have the whole Sacrament.[83]

The Number of Sacraments

Q. 164: How many sacraments hath Christ instituted in his church under the New Testament?

A.: Under the New Testament Christ hath instituted in his church only two sacraments, baptism and the Lord's Supper.

What Constitutes a Sacrament?

Only two sacraments have been instituted by Christ, the Head of the Church, as ordinances of worship in His Church until the end of the world: baptism and the Lord's Supper. Only baptism and the Lord's Supper are sacraments because only these two: (1) were instituted by Christ as holy ordinances for His Church (Matt. 28:19–20; Matt. 26:26f–29); and (2) represent, seal and convey Christ and the benefits of redemption to believers. Only Jesus Christ, the Head of the Church has the prerogative to determine how He is to be worshiped in His Church; and He has prescribed how He is to be worshiped in His Word. If Jesus Christ has not commanded a certain rite, practice or ordinance of worship, it is not to be used in the worship of God (Deut. 12:32; Mark 7:1–13).

Not all symbols are sacraments. Only God in Christ can institute a sacrament.

> The decision to establish a sacrament rests with God alone. Indeed, a sacrament ought, by God's sure promise, to encourage and comfort believers' consciences, which could never receive this certainty from man. A sacrament ought to be for us a testimony of God's good will toward us.... A sacra-

83. Bruce, *The Mystery of the Lord's Supper*, 62.

> ment is a seal by which God's covenant, or promise, is sealed. But it could not be sealed with physical things and the elements of this world, unless it were shaped and designed for this by God's power. Therefore, man cannot establish a sacrament, because it is not in man's power to cause such great mysteries of God to be concealed under such humble things.[84]

The Minister of the Word and Sacraments

The Westminster Confession of Faith says that neither of these sacraments "may be dispensed by any but by a minister of the word, lawfully ordained"[85] (XXVII, iv). To the apostolic office-holders in the church, Jesus said, "Go, therefore, and make disciples of all nations, baptizing them" (Matt. 28:19). In 1 Corinthians 11:23, Paul the apostolic office-holder said, "For I have received from the Lord that which also I delivered unto you, that the Lord Jesus in the same night in which He was betrayed, took bread." In 1 Corinthians 4:1, official "ministers of Christ" are called "stewards of the mysteries of God," *i.e.*, of the word and sacraments. And in Hebrews 5:4, we are told regarding offices in the church, "no man taketh this honor unto himself, but he that is called of God, as was Aaron." Notice several principles in these verses: (1) To those officers who have been assigned the responsibility of preaching and teaching has also been assigned the responsibility to baptize; (2) There is no instance in the New Testament of the sacraments of baptism and the Lord's Supper being administered by anyone except ministers of the Word and Sacraments; (3) Those who are ordained as ministers are the ones who are stewards of the "mysteries" of God, *i.e.*, that which God has revealed, which is otherwise unknown, which includes Word and Sacraments; (4) No one may take up an office in the church and carry out its responsibilities, unless he has been called by God, and sent by Christ (Rom. 10:15).

84. Calvin, *Institutes of the Christian Religion*, 2:1450.

85. This statement in the Westminster Confession is in direct and conscious opposition to the doctrine and practice of the Roman Catholic Church, which allows laymen and women to administer the sacrament of baptism in emergency situations.

Consider again the arguments of George Gillespie in *The Works of George Gillespie:*

FIRST,

> God hath appointed the ministers of the word, lawfully called and ordained, and no other, to be the stewards and dispensers of the mysteries of Christ—1 Cor. iv:1, 'Let a man so account of us, as of the ministers of Christ, and stewards of the mysteries of God. Moreover it is required of stewards that a man be found faithful;'—which the Apostle doth not only apply to himself and Apollos, ver. 6, (where, by the way, it may be remembered that Apollos was neither an apostle, nor evangelist, but a powerful minister of the gospel,) and to Sosthenes (as appeareth by comparing the text now cited with 1 Cor. i:1), but he also applieth the same to every lawful bishop, or ordinary minister, Tit. i:7, for a bishop must be blameless as the steward of God, and this steward is ordained, ver. 5.
>
> So Luke xii:42: 'Who then is that faithful and wise steward, whom his Lord shall make ruler over his household, to give them their portion of meat in due season?' It is not Christ's will that any one of the household who is faithful, wise and discreet, may take upon him the steward's office, to dispense meat to the rest; but there is a steward constituted and appointed for that purpose; there are stewards appointed in the church, which is the house of the living God, and those to continue till the coming of Christ... ver. 43, 46.[86]

SECOND,

> "Ministers lawfully called and ordained, and none other, hath Christ appointed to be pastors and shepherds, to feed the flock of God, Jer. iii:15; Eph. iv:11; Acts xx:28; 1 Pet. v:2."[87]

86. George Gillespie, "A Treatise of Miscellany Questions," *The Works of George Gillespie*, 2 vols. (Edinburgh: Robert Ogle and Oliver & Boyd, 1846; reprint Canada: Still Waters Revival Books, 1991), 2:37.

87. Gillespie, *The Works of George Gillespie,* 2:37.

THIRD,

> Ezekiel's vision concerning the new temple is generally acknowledged to be an evangelical prophecy... Now, among other things, it is there prophesied concerning the ministers of the gospel, Ezek. xliv:16, 'They shall enter into my sanctuary, and they shall come near unto my table to minister unto me; and they shall keep my charge,' whereof we can make no gospel sense, except it belong to the charge of ministers, lawfully called and entered into that work, to administer the sacraments, and namely, that of the Lord's supper at His table. These ministers are also in that chapter plainly distinguished from the people, or children of Israel, ver. 15, 19, 22, 23, 28.[88]

FOURTH,

> Christ gives a commission to the apostles to teach, and baptize, and extends the same commission to all teaching ministers to the end of the world, Matt. xxviii:19, 20, from which place it is plain, 1. That Jesus Christ would have the distinction of teachers and taught, baptisers and baptised, to have place in the church alway, even unto the end. 2. That the commission to teach and baptise was not given to all who believe in Jesus Christ, but to some only. 3. That these some who received this commission are not only the apostles but ordinary ministers, as is manifested by the explaining of the commission, and promise to the end of the world.[89]

FIFTH,

> Christ hath distinguished between magistracy and ministry, between civil and sacred vocations, Mat. xxii:21; xvi:19; xviii:18; xxviii:19; John xx:23; Rom. xiii:1, 7; 1 Tim. ii:2; 1 Pet. ii:13, 14; compared with Rom. xii:6–8; 1 Cor. xii:28; Eph. iv:11; 1 Thess. v:12; Heb. xiii:7, 17. So that, as ministers may not assume civil dignities and administrations, nor exercise

88. Gillespie, *The Works of George Gillespie,* 2:37.
89. Gillespie, *The Works of George Gillespie,* 2:38.

secular power, Lk. xii:14; xxii:25, 26; John xviii:36; 2 Cor. x:4; 2 Tim. ii:4, it is no less contrary to the ordinance of Christ that magistrates (or any other civil persons) stretch themselves beyond their line, and get, with Pompey, into the holy of holies, or, with Uzziah, to the burning of incense; in both which examples such intrusion was exemplarily punished. As it may be said to a secularized minister, Who made thee a judge, or a civil magistrate? So it may be said to a ministerialised civil person, Who made thee a dispenser of the word and sacraments?[90]

SIXTH,

We have clear and convincing examples in the New Testament, that [preaching and] the sacraments were administered by public ministers, called and appointed thereunto, as baptism by John (John i:33, 'He hath sent me to baptise'), and frequently by the apostles, in the story of the Acts. The Lord's supper, administered by Christ himself... and by the Apostle Paul, Acts xx:7, 11. So 'the breaking of bread' is joined with 'the apostles' doctrine and fellowship,' Acts ii:42; ministers being also called the stewards and dispensers of the mysteries of God.... *So that a lawful minister may in faith administer, and the receivers receive from him in faith, the sacraments, having Scripture warrants for so doing; but there is neither any commission from Christ to such as are no church officers to administer the sacraments, nor can there any clear example be found in the New Testament, of administering either the one sacrament or the other by any person who can be proved not to have been a minister lawfully called and ordained. Therefore such persons cannot in faith administer, nor others in faith receive from them, either baptism or the Lord's supper.*[91]

SEVENTH,

---

90. Gillespie, *The Works of George Gillespie,* 2:38.
91. Gillespie, *The Works of George Gillespie,* 2:38. Emphasis added.

> That one text, Eph. iv:11–13, is enough to put to silence the gainsayers, 'And He gave some apostles, and some prophets, and some evangelists, and some pastors and teachers, for the perfecting of the saints...' Is not the administration of the sacraments a perfecting of the saints...? Are we not told that this shall continue till the whole number of the elect be fulfilled? And whom hath Christ given to his church for this work? Hath he given any other but pastors and teachers (setting aside the extraordinary offices), and who are the pastors and teachers appointed hereunto? All, or whosoever will? Nay, not all, but some, saith the text.[92]

Along with these, Robert L. Dabney adds additional strong arguments in his book, *Lectures in Systematic Theology*:

> [1] Since the sacraments are a solemn and formal representation of Gospel truth by symbols, a sort of pantomimic Word, it seems most reasonable that the exhibition of them should be reserved to the same class [of officers] to whom is committed the authoritative preaching of the Word. And it may be urged, with yet more force, that since the presbyters, and especially the pastor of the church, are the guardians of the sealing ordinances, responsible for their defence against abuse and profanation, it is reasonable, yea, necessary, that they should have the control of their administration. This consideration seems to me to have the force of a just and necessary inference.... [2] The sacraments have this use among others, to be badges and pledges of Church membership. The control of them cannot therefore be given to others than the appointed rulers of the Church: to do so is utter disorganization.[93]

The Sacraments of the Old Testament

"The sacraments of the Old Testament, in regard of the spiritual things thereby signified and exhibited, were, for substance, the

---

92. Gillespie, *The Works of George Gillespie*, 2:38.
93. Dabney, *Lectures in Systematic Theology*, 746–47.

same with those of the New" (WCF, XXVII, v). 1 Cor. 10:1–4 makes this point:

> Moreover, brethren, I would not that ye should be ignorant, how that all our fathers were under the cloud, and all passed through the sea; and were all baptized unto Moses in the cloud and in the cloud and in the sea; and did all eat the same spiritual meat; and did all drink from the same spiritual drink; for they drank of that spiritual Rock that followed them; and that Rock was Christ.

The ordinary sacraments of the Old Testament were circumcision and Passover. In the New Testament, baptism fulfills circumcision and the Lord's Supper fulfills Passover. The Old Testament sacraments represented Christ to come (1 Cor. 10:1–4), and the New Testament sacraments represent Christ as having come and being present (1 Cor. 11:23–26). However, the New Testament sacraments are set forth with greater clarity and plainness than the Old Testament sacraments. Roman Catholicism errs when it asserts that the Old Testament sacraments were only empty shadows of the grace conferred in the New Testament sacraments. Rather, the Bible teaches that, with respect to the spiritual blessings signified and conveyed in the sacraments of the Old Testament, they were substantially the same with those of the New Testament.[94] Both Old Testament sacraments and New Testament sacraments were signs and seals of the same righteousness of faith (Rom. 4:11), and of the covenant promises (Gen. 17:7; Acts 2:38, 39).

The Biblical reasons for believing the above paragraph from the Westminster Confession of Faith are:

---

94. "This covenant [of grace] was differently administered in the time of the law, and in the time of the gospel [2 Cor. 3:6–9]: under the law it was administered by promises, prophecies, sacrifices, circumcision, the paschal lamb, and other types and ordinances delivered to the people of the Jews, all foresignifying Christ to come [Heb. 8, 9, 10; Rom. 4:11; Col. 2:11, 12; 1 Cor. 5:7], which were for that time sufficient and efficacious, through the operation of the spirit, to instruct and build up the elect in faith in the promised Messiah [1 Cor. 10:1–4; Heb. 11:13; John 8:56], by whom they had full remission of sins, and eternal salvation; and is called the Old Testament [Gal. 3:7–9,14]" (WCF, VII, v).

(1) The covenant of grace is the same under the two testaments, offering the same blessing, redemption; through the same agencies, justification and sanctification through the work of Christ and the Holy Ghost. Hence, it is natural to suppose that sacraments, especially when sealing the same covenant graces, should operate in substantially the same way.[95]

(2) 1 Corinthians 10:1–4 teaches us that

> there was a sense in which the Hebrew Church possessed baptism and the Lord's Supper.... The scope of the Apostle is, to show that participation in sealing ordinances and ecclesiastical privileges does not ensure salvation. For Israel all shared these wondrous sealings to God, yet many of them perished. And to strengthen the analogy he compares them to the New Testament sacraments. Now, if Israel's consecration to God in this Exodus was virtually a baptizing and a Eucharist, we infer that the spirit of the Israelitish ordinances was not essentially different from that of the New Testament. The scope of the Apostle necessitates this view. His design was, to stimulate to watchfulness, by showing that sacraments alone do not guarantee our salvation. This premise he proves, from the case of the Israelites who, though enjoying their sacraments, perished by unbelief.[96]

(3) The Supper is the fulfillment of Passover (1 Cor. 5:7, 8); and baptism is declared to be New Testament circumcision (Col. 2:11, 12). (4) The Supper came in the place of the Passover, as is evident from the circumstances surrounding its institution in "the Last Supper"; and baptism came in the place of circumcision. Compare Gen. 17:11 with Matt. 28:19. See Acts 2:38, 39. (5) Circumcision and baptism signify and seal the same graces. This will be obvious from a comparison of Gen. 17:13, 14 with Acts 2:41; Deut. 10:16 or 30:6 with John 3:5 or with Tit. 3:5, and Eph. 5:26; Acts 7:8 with Rom. 6:3, 4; Rom. 4:11 with Acts 2:38, and 22:16.

---

95. Dabney, *Lectures in Systematic Theology*, 735.
96. Dabney, *Lectures in Systematic Theology*, 735–36.

The Westminster Confession of Faith also makes this statement:

> Under the gospel, when Christ the substance [Col. 2:17], was exhibited, the ordinances in which this covenant is dispensed are the preaching of the Word, and the administration of the sacraments of Baptism and the Lord's Supper [Matt. 28:19–20; 1 Cor. 11:23–25]; which, though fewer in number, and administered with more simplicity and less outward glory, yet in them it is held forth in more fulness, evidence, and spiritual efficacy [Heb. 12:22–27; Jer. 31:33, 34], to all nations [Matt. 28:20; Eph. 2:15–19] (VII, 6).

This paragraph tells us that, as glorious as the Old Testament age was, the New Testament age is greatly superior in many ways.

> The present dispensation exceeds the past, in the superior clearness of its manifestations—in its substantial ratification by the death of Christ—in the more abundant outpouring of the Holy Spirit—in the introduction of a more spiritual form of worship, and in its extension to all nations.[97]

"When Christ was revealed, sacraments were instituted, fewer in number, more majestic in signification, more excellent in power."[98]

The Seven Sacraments of Roman Catholicism

The Roman Catholic Church has added five more sacraments to the two sacraments instituted in the Bible; and they have done so without divine warrant, and in disobedience to the Bible, which commands us neither to add to nor to subtract from what God has commanded us in the Bible (Deut. 4:2; Mat. 28:20). Those Roman pseudo-sacraments are: (1) ordination, (2) confirmation, (3) penance, (4) extreme unction, and (5) marriage.

> None of these have any divine appointment *as sacraments*; and the three last, as used by Papists, have no warrant at all from Scripture. None of them are seals of the covenant of

97. Shaw, *The Reformed Faith*, 94.
98. Calvin, *Institutes of the Christian Religion*, 2:1303.

> grace, and therefore, they are no sacraments, but are to be considered as gross corruptions of the purity and simplicity of the Christian ritual.[99]

The arguments against Rome's doctrine of the seven sacraments are many: (1) Only baptism and the Lord's Supper are instituted by Christ for His Church in the Bible; (2) Rome's doctrine of baptism and the Lord's Supper is not the Bible's doctrine; (3) The effect of Rome's sacramental system is "a serious devaluation and misappreciation of the significance of baptism… this impoverishment of baptism."[100] Rome "views baptism as an incidental event, which to be sure infuses supernatural grace but which cannot function decisively in the struggles of life."[101] Baptism, according to their view, infuses grace into a person, but the other six sacraments are needed to complete and supplement baptism, which deals with sins committed prior to baptism, but which is inadequate to deal with sins committed after baptism, for which other sacraments are needed. Furthermore, the grace infused in baptism could be lost after baptism. The Bible and the Reformers have a much higher view of baptism than Roman Catholicism. "There is 'no separate grace needed in confirmation, penance, and extreme unction for through Word, baptism, and the Lord's Supper man receives all the grace he needs in life and death, for time and eternity' [Herman Bavinck]."[102]

Roman Catholicism teaches that in baptism we are regenerated unto life and in confirmation we are equipped for the battles of life. John Calvin's critique of their doctrine is to the point:

> And they are so shameless as to deny that baptism can be duly completed without confirmation! What wickedness! Have not we then been buried in baptism with Christ, made partakers in his death, that we may also be sharers in his resurrection [Rom. 6:4–5]? Moreover, this fellowship with Christ's death and life Paul explains to be the mortifying of

99. Shaw, *The Reformed Faith,* 282.
100. Berkouwer, *Studies in Dogmatics: The Sacraments*, 37.
101. Berkouwer, *Studies in Dogmatics: The Sacraments*, 37.
102. Berkouwer, *Studies in Dogmatics: The Sacraments*, 39.

> our flesh and the quickening of the Spirit, because "our old man has been crucified" [Rom. 6:6], in order that "we may walk in newness of life" [Rom. 6:4]. What is it to be equipped for battle, but this? ... You who are of God observe here Satan's malicious and dangerous fraud. In order stealthily to draw the unwary from baptism, he lies in saying that what was truly given in baptism is given in his confirmation. Who now can doubt that this is a doctrine of Satan, which, cutting off from baptism the promises proper to baptism, conveys and transfers them elsewhere?[103]

> It is usually said that Rome esteems baptism more highly than did the Reformation, because it sees in baptism the cause of regeneration; but in the time of the Reformation itself we see the actual situation more profoundly, with Calvin reproaching Rome for seriously underestimating baptism in its doctrine of the sacraments as a whole, and of penance in particular.[104]

For helpful explanations and refutations of the five additional sacraments of the Roman Catholic Church see: (1) John Calvin, *Institutes of the Christian Religion*, IV, xviii & xix; (2) Robert L. Dabney, *Lectures in Systematic Theology*, pgs. 732–36; and (3) Thomas Ridgeley, *Commentary on the Larger Catechism*, Vol. II, pgs. 488–91.

The Sacrament of Baptism

The Meaning of Baptism

Q. 165: What is Baptism?

A.: Baptism is a sacrament of the New Testament, wherein Christ hath ordained the washing with water in the name of the Father, and of the Son,

103. Calvin, *Institutes of the Christian Religion*, 2:1456.

104. Berkouwer, *Studies in Dogmatics: The Sacraments*, 37.

> and of the Holy Ghost, to be a sign and seal of ingrafting into himself, of remission of sins by his blood, and regeneration by his Spirit; of adoption, and resurrection unto everlasting life; and whereby the parties baptized are solemnly admitted into the visible church, and enter into an open and professed engagement to be wholly and only the Lord's.

The Ordinance of Christ

Baptism is a sacrament in the Christian Church for one reason: it was instituted to be such by the Head of the Church, Jesus Christ (1 Cor. 1:17; Matt. 28:19–20). Furthermore, it is a permanent sacrament in the Church until the very end of history. In the Great Commission, Jesus commanded His church to baptize disciples of Christ, until all the world's nations become Christ's disciples, for Jesus will be present with His church always, even to the end of the age (Matt. 28:20). And the sacraments of baptism and the Lord's Supper are to be signs and seals of His presence with His Church until the end of the age.

> If baptism were nothing more than one of several customs and rites instituted by man to express certain religious thoughts and concepts, it could boast of a venerable tradition and would fit nicely into certain anthropological theories, but it would have no decisive significance for the Christian faith. For that decisive element cannot lie in what man does, but in what God does and grants. Precisely because throughout the centuries baptism has been directly connected with admonition, sealing, and assurance, the institution of baptism is of primary importance, for here the question arises wheither it is man who speaks, or whether it is God who comes to meet man with his divine authority.[105]

---

105. Berkouwer, *Studies in Dogmatics: The Sacraments*, 90.

The Essential Elements in a Baptism

A valid baptism will include three elements: (1) The application of water, which represents the blood and Spirit of Christ (Rev. 1:5; Tit. 3:5; Luke 3:16). "As water has a cleansing virtue [power] for removing defilements from the body, so the blood of Christ removes the guilt of sin and cleanses the defiled conscience, and the Spirit of Christ purifies the soul from the pollution of sin."[106] This does not mean that "our cleansing and salvation are accomplished by water, or that water contains in itself the power to cleanse, regenerate, and renew; nor that here is the cause of salvation, but only that in this sacrament are received the knowledge and certainty of such gifts."[107] (2) In the name of the Trinity (Matt. 28:19).

> To be baptized in the name of the Father, and of the Son, and of the Holy Ghost, signifies that we are baptized by the authority of the persons of the Holy Trinity; that we are baptized into the faith and profession of the blessed Trinity; and that we are solemnly devoted to the service of these divine persons.[108]

(3) By a minister duly ordained (1 Cor. 1:17). "They only have authority to administer baptism who have received a commission from Christ to preach the gospel."[109] We find these elements in the New Testament, and no other rituals or elements, involved in baptism.[110] Only water is used. Only the name of the Trinity is used. And no one baptized in the New Testament but ministers of the gospel.

Therefore, we must conclude, that if a person has received a valid baptism, he should never be re-baptized. "The sacrament of baptism is but once to be administered unto any person" (WCF,

---

106. Shaw, *The Reformed Faith*, 285.
107. Calvin, *Institutes of the Christian Religion*, 2:1304.
108. Shaw, *The Reformed Faith*, 285.
109. Shaw, *The Reformed Faith*, 286.
110. The Roman Catholic Church has added to baptism several superstitious rites, several of which are practiced by Episcopal Churches: blessing the water in the font, renouncing Satan, anointing in the form of a cross, anointing the eyelids and ears with saliva, breathing on the person baptized, putting on a white robe, tasting salt and honey, taking hold of a white cloth, the appointment of god-parents, and the completion of baptism in the sacrament of confirmation.

XXVIII, vii). This is true for three reasons: (1) God takes all valid baptisms seriously, just as He took all valid circumcisions seriously in the Old Testament Baptism, like circumcision, places the person baptized in the realm of God's special covenant blessings and special covenant curses (Deut. 28; Lev. 26). If the person is faithful in his life to what baptism signifies, he will receive God's special blessings; but, if he apostatizes from the covenant, his baptism is still effective in sealing to him God's special covenant curses. To re-baptize is to say that God did not take the first baptism seriously, which thought is contradicted by the Word of God. (2) Since baptism is the fulfillment of circumcision, as we will see, then re-baptism is as impossible as re-circumcision. (3)

> This is plain from the nature of the ordinance. It is a solemn admission of the person baptized as a member of the visible Church; and though those that "walk disorderly" are to be cast out, yet there is no hint in Scripture that, when re-admitted, they are to be baptized again. The thing signified by baptism [*i.e.* regeneration], cannot be repeated, and the engagements come under can never be disannulled.[111]

> We must realize that at whatever time we are baptized, we are once for all washed and purged for our whole life. Therefore, as often as we fall away, we ought to recall the memory of our baptism and fortify our mind with it, that we may always be sure and confident of the forgiveness of sins.... There is no doubt that all pious folk throughout life, whenever they are troubled by a consciousness of their faults, may venture to remind themselves of their baptism, that from it they may be confirmed in assurance of that sole and perpetual cleansing which we have in Christ's blood.[112]

> Baptism is never repeated. It is a sign given once to each believer. But the sign given on that one occasion can in later years still remain continually efficacious if it is properly used

111. Shaw, *The Reformed Faith*, 292.
112. Calvin, *Institutes of the Christian Religion*, 2:1304, 1306–07.

> and continually "connected with its truth and efficacy."... The power of Baptism never 'becomes obsolete'... in a believer.
>
> Thus even though the believer cannot with any vividness remember the occasion of his Baptism, nevertheless in remembering the simple fact that at one time he was baptized his Baptism can in his time of need yield all the efficacy attached to the sacrament by the promises of God. "Though the visible figure immediately passes away, the grace which it testifies still remains."... The spiritual grace of which Baptism is a sign, namely mortification, is not given simply in one great crisis but is 'a continued process' taking place throughout all the length of the Christian life.[113]

The Trinitarian Nature of Baptism

Christ has mandated His Church to make the world's nations Christ's disciples, and to "baptize them in the name of the Father, the Son and the Holy Spirit" (Matt. 28:19; 1 Cor. 1:13). This reminds us that baptism signifies, seals and conveys to us union and communion with the Trinity in the deepest of covenant relationships.

> Baptism is an act of religious worship; in which God's right to the persons baptized is publicly owned; and in which an intimation is made, that all saving blessings which are desired or expected in the ordinance, are given by the Father, through a Mediator, purchased by the Son, and applied by the Holy Spirit.... Being baptized in the name of the Father, Son and Holy Ghost signifies more than this, namely, a person's being dedicated to them. In this dedication, a solemn profession is made that these divine persons have a right to all religious worship, which we are obliged to perform, as well as that all our hope of salvation is from them.[114]

113. Wallace, *Calvin's Doctrine of the Word and Sacrament*, 187–88.
114. Ridgeley, *Commentary on the Larger Catechism*, 493.

However, Ridgeley emphasizes the secondary purpose of the sacraments, whereas the primary purpose of both sacraments is to represent, signify, seal and convey saving grace to those in union and communion with the triune God.

The phrase, "baptizing them INTO the Name of the Father, the Son and the Holy Spirit" in Matthew 28:19 helps us understand the meaning of the sacrament of baptism. The idea of "baptized into" must be appreciated and understood. Matthew 28:19 says we are "baptized into the name of the Trinity;" 1 Corinthians 10:2 speaks of the Israelite fathers as being "baptized into Moses;" in 1 Corinthians 1:13 Paul uses the phrase, "baptized into the name of Paul;" and in Romans 6:3 believers are said to be "baptized into Christ." Obviously, this idea expresses a relationship to the person into whom persons are baptized. The focus is on this relationship. Other passages clarify its nature (Rom. 6:3–6; 1 Cor. 12:13; Gal. 3:27, 28; Col. 2:11, 12). All of these passages indicate clearly that union with Christ is the governing idea of the phrase "baptized into," when its object is Christ or the Trinity. The point is that *baptism signifies union with the Triune God, and more particularly with Christ in His death, burial and resurrection.* Because believers are united to Christ in His redemptive work in history, they are united to the power of that death and the fellowship it creates in the one Body of Christ. Baptism is the sign and seal of this union.

> The relationship which baptism signifies is therefore that of union, and union with Christ [and the Trinity] is its basic and central import.... Baptism is into the name of the Father, and of the Son, and of the Holy Ghost. It means therefore that a relation of union to the three persons of the Godhead is thereby signified [John 14:16, 17, 23; 17:21–23].... Consequently baptism, by the very words of institution, signifies union with the Father and the Son and the Holy Ghost, and this means with the three persons of the trinity, both in the unity expressed by their joint possession of the one name and in the richness of the distinctive relationship which each person of the Godhead sustains to the people of God in the economy of the covenant of grace.[115]

115. John Murray, *Christian Baptism* (Philadelphia: Presbyterian & Reformed Publishing Co., 1962), 6–7.

> All the gifts of God proffered in baptism are found in Christ alone. Yet this cannot take place unless he who baptizes in Christ invokes also the names of the Father and the Spirit. For we are cleansed by his blood because our merciful Father, wishing to receive us into grace in accordance with his incomparable kindness, has set this Mediator among us to gain favor for us in his sight. But we obtain regeneration by Christ's death and resurrection only if we are sanctified by the Spirit and imbued with a new and spiritual nature. For this reason we obtain and, so to speak, clearly discern in the Father the cause, in the Son the matter, and in the Spirit the effect, of our purgation and our regeneration.[116]

The Mode of Baptism

The Bible teaches that "baptism is rightly administered by pouring or sprinkling water upon a person" (WCF, XXVIII, iii). Sprinkling or pouring (affusion), was the mode of baptism in the Old Testament, of John the Baptist, and of Christ's apostles in the New Testament, not immersion, as has been proven time and again.

The Old Testament Roots of Baptism

Several ceremonial ablutions (symbolic cleansings) were practiced in the Old Testament. Hebrews 9:10 speaks of these "various washings," (literally "baptisms" in Greek), as in some way pointing to Christ and His redemptive work which cleanses us from sin (Lev. 14:4–7, 16, 49–53; 16:19; Numbers 8:5–7; 19:18,19).[117] In the rest of

116. Calvin, *Institutes of the Christian Religion*, 2:1308.

117. John Murray has written in his book, *Christian Baptism*, 22 (ftnt. 12), "There are so many instances of sprinkling in the ritual of the Mosaic economy that it is not necessary to give the citations. In connection with the blood of the sacrifices no action of the priest was more prominent than the sprinkling of the blood. And the significance of sprinkling is shown by nothing more than by the fact that when the high priest went into the holiest of all once a year on the great day of atonement he sprinkled the blood of the sin-offerings seven times before the mercy-seat and upon the mercy-seat (Lev. 16:14,15).... Ezekiel 36:25 indicates as clearly as any text in the Old Testament the purificatory significance of sprinkling and the adequacy of sprinkling as a mode of purification."

Hebrews 9, the author specifically refers to THREE of these Old Testament BAPTISMS: (1) In 9:13, he speaks of the "sprinkling" of the blood on those who had been defiled (Num. 19:9, 17–19); (2) In 9:19, he speaks of the "sprinkling" of the book of the Law and all the people with blood and water (Ex. 24:7, Lev. 14:4, 7; Num. 19:6, 18); and (3) In 9:21 he speaks of the "sprinkling" of the tabernacle and its vessels with blood (Ex. 24:8; Lev. 5:11–13; 17:11). Immersionists should take note that the Old Testament baptisms were performed by sprinkling![118]

The Greek Words for "Baptize" in the Septuagint

In the Greek Old Testament, (Septuagint), which was commonly used in Jesus' day, the word *bapto* occurs frequently. In Isaiah 21:4 it is used in a figurative sense to translate the Hebrew word meaning "to terrify, startle, or fall upon." In 2 Kings 5:14 it is used with reference to Naaman's "baptizing" himself seven times in the Jordan River

118. George Armstrong, in his book, *The Sacraments of the New Testament as Instituted by Christ*, has shown convincingly that not only is there "no evidence that personal purifications (in the Old Testament) were ever by immersion"; but that "the Scriptures give us good reason to believe that immersion was never resorted to for such a purpose." He gives three reasons for this conclusion: (1) The words used in the Hebrew Old Testament and in the Greek New Testament and translated in our English versions by the words, bathe and wash, are words having no reference to mode. For instance in Leviticus 15:5 the words, wash and bathe are used, without reference to how the washing and bathing were performed. (2) THE ORIENTAL MANNER OF WASHING THE HANDS AND FEET WAS NOT BY PUTTING THEM INTO WATER, BUT BY POURING WATER OVER THEM ACCORDING TO II Kings 3:11. (3) A fundamental principle in the Mosaic law of purification, *i.e.*, the principle of defilement by contact, FORBIDS WASHING OR BATHING BY IMMERSION, when performed for purposes of purification (Lev. 11:33, 34, 35). Armstrong writes: "Upon the Mosaic principle of defilement by contact, had a person bathed by immersion, or washed his hands by dipping them in any ordinary household water-vessel or bath, or even cistern, he would thereby have defiled the whole body of water, and the vessel which contained it; and these, in their turn, unless first purified, would have defiled any water which might subsequently have been put in them." Armstrong does concede that, perhaps, the only instance in which immersion may have been resorted to was in the case of Leviticus 11:32; but he immediately adds that "The quantity of water defiled in immersing such things would be small, and the Mosaic Law, in its principles, might be observed without great inconvenience" (Richmond, VA: Presbyterian Committee of Publication, 1884, 23, 24).

to cure his leprosy. It translates the Hebrew word *tabal* which means "to be moistened with." What Naaman was doing at this point was applying the cleansing ritual for lepers to himself as commanded in the Mosaic Law (Lev. 16:6, 16, 21): "He shall then SPRINKLE seven times the one who is to be cleansed from leprosy" (Lev. 14:7).

The point is that *bapto* and *baptizo* in the Greek Old Testament do not and cannot mean immersion. Consider Leviticus 14:6, 51 where a ritual is prescribed for the cleansing of a leper and of a house in which leprosy has appeared. Two lives birds were taken. One was slain and its blood caught in an earthenware vessel (vs. 5). Then the live bird, along with cedar wood, a scarlet string, and hyssop, were "baptized" (literally) in the blood of the slain bird which had been caught in the clay dish (vs. 6). It is obvious that a living bird cannot be immersed in the blood of another bird. It is biologically impossible. Furthermore, consider the ritual in Leviticus 14:16, where the priest is said to "dip,"[119] or literally baptize, the finger of his right hand into the oil that is in his left hand, and with his finger "sprinkle" some of the oil seven times before the Lord. Not even here is immersion required. "All that is prescribed is dipping of the right finger in the oil which is in the palm of the left hand, and it is quite unreasonable to suppose that [total] immersion of that right finger was required."[120] See also Ruth 2:14 and 1 Samuel 14:27.

> What we have found is this: there is one case where βαπτω and even βαπτω εισ does not mean and cannot mean immersion (Lev. 14:6, 51); there is another case where it is unreasonable to suppose that immersion was required or took place (Lev. 14:16); there is still another instance where dipping but not immersion is the reasonable and natural supposition (Ruth 2:14); finally, in the case of 1 Samuel 14:27 immersion is not unreasonable, but it is not by any means necessary to the action denoted. Hence we have no reason

119. It should be pointed out that dipping is not immersion. "This fact that dipping is not equivalent to immersion needs to be stressed at the outset. Far too often in anti-baptist discussions this fact is overlooked and a good deal of unnecessary argumentation arises from the oversight" (Murray, *Christian Baptism*, 11).

120. Murray, *Christian Baptism*, 12.

to suppose that in a great many other instances immersion is the action denoted by βαπτω. In other words, we have no ground upon which to insist that in Exodus 12:22; Leviticus 4:6, 17; 9:9; Numbers 19:18; Deuteronomy 33:24; 2 Kings 8:15 immersion is the mode of action referred to in the respective cases. There is nothing in the Hebrew word used nor in the context of the passages concerned which requires immersion.[121]

The New Testament Use of the Word, Baptizo

In the New Testament, the word *bapto* recedes into the background and *baptizo* comes to the foreground. *Bapto* occurs only four times (Luke 16:24; twice in John 13:26; Rev. 19:13), whereas *baptizo* occurs around eighty times. A study of this word shows that "*the Baptist contention that βαπτιζω and its cognates mean immersion is not borne out by the evidence* and that *βαπτιζω* can be used to denote an action which neither indicates nor implies immersion."[122] (For Murray's defense of this claim see pages 15–23 in his book, *Christian Baptism*) This claim can be defended not only by (1) Heb. 9:10–23 as we have seen, but also by (2) Matt. 3:11; Mark 1:8; Luke 3:16; Acts 1:5; 11:16; (3) Heb. 9:13, 14, 22; 10:22; 12:24; 1 Pet. 1:2; (4) 1 Cor. 10:2; and (5) Matt. 15:2; Mark 7:2–5; Luke 11:38. "*βαπτιζω*... is one of those words which indicate a certain effect without itself expressing or prescribing the particular mode by which this effect is secured."

The last three texts mentioned in the previous paragraph, Matthew 15:2; Mark 7:2–5 and Luke 11:38 are concerned with the extra-biblical religious practices of the Pharisees. (1) They would not eat until they had "washed their hands" (Matt. 15:2). The Jewish custom of washing at the time was in pouring water over the hands, according to the Talmud. (2) Luke 11:38 tells us that the Pharisees were shocked that Jesus "had not first baptized himself before dinner." There is no reason at all to believe that Luke is referring to anything other than the practice described in Matthew 15:2, of

121. Murray, *Christian Baptism,* 13.
122. Murray, *Christian Baptism,* 15.

pouring water over the hands up to the wrists. In Luke 11:38 the word *ebaptisthe* is used showing that washing the hands by pouring water over them can be called baptism. The significant thing is that such washing is referred to as a baptizing oneself. (3) In Mark 7:4 we are told that whenever the Pharisees returned home from the market they would not eat until they had washed themselves. In this verse, some manuscripts use the word, *baptizo,* and others, *hrantizo,* meaning "sprinkle." Verse 4 also speaks of the "baptism of cups and pots and brazen vessels," which statement some use to prove immersion. However, some manuscripts of Mark 7:4 include the words, "And many other things there be, which they received to hold, as the washing (baptizing) of cups and pots and brazen vessels AND TABLES" (KJV). Did the Pharisees immerse their tables and other furniture every time they returned from the market? No. But they could have very easily sprinkled them in a symbolic cleansing.

The Mode of Baptism by John the Baptist

The Use of the Word "Baptizo" by John the Baptist

John the Baptist contrasted his baptism with that of Christ when he said: "I indeed baptize you with water unto repentance... He shall baptize you with the Holy Spirit and fire" (Luke 3:16; Matt. 3:11; Mark 1:8). John is prophesying the Day of Pentecost, as Acts 1:5 and 11:16 prove. The coming of the Holy Spirit on the disciples on the Day of Pentecost recorded in Acts 2 is undoubtedly Christ's baptism of His church with His Spirit, promised by John the Baptist.

> If baptism means immersion then the statement of John that Jesus would baptise with the Holy Spirit and fire must mean strictly, 'he shall immerse in the Holy Spirit and fire,' and any language used with reference to the baptism of the Spirit, however figurative it may be, cannot depart from or violate this basic meaning.... But what we actually find is that the baptism of the Spirit is referred to in terms that are quite contrary to the idea of immersion and in fact preclude it. In Acts 1:8 the Holy Spirit is represented as *coming upon* the disciples: 'Ye shall receive power *after that the Holy Spirit has*

> *come upon you.'* The [Greek] verb is επερχομαι and conveys the notion of 'coming down upon.' In Acts 2:17, 33 the Holy Spirit is represented as having been poured out, and the verb is ἐκχέω. In Acts 10:44; 11:15 the Holy Spirit is represented as having fallen upon the persons concerned, and the verb is ἐπιπίπτω.
>
> It is surely significant that the terms in each case are those of affusion [*i.e.*, pouring or sprinkling] and not of immersion. Yet it is precisely this affusion that is called the baptism of the Holy Spirit.... It is not without relevance in this same connection that in the Old Testament the giving of the Spirit, in some cases explicitly referring to Pentecost, is promised in terms of pouring out, shedding forth and sprinkling (Isa. 32:15; Joel 2:28; Prov. 1:23; Ezek. 36:25–27).... The language of the Old Testament provides the imagery of the New Testament and is quite foreign to the notion of immersion.[123]

The Practice of Baptism by John the Baptist

The baptizing work of John the Baptist is said to have been in the Jordan River, (*en to Jordane potamo* (Mat. 3:6; Mark 1:5); and *eis ton Jordanan* (Mark 1:9)); and in *Ænon* near *Salim* because there was "much water" there, (*hudata polla en ekei*) (John 3:23). None of these phrases require immersion or imply immersion. "In the Jordan River" is nothing more than a designation of location, as is "baptizing in *Ænon.*" Neither "into the Jordan" or "going down into the water" or "coming up out of the water" imply immersion, as far as the meaning of the Greek words and phrases are concerned. Standing in the water or on the edge of the river would satisfy completely the idea expressed. The phrase "because there was much water there" is more literally translated, as the NASB does, "many waters" or "many springs". Consider the need for "much water" and "many springs" in connection with John's ministry. Besides the need of water for baptizing, there would be the need for abundant resources of water for the families and animals of those multitudes of

123. Murray, *Christian Baptism*, 23–24.

people who came out in the hot, dry wilderness to hear John's preaching and to be baptized by him.

Further, John himself said, "I baptize you *with water*," and that Jesus Himself would "baptize you *with the Holy Spirit*" (Luke 3:16). The first phrase is a dative of means with the preposition implied, expressing instrumentality, *i.e.*, John used water with which to baptize people. The second phrase is a prepositional phrase following the preposition "*en*," meaning "with the Holy Spirit." Neither Jesus nor John would baptize people *into* the water or *into* the Spirit, which might be interpreted by some to imply immersion; instead they would baptize people *with* or *by means of*, the application of water and of the Holy Spirit.

The comments of Lenski, the great Lutheran commentator of the New Testament, are wise and to the point:

> Matthew's [use of '*ebaptidzonto*'] says absolutely nothing regarding the mode of baptism which the Baptist employed. Nothing regarding the mode can be obtained from the added proposition εν, 'in the river Jordan', for which Mark 1:9 uses εις, with no difference in meaning. This εν is locative...stating where the baptism took place; it denotes place...and nothing more. The readiness with which the multitudes submitted to baptism is explained by the fact that purificatory rites by the application of water were not new nor strange to the Jews; and these rites were not administered by immersion (Lev. 14:7, 27; Num. 8:7; 19:13; Heb. 9:13; Ex. 19:10; Lev. 15; 16:26, 28; 22:6; Deut. 23:10). These were washings, rinsings, and bathings and *not* immersions. The Jews expected that, when the Messiah came, He would use a purificatory rite such as this; see the question on this point put to the Baptist by the Pharisees in John 1:25. Instead, therefore, of seeking to explain Matthew's verb 'were being baptized' by some later fixed practice obtaining in the Christian Church at the time when Matthew wrote, the Christian practice must be explained by the purificatory rites used by the Jews since the days of Moses. Since none of these were immer-

sions, immersion was not the mode of either the Baptist's or Jesus' baptism.

The verb [*baptizo*], as all lexicons agree refers to any mode of applying water. It is linguistically unwarranted to restrict it to one mode to the exclusion of all other modes, and that a mode for which Jewish practice furnishes no evidence. How could immersions be administered on the desert journey and in a city like Jerusalem, where water was never abundant? But did not the Baptist labor near the river Jordan? If his baptism was administered by immersion, then, since the estimated number he baptized during the brief period of a little over a year in which he labored was between 200,000 and 500,000, he must have lived an aquatic life. We have no evidence that he used his disciples as his assistants when baptizing. Moreover, he also baptized at Ænon (John 3:23), the very name of which means 'Springs.' The [*polla hudata*], literally, "many waters," rivulets flowing from these springs, made the place suitable for his work, not by furnishing water for immersions, but by providing water for drinking, a great necessity where many people were gathered. Of course, he could use these 'waters' also to pour or to sprinkle when baptizing.

Yet the idea prevails that the Baptist immersed. This is plainly traditionalism. It is well illustrated in the case of Zahn, who admits that there are no indications of the mode of baptism in Matthew's words and yet, when he tries to imagine how the Baptist baptized, speaks of a *Vollbad* [full bath]. Some refer to the baptism of Jewish proselytes, but they fail of proof regarding two points. This rite is not mentioned until the second century, and no one can show that it was practiced at the time of the Baptist; still more vital, no evidence is at hand that the baptism of proselytes was more than a washing, it was like similar Jewish rites. We may add that nowhere does it appear that the Baptist thought that he was making proselytes of the Jews whom he baptized.[124]

124. R. C. H. Lenski, *The Interpretation of St. Matthew's Gospel* (Minneapo-

The Mode of Baptism in the Rest of the New Testament

First, baptism is a sign and seal of our cleansing from sin's pollution by the Holy Spirit, who has been *poured out* abundantly on us from on high (Acts 2:1–4, 32, 33; 10:44–48; 11:15,16; Isa. 44:3; 52:15; Ezek. 36:25–27; Joel 2:28, 29). These passages present the baptism with the Holy Spirit always as a pouring and a sprinkling, but never as an immersion. Therefore, since a natural similarity exists between the visible sign and that spiritual reality which it signifies, so that the actions and elements in the sign remind us of the nature of the spiritual blessing it signifies, there should be nothing in the sign that misrepresents the thing signified. Hence, water baptism is by "pouring" or "sprinkling" of water down upon the head, just as the Holy Spirit comes down from above, *i.e.*, from God, just as the dove-like descent of the Holy Spirit from above onto Jesus. The idea that we are immersed into the Person of the Holy Spirit is neither Biblical nor rational.

Second, baptism is a sign and seal of our cleansing from sin's guilt by the application of the blood of Jesus, which the Bible represents as a *sprinkling* of the blood of Jesus: "that you may obey Jesus Christ and be sprinkled with His blood" (1 Pet. 1:2). "Let us draw near with a sincere heart in full assurance of faith, having our hearts sprinkled clean from an evil conscience" (Heb. 10:22).

> For if the blood of goats and bulls and the ashes of a heifer sprinkling those who have been defiled, sanctify for the cleansing of the flesh, how much more will the blood of Christ, who through the eternal Spirit offered Himself without blemish to God, cleanse your conscience from dead works to serve the living God? (Heb. 9:13–14).

See also Hebrews 9:22 and 12:24. "It would be strange if the baptism with water which represents the sprinkling of the blood of Christ could not properly and most significantly be performed by sprinkling."[125] In the Bible, the blood is applied to us; we are not im-

lis, MN: Augsburg Publishing House, [1943] 1964), 100–101.

125. Murray, *Christian Baptism*, 24.

mersed in the blood. Baptism by immersion contradicts the spiritual reality it signifies.

Third, 1 Corinthians 10:2 says concerning Old Testament Israel that "all were baptized unto Moses in the cloud and in the sea." If the immersionist argument is correct, since the word, baptized, is used, which, according to their view, always of necessity means immersion, then there must be in this verse an allusion to the mode of baptism. In this view, "the children of Israel would have to be regarded as having been immersed in the cloud and in the sea. Now it is only too apparent that they were not immersed in the sea—they passed through the sea upon dry ground. They did not enter the water nor did the water come upon them (cf. Exod. 14:22)."[126] The cloud led them. They did not come into contact with the cloud, nor were they immersed in it. The only people immersed in the Red Sea that day were the Egyptian chariots and their riders! They were immersed in the Red Sea, while the children of Israel, not immersed in the Red Sea, were nevertheless "baptized unto Moses". The point is that the word "*baptizo*" does not express mode, nor does it mean immersion. Rather it means "to be made one with," "to be bound to"—the children of Israel were bound to Moses in the covenant of which he was the mediator.

Fourth, 1 Peter 3:20–21 says that "when the patience of God kept waiting in the days of Noah, during the construction of the ark, in which a few, that is, eight persons, were brought safely through the water. And corresponding to that, baptism now saves you." Corresponding to what? Corresponding to the water of Noah's flood, which water "brought" Noah and his family, "safely through the water" (3:20), *i.e.*, which water "saved" Noah and his family from cultural pollution and divine judgment, and was a type or symbol of Christian baptism which *saves* us from divine judgment and sinful pollutions as a sign and seal of Christ and the benefits of redemption. The point is that *Noah was baptized unto salvation and corresponding to that Christians are baptized unto salvation.* The flood was for Noah a baptism; BUT (!), Noah and his family were the only people in the world who were not im-

126. Murray, *Christian Baptism*, 25.

mersed! The world was immersed in Noah's flood; but Noah and his family were baptized by the flood, without being immersed, *i.e.*, God separated and saved them for Himself from the depravity and condemnation of the world.

Fifth, after Paul's conversion on the road to Damascus (Acts 9:1–9), he was baptized by a man named Ananias (Acts 9:10–19). After both men had entered the "house" (9:17), Ananias said to Paul, "And now why do you delay? ARISE and be baptized, and wash away your sins, calling on His name" (22:16). And then the Bible simply says, "and he arose and was baptized" (9:18). In these accounts of Paul's baptism, there is not the slightest hint of immersion. Rather, there is a strong implication of affusion.

> This is the only instance in the New Testament where any physical preparation is directed preliminary to baptism, and that preparation was just to arise.... No impartial reader could receive any other impression than that Paul stood up and was baptized right there in the apartment where Ananias found him.[127]

Sixth, as Peter was preaching in the home of Cornelius to an assembly of his family and friends, something amazing happened:

> While Peter was still speaking these words, the Holy Spirit fell upon all those who were listening to the message.... Then Peter answered, "Surely no one can refuse the water for these to be baptized who have received the Holy Spirit just as we did, can he?" And he ordered them to be baptized in the name of Jesus Christ (Acts 10:44, 46–48).

Nothing here suggests immersion. On the contrary,

> the language used and the clear reference to the mode of the Spirit's baptism both evidently suggest affusion. "Can any man forbid water...?" This would sound foolish if the candidates had to go out of the house to a stream or a pool to be

127. Robert Rayburn, *What About Baptism?* (St. Louis, MO: The Covenant College Press, 1957), 37.

> baptized. Such language suggests that certainly no one would refuse to bring a little water in an appropriate vessel in order that the believers might be baptized.[128]

Notice several things in this incident: (1) It was because the Holy Spirit "fell" down on those present, as He did on the Day of Pentecost, when He was "poured out" on His disciples, that Peter ordered those upon whom the Spirit came to be baptized, which is a sign and seal of the COMING DOWN of the Spirit on us, just as water comes down on the candidate when baptism is practiced by affusion. (2) Peter's question implies that he wants someone to bring him a little water right at that very moment. (3) There is a strong implication that these people were baptized in the home of Cornelius, which would not have had a baptistery.

Seventh, after the miraculous release of Paul and Silas from prison, the baptism of the Philippian jailor and his entire family took place in a prison shortly after midnight (Acts 16:25–34). There would have been no baptism pool in a prison! That Paul baptized them in the prison is obvious from three facts: (1) "that very hour of the night," *i.e.*, the hour of the great earthquake, the shaking of the prison, the opening of the doors and the unfastening of everyone's chains by a miracle, the jailor began washing the wounds of Paul and Silas, "and immediately he was baptized, he and all his household" (16:33); and (2) that Paul and Silas, whose prison bars were miraculously broken, refused to leave the prison until the magistrates themselves came and released them (16:35–40). (3) The baptism of the jailor and his family is mentioned in verse 33, but Paul and Silas did not leave the prison until verse 40!

Eighth, there is every reason to believe that Jesus Himself was baptized by sprinkling or pouring, and no reason to believe that he was immersed by John the Baptist. Why do we say this? First, because of what we explained above regarding the mode of John's baptism, *i.e.*, affusion, following the example of the purification rites of the Old Testament. Second, because of the purpose behind Jesus' baptism. Since Jesus' baptism was His public ordination into the office of our High Priest, and His Spiritual equipping for that office,

128. Rayburn, *What About Baptism?*, 38.

we would expect that this public ordination would fit the pattern of the Old Testament regarding the ordination of the High Priest, which included these three elements: (1) the priest to be ordained had to be 30 years of age, as Jesus was at the time of His baptism (Luke 3:23; Num. 4:3, 47); (2) he had to be "anointed," not immersed, with oil and "sprinkled," not immersed, with sacrificial blood: "Then you shall take some of the blood that is on the altar and some of the anointing oil, and *sprinkle* it on Aaron and his garments, and on his sons and on his sons' garments with him; so he and his garments shall be consecrated, as well as his sons and his sons' garments with him" (Ex. 29:21), just as Jesus was presumably "anointed" or "sprinkled" by John the Baptist. And (3) he had to be personally called by God to this office, as was Jesus when God spoke out of the heavens at His baptism: "Thou art My beloved Son, in Thee I am well pleased" (Luke 3:22) which statement is taken from Isaiah 42 and Psalm 2. In Psalm 2, Jehovah speaks of inaugurating and installing His Son "upon Zion, My holy mountain," which was holy because that was the location of the Temple where the Lord's PRIESTS ministered. So then, at His baptism, Jesus was ordained and "anointed" as the Christ, which means "*the anointed one*," not "the immersed one." At His baptism, He was *certainly anointed by God* with the Holy Spirit who *came down* upon Him like a dove, and He was PRESUMABLY ANOINTED by John the Baptist with water from the Jordan River. If Christ, "the Anointed One," was not anointed at His baptism, when was He anointed?

The Purpose of Baptism

Not a Commemoration of Christ's Burial and Resurrection

Presbyterians differ from Baptists, not only regarding the mode of baptism, but regarding the meaning and purpose of baptism. Most Baptists, departing from the Bible and the united testimony of historical evangelical Christianity, say that baptism is primarily a symbol of Christ's burial and resurrection, as the Lord's Supper is a symbol of His death. The texts they use in an attempt to support their view are usually Romans 6:3–5; Colossians 2:12; and 1 Corinthians 15:29.

However, there are many objections to this view. First, it lacks any actual Biblical support whatever.

> He would be a hardy man, who would base any theory on the exposition of a passage so obscure as 1 Cor. xv:29. The most probable explanation is, that the Apostle here refers to the Levitical rule of Num. xix:14–19. Were there no resurrection, a corpse would be like any other clod; and there would be no reason for treating it as a symbol of moral defilement, or for bestowing on it, so religiously, the rites of sepulture. But this exposition presents not a particle of reason for regarding Christian baptism as a commemoration of Christ's burial.[129]

The other two passages, Romans 6:3–5 and Colossians 2:12, make substantially the same point:

> Therefore we have been buried with Him through baptism into death, in order that as Christ was raised from the dead... so we to might walk in newness of life.... Having been buried with Him in baptism, in which you were also raised up with Him through faith in the working of God, who raised Him from the dead.

A careful study of these two passages will show, first that they cannot be used to support the Baptist view, and second, that there is no allusion here to the mode of baptism.

Rather than commemorating the burial and resurrection of Christ, baptism signifies the believer's union with Christ in His death, burial and resurrection (Rom. 6:5–6). Everyone who is united to Christ is, by virtue of the effectiveness of Christ's death and the power of His resurrection, freed from the tyranny of sin, lives a new resurrection life, and therefore, cannot use His new life in Christ as an excuse for continuing sinning.

---

129. Dabney, *Lectures in Systematic Theology*, 760.

It is very easy to point to the expression, "buried with him" in verse 4 and insist that only immersion provides any analogy to burial. But such procedure fails to take account of all that Paul says here. It should be noted that Paul not only says "buried together,"... but also "planted together"... and "crucified together."... These latter expressions indicate the union with Christ which is symbolized and sealed by baptism just as surely as does buried together. But it is only too apparent that they do not bear any analogy to immersion.... [By the phrase, "crucified together"] we are represented as having been hung on the cross together with Christ, and that phase of union with Christ is represented by our baptism into Christ not one whit less than our death in him and our burial with him.... When all of Paul's expressions are taken into account, we see that burial with Christ can be appealed to as providing an index to the mode of baptism no more than can crucifixion with Him.... The fact is that there are many aspects to our union with Christ. It is arbitrary to select one aspect and find in the language used to set it forth the essence of the mode of baptism.... Confirmatory of this conclusion is Galatians 3:27.... In Romans 6:3 Paul says: "As many as were baptized into Christ were baptized into His death" and in Galatians 3:27: "For as many as were baptized into Christ did put on Christ"... in Galatians 3:27, the figure used by the apostle to set forth the import of baptism into Christ has no resemblance to immersion. It is the figure of putting on a garment. The plain inference is that Paul is not alluding to the mode of baptism at all. And neither may we suppose that he is in Romans 6:2–6.... In 1 Corinthians 12:13, we have the same effect: "For by one Spirit have we all been baptized into one body." The figure here is the making up of one unified organism and is quite foreign to the notion of immersion. The only sane conclusion is that in none of these cases is reference made to the mode of baptism. The emphasis is plainly upon the meaning of baptism into Christ, that is to say, of union with Him.... In such expressions as "baptized into Christ," "baptized into his death" (Rom. 6:3;

> Gal. 3:27), and "baptized into one body" (1 Cor. 12:13), it is not the rite of baptism that is in the foreground but rather the idea of union with Christ. *"Being baptized into" is a way of expressing "union with."* To be "baptized into Moses" (1 Cor. 10:2) is to be bound to Moses in the fellowship of that covenant of which Moses was the mediator.... To be "baptized into Christ" is to be bound to him in the bonds of that union that makes us the beneficiaries of all the blessings of redemption and pledges us to his Lordship. The rite of baptism is the sign and seal of this union.[130]

> "Our faith receives from baptism the advantage of its sure testimony to us that we are not only engrafted into the death and life of Christ, but so united to Christ himself that we become sharers in all His blessings."[131]

> Second, "by making baptism the commemoration of Christ's burial, and resurrection, the sacramental analogy... is totally lost. This analogy is not in the element to the grace; for in that aspect, there can be no resemblance. Water is not like a tomb.... The use of water is to cleanse."[132]

Third,

> sacraments (always few) are only adopted by God to be commemorative of the most cardinal transactions of redemption. Christ's burial was not such. Christ's burial is nowhere proposed to us as an essential object of faith. His death and the Spirit's work are. His death and resurrection are.... And besides: it would seem strange that the essential work of the Holy Ghost should be commemorated by no sacrament.... In the old dispensation the altar and the laver stood side by side.[133]

130. Murray, *Christian Baptism*, 29–33.
131. Calvin, *Institutes of the Christian Religion*, 2:1307.
132. Dabney, *Lectures in Systematic Theology*, 760–61.
133. Dabney, *Lectures in Systematic Theology*, 761.

Fourth, this theory involves those who believe it in intense confusion. "In the gospel history, Christ's death preceded his burial and resurrection: so the commemoration of the death ought to precede. But the immersionist makes it follow, with peculiar rigidity."[134]

A Sign and Seal of the Covenant of Grace

Baptism is a sign and seal of the covenant of grace, *i.e.*, that eternal bond of friendship, communion of life, and sovereignly-dictated order of life, which God has graciously established with His chosen people in Christ, wherein He is their Sovereign-Friend and they are His servant-friends (Gen. 3:15; Gen. 7–9; 12–17; Ex. 19–24; 2 Sam. 7; Heb. 7–9). It signifies and confirms all the privileges and obligations of that covenant, together with all its promises and benefits, which include our ingrafting into Christ, the remission of sins by the blood of Christ, regeneration by the Holy Spirit, adoption into the family of God, and resurrection unto everlasting life. The covenant of grace contains all the promises included in our salvation, and of these, one comprehends all the rest: union and communion with the triune God, wherein God will be "a God to His people" (Gen.17:7), "their shield and exceeding great reward" (Gen. 15:1), who will "put [His] laws into their minds, and write them on their hearts, and will be to them a God, and they shall be to Him a people" (Heb. 8:10).

> There are very great privileges contained in this relation—namely, our being under the special care and protection of Christ; having a right to what he has purchased, and to that inheritance which he has laid up in heaven for his children; and enjoying communion with him here, and being made happy with him hereafter.[135]

(What the covenant of grace is, what its blessings are, and how the grace of God is manifested in it, are explained in the Westminster Confession of Faith, Chapter 7, and in the Larger Catechism Questions 31 and 32.)

---

134. Dabney, *Lectures in Systematic Theology*, 761.

135. Ridgeley, *Commentary on the Larger Catechism*, 2:495.

A Sign and Seal of Our Ingrafting into Christ

For you are all sons of God through faith in Christ Jesus. For as many of you as have been baptized into Christ have put on Christ (Gal. 3:26, 27).

The Necessity of Union with Christ

It is impossible to receive the benefits of salvation which Christ gives unless we receive the person of Christ, who is the Giver of these benefits: "But as many as received HIM, to them He gave the right to become the children of God, even to those who believe in His name" (John 1:12; emphasis added).

> It is impossible for me to get the juice and virtue that flow out of Christ without first getting the substance, that is, Christ Himself.... Therefore, in order that the Sacrament may nourish you to life everlasting, you must get in it your whole Savior, the whole Christ, God and man, with all His graces and benefits.... And how do I get Him? Not by my mouth.... We get Him by faith.... So, if ever you are to get good out of the Sacrament, you must get the whole Christ. Moreover, there is no instrument with which you may lay hold of Him, but faith.[136]

> "Our faith receives from baptism the advantage of its sure testimony to us that we are not only engrafted into the death and life of Christ, but so united to Christ himself that we become sharers in all his blessings."[137]

The Comprehensiveness of Our Union with Christ

Our union in Christ is the central truth of the whole doctrine of salvation. From this union and because of this union, all the blessings and powers of salvation flow into our lives. From eternity to eternity the people of God are "in Christ." Before the universe was created, we were chosen by God *in Christ* (Eph. 1:3, 4).

---

136. Bruce, *The Mystery of the Lord's Supper*, 46–47.
137. Calvin, *Institutes of the Christian Religion*, 2:1307.

When Jesus gave His life as a ransom for us and redeemed us from our sins by His blood, arose triumphantly from the grave, and ascended to God's right hand, His own were *in Christ* (Rom. 6:2–11; Eph. 2:4–6; Col. 3:3, 4). The people of God are recreated spiritually IN CHRIST (Eph. 2:8–10). Not only does our new life in Christ begin IN CHRIST, it continues and is sustained by the power of that relationship to Him. The Christian life is lived IN CHRIST (Rom. 6:4; 1 Cor. 1:4, 5; 1 Cor. 6:15–17). Believers die and their bodies are buried IN CHRIST (1 Thess. 4:14, 16). And it is IN CHRIST that they will be raised from the dead to eternal glory and bliss (1 Cor. 15:22; Rom. 8:17).

> We thus see that union with Christ has its source in the election of God the Father before the foundation of the world and it has its fruition in the glorification of the sons of God.... What is it that binds past and present and future together in the life of faith and in the hope of glory? Why does the believer entertain the thought of God's determinate counsel with such joy? Why can he have patience in the perplexities and adversities of the present? Why can he have confident assurance with reference to the future and rejoice in hope of the glory of God? *It is because he cannot think of past, present, or future apart from union with Christ.*[138]

The Meaning of "Ingrafting" into Christ

Baptism is the sign and seal of our ingrafting into Christ in order that we may be counted as being among the children of God. "Ingrafting" is a horticultural word. It means to insert a twig or sprout of a tree or other plant, or specifically a cutting of a twig into the stock or trunk of another tree or plant for propagation. In the Bible, Christ is the stock or trunk, and we are the ingrafted branches, that live and bear fruit, because of our ingrafting onto the trunk, from which we draw their life-giving, life-sustaining, fruit-producing, vital sap. Separated from the trunk, the branches

---

138. John Murray, *Redemption Accomplished and Applied* (Grand Rapids, MI: William B. Eerdmans Publishing Co., 1955), 164. Emphasis added.

dry up and die. It is only as we are "ingrafted" into Christ, made one with Him in His Body, drawing strength from Him to enjoy intimate communion with Him, to glorify Him and to mature in love and Christ-likeness (Eph. 4:15–16). Jesus said,

> I am the true vine.... Abide in Me, and I in you. As a branch cannot bear fruit of itself, unless it abides in the vine, so neither can you, unless you abide in Me. I am the vine, you are the branches; he who abides in Me, and I in him, he bears much fruit; for apart from Me you can do nothing" (John 15:1–5).

In Romans 11, Paul speaks of the covenant community, rooted in the covenant promises of Christ, the "Seed" (Gal. 3:16), to Abraham (Gen. 12–17), as the holy root of the Christian Church (Rom. 11: 16–17). He describes the believing Gentiles as branches of a "wild olive tree," who "were grafted into" the covenant stock, and became partakers with the believing Jews "of the rich root of the olive tree" (11:17). This is not a basis for pride but for gratitude, realizing that "it is not you who supports the root, but the root supports you" (11:18).

The Exposition of Galatians 3:26–27

> For you are all sons of God through faith in Christ Jesus. For all of you who were baptized into Christ have clothed yourselves with Christ.

We Are Adopted into God's Family Through Faith in Christ

Faith is the Means of Adoption

Verse 26 makes absolutely clear that we are adopted into God's family as His dearly loved sons and daughters only through faith in Jesus Christ as our Lord and Savior (John 1:12).

> Our believing in Jesus Christ is not as the crediting of some story when we hear it or read it, but a receiving and con-

> ceiving of him inwardly with full assuredness as he is offered us by God his father. Therefore when we embrace our Lord Jesus Christ, as the party that hath made amends for our sins to reconcile us to God, so as we repose the whole trust of our welfare in him, not doubting but that he hath brought us all that is for the inheriting of heaven.... By this word *Faith* Saint Paul meaneth to exclude all the desert and worthiness that men suppose or imagine themselves able to bring with them to God.[139]

Grace is the Cause of Adoption

Faith is not the cause of our adoption, nor is it the basis of our adoption. God did not adopt us because of faith or on account of faith or on the basis of faith, as if there were some merit to our believing. Rather, faith is only the instrument, the means, that receives the gift of adoption (John 1:12). We are God's children, and freely adopted into His family solely because of His grace and generosity. It pleased Him to have mercy on us and so He adopted us. Faith, which itself is a gift of God, merely receives what God graciously gives.

We are Adopted into God's Family Because of Our Union with Christ

How is it even possible that we, sinners, should become the children of God, especially since Jesus is the "only begotten" Son of God? He alone holds that title and that dignity. Since Jesus is the only Son of God, how does this title apply to us who believe? Jesus said it was because of the union between Christ and believers: "I in them, and Thou in Me, that they may be perfected in unity, that the world may know that Thou didst send Me, and didst love them, even as Thou didst love Me" (John 17:23). (See "The Comprehensiveness of our Union with Christ.")

Paul can speak of our being "baptized INTO Christ" and of our "clothing ourselves with Christ," or "putting on Christ" as a garment.

---

139. John Calvin, *Sermons on Galatians* (Audubon, NJ: Old Paths Publications, 1995), 480, 482.

> Jesus Christ is our apparel or raiment, whereby all is covered and buried that might make us to be rejected at God's hand, and grace is purchased unto us, so as he doth not anymore sift us and search us in ourselves, but accepteth us as if we came in the very person of his own Son.[140]

> "To put on Christ" is to become as Christ, to have his standing; in this context to become objects of the divine favour, sons of God, as he is the Son of God.[141]

> The putting on of Christ, according to the gospel, consisteth not in an imitation, but in a new birth, and a new creation; that is to say, in putting on Christ's innocency, His righteousness, His wisdom, His power, His saving health, His life, and His Spirit.... Wherefore to be appareled with Christ... [is to be appareled]... with an incomparable gift; that is to say, with remission of sins, righteousness, peace, consolation, joy of spirit, salvation, life and Christ Himself.[142]

Our Union with Christ is Signified, Sealed and "Exhibited" to Us in Baptism

By faith, signed and sealed by baptism, we are so intimately, spiritually, mystically, and eternally united to Christ, that, in God's sight, we "bear the name and character of Christ[143], and are viewed

140. Calvin, *Sermons on Galatians*, 483.

141. Ernest De Witt Burton, *A Critical and Exegetical Commentary on the Epistle to the Galatians* (Edinburgh: T & T Clark, [1921] 1968), 203.

142. Martin Luther, *Commentary on Galatians*, trans. by Erasmus Middleton, ed. by John Prince Fallowes (Grand Rapids, MI: Kregel Publications, 1979), 221–22.

143. In Jeremiah 33:16, we read the Messianic promise that "in those days (*i.e.*, during the reign of the Messiah) Judah shall be saved, and Jerusalem shall dwell in safety; and this is the name by which SHE shall be called: The LORD our Righteousness!" What a promise! The covenant people of Jehovah will be saved from sin and judgment, and will live in security under God's blessing, for one reason: "SHE", *i.e.*, the faithful people of God, or the church, will be given God's own name: "Jehovah our righteousness", and in that divine name, "SHE" will find salvation (Acts 4:12). Jehovah's name and righteousness imputed to believers on the basis of the finished work of Christ through faith in Him alone is the essence

in him rather than in [ourselves]."[144]

Because God has freely bestowed His grace on us "in the Beloved" (Eph. 1:6), we are accepted with God "in the Beloved." Our lives as baptized believers are "hidden with Christ in God" (Col. 3:3).

> Just as a garment which one puts on... quite envelops the person wearing it, and identifies his appearance and his life, so the person baptized in Christ is quite entirely taken up in Christ and in the salvation brought by Him.... What happens at baptism is a confirmation and sealing, a visible manifestation of what is given to the church by faith.[145]

> When Saint Paul speaketh of Baptism, he presupposeth that we receive the thing that is offered unto us in it. Many that are baptized do wipe away the grace of God: and notwithstanding that it be offered them, yet they make themselves unworthy of it through their unbelief, lewdness, and rebellion.... And so the thing that maketh us God's children and clothed us with Jesus Christ, is that God draweth us out of the corruption wherein we were by nature, and will have Jesus Christ to be our head, and us ingrafted into him to be partakers of his goods. Therefore look when we receive that, then is all accomplished that is figured by baptism.[146]

> For as much as God has "knit us into the body of our Lord Jesus Christ, we be no more considered in our own kind, neither doth God look what we be of ourselves, nor what we have deserved: but accepteth us as if Jesus Christ were in us, as in deed we must not be separated from him."[147]

---

of the New Testament's doctrine of justification by faith.

144. John Calvin, *Commentaries on the Epistles of Paul to the Galatians & Ephesians*, trans. by Rev. William Pringle (Edinburgh: Calvin Translation Society, 1843; reprint Grand Rapids, MI: Baker Book House, 1979), 111.

145. Herman N. Ridderbos, *New International Commentary on the New Testament: The Epistle of Paul to the Churches of Galatia*, trans. by Henry Zylstra (Grand Rapids, MI: William B. Eerdmans Publishing Co., [1953] 1965), 148.

146. Calvin, *Sermons on Galatians*, 485.

147. Calvin, *Sermons on Galatians*, 492.

The Corroboration of Romans 6:3–5 & Colossians 2:12

> Therefore we have been buried with Him through baptism into death, in order that as Christ was raised from the dead… so we too might walk in newness of life (Rom. 6:4).

> Having been buried with Him in baptism, in which you were also raised up with Him through faith in the working of God, who raised Him from the dead (Col. 2:12).

The Meaning of Romans 6:3–5

Romans 6:2 says that the reason the true Christian is not a slave to sin is because he has *died*. This verb is in the aorist tense, denoting a once-for-all happening in past time, a once-for-all, definite breach with sin. It happened once and was concluded. Paul is not speaking of a process, or of something the Christian should do, but of an accomplished fact, true of all Christians.

In what sense, then, has the Christian "died"? He has died in Christ to the reign and mastery of sin over his life and thoughts. A radical breach with sin has taken place for the Christian. This is the object of the reign of grace mentioned in Rom. 5:21.

How, therefore, did we die to sin? Answer: By virtue of our union with Jesus Christ. To say that we are "baptized into Christ" is to say that we have been brought into union and communion with Him. It signifies our intimate identification and solidarity with Christ. Union with Christ means union with Him in all that He is and in all phases of His work as our Mediator. As Christians, we are no longer "in Adam," we are in union with Christ. We are so closely united with Him that whatever happened to Him happens to us; whatever was true of Him, will be true of us.

Our victory over sin is based on the reality of our union with Christ in His death, burial and resurrection. Notice the phrases, "into HIS death" and "buried *with* Him." The point is this: this passage is concerned with the experiential effects in our individual life histories of our union with Christ *when* He died, was buried and was raised from the death. It refers to a "baptism" into those historical events of the gospel, of which water baptism is a sign and a seal.

We died in Christ *when* Christ died (Gal. 2:20). We were buried in Christ *when* Christ was buried, emphasizing the completion and finality of death. Burial proclaims that a person is finished with life as a slave of sin. And we were raised from the dead in Christ *when* Christ was raised from the dead. Christ's resurrection is the ultimate proof that He conquered the reign of sin and death. We are not left in the grave, because Christ was not left in the grave. God raised him, and God raised us in Him: "But now Christ has been raised from the dead, the firstfruits of those who are asleep.... For as all in Adam die, so also all in Christ shall be made alive" (1 Cor. 15:20, 22). Therefore, all we were in Adam was crucified in Christ, the mastery of sin over us has been broken, we are no longer slaves to sin, and we walk in newness of life, presenting ourselves day by day to God as His grateful servants.

The Significance of Baptized Into

Everyone who is united to Christ is, by virtue of the effectiveness of Christ's death and the power of His resurrection, freed from the tyranny of sin, lives a new resurrection life, and therefore, cannot use His new life in Christ as an excuse for continuing sinning.

Time and again Paul makes this point with the phrase, "baptized into." He says we have been "baptized into Christ" (Gal. 3:27), "baptized into His death" (Rom. 6:3), "baptized into one body" (1 Cor. 12:13). The Old Testament believers were "baptized into Moses" (1 Cor. 10:2). *Being baptized into is a way of expressing union with.* To be baptized into Moses is to be united and bonded to Moses in the fellowship of that covenant of which he was the mediator. To be "baptized into Christ" is not a reference to the mode of baptism (immersion),[148] but rather means to be united

148. "When the believer is said to be baptized into (or unto) Christ, or into His one body, and thus to have put on Christ, there can be no allusion to mode, because then it would be the preposterous idea of immersing into Christ, or into His mystical body, instead of into water. The exact idea expressed is that of a consecrating separation. Baptism is here conceived by the Apostle as our separation

and bonded to Christ "in the bonds of that union that makes us the beneficiaries of all the blessings of redemption and pledges us to his Lordship. The rite of baptism is the sign and seal of this union."[149] "Our faith receives from baptism the advantage of its sure testimony to us that we are not only engrafted into the death and life of Christ, but so united to Christ himself that we become sharers in all his blessings."[150]

This invaluable union with Christ is represented, signified, sealed, conveyed, sustained and perfected by the sealing of the Holy Spirit (Eph. 1:13), using the Word of God and "the sealing ordinances" of baptism and the Lord's Supper in the life of believers in Jesus.

A Sign and Seal of Our Remission of Sins By His Blood

> John did baptize in the wilderness, and preached the baptism of repentance for the remission of sins (Mark 1:4). Repent and let each of you be baptized in the name of Jesus Christ for the forgiveness of your sins (Acts 2:38).

The Call to Baptism in Acts 2:38

This is Peter's answer to the inquiry of the 3,000 people who had just been convicted of their sins by Peter's sermon. He calls upon them to repent and to be baptized, and in so doing they are promised forgiveness of sins and the gift of the Holy Spirit. Repentance is a complete change of mind and heart, leading to a change of life and behavior—a turning from sins and a turning to God in submission, which is rooted in faith in Jesus Christ as Lord and Savior. Forgiveness of sins, along with the cleansing renewal of the Holy Spirit, is the "sending away," literally, of sins. The sins of the believing, repentant sinner are taken away and sent far from him, along with their guilt and punishment, in such a way that God will never use them against him again (Ps. 103:12; Isa. 43:25; Mic. 7:19).

---

from the ruined mass of mankind and annexation to the Saviour in our mystical union" (Dabney, *Lectures in Systematic Theology*, 772).

149. Murray, *Christian Baptism*, 33.

150. Calvin, *Institutes of the Christian Religion*, 2:1307.

Now, the call to repentance, which is Peter's basic and primary command, is to be expected. But to join a call to baptism with a call to repentance for the forgiveness of sins is difficult to understand, and has been misunderstood, unless one understands the nature of sacraments as signs and seals, and the sacramental union between the visible sign and the grace signified. In that light, it is understandable that Peter issued this twin call. Forgiveness of sins comes with faith in Christ (Acts 5:32; 15:9; 26:18). Baptism signifies, seals and conveys forgiveness of sins to the believer.

> Although in the text and order of the words, baptism doth here go before remission of sins, yet doth it follow it in order, because it is nothing else but a sealing of those good things which we have by Christ, that they may be established in our consciences.... Let us know, therefore, that forgiveness of sins is grounded in Christ alone, and that we must not think upon any other satisfaction [expiatory sacrifice that we make in any way] save only that which he hath performed by the sacrifice of his death.... Although God hath once reconciled men unto himself in Christ,... and doth now imprint in our hearts the faith thereof by his Spirit; yet, notwithstanding, because baptism is the seal whereby he doth confirm unto us this benefit, and so, consequently, the earnest [guarantee] and pledge of our adoption, it is worthily said to be given us for the remission of sins. For because we receive Christ's gifts by faith, and baptism is a help to confirm and increase our faith, remission of sins, which is an effect of faith, is annexed unto it as unto the inferior mean.[151]

The Baptism of John in Mark 1:4

John the Baptist also preached repentance-baptism for the forgiveness of sins. He called the people to faith and repentance, and then he baptized those who repented in faith, assuring them that

151. John Calvin, *Commentary Upon the Acts of the Apostles,* trans. by Christopher Fetherstone; ed. by Henry Beveridge, 2 vols. (Edinburgh: Calvin Translation Society, 1843; reprint Grand Rapids, MI: Baker Book House, 1979), 1:118–19.

God forgives all those who repent and believe in Jesus as the Messiah. Therefore, John's baptism is also an outward sign and seal of the forgiveness of sins by God in Christ. This forgiveness was not given by John, nor by the water of baptism, but by God Himself through the preaching of His Word and the administration of baptism to those who receive that Word and submit to that baptism in faith.

By John's words we learn that his baptism was a true means of grace. His baptism was "of repentance" and "for the forgiveness of sins." Every such baptism administered by John to the truly repentant believer actually conveyed forgiveness of sins to the person baptized. Furthermore, by means of baptism, God powerfully stimulates and sustains true conversion in the hearts and lives of His people. The designation of John's baptism as a "baptism of repentance" may by taken as a genitive of purpose, indicating that the baptism, as a means of grace, was intended to produce and stimulate repentance, which view agrees with Matthew 3:11.

> If repentance was the expected result of the act, it is clear that the rite cannot have been a mere piece of symbolism, but must have constituted a true sacrament, intended to convey some form of grace. And with this also agrees John's urging the people "to bring forth fruit worthy of repentance."[152]

A Sign and Seal of the Righteousness Which is By Faith

> And he received the sign of circumcision, a seal of the righteousness of the faith which he had yet being uncircumcized; that he might be the father of all them that believe (Rom. 4:11).

The Point of Romans 4:11

Here we have a definition of two things: (1) the relation of faith and circumcision, and baptism, since baptism has fulfilled circumcision (Col. 2:11–12), and is the New Testament form of circumci-

---

152. Geerhardus Vos, *Biblical Theology* (William B. Eerdmans Publishing Co., 1948), 317.

sion (Phil. 3:2–3); and (2) that blessing which is signified and sealed to the believer in circumcision or baptism.

The Relation of Faith and Baptism

Baptism does not contribute to the justification of the believer, which is based on the finished work of Christ. Neither does baptism create justifying faith, although it does sustain a definite relationship to faith and to justification. Baptism signifies and seals faith in the believer, which indicates that faith existed in the believer prior to the baptism, since "a seal or authentication presupposes the existence of the thing sealed and the seal does not add to the content of the thing sealed."[153]

> A sign points to the existence of that which it signifies, whereas a seal authenticates, confirms, and guarantees the genuineness of that which is signified.... And the seal is that which God himself appended to assure Abraham that the faith he exercised in God's promise was accepted by God to the end of fulfilling to Abraham the promise which he believed. In Genesis 17:10–14 circumcision is clearly stated to be the sign of the covenant. There is no incompatibility. As the sign and seal of the covenant it was also the seal of that faith and of the justification by faith apart from which the covenant is meaningless.[154]

(See Genesis 12:1–3; 15:4–6, 18–21; 17:1–21.)

The Blessing Sealed to the Believer in Baptism

The divine blessing signified and sealed to believer in baptism is "the righteousness of the faith which he had while uncircumcized." From this statement we learn that: (1) Abraham did receive the sign of circumcision; (2) circumcision was a seal of the faith he had before he was circumcized; and (3) circumcision sealed "the

153. John Murray, *New International Commentary on the New Testament: The Epistle to the Romans* (Grand Rapids, MI: William B. Eerdmans Publishing Co., 1959), 1:137.

154. Murray, *The Epistle to the Romans*, 1:138.

righteousness" which his faith had received to Abraham. And, as we have shown, this statement can be properly applied to baptism; and just as there was only one circumcision in the Old Testament, signifying the same thing to all who were circumcized; so in the New Testament there is only one baptism, signifying the same thing to all who are baptized. Therefore, we can conclude: (1) Believers and their children are to receive the sign of baptism, just as Old Testament believers and their children received the sign of circumcision, Genesis 17; (2) Baptism as a seal of faith presupposes faith, produced by the Spirit, in those being baptized; and (3) Baptism seals the righteousness of faith, "which HE HAD" while unbaptized, presupposing the actual possession of that righteousness in the one baptized prior to his baptism. Since there is only one baptism, this would be true of adults and children receiving baptism.

"The righteousness of faith," or received by faith in Christ alone, is Christ's righteousness imputed to us in justification as the basis of our acceptance with God (Rom. 4:1–9), and imparted to us by His Spirit in regeneration and sanctification (Rom. 6:1–22). This is the case because the righteousness, which is the basis of our acceptance with God, is Christ's complete and perfect righteousness, both active and passive, *i.e.*, both throughout His life in obedience to God's Law and in His death in which He submitted to God's will. Christ's righteousness is received by faith and sealed to the believer in baptism. Baptism is the sign and seal of our union and communion with the whole Christ, His complete righteousness and His comprehensive salvation: "But now apart from the Law, the righteousness of God has been manifested, being witnessed by the Law and the Prophets; even the righteousness of God through faith in Jesus Christ for all those who believe" (Rom. 3:21–22). "For I am not ashamed of the gospel, for it is the power of God for salvation to everyone who believes, to the Jew first and also to the Greek. For in it the righteousness of God is revealed from faith to faith; as it is written, 'But the righteous man shall live by faith.'" (Rom. 1:16–17). This righteousness of God in Christ given by divine omnipotence to all who believed includes justification (Rom. 3–5) and sanctification (Rom. 6–8). *Both imputed righteousness and imparted righteousness are sealed to us in baptism, the water of which is a symbol of God's purification of us from the guilt of sin by the blood of Christ and from the pollution of sin by the cleansing renewal of the Holy Spirit.* Baptism as the sign and seal of the purification of the guilt of sin is seen in such passages as Matthew 3:6; Mark 1:4; Luke 3:3; Acts 2:38; 22:16; 1 Peter 3:21. "We may therefore conclude that baptism represents the remission of sins or, in other words, purification from the guilt of sin by the sprinkling of the blood of Christ."[155] Baptism as the sign and seal of the purification of the defilement of sin is seen in such passages as John 3:5; Titus 3:5; 1 Corinthians 6:11, because

> since baptism is washing with water, since it involves a religious use of water, and since regeneration is expressed elsewhere in terms of washing... it is difficult, if not impossible, to escape the conclusion that this washing with water involved in baptism represents that indispensable purification which is presupposed in union with Christ and without which no one can enter the kingdom of God.[156]

In summary, we have learned that *baptism has a three-fold meaning:*

> we may say then that baptism signifies union with Christ in the virtue of his death and the power of his resurrection, purification from the defilement of sin by the renewing grace of the Holy Spirit, and purification from the guilt of sin by the sprinkling of the blood of Christ. The emphasis must be placed, however, upon union with Christ.[157]

The Point of Colossians 2:11–12: The Fulfillment of Circumcision in Baptism

> And in Him [Christ] you were also circumcised with a circumcision made without hands, in the removal of the body

155. Murray, *Christian Baptism*, 8.
156. Murray, *Christian Baptism*, 7–8.
157. Murray, *Christian Baptism*, 8.

> of the flesh by the circumcision of Christ; having been buried with Him in baptism, in which you were also raised up with Him through faith in the working of God, who raised Him from the dead.

We have been pointing out that circumcision, the sign of the covenant in the Old Testament, has been fulfilled in baptism, the sign of the covenant in the New Testament. Now, we should consider this claim and the nature of the relation between circumcision and baptism.

The Meaning of Circumcision

It was instituted by Jehovah to be a sign and seal of the highest spiritual blessings of the covenant He established with His people (Gen. 17:10; Deut. 30:6; Roma. 4:11; Acts 7:8, 38). It was not a badge of national identity. It was (1) a sign and seal of the believer's union and communion with Jehovah: "This is My covenant, which you shall keep, between Me and you and your descendants after you: every male among you shall be circumcised" (Gen. 17:10); (2) a sign and seal of Spiritual rebirth and sanctification, *i.e.,* the cleansing of sin's defilement: "the Lord your God will circumcise your heart and the heart of your descendants, to love the Lord your God with all your heart" (Deut. 30:6); and (3) it was a sign and seal of justification by faith, *i.e.,* the removal of sin's guilt: "he received the sign of circumcision, a seal of the righteousness of the faith which he had while uncircumcised" (Rom. 4:11).

The Function of Circumcision

Circumcision functioned as: (1) a sign and seal of God's gracious covenant and its blessings (Rom. 4:11); (2) a means of distinguishing God's people from the world (Ex. 12:48; Gen. 34:14); and (3) a public admission into the visible congregation of the Lord, *i.e.,* the covenant community (Gen. 17:4).

The Rules for Administering Circumcision

God gave Israel two rules for administering circumcision: (1) Adult males upon profession of faith in the covenant Lord and Savior should be circumcised. They must know what the covenant is and bow before its Lord, before they may receive the sign of the covenant (Gen. 34:14, 17, 22). (2) All males in a believer's household, being joint-heirs with him of the covenant (Gen. 17:7), are to receive the sign, including those who neither understand nor profess covenant religion, *i.e.*, infants (Gen. 17:10). Though there were two recipients of circumcision, there were not two *kinds* of circumcision, *i.e.*, adult circumcision and infant circumcision. There was ONE CIRCUMCISION, the same in mode, meaning and function, for adults and for children. Whatever it signified and sealed to elect adults, it signified and sealed to elect infants.

The Permanence of the Sign of the Everlasting Covenant

> And I will establish My covenant between Me and you and your descendants after you throughout their generations for an EVERLASTING COVENANT, to be God to you and to your descendants after you.... This is My covenant, which YOU SHALL KEEP, between Me and you and your descendants after you: every male among you shall be circumcised....It shall be the sign of the covenant between Me and you (Gen. 17:7, 10–11; emphasis added).

The divine command to bear and to have your descendants to bear "the sign of the covenant," which is "an everlasting covenant," signifying and sealing an everlasting union and communion between God and His people, is *a permanent command.* This command is nowhere in the Old Testament or New Testament abrogated or annulled. Therefore, since it is the Law of God, we must assume it is still in force, and it remains our duty and privilege to obey it. So that, if any one refuses to obey it with reference to himself or his children, he is living in disobedience to God. 1 Corinthians 7:19 and Galatians 3:2 are sometimes used to prove that the Old Testament laws have been abrogated, but both of these passages deal with circumcision and law from the Judaizer's legalistic point of view. (A little later in this chapter we will see how this relates to baptism.)

The Fulfillment of Circumcision in Baptism

In the New Testament, circumcision fades out of the picture, and baptism comes to the forefront. The apostles use baptism in the New Testament as the patriarchs used circumcision in the Old Testament. (1) Baptism has the same meaning in the New Testament as circumcision does in the Old Testament. (2) Baptism has the same functions as circumcision. (3) Baptism has the same rules of administration as circumcision. (4) Baptism signifies no higher blessings than circumcision signified.

Baptism has fulfilled and replaced circumcision as the sign of the covenant. This is a historical fact as well as a doctrinal truth. In the New Testament church, baptism did replace circumcision. Adult converts were now baptized not circumcised (Acts 16:31–34). The households of converts were now baptized not circumcised (Acts 16:33). Baptism upon profession of faith in adulthood or adolescence of those children born of Christian parents lacks any kind of support in the New Testament.

Colossians 2:11–12 confirms that baptism is the fulfillment of circumcision. As circumcision in the Old Testament, baptism is now the sign and seal of regeneration, *i.e.*, the cleansing of sin's defilement by the Spirit. "*Just as physical circumcision indicated a circumcision of the heart, so now physical baptism indicates a circumcision of the heart.*"[158] Just as Deuteronomy 30:6 says that "the Lord your God will circumcise your heart and the heart of your descendants" so Colossians 2:11 speaks of the Christians in Corinth as being "circumcised with a circumcision made without hands, in the removal of the body of the flesh by the circumcision of Christ." Furthermore, Paul is telling the Corinthian Church that *Christians are "circumcised" when they baptized*: "you were also circumcised ... having been buried with Him in baptism." The circumcision of their hearts, made without hands, *i.e.*, not produced by man in any sense, was performed by the living Christ Himself by His Spirit. Hence, Paul can speak of all the members of the church saved by grace—men and women, young and old: "we are the true circumci-

158. Robert R. Booth, *Children of the Promise: The Biblical Case for Infant Baptism* (NJ: Presbyterian & Reformed Publishing Co., 1995), 107.

sion, who worship in the Spirit of God and glory in Christ Jesus and put no confidence in the flesh" (Phil. 3:3).

When Paul says "that you were also circumcised ... having been buried with Him in baptism," he is using "sacramental language." He frequently uses the name of the external symbol in the place of the internal, Spiritual reality. So that, when he speaks of us as being "buried" with Christ and "raised up" with Christ in verse 12, he is referring to our union with Christ in His death and resurrection, which union is signified and sealed to us in baptism. And baptism signifies and seals this vital union to those who believe: "through faith in the working of God," verse 12, *i.e.*, as the visible signs are received externally, the Spiritual reality they signify is received by faith, at that point in time or later.

So then, what can we learn about baptism from Colossians 2:11–12? (1) The true, inner circumcision of the heart is accomplished by Christ, manifested in faith, and sealed, sacramentally, by baptism. (2) Baptism is the sign and seal of that Spiritual circumcision which has been wrought in every believer in Christ, which the New Testament describes as being "born of God" (John 1:12–13). (3) Water baptism has appropriately succeeded circumcision as the sign of the covenant. *"Circumcision looked forward to the saving work of the Redeemer; baptism looks back on his completed work on the cross."*[159] (5) As we shall discuss more fully later, children of believers, being heirs of the covenant, have a right to baptism, as they did to circumcision in the Old Testament. *"Any argument against infant baptism is necessarily an argument against infant circumcision."*[160]

Why was the sign of the covenant changed from circumcision to baptism? The New Covenant in Christ brought significant changes to the history and life of the human race, and yet not so as to invalidate the principles of the older "covenant of promise." However,

> the new covenant did *expand* upon the previous covenant administrations and usher in a *greater degree* of blessing,

159. Booth, *Children of the Promise*, 106.
160. Booth, *Children of the Promise*, 109.

> thus *extending* the application of these blessings to *more people* than before. There was a *greater outpouring* of the Holy Spirit (Acts 2: 17). *Gentiles* were now included on a par with Jews (Gal. 3:14), and *women* now received equal covenant privilege (Gal. 3:28). These and other blessings were not minor changes; they called for fresh signs that would draw attention to the new circumstances. Many of the burdensome rites of the Old Testament were changed under the new covenant to reflect the completed work of Christ, (*e.g.*, no more animal sacrifices). Thanks to the work of Christ, a few simple ordinances were put in their place. Water baptism replaced the bloody rite of circumcision, just as the bread and wine replaced the bloody Passover lamb. The shed blood of Christ meant that there was no longer any need for blood to be shed in order for his people to be cleansed and made pure.... It pleased God for the water of baptism, and the bread and wine of the Lord's Supper, to mark the fact that his redemptive work was now completed and that there was no longer any need for blood to be shed.[161]

A Sign and Seal of Our Regeneration by His Spirit

Not by works of righteousness which we have done, but according to His mercy He saved us, by the washing of regeneration, and renewing of the Holy Spirit (Tit. 3:5). That He might sanctify and cleanse her [the church] with the washing of water by the Word (Eph. 5:26).

God in Christ "washes" His Church clean from the defilement of sin by the regenerating, renewing, sanctifying work of the "Holy Spirit" and the "Word" of God. In these two verses (Tit. 3:5 and Eph. 5:26) Paul is using "sacramental language," which, as we have seen, is proper because of the nature of the "sacramental union" of visible sign and Spiritual blessing signified. In other words, it is proper to call the Spiritual reality signified by the sign and conveyed to believers in the sign, by the name of the visible sign itself. Hence, the Holy Spirit "washes" and the church is "cleansed" by

161. Booth, *Children of the Promise*, 111–12. Emphasis added.

"the washing of water by the Word." This sanctifying work of the Spirit and the Word is signified, sealed and conveyed to us in the sacrament of baptism.

> Paul did not mean to signify that our cleansing and salvation are accomplished by water, or that water contains in itself the power to cleanse, regenerate, and renew; nor that here is the cause of salvation, but only that in this sacrament are received the knowledge and certainty of such gifts. This the words themselves explain clearly enough. For Paul joins together the Word of life and the baptism of water, as if he had said: "Through the gospel a message of our cleansing and sanctification is brought to us; through such baptism the message is sealed."[162]

Paul makes this same point in Romans 6:4: "Therefore we have been buried with Him through baptism into death, in order that as Christ was raised from the dead through the glory of the Father, so we too might walk in newness of life."

> By these words he not only exhorts us to follow Christ as if he had said that we are admonished through baptism to die to our desires by an example of Christ's death, and to be aroused to righteousness by the example of his resurrection. But he also takes hold of something far higher, namely, that through baptism Christ makes us sharers in his death, that we may be engrafted in it (Rom. 6:5). And, just as the twig draws substance and nourishment from the root to which it is grafted, so those who receive baptism with right faith truly feel the effective working of Christ's death in the mortification of their flesh, together with the working of his resurrection in the vivification of the Spirit.[163]

"Mortification[164]" means the "putting to death" of our old totally depraved human nature, that comes with the new heart the

---

162. Calvin, *Institutes of the Christian Religion*, 2:1304.
163. Calvin, *Institutes of the Christian Religion*, 2:1307.
164. The mortification of the Spirit sealed in baptism is continual and life-

Spirit creates within us in the place of the old, stony heart (Ezek. 36:26; Jer. 31:31–34). "Flesh" refers to our fallen human natures, totally depraved and condemned by God. "Vivification" means the Spiritual resurrection of the chosen of God out of death into life that comes with regeneration (John 5:21–26).

A Sign and Seal of Our Adoption into the Family of God

"For you are all sons of God through faith in Christ Jesus.... And because you are sons, God has sent forth the Spirit of His Son into our hearts, crying, 'Abba! Father!'" (Gal. 3:26 and 4:6). The new life believers have in Christ, sealed and "exhibited" to them in baptism and the Lord's Supper, is

> the life of sonship of the Father in union with Christ, who was declared the son of God by the resurrection from the dead. *Baptism is thus a sign of adoption into the family of God.* "In Baptism, the *first* thing to be considered is, that God the Father, by planting us in His Church in unmerited goodness, receives us by adoption into the number of His sons. *Secondly,* as we cannot have any connection with Him except by means of reconciliation, we have need of Christ to restore us to the Father's favour by His blood. *Thirdly,* as we are by Baptism consecrated to God, we need also the interposition of the Holy Spirit whose office it is to make us new creatures." "In Baptism, we have to do with God, who, not only by testifying His paternal love, pledges His faith to us, so as to give us a sure persuasion of salvation, but also inwardly ratifies by His divine agency that which He figures by the hand of the minister." "By what title can He be their Father if they in no way belong to the Church?" The Church is for Calvin the sphere of the Fatherhood of God, and entrance into [it] is an

---

long. "Christ kills sin in His, by the effect of Baptism, whereby we are incorporated into His faith [Calvin]" (Ronald Wallace in *Calvin's Doctrine of the Word and Sacrament,* 178). "This we must believe: we are baptized into the mortification of our flesh, which begins with our baptism and which we pursue day by day and which will, moreover, be accomplished when we pass from this life to the Lord" (Calvin, *Institutes of the Christian Religion,* 2:1312).

> entrance into the family of God, Baptism being the sign of adoption. "When we are baptized in the name of our Lord Jesus Christ, we are brought into God's household: it is the mark of our adoption. Now, He cannot be our Father, unless we are under His divine protection and governed by His Holy Spirit: as we have an evident witness in Baptism and a greater in the Lord's Supper."[165]

A Sign and Seal of Our Resurrection Unto Everlasting Life

"All of us who have been baptized into Christ Jesus have been baptized into His death... For if we have become united with Him in the likeness of His death, certainly we shall be also in the likeness of His resurrection" (Rom. 6:3, 5). The sacrament of baptism signifies and seals to us a union with Christ, which has already begun, and which is moving more and more toward perfection, but which can only be completed in heaven: "For I am confident of this very thing, that He who began a good work in you will perfect it until the day of Christ Jesus" (Phil. 1:6). We have experienced Spiritual death and resurrection by virtue of our union with Christ in His life, death and resurrection. We have died to sin's tyranny and have been raised to walk in newness of life; although not perfectly yet.

Someday, at Christ's second coming, we shall see Him as He is and be made like Him by that power of His that makes Him the Master of everything that is (Phil. 3:21). On "the day of Christ Jesus," this continuous and life-long work of God within us, which began with our *Spiritual resurrection from the dead* will be consummated and perfected in our *physical resurrection from the dead* (John 5:28–29; 1 Cor. 15). Then, we will be completely and perfectly "in the likeness of His resurrection" (Phil. 3:21; 1 John 3:2). We have been raised from the dead in regeneration (John 5:21–25). Our resurrected life in Christ is advanced day by day in sanctification (Rom. 6–8). And it will be perfected in glorification (Rom. 8:30). The new birth is our First Resurrection and our physical resurrection from

165. Wallace, *Calvin's Doctrine of the Word and Sacrament*, 180–81.

the dead at the return of Christ is our Second Resurrection (John 5:21–29). The First Resurrection saves us from spiritual death, and the Second Resurrection saves us from physical death. Moreover, our Spiritual resurrection, or new birth by the Spirit, is a sure guarantee that God's Spirit will raise our bodies from the dead on the Last Day:

> And if Christ is in you, though the body is dead because of sin, yet the SPIRIT is alive because of righteousness. But if the Spirit of Him who raised Jesus from the dead dwells in you, He who raised Christ Jesus from the dead will also give life to your MORTAL BODIES through His Spirit who indwells you (Rom. 8:10–11).

Therefore, baptism, which is a sign and seal of our union with Christ in His life, death, resurrection and consummation is an "eschatological sign," in that it signifies and seals something that has begun in us, which is being advanced in us, and which will not be complete until the Last Day. The fact that it has begun, and is being sealed to us in the sacraments, is proof that it will reach its destiny of total perfection in the immediate presence of God. Baptism is a pledge of a present reality and a future certainty. Therefore we can be certain that this union with Christ, signified in Baptism, "*is a pledge not only of the redemption of our souls but also of our bodies, which through the sacraments have the sign engraven on them that they also, as well as our souls, are united into the body of Christ.*"[166] As the Bible says, "For the Lord Himself will descend from heaven with a shout... and the dead in Christ shall rise first" (1 Thess. 4:16). The "dead in Christ" in this verse has reference to the physical resurrection of the bodies in the grave of those who have died and who are in spirit present with the Lord (2 Cor. 5:8). "Do you not know that your bodies are members of Christ?" (1 Cor. 6:15). Therefore *by the Holy Spirit's work in baptism, believers in Christ are sealed for the day of redemption* (Eph. 4:30; 1:13–14).

166. Wallace, *Calvin's' Doctrine of the Word and Sacrament*, 156.

A Public Initiation and A Public Confession

A Public Initiation into the Visible Church

For by one Spirit are we all baptized into one body, whether we are Jews or Gentiles, whether we are bond or free; and have been all made to drink into one Spirit (1 Cor. 12:13).

Being "baptized into Christ Jesus" by the Holy Spirit (Rom. 6:3), is also being "baptized into one body" of Christ by the Holy Spirit (1 Cor. 12:12–13); therefore, since the church is the body of Christ, water-baptism is our public admittance or public initiation into the visible church. It signifies, seals and confers our membership in Christ and His Body. There are some passages in Calvin's writings

> where it is difficult to decide whether Calvin, when he speaks of the body of Christ, means the actual glorified body now in heaven or the Church.... Calvin can thus speak of admission into the Church and ingrafting into the body of Christ as the same thing.... These quotations may serve to show how close, in Calvin's thought, is the relationship between Christ and the Church.[167]

In fact, the Apostle Paul can go so far as to say that "For even as the body is one and yet has many members, and all the members of the body, though they are many, are one body, *so also is Christ*" (1 Cor. 12:12). In this verse, Paul not only refers to the church as the body of Christ, with Christ as the head; but he refers to both body and head as Christ, so close is their union and communion.

Now, water-baptism does not make a person a member of Christ's church, it is his public initiation or public admittance into the church. We are made members of the body of Christ by the baptism of the Holy Spirit (1 Cor. 12:13), through faith in Christ. Baptism is "a solemn admission of the party baptized into the visible Church, and to all its privileges. 'It supposes the party to have a right to these privileges before, and does not *make* them members of the visible Church, but *admits* them solemnly thereto' [Thomas

167. Wallace, *Calvin's Doctrine of the Word and Sacrament*, 154–55.

Boston]."[168] Why does baptism presuppose actual membership in Christ's Church? "Because the seals of the Covenant can never be applied to any, but such as are supposed to be in the covenant; nor can the privileges of the church be confirmed to any that are without the church."[169]

If the above paragraph is true, why does our Larger Catechism speak of the people who are baptized as being solemnly admitted into the visible church by baptism?

> Because there is a vast difference between making a person a church-member, who was none before, and the solemnity of the admission of one, who is already a member. All that our Confession and Catechism affirm, is, that, by baptism, we are solemnly admitted into the visible church; that is, by baptism we are publicly declared to be church-members before, and thus have our membership solemnly sealed to us... 1 Cor. xii:13.[170]

A Public Covenanting to be Wholly and Only the Lord's

> Therefore we are buried with Him by baptism into death; that like as Christ was raised up from the dead by the glory of the Father, even so we also should walk in newness of life (Rom. 6:4).

The Token of Our Confession Before Men

> Baptism serves as our confession before men. Indeed, it is the mark by which we publicly profess that we wish to be reckoned God's people; by which we testify that we agree in worshipping the same God, in one religion with all Christians; by which finally we openly affirm our faith. Thus not only do our hearts breathe the praise of God, but our tongues also

168. Shaw, *The Reformed Faith*, 284.

169. James Fisher, *Fisher's Catechism* (Presbyterian Board of Publishing and Sabbath School Work, 1911), 189.

170. Fisher, *Fisher's Catechism*, 190.

> and all members of our body resound his praise in every way they can.... Paul had this in mind when he asked the Corinthians whether they had not been baptized in Christ's name (1 Cor. 1:13). He thus implied that, in being baptized in his name, they had devoted themselves to him, sworn allegiance to his name, and pledged their faith to him before men. As a result, they could no longer confess any other but Christ alone, unless they chose to renounce the confession they had made in baptism.[171]

"Or were you baptized in the name of Paul?" (1 Cor. 1:13). "Do... not blaspheme the fair name which has been called upon you [or by which you have been called]" (James 2:7). (James seems to have been thinking of baptism in this verse.)

The Necessity of Baptism

As a token and pledge of our confession,

> baptism is the established means whereby a man declares publicly that he is a Christian. It is the mark of his Christian profession before men; it assures to him the privileges of membership in the visible Church and, if he is sincere and faithful, it is the pledge given by God that he will participate in all the blessings of redemption.[172]

Therefore, we must conclude that,

> as we have seen when studying the sacraments in general, *baptism has the necessity of precept, not the necessity of means.* Our Lord has not said that he who has not been baptized will be condemned: that is the lot of those who will not believe.[173]

If God has graciously given us the sacraments as signs and seals of His love for us in Christ,

---

171. Calvin, *Institutes of the Christian Religion*, 2:1313–14.
172. Marcel, *The Biblical Doctrine of Infant Baptism*, 178–79.
173. Marcel, *The Biblical Doctrine of Infant Baptism*, 178.

> it is impossible for men to dispense with sacraments and visible signs.... Let us carefully observe, then, when we wish to use the sacraments as God has ordained, that they should be like ladders for raising us on high: for we are heavy and cumbrous and held down by earthly things. Thus, because we are unable to fly high enough to draw near to God, He has ordained sacraments for us, like ladders. If a man wishes to leap on high, he will break his neck in the attempt; but if he has steps he is able to proceed with confidence. So also, *if we are to reach our God, we must use the means which He has instituted for us,* since He knows what is suitable for us.... Thus *let us carefully observe that it is God who holds out His hand to us, when we have the sacraments to lead us to Him* [Calvin]. Consequently, baptism is a duty. If a man desires to be a disciple of Jesus Christ, and to be regarded as such, he is bound to be baptized, thus submitting himself to the commandment of Christ, as well as to the invariable practice of the Apostles and to the constant and universal usage of the Christian Churches in all ages and in all parts of the world.[174]

Or as our Westminster Confession of Faith says, "Although it be a GREAT SIN to condemn or neglect this ordinance [of baptism], yet grace and salvation are not so inseparably annexed unto it, as that no person can be regenerated or saved without it; or that all that are baptized are undoubtedly regenerated" (WCF, XXVIII, v; emphasis added). Such neglect is a "great sin" because "it consists in despising an express and positive institution of Christ, appointed to be administered in his church to the end of the world (Matt. xxviii:19, 20); and in slighting all the great and glorious benefits and privileges signified and sealed by it (Luke vii:30)."[175]

> Clearly, in the light of their divine institution by Christ, one will not easily speak of the sacraments' non-necessity. Granted that sacramentalism[176] is an error, we should not allow

174. Marcel, *The Biblical Doctrine of Infant Baptism,* 179–80.

175. Fisher, *Fisher's Catechism,* 190.

176. Roman Catholic sacramentalism, (which is also held by some Protestant churches), teaches that the sacraments are a prerequisite for salvation, and there-

polemical interests to threaten our vision of the whole truth. And we can escape that danger by speaking without hesitation of the necessity of the sacraments in the light of their institution by Christ. Even in those churches where the non-necessity of the sacraments for salvation is emphasized, men continue to speak of the command of God and of our calling to use the sacraments. Furthermore, neglect of the sacraments led to the use of the term 'disobedience,' which presupposes a certain necessity of the sacraments. Only if we honor their institution by Christ fully, can we speak polemically of the non-necessity of the sacraments.

The danger of devaluation is not imaginary, since believers always run the danger of stressing what is immediately 'necessary' for their salvation; and if they are told that the sacraments are not necessary for salvation, they might easily conclude that they are relatively unimportant. We must therefore be careful. On the one hand, we must maintain the polemic against Rome; but on the other hand we must speak emphatically of the necessity of the sacraments in the light of the institution by God.... When we consider that the sacraments are pledges of God's grace and signs of His promise, we shall be able to speak all the more seriously of the necessity of the sacraments, for this necessity is directly connected with our weakness, smallness of faith, and unbelief, the very reasons for which God has ordained the sacraments....

Baptism is not left up to the whim of the believers, who then determine whether they need this condescending act of God's strengthening and sealing. On the contrary, when God institutes the sacrament for the strengthening of faith he thus ends all dispute. The question whether this sacrament is necessary is illegitimate in the eyes of Christian faith. The only proper question is that uttered by the eunuch: "What doth hinder me to be baptized?" (Acts 8:36). This is no nega-

---

fore, are necessary, not simply because Christ instituted them, but also because salvation is absolutely impossible without them.

tive approach to 'unimportant' baptism, but an eager seeking of the sign of God through which one can travel his way with gladness.

In the... verse (8:37) that follows, Philip replies, "If thou believest with all thy heart, thou mayest." This does not warrant the conclusion that the ancient Christian Church left baptism to arbitrary decision. Rather, it points to the fact that no obstacle prevented executing the unbreakable and meaningful connection between believing and being baptized.

Because of this connection by virtue of God's command, one can and must speak of the necessity of baptism. The desire for God's sign is not dependent on the state of one's belief, whereby the believer himself determines whether he needs strengthening of faith through the sacrament. The seeking of the sign corresponds to the granting of the pledge of God's goodness in the struggle with man's heart. One can ask for a sign out of unbelief, as the Pharisees did who wanted to try Jesus, but one can also desire the sign in order to honor in it God's institution and to rest in God's salvation. To be sure, we shall have to maintain our protest against every evaluation of baptism that pushes the Word of promise to the background; but those who see baptism in its institution and in connection with the progress of the life of faith, will have to speak emphatically of the necessity of baptism.... To say that baptism is more or less superfluous is to reveal one's failure to appreciate the richness of God's institution.

The basic issue concerning the doctrine and practice of baptism is not simply whether one acknowledges that baptism has been instituted by Christ, but whether one wishes to continue speaking with joy and gladness of the necessity of the sacraments. This is the real touchstone.... It is faith, desiring the sacraments and making use of them, that will speak of the necessity of the sacraments. The man of faith

> does not attempt to be wiser than God, who cannot be separated from his mercy and who in mercy has granted the sacrament to weak, sinful man. Only thus will the institution of the sacrament be honored and the way of faith traveled gladly, also because of the sign.[177]

The Pledge to God for a Good Conscience

In 1 Peter 3:21 we are told that "baptism now saves you—not the removal of dirt from the flesh, BUT AN APPEAL [or pledge] TO GOD FOR A GOOD CONSCIENCE—through the resurrection of Jesus Christ" (emphasis added). This verse confirms that the sign and seal of baptism is also the means by which we make a public profession of faith before the world. "When the candidate is baptized, he pledges to serve the Lord with a good conscience. If the water of baptism symbolizes the washing away of sins, then the believer's response to God is to live conscientiously to his honor and glory."[178]

The Meaning of "Wholly and Only the Lord's"

It should also be pointed out that when we publicly confess our allegiance to the Living God, and publicly covenant with Him to be His faithful servant-friends, we are promising that we will be "wholly and only the Lord's." "Wholly" means "to be His, in all that we are, soul, spirit, and body, 1 Cor. vi:19–20; and in all that we have, whether gifts, graces or worldly comforts, 1 Chron. xxix:14."[179] As Paul said, "Or do you not know that your body is a temple of the Holy Spirit who is in you, whom you have from God, and THAT YOU ARE NOT YOUR OWN? For you have been bought with a price: therefore glorify God in your body" (1 Cor. 6:19–20; emphasis added). "Only"

---

177. Berkouwer, *Studies in Dogmatics: The Sacraments*, 106–09.

178. Simon Kistemaker, *New Testament Commentary: Exposition of the Epistles of Peter and the Epistle of Jude* (Grand Rapids, MI: Baker Book House, 1987), 149.

179. Fisher, *Fisher's Catechism*, 189.

means "to be his in opposition to all his rivals and competitors, every one of whom we profess to renounce in baptism, Hos. xiv:8."[180]

The Recipients of Baptism

Q. 166: Unto whom is baptism to be administered?

A.: Baptism is not to be administered to any that are out of the visible church, and so strangers from the covenant of promise, till they profess their faith in Christ, and obedience to him, but infants descending from parents, either both, or but one of them, professing faith in Christ, and obedience to him, are in that respect within the covenant, and to be baptized.

The Biblical Truth Packed in Larger Catechism Question 166

(a) Baptism is not to be administered to those outside the visible church (Eph. 4:4–6; 1 Cor. 11:18–19). Baptism is a sign and seal of salvation; but, since the visible church[181] is "the house and family of God, out of which there is no ordinary possibility of salvation" (WCF, XXV, ii), therefore, baptism should not be given to those outside the visible church. See Ephesians 2:19; 3:15 and Acts 2:47.

> Baptism is not an addendum to discipleship but that by which discipleship is consummated.... Since discipleship is not consummated without baptism we must regard baptism

---

180. Fisher, *Fisher's Catechism*, 189.

181. "The very constitutive idea of the church, namely, union with Christ and the union of believers with one another in the body of Christ, as an idea realised in the history of this world, necessarily involves *visible* union and communion." (Murray, *Christian Baptism*, 37. Emphasis added.). See Rom. 16:5; 1 Cor. 16:19; Acts 8:1; 11:22; 9:31; 14:23; 15:41; 16:4, 16.

> as an indispensable mark of the church. The person who refuses baptism and declines the reproach of Christ, which it entails, cannot be received as a member of Christ's body.[182]

(b) Those who are outside the visible church are "strangers from the covenant of promise" (Eph. 2:12). The promises of God are addressed to the covenant community, *i.e.*, those who have entered into covenant with God through faith in Him as their Lord and Savior and submission to His sovereignly dictated order of life (Deut. 6:13–15; 29:9–13; Rom. 10:9; Gen. 15:6; 18:19).

(c) A credible profession of faith in Jesus Christ makes one, together with his household, a member of the visible church, which is God's covenant community (Acts 16:31; Rom. 10:9; Deut. 6:13).

> What we find in the New Testament is that the constituting bond of communion was common faith in Christ and that the condition of admission to the fellowship was this same common faith (cf. Acts 2:38–42; 8:13, 35–38; 10:34–38; 16:14, 15, 31–33). This faith, however, did not have any automatic way of evidencing itself and, consequently, could become effective in gaining admission to the fellowship of the saints only by confession or profession [Rom. 10:9].... It is not the prerogative of man to search the heart of another. But it is the prerogative of man to judge in reference to public confession or profession.... It is by divine institution that the church, as a visible entity administered by men in accordance with Christ's appointment, must admit to its fellowship those who make a credible profession of faith in Christ and promise of obedience to him.... This profession, though it is a profession that only a true believer can honestly and truly make, is, nevertheless, of such a nature that those who do not have true faith may make it to the satisfaction of those responsible for that administration whereby admission is secured into the fellowship of the church (cf. Acts 8:13, 20–23).[183]

182. Murray, *Christian Baptism*, 45.
183. Murray, *Christian Baptism*, 38–39.

To profess faith in Christ is, resting in Christ alone for salvation, to profess a belief of "the whole doctrines of the Christian religion, Acts viii:37."[184] To profess obedience to Christ is "to yield an external subjection to all the ordinances and institutions of Christ, Acts ii:46."[185] A "credible" profession is a believable profession of faith because: [1] the profession appears to be knowledgeable; [2] it appears to be accurate, *i.e.*, in accord with the Bible; and [3] a correspondence exists between profession and life, *i.e.*, "faith without works is dead." The Larger Catechism Question 62 identifies the members of the visible church of Christ as "all such as profess the true religion, and their children." So then, to "profess faith in Christ" and to "profess the true religion" mean for the writers of the Larger Catechism one and the same thing. By "true religion" they meant "the whole of those doctrines deduced from the holy scriptures, which are contained in our Confession of Faith, and Catechisms, as agreeing, in the main, with the Confessions of other reformed churches, 2 Tim. i:13: 'Hold fast the form of sound words.'"[186] Therefore, to profess the true religion is "openly to acknowledge, on all proper occasions, a steadfast adherence to the whole of divine truth, without espousing or countenancing any opposite error (Ps. 119:1, 5; Rom. 10:10).

(d) A credible profession of faith in Christ also includes a commitment to live in obedience to Him (Deut. 6:13–19; 29:9–13). A bare profession is an empty profession. A profession that one is trusting in Jesus as Savior must include a commitment to bow before Him as Lord, for no one can enjoy the benefits of Christ's cross without bowing before the claims of Christ's crown. Paul told the Philippian jailor, who wanted to know how to be saved, "Believe in the LORD Jesus, and you shall be saved" (Acts 16:31). "Faith without works is dead" (James 2:26). Jesus, following Isaiah, strongly condemned profession of faith without a life of obedience: "This people honors Me with their lips, but they heart is far away from Me. But in vain do they worship Me" (Mark 7:6–7a).

---

184. Fisher, *Fisher's Catechism*, 193.
185. Fisher, *Fisher's Catechism*, 193.
186. Fisher, *Fisher's Catechism*, 194.

(e) Those who make a profession of faith in Christ, having been strangers to the covenant of promise, should be baptized (Acts 8:36, 37; Acts 2:38). Those who profess faith in Christ, having never been raised in the Christian Church, and therefore, never baptized as infants or children, should be baptized, because baptism is the public initiation into the visible church, and the means by which we declare ourselves to be wholly and only the Lord's. Public confession of the Lordship of Christ over us accompanies, of necessity, faith in Christ's Saviorhood in the heart (Rom. 10:9).

(f) No one capable of making a profession of faith in Christ and living a life of deliberate obedience to Him, and who has not done so, should be baptized (Acts 16:31). The sign and seal of salvation should not be given to those who do not profess to possess salvation in Christ, and who are capable of doing so. Baptism signifies, seals and nourishes our union with Christ the Lord and Savior; hence, it would be a total contradiction of the meaning and purpose of the sign to give it to someone whom we have no reason to believe that Christ is His Savior. Baptism is in the NAME of the Triune God, and "there is salvation in no one else; for there is no other name under heaven that has been given among men, by which we must be saved" (Acts 4:12).

(g) The children of those who profess faith in Jesus Christ are also to be considered as being "within the covenant" and the church from infancy, and therefore should be baptized (Gen. 17:7, 9; Acts 2:39; Rom. 4:11, 12; Luke 18:15, 16; Rom. 11:16; Deut. 29:9–13). The Westminster Directory for the Publick Worship of God affirms this as well. It says that the infants of believers should be baptized because "they are Christians, and federally [or covenantally] holy BEFORE BAPTISM, and therefore are they baptized." We shall spend much more time establishing and explaining this point a little later; but, suffice it to say for the present, that *the children of believers are not brought into the covenant and church by baptism but are baptized because they are already in the covenant and church, because they are already Christians*: "Believe in the Lord Jesus and you shall be saved; YOU AND YOUR HOUSEHOLD" (Acts 16:31). Because they are in the covenant, they have the right to the sign of the covenant! If, as the Bible says, children of believers are within the covenant from the moment they become children of believers, *i.e.*, conception, then they must always be thought of and treated as within the covenant, unless and until they apostatize from the faith.

> The children of believers are baptized not in order that they who were previously strangers to the church may then for the first time become children of God, but rather that, because by the blessing of the promise they already belonged to the body of Christ, they are received into the church with this solemn sign.[187]

> Upon what ground have the infants of such as are members of the visible church a right to baptism? Upon the ground of the grace and goodness of God in the promise, including them in the same covenant with their parents; as in the promise made to Abraham, Gen. xvii:7: "I will establish My covenant with Me and thee, and thy seed after thee—to be a God unto thee, and to thy seed after thee."[188]

Is this a promise to Abraham's biological descendants, or is it broader in scope? Both Peter and Paul tell us it is broader, and is not to be taken in a racial sense. On the Day of Pentecost, Peter declared that this promise of God's covenant of grace extended to Gentiles as well as to Jews: "For the promise is unto you, and *to your children*, and *to all that are afar off*, even as many as the Lord our God shall call" (Acts 2:39; emphasis added). And in Galatians 3:28–29 Paul makes absolutely clear that the promises of the covenant are not to be defined racially or ethnically.

Why should infants be baptized, when they are incapable of making a profession of faith in Christ?

> An explicit or formal profession of faith, is required only of them that are adult, or come to age, when they are to be baptized: but not of infants now, any more than when they were circumcised of old, on the eighth day after their birth. Are infants capable of the blessings signified and sealed in bap-

187. Calvin, *Institutes of the Christian Religion*, 2:1323.
188. Fisher, *Fisher's Catechism*, 194.

> tism? Undoubtedly they are; for some of them have been filled with the Holy Ghost even from their mother's womb, Luke i:15; and, consequently, by grace capable of regeneration, pardon, and eternal life; wherefore the sign and seal of these blessings ought not to be withheld.[189]

(h) If only one parent professes faith in Christ, even then his/her children are to be considered as "within the covenant" from infancy and therefore should be baptized (1 Cor. 7:14; Acts 16:31–34). "For the unbelieving husband is sanctified through his wife, and the unbelieving wife is sanctified through her believing husband; *for otherwise your children are unclean, but now they are holy"* (1 Cor. 7:14; emphasis added). To be unclean is to be outside the covenant, its life, and its blessings. (Ezra 9:2) To be holy is to be consecrated to God and to be inside His covenant, enjoying its life and blessings (Isa. 6:13). How does this covenantal holiness entitle an infant of even one believing parent to baptism? Covenantal holiness "necessarily supposes a being within the covenant, in virtue of the credible profession of the parent, and, consequently, a right to the initiatory seal of it."[190]

The Baptism of Households of Believers

The Bible teaches that, not only should adults be baptized upon profession of faith in Christ, but that also the households, or families, including infants, of those professing faith in Christ should also be baptized: "Believe in the Lord Jesus and you shall be saved; *you and your household*" (Acts 16:31).

The Antiquity and Perpetuity of the Membership of Children of Believers in God's Covenant of Grace

The Biblical basis for the baptism of the households or families of believers, including their infants is a strong one. Since the beginning of the human race, every covenant relationship which God established with His people always included their children. This was

189. Fisher, *Fisher's Catechism*, 196.
190. Fisher, *Fisher's Catechism*, 196.

obviously true in the covenant made with ADAM and EVE, when God said to the serpent, "And I will put enmity between you and the woman, and between your seed and her seed" (Gen. 3:15). When God made a covenant with NOAH, after the flood, He said, "Behold, I establish My covenant with you and with your seed" (Gen. 9:9). To ABRAHAM God covenanted, "I will establish My covenant between Me and you and your descendants after you throughout their generations for an everlasting covenant, to be God to you and to your descendants after you" (Gen. 17:7). MOSES addressed the people of God as "standing before the Lord their God, with their little ones, and their wives, to enter into covenant with the Lord their God" (Deut. 29:10–12). With reference to the covenant God made with him, David said, "Now therefore may it please Thee to bless the house of Thy servant, that it may continue forever before Thee" (2 Sam. 7:29a). And in the New Covenant, Peter tells his hearers to repent and be baptized, "for the promise is to you and your children" (Acts 2:39).

The Universal and Unopposed Practice of Infant Baptism in the Church for Its First Fifteen Hundred Years

Furthermore,

> *the history of the Christian Church from the apostolic age,* furnishes an argument of irresistible force in favor of the divine authority of infant baptism.... *for more than fifteen hundred years after the birth of Christ, there was not a single society of professing Christians on earth, who opposed infant baptism on any thing like the grounds which distinguish our modern Baptist brethren.* It is an undoubted fact, that the people known in ecclesiastical history under the name of the Anabaptists, who arose in Germany, in the year 1522, were the very first body of people, *in the whole Christian world,* who rejected the baptism of infants, on the principles now adopted by the [anti-infant-baptism] body.... It is not only certain, that we hear of no society of [anti-infant-baptists] resembling our present Baptist brethren, for more than fifteen hundred years after Christ; but

> we have positive and direct proof that, during the whole of that time, infant baptism was the general and unopposed practice of the Christian Church.[191]

Both the great Augustine and the heretic Pelagius declared "about three hundred years after the apostolic age, that they never saw or heard of any one who called himself a Christian, not even the most impious heretic, no nor any writer who claimed to believe in the Scriptures, who denied the baptism of infants."[192]

> For fifteen hundred years after Christ, the practice of infant baptism was universal; that to this general fact there was absolutely no exception, in the whole Christian church, which, on principle, or even analogy, can countenance in the least degree, modern [anti -infant-baptists]; that from the time of the Apostles to the time of Luther, the general, unopposed, established practice of the church was to regard the infant seed of believers as members of the church, and, as such, to baptize them. But this is not all. If the doctrine of our Baptist brethren be correct; that is, if infant baptism be a corruption and a nullity; then it follows, from the foregoing historical statements, most inevitably, that the ordinance of baptism was lost for fifteen hundred years: yes, entirely lost, from the apostolic age til the sixteenth century.[193]

Now, the question is was the Church in error in baptizing children of believers for the first fifteen centuries of her history? Have the Presbyterian, Reformed, Methodist, Lutheran and Episcopal churches been in error for the past five centuries? Or are the modern Baptists correct? These questions are to be submitted to the Bible to be answered, because "the supreme Judge, by which all controversies of religion are to be determined, and all decrees of councils, opinions of ancient writers, doctrines of men, and private spirits, are to be exam-

---

191. Samuel Miller, *Baptism and Christian Education* (Dallas TX/ Jackson MS: Presbyterian Heritage Publications, 1984), 21, 23.

192. Miller, *Baptism and Christian Education*, 26.

193. Miller, *Baptism and Christian Education,* 31.

ined, and in whose sentence we are to rest, can be no other but the Holy Spirit speaking in the scripture" (WCF, I, x).

The Biblical Basis for the Baptism of Children of Believers

The Summary of the Basic Pillars of Infant Baptism

Randy Booth, in his book, *Children of the Promise*, has clearly summarized the basic elements of the case for infant baptism under five compelling headings:

> 1. *Covenant Theology.* Throughout the Bible, God relates to his people by way of a covenant of grace [Eph. 2:12]. Covenant theology provides the basic framework for rightly interpreting Scripture.[194] 2. *Continuity of the Covenant of Grace.* The Bible teaches one and the same way of salvation in both the Old and the New Testaments, despite some different outward requirements[195] [Rom. 4:1–9]. 3. *Continuity of the People of God.* Since there is one covenant of grace between God

194. The Biblical, or covenantal, method of interpreting the Bible sees "*...a basic continuity between the Old and New Testaments, with the New Testament flowing out of the Old and building on its foundation.* The New Testament offers a greater revelation of God and his redemptive work, but it does not abruptly do away with the Old Testament and start all over" (Booth, *Children of the Promise*, 16–17). See Matthew 5:17–19 and 2 Timothy 3:15–17.

195. "The fallacy of your young friend,... so far as the Scriptures are concerned, lies in setting the New Testament over and above the Old, whereas both are equally the Word of God, equally authoritative, and form *one* perfect revelation, one perfect rule of faith and practice. They are not in any respect antagonistic, but consonant, and mutually support the one the other. Nothing is set aside in the Old Testament in and by the New save the types and shadows and ceremonial laws, all which find their fulfillment in our Lord and savior Jesus Christ and expire, as the lawyers would say, but the statute of their own limitation. But all the laws of God that embody our duties to God and men, whether socially or civilly, remain ever in force. These laws are recognized in the New Testament, but not repeated *in extenso*, there being no necessity for it.... The New Testament is built up out of and upon the Old, and is not contrary to it in any thing whatever. It ever recognizes and then supports the Old [Charles Colcock Jones]" (Booth, *Children of the Promise*, 21–22), and found originally in the book *A Georgian At Princeton* by Robert Manson Myers, (New York: Harcourt Brace Jovanovich, 1976), 89–90.

> and man, there is one continuous people of God (the church) in the Old and New Testaments [Heb. 3:1–6]. 4. *Continuity of Covenant Signs.* Baptism is the sign of the covenant in the New Testament, just as circumcision was the sign of the covenant in the Old Testament [Col. 2:11–12]. 5. *Continuity of Households.* Whole households are included in God's redemptive covenant [Acts 16:31].

The Case for the Baptism of Children of Believers

The Unity and Continuity of the Covenant

A careful study of "the covenants of promise" (Eph. 2:12) will show that they are one great covenant running throughout the Bible and the history of redemption. That covenant of grace is a bond of eternal friendship between God and His people in Christ in which He is their Sovereign-Friend and they are His servant-friends. It is a communion of life and a sovereignly dictated order of life. God sovereignly and graciously established it, sustains it and administers it, determining who will participate in it, its promises and demands, blessings and curses.

It is true that there is a variety of historical expressions of this relationship: "the covenants." But they all are united together into one, building upon each other as history proceeds; and the bond that unifies them, which they advance and develop as time goes on is the one "promise" that pervades them all, that of union and communion with God in Christ (Gen. 17:7; Matt. 1:21). All these covenants reach a climax, and are consummated in Jesus Christ and the New Covenant (Heb. 8).

> The Lord held to this orderly plan in administering the covenant of His mercy: as the day of full revelation approached with the passing of time, the more He increased each day the brightness of its manifestation. Accordingly, at the beginning when the first promise of salvation was given to Adam it glowed like a feeble spark. Then, as it was added to, the light grew in fullness, breaking forth increasingly and shed-

> ding its radiance more widely. At last—when all the clouds were dispersed—Christ, the Sun of righteousness, fully illuminated the whole earth.[196]

The various covenants of Biblical history—Edenic, Adamic, Noahic, Abrahamic, Davidic, and New Covenant—unite into one over-arching covenant from creation to the consummation at the end of the world. This one covenant is eternal. It began in eternity in the covenant of redemption in the Trinity. It embraces all history, and it continues in its blessings and curses throughout all eternity. This unity and oneness is evident in the Bible from two perspectives: (1) God's covenants of promise manifest a *structural* unity in the Bible, a *framework* within which all events take place and all revealed truths must be understood. (2) God's covenants of promise manifest a *thematic* unity in the Bible. "God's multiple bonds with his people ultimately unite into a single relationship. Particular details of the covenants may vary. A definite line of progression may be noted. Yet the covenants of God are one,"[197] in theme and promise.

The Unity of the Covenantal Structure of the Bible

The Unity of the Abrahamic, Mosaic and Davidic Covenants

The unity of the Abrahamic Covenant (Gen. 12–17), the Mosaic Covenant (Ex. 19–24), and the Davidic Covenant (2 Sam. 7), is evident in two ways: FIRST, it is evident in *the history and experience of God's people* from Abraham to David. (a) According to Exodus 2:24 and 6:4–8, the Exodus, the redemptive basis of the Mosaic Covenant, and possession of Canaan by Israel, the promised effect of the Mosaic Covenant, are fulfillments of the Abrahamic Covenant. (b) The history of Israel after Moses' receiving of the Law on Mt. Sinai continues to focus on the promises of Abraham (Ex. 32:13, 14; Gen. 15:18; Ex. 23:31; Josh. 1:3). (c) The Mosaic Covenant is rooted in the Abra-

196. Calvin, *Institutes of the Christian Religion*, 1:446.

197. O. Palmer Robertson, *The Christ of the Covenants* (Phillipsburg, NJ: Presbyterian and Reformed Publishing Co., 1980), 28.

hamic Covenant (Ex. 6:1–8; Deut. l:l–11; Ex. 32:13; Ps. 105:8–10; Lev. 26:42). (d) The Mosaic Covenant in no way annulled or interrupted the Abrahamic Covenant (Gal. 3:17–19). (e) The Davidic Covenant also is rooted in the Abrahamic Covenant (2 Sam. 7:8–16; 23:5); and is a development of the Mosaic Covenant (2 Sam. 7:6, 23; 1 Kings 2:3–4). The centralization of worship under King David was anticipated by Moses (Deut. 12:5, 11, 14, 18). The ark brought to Jerusalem with the coronation of King David and the establishment of God's throne in Jerusalem were in fulfillment of the Abrahamic Covenant (1 Chron. 16:15–18). SECOND, the unity of these covenants is evident in *the development of the covenants genealogically, i.e.*, in the line of continued generations. (a) This is seen in a study of the seed concept in the Abrahamic Covenant (Gen. 15:18) and the Mosaic Covenant (Ex. 20:5, 6; Deut. 7:9); and the Davidic Covenant (2 Sam. 7:12), which promises that David's son will be the heir of the promises to Moses and Abraham. See also Deuteronomy 5:2, 3; 29:14–15; Psalm 105:8–10; Isaiah 59:21; Acts 3:25. (b) Deuteronomy 7:9 shows us that covenant promises extend to a thousand generations, not only reminding us that this is an eternal covenant, but also that it involves *a continuous succession of generations.*[198]

The Unity of the Old Testament Covenants and the New Covenant in Christ

A clear and profound unity exists between all the Old Testament covenants and the New Covenant in Christ. (a) The New Covenant may be understood in no other way than as a realization and fulfillment of the projections and promises of the Old Testament covenants. (b) Jeremiah 31:31–33 and 32:39–41 show the intertwining of the Abrahamic and Mosaic Covenants in the New Covenant. (c) Ezekiel 34:20–24 shows the fulfillment of the Davidic Covenant

198. Two important principles must be kept in mind at this point. (1) The "grafting" principle (Gen. 17:12, 13). Any definition of the significance of "Israel" must include this dimension. "Israel" cannot be restricted to a closed ethnic community (Rom. 11:17, 19). By "ingrafting" the Gentile became an Israelite in the full sense of the word. His line stands as legal heirs of genealogical promises. (2) The "pruning" principle (Rom. 11:13; Mal. 1:2, 3; Gen. 25:23). This must also be included in identifying "Israel" (Rom. 9:6).

in the New Covenant. (d) Ezekiel 37:24–26 combines the Abrahamic, Mosaic and Davidic Covenants in the New Covenant.[199] See also Luke 22:20; 1 Cor. 11:25; Heb. 8:6–13; 10:15–18; 2 Cor. 1:20.

The Unity of the Covenantal Theme in the Bible

The "promise" which unites all the historical "covenants" (Eph. 2:12), and which is fulfilled in the New Covenant is union and communion with God in Christ by all believers: "And I will establish My covenant between Me and you and your descendants after you throughout their generations for an everlasting covenant, to be God to you and to your descendants after you" (Gen. 17:7). This is the heart of all Biblical covenants, from Genesis through Revelation (Gen. 17:7; Ex. 6:6,7; 19:4, 5; Lev. 11:45; Deut. 4:20; 29:13; 2 Kings 11:17; 2 Chron. 23:16; Ezek. 34:24; Jer. 24:7; 31:33; 32:37–39; Zech. 2:11; 8:8,16; Matt. 1:21; Eph. 4:25; Heb. 8:10; 2 Cor. 6:16; 1 John 1:3; Rev. 21:3). This has been called "THE IMMANUEL-PRINCIPLE" because of the realization of this promise in Jesus Christ: "Behold, the virgin shall be with child, and shall bear a Son, and they shall call His name *immanuel,* which translated means, 'GOD WITH US.'" (Matt. 1:23). In the Old Testament, this principle is developed in terms of God's actual dwelling in the Tabernacle in the midst of His people, enjoying reconciled fellowship with them (Ex. 25:8; 29:42–45; Lev. 26:9–13; Deut. 12:5, 11, 14; 14:2; 16:2–11; Ezek. 37:26–28). Christ as "Immanuel" is God incarnate dwelling, (literally "tabernacling," in John 1:14), with us, once upon the earth and now by His Spirit (Eph. 2:21–22; Rev. 7:15; 21:3). In Christ the heart-theme of the Old Testament reaches a climax in that the promise of God dwelling with His people is embodied in a single person (Isa. 42:6; 49:8; 55:3, 4).

The Content of This Covenantal Unity

Because of the unity and continuity of the covenantal framework and theme in the Bible, all the Old Testament covenants and the New Covenant have the same GOAL—the establishment of a

---

199. There is even a firm unity of the Adamic and Noahic Covenants with the New Covenant (Gen. 8:21–22; Rom. 16:20; Gen. 3:15).

kingdom of priests and a holy nation (Ex. 19:5–11; 1 Pet. 2:9). "The covenants of promise" and the New Covenant are all covenants of grace (Ex. 14:13; 15:2; 19:4; 20:2; John 3:14; Ex. 32:13; Deut. 20:3–4; Heb. 11:24–29). Both the Old Testament covenants and the New Covenant define sin as transgression of Biblical Law (Josh. 7:11; Isa. 24:5; Hos. 6:7; 1 John 3:4). And all Biblical covenants have the same definitions, principles, operating power and foundation. "Grace is the foundation, and holiness the character, of all covenant relationships with God."[200]

The Family in the Biblical Covenants

As we have seen, in all the Biblical covenants, God establishes a bond of friendship with *believers and their households* (Gen. 3:15; 9:9; 17:7; Deut. 29:10–12; 2 Sam. 7:29; Acts 2:39; 11:14; and 16:31): "Believe on the Lord Jesus, and you shall be saved, YOU AND YOUR HOUSEHOLD.... the PROMISE is for YOU AND YOUR CHILDREN" (Acts 2:39).

> In the whole history of our race, God's covenanted dealings with His people, with respect to spiritual blessings, have had regard to their children as well as to themselves; so that the children as well as the parents have been admitted to the spiritual blessings of God's covenants, and to the outward signs and seals of these covenants;... there is no evidence that this general principle, so full of mercy and grace, and so well fitted to nourish faith and hope, was to be departed from, or laid aside, under the Christian dispensation; but, on the contrary, [there is] a great deal [of evidence] to confirm the conviction that it was to continue to be acted on.[201]

200. Greg Bahnsen, *Theonomy in Christian Ethics* (Nutley, NJ: The Craig Press, 1977), 187.

201. William Cunningham, *Historical Theology*, 2 vols. (London: The Banner of Truth Trust, [1862] 1960), 2:149.

The Meaning of Household in the Old Testament

The New Testament references to "households" must be understood in the light of the Old Testament concept of "household," which includes everybody who is under the authority of the head of the family unit, which could include a husband, wife, their children, (adopted and natural born), and any slaves (Gen. 7:1; Gen. 12:17). In Genesis 17:12–13, 23, 27, all the males in Abraham's household were to be given "the sign of the covenant," *i.e.*, "all" who were "born in Abraham's house" or who were "bought with his money." See also Gen. 19:16; 20:17–18; 34:30; Ex. 12:27; Num. 3:15; Josh. 24:15; 1 Sam. 3:12–14; 2 Sam. 12:10. "In the Old Testament (and in the New), the parent-child relationship is organic; that is, God views parents and children not simply as individuals that happen to be related but as a divinely created unit or organism. This organism extends through the generations."[202] "Know therefore that the Lord your God, He is God, the faithful God, who keeps His covenant and His lovingkindness TO A THOUSANDTH GENERATION with those who love Him and keep His commandments" (Deut. 7:9).

The Meaning of Household in the New Testament

The Old Testament concept of "household" continues in the New Testament. For example, an elder "must be one who manages His own *household* well, keeping *his children* under control with all dignity" (1 Tim. 3:4). See also 1 Timothy 3:12; Titus 1:6; Acts 16:31.

> When the Bible speaks of a household, it includes every member of the family—husband, wife, children, (including infants), and slaves. Kenneth Gentry expresses the biblical principle of family solidarity in God's covenantal dealings when he observes, "There is *nothing* in the New Testament that undermines and invalidates the Old Testament covenantal principle of family solidarity. In fact, everything confirms its continuing validity. Thus, a covenantal understanding of baptism leads inexorably to infant baptism."[203]

202. Booth, *Children of the Promise*, 123.
203. Booth, *Children of the Promise*, 126.

The Implications of This Fact for Infant Baptism

> The inclusion of the children of believers in the covenant of grace is predicated on the continuity of the various covenantal administrations of that covenant of grace. God demonstrated in each of the covenants, his redemptive concern for the individual believer, the believer's household, and the believer's society. This comprehensive redemptive plan extends to, and expands in, the new covenant, with all the blessings of the past and more....
>
> The households of believers in the Old Testament, including their infants, received the special privilege of God's redemptive covenants. These "little ones" of believers were marked out by God and set apart or sanctified from the rest of the fallen world. This inclusion of the children of believers in the covenant of grace was not a mere footnote in redemptive history. Rather, the children of God's people played a central role in God's redemptive plan from generation to generation. They continue to do so.[204]

The Unity and Continuity of the Church

The Fact of the Unity and Continuity of the Church

"There is only one people of God, the church, established in the Old Testament and brought to maturity in the New Testament."[205] "*The Bible teaches that the people of God in the Old Testament and the people of God in the New Testament are one and the same people.... Since God has not changed the terms of church membership, new covenant believers and their children are likewise included in his church,*" just as they were in the Old Testament covenants.[206]

---

204. Booth, *Children of the Promise*, 46.
205. Booth, *Children of the Promise*, 82.
206. Booth, *Children of the Promise*, 73.

That children of believers, including infants, were members of the visible church, or congregation of the Lord, in the Old Testament is obvious and indisputable.

> Whatever else may be doubtful, it is certain that infants were, in fact, members of the church under the former dispensation; and as such, were the regular subjects of a covenant seal. When God called Abraham, and established his covenant with him, he not only embraced his infant seed, in the most express terms, in that covenant, but he also appointed an ordinance by which this relation of his children to the visible church was publicly ratified and sealed, and that when they were only eight days old. If Jewish adults were members of the church of God, under that economy, then, assuredly, their infant seed were equally members, for they were brought into the same covenant relation, and had the same covenant seal impressed upon their flesh as their adult parents.... This covenant seal was solemnly appointed by God to be administered, and was actually administered, for nearly two thousand years, to infants of the tenderest age, in token of their relation to God's covenanted family, and of their right to the privileges of that covenant.... If infinite wisdom once saw that it was right and fit that infants should be made the subjects of "a seal of the righteousness of faith," before they were capable of exercising faith, surely a transaction the same in substance may be right and fit now.[207]

The Biblical Basis for the Unity and Continuity of the Church

Hebrews 3:2–6

Here the unity and continuity of the Church in the Old Testament and New Testament is pictured in the figure of a "house" that is being built. Moses is one of the builders of this "house", and so is "Jesus." Several important parts of this figure must be noticed: (1) Both

207. Miller, *Baptism and Christian Education*, 8–9.

Moses and Jesus are building ONE house, not two. (2) The house Moses and Jesus are building is "His house," *i.e.*, Jesus' house (3:2). (3) Although both Moses and Jesus are builders of this one house, Jesus is far superior to Moses, because Moses is only a faithful "servant" in the house, and Jesus is the owner, "the Son over His house" (vs. 6), and the ultimate "builder" of the house, with Moses as his instrument and tool (vs. 3–4). (4) Jesus' one house, built by Jesus Himself for Himself using Moses as his instrument, is the Church: "Christ was faithful as a Son over His House, whose House we are, if we hold fast our confidence and the boast of our hope firm unto the end" (vs. 6). Once again, we are being taught that the Church of Christ is one in the Old Testament and the New Testament.

Acts 7:38

The organization of the covenant people of God in the Old Testament is expressly called "the church in the wilderness" (*ekklesia*), in this passage. God does not have two churches; He has one visible catholic church, comprised of all those who profess faith in the true religion in Christ, along with their children.

Romans 9:24–26 And Hosea 1:10–11

In Hosea 1:10–11, we are given a prophecy regarding "the sons of Israel"; and in Romans 9:24–26 Paul, without hesitation, applies this very passage to the church of Christ! He can do this, because the church of God is one in Old Testament and New Testament alike.

Hebrews 8:6–13 and Jeremiah 31:31–34

In Jeremiah 31:31–34, the prophet speaks of a New Covenant that Jehovah will make with "the house of Israel and with the house of Judah." Hebrews 8:6–13 quotes this passage, "which speaks so plainly and specifically of Israel and Judah, and applies it to the church of the new covenant."[208] Why does the writer to the Hebrews do this? Because of the unity and continuity of the church in the

208. Booth, *Children of the Promise*, 84.

Old Testament and New Testament The house of Israel and Judah in the Old Testament was the church. The church in the New Testament is the renewed house of Israel and Judah, *i.e.*, the renewed covenant community in Christ, the Mediator of the New Covenant. Therefore, we must conclude that the membership of this one church remains the same—for believers and their children.

Romans 11:17–24

Paul uses the imagery of an olive tree to show us that the Old Testament church continues under the New Covenant. "The good olive tree was not uprooted, but pruned [apostate Jews], and new branches [Gentiles] were grafted in."[209] The church of God is an olive tree with a rich root. Many Jews were pruned off this tree, because of their apostasy, but that did NOT result in the cutting down of the Old Testament olive tree and the planting of a New Testament tree. "In fact, the tree remained healthy and the Gentile branches of a wild olive tree were grafted into it. This is a beautiful picture of the fact that the New Testament church was a continuation of the Old Testament church."[210] If the church continues, then its membership continues as well—believers and their children.

The church, as it exists throughout the Old Testament and into the New Testament is not two organisms, but one. It is compared, in this passage, "to one tree with many branches, all of which grow from one root and stock and form one organic life."[211] This passage also teaches us that the New Testament church is founded on the covenant God made with Abraham, and is an unfolding of that covenant. It is the root onto which the branches are grafted and from which the branches grow. To become one of the people of God today, one must be grafted by faith on the stock of the tree that is rooted deeply in the Old Testament covenants. Hence, Paul can say that "those who are of faith are blessed with faithful Abraham" (Gal. 3:9).

---

209. Booth, *Children of the Promise*, 85.
210. Booth, *Children of the Promise*, 86.
211. Murray, *Christian Baptism*, 46.

Exodus 19:5–6 and 1 Peter 2:9

In Exodus 19–24, God reaffirms His covenant through Moses "to the house of Jacob and the sons of Israel" (vs. 3). In verses 5 and 6, He sets forth the purposes of the Mosaic Covenant: "if you will indeed obey My voice and keep My covenant, then you shall be My own possession among all the peoples, for all the earth is Mine; and you shall be to Me a kingdom of priests and a holy nation." In 1 Peter 2:9, the apostle applies this verse to all "those who are chosen to obey Jesus Christ and be sprinkled with His blood," who are scattered throughout the world (1:1–2), *i.e.*, the visible catholic church: "you are a chosen race, a royal priesthood, a holy nation, a people for God's own possession, that you may proclaim the excellencies of Him who has called you out of darkness into His marvelous light." Again, the church of God is one.

Galatians 3:15–22

The Abrahamic Covenant still stands. Nothing has happened in history since the establishment of that covenant to abrogate it. Christ came to fulfill its promises in His Church.

> The ecclesiastical covenant made with Abraham still subsists unrepealed, and all Christians are brought under it. As children were members of that covenant, the inference is irresistible that they are members still, unless their positive exclusion can be pointed out in the New Testament.[212]

Galatians 3:28–29; 6:16

Here again the New Testament gives the Church of Christ names and descriptions that originally were applied to the covenant people of God in the Old Testament. After declaring that the Christian Church makes no racial distinctions in its membership (3:28), Paul says to "the churches of Galatia" (1:2): "if you belong to Christ, then you are Abraham's offspring (seed), heirs according to promise" (3:29). The phrase, taken from the Abrahamic Covenant, "seed

212. Dabney, *Lectures in Systematic Theology*, 783.

of Abraham," is applied to the Church, whose membership, by faith, are heirs of the covenant "promise" (Eph. 2:12). This means that, as under the Abrahamic Covenant, the "spiritual seed" is to be found among the "physical seed" of believers, hence, as in the Old Testament, believers and their children are taken into covenant with God in the New Testament Church. For this reason, the Church of Christ is called "the Israel of God" (Gal. 6:16).

> 'All who walk by this rule and the Israel of God,' [in 6:16], are not two groups, but one. The connecting [Greek] participle, *kai*, should be translated 'even', not 'and', or be omitted (as in RSV). The Christian Church enjoys a direct continuity with God's people in the Old Testament. Those who are in Christ today are 'the true circumcision' (Phil. 3:3), 'Abraham's offspring' (Gal. 3:29), and 'the Israel of God.'[213]

The Church is the *new* Israel of God, reformed by the Word of God and revitalized by the Baptism of the Holy Spirit (Acts 2). Therefore, because of this unity and continuity of the Church of the Bible, we have no reason to believe that the membership has changed, *i.e.*, believers and their children.

Hebrews 12:22

No verse brings out the unity and continuity of the church in both Testaments as this verse. Addressing New Testament Christians, the author of Hebrews says, "You have come to Mount Zion and to the city of the living God, the heavenly Jerusalem, and to myriads of angels, to the general assembly and church of the firstborn... and to Jesus the mediator of a New Covenant."

Ephesians 2:12, 19, 20

Until reconciled to God by the blood of Christ (2:13), unbelievers today, as unbelieving Gentiles in the Old Testament, are outside the church of God, which is "God's household, having been built

---

213. John R.W. Stott, *The Message of Galatians* (London: Inter-Varsity Press, 1968), 180.

upon the foundation of the apostles and prophets, Christ Jesus Himself being the cornerstone, in whom the whole building, being fitted together is growing into a holy temple in the Lord" (2:19–22). Therefore, to use Paul's own words, to be outside the Christian Church is to be "separate from Christ, excluded from the commonwealth of Israel, and strangers to the covenants of promise, having no hope and without God in the world" (2:12). In the Old Testament, the commonwealth of Israel was the Church; and in the New Testament, the Church is the commonwealth of Israel, because the Church is one, and therefore, its membership is one—believers and their children.

The Implications of This Doctrine for Infant Baptism

There is but one church—one people of God—extending from the beginning to the end of time. Its membership consists of believers and their households. Charles Hodge sums it up well: "This is really the turning point in the controversy concerning infant church-membership. If the Church is one under both dispensations; if infants were members of the Church under the theocracy, then they are members of the Church now, unless the contrary can be proved."[214]

> Having seen that the infant seed of the professing people of God *were* members of the church under the Old Testament economy; and having seen also that the church under that dispensation and the present is *the same*; we are evidently prepared to take another step, and to infer, that *if infants were once members and if the church remains the same, they undoubtedly are still members unless some positive divine enactment excluding them, can be found....* But can such an act of repeal and exclusion, I ask, be produced? It cannot. It never has been, and it never can be. The introduction of infants into the church by divine appointment, is undoubted. The identity of the church, under both dispensations, is undoubted. The perpetuity of the Abrahamic covenant, in which not

214. Booth, *Children of the Promise*, 92.

> merely the lineal descendants of Abraham, but *'all the nations of the earth were to be blessed'* is undoubted. And we find no hint in the New Testament of the high privileges granted to the infant seed of believers being withdrawn.... The advocates of infant baptism are not bound to produce from the New Testament an express warrant for the membership of the children of believers. The warrant was given most expressly and formally, two thousand years before the New Testament was written; and having never been revoked, remains firmly and indisputably in force.[215]

The Unity and Continuity of the Sign of the Covenant

The Fulfillment of Circumcision in Baptism

For an explanation of the meaning of circumcision in the Old Testament, and of how baptism fulfills, and thus replaces, circumcision as the sign of the covenant in the New Testament, see pages 341-346.

The Meaning of Circumcision

In light of the previous explanation of circumcision, we can conclude that

> circumcision signified God's promise of a Redeemer, the Lamb of God, who was to come and take away the sins of his people. Circumcision was a sign and seal of God's covenant promise to believers that he was their God and that they were his people. Only in covenant faithfulness could such spiritual blessings be appropriated by the one who was circumcised.... Calvin saw this when he said, We have, therefore, a spiritual promise given to the patriarchs in circumcision such as is given us in baptism, since it represented for them forgiveness of sins and mortification of flesh. Moreover, as we have taught that Christ is the foundation of bap-

215. Miller, *Baptism and Christian Education,* 12–13.

> tism, in whom both of these reside, so it is also evident that he is the foundation of circumcision. For he is promised to Abraham, and in him the blessing of all nations (Gen. 12:2–3). To seal this grace, the sign of circumcision is added.[216]

The Meaning of Baptism

Also, in the light of our study thus far, we can conclude that

> baptism, like circumcision, is essentially a spiritual sign and seal that sets us apart as God's people. It too signifies the need for, and God's gracious provision of, a renewed and cleansed heart. It points to the necessity of spiritual regeneration. Baptism unites believers and their children with God's promised Redeemer, Jesus Christ, and secures their position as His people. Baptism must also be responded to by faith before covenant blessings may be appropriated. Failure to faithfully respond to one's baptism brings covenant curses rather than blessings.[217]

The Similarity of Circumcision and Baptism

In the light of Colossians 2:11–12, John Calvin can conclude:

> Now we can see without difficulty the similarity and difference[218] of these two signs. The promise (in which we have shown the power of the signs to consist) is the same in both, namely, that of God's fatherly favor, of forgiveness of sins, and of eternal life. Then the thing represented is the same, namely, regeneration. In both there is one foundation upon which the fulfillment of these things rests.... What dissimilarity remains in the outward ceremony, which is a very slight factor, since the most weighty part depends upon the promise and the thing signified. We therefore conclude that,

---

216. Booth, *Children of the Promise*, 103–04.

217. Booth, *Children of the Promise*, 107.

218. John Calvin points out that the differences between circumcision are only external, and not substantial, in *Institutes of the Christian Religion*, 2:1327–29.

apart from the difference in the visible ceremony, whatever belongs to circumcision pertains likewise to baptism.... And the thing is so true we can almost touch it. For circumcision was for the Jews their first entry into the church, because it was a token to them by which they were assured of adoption as the people and household of God, and they in turn professed to enlist in God's service. In like manner, we also are consecrated to God through baptism, to be reckoned as His people, and in turn we swear fealty to him. By this it appears incontrovertible that baptism has taken the place of circumcision to fulfill the same office among us.[219]

The Inescapable Conclusion

It is most evident that the covenant which the Lord once made with Abraham (cf. Gen. 17:14), is no less in force today for Christians than it was of old for the Jewish people, and that this word relates no less to Christians than it then related to the Jews. Unless perhaps we think that Christ by his coming lessened or curtailed the grace of the Father—but this is nothing but execrable blasphemy! Accordingly, the children of the Jews also, because they had been made heirs of his covenant and distinguished from the children of the impious, were called a holy seed (Ezra 9:2; Isa. 6:13). For this same reason, the children of Christians are considered holy... (1 Cor. 7:14). Now seeing that the Lord, immediately after making the covenant with Abraham, commanded it to be sealed in infants by an outward sacrament (Gen. 17:12) what excuse will Christians give for not testifying and sealing it in their children today?[220]

---

219. Calvin, *Institutes of the Christian Religion*, 2:1327.
220. Calvin, *Institutes of the Christian Religion*, 2:1328–29.

Answering Objections

> *"Any argument against infant baptism is necessarily an argument against infant circumcision."*[221]

> For it is very clear from many testimonies of Scripture that circumcision was also a sign of repentance (Jer. 4:4; 9:25; cf. Deut. 10:16; 30:6). Then Paul calls it the seal of the righteousness of faith (Rom. 4:11). Therefore, let a reason be required of God Himself why He commanded it to be impressed on the bodies of infants. For since baptism and circumcision are in the same case, our opponents cannot give anything to one without conceding it to the other.... (S)ince God communicated circumcision to infants as a sacrament of repentance and of faith, it does not seem absurd if they are now made participants in baptism.... God's command concerning circumcision of infants was either lawful and not to be trifled with, or it was deserving of censure. If there was in it nothing incongruous or absurd, neither can anything absurd be found in the observance of infant baptism.[222]

The Attitude of Jesus Christ Toward Covenant Children

> "Then some children were brought to Him so that He might lay His hands on them and pray; and the disciples rebuked them. But Jesus said, 'Let the children alone, and do not hinder them from coming to Me; for the kingdom of heaven belongs to such as these.' And after laying His hands on them, He departed from there" (Matt. 19:13–15).

"And He took them in His arms and began blessing them, laying His hands upon them" (Mark 10:16). "And they were bringing even their babies to Him." (Luke 18:15). Notice several important points in these texts: (1) The little children were brought to Jesus, they did not come on their own initiative. (2) These children were, according to

221. Booth, *Children of the Promise*, 109.

222. Calvin, *Institutes of the Christian Religion*, 2:1342–44.

the Greek words used, newborns (*brephe*), and young children (*paidia*). (3) Their parents must have been faithful covenant members, who believed that Jesus is the Messiah, for they brought their children to Him for the express purpose of having Him bless them. (4) When Jesus said, "For the kingdom of heaven belongs to such as these," He is specifically referring to the newborns and young children brought to Him, and not to those who come to Him in faith AS little children. The grammar of His statement does not allow for this interpretation. The Greek pronoun translated "of such" or "to such" is *toioutos* meaning "of this kind, sort or class," *i.e.*, of the infant-kind. "The usage of the New Testament will show also that the force of τοιουτος is not to institute a comparison but rather to specify a class, and the class specified is defined by the context."[223] And in the context we see that the infants brought to Him were incapable of demonstrating faith in Christ; that Jesus was angered that His disciples had kept these newborns and young children away from Him; and that Matthew 19:13, 14 does not even mention "faith as a little child." Therefore, we must conclude that, when Jesus says "to such," He is referring to the little children themselves and not to those who resemble little children, thereby affirming unmistakably that little children are citizens in the Kingdom of God. (5) Jesus, the God-man, actually performed a Spiritual act in their behalf, calling down God's rich and covenantal blessings upon them (Matt. 19:13–15).

In Mark 9:36–37, 42 we read that

> taking a child, He stood him in the midst of them; and taking him in His arms, He said to them. "Whoever receives one child like this in My name is receiving Me.... For whoever gives you a cup of water to drink because of your name as followers of Christ [or literally, in a name that you are Christ's], truly I say to you, he shall not lose his reward."
>
> In Mark 9:41 the expression "in my name" is explained by the qualifying clause, "because you belong to Christ" [(or "in a name that you are Christ's")]. To receive them in Christ's name is therefore equivalent to receiving them as belonging

223. Murray, *Christian Baptism*, 64.

to Christ. This, in turn, is but a variation of expression which has the same effect as saying that they belong to the kingdom of God. To conclude: these two assertions: (1). that little children belong to the kingdom of God; (2). that they are to be received in Christ's name... supply us with certain principles which lie close to the argument for infant baptism and without which the ordinance of infant baptism would be meaningless. These principles are: (1). that little children, even infants, are among Christ's people and are members of his body; (2). that they are members of his kingdom and therefore have been regenerated; (3). that they belong to the church, in that they are to be received as belonging to Christ, that is to say, received into the fellowship of the saints.... *If little children belong to the kingdom of God, if they belong to Christ, if they are to be received into the fellowship of believers, if they are to be reckoned as possessing the qualities and rights that constitute them members of the kingdom of God and of the church, is there any reason why they should not receive the sign of that membership?*[224]

The Lord Jesus, wishing to give an example by which the world would understand that he came to enlarge rather than to limit the Father's mercy, tenderly embraces the infants offered to him, chiding his disciples for trying to deny them access to him, because they were leading away from him those to whom the Kingdom of Heaven belonged. But (someone will say) what does baptism have in common with Christ's embracing the children? For it is not related that he baptized them, but that he took them, embraced them, and blessed them. Accordingly, they assert, if we would follow his example, let us help infants with prayers, but not baptize them. Let us, however, weigh Christ's acts a little more carefully than such men do. For we must not lightly pass over the fact that Christ commands that the infants be presented to him, adding the reason, "for of such is the Kingdom of Heaven" (Matt. 19:14). And thereupon he attests his will by his act

224. Murray, *Christian Baptism*, 65–66.

> when, embracing them, he commends them with his prayer and blessing to his Father. *If it is right for infants to be brought to Christ, why not also to be received into baptism, the symbol of our communion and fellowship with Christ? If the Kingdom of Heaven belongs to them, why is the sign denied which, so to speak, opens to them a door into the church, that, adopted into it, they may be enrolled among the heirs of the Kingdom of Heaven?* How unjust of us to drive away those whom Christ calls to himself! To deprive those whom he adorns with gifts! To shut out those whom he willingly receives! But if we wish to make an issue of the great difference between baptism and this act of Christ, how much more precious shall we regard baptism, by which we attest that infants are contained within God's covenant than the receiving, embracing, laying on of hands, and prayer, by which Christ himself present declares both that they are his and are sanctified by Him? In other niggling arguments... they argue from this saying of Christ, "Let the little ones come unto me," that these were already somewhat grown and now fit to come. But the Evangelists call them "babes and children" (Luke 18:15; Matt. 19:14; Mark 10:13); by these words the Greeks mean infants at the breast. Therefore, the word "to come" is used simply in the sense of "to have access."... When he commands that infants be allowed to come to him, nothing is clearer than that true infancy is meant. Lest this seem absurd, he adds, "For of such is the Kingdom of Heaven" (Matt. 19:14). If infants must be included in it, it will be perfectly clear that by the expression "of such" the infants themselves and those like them are designated.[225]

The Baptism of Households in the New Testament

Twelve instances of actual baptism are recorded in the New Testament (Acts 2:41; 8:12, 13, 38; 9:18; 10:48; 16:15, 33; 18:8; 19:5; 1 Cor. 1:14, 16). Those that refer to the baptism of whole households

225. Calvin, *Institutes of the Christian Religion*, 2:1329–31. Emphasis added.

are Acts 10:2, 47–48, which refer to the household of Cornelius; (16:15), which refers to the household of Lydia; (16:33), which refers to the household of the Philippian jailor; (Acts 18:8), which refers to the household of Crispus; and 1 Cor. 1:16, which refers to the household of Stephanas. Thus, almost half of the instances of baptism are the baptism of households, and not simply of individuals who profess faith in Christ. Furthermore, it must not be forgotten what we have learned, that in the Old Testament and the New Testament, "household" means everybody that is under the authority of a covenantal head of a family unit—wife, children, slaves. If someone objects by saying that in the baptism of "households" recorded in the New Testament there are no explicit references to infants in those "households," the answer to that objection is twofold: (1). there are not explicit references to adults in those households either; and (2). the issue is not infant baptism but household baptism—whole households were baptized, whether they included infants or whether they did not. The point is that Christian baptism is covenant baptism—it is to be administered to entire families, if the head of that family is a professed believer.

Now we must establish Scripturally the last point of the previous paragraph, namely that baptism is to be administered to the entire family of the believing head of that family. Let us consider three instances of household baptism: that of Lydia's household in Acts 16:14–15; that of the Philippian jailor in Acts 16:33; and that of Crispus in Acts 18:8.

The Baptism of Lydia's Household (Acts 16:14–15)

> And a certain woman named Lydia, from the city of Thyatira, a seller of purple fabrics, a worshiper of God, was listening, and the Lord opened her heart to respond to the things spoken by Paul. And when she and her household had been baptized, she urged us, saying, "If you have judged me to be faithful to the Lord, come into my house and stay." And she prevailed upon us.

Our text informs us that *only* Lydia's heart was opened by the Lord, *only* Lydia had been judged faithful to the Lord by the apostles; and yet Paul baptized Lydia's *entire family!* "The only conclusion we can draw about the baptism of the other members of Lydia's household is that they were baptized because they were members of the household of the believer Lydia."[226]

The Baptism of the Jailor's Household (Acts 16:31–34)

> And they [Paul and Silas] said, "Believe in the Lord Jesus, and you shall be saved, YOU AND YOUR HOUSEHOLD." And they spoke the word of the Lord to him together with all who were in his house. And he (the jailor) took them that very hour of the night and washed their wounds, and immediately he was baptized, he and ALL HIS HOUSEHOLD. And he brought them into his house and set food before them, and rejoiced greatly, having believed in God, with his whole household [emphasis added].

After having proclaimed to the Philippian jailor that through faith in the Lord Jesus, both he and his household would be saved from sin, the jailor believed, and immediately, in the prison, the jailor and his entire family, "all his household", were baptized by Paul. Then, in verse 34 we read that the jailor brought the apostles, whose wounds he had just cared for, into his own home, served them a meal, and, according to the translation of the New American Standard Version, "rejoiced greatly, having believed in God with his whole household." However, this translation of verse 34 is misleading, for it leaves the impression that the jailor and his whole family rejoiced, because he AND his whole family "believed in God." The original Greek is quite clear and not at all misleading, making the interpretation impossible that others in the family believed beside the jailor. "Rejoiced" is a third person, singular verb, referring ONLY to the jailor, and not to his entire family. The Greek participle, "having believed," is in the SINGULAR, referring ONLY to the jailor, not the plural, which would have been necessary if Paul

226. Booth, *Children of the Promise*, 147.

were referring to the jailor and his family. So that, a more accurate translation of verse 34 would be: "And he, having believed in God, rejoiced greatly with all his household"! Here again, we have an instance of an entire family being baptized, because the head of the family believed in Jesus Christ.

The Baptism of Crispus' Household (Acts 18:8)

"And Crispus, the leader of the synagogue, believed in the Lord with all his household, and many of the Corinthians when they heard were believing and being baptized." Although it is possible, in this particular case, that Crispus and every member of his family were professed believers in the Lord Jesus Christ, nevertheless,

> since Crispus was the leader of the synagogue, his entire household, including his children, would have belonged to the synagogue. It seems likely, then, that Crispus, as the head of his house, would have brought his entire family for household baptism.... We should expect that a first-century Jewish family would similarly have followed the lead of its covenantal head. This text should be interpreted in accordance with the Jewish culture of the times, not the individualistic assumptions of our own culture.... The New Testament culture arose from the Old Testament culture, and therefore it is not surprising to find whole households believing because the head of the household believes. Consider the similarly covenantal thinking in what Ruth says to Naomi in Ruth 1:16–17: "Do not urge me to leave you or turn back from following you; for where you go, I will go, and where you lodge, I will lodge. Your people shall be my people, and your God, my God. Where you die, I will die, and there I will be buried. Thus may the Lord do to me, and worse, if anything but death parts you and me."[227]

227. Booth, *Children of the Promise*, 147–48.

The Significance of Missing Adult Baptisms

There are NO instances in the New Testament of a child growing up in a Christian home, being baptized on profession of faith as an adult.

> Those who dispute the Biblical character of infant Baptism have therefore to reckon with the fact that *adult Baptism for sons and daughters born of Christian parents, which they recommend, is even worse attested by the New Testament than infant baptism* (for which certain possible traces are discoverable) and indeed LACKS ANY KIND OF PROOF.[228]

The Solemnity and Sanctity of the Baptism of the Children of Believers

To The Believing Parents Who Have Their Children Baptized

> Oh, that [this] sentence could be made to thrill through every parent's heart in Christendom: *THE BAPTISM OF A CHILD IS ONE OF THE SOLEMN TRANSACTIONS PERTAINING TO OUR HOLY RELIGION.* A human being, just opening its eyes to the world; presented to that God who made it, devoted to that Saviour without an interest in whose atoning blood, it had better never have been been born; and consecrated to that Holy Spirit, who alone can sanctify and prepare it for heaven; is indeed a spectacle adapted to affect every pious heart. In death, our race is run; worldly hope and expectation are alike extinct; and the destiny of the immortal spirit is forever fixed. But the child presented for baptism, if it reach the ordinary limit of human life, has before it many a trial, and will need all the pardoning mercy, all the sanctifying grace, and all the precious consolations which the

228. Oscar Cullman, quoted in Murray, *Christian Baptism*, 69 (ftnt. 38). Emphasis added.

blessed Gospel of Christ has to bestow. And even if it die in infancy, it still needs the pardoning mercy and sanctifying grace which are set forth in this ordinance. On either supposition, the transaction is important. A course is commenced which will be a blessing or a curse beyond the power of the human mind to estimate. And the eternal happiness or the misery of the young immortal will depend, under God, upon the training it shall receive from the hands of those who offer it.

Let those, then, who bring their children to the sacred font to be baptized, ponder well what this ordinance means, and what its reception involves, both in regard to parents and children. Let them remember that in taking this step, we make a solemn profession of belief, that our children, as well as ourselves, are born in sin, and stand in indispensable need of pardoning mercy and sanctifying grace. We formally dedicate them to God, that they may be "washed and justified, and sanctified in the name of the Lord Jesus, and by the Spirit of our God." And we take upon ourselves solemn vows to train them up in the knowledge and fear of God; to instruct them, from the earliest dawn of reason, in the principles and duties of our holy religion; to consider and treat them as ingrafted members of the family of Christ, and to do all in our power, by precept and example, by authority and by prayer, to lead them in the ways of truth, of holiness, and of salvation.... Surely if there be a transaction, among all the duties incumbent on us as Christians—if there be a transaction which ought to be engaged in with reverence, and godly fear: with penitence, faith, and love; with bowels of Christian compassion yearning over our beloved offspring; with humble and importunate aspirations to the God of all grace for His blessing on them and ourselves; and with solemn resolutions, in the strength of His grace, that we will be faithful to our vows,—this is that transaction![229]

229. Miller, *Baptism and Christian Education*, 55, 56.

To The Baptized Children of Believing Parents

> *How responsible, and how solemn is the situation of those young persons who have been in their infancy dedicated to God in holy baptism!...* It is generally conceded, and extensively felt, that parents, by dedicating their children to God in this ordinance, are brought under very weighty obligations, which cannot be forgotten by them, without incurring great guilt. But young people seldom lay to heart as they ought, that their early reception of the seal of God's covenant, in consequence of the act of their parents, places them in circumstances of the most solemn and responsible kind.... Baptized young people! Think of this. You have been in the bosom of the church ever since you drew your first breath. The seal of God's covenant has been placed upon you. You cannot, if you would, escape from the responsibility of this relation. You may forget it; you may hate to think about it; you may despise it; but still the obligation lies upon you; you cannot throw it off. Your situation is solemn beyond expression.[230]

The "Improvement" of Baptism

Q. 167: How is our baptism to be improved by us?

A.: The needful but much neglected duty of improving our baptism, is to be performed by us all our life long, especially in the time of temptation, and when we are present at the administration of it to others; by serious and thankful consideration of the nature of it, and of the ends for which Christ instituted it, the privileges and benefits conferred and sealed thereby, and our solemn vow made therein; by

230. Miller, *Baptism and Christian Education,* 57, 58.

being humbled for our sinful defilement, our falling short of, and walking contrary to, the grace of baptism, and our engagements; by growing up to assurance of pardon of sin, and of all other blessings sealed to us in that sacrament; by drawing strength from the death and resurrection of Christ, into whom we are baptized, for the mortifying of sin, and quickening of grace; and by endeavouring to live by faith, to have our conversation in holiness and righteousness, as those that have therein given up their names to Christ; and to walk in brotherly love, as being baptized by the same Spirit into one body.

The Meaning of "Improving Our Baptism"

"Improving our baptism" means using our baptism for beneficial purposes, practically applying our baptism to our lives so that it grows more valuable to us, and so that we can make progress in our Christian life.

> As baptism is an ordinance or means of grace for our attaining spiritual blessings, we are not only guilty of a sinful neglect, but we lose the advantage which might otherwise be expected, if we do not improve it so as to answer its valuable end. And when we consider it as a professed dedication to God, or as a bond and obligation laid on us to be entirely and for ever his, it cannot but be reckoned the highest affront offered to the divine Majesty, and a being unsteadfast in his covenant, for us practically to disown the engagement, or, in effect, to deny his right to us.[231]

231. Ridgeley, *Commentary on the Larger Catechism*, 2:513–14.

The Time to Improve Our Baptism

We should "improve" or make the best use of our baptism at many important junctures in our lives: when we are present at the baptism of others; when we are facing temptation, in order to resist it and prevent our being entangled in and overcome by it; at any time in our Christian life, in order to grow in Christ, especially if we are beginning to grow cold spiritually or are beginning to lose our zeal and diligence. In the whole course of life,

> it will be of use for promoting the life of faith, which consists in an entire dependence on him as those who are sensible that we can do nothing without him, to consider that, when we were first devoted to him, it was acknowledged, and from the time when we were enabled to give ourselves up to him by faith, we have been always sensible, that we stand in need of daily supplies of grace from him.[232]

The Method of Improving our Baptism

FIRST, use your baptism as a shield against temptations.

> Satan, I have given up myself to God by a sacred vow in baptism; I am not my own, I am Christ's; therefore I cannot yield to thy temptations, for I should break my oath of allegiance which I made to God in baptism. [Martin] Luther tells us of a pious woman, who, when the devil tempted her to sin, answered, "Satan,... I am baptized;" and so beat back the tempter.[233]

SECOND, use your baptism as a spur to holiness. In remembering your baptism, remember the vows you made or which were made by your parents, when you were baptized, by which you renounced this evil world and devoted yourself to the worship and service of Christ. "To be baptized into the name of the Father, Son,

232. Ridgeley, *Commentary on the Larger Catechism*, 2:516.

233. Thomas Watson, *A Body of Divinity* (Grand Rapids, MI: Sovereign Grace Publishers, n.d.), 383.

and Holy Ghost, implies a solemn dedication of ourselves to the service of all the Three Persons in the Trinity."[234]

THIRD, use your baptism as a spur to courage. We should be ready at all times and in all circumstances to confess the Holy Trinity into whose Name we were baptized. "Whosoever shall confess Me before men, him shall the Son of man also confess before the angels of God" Jesus said. "He that dare not confess the Holy Trinity, shames his baptism, and God will be ashamed to own him at the day of judgment."[235]

The Sacrament of the Lord's Supper

The Meaning and Purpose of the Lord's Supper

Q. 168: What is the Lord's supper?

A.: The Lord's supper is a sacrament of the New Testament, wherein, by giving and receiving bread and wine according to the appointment of Jesus Christ, his death is shewed forth; and they that worthily communicate feed upon his body and blood, to their spiritual nourishment and growth in grace; have their union and communion with him confirmed; testify and renew their thankfulness, and engagement to God, and their mutual love and fellowship each with other, as members of the same mystical body.

The Names of This Ordinance

This sacrament is given several names in the Bible to help us understand its full meaning. It is called "the body and blood of Christ," because in it we are spiritually nourished on Christ and the

234. Watson, *A Body of Divinity*, 383.
235. Watson, *A Body of Divinity*, 383.

accomplishments of His redemptive work. It is called "the Supper of the Lord," not only to distinguish it from ordinary meals, but also to remind us that it is a holy supper, "a Supper appointed for the increase of holiness, for the food of the soul in holiness, to feed the soul for the life everlasting."[236] It is "the Table of the Lord," around which we fellowship with the living Lord and receive His bounties from His own hand. It is called "the Communion of the body and blood of Christ," because by partaking of this sign and seal by faith we commune with Christ and participate in the benefits of His redemption. The Lord's Supper is never called "an altar" in the Bible.

The Lord's Supper is

> The Communion; having in it communion with Christ and with the universal church;... The Eucharist; Christ in the institution of it gave thanks, and we in the participation;... The Feast; a royal feast, a marriage feast, a feast of memorial, a feast of dedication, a feast upon a sacrifice, and a feast upon a covenant.[237]

The Ordinance of Christ

The Reality of the Ordinance

The Lord's Supper was instituted for the Church by the Lord Jesus Christ Himself; and therefore, being founded on divine command, is of divine authority (Matt. 26:26–29; Mark 14:22–25; Luke 22:19–20; 1 Cor. 11:23–26). Jesus Christ is the Head of the church, and therefore, it is His royal prerogative, and His alone, to institute ordinances and practices by which He is to be worshiped and His church edified. And no individual or group of individuals, neither elders nor church, has the liberty to add to or subtract from His ordinances (Deut. 12:32). As we have seen, the regulative principle of the church in its worship is: (1) Whatever is commanded is required; (2) Whatever is forbidden is prohibited; (3) Whatever is not commanded is forbidden.

---

236. Bruce, *The Mystery of the Lord's Supper,* 70.

237. Matthew Henry, *How To Prepare for Communion* (MacDill AFB, FL: MacDonald Publishing Co., n.d.), 8.

"Only God may make a Sacrament,"[238] for no one has the power to give Christ, who is signified in the sacrament, but the Father or Christ Himself. Therefore, since the Lord's Supper is God's institution, it must be observed exactly as He has commanded.

> If you leave undone one jot of what He commanded you to do, you pervert the institution, for there is nothing in the register of the institution but what is essential. Thus in the celebration of Christ's institution, we must pay attention to whatever He said, did or commanded to be done. We must first say whatever He said, and then do whatever He did, for the administration of the Sacrament must follow upon the Word. You must first teach what Christ commanded you to teach, and then administer the Sacrament faithfully keeping to this institution.... Thus if we leave any particular point or ceremony belonging to this institution undone, we pervert the whole action.[239]
>
> It is God alone who makes a thing that is common to be holy. By His will and ordinance, declared and set down in His Word, God has made the things that were common, by His appointment, to be holy. In answer to the question as to the way and means whereby they are made holy, we say it is the Word of God, the institution of Christ, the will of Christ declared in His institution, that makes them holy. For the preaching and exposition of the Word and institution of Christ shows us that God has made these things holy, and not only that He has made them holy, but it shows us a holy way in which they are to be used, in what place, at what time, with what heart, and to what end.[240]

---

238. Bruce, *The Mystery of the Lord's Supper,* 109.
239. Bruce, *The Mystery of the Lord's Supper,* 110.
240. Bruce, *The Mystery of the Lord's Supper, 115.*

The Time of Institution

> The Lord Jesus, in the night in which He was betrayed, took bread (1 Cor. 11:23).
>
> When we reflect on the time of the institution of this ordinance, we have a striking view of the fortitude with which Jesus met his unparalleled sufferings, and of the singular love which He cherished toward his people; and we ought to feel the sacred obligation laid upon us to keep the feast. On that night the Jewish rulers and the chief priests were met in close cabal, to concert measures for apprehending Jesus, and bringing him to an ignominious death. In that night he was to be perfidiously betrayed by one of his own disciples, denied by another, and abandoned by them all to the rage of his malicious foes. He was to be smitten by the sword of Justice, and forsaken of his God—to be cruelly mocked and scourged—to be led away to a cross, and there to pour out His soul unto death. Of all this Jesus was fully apprized; yet in the immediate view of the dreadful sufferings He was about to undergo, such was the calm serenity of his mind, such his matchless love to his people, and such his concern for their spiritual benefit, that he instituted this ordinance for their encouragement and consolation in all succeeding ages. Did he remember them in such affecting circumstances?—and shall not this engage them to remember him?—shall they undervalue, by a wilful neglect, an ordinance which he settled immediately before his death, and disregard the dying command of that friend who laid down his life for them?[241]

The Permanence of the Ordinance

The sacrament of the Lord's Supper is to be observed in Christ's Church until the very end of the world: "as often as you eat this

241. Shaw, *The Reformed Faith*, 293–94.

bread and drink this cup, you show forth the Lord's death until He comes" (1 Cor. 11:26).

The Nature of this Ordinance

Being a sacrament instituted by Jesus Christ for His Church, the Lord's Supper, like Baptism, is a sign and seal of the blessings of the covenant of grace secured for us by the redemptive work of Christ, and applied to us by the risen Christ with His Holy Spirit.

The Lord's Supper is

> (i)....a commemorating ordinance, in remembrance of the person of Christ...and [of the death of Christ].... (ii). It is a confessing ordinance; we profess our value and esteem for Christ crucified, and our dependence upon, a confidence in Christ crucified. (iii). It is a communicating ordinance; Christ and all his benefits are here communicated to us, and are here to be received by us. (iv). It is a covenanting ordinance; it is... the new covenant, opened distinctly; God seals to us to be to us a God, and we seal to him to be to him a people.[242]

The Purpose of the Lord's Supper

To Show Forth His Death Until He Comes Again

In the Lord's Supper, God not only recalls to our memory the death of Christ and what it accomplished, He places in the hand of faith its benefits. Therefore, to show out gratitude to Him, He calls us in the Lord's Supper to celebrate that accomplished and applied redemption in Christ with thanksgiving and with fitting praises. He commands us that "as often as you eat this bread and drink the cup, YOU PROCLAIM THE LORD'S DEATH UNTIL HE COMES" (1 Cor. 11:26). In these words God calls us

> with a single voice to confess openly before men that for us the whole assurance of life and salvation rests upon the Lord's

242. Henry, *How To Prepare for Communion*, 13.

> death, that we may glorify him by our confession, and by our example exhort others to give glory to him. Here again the purpose of the Sacrament is made clear, that is, to exercise us in the remembrance of Christ's death. For the command to us to "declare the Lord's death til he comes" (1 Cor. 11:26) in judgment means nothing else than that we should by the confession of our mouth declare what our faith recognizes in the Sacrament: that the death of Christ is our life.[243]

To Be Spiritually Nourished on Christ

> God has received us, once for all, into his family, to hold us not only as servants but as sons. Thereafter, to fulfill the duties of a most excellent Father concerned for his offspring, he undertakes also to nourish us throughout the course of our life. And not content with this alone, he has willed, by giving his pledge, to assure us of this continuing liberality. To this end, therefore, he has, through the hand of his only-begotten Son, given to his church another sacrament, that is, a spiritual banquet, wherein Christ attests himself to be the life-giving bread, upon which our souls feed unto true and blessed immortality.[244]

Jesus said, "I am the living bread that came down out of heaven; if any one eats of this bread, he shall live forever; and the bread also which I shall give for the life of the world is My flesh" (John 6:51).

> Now Christ is the only food of our soul, and therefore our Heavenly Father invites us to Christ, that, refreshed by partaking of him, we may repeatedly gather strength until we shall have reached heavenly immortality, Since, however, this mystery of Christ's secret union with the devout is by nature incomprehensible, he shows its figure and image in visible signs best adapted to our small capacity. Indeed, by giving guarantees and tokens, he makes it as certain for us as

243. Calvin, *Institutes of the Christian Religion*, 2:1414.
244. Calvin, *Institutes of the Christian Religion*, 2:1359–60.

> if we had seen it with our own eyes.... Just as bread and wine sustain physical life, so are souls fed by Christ.[245]

To Confirm Our Union and Communion with Christ

"Is not the cup of blessing which we bless a sharing [communion] in the blood of Christ? Is not the bread which we break a sharing [communion] in the body of Christ?" (1 Cor.10:16). As we have seen, the sacrament of the Lord's Supper signifies, seals and conveys Christ and the benefits of His accomplished salvation to believers. In the sacraments, as signs and seals of salvation, Christ attests and confirms Himself to be "the life-giving bread, upon which our souls feed unto true and blessed immortality."[246] Therefore, as we partake of the Lord's Supper in faith, we may assure ourselves that we are truly and savingly in Christ, enjoying communion with Him, participating afresh in the benefits of His death and resurrection. As our text says, in taking the Lord's Supper we actually, truly and Spiritually commune, fellowship, participate, share in the body and blood of Christ, *i.e.*, in the living Christ and the benefits of His redemptive work.

> Now, that sacred partaking of his flesh and blood, by which Christ pours his life into us, as if it penetrated into our bones and marrow, he also testifies and seals in the Supper—not by presenting a vain and empty sign, but by manifesting there the effectiveness of his Spirit to fulfill what he promises. And truly he offers and shows the reality there signified to all who sit at that spiritual banquet, although it is received with benefit by believers alone, who accept such great generosity with true faith and gratefulness of heart.
>
> In this manner the apostle said, "The bread which we break is a participation in the body of Christ; the cup which we consecrate to this by word and prayers is a participation in His blood" (1 Cor. 10:16p., order changed). There is no reason for anyone

245. Calvin, *Institutes of the Christian Religion*, 2:1360–61.
246. Calvin, *Institutes of the Christian Religion*, 2:1360.

to object that this is a figurative expression by which the name of the thing signified is given to the sign. I indeed admit that the breaking of bread is a symbol; it is not the thing itself. But, having admitted this, we shall nevertheless duly infer that by the showing of the symbol the thing itself is also shown. For unless a man means to call God a deceiver, he would never dare assert that an empty symbol is set forth by him. Therefore, if the Lord truly represents the participation in his body through the breaking of bread, there ought not to be the least doubt that he truly presents and shows his body. And the godly ought by all means to keep this rule: whenever they see symbols appointed by the Lord, to think and be persuaded that the truth of the thing signified is surely present there. For why should the Lord put in your hand the symbol of his body, except to assure you of a true participation in it? But if it is true that a visible sign is given us to seal the gift of a thing invisible, when we have received the symbol of the body, let us no less surely trust that the body itself is also given to us.[247]

To Testify and Renew our Thankfulness to God

"And when He had given thanks, He broke it, and said, 'Take eat'" (1 Cor. 11:24). "Through Him [Jesus] then let us continually offer up a sacrifice of praise to God, that is, the fruit of our lips that give thanks to His name. And do not neglect doing good and sharing; for with such sacrifices God is pleased" (Heb. 13:15–16). We know that there is nothing meritorious or propitiatory about these sacrifices of praise, thanksgiving and good deeds, for they are all offered to God "through Him," *i.e.*, through the redemption we have in Christ accomplished by His life, death and resurrection, and are offered to God with "thankfulness to His Name," *i.e.*, in heart-felt gratitude to the revelation of God's grace and glory in our salvation from sin in Christ.

Reformed Christianity can speak of the Lord's Supper as the Eucharist, *i.e.*, a Thanksgiving, and as a sacrifice, as does Roman Catholicism; but the similarity is only semantic. In Roman Catholi-

247. Calvin, *Institutes of the Christian Religion*, 2:1370–71.

cism the sacrifice of the Mass is offered up to God on the altar in the front of the sanctuary. In Reformed Christianity the Eucharist is a holy meal based on Christ's once-for-all, unrepeatable sacrifice on Calvary, the benefits of which are received by faith at the table in the front of the sanctuary. The sacrifices offered by Rome in the Eucharist are expiatory, atoning and meritorious. The sacrifices offered by Reformed Christians at the Lord's Table are sacrifices of praise and thanksgiving for the accomplished redemption in Christ.

> After Christ's sacrifice was accomplished, the Lord instituted another method for us, that is, to transmit to the believing folk the benefit of the sacrifice offered to himself by his Son. He has therefore given us a Table at which to feast, not an altar upon which to offer a victim; He has not consecrated priests to offer sacrifice, but ministers to distribute the sacred banquet.[248]

In the Old Testament there were two kinds of sacrifices offered to God: those offerings made for sin by some kind of satisfaction, by which guilt was atoned before God, or those which were symbols of divine worship and confessions of faith and thanksgiving to God, by which the offerer would beseech God for continued favor and renew his covenant obligations to the Lord. In the New Testament these are called "sacrifices of praise" and "sacrifices of thanksgiving," while the first type we can refer to as sacrifices of propitiation.

> The sacrifice of expiation [or propitiation] is that which is intended to appease God's wrath, to satisfy his judgment, and so to wash sins and cleanse them that the sinner, purged of their filth and restored to the purity of righteousness, may return into favor with God. The sacrificial victims which were offered under the law to atone for sins (Ex. 29:36) were so called, not because they were capable of recovering God's favor or wiping out iniquity, but because they prefigured a true sacrifice such as was finally accomplished in reality by Christ alone.... And it was done but once, because the effec-

248. Calvin, *Institutes of the Christian Religion*, 2:1440.

> tiveness and force of that one sacrifice accomplished by Christ are eternal.... And so perfect was it that no place was left afterward for any other sacrificial victim. Therefore I conclude that it is a most wicked infamy and unbearable blasphemy, both against Christ and against the sacrifice which he made for us through his death on the cross, for anyone to suppose that by repeating the oblation he obtains pardon for sins, appeases God, and acquires righteousness, [as is claimed by Roman Catholicism for the Mass].[249]

Hebrews 13:15–16 also teaches us that sacrifices of praise and thanksgiving also include "doing good and sharing, for with such sacrifices God is pleased." This means that included in these sacrifices are

> all the duties of love. When we embrace our brethren with these, we honor the Lord himself in his members. Also included are all our prayers, praises, thanksgivings, and whatever we do in the worship of God. All these things finally depend upon the greater sacrifice, by which we are consecrated in soul and body to be a holy temple to the Lord (1 Cor. 3:16).... This kind of sacrifice has nothing to do with appeasing God's wrath, with obtaining forgiveness of sins, or with meriting righteousness; but is concerned solely with magnifying and exalting God. For it cannot be pleasing and acceptable to God, except from the hands of those whom he has reconciled to himself by other means, after they have received forgiveness of sins.... But this is so necessary for the church that it cannot be absent from it [Mal. 1:11; Rom. 12:1; 1 Pet. 2:5–6; Phil. 4:18; Ps. 141:2; Hos. 14:2; Ps. 50:23; 51:19].... The Lord's Supper cannot be without a sacrifice of this kind, in which, while we proclaim his death (1 Cor.11:26) and give thanks, we do nothing but offer a sacrifice of praise. From this office of sacrificing, all Christians are called a royal priesthood (1 Pet. 2:9), because through Christ we offer that sacrifice of praise to God of which the apostle speaks: "the

249. Calvin, *Institutes of the Christian Religion*, 2:1441–42.

> fruit of lips confessing His name" (Heb. 13:15). And we do not appear with our gifts before God without an intercessor. The Mediator interceding for us is Christ, by whom we offer ourselves and what is ours to the Father. He is our Pontiff, who has entered the heavenly sanctuary (Heb. 9:24), and opens a way for us to enter (cf. Heb. 10:20).[250]

To Testify and Renew Our Engagement to God

> Therefore, my beloved, flee from idolatry. I speak as to wise men; you judge what I say. Is not the cup of blessing which we bless a sharing in the blood of Christ? Is not the bread which we break a sharing in the body of Christ? ... You cannot drink the cup of the Lord, and the cup of demons; you cannot partake of the table of the Lord, and the table of demons (1 Cor. 10:14–16, 21).

This covenant meal is a time of renewal, a time for rededication of ourselves and our families to the covenant privileges and responsibilities which God gives us in Christ. At the sacrifices and holy festivals in the Old Testament, Israel not only rejoiced in Her Savior and Covenant Lord, but also renewed her covenant vows and obligations to the Lord. On the threshold of entering the Promised Land, we see such a ceremony in Deuteronomy 26–32:

> You have today declared the Lord to be your God, and that you would walk in His ways and keep His statutes, His commandments and His ordinances, and listen to His voice. And the Lord has today declared you to be His people, a treasured possession, as He promised you... that you shall be a consecrated people to the Lord your God (Deut. 26:17–19).

The Lord's Supper is such a covenant meal by which believers in Jesus testify to and rededicate themselves to be engaged in covenant with the Lord in a communion of life with Him, living faithfully according to His sovereignly dictated order of life out of gratitude to

250. Calvin, *Institutes of the Christian Religion*, 2:1443–45.

Jesus for saving them. Those who eat the Lord's Supper do thereby dedicate themselves to the Lord's service, and *this dedication must be total, comprehensive and exclusive*: "You cannot drink the cup of the Lord, and the cup of demons; you cannot partake of the table of the Lord, and the table of demons." It is impossible to be a friend of Christ and friend of devils at the same time! It is impossible to enjoy communion with Christ and with the devil and his people at the same time! It is impossible to live for Christ and live for Satan at the same time! The break with evil must be clean and total! Those who partake of the Lord's Supper worthily promise the Lord that they will "flee from idolatry." This command to "flee from idolatry"

> includes two things; first, avoiding what is questionable; that is, everything which lies upon the border of what is allowable, or which approaches the confines of sin; and secondly, avoiding the occasion and temptations to sin; keeping at a distance from everything which excites evil passion, or which tends to ensnare the soul.[251]

To Testify and Renew Our Mutual Love for Each Other in the Body of Christ

The Lord's Supper is a kind of exhortation from the Lord to us,

> which can more forcefully than any other means quicken and inspire us both to purity and holiness of life, and to love, peace and concord. For the Lord so communicates his body to us there that he is made completely one with us and we with him. Now, since he has only one body, of which he makes us all partakers [1 Cor. 12:13], it is necessary that all of us also be made one body by such participation. The bread shown in the Sacrament represents this unity. As it is made of many grains so mixed together than one cannot be distinguished from another, so it is fitting that in the same way we should be joined and bound together by such great agreement of minds that no sort of disagreement or division may

251. Hodge, *A Commentary on The First Epistle to the Corinthians*, 184–85.

intrude. I prefer to explain it in Paul's words: "The cup of blessing which we bless is a communicating of the blood of Christ; and the bread of blessing which we break is a participation in the body of Christ.... Therefore... we... are all one body, for we partake of one bread" (1 Cor. 10:16–17).

We shall benefit very much from the Sacrament if this thought is impressed and engraved upon our minds: that none of the brethren can be injured, despised, rejected, abused, or in any way offended by us, without at the same time, injuring, despising and abusing Christ by the wrongs we do... that we cannot love Christ without loving Him in the brethren; that we ought to take the same care of our brethren's bodies as we take of our own; for they are members of our body; and that, as no part of our body is touched by any feeling of pain which is not spread among all the rest, so we ought not to allow a brother to be affected by any evil, without being touched with compassion for him. Accordingly, Augustine with good reason frequently calls this Sacrament "the bond of love." For what sharper goad could there be to arouse mutual love among us than when Christ, giving himself to us, not only invites us by his own example to pledge and give ourselves to one another, but inasmuch as he makes himself common to all, also makes all of us one in himself.[252]

The Supper is no personal affair between the individual believer and Christ. It is the covenant meal, the congregational meal, *par excellence*. And it points to the sacrifice made by Christ, the reconciliation that has taken place in his blood, as the only ground of this communion between God and his people and of the unity of the church. Only in the eating of the body thus understood and in the drinking of this cup representing the reconciling power of his blood is the church one. In that sense, therefore, the Supper is the foundation and criterion for the unity of the church as the new people of

252. Calvin, *Institutes of the Christian Religion*, 2:1414–16.

> God.—The continued observance of the Supper is the incomparable means for bringing the unity of spiritual Israel and of the body of Christ to revelation in its deepest and only ground: communion in the body and blood of Christ.... Both [Sacraments, in relation to the Word], establish contact with the death of Christ—baptism as baptism-into-his-death and the Supper as communion with the body and blood of Christ. As such the unity of the church as the body of Christ attaches to both,—baptism as entrance to and incorporation into the body and the supper as the unity of the body repeatedly received and manifested afresh in eating one bread.[253]

The Presence of Christ in the Lord's Supper

The Location of the Physical Body of Jesus Christ Today

At His incarnation, the Son of God took to Himself our humanity, and became fully human, without ceasing to be fully divine. When the women went to the tomb to anoint the body of Jesus, His body was gone! God had raised Him from the dead in the same body in which He suffered. Forty days after His resurrection, He physically ascended to God's right hand, where He is seated and reigning until His second physical coming to earth. The point of all this is that this very moment, Jesus, who is the same yesterday, today, and forever, in His humanity is in Heaven at the right hand of God. As God the Son, He is wholly present everywhere, *i.e.*, He is omnipresent; but His humanity is not omnipresent, occupying many places and many times, without being limited to one place at a time, without form. To say such things is to deny His real humanity, because "such is the condition of flesh that it must subsist in one definite place, with its own size and form."[254] The physical body of a human being is not omnipresent nor invisible. Jesus is fully and truly human, physically and spiritually. Therefore, Jesus, in His hu-

253. Herman Ridderbos, *Paul: An Outline of His Theology*, trans. by John Richard DeWitt (Grand Rapids, MI: William B. Eerdmans Publishing Co., 1975), 423–24.

254. Calvin, *Institutes of the Christian Religion*, 2:1391.

manity is not infinite and omnipresent; but His invisible Deity is omnipresent.

The Bible teaches us unequivocally that "the body of Christ from the time of his resurrection [and from His incarnation] was finite, and is contained in heaven even to the Last Day (Acts 3:21)."[255] Jesus Himself declared to His disciples that He would not always be in the world physically with them, but that after His ascension and the day of Pentecost, His presence would be with them in an even more glorious manner, Spiritually, *i.e.*, by the Holy Spirit (Matt. 26:11; John 12:8; John 14:12, 28; 16:7, 28). As Augustine said,

> When Christ said, "You will not have Me with you always" he was speaking of the presence of the [physical] body. For with regard to his majesty, to his providence, to his ineffable and invisible grace, he fulfilled what he said, "Behold, I am with you even to the end of the age" (Matt. 28:20). But with regard to the flesh that the Word assumed, the fact that he was born of the virgin, the fact that he was seized by the Jews, was fastened upon the tree, taken down from the cross, wrapped in linen, laid in the tomb, manifested in the resurrection: "You will not always have Me with you." Why? Because according to his bodily presence, he had fellowship for forty days with his disciples; and while they accompanied him, seeing but not following, he ascended (Acts 1:3, 9). "He is not here" (Mark 16:6): for he sits there at the right hand of the Father (Mark 16:19). And yet he is here, for the presence of his majesty has not departed (Heb. 1:3). According to the presence of his majesty, we have Christ always; but according to the presence of the flesh, it is rightly said, "You will not always have me" (Matt. 26:11). For the church had him according to the presence of the flesh for only a few days; now it holds him by faith, but does not see him with the eyes.[256]

255. Calvin, *Institutes of the Christian Religion*, 2:1393.
256. Calvin, *Institutes of the Christian Religion*, 2:1393–94.

> *Christ withdrew his bodily presence from his disciples in order to be with them in spiritual presence.* There it is clear that he distinguishes the essence of the flesh from the power of the Spirit, by which we are joined to Christ, though we are otherwise separated from him by a great distance in space.[257]

As Jesus teaches His disciples about His imminent death, resurrection and ascension in John 14–16, His actual promise is that when He has ascended to His Father ("because I go to the Father" 14:12),

> I will ask the Father, and He will give you another Helper, that He may be with you forever; that is the Spirit of truth... you know Him because He abides with you, and will be in you. I will not leave you as orphans; I WILL COME TO YOU. After a little while the world will behold Me no more; but you will behold Me; because I live, you shall live also. In that day you shall know that I am in My Father, and you in Me, and I in you. He who has My commandments, and keeps them, he it is who loves Me; and he who loves Me shall be loved by My Father, and I will love Him, and will DISCLOSE MYSELF to him (John 14:16–21; emphasis added).

Notice several important things in this text. (1) This promise hinges upon Jesus dying, rising and ascending to the Father. (2) When He ascends to the Father, He will no longer be physically in the world, nor will He be seen with physical eyes. (3) When He ascends to the Father, then He will pour out His Holy Spirit on His Church. (4) The presence of the Holy Spirit will abide within Christ's disciples. (5) *In sending the Holy Spirit to us and in the Spirit's indwelling of us, Christ Himself will come to us*: "I will come to you!" *The Holy Spirit brings the spiritual presence of Jesus Christ into our lives, while Jesus sits at God's right hand in Heaven.* (6) When that happens, although the world will not see Jesus with its physical eyes, Jesus' disciples will "behold" Him by faith, for He lives in them and for them, and they live in Him, (John 17). (7) The Spirit brings the presence of Jesus so

257. Calvin, *Institutes of the Christian Religion*, 2:1397–98.

close to His disciples that, as they live for Him, He Himself, with His Father, will love them, and Jesus personally by the Spirit "will disclose" Himself to them. *Where the presence of the Spirit is, there is the presence of Jesus Christ. Although the persons of the Spirit and of Christ are distinct, their presence is the same!* But it must be emphasized again, that the presence of Jesus Christ with His disciples is Spiritual, not physical, and therefore, incomprehensible.

The disciples asked Jesus specifically about His statements, "A little while, and you will not behold Me; and again a little while, and you will see Me; and, Because I go to the Father" (John 16:19).

We have spent some time making this point about the presence of the physical body of Jesus in heaven and not on earth, because of the monstrous teaching of Roman Catholicism called transubstantiation, which teaches that Jesus Christ is physically present in the Lord's Supper and that His physical body and blood are physically eaten by participants in the Supper. It teaches that, when Jesus said concerning the bread, "This is My body", that it was a literal and physical statement—the bread is literally His body and the wine is literally His blood, although it has the appearance of bread and wine. However,

> unless the body of Christ can be everywhere at once, without limitation of place, it will not be credible that he lies hidden under the bread in the Supper. To meet this necessity, they [Roman Catholics] have introduced the monstrous notion of ubiquity. But as we have proved by firm and clear testimonies of Scripture, Christ's body was circumscribed by the measure of a human body. Again, by his ascension into heaven he made it plain that it is not in all places, but when it passes into one, it leaves the previous one.... Although the whole Christ is everywhere, still the whole of that which is in Him is not everywhere.... Therefore, since the whole Christ is everywhere, our Mediator is ever present with His own people, and in the Supper reveals himself in a special way, yet in such a way that the whole Christ is present, but not in his wholeness. For, as has been said, in his flesh he is contained in heaven until he appears in judgment.... They [Roman Catho-

> lics] place Christ in the bread, while we do not think it lawful for us to drag him from Heaven."[258]

> From what Word have they inferred that the body of Christ is visible in heaven, but lies hidden invisible on earth under innumerable crumbs of bread?[259]

The Spirit of Christ and the Presence of Christ

The risen Christ is truly present with His people at the Lord's Supper by His Holy Spirit (John 14:16–18). During the Supper He gives Himself to His people and communes with them as friend with friend, building them up in their faith and reassuring them of their salvation. We know this to be true because the Bible teaches us to understand that the Lord's Supper signifies, seals and conveys Christ and His benefits of salvation to believers, as we have seen.

> Now Christ is the only food of our soul, and therefore our Heavenly Father invites us to Christ, that, refreshed by partaking of him, we may repeatedly gather strength until we shall have reached heavenly immortality. Since, however, this mystery of Christ's secret union with the devout is by nature incomprehensible, he shows its figure and image in visible signs best adapted to our small capacity. Indeed by giving guarantees and tokens he makes it as certain for us as if we had seen it with our own eyes. For this very familiar comparison penetrates into even the dullest minds: just as bread and wine sustain physical life, so are souls fed by Christ.[260]

In the Lord's Supper by faith we embrace Jesus Christ, "not as appearing from afar but as joining himself to us that he may be our head, we his members."[261] Christ is "a rich and inexhaustible foun-

258. Calvin, *Institutes of the Christian Religion*, 2:1402–03.
259. Calvin, *Institutes of the Christian Religion*, 2:1392.
260. Calvin, *Institutes of the Christian Religion*, 2:1360–61.
261. Calvin, *Institutes of the Christian Religion*, 2:1366.

tain that pours into us the life springing forth from the Godhead into itself [John 5:26]."[262]

> Even though it seems unbelievable that Christ's flesh, separated from us by such great distance, penetrates to us, so that it becomes our food, let us remember how far the secret power of the Holy Spirit towers above all our senses, and how foolish it is to wish to measure his immeasurableness by our measure. What, then, our mind does not comprehend, let faith conceive: that the Spirit truly unites things separated in space.[263]

> Now, that sacred partaking of his flesh and blood, by which Christ pours His life into us, as if it penetrated into our bones and marrow, he also testifies and seals in the Supper—not by presenting a vain and empty sign, but by manifesting there the effectiveness of his Spirit to fulfill what he promises. And truly he offers and shows the reality there signified to all who sit at that spiritual banquet, although it is received with benefit by believers alone, who accept such great generosity with true faith and gratefulness of heart.[264]

The Biblical basis for saying this is 1 Corinthians 10:16: "Is not the cup of blessing which we bless a sharing in the blood of Christ? Is not the bread which we break a sharing in the body of Christ?" Therefore we know that

> by the showing of the symbol the thing [symbolized] itself is also shown. For unless a man means to call God a deceiver, he would never dare assert that an empty symbol is set forth by him. Therefore, if the Lord truly represents the participation in his body through the breaking of bread, there ought

262. Calvin, *Institutes of the Christian Religion*, 2:1369.

263. These sentences express "Calvin's sense of the mystery of the sacramental participation in Christ's body through the activity of the Holy Spirit, despite distance... and separation,... a thing incredible until we realize the transcendent hidden power... of the Holy Spirit" (footnote by editor in *Institutes of the Christian Religion*, 2:1370).

264. Calvin, *Institutes of the Christian Religion*, 2:1370.

> not to be the least doubt that he truly presents and shows his body. And the godly ought by all means to keep this rule: whenever they see symbols appointed by the Lord, to think and be persuaded that the truth of the thing signified is surely present there. For why should the Lord put in your hand the symbol of his body, except to assure you of a true participation in it? But if it is true that a visible sign is given us to seal the gift of a thing invisible, when we have received the symbol of the body, let us no less surely trust that the body itself is also given to us.[265]

The Role of Faith in the Lord's Supper

> For he who eats and drinks, eats and drinks judgment to himself, if he does not judge the body rightly (1 Cor. 11:29).

There are no Roman Catholic doctrines of transubstantiation or *ex opere operato* in the Biblical doctrine of the Lord's Supper. The bread remains bread, although holy bread; and the wine remains wine, although holy wine. The blessings of the Supper are not operative in the recipient merely because he receives the bread and wine, but because he comes to the Table with faith. *The blessings offered and given at the Lord's Table by the Holy Spirit are always and only received by faith in Christ.* "The Flesh and Blood of Christ, or Christ Himself, cannot be perceived, except by the eye of faith, or be received, except by the mouth of faith; nor He be laid hold of, except by the hand of faith."[266] If a person has true faith, however small or weak, he gets some hold on Christ; but if he is without faith, however clear his understanding of the sacrament, it is impossible for him to get any hold of Christ, because *Christ is received by faith alone.* As Augustine said, *A person cannot carry away from this sacrament more than he can collect in the vessel of faith.* John 6:51–58 makes unmistakably clear that "eating" Christ is believing in Christ and being nourished upon Him by faith.

---

265. Calvin, *Institutes of the Christian Religion*, 2:1371.
266. Bruce, *The Mystery of the Lord's Supper*, 97.

Therefore, to benefit from the Lord's Supper, we must bring to the Table TWO MOUTHS: the mouth of the physical body by which we receive the visible signs, and the mouth of the soul, which is faith in Christ, by which we receive Christ and His blessings.

What must faith do in the Lord's Supper, if the believer is to commune with Christ as he eats the bread and drinks the wine?

FIRST, faith must rest on the finished work of Jesus Christ and glory in the exalted Person of Jesus Christ, who is present by His Spirit to bless him as he partakes.

SECOND, faith must "remember the Lord's death" and "discern the Lord's body" in the holy meal. He must meditate on the person and work of Christ for him.

THIRD, faith moves us to prayer during the Lord's Supper. In our prayers we are full of gratitude and praise to God. We confess our sins discovered during our self-examination prior to coming to the Table, asking God to take them from us and to replace them with the fruit of the Spirit, which are the virtues of the humanity of Christ. We supplicate God to meet with us at the Table. And we intercede for one another around the Holy Table.

FOURTH, faith comes to the Table with an "ardent love for Him who first loved us; with deep contrition for our sins; with holy joy in God and with the warmest gratitude to Christ, believing that Christ is mine and I am his forever." In the Lord's Supper, Christ offers Himself and all His benefits to us, and we receive Him by faith.

> Therefore, the Sacrament does not cause Christ to begin to be the bread of life; but when it reminds us that he was made the bread of life, which we continually eat, and which gives us a relish and savor of that bread, it causes us to feel the power of that bread. For it assures us that all that Christ did or suffered was done to quicken us; and again, that this quickening is eternal, we being ceaselessly nourished, sustained, and preserved throughout life by it.[267]

---

267. Calvin, *Institutes of the Christian Religion*, 2:1364.

"By faith we embrace Christ not as appearing from afar, but as joining himself to us that he may be our head, we his members."[268]

The Administration of the Lord's Supper

Q. 169: How hath Christ appointed bread and wine to be given and received in the sacrament of the Lord's supper?

A.: Christ hath appointed the ministers of his word, in the administration of this sacrament of the Lord's supper, to set apart the bread and wine from common use, by the word of institution, thanksgiving, and prayer; to take and break the bread, and to give both the bread and the wine to the communicants; who are, by the same appointment, to take and eat the bread, and to drink the wine, in thankful remembrance that the body of Christ was broken and given, and his blood shed, for them.

The Administration of the Lord's Supper by Minister Only

We have already sufficiently proven this point from the convincing arguments of George Gillespie.

During the Old Testament period, the worship services at the Temple,

> being significant signs of Christ and the benefits of the covenant of grace, were to be administered by none but those who were qualified, called, and lawfully set apart to the work; as the apostle says, 'No man taketh this honor unto himself, but he that is called of God, as was Aaron' (Heb. 5:4). And we

268. Calvin, *Institutes of the Christian Religion,* 2:1366.

may conclude that the moral reason of the thing extends itself to the administration of the seals of the covenant under the gospel-dispensation. It is certain that some must be appointed or set apart to the work of dispensing the ordinance, otherwise it would belong to everybody, and there would be no determinate administrators of these ordinances, who might be said to have a special call to this work from God and man. The point may be inferred also from those scriptures which speak of 'pastors after God's own heart,' who are to 'feed' His people 'with knowledge and understanding,' as being his special 'gift,' [Jer. 3:15]; and from what the apostle says concerning gospel–ministers, whether extraordinary or ordinary, that they were Christ's 'gift' when He 'ascended up on high' [Eph. 4:8, 11].[269]

The Method of Administering the Lord's Supper

"The Last Supper" of The First Lord's Supper

And while they were eating, Jesus took some bread, and after a blessing, He broke it and gave it to the disciples, and said, "Take, eat; this is My body." And He took a cup and gave thanks, and gave it to them, saying, "Drink from it, all of you; for this is My blood of the covenant, which is to be shed on behalf of many for forgiveness of sins. But I say to you, I will not drink of this fruit of the vine from now on until that day when I drink it new with you in My Father's kingdom." And after singing a hymn, they went out to the Mount of Olives (Matt. 26:26–30).

And when the hour had come He reclined at table, and the apostles with Him.... And having taken a cup, when He had given thanks, He said, "Take this and share it among yourselves." And having taken some bread, when He had given thanks, He broke it, and gave it to them, saying, "This is My

269. Ridgeley, *Commentary on the Larger Catechism*, 2:551.

> body which is given for you; do this in remembrance of Me." And in the same way He took the cup after they had eaten, saying, "This cup which is poured out for you is the new covenant in My blood" (Luke 22:14–20). (See also 1 Cor. 11:23–26.)

The Administration of the Lord's Supper According to the Westminster Standards

The simplicity of the administration of the supper should be noted. Our Standards shave off all rituals and rites in the Lord's Supper not commanded by the Word of God. FIRST, the minister reads from the Biblical texts on the institution of the Lord's Supper to the congregation, to pray, and bless[270] the elements of bread and wine, thereby setting them apart from a common to a holy use (Matt. 26:26; 1 Cor. 10:16). SECOND, the minister takes and breaks the bread[271] (Acts 2:42; 20:7), intimating that

> the broken bread is a figure of his body as wounded, bruised, and crucified, to make atonement for our sins. As an unbroken Christ could not profit sinners, so unbroken bread cannot fully represent to faith the food of the soul. Wherefore, to divide the bread into small pieces called wafers, and put a wafer into the mouth of each of the communicants, as is

270. In blessing the elements they are consecrated to a holy use as sacraments. Roman Catholicism teaches that with the consecration of the elements, there is a total change of the substance of the bread and wine into the literal body and blood of Christ. "But the only change which Protestants admit in a consecration of the elements is the simple change of their use, from a common, to a sacred and sacramental one. And this consecration we believe to be wrought, *not* by pronouncing the words, 'This is My body', but by the eucharistic act of worship which introduces the sacrament [*i.e.*, the blessing]" (Dabney, *Lectures in Systematic Theology*, 802).

271. "The breaking of the bread is plainly one of the sacramental acts, and should never be done beforehand, by others, nor omitted by the minister.... Further, Christ brake the bread in distributing it; and commanded us to imitate Him saying: 'This do.'... The Apostles undoubtedly made the breaking one of the sacramental acts; for Paul says, 1 Cor. 10:16, 'The bread which we break.'... Last, when the sacrament itself is more often called, 'the breaking of bread', than any other one name, it can hardly be supposed that the breaking is not a proper part of the ceremonial" (Dabney, *Lectures in Systematic Theology*, 802).

> done in the Church of Rome, is grossly to corrupt this ordinance, for it takes away the significant action of breaking the bread.[272]

THIRD, the minister is to take the cup of wine, and give both the bread and the wine to the communicants, because the command to drink the wine is as explicit as the command to eat the bread (Matt. 26:26, 27).

Robert L. Dabney thinks that

> there is also a significancy in the taking of the wine after the bread, in a distinct act of reception, because it is the blood as separated from the body by death, that we commemorate. Hence the soaking of the bread in the cup is improper, as well as the plea by which Rome justifies communion in one kind; that as the blood is in the body, the bread conveys alone a complete sacrament. As we should commemorate it, the blood is not in the body, but poured out.[273]

The Administration of the Lord's Supper in Calvin's Geneva

> First, then, it should begin with public prayers. After this a sermon should be given. Then, when bread and wine have been placed on the Table, the minister should repeat the words of institution of the Supper. Next, he should recite the promises which were left to us in it; at the same time, he should excommunicate all who are debarred from it by the Lord's prohibition. Afterward, he should pray that the Lord, with the kindness wherewith he has bestowed this sacred food upon us, also teach and form us to receive it with faith and thankfulness of heart, and, inasmuch as we are not so of ourselves, by His mercy make us worthy of such a feast. But here either psalms should be sung, or something be read, and in becoming order the believers should partake of the most

272. Shaw, *The Reformed Faith*, 300.
273. Dabney, *Lectures in Systematic Theology*, 803.

holy banquet, the ministers breaking the bread and giving the cup. When the Supper is finished, there should be an exhortation to sincere faith and confession of faith, to love and behavior worthy of Christians. At the last, thanks should be given, and praises sung to God. When these things are ended, the church should be dismissed in peace.[274]

The Celebration of the Lord's Supper According to the Westminster Directory for the Publick Worship of God

The communion, or supper of the Lord, is frequently to be celebrated; but how often, may be considered and determined by the ministers, and other church-governors [elders] of each congregation, as they shall find most convenient for the comfort and edification of the people committed to their charge. And, when it shall be administered, we judge it convenient to be done after the morning sermon.

The ignorant and the scandalous are not fit to receive the sacrament of the Lord's Supper.

Where this sacrament cannot with convenience be frequently administered, it is requisite that publick warning be given the sabbath-day before the administration thereof: and that either then, or on some day of that week, something concerning that ordinance, and the due preparation thereunto, and participation thereof, be taught; that, by the diligent use of all means sanctified of God to that end, both in publick and private, all may come better prepared to that heavenly feast.

When the day is come for administration, the minister, having ended his sermon and prayer, shall make a short exhortation:

Expressing the inestimable benefit we have by this sacrament, together with the ends and use thereof: setting forth the great necessity of having our comforts and strength renewed thereby in this our pilgrimage and warfare: how nec-

274. Calvin, *Institutes of the Christian Religion*, 2:1421–22.

essary it is that we come unto it with knowledge, faith, repentance, love, and with hungering and thirsting souls after Christ and His benefits: how great the danger to eat and drink unworthily.

Next, he is, in the name of Christ, on the one part, to warn all such as are ignorant, scandalous, profane, or that live in any sin or offence against their knowledge or conscience, that they presume not to come to that holy table; shewing them, that he that eateth and drinketh unworthily, eateth and drinketh judgment unto himself: and, on the other part, he is in an especial manner to invite and encourage all that labour under the sense of the burden of their sins, and fear of wrath, and desire to reach out unto a greater progress in grace than yet they can attain unto, to come to the Lord's table; assuring them, in the same name, of ease, refreshing, and strength to their weak and wearied souls.

After this exhortation, warning, and invitation, *the table* being before decently covered, and so conveniently placed, *that the communicants may orderly sit about it,* or at it, the minister is to begin the action with sanctifying and blessing the elements of bread and wine set before him, (the bread in comely and convenient vessels, so prepared, that, being broken by him, and given, it may be distributed amongst the communicants; *the wine also in large cups,*) having first, in a few words, shewed that those elements, otherwise common, are now set apart and sanctified to this holy use, by the word of institution and prayer.

Let the words of institution be read out of the Evangelists, or out of the first Epistle of the Apostle Paul to the Corinthians, Chap. xi. 23. *I have received of the Lord &c.* to the 27th Verse, which the minister may, when he seeth requisite, explain and apply.

Let the prayer, thanksgiving, or blessing of the bread and wine, be to this effect:

"With humble and hearty acknowledgment of the greatness of our misery, from which neither man nor angel was able to deliver us, and of our great unworthiness of the least of all God's mercies; to give thanks to God for all his benefits, and especially for that great benefit of our redemption, the love of God the Father, the sufferings and merits of the Lord Jesus Christ the Son of God, by which we are delivered; and for all means of grace, the word and sacraments; and for this sacrament in particular, by which Christ, and all his benefits, are applied and sealed up unto us, which, notwithstanding the denial of them unto others, are in great mercy continued unto us, after so much and long abuse of them all.

"To profess that there is no other name under heaven by which we can be saved, but the name of Jesus Christ, by whom alone we receive liberty and life, have access to the throne of grace, are admitted to eat and drink at his own table, and are sealed up by his Spirit to an assurance of happiness and everlasting life.

"Earnestly to pray to God, the Father of all mercies, and God of all consolation, to vouchsafe his gracious presence, and the effectual working of his Spirit in us; and so to sanctify these elements both of bread and wine, and to bless his own ordinance, that we may receive by faith the body and blood of Jesus Christ, crucified for us, and so to feed upon him, that he may be one with us, and we one with him; that he may live in us, and we in him, and to him who hath loved us, and given himself for us."

All which he is to endeavour to perform with suitable affections, answerable to such an holy action, and to stir up the like in the people.

The elements being now sanctified by the word and prayer, the minister, being at the table, is to take the bread in his hand, and say, in these expressions, (or other the like, used by Christ or his apostle upon this occasion):

> "According to the holy institution, command, and example of our blessed Saviour Jesus Christ, I take this bread, and, having given thanks, break it and give it unto you; (there the minister, who is also himself to communicate, is to break the bread, and give it to the communicants); *Take ye, eat ye; this is the body of Christ which is broken for you: do this in remembrance of him.*"

In like manner the minister is to take the cup, and say, in these expressions, (or other the like, used by Christ or the apostle upon the same occasion):

> "According to the institution, command, and example of our Lord Jesus Christ, I take this cup, and give it unto you; (here he giveth it to the communicants): *This cup is the new testament in the blood of Christ, which is shed for the remission of the sins of many: drink ye all of it.*"

After all have communicated, the minister may, in a few words, put them in mind,

> "Of the grace of God in Jesus Christ, held forth in this sacrament; and exhort them to walk worthy of it."

The minister is to give solemn thanks to God,

> "For his rich mercy, and invaluable goodness, vouchsafed to them in that sacrament; and to entreat for pardon for the defects of the whole service, and for the gracious assistance of his good Spirit, whereby they may be enabled to walk in the strength of that grace, as becometh those who have received so great pledges of salvation."

The collection for the poor is so to be ordered, that no part of the public worship be thereby hindered.

The Content and Significance of the Words of Institution

> Take, eat; this is My body.... Drink from it, all of you; for this is My blood of the covenant, which is to be shed on behalf of many for forgiveness of sins (Matt. 26:26–28). (See also Mark 14:22–25 and 1 Cor. 11:24–26.)

The Roman Catholic Interpretation

Roman Catholicism interprets Jesus' words of institution literally, meaning that this form of bread and wine, being consecrated by the priest, and thereby transubstantiated, is literally, in substance,[275] the physical body and physical blood of Jesus, so that the communicant, in eating the Lord's Supper, chews with teeth, tongue and mouths the literal flesh and blood of Jesus. As the Roman Catholic *Basic Catechism* states:

> The words of consecration... tell us that the Eucharist is the body and blood of Jesus, and that Christ is offered in sacrifice.... Transubstantiation is the changing of the entire substance of bread and wine into Christ's body and blood. This takes place at Mass at the words of Consecration.[276]

275. "According to Rome, when the priest canonically, and with proper intention, pronounces the words in the mass: *Hoc est corpus meum* ['This is My body'], the bread and wine are changed into the very body and blood of the living Christ, including, of course, His soul and divinity; which mediatorial person, the priest does then truly and literally break and offer again, as a proper sacrifice for the sins of the living and the dead; and he and the people eat Him. True, the accidents, or material qualities of bread and wine remain, but in and under them, the substance of bread is gone, and the substance really existing is Christ's person. But in this condition of things, it exists without the customary material attributes of locality, extension and divisibility; for He is none the less in heaven, and in all the 'hosts' all over the world at once; and into however small parts they may be divided, each is a perfect Christ! Hence, to elevate, and carry this host in procession, and to worship it with *Latreia* is perfectly proper. Whether such a batch of absurdities is really believed by any reflecting mind, it is not for us to decide" (Dabney, *Lectures in Systematic Theology*, 804).

276. The Daughters of St. Paul, *Basic Catechism* (Boston, MA: St. Paul Books & Media, [1987] 1993), 89.

Notice the two erroneous and monstrous teachings here: (1) The bread and wine are literally and miraculously transubstantiated into the physical body and blood of Jesus. (2) In the Eucharist "Christ is offered in sacrifice," which is the reason they refer to the table as "the altar." Their *Basic Catechism* adds:

> The Mass or Eucharistic Celebration is: the sacrifice of the cross taking place today on our altars.... Christ renews the sacrifice of the cross in the Mass in an unbloody manner [?] for our sake.... By the sacrifice of Calvary we mean Jesus' death on the cross, for our sins, which is renewed in every Eucharistic Celebration.... The main purposes of the Mass are:... to ask His forgiveness and atone [make up] for sin."[277]

This literalistic interpretation imposed upon Christ's words of institution has been refuted from the Bible time again through the centuries.

> All men agree that the whole Christ is offered us in the Supper. But it is an intolerable blasphemy to declare literally of an ephemeral and corruptible element that it is Christ. Now I ask of them whether these two propositions amount to the same thing: 'Christ is the Son of God' and 'The bread is the body of Christ.' If they should admit that these are different (which they will be compelled unwillingly to grant), let them answer where lies the difference. They will bring forward no other reason, I think, than that bread is called the body in a sacramental sense. For this it follows that Christ's words are not subject to the common rule and ought not to be tested by grammar.[278]

In order for Roman Catholicism to base its doctrine of transubstantiation on the words of institution, it must interpret the verb "is" as meaning "to be transubstantiated," thereby taking refuge

277. The Daughters of St. Paul, *Basic Catechism*, 90–92.
278. Calvin, *Institutes of the Christian Religion*, 2:1384.

> in a more forced and violently distorted gloss. There is therefore no reason why they should pretend to be moved by reverence for words. For it is something unheard of in all nations and languages that the word *est* ["is"] should be taken to mean "to be converted into something else."[279]

> The doctrine of transubstantiation contradicts the analogy of faith. It is incompatible with our Savior's professed attitude and intention, which was then to institute a sacrament. But Rome herself defines a sacrament as an outward sign of an invisible grace. Hence Christ's attitude and intention naturally lead us to regard the elements as only signs.... Transubstantiation would utterly destroy the nature of a sacrament; because, if the symbols are changed into the Christ, there is no sign. It contradicts also the doctrine of Christ's ascension and second advent. For these teach us, that He is at the Father's right hand now, and will only come thence at the final consummation. It contradicts the doctrine of atonement, substituting a loathsome form of sacred (literal) cannibalism, for that faith of the soul, which receives the legal effects of Christ's atoning suffering as its justification.[280]

The doctrine that the Mass or Eucharist includes the repetition or "renewal" of Christ's atoning sacrifice on the "altar," is dishonoring to Christ and a blatant contradiction of the repeated emphasis in the book of Hebrews, which teaches us that Christ, the Mediator of the New Covenant, is not like the Old Testament priests who offered sacrifices repeatedly and daily, because He offered Himself as our atoning sacrifice "once for all when He offered up Himself" (7:27). Christ "entered the holy place once for all, having obtained eternal redemption" (9:12).

> Nor was it that He should offer Himself often, as the high priest enters the holy place year by year with blood not his own. Otherwise, He would have needed to suffer often since

279. Calvin, *Institutes of the Christian Religion*, 2:1383.
280. Dabney, *Lectures in Systematic Theology*, 807.

> the foundation of the world; but now once for all at the consummation He has been manifested to put away sin by the sacrifice (not sacrifices) of Himself.... So Christ, having been offered once for all to bear the sins of many, shall appear a second time" (9:25–28).

"By this will we have been sanctified through the offering of the body of Jesus Christ once for all.... But He, having offered ONE SACRIFICE for sins for all time, sat down at the right hand of God" (10:10–12).

The Reformed Interpretation

> On account of the affinity which the things signified have with their symbols, the name of the thing was given to the symbol—figuratively, indeed—but not without a most fitting analogy.... This expression [*i.e.*, the words of institution], is a metonymy[281], a figure of speech commonly used in Scripture when mysteries are under discussion. For you could not otherwise understand such expressions as "circumcision is a covenant," (Gen. 17:13), "the lamb is the passover," (Ex. 12:11), "the sacrifices of the law are expiations" (Lev. 17:11; Heb. 9:22), and finally, "the rock from which water flowed in the desert" (Exodus 17:16), "was Christ," (1 Cor. 10:4), unless you were to take them as spoken with meanings transferred. Not only is the name transferred from something higher to something lower, but, on the other hand, the name of the visible sign is also given to the thing signified: as when God is said to have appeared to Moses in the bush (Ex. 3:2); the Ark of the Covenant is called God and God's face (Ps. 84:8), and the dove, the Holy Spirit (Matt. 3:16). For though the symbol differs in essence from the thing signified (in that the latter is spiritual and heavenly, while the former is physical and visible) still, because it not only symbolizes the thing that it has

281. Metonymy: A figure of speech in which a person, place, or thing is referred to by something closely associated with it. Referring to a king as 'the crown' is an example of metonymy, as is calling a car 'wheels' (*American Heritage Dictionary*).

> been consecrated to represent as a bare and empty token, but also truly exhibits it, why may its name not rightly belong to the thing? ... Those things ordained by God borrow the names of those things of which they always bear a definite and not misleading signification, and have the reality joined with them. So great, therefore, is their similarity and closeness that transition from one to the other is easy.[282]

> If sacraments... did not have a certain likeness to those things of which they are sacraments, they would not be sacraments at all. Moreover, from this likeness they often also take the names of the things themselves.[283]

For those who insist that "is," in the words of institution, being a copulative verb, does not allow for a figure of speech, are clearly refuted by the statement of Paul that *the church IS Christ.* After comparing the church with the human body, he adds, "So is Christ" (1 Cor. 12:12). He is not referring to the only-begotten Son of God in Himself but in the members of His body, the church.

Figurative statements are frequent in the Bible (Gen. 41:26, 27; Ezek. 37:11; Dan. 7:24; Ex. 12:11; Matt. 13:38, 39; Rev. 1:20; 17:9, 12, 18). Jesus Himself said of Himself, "I am the way, the truth and the life" (John 14:6), or "I am the vine" (John 15:1), or "I am the door" (John 10:9). And it is obvious that Jesus meant His words of institution of the Lord's Supper in this figurative sense. "This" is

> demonstrative of bread, and equivalent to, this bread ("is My body"); because bread is the nearest antecedent, the whole series of the narrative shows it; in the parallel case of the wine, cup is, in one narrative, expressed: and the allusion of Paul, 1 Cor. x:16, "The bread which we break" shows it. So, the "soma", [Greek for body], means evidently the body dead (corpse), as is proved by the expression "broken for you," and by the fact that the blood is separated from it: as well as by current usage of narratives. Now paraphrase the sentence:

282. Calvin, *Institutes of the Christian Religion*, 2:1385–86.
283. Augustine, quoted in Calvin, *Institutes of the Christian Religion*, 2:1386.

> "This bread is My dead body," and any other than a tropical [figurative] sense is impossible. For (a). The predication is self-contradictory; if it is bread, it is not body; if body, it is not bread, subject or predicate is out of joint. (b). The body was not yet dead, by many hours. (c). Incompatibles cannot be predicated of each other. A given substance A. cannot be changed into a substance B. which was pre-existent before the change, because the change must bring B. into existence. Again: all will admit that the proper sense is that in which the disciples comprehended the words as first spoken. It is impossible that they should have understood the bread as truly the body: because they saw the body handling the bread! The body would have been wholly in its own hand! Scripture calls it bread still after it is said, by Papists, to be transubstianted, 1 Cor. x:17.[284]

The Method of Receiving the Lord's Supper

Coming forward to receive the Lord's Supper from the minister, and coming forward and kneeling to receive the Lord's Supper are "hang-overs" of Roman Catholic ritual. It is not commanded of us in the Word of God. It was unknown in the Christian Church for several centuries after the apostolic age. In fact, in the second, third and fourth centuries it was considered unlawful to kneel in worship on the Lord's Day, since kneeling was the posture of solemn fasting and not of the celebration and joy of worship in the presence of the risen Lord. Even the famous Council of Nicea (AD 381) forbade kneeling on the Lord's Day! Coming forward and kneeling to receive the Lord's Supper was not introduced until the doctrine of transubstantiation made its appearance in the Roman Catholic Church.

> It is granted, on all hands, that the posture in which the Lord's Supper was first administered by the Saviour himself was that in which it was customary to receive ordinary meals.... The Evangelist Matthew declares: Now when the

284. Dabney, *Lectures in Systematic Theology*, 805–06.

> evening was come, He *sat down* with the twelve. And as they were eating, Jesus took bread and blessed it, and brake it, and gave it to His disciples.[285]

"The Directory for Publick Worship" of the Westminster Assembly states: "After this exhortation, warning, and invitation, the table being before decently covered, and so conveniently placed, that the communicants may ORDERLY SIT ABOUT IT, OR AT IT."

> The essential nature of the Eucharist renders the attendance upon it in a kneeling posture incongruous, and, of course, unsuitable. This ordinance is a feast, a feast of love, joy and thanksgiving. The very name, Eucharist, implies as much. It is intended to be a sign of love, confidence and affectionate fellowship between each communicant and the Master of the feast, and between all the members of His Body. It is also intended to be an emblem, and a means of that spiritual nourishment which is found in feeding by faith, and, in a spiritual sense, on the body and blood of the Redeemer, set forth in this ordinance as crucified for us.[286]

The Westminster Assembly had an extended debate as to whether people should come to the table or whether the elements could be taken from the table to where they were seated. It was finally decided that they could "sit about it, or at it," which allowed either....

However, in its Act "for the Establishing and putting in Execution of the Directory for the Publick Worship of God," the General Assembly of the Church of Scotland, on February 3, 1645, approved this section of the Directory with the provision "that the clause in the Directory, of the administration of the Lord's Supper, which mentioneth the communicants sitting about the table, or at it, be not interpreted, as if in judgment of this Kirk [Scottish Church] it

285. Samuel Miller, *Presbyterianism: The Truly Primitive and Apostolic Constitution of the Church of Christ* (Philadelphia: Presbyterian Board of Publication, 1835), 86.

286. Miller, *Presbyterianism: The Truly Primitive and Apostolic Constitution of the Church of Christ,* 87.

were indifferent and free for any of the communicants not to come to and receive at the table; or as if we did approve the distributing of the elements by the minister to each communicant, and not by the communicants among themselves."[287]

For a historical study of this subject see Benjamin B. Warfield's article, "The Posture of the Recipients at the Lord's Supper" in *Selected Shorter Writings of Benjamin B. Warfield,* ed. by John E. Meeter, 2 vols. (Nutley, NJ: Presbyterian and Reformed Publishing Co., 1973), 2:351–69.

The Frequency of the Celebration of the Lord's Supper

The Larger Catechism says that the Lord's Supper is to be celebrated "often." John Calvin was of the opinion that "the Lord's Table should have been spread AT LEAST ONCE A WEEK for the assembly of Christians," and that "all, like hungry men, should flock to such a bounteous repast."[288] His reasons for holding this viewpoint were two: (1) According to passages like Acts 2:42, we learn that

> it became the unvarying rule that no meeting of the church should take place without the Word, prayers, partaking of the Supper, and almsgiving. That this was the established order among the Corinthians also, we can safely infer from Paul [cf. 1 Cor. 11:20]. And it remained in use for many centuries after.[289]

(2) The Lord's Supper

> was ordained to be frequently used among all Christians in order that they might frequently return in memory to Christ's Passion, by such remembrance to sustain and strengthen their faith, and urge themselves to sing thanksgiving to God and to proclaim his goodness; finally, by it to

287. Kerry W. Hurst, "The Administration of the Sacraments," *Worship in the Presence of God,* ed. by David Lachman and Frank J. Smith (Greenville, SC: Greenville Seminary Press, 1992), 250–51.

288. Calvin, *Institutes of the Christian Religion,* 2:1424.

289. Calvin, *Institutes of the Christian Religion,* 2:1422.

nourish mutual love, and among themselves give witness to this love, and discern its bond in the unity of Christ's body.[290]

The Elements to be Used in the Lord's Supper

The Bread

> Common leavened bread was used before the time of the Roman Bishop Alexander, who was the first who delighted in unleavened bread. But I see no reason for this, unless to draw the eyes of the common people to wonderment by a new spectacle, rather than to instruct their minds in sound religion.[291]

The Eastern Orthodox Church says that the bread in the Lord's Supper must be leavened, and the Roman Catholic Church says it must be unleavened. The bread used in "the Last Supper," was probably the unleavened bread used in Passover, since "the Last Supper" was celebrated in connection with the Passover.

> But it was not Christ's intention to give ritually a paschal character to the new sacrament; and bread is employed as the material element of nutrition, the one most familiar and universal. Hence, we regard all the disputes as to leaven, and the other *minutiae* made essential by the Romish rubrick...as non-essential.[292]

> Christ used unleavened bread because it was present at the Passover. The early Christians celebrated the Communion at a common meal, with the bread of common life, which was leavened.... The Reformed Church... regards the use of leavened bread, as the food of common life, to be most proper, since bread in the Supper is a symbol of spiritual nourishment.[293]

---

290. Calvin, *Institutes of the Christian Religion*, 2:1422.
291. Calvin, *Institutes of the Christian Religion*, 2:1420–21.
292. Dabney, *Lectures in Systematic Theology*, 801–02.
293. Archibald A. Hodge, *Outlines of Theology* (Grand Rapids, MI: Zonder-

The Wine

There can be no doubt that the first Lord's Supper, (*i.e.*, the Last Supper of Jesus with His apostles) was instituted with wine, and not mere grape juice. This is easily demonstrated exegetically and culturally. When Jesus spoke of "the cup," He had reference to its contents: "the fruit of the vine" (Matt. 26:29; Mark 14:25; Luke 22:18). These terms were functional equivalents for "wine."

> Fruit of the vine, the designation used by Jesus at the institution of the Lord's Supper... is the expression employed by the Jews from time immemorial for the wine partaken of on sacred occasions, as at the passover and on the evening of the Sabbath (Mishna, *Berakoth*, vi.1). The Greeks also used the term as a synonym of wine which was capable of producing intoxication (Herod i. 211, 212).[294]

Calvin makes the point that "when we see wine set forth as a symbol of blood, we must reflect on the benefits which wine imparts to the body, and so realize that the same are spiritually imparted to us by Christ's blood. These benefits are to nourish, refresh, strengthen, and GLADDEN."[295]

The Meaning of "Feeding Upon the Body and Blood of Christ"

Q. 170: How do they that worthily communicate in the Lord's supper feed upon the body and blood of Christ therein?

A.: As the body and blood of Christ are not corporally or carnally present in, with, or under the

---

van Publishing House, [1860] 1976), 633.

294. Davis' Dictionary, quoted in Kenneth Gentry, Jr., *The Christian and Alcoholic Beverages: A Biblical Perspective* (Grand Rapids, MI: Baker Book House, [1986] 1990), 55.

295. Calvin, *Institutes of the Christian Religion*, 2:1363. Emphasis added.

> bread and wine in the Lord's supper, and yet are spiritually present to the faith of the receiver, no less truly and really than the elements themselves are to their outward senses; so they that worthily communicate in the sacrament of the Lord's supper, do therein feed upon the body and blood of Christ, not after a corporal and carnal, but in a spiritual manner; yet truly and really, while by faith they receive and apply unto themselves Christ crucified, and all the benefits of his death.

The Teaching of the Larger Catechism

In what sense do we "eat Christ's body" and "drink Christ's blood," that is, "feed upon the body and blood of Christ," in the Lord's Supper? Our catechism carefully, and Biblically, answers this question by telling us in what sense Christ is present in the Supper, and then by telling us in what sense He is "eaten" in the Supper. FIRST, the body and blood of Christ are not literally or physically ("corporally or carnally"), present "in, with, or under" the bread and wine; rather, they are "spiritually present to the faith of the believer." This is not to say that Christ is only wishfully present, or less present with us because He is not physically present with us; for in the Lord's Supper the body and blood, (*i.e.*, the Son of God incarnate in person), are no less "truly and really" present than the bread and wine themselves (Matt. 26:26). SECOND, Because the physical body of Jesus is at the right hand of God (Heb. 12:2), and mystically present by the Holy Spirit, (*i.e.*, Spiritually), at the Lord's Supper, those who receive the Supper worthily do "feed," *i.e.*, nourish themselves Spiritually, upon "the body and blood of Christ," *i.e.*, Christ in person and the benefits of His broken body and shed blood, not in a literal and physical sense, but "in a Spiritual manner; YET TRULY AND REALLY" (1 Cor. 11:24–29), as they, *by faith*, receive and apply to themselves Christ and all the benefits of His death: "The cup of blessing which we bless, is it not the communion of the blood of Christ? The bread which we break, is it not the communion of the body of Christ?"

What we are to understand by feeding upon Christ in the Lord's Supper is this:

> our graces [*i.e.*, the gifts and fruit of the Spirit], being farther strengthened and established, our being enabled to exercise them with great vigour and delight, and our deriving these blessings from Christ, particularly as founded on his death. Our being said to feed upon him, in particular, denotes the application of what he has done and suffered, to ourselves; and, in order to this, we are to bring our sins, with all the guilt which attends them, as it were, to the foot of the cross of Christ, confess and humble our souls for them before him, and by faith plead the virtue of his death, in order to our obtaining forgiveness, and, at the same time, renew our dedication to him, while hoping and praying for the blessings and privileges of the covenant of grace which were purchased by him.[296]

The point is this: *we really and truly receive Christ and the benefits of His death in the Lord's Supper, and we really and truly are nourished upon Him by the Holy Spirit through faith and not physically or literally. The living Christ is present at His Table by His Spirit to bless and to keep saving the people He loves and for whom He laid down His life. We meet Him at the Table and enjoy intimate communion with Him there through faith.* TO EAT CHRIST IS TO BELIEVE IN CHRIST AND TO RECEIVE HIM AS HE OFFERS HIMSELF TO US.

The Feeding Upon the Whole Christ: Human and Divine

The Lord's Supper takes us by the hand and leads us to Jesus Christ.

> "The sacraments direct our faith to the whole, not to a part of Christ." Union with Christ... means a participation in the whole Christ. It means union with His human nature as well as His divine nature. "He is both God and man in us," says Calvin, "for, in the first place, He makes us alive by the power

296. Ridgeley, *Commentary on the Larger Catechism*, 2:524.

> of His Holy Spirit: then He is man within us, for He makes us participate in the sacrifice He offered for our salvation, and declares to us that it is not without cause that He has appointed His flesh to be our food indeed, and His blood our drink indeed." The communion which we have with Christ in the Lord's Supper is thus communion with the whole Christ in both His natures—divine and human.... "Two things are to be sought for in Christ, that we may find salvation in Him: His divinity and His humanity. His divinity contains in itself His power, righteousness and life which are communicated to us by His humanity." Thus everything we need for our sanctification and righteousness is to be found near to us, in our own nature, in the humanity of the Son of God, "in our own flesh." Where the humanity of Christ is, there is the divinity; but apart from the humanity we cannot communicate with the divinity. *What is therefore effected in the Lord's Supper is communion with the whole Christ with all His gifts so that He becomes wholly ours, and we are pledged as wholly His....* The whole Christ is *really given* in the sacrament.... Since the gift in the sacrament is the whole Christ, there is given along with Him those benefits that He has won for His people through His death and resurrection. Thus through our participation in the body of Christ through the Supper there flows to us righteousness, forgiveness, sanctification, indeed all the blessings that are the fruit of His death.[297]

"But by His doing you are in Christ who became to us wisdom from God, and righteousness and sanctification and redemption" (1 Cor. 1:30).

The Mystery of the Presence of Christ in the Lord's Supper

The mystery of the presence of Christ in the Lord's Supper and of our "feeding" upon Him by faith will never be fully comprehended by our minds.

297. Wallace, *Calvin's Doctrine of the Word and Sacrament,* 200–01.

> I therefore freely admit that no man should measure its sublimity by the little measure of my childishness. Rather, I urge my readers not to confine their mental interest within these too narrow limits, but to strive to rise much higher than I can lead them. For, whenever this matter is discussed, when I have tried to say all, I feel that I have as yet said little in proportion to its worth. And although my mind can think beyond what my tongue can utter, yet even my mind is conquered and overwhelmed by the greatness of the thing. Therefore, nothing remains but to break forth in wonder at this mystery, which plainly neither the mind is able to conceive nor the tongue to express.[298]

The Meaning of John 6:48–58

> I am the bread of life. Your fathers ate the manna in the wilderness, and they died. This is the bread which comes down out of heaven, so that one may eat of it and not die. I am the living bread that came down out of heaven; if anyone eats of this bread, he shall live forever; and the bread also which I shall give for the life of the world is My flesh.... Truly, truly I say to you, unless you eat the flesh of the Son of Man and drink His blood, you have no life in yourselves. He who eats My flesh and drinks My blood has eternal life; and I will raise him up on the last day. For My flesh is true food, and My blood is true drink. He who eats My flesh and drinks My blood abides in Me, and I in him. As the living Father sent Me, and I live because of the Father; so he who eats Me, he also shall live because of Me. This is the bread which came down out of heaven; not as the fathers ate, and died; he who eats this bread shall live forever.

Although Jesus may have had these words in mind at the Last Supper, when He instituted the Lord's Supper, Jesus is not referring to the Lord's Supper in John 6, when He first spoke these words, for

298. Calvin, *Institutes of the Christian Religion*, 2:1367.

two simple reasons: (1) that is not the concern of the context as we shall see; and (2) the Lord's Supper was not as yet instituted.

The Bread We are to Eat

After having miraculously fed the five thousand with five loaves and two fish to draw the multitudes to Himself, Jesus exhorts them: "Do not work for the food which perishes, but for the food which endures to eternal life, which the Son of Man shall give to you, for on Him the Father, even God, has set His seal" (John 6:27). This draws from the crowds this response: "What shall we do, that we may work the works of God?" (6:28). And Jesus answers: "This is the work of God, that you BELIEVE IN HIM whom He has sent" (6:29). The crowds then ask Jesus if He is calling them to believe in Him, since they have Moses, who gave manna to their fathers in the wilderness (6:30–31). And Jesus answers: "Truly, truly, I say to you it is not Moses who has given you the bread out of heaven, but it is My Father who gives you the TRUE bread out of heaven. For the bread of God is that which comes down out of heaven, and gives life to the world" (6:32–33). The crowds ask Jesus for this true, life-giving bread from God; and Jesus proclaims to them: "I am the bread of life; he who comes to Me shall not hunger, and he who believes in Me shall never thirst" (6:34–35). Time and again in John 6, Jesus identifies Himself as the bread of life from God (6:35, 41, 48, 51, 58).

The Benefits of Eating This Bread

If we do not eat the Bread of life from God, we will die forever; but if we eat that Bread we will live forever. This is the great, central truth Jesus is bringing out in this discourse in John 6. Those who receive Christ as the Bread of Life from God, will be given Life in the fullest sense of the word, since He is the Bread "of Life." The genitive "of Life" denotes that Christ is living, that He is the source of life, and that He is life itself. The life He gives to those who receive Him is "eternal life." Those who ate the manna of Moses died; but those who eat the Bread of life do not die. Furthermore, the person who has this eternal life will never be hungry or thirsty again for anything other than this Living Bread, because the bread which Jesus gives and which is Jesus Christ Himself is completely satisfying.

> When our soul's deep need has been satisfied we are delivered forever from the emptiness and dissatisfaction that are an inevitable part of the life of the worldly.... As Augustine put it in his prayer: "Thou hast made us for Thyself and our hearts are restless till they rest in Thee." It is in this sense that our need is met in Christ. We still long for more and more knowledge of him. But the world's restlessness has gone forever.[299]

The Nature of Eating This Bread

The Necessity of Eating Jesus' Flesh and Drinking Jesus' Blood to Receive Eternal Life

The Bread of Life and all its benefits is received by those who eat Jesus' flesh and drink Jesus' blood, because "unless you eat the flesh of the Son of Man and drink His blood, you have no life in yourselves" (6:53). Because Jesus' "flesh" is "true food" and His "blood" is "true drink," He said that "He who eats My flesh and drinks My blood has eternal life; and I will raise him up on the last day" (6:54–55). "He who eats My flesh and drinks My blood abides in Me, and I in Him" (6:56). In this powerful metaphorical language we are made to see that if we receive Christ into our lives by faith as the Gift of God and the Giver of life and salvation, we will be satisfied and nourished in Him, we will live forever, and we will enjoy intimate, life-sustaining union and communion with Him, making our home in Him, as He makes His home in us.

---

299. Leon Morris, *Reflections on the Gospel of John*, 2 vols. (Grand Rapids, MI: Baker Book House, [1987] 1989), 2:230.

The Metaphorical Language for Faith in Christ

Obviously Jesus' words are not to be taken literally. He is not teaching us to literally cannibalize His physical flesh and, like vampires, drink His literal blood. The context of these verses clearly teach us that the figure of eating Jesus' flesh and drinking Jesus' blood is to represent receiving Him—*eating is believing.* Jesus begins this discourse by encouraging His hearers not to work for perishable food that does not satisfy the heart nor prevent death, but to work for imperishable food that endures to eternal life, which only He, as the Son of Man, can give (6:27). He gives this imperishable food and eternal life to all those who "believe in Him whom He has sent," *i.e.*, Himself upon whom "the Father, even God, has set His seal" (6:27, 29). In 6:35, Jesus tells us: "I am the bread of life; he who COMES TO ME shall not hunger, and he who BELIEVES IN ME shall never thirst." In 6:37, once again He identifies coming to Him as believing in Him: "All that the Father gives Me shall come to Me." *Saving faith is believing to be true whatever the Bible says about Jesus Christ and coming to Him trusting Him with our hearts to be to us what the Bible says He is in fact.* Believing is called "coming" to Christ, because true faith is the movement of the whole heart and soul toward Christ in trust, dependence and submission.

In 6:40 we are told that "everyone who beholds the Son, and believes in Him, may have eternal life." In 6:45 Jesus says that "everyone who has heard and learned from the Father, comes to Me." In 6:47, He says, "he who *believes* has eternal life." Immediately after this verse, He says again that He is the bread of life (6:48), and in 6:50–51, He declares that "this is the bread which comes down out of heaven, so that one may eat of it and not die. I am the living bread that came down out of heaven; if any one eats of this bread, he shall live forever." Notice the parallel: he who believes in Jesus has eternal life and he who eats the Bread of Life lives forever. It could not be made any plainer—*EATING IS BELIEVING.*

The Flesh of Jesus Given For the Life of the World

In the last part of 6:51, Jesus adds this thought: "the bread also which I shall give for the life of the world is My flesh." In these words He makes His transition from the metaphor of eating bread to the metaphor of eating His flesh and drinking His blood. With these final words in 6:51, Jesus introduces the fact that it is specifically by the giving of His "flesh, for the life of the world," that He gives to those who believe in Him the bread of eternal life and salvation from sin and death. "Flesh" in 6:51 has reference to Jesus' actual human life, His incarnate life. It was His own human life, His body of flesh, that Jesus would give for the life of the world. "For" is *hyper* in Greek, meaning not only "on behalf of," but also "in the place of," as when someone does something in the place of someone else (Philem. 13). John himself often uses this word in this way. He recounts that the Good Shepherd gives His life "for the sheep" (John 10:11, 15). He reports the words of Caiaphas that it is expedient that one man die "in the place of the people" (11:50). He explains that in this way the high priest prophesied that Jesus would die "for the people" (11:51–52). Therefore when Jesus says that "the bread which I shall give for the life of the world is My flesh," we should understand by these words that *Jesus gives eternal life to those who believe in Him by sacrificing His own human life on the cross in the place of sinners.* "When Jesus gives his flesh 'for' the life of the world he is speaking of his death in the place of sinners, that death that would give life to the world."[300]

The Clarification of Jesus about Eating His Flesh and Drinking His Blood

When the Jews heard this it confused them. They argued among themselves whether Jesus was speaking literally about eating His physical body with physical mouths in order to have life (6:52). Therefore, beginning in 6:53 Jesus clarifies exactly what He means about eating and benefiting from the Bread of Life.

The Repeating of Christ's Emphasis in Stronger Form

This comment in 6:51 led Jesus to repeat what He had just said, but in a stronger form. In 6:53 He begins His clarification with the

300. Morris, *Reflections on the Gospel of John*, 2:237.

words, "Truly truly, I say to you." This was His common way of putting emphasis on what follows as something of vital importance. He then goes on to speak, not simply of the giving of His "flesh" or of the eating of the "bread of life," but of eating His flesh and drinking His blood. "This is the sort of thing that would arouse horror in a pious Jew, who would not even eat meat in his daily food unless the blood had been drained from the carcass. But Jesus says that apart from this eating and drinking there is no life. It is a strong and emphatic statement."[301]

The Misapplication of this Text to the Lord's Supper

Although some would see in Jesus' words in 6:53–56 a reference to the Lord's Supper, Jesus makes no reference to the Lord's Supper in this discourse, because, as we have said, the Lord's Supper is not yet instituted. Moreover,

> despite the confident assertions, the language is not that of the Holy Communion. There one reads of eating the body, here of eating the flesh. The difference may not be great but it is real.... We cannot take the use of "flesh" in John 6 as obviously a reference to the communion. It would be a most unusual way of referring to the sacrament, one completely without parallel in the New Testament.... Even more significant is the strength of Jesus' language. He says that without the eating and drinking of which he speaks "you have no life." It is very difficult indeed to think that Jesus is saying that the one thing necessary for eternal life is to receive the Holy Communion. That would be out of harmony with his teaching in all four Gospels. *But here his language is unqualified in any way. He allows of no exception. This is the one way into life.*[302]

---

301. Morris, *Reflections on the Gospel of John,* 2:237.
302. Morris, *Reflections on the Gospel of John,* 2:238. Emphasis added.

The Meaning of Eating Jesus' Flesh and Drinking His Blood

So then, what is Jesus saying in these strong words? In context He can mean only that we are to believe in Him, receive Him by faith, resting upon His substitionary sacrifice in our behalf for the benefits of salvation. After speaking of eating His flesh and drinking His blood in 6:53–57, Jesus goes back to the subject of the bread of life which gives eternal life to all who eat it, as we have seen, by faith in Him (6:58). Since eating the Bread of Life by faith in Christ gives eternal life, and eating Jesus' flesh and drinking His blood gives eternal life (6:54), therefore eating the Bread of Life, which is believing in Christ and coming to Christ, is also described as eating Christ's flesh and drinking Christ's blood.

> Jesus is saying, then, that his death is the one means of salvation and that we appropriate his dying for us when we come to him in faith. That is the one way of salvation, for unless we receive him in this way we "have no life" in us (v. 53). This is a strong and emphatic statement. The cross is at the heart of the Christian way, and it is only by the death of Jesus that we are able to enter into the life he died to bring.[303]

What must we do to live forever at home with God in complete satisfaction? We must receive Jesus Christ as our Lord and Savior, depending solely upon His "flesh," broken in death for us, and His "blood," spilt in our place to redeem us from our sins, for those great benefits of salvation He died to purchase for us: forgiveness of sins, adoption into God's family, righteousness, sanctification by the Holy Spirit, and eternal life in union and communion with the triune God.

Notice Jesus' change of phraseology in 6:57: "As the living Father sent Me, and I live because of the Father; so HE WHO EATS ME, he shall live because of Me." The living Father, who is the living God and the source of all life, sent Jesus Christ to give the world life and salvation by His death through faith in Him.

---

303. Morris, *Reflections on the Gospel of John*, 2:240.

We are alive physically only because the living God gives us physical life, and we are alive spiritually only because the living God gives us spiritual life. That living Father is so interested in giving us spiritual life that He sent His Son into the world to live and to die for us.

Jesus says that he lives "because of the Father." This may be understood in more ways than one. There is the sense that it is the Father who has life in himself and he has given to his Son also to have life in himself (5:26). The life of the Father and the life of the Son are inseparable.... There is also the sense that on earth the incarnate Son lived to do the will of the Father. That is his necessary food (4:34)....

Notice that Jesus speaks now not of eating his flesh and drinking his blood but of eating him, but the difference in meaning is not great. There is still the thought of taking him into our innermost being. When we do that we will enter into the experience of living for Christ in the same kind of way that he lives for the Father. Both aspects will be true for us. We owe our spiritual life to him; it is not something we achieve by our own efforts. And when we have that gift of life we will live to do service to Christ. We will live "because of" him.[304]

The Helpful Comments of Matthew Henry

What is meant by the *flesh and blood of Christ*? It is called (*v.*53), *the flesh of the Son of man, and his blood, his* as Messiah and Mediator: the *flesh and blood* which he *assumed* in his incarnation (Heb. 2:14), and which he *gave up* in his *death and suffering....* So that *the flesh and blood of the Son of Man denote the Redeemer incarnate and dying*: Christ and *him crucified*, and the redemption wrought out by him, with all the precious benefits of redemption: pardon of sin, acceptance with God, the adoption of sons, access to the throne of grace, the promises of the covenant, and eternal life; *these*

304. Morris, *Reflections on the Gospel of John*, 2:241–42.

are called the flesh and blood of Christ, 1. Because they are purchased by his flesh and blood, by the breaking of his body and shedding of his blood.... 2. Because they are meat and drink to our souls... the privileges of the gospel are as flesh and blood to us, prepared for the nourishment of our souls....

What is meant by *eating this flesh and drinking this blood,* which is so necessary and beneficial: it is certain that it means neither more nor less than believing in Christ. As we partake of meat and drink by eating and drinking, so we partake of Christ and his benefits by faith: *and believing in Christ includes these four things, which eating and drinking do:—First,* it implies an *appetite* to Christ. This spiritual eating and drinking begins with *hungering* and *thirsting* (Matt. 5:6), earnest and importunate desires after Christ.... *Secondly,* An *application* of Christ to ourselves. *Meat looked upon will not nourish us, but meat fed upon, and so made our own and as it were one with us.* We must so accept of Christ as to appropriate him to ourselves.... *Thirdly,* A *delight* in Christ and his salvation. The doctrine of Christ crucified must be *meat and drink* to us, most pleasant and delightful.

We must feast upon the dainties of the *New Testament in the blood of Christ.... Fourthly,* A *derivation of nourishment* from him and a dependence upon him for the support and comfort of our spiritual life, and the strength, growth and vigor of the new man. To *feed upon Christ* is to do all *in his name,* in union with him, and by virtue drawn from him; it is to live upon him as we do upon our meat. How our bodies are nourished by our food we cannot describe, but that they are so we know and find; so it is with this spiritual nourishment.[305]

305. Matthew Henry, *Matthew Henry's Commentary on the Whole Bible,* 6 vols. (Peabody, MA: Hendrickson Publishers, [1991] 1992), 5:770. Emphasis added.

The Added Interpretation of John Calvin

There are some who define the eating of Christ's flesh and the drinking of his blood as, in one word, nothing but to believe in Christ. But it seems to me that Christ meant to teach something more definite, and more elevated, in that noble discourse in which he commends to us the eating of his flesh (John 6:26f). It is that we are quickened by the true partaking of him; and he has therefore designated this partaking by the words "eating" and "drinking," in order that no one should think that the life that we receive from Him is received by mere knowledge. As it is not the seeing but the eating of bread that suffices to feed the body, so the soul must truly and deeply become partaker of Christ that it may be quickened to spiritual life by his power.

We admit indeed, meanwhile, that this is no other eating than that of faith, as no other can be imagined. But here is the difference between my words and theirs: for them to eat is only to believe; I say that we eat Christ's flesh in believing, because it is made ours by faith, and that this eating is the result and effect of faith. Or if you want it said more clearly, for them eating is faith; for me it seems rather to follow from faith.... For even though the apostle teaches that "Christ dwells in our hearts through faith" (Eph. 3:17), no one will interpret this indwelling to be faith, but all feel that he is there expressing a remarkable effect of faith, for through this believers gain Christ abiding in them. In this way the Lord intended, by calling himself the "bread of life" (John 6:51), to teach not only that salvation for us rests on faith in His death and resurrection, but also that, *by true partaking of Him, His life passes into us and is made ours—just as bread when taken as food imparts vigor to the body.*[306]

306. Calvin, *Institutes of the Christian Religion*, 2:1365.

The Preparation for Receiving the Lord's Supper

Q. 171: How are they that receive the sacraments of the Lord's supper to prepare themselves before they come unto it?

A.: They that receive the sacrament of the Lord's supper are, before they come, to prepare themselves thereunto, by examining themselves of their being in Christ, of their sins and wants; of the truth and measure of their knowledge, faith, repentance; love to God and the brethren, charity to all men, forgiving those that have done them wrong; of their desires after Christ, and of their new obedience; and by renewing the exercise of these graces, by serious meditation, and fervent prayer.

> No man can hear the Word of God fruitfully without in some measure preparing his soul, and preparing the ear of his heart to hear, but preparation is always just as necessary for the receiving of the visible Sacrament as for the hearing of the simple Word.... Since we go to the Table of the King of heaven, it becomes us to put on our best apparel.[307]

It is for this reason that the Apostle Paul writes:

> Therefore whoever eats the bread or drinks the cup of the Lord in an unworthy manner, shall be guilty of the body and the blood of the Lord. But let a man examine himself, and so let him eat of the bread and drink of the cup. For he who eats and drinks, eats and drinks judgment to himself, if he does not judge the body rightly. For this reason many among you are weak and sick, and a number sleep. But if we judged ourselves rightly, we should not be judged. But when we are

---

307. Bruce, *The Mystery of the Lord's Supper*, 139.

judged, we are disciplined by the Lord in order that we may not be condemned along with the world (1 Cor. 11:27–32).

The Difference Between Worthy Eating and Unworthy Eating

Because the Lord's Supper is a proclamation of the death of the Lord Jesus Christ, it is not an ordinary meal, and it must not be treated as such. Those who sit at the Lord's Table must do so in a reverent manner, participating in this holy meal for the purpose for which it was instituted, and having adequately prepared themselves beforehand by self-examination, rededication of themselves to God, serious meditation on the meaning of the Supper, with fervent prayer for God's blessing in the Supper. This is what is meant by "worthy eating." Notice Paul does not speak of the worthy eater, for no one is worthy to come to this Table, but of "worthy eating," *i.e.*, preparing oneself adequately to take the meal in a right attitude. Eating with a consciousness of our own unworthiness is not unworthy eating; it is worthy eating. "Unworthy eating" is participation in the Lord's Supper in a careless, irreverent manner, without any intention or desire to commemorate the death of Christ, to commune with Christ, to receive the benefits of His redemption, or to rededication ourselves to more consistent service to Him. "Unworthy eating" is not timid and doubtful eating, it is careless and profane eating.

> We see that this sacred bread of the Lord's Supper is *spiritual food, as sweet and delicate as it is healthful for pious worshipers of God*, who, in tasting it, feel that Christ is their life, whom it moves to thanksgiving, for whom it is an exhortation to mutual love among themselves. On the other hand, *it is turned into a deadly poison for all those whose faith it does not nourish and strengthen*, and whom it does not arouse to thanksgiving and to love.... Men of this sort who, without any spark of faith, without any zeal of love, *rush like swine to take the Lord's Supper do not discern the Lord's body.*[308]

308. Calvin, *Institutes of the Christian Religion*, 2:1417.

The Meaning of Being "Guilty of the Body and Blood of the Lord"

When someone eats the Lord's Supper in an unworthy and unprepared manner, he is "guilty of the body and blood of the Lord." Because he treats the signs and seals of Christ's body and blood in an irreverent manner, he is guilty of irreverence toward Christ Himself. To "profane" the meal that was meant to proclaim the Lord's death, is to place oneself "under the same liability as those responsible for the death in the first place. Thus, to be 'guilty of his body and blood' means to be 'liable for his death.'"[309]

But, in the light of all that has been said about the sacraments as signifying, sealing and conveying Christ and His blessings to the believer, how can it be said that unbelievers are guilty of the body and blood of the Lord, if they do not also receive the physical body and blood of Christ in the sacrament, as Roman Catholicism teaches in its doctrines of transubstantiation and '*ex opere operata*'? Answer: by treating these divinely instituted signs and seals, which were given to signify, seal and convey Christ to the believer's heart, with irreverence. "It is not necessary, therefore, in order to the guilt spoken of here, either that the body of Christ should be locally present, or that the unworthy receiver be a partaker of that body, which is received by faith alone."[310, 311] Just as a man who

---

309. Fee, *The First Epistle to the Corinthians*, 561.

310. Consider these quotations of Augustine, explaining that Christ and His blessings offered in the Lord's Supper, are received by the mouth of faith and not by the mouth of the physical body: (1) "I hold that men bear away from this Sacrament no more than they gather with the vessel of faith." (2) "He who does not abide in Christ and in whom Christ does not abide, doubtless does not spiritually eat His flesh or drink His blood, although he may carnally and visibly press the sign of the body and blood with his teeth." (3) "The rest of the disciples ate the bread which was the Lord, but Judas ate the bread of the Lord." (4) The person who 'eats Christ's flesh and drinks Christ's blood' (John 6:54, 55), is "He who received the power of the Sacrament, not only the visible Sacrament; and indeed inwardly, not outwardly; and *who eats with the heart, not who presses with the teeth.*" (5) "Do not prepare your jaws but your heart: for this the Supper is commended. Behold, we believe in Christ when we receive him in faith.... It is not what is seen, then, but what is believed, that feeds" (Calvin, *Institutes of the Christian Religion*, 2:1407, 1409).

311. Hodge, *A Commentary on The First Epistle to the Corinthians*, 230.

tramples the flag of his country, dishonors and insults his country; so, in a similar way, he who treats the sacraments with disrespect, dishonors and insults Christ, trampling under foot the signs and seals of His body and blood.

In the Lord's Supper,

> Christ proffers this spiritual food and gives this spiritual drink to all. Some feed upon them eagerly, others haughtily refuse them. Will the latters' rejection of them cause the food and drink to lose their nature? ... I hold that men bear away from this Sacrament no more than they gather with the vessel of faith. Thus nothing is taken away from the Sacrament; indeed, its truth and effectiveness remain undiminished, although the wicked go away empty after outward participation in it.
>
> If they object again that the word—"This is My body"—loses meaning if the wicked receive corruptible bread and nothing besides, there is a ready reply: God's will is that His truthfulness be acknowledged not in the reception itself, but in the constancy of His goodness, in that *He is ready to give to the unworthy what they reject, indeed, offers it freely.* And this is the wholeness of the Sacrament, which the whole world cannot violate: that the flesh and blood of Christ are no less truly given to the unworthy than to God's elect believers. At the same time, it is true, however, that, *just as rain falling upon a hard rock flows off because no entrance opens into the stone, the wicked by their hardness so repel God's grace that it does not reach them. Besides, to say that Christ may be received without faith is as inappropriate as to say that a seed may germinate in fire.*[312]

312. Calvin, *Institutes of the Christian Religion*, 2:1406–07.

The Way to Avoid Eating and Drinking Judgment to Oneself

Everyone without exception, who participates in the Lord's Supper receives something from the Lord Jesus Christ! If they participate in a worthy manner, they will receive Him and His rich blessings of salvation. If they participate in an unworthy manner, not discerning the Lord's body by faith, they "eat and drink divine judgment" unto themselves. In other words, in the Lord's Supper, the resurrected Christ administers the blessings and curses of His Covenant—blessings to those who have faith, curses to those who come irreverently. By eating and drinking unworthily, that person "incurs the manifestation of God's displeasure by the act of eating."[313] And the only way to avoid this manifestation of God's displeasure is by "examining himself" and "judging" or "discerning the Lord's body rightly," *i.e.*, to value the Lord's Supper properly, receiving it with reverence, and for the purpose for which it was intended: to signify, seal and convey Christ and the benefits of His broken "body" and shed blood to the heart. Those who do "not discern the Lord's body rightly" in the bread and wine, are those who

> do not believe that that body is their life, so far do they dishonor it, robbing it of all its dignity; and finally they profane and pollute it by so receiving it.... Therefore, they are deservedly held guilty of the Lord's body and blood, which they so foully defile with sacrilegious impiety. Hence, by this unworthy eating they bring condemnation upon themselves. For while they have no faith fixed upon Christ, yet, in receiving the Sacrament, they profess that their salvation is nowhere but in him and abjure all other assurance. Therefore, they are their own accusers; they bear witness against themselves and seal their own condemnation.[314]

313. Hodge, *A Commentary on the First Epistle to the Corinthians*, 232.
314. Calvin, *Institutes of the Christian Religion*, 2:1417–18.

The Nature and Purpose of the Discipline of the Lord Upon Those Who Eat Unworthily

In the church at Corinth, because several people were not taking the Lord's Supper in a worthy manner, failing to be at peace with one another, loving one another, and failing to treat the Lord's Supper as a holy meal, 1 Corinthians 11:30 tells us, "many are weak and sick, and a number sleep," *i.e.*, are dead. This shows us how serious and holy the Lord's Supper is to God and how serious we ought to be when we take it. The many sicknesses and the frequent deaths among the Christians at Corinth were a disciplinary judgment from God because they celebrated the Lord's supper in an unworthy manner, *i.e.*, without faith, self-examination, meditation, rededication and prayer. "But if we judged ourselves rightly, we should not be judged" (11:31). "It is because we do not sit in judgment on ourselves, that God judges us."[315]

This "judgment" upon members of the church is the FATHERLY DISCIPLINE of the Lord on His unfaithful children who eat the Lord's Supper unworthily: "But when we are judged, we are disciplined by the Lord in order that we may not be condemned along with the world" (11:32).

> These judgments were chastisements designed for the benefit of those who suffered, to bring them to repentance, that they might not be finally condemned with the world; that is, with unbelievers. The world often means mankind as distinguished from the church, or those chosen out of the world [John 17:16]. What Paul says of the design of these judgments, proves that even the extreme irreverence with which he charges the Corinthians in reference to the Lord's supper, was not an unpardonable sin.[316]

315. Hodge, *A Commentary on the First Epistle to the Corinthians*, 234.
316. Hodge, *A Commentary on the First Epistle to the Corinthians*, 234.

The Preparation for Receiving the Lord's Supper

Self-Examination

"But let a man examine himself, and so let him eat of the bread and drink of the cup" (1 Cor. 11:28). Adequate preparation for the reception of the Lord's Supper, so that we will eat and drink in a worthy manner, and not be guilty of the body and blood of the Lord, involves thorough and honest SELF-EXAMINATION. "This is not a call for deep personal introspection to determine whether one is worthy of the Table,"[317] for none are worthy because of sin. A sense of unworthiness is essential for taking the Lord's Table; and a sense of worthiness means that the eating and drinking is in an unworthy manner. Rather, this call to self-examination stands in contrast to God's "examination" or judgment of those who eat and drink unworthily. The word, "examine," denotes "to put to the test." Elsewhere, Paul calls upon believers to "examine" themselves in relation to their "works" (Gal. 4:6) and "to the faith" (2 Cor. 13:5). Here, in 11:28, he calls upon them to "test" themselves with reference to two things: (1) their attitude toward the Lord's Supper; and (2) their behavior and attitude while taking the Lord's Supper.

> In other words, let him ascertain whether he has correct views of the nature and design of the ordinance, and whether he has the proper state of mind. That is, whether he desires thankfully to commemorate the Lord's death, renewedly to partake of the benefits of that death as a sacrifice for his sins, publicly to accept the covenant of grace with all its promises and obligations, and to signify his fellowship with his brethren as joint members with himself of the body of Christ.[318]

By SELF-EXAMINATION Paul means that each participant

> descend into himself, and ponder with himself whether he rests with inward assurance of heart upon the salvation purchased by Christ; whether he acknowledges it by confession

317. Fee, *The First Epistle to the Corinthians*, 561.
318. Hodge, *A Commentary on the First Epistle to the Corinthians*, 232.

> of mouth; then, whether he aspires to the imitation of Christ with the zeal of innocence and holiness; whether, after Christ's example, he is prepared to give himself for his brethren and to communicate himself to those with whom he shares Christ in common; whether, as he is counted a member by Christ, he in turn so holds all his brethren as members of his body; whether he desires to cherish, protect, and help them as his own members.[319]

Or, as our Larger Catechism says, we are to examine ourselves with reference to: our being in Christ, our sins and needs, the truth and measure of Spiritual graces, and the intensity of our desire for Christ and the consistency and constancy of our new obedience.

"Of Their Being in Christ"

Since a person must first be in union with Christ before he can enjoy communion with Him, it is important that we examine our personal relationship to Jesus Christ. "Test yourselves to see if you are in the faith; examine yourselves! Or do you not recognize this about yourselves, that Jesus Christ is in you—unless indeed you fail the test?" (2 Cor. 13:5) In this verse Paul "appeals to their self knowledge, which of all knowledge is the most intimate and indisputable: if they know Jesus Christ to be in themselves, then they know... that He is in the one [Paul] who proclaimed Jesus Christ to them."[320] (Ridgeley gives some helpful counsel to help us see if we have any reasons in us to think we are truly "in Christ," in *Commentary on the Larger Catechism,* Vol. 2, pg. 528.)

"Of Their Sins and Wants"

To prepare ourselves for taking the Lord's Supper we should examine ourselves to see how sensitive and convicted we are to sin in our lives, whether such awareness humbles us, and whether and

319. Calvin, *Institutes of the Christian Religion,* 2:1417–18.

320. Philip E. Hughes, *New International Commentary on the New Testament: Paul's Second Epistle to the Corinthians* (Grand Rapids, MI: William B. Eerdmans Publishing Co., 1962), 480.

how intensely we desire to be delivered from sin. Furthermore, we should see what it is about ourselves we lack and are in need of to be complete, mature believers in Jesus Christ. "These things we are to examine ourselves concerning, that we may spread our wants [*i.e.*, needs] before the Lord at his Table."[321] "Purge out therefore the old leaven, that you may be a new lump, as you are unleavened. For even Christ our Passover is sacrificed for us" (1 Cor. 5:7).

"Of The Truth and Measure of Their Knowledge, Faith, Repentance, Love to God and the Brethren, Charity to All Men, Forgiving Those that Have Done Them Wrong"

We should examine ourselves regarding the truth, strength, degree and maturity of our faith, along with all the other Spiritual virtues, (*i.e.*, "fruit of the Spirit") which are inseparably connected with true faith, such as: knowledge (1 Cor. 11:29); faith (1 Cor. 13:5, Matt. 26:28); repentance (Zech. 12:10, 1 Cor. 11:31); love to God and the brethren (1 Cor. 10:16, 17; Acts 2:46, 47); charity to all people (1 Cor. 5:8, 1 Cor. 11:18, 20); forgiving those who have done us wrong (Matt. 5:23–24): "Therefore, if you bring your gift to the altar, and there remember that your brother has something against you; leave your gift there before the altar, and go your way; first be reconciled to your brother, and then come and offer your gift." (See Ridgeley's counsel in *Commentary on the Larger Catechism*, Vol. 2, pgs. 531–532.)

"Of Their Desires After Christ, and Of Their New Obedience"

We must ask ourselves whether that which motivates and moves us is our desire for a close relationship with Him, living for His pleasure, glorifying and enjoying Him; or whether we desire only the good things He can give us, with no regard for the Giver, or only that we escape hell when we die? Do we love Him so much that we

321. Ridgeley, *Commentary on the Larger Catechism*, 2:530. (See Ridgeley's counsel in *Commentary on the Larger Catechism*, Vol. 2, pgs. 528–530.)

are willing to suffer reproach and experience the loss of everything for His sake? Can we say with Paul, in Philippians 3:8, 10,

> I count all things to be loss in view of the surpassing value of knowing Christ Jesus my Lord, for whom I have suffered the loss of all things, and count them but rubbish in order that I may gain Christ... that I may know Him, and the power of His resurrection and the fellowship of His sufferings?

Rededication

The Lord's Supper is a covenant meal, a covenanting meal, wherein God reassures us of His faithfulness to His promises to us as our great Sovereign-Friend, and wherein we vow to God to be His faithful servant-friends. It is a time for us to renew our covenant with God and our covenant responsibilities and obligations, as He gives us the strength to do so (Deut. 29:10, 12–13): "You stand today, all of you, before the Lord your God... that you may enter into the covenant with the Lord your God, and into His oath, which the Lord your God is making with you today, in order that He may establish you today as His people and that He may be your God, just as He spoke to you and as He swore to your fathers."

In our renewal of the covenant with God:

> (i). We must repent of our sins, by which we have rendered ourselves unworthy to be taken into covenant.... (ii). We must renounce the devil, the world, and the flesh.... (iii). We must receive Christ as offered to us, consenting to his grace, and to his government. (iv). We must resign, and give up ourselves to God in Christ; devote ourselves to his praise, and submit ourselves to his power.... (v). We must resolve to abide in it.... (vi). We must rely on the righteousness and strength of Christ herein.... And we must renew our covenant intelligently, considerately, humbly, cheerfully, and in sincerity.[322]

322. Henry, *How To Prepare for Communion*, 41.

Serious Meditation

"This is My body, which is for you; do this in remembrance of Me... as often as you drink it, in remembrance of Me" (1 Cor. 11:24, 25). In the Lord's Supper we are to remember Christ—His glorious person, His redemptive work, and His mediatorial offices of prophet, priest and king. We are to focus our hearts, our minds and our faith on Him in serious meditation on His glory and greatness.

Meditation is thought engaged and thought inflamed. It is THOUGHT ENGAGED because the heart is fastened and fixed upon Christ, dwelling on His greatness, considering and adoring all His perfections and works. It is THOUGHT INFLAMED because, to meditate on Christ is not only to think seriously about Him, it is also to think of Him with passion, love, adoration, worship, and all those affections that stir up the soul to worship the living and true God.

Meditation on Christ in the Lord's Supper has several effects on us: (1) It elevates our spirits and expands our minds. (2) It sanctifies us and increases our faith. The spirit of a person takes its character from the themes of his meditation. (3) It blesses us and brings us indescribable pleasure intellectually, emotionally, and spiritually.

As we prepare ourselves for the Lord's Supper by serious meditation:

(i). Let us set ourselves to think of the sinfulness and misery of man's fallen state, that we may be taught to value our recovery and restoration by the grace of the second Adam....

(ii). Let us set ourselves to think of 'the glory of the divine attributes, shining forth in the work of our redemption and salvation.'...

(iii). Let us set ourselves to think of the 'person of the Redeemer, and his glorious undertaking of the work of our salvation.'...

(iv). Let us set ourselves to think of the 'cross of our Lord Jesus Christ, the dishonors done to Him, and the honours done to us by it.'...

(v). Let us set ourselves to think of the present glories of the exalted Redeemer.—When we meditate on the cross he bore, we must not forget the crown he wears within the veil. Think, my soul, think where he is at the right hand of the Father....

(vi). Let us set ourselves to think of the unsearchable riches of the new covenant, made with us in Jesus Christ, and sealed to us in the sacraments....

(vii). Let us set ourselves to think of the communion of the saints.... Enlarge thy thoughts, then, O my soul, and let it be a pleasure to thee to think of the relation thou standest in to the whole family, both in heaven and earth....

(viii). Let us set ourselves to think of the happiness of heaven.... Raise thy thoughts, then, O my soul, to the joyful contemplation of the glory to be revealed.[323]

Fervent Prayer

When we have done our best in preparing for the Lord's Supper, we recognize that we still are too much unprepared for it, and so we cry out to God in fervent prayer, because we know that without His assistance, we can do nothing that is pleasing to Him (John 15:5; 2 Chron. 30:18–19).

> In prayer, the soul ascends to God, and converses with him; and thereby the mind is prepared to receive the visits of his grace, and habituated to holy exercises.... The greatest blessings are promised to the prayer of faith, but God will not give, if we will not ask: why should he?[324]

We must earnestly pray that our preparations and performances will be accepted because of the merits of Christ; that our preparations and performances will be sanctified by the Holy Spirit; that the sacraments will be everything they were intended

323. Henry, *How To Prepare for Communion*, 52–56.
324. Henry, *How To Prepare for Communion*, 57.

to be to us—signs and seals bringing Christ and His covenant blessings to us.

In our prayers we are full of gratitude and praise to God. We confess our sins discovered during our self-examination, asking God to take them from us and to replace them with the fruit of the Spirit, which are the virtues of the humanity of Christ. We supplicate God to meet with us at the Table. And we intercede for one another around the Holy Table.

The Question of the Doubter: Should He Partake?

Q. 172: May one who doubteth of his being in Christ, or of his due preparation, come to the Lord's supper?

A.: One who doubteth of his being in Christ, or of his due preparation to the sacrament of the Lord's supper, may have true interest in Christ, though he be not yet assured thereof; and in God's account hath it, if he be duly affected with the apprehension of the want of it, and unfeignedly desires to be found in Christ, and to depart from iniquity: in which case (because promises are made, and this sacrament is appointed, for the relief even of weak and doubting Christians) he is to bewail his unbelief, and labour to have his doubts resolved; and, so doing, he may and ought to come to the Lord's supper, that he may be further strengthened.

This answer shows the deep pastoral concern the Westminster fathers had for the members of their congregations. They took the Bible's theology seriously, seeking to apply it consistently and faithfully to every individual situation. Here their concern is for the Christian who is experiencing serious doubts regarding his true spiritual condition—should he take the Lord's Supper? Their answer is a wise one. (1) True Christians may have serious doubts about their spiritual standing with God, and still be true Christians (Isa. 50:10; 1 John 5:13; Ps. 88; 77:1–12). (2) Doubting Christians will find evidences that they are truly Christian: (a) they are apprehensive because of their lack of assurance of salvation (Isa. 54:7, 8, 9, 10; Matt. 5:3, 4; Ps. 31:22; 73:13, 22, 23); (b) they sincerely desire to be found in Christ (Phil. 3:8, 9; Ps. 10:17; Psalm 42:1, 2, 5, 11); (c) they sincerely desire to depart from iniquity (2 Tim. 2:19; Isa. 50:10; Psalm 66:18, 19, 20). (3) The sacrament and its promise were appointed for the relief of doubting Christians (Isa. 40:11, 29, 31; Matt. 11:28; Matt. 12:20; 26:28). (4) As the doubting Christian bewails his unbelief (Mark 9:24), and labors to have his doubts resolved (Acts 2:37; Acts 16:30), he may and should partake of the Lord's Supper. (5) The Lord's Supper, taken in faith by the doubting Christian, will strengthen his faith and kill his doubts (Rom. 4:11; 1 Cor. 11:28).

> Though his being duly prepared for the Lord's Supper is a matter of doubt to him, he being destitute of assurance of his being in Christ; yet he may be mistaken in the judgment which he passes concerning himself.... Many have reason to complain of the weakness of their faith, and the great resistance and disturbance which they meet with from the corruption of nature. Others, too, who at present have assurance of their interest in Christ, may afterwards, through divine desertion, lose the comfortable sense of it. Hence, we must not conclude that every doubting believer is destitute of faith. Those are to be tenderly dealt with, and not discouraged from attending on the Lord's Supper.[325]

325. Ridgeley, *Commentary on the Larger Catechism,* 2:535. On pages 535–537, Ridgeley offers good and practical counsel to the doubting Christian.

The Question of the Ignorant or Scandalous: Should They Partake?

Q. 173: May any who profess the faith, and desire to come to the Lord's supper, be kept from it?

A.: Such as are found to be ignorant or scandalous, notwithstanding their profession of faith, and desire to come to the Lord's Supper, may and ought to be kept from that sacrament, by the power which Christ hath left in His church, until they receive instruction, and manifest their reformation.

This answer from our Catechism is concerned with church discipline. Do the elders of the church have the authority from Christ to bar an ignorant or scandalous person from taking the Lord's Supper until he has shown repentance, even though he has made profession of faith and is a member of the church? The Larger Catechism answers, Yes, and gives as its Scriptural support 1 Cor. 11:27–31; Matt. 7:6; 1 Cor. 5; Jude 23; 1 Tim. 5:22; and 2 Cor. 2:7. Those who are "ignorant" are those who are "ignorant of the great doctrines of the gospel, and consequently unacquainted with Christ, whom they never truly applied themselves to, nor received by faith."[326] This would include non-communing members of the church, *i.e.*, the infants and young of the church, who are to be admitted to the Lord's Supper by the elders, upon their credible profession of faith in Christ, after catechetical instruction. The "scandalous" are those who are

> scandalous or immoral in their practice, whatever pretensions they make to the character of Christians. These are described by the apostle as persons who 'profess that they know

326. Ridgeley, *Commentary on the Larger Catechism,* 2:538.

> God, but in works deny him, being abominable, and disobedient, and unto every good work reprobate' [Tit.1:16]. Such ought not to have communion with those whom the apostle describes as 'called to be saints' [Rom. 1:7]. Nor can they partake of this ordinance aright; for they are not apprized of the end and design of it, and they are not able, as the apostle expresses it, to 'discern the Lord's body' [1 Cor. 11:27].[327]

The issue of church discipline is an important one, not only because church discipline was instituted by Jesus Christ for His Church, but because the loving practice of church discipline, along with the faithful preaching of the Word of God, and the faithful administration of the sacraments are the three marks of a true church. Moreover, church discipline is the "keys of the kingdom," which Christ Himself places into the hands of His Church to be used by the ruling officers of the Church, so that "whatever you bind on earth shall have been bound in heaven, and whatever you shall loose on earth shall have been loosed in heaven" (Matt. 16:18–19; 18:15–18; 1 Cor. 5:1–7).

The Westminster Confession of Faith carefully explains the meaning and practice of church discipline in its chapter entitled, "Of Church Censures" (Chapter XXX):

1. The Lord Jesus, as king and head of his church, hath therein appointed a government in the hand of Church-officers, distinct from the civil magistrate [Isa. ix:6, 7; 1 Tim. v:17; 1 Thess. v:17; Acts xx:17; Heb. xiii:7, 17, 24; 1 Cor. xii:28; Matt. xxviii:18–20].
2. To these officers, the keys of the kingdom of heaven are committed by virtue whereof, they have power respectively to retain, and remit sins, to shut that kingdom against the impenitent, both by the word and censures; and to open it unto penitent sinners, by the ministry of the gospel, and by absolution from censures, as occasion shall require [Matt. xvi:19; Matt.xviii:17, 18; John xx:21, 22, 23; 2 Cor. ii:6, 7, 8].

327. Ridgeley, *Commentary on the Larger Catechism*, 2:538

3. Church censures are necessary for the reclaiming and gaining of offending brethren; for deterring of others from the like offences; for purging out of that leaven which might infect the whole lump; for vindicating the honour of Christ, and the holy profession of the gospel; and for preventing the wrath of God, which might justly fall upon the church, if they should suffer his covenant, and the seals thereof, to be profaned by notorious and obstinate offenders [1 Cor. v:1 ff; 1 Tim. v:20; Matt. vii:6; 1 Tim. i:20; 1 Cor. xi:27–34; Jude 23].

4. For the better attaining of these ends, the officers of the church are to proceed by admonition, suspension from the sacrament of the Lord's Supper for a season, and by excommunication from the church, according to the nature of the crime, and demerit of the person [1 Thess. v:12; 2 Thess. iii:6, 14, 15; 1 Cor. v:4, 5, 13; Matt. xviii:17; Tit. iii:10].

The Attitude of Heart and Mind During the Receiving of the Lord's Supper

---

Q. 174: What is required of them that receive the sacrament of the Lord's supper in the time of the administration of it?

A.: It is required of them that receive the sacrament of the Lord's supper, that, during the time of the administration of it, with all holy reverence and attention they wait upon God in that ordinance, diligently observe the sacramental elements and actions, heedfully discern the Lord's body, and affectionately meditate on his death and sufferings, and thereby stir up themselves to a vigorous exercise of their graces; in judging themselves, and sorrowing for sin; in earnest

> hungering and thirsting after Christ, feeding on him by faith, receiving of his fulness, trusting in his merits, rejoicing in his love, giving thanks for his grace; in renewing of their covenant with God, and love to all the saints.

"With All Holy Reverence and Attention They Wait Upon God in That Ordinance"

We are to wait upon God in faith, confidence, submission and patience to bless us in the sacrament

> with an holy reverence arising from a becoming sense of his divine perfections, and the infinite distance we stand at from him; and we are to impress on our souls an awful sense of His omniscience and omnipresence. For he knows better than we do ourselves, with what frame of spirit we draw nigh to him; and highly resents everything which is contrary to his holiness, or unbecoming the character of those who are worshipping at his footstool.[328]

"Wherefore, we receiving a kingdom which cannot be moved, let us have grace, whereby we may serve God acceptably with reverence and godly fear" (Heb. 12:28). "But as for me, I will come into Thy house in the multitude of mercy; and in Thy fear will I worship toward Thy holy temple" (Ps. 5:7).

"Diligently Observe the Sacramental Elements and Actions"

The sacramental elements of bread and wine, and the sacramental actions of the minister in the distribution of the elements, are by Christ's appointment, and are significant and instructive signs of His death and of the benefits purchased for us by it. Therefore, close attention must be paid to every part of the service of Communion. "And Moses took the blood, and sprinkled it on the

---

328. Ridgeley, *Commentary on the Larger Catechism,* 2:541.

people, and said, 'Behold the blood of the covenant, which the Lord hath made with you concerning all these words'" (Ex.24:8). See also Matthew 26:28.

"Heedfully Discern the Lord's Body"

As we have seen, to avoid God's judgment on us in an unworthy eating and drinking of the Lord's Supper, we must "discern the Lord's body rightly" in the Supper (1 Cor. 11:29). To "discern the Lord's body rightly" in the Lord's Supper is to value the Supper properly, receiving it with reverence and for the purpose for which it was intended: to signify, seal and convey Christ and all His benefits to the believer. It is to believe that the Lord's body, that is the Lord Jesus Christ Himself, and all the benefits of His broken body and shed blood, are given to us in the Lord's Table as we come to the Table in faith.

"Affectionately Meditate on His Death and Sufferings"

If we are to receive the Supper "in remembrance" of Christ, as He commanded, then we must "affectionately meditate on His death and sufferings" in our behalf, by which He "obtained eternal redemption" for us.

> We are to consider his condescending love in giving his life a ransom for us; and... the divine excellency and glory of his Person, which adds an infinite value to every part of his obedience and sufferings. We must consider also the kind of death he died... the character of the persons for whom he laid down his life... that he died in our room and stead, 'bearing our griefs and carrying our sorrows'... the great ends designed: that God is glorified and his holiness and justice demanding and receiving a full satisfaction for sin, illustrated in the highest degree... the great advantage which we hope to receive: that 'being justified by His blood, we shall be saved from wrath through Him.'[329]

329. Ridgeley, *Commentary on the Larger Catechism*, 2:542.

"Thereby Stir Up Themselves to a Vigorous Exercise of Their Graces"

As we take the Lord's Supper properly, we will stir up ourselves to a vigorous and zealous and constant performance of those responsibilities and manifestation of those virtues and dispositions, which the nature of this sacrament requires. See 1 Cor. 11:26; 1 Cor. 10:3, 4, 5, 11, 14.

"In Judging Themselves and Sorrowing For Sin"

As we have seen, *if we judge ourselves, sorrowing over our sin and rejoicing in Christ, we will not be judged by God.* "This we ought to do, by accusing, condemning and passing sentence against ourselves, for those sins which we have committed against Christ, whereby we were plunged into the utmost depths of misery, in which we should for ever have continued, had he not redeemed us by his blood."[330] This sorrow for sin is, to use Paul's words, "a godly sorrow that leads to repentance." This self-judgment (1 Cor. 11:31), and sorrowing for sin (Zech. 12:10), should also produce in us

> an holy 'indignation', and a kind of 'revenge' against sin, as that which has been so prejudicial to us; likewise a 'fear' of offending, a 'zeal' for the glory of God, whom we have dishonoured, and 'a vehement desire' of those blessings which we have forfeited. It ought to proceed from an inward loathing and abhorrence of sin.... To feel in this way is very agreeable to the nature of the ordinance we are engaged in, since nothing tends more to enhance the vile and heinous nature of sin, than the consideration of its having crucified the Lord of glory. The fact, too, of Christ having died on account of sin, is to be the immediate subject of our meditation in observing the ordinance.[331]

330. Ridgeley, *Commentary on the Larger Catechism,* 2:542.
331. Ridgeley, *Commentary on the Larger Catechism,* 2:542–43.

"In Earnest Hungering and Thirsting After Christ"

The most ardent desire of the believer's heart is for the enjoying of communion with Jesus Christ. "As the mountain goat pants after the mountain brooks," so the believer's heart pants after Christ. Our hearts are restless until they rest in Him. We can say, "With my soul have I desired Thee in the night; yea, with my spirit will I seek Thee early" (Isa. 26:9). "This desire arises from a deep sense of our need of Christ, and of [additional] supplies of grace from him; and is [accompanied] with a firm resolution that nothing short of him shall satisfy us."[332] See also Rev. 22:17.

"Feeding On Him By Faith"

Jesus is "the bread of life" (John 6:35), "the food that does not perish, but endures to everlasting life" (John 6:27). The table He sets for His disciples is "a feast of fat things, the feast of wines on the lees, of fat things full of marrow, of wines on the lees well-refined" (Isa. 25:6). All we need we find in Him by faith, so that we are complete in Him, Who is our all in all. The Lord Jesus truly is our Shepherd; we have no needs which He does not, of Himself, fill. And so, in the Lord's Supper, which signifies, seals and conveys Christ and His benefits to believers, we feed on Christ, Spiritually, and thus find ourselves Spiritually nourished on and edified by Him. "And Jesus said unto them, I am the bread of life; he that comes to Me shall never hunger; and he that believes on Me shall never thirst" (John 6:35).

"Receiving of His Fulness"

"And of His fulness have all we received, and grace for grace" (John 1:16).

> Thus, when drawing nigh to Christ in this ordinance, we are to consider that fulness of grace which is in him, of merit for our justification, of strength to enable us to mortify sin and resist temptations, of wisdom to direct us in all emergencies

---

332. Ridgeley, *Commentary on the Larger Catechism*, 2:543.

> and difficulties, of peace and comfort to revive and encourage us under all our doubts and fears, and to give us suitable relief when we are ready to faint under the burdens we complain of. All these blessings are to be apprehended and applied by faith.[333]

"Trusting in His Merits"

As we take the Lord's Supper, as well as throughout life, we are to rest in Christ alone for salvation, who has perfectly accomplished our eternal salvation in His life, death and resurrection. Our standing with God depends entirely on His merits, not on our merit, since we have none. In Christ God gives believers, not what they deserve, which is condemnation, but what Christ deserves, which is life. We are deserving only of God's fierce anger because of our sins, but Christ has fully satisfied God's justice and turned away God's wrath as our sacrificial substitute, and by His death has purchased for us all the blessings of God, which, because of our sin, we had lost in Adam (Rom. 5:12–15). "But by His doing you are in Christ Jesus, who became to us wisdom from God, and righteousness and sanctification and redemption, that, just as it is written, 'Let him who boasts, boast in the Lord'" (1 Cor. 1:30–31).

Salvation cannot be merited, earned or bought by us. It is not deserved. It cannot be produced by anything in us. "Salvation is of the Lord!" As Charles Spurgeon said, not one stitch of our salvation garments has been sewn by our own hand. It is all of God. "For by grace are you saved through faith." It is all of grace, of God's free and undeserved favor shown in Christ, from beginning to end. And it is all received by faith in Christ alone: "For we maintain that a man is justified by faith apart from works of the Law" (Rom. 3:28). The believer in Jesus understands that "not having a righteousness of my own derived from the Law" his acceptance with God is based on the righteousness "which is through faith in Christ, the righteousness which comes from God through faith" (Phil. 3:9).

333. Ridgeley, *Commentary on the Larger Catechism*, 2:543.

"Rejoicing In His Love"

Because the Lord's Supper is a confirmation of the bond of love the believer has with His Lord and Savior, as he takes the Supper, being assured of Christ's love for Him, he rejoices in that love (Ps. 63:4, 5; 2 Chron. 30:21). The prayer and heart-desire of the true believer is to "be able to comprehend with all the saints what is the breadth and length and height and depth, and to know the love of Christ which surpasses knowledge," that he "may be filled up to all the fulness of God" (Eph. 3:18–19). "Therefore when we once know how well God loves us, and how inestimable is the mercy of which he has given us so good a pledge in the person of his only Son, we have everything."[334]

"Without being strengthened by the Spirit in the inner man [Eph. 3:16], without the indwelling of Christ [3:17], without being rooted and grounded in love [3:17], it is impossible to have any adequate apprehension of the gospel or of the love of Christ therein revealed."[335] Therefore the believer earnestly prays to know fully and in his own experience the unparalleled and infinite love of God in Christ for him. He prays that he may know truly what cannot be known fully by man—to comprehend the incomprehensible. The love of Christ "surpasses knowledge." "It is infinite; not only because it inheres in an infinite subject, but because the condescension and sufferings to which it led, and the blessings which it secures for its objects, are beyond our comprehension."[336]

The believer rejoices with all his heart and soul in this infinite and wonderful love of God for him in Christ, because it keeps pouring into his life the "fullness of God," *i.e.*, "that fullness with which God is full." "'The fulness of God' is then the abundance of gifts and grace which flows from God;... 'He who has Christ,' says Calvin, 'has everything that is required to our perfection in God,

334. John Calvin, *Sermons on the Epistle to the Ephesians*, trans. and published by Arthur Golding, 1577 (reprint Edinburgh: The Banner of Truth Trust, 1973), 296.

335. Charles Hodge, *Commentary on the Epistle to the Ephesians* (Grand Rapids, MI: William B. Eerdmans Publishing Co., n.d.), 187.

336. Hodge, *Commentary on the Epistle to the Ephesians*, 189.

for this is what is meant by the *fulness of God*.'"[337] Therefore, he particularly rejoices in Christ's love as he takes the Lord's Supper, for there, sacramentally, God pours His "fullness" into the believer's heart and life.

"Giving Thanks for His Grace"

As we take the Lord's Supper we are to adore, praise and thank God that He has been pleased to look upon us with favor and compassion, and graciously bestows on us those rich blessings which are the the gifts of His sovereign grace. "The meek shall eat and be satisfied; they shall praise the Lord that seek Him: your heart shall live forever" (Ps. 22:26). "Through Him [Christ] then let us continually offer up a sacrifice of praise to God, that is, the fruit of lips that give thanks to His name" (Heb. 13:15). Animal sacrifices have been rendered obsolete by the atoning death of Christ, but sacrifices of thanksgiving are still to be offered to God "continually" by all who appreciate the perfect sacrifice of Christ. "The gratitude which is the motive force of the whole life of a Christian cannot fail to burst forth from his lips."[338] "Offer unto God the sacrifice of thanksgiving; and pay thy vows unto the Most High; And call upon Me in the day of trouble; I will deliver thee, and thou shalt glorify Me" (Ps. 50:14–15).

"Renewing of Their Covenant with God"

As we have seen, because the Lord's Supper is a covenant meal, in which God reassures us of His covenant faithfulness to His promises, we, as God's covenant people, are to reaffirm and renew our vow and obligation to covenant faithfulness to God and to His Word. It is the appointed time to renew our covenant with God. "Come, let us join ourselves to the Lord in a perpetual covenant that shall not be forgotten" (Jer. 50:5). "Gather My saints together unto Me; those that have made a covenant with Me by sacrifice" (Ps. 50:5). This renewal of our covenant with God

337. Hodge, *Commentary on the Epistle to the Ephesians*, 191.

338. Philip E. Hughes, *A Commentary on the Epistle to the Hebrews* (Grand Rapids, MI: William B. Eerdmans Publishing Co., 1977), 583.

> consists in our making a surrender of ourselves to Christ, and depending on Him for the [full provision of all our needs], humbly hoping and trusting that he will enable us to adhere steadfastly to him, working in us all that grace which he requires of us; and if he is pleased to grant us this blessing, we shall be enabled to perform all the duties which are incumbent on us, [however difficult] they may be.... Moreover, to renew our covenant, is to declare that, through his grace, we are inclined steadfastly to adhere to our solemn dedication to him.... Accordingly, while we express our earnest desire to be steadfast in his covenant, we depend on his promise that he will never fail us, nor forsake us.[339]

"You stand today, all of you, before the Lord your God... that you may enter into the covenant with the Lord your God, and into His oath which the Lord your God is making with you today, in order that He may establish you today as His people and that He may be your God" (Deut. 29:10, 12–13). "See, I have set before you today life and prosperity, and death and adversity; in that I command you today to love the Lord your God, to walk in His ways and to keep His commandments,... that you may live and multiply, and that the Lord your God may bless you" (Deut. 30:15–16).

"And Love To All the Saints"

In the Lord's Supper, we primarily enjoy His love for us, and reaffirm our love for Him; but we also enjoy the love that believers share with each other in the Body of Christ: "we who are many, are one body in Christ, and individually members one of another" (Rom. 12:5), and "Since there is one bread, we who are many are one body; for we all partake of the one bread" (1 Cor. 10:17). "Everyone who comes to the Lord's supper enters into communion with all other communicants. They form one body in virtue of their joint participation of Christ."[340] Therefore, at the Supper, we should pray for our brothers and sisters in Christ around the

339. Ridgeley, *Commentary on the Larger Catechism*, 2:545.
340. Hodge, *A Commentary on The First Epistle to the Corinthians*, 190.

world, for ourselves, that our love for them would increase. We should pray that God would strengthen the unity we share in the Body of Christ, that peace and love may abound in us, and that we would be concerned and show concern for one another's spiritual and physical welfare.

> This love to all Christians is to be expressed, more especially in the ordinance of the Lord's Supper; inasmuch as we are to consider all saints as members of Christ's mystical body, children of the same God and Father, partakers of the same grace with us, fellow-travellers to the same heavenly country, where we hope to meet them at last, though now they are liable to the same difficulties with ourselves, and exposed to those assaults and temptations which we often meet with from our spiritual enemies.[341]

The Duties of Christians After They Have Received the Lord's Supper

---

Q. 175: What is the duty of Christians, after they have received the sacrament of the Lord's supper?

A.: The duty of Christians, after they have received the sacrament of the Lord's supper, is seriously to consider how they have behaved themselves therein, and with what success; if they find quickening and comfort, to bless God for it, beg the continuance of it, watch against relapses, fulfil their vows, and encourage themselves to a frequent attendance on that ordinance: but if they find no present benefit, more exactly to review their preparation to, and carriage at, the sacrament; in both which, if they can approve themselves to God and their own consciences,

---

341. Ridgeley, *Commentary on the Larger Catechism*, 2:545.

they are to wait for the fruit of it in due time: but, if they see they have failed in either, they are to be humbled, and to attend upon it afterwards with more care and diligence.

After we have received the Lord's Supper we are to ask ourselves whether: (1) we behaved properly while we were receiving it; and (2) we have any good reasons to believe that we were favored with the special presence and gifts of Christ in our taking of it, so that it was a means of grace to us.

The Reflection on Our Behavior While Taking the Supper

> Thus we have sometimes reason to reflect, with grief and sorrow of heart, on our behaviour at the Lord's supper, as what has been disagreeable to the nature of the ordinance. But, on the other hand, we may sometimes, in taking a view of our behaviour at the Lord's supper, find matter of encouragement; when, abating for human frailties, and the imperfection of grace, which inseparably attend the present state, we can say, to the glory of God, that we have, in some measure, behaved ourselves as we ought to do.[342]

> If our hearts have been duly affected with the love of Christ, and we have had the exercise of corresponding graces; and if we can say that we have had some communion with him, and have not been altogether destitute of his quickening and comforting presence, and the witness of his Spirit with ours that we are the children of God; then we may conclude that we have engaged in this ordinance in a right manner;—and if we have found that it has been thus with us, we are to bless God for it; considering that He alone can excite grace in us, who wrought it at first. Such acts of grace, too, will be a good evidence of its truth and sincerity, and will tend to establish

342. Ridgeley, *Commentary on the Larger Catechism*, 2:546.

our comfort, and to enable us to walk more closely and thankfully with God.[343]

The Assessment on Whether in the Supper We Received the Special Favor and Blessing of God

After taking the Supper, we should ask ourselves: With what success did I receive the Lord's Supper? Did I receive the Lord in the Supper? Was it a true means of God's grace to me? Were Christ and His benefits sealed and conveyed to me in the Lord's Supper? Was I a worthy eater, and therefore, a successful eater? Did God favor me with His special presence in Christ by His Spirit as I partook of the holy meal?

The psalmist reflected on his experience and was able to say, "The Lord is my strength and my shield; my heart trusted in Him, and I am helped; therefore my heart greatly rejoiceth; and with my song will I praise Him" (Ps. 28:7). He could say that, by God's grace, his heart trusted the Lord, and through that trust, God helped him and continues to help him, thus producing in Him rejoicing and praise to God.

How could he be so certain that he was "helped" by God? His inner frame of mind was changed as he prayed from one of anxious fear (28:1–5), to one of peace, security and praise. How can we know if God favored us with His special presence and blessing in the Lord's Supper? Has God used the Lord's Supper to bring us into a new frame of mind, motivating and enabling us to walk more closely with Him and in continual gratitude and praise to Him for all we have in Christ? Are we motivated to live to praise, glorify and honor Him with all we are and all we do? See 1 Cor. 10:31; 6:19–20; Acts 2:42, 46, 47; 2 Chron. 30:21–26.

343. Ridgeley, *Commentary on the Larger Catechism*, 2:546.

The Responsibilities of One Who Upon Reflection Believes, As A Worthy Eater, He Has Been Blessed of God in the Supper, After He Has Partaken of the Supper

> (i). We must come from this ordinance admiring the condescension of the divine grace to us; considering our meanness by nature, and our vileness by sin; (ii). Lamenting our manifold defects either trembling, or at least blushing; (iii). Rejoicing in Christ, and the great love wherewith He has loved us; expressing itself in praises to God, and encouragements to ourselves; (iv). Much quickening to every good work; (v). With a watchful fear of Satan's wiles, and a firm resolution to stand our ground against them,... (vi). Praying that God will fulfill his promises to us, and enable us to fulfill ours to him. (vii). With a charitable disposition,... love our fellow Christians,... give to the poor and forgive injuries, (viii). Longing for heaven.[344]

He Blesses God for His Quickening and Comforting of Us During the Lord's Supper

As we have pointed out, if we have concluded that we were worthy eaters of the Supper and that God did show us His favor and blessing as we partook of the meal, then we are to praise God for it, because only He can enable us to eat in a worthy manner, and only He can work grace and its effects in our hearts and lives. Once again we must say that, from first to last, "salvation is of the Lord!"

He Begs God to Continue His Work Within Him

If we conclude that God has Spiritually "quickened and comforted" us in the Supper, giving us a new frame of mind marked by praise, then, we should earnestly plead with God to continue his work and to maintain this new disposition He has placed within us. We should pray with the psalmist, "O continue Thy lovingkindness unto them that know Thee; and Thy righteousness to the upright in

---

344. Henry, *How to Prepare for Communion*, 100.

heart" (Ps. 36:10). The bride of Christ can say, "I found Him whom my soul loveth; I held Him and would not let Him go" (Song of Solomon 3:4). And from our lips should continually go this prayer, "O Lord God of Abraham, Isaac and of Israel, our fathers, keep this (God-centered frame of heart) forever in the imagination of the thoughts of the heart of Thy people, and prepare their heart unto Thee" (1 Chron. 29:18).

> The best frame of spirit will be no longer abiding than it pleases God to keep up the lively exercise of faith and other graces; and this, being so valuable a blessing, is to be sought for by fervent prayer and supplication, that our good frames may not be like the morning cloud, or early dew, that soon passes away.[345]

He Watches Against Relapses

Christians are always sinners: "Prone to wander, Lord I feel it." Before we were Christians we were slaves to sin and Satan; but in Christ we have been freed from sin's condemnation and slavery, and we now abhor that which we once loved. And yet, it still is possible for us to fall back into old sins, if we are not careful. Even then, we will not be totally free until death when we are perfected in holiness. "Let him who thinks he stands, take heed lest he fall" (1 Cor. 10:12). "Neither the members of the church nor the elect can be saved unless they persevere in holiness [Heb. 11:14]; and they cannot persevere in holiness without continual watchfulness and effort [1 Cor. 16:13]."[346] "Brethren, even if a man is caught in any trespass, you who are spiritual, restore such a one in a spirit of gentleness; looking to yourself, lest you too be tempted" (Gal. 6:1). Notice three things in this verse: (1) Sometimes true Christians can get "caught" in or "overtaken" by a sin. The sinning Christian did not deliberately and consciously plan to perform a wicked deed; but before he had even realized the full extent of the ethical reprehensibility and injurious nature of the sin, he had already committed it. (2) This

345. Ridgeley, *Commentary on the Larger Catechism*, 2:547.
346. Hodge, *A Commentary on The First Epistle to the Corinthians*, 181.

one should be restored with gentleness, because, even those Christians who are mature enough to restore the fallen are capable of being "tempted" and falling into sin themselves. (3) The only way any Christian is going to keep from giving in to temptation and being "overtaken" by sin is by "looking to yourself," *i.e.*, by "constantly looking to yourself."

> There is no man, no, not the most spiritual, who can promise unto himself immunity from being set upon with strong temptations unto gross and scandalous evils, or that he shall stand when he is tempted, if he be left of God under the temptation; for he biddeth even the *spiritual* man consider himself, "lest he also be tempted;" whereby he holdeth forth not only a possibility that the spiritual man may be tempted, but also of his yielding to the temptation, when it should be presented.[347]

He Fulfills His Vows to God

Once again our Catechism reminds us that the Lord's Supper is a covenant meal in which we renew our vows of faithfulness to God, as He reassures us of His faithfulness to His covenant promises. The Bible commands us to "offer to God a sacrifice of thanksgiving, and pay your vows to the Most High; And call upon Me in the day of trouble; I shall rescue you, and you will honor Me" (Ps. 50:14, 15). In this vow at the Lord's Table we devote ourselves entirely to Christ, hoping and trusting that He will give us the strength to fulfill that vow, for we know that we cannot fulfill it in our own strength. Now having made the vow, in His strength we are able and obligated to keep it.

> Having at God's [Table] sworn that we will keep his righteous judgments [laws], we must conscientiously perform it [the oath] in all the evidences of a holy, righteous and sober conversation [way of life]. The vows we have made, express

347. James Fergusson, *An Exposition of the Epistles of Paul to the Galatians, Ephesians, Philippians, Colossians, Thessalonians* (Indiana: Sovereign Grace Publishers, n.d.), 102.

> or implicit, must be carefully made good by a constant watchfulness against all sin, and a constant diligence in all duty; because, 'better it is not to vow, than to vow and not to pay' [Eccl. 5:5].
>
> When we are at any time tempted to sin, or in danger of being surprised into any ill thing, let this be our reply to the tempter, and with this let us quench his fiery darts, 'Thy vows are upon me, O God.' Did I not say, 'I would take heed to my ways, that I sin not with my tongue?' I did say so, and therefore, 'I will keep my mouth as with a bridle.' Did I not make a 'covenant with my eyes?' I did; that therefore shall be to me a covering of the eyes, that they may never be either the inlets or outlets of sin. Did I not say, 'I will not transgress?' I did so; and therefore, by the grace of God, I will 'abstain from all appearances of evil, and have no fellowship with the unfruitful works of darkness.' An honest man is as good as his word.[348]

He Encourages Himself to Take the Lord's Supper Regularly and Frequently

Jesus told His disciples, "This do *as often* as you drink it, in remembrance of Me. For *as often* as you eat this bread, and drink this cup, you proclaim the Lord's death until He comes" (1 Cor. 11:25, 26). And in the early church we find that the believers and their families "*continued steadfastly* in the apostles' doctrine and fellowship, and in breaking of bread, and in prayers. And they, continuing *daily* with one accord in the temple, and breaking bread from house to house, did eat their meat with gladness and singleness of heart" (Acts 2:42, 46).

Once we have tasted the goodness of God in the Lord's Supper, we hunger and thirst for more. Having experienced the favor and blessing of God signified, sealed and conveyed to us in the sacrament, we long to take it regularly and as frequently as possible. We

348. Henry, *How To Prepare for Communion*, 112–13.

not only discipline ourselves to receive the Word and sacrament regularly, we also encourage ourselves to do so.

> Our having experienced God's comforting and quickening presence in our attending on the Lord's supper, will effectually remove all those doubts and scruples which discourage us from engaging in it, [such as] fearing that we shall not behave ourselves in a right manner in it, that we are not sufficiently prepared for it, and that we shall be disowned by Christ when we engage in it.[349]

The Responsibilities of One Who Upon Reflection Concludes That, As An Unworthy Eater, He Was Not Blessed of God in the Lord's Supper, After He Has Partaken of the Supper

He Should Review More Exactly His Preparation for and Behavior During the Lord's Supper

> Guard your steps as you go to the house of God, and draw near to listen rather than to offer the sacrifice of fools; for they do not know they are doing evil. Do not be hasty in word or impulsive in thought to bring up a matter in the presence of God. For God is in heaven and you are on the earth; therefore let your words be few. For the dream comes through much effort, and the voice of a fool through many words. When you make a vow to God, do not be late in paying it, for He takes no delight in fools. Pay what you vow! It is better that you should not vow than that you should vow and not pay. Do not let your speech cause you to sin and do not say in the presence of the messenger of God that it was a mistake. Why should God be angry on account of your voice and destroy the work of your hands? (Eccl. 5:1–6).

349. Ridgeley, *Commentary on the Larger Catechism*, 2:548.

Unworthy eaters, who have concluded regretfully that they missed the blessing of the Lord's Supper should apply the warnings of the inspired Preacher to their own lives:

(1) How did I fail in my participation in public worship, including the Lord's Supper, so that I failed to received the favorable presence of God and His blessing in my life? Was my involvement in public worship merely an "external," or intellectual or emotional thing, rather than being rooted in my heart? I attended public worship regularly and strictly, but was it only formally, and not spiritually?

(2) Did I involve myself in the worship services with all possible seriousness and care? Did I keep my thoughts from wandering?

(3) Was the sacrifice I offered "the sacrifice of fools," that is, one not accepted with God, because offered for the wrong motives, even though offered according to correct forms? Was I placing my faith in some imagined merit of my worship performances, and resting in them, rather than resting in God's grace for acceptance of myself and my worship before Him? Was I foolish enough to believe that just going through the correct religious motions is all that matters, although my heart was not in it and I did not enact my worship to the glory of God?

(4) Were there sinful attitudes and desires that filled my heart as I worshipped that even I was not fully aware of?

(5) Did I attend worship and partake of the Lord's Table with my heart ready and willing to know and to do whatever God commanded me in His Word?

(6) Was I cautious, deliberate, and reverent, as I approached worship and the Lord's Supper?

(7) Was I careless, rash, hypocritical and shallow in my vows and commitments to God? Did I make resolutions and promises to God with mental reservations?

(8) Have I been slow and unfaithful in the fulfillment of my vows and promises to God? Were they all lies?

(9) Did I give the Word of God, both preached and visualized in the sacraments the best attention I was capable of giving it? (See also Song of Solomon 5:1–6, which is one of the footnotes supporting this phrase in the Larger Catechism.)

He Should Repent of His Inadequate Preparations and His Sinful Participation and Unworthy Eating of the Lord's Supper, and Make More Diligent Effort at Preparation and Participation, Waiting Upon God to Bring Fruit and Blessing to His Labor of Faith

"Unto Thee lift I up mine eyes, O Thou that dwellest in the heavens. Behold, as the eyes of servants look unto the hand of their masters, and as the eyes of a maiden unto the hand of her mistress; SO OUR EYES WAIT UPON THE LORD OUR GOD, UNTIL THAT HE HAVE MERCY UPON US" (Ps. 123:1, 2). Because we are totally without strength, hope and protection in and of ourselves, we must constantly look trustingly and dependently to God in prayer to supply what we lack and to bless us, for we cannot bless ourselves. And if He does not answer as quickly as we expect, we are to continue to look to Him and not stop looking to Him until He has mercy on us.

> God... purposely disarms us and strips us of all worldly aid, that we may learn to rely upon his grace, and to be contented with it alone....
>
> Nor can it be doubted that God, when he sees us placing an exclusive dependence upon his protection, and renouncing all confidence in our own resources, will as our defender encounter, and shield us from all the molestation that shall be offered to us.[350]

---

350. John Calvin, *Commentary Upon the Book of Psalms,* trans. by Rev. James Anderson, 5 vols.(Edinburgh: Calvin Translation Society, 1843; reprint Grand Rapids, MI: Baker Book House, 1979), 5:81.

> Why art thou cast down, O my soul? And why are thou disquieted in me? HOPE THOU IN GOD; FOR I SHALL YET PRAISE HIM for the help of His countenance.... YET the Lord will command His lovingkindness in the daytime, and in the night His song shall be with me, and my prayer unto the God of my life (Ps. 42:5, 8).

> By the term *yet,* he confesses that for the present, and in so far as the praises of God are concerned, his mouth is stopped, seeing he is oppressed and shut up on all sides. This, however, does not prevent him from extending his hope to some future distant period; and, in order to escape from his present sorrow, and, as it were, get beyond its reach, he promises himself what as yet there was no appearance of obtaining. Nor is this an imaginary expectation produced by a fanciful mind; but, relying upon the promises of God, he not only encourages himself to cherish good hope, but also promises himself certain deliverance.[351]

> O send out Thy light and Thy truth; let them lead me, let them bring me unto Thy holy hill, and to Thy tabernacles. Then will I go unto the altar of God, unto God my exceeding joy; yea, upon the harp will I praise Thee, O God, my God. Why art thou cast down, O my soul? And why art thou disquieted within me? Hope in God, for I shall YET praise Him, who is the health of my countenance, and my God (Ps. 43:3–5).

"In order... to encourage himself in the hope of obtaining the grace of God, David rests with confidence in this, that God, who is true, and cannot deceive any, has promised to assist his servants."[352] And so as David perseveres in well-doing, he hopes and patiently praises God, trusting and waiting for God to do what He has promised, confident that He will.

351. Calvin, *Commentary Upon the Book of Psalms,* 2:135.
352. Calvin, *Commentary Upon the Book of Psalms,* 2:146.

He Should Be Humbled and Partake of the Lord's Supper in the Future with More Care and Diligence

If we participated in the Lord's Supper depending upon our own merit or actions, or with self-confidence and high self-esteem, not looking to Christ alone for salvation, provoking the Lord to withhold His blessing and to withdraw His presence from us, we should be deeply and sadly humbled and humiliated in His sight, confessing our sins and repenting of them. Then we may hope that He will enable us to wait upon Him reverently in the Lord's Supper in the future, being sure to participate with more care and diligence, so as not to miss His blessings. See 2 Chronicles 30:18–19 and Isaiah 1:16–18.

The Apostle Paul describes the effects of this humbled attitude in 2 Corinthians 7:10–11,

> For the sorrow that is according to the will of God produces a repentance without regret, leading to salvation, but the sorrow of the world produces death. For behold what earnestness this very thing, this godly sorrow, has produced in you, what vindication of yourselves, what indignation, what fear, what longing, what zeal, what avenging of wrong!

> Paul's concern here is not with the ground of salvation, which is the pure grace of God in Christ, but with the commendation of repentance, itself a sign of the grace of God in operation, because of the fruit which it produces.... Besides godly sorrow, however, there is a different kind of sorrow which Paul calls "the sorrow of the world," and which works out its fulfilment in death.... It is not sorrow because of the heinousness of sin as rebellion against God, but sorrow because of the painful and unwelcome consequences of sin. Self is its central point; and self is also the central point of sin, Thus the sorrow of the world manifests itself in self-pity rather than in contrition and turning to God for mercy.... His [David's in Psalm 51] was truly godly sorrow—centered in God

> and His holiness. And such godly sorrow is transmuted into godly joy—the joy of God's salvation and the praise of His goodness (Ps. 51:12f).[353]

See also 1 Chronicles 15:12–14.

The Similarities of Baptism and the Lord's Supper

Q. 176: Wherein do the sacraments of baptism and the Lord's supper agree?

A.: The sacraments of baptism and the Lord's supper agree, in that the author of both is God; the spiritual part of both is Christ and his benefits; both are seals of the same covenant, are to be dispensed by ministers of the gospel, and by none other; and to be continued in the church of Christ until his second coming.

Baptism and the Lord's Supper are similar in five ways: (1) They have the same Author, who is God in Christ (Matt. 28:19; 1 Cor. 11:23); (2) They signify, seal, and communicate Christ and His benefits to believers. (Rom. 6:3, 4; 1 Cor. 10:16); (3) They are seals of the same covenant of grace (Rom. 4:11; Col. 2:12; Matt. 26:27, 28); (4) They are both dispensed by ministers of the gospel, and by no one else (John 1:33; Matt. 28:19; 1 Cor. 11:23; 1 Cor. 4:1; Heb. 5:4); and (5) They are both to be continued in the church until the second coming of Christ (Matt. 28:19, 20; 1 Cor. 11:26).

> Though we look and hope for more of the presence of God in them, and a greater effusion of his Spirit, to make them more effectual, and render the church more bright and glorious, as being favored with greater degrees of the communications of divine grace; yet we have no ground to expect new ordinanc-

---

353. Hughes, *Paul's Second Epistle to the Corinthians,* 272–73.

es, or a new dispensation to succeed this which we are under, till Christ's second and most glorious coming.[354]

How Baptism and the Lord's Supper Differ

Q. 177: Wherein do the sacraments of baptism and the Lord's supper differ?

A.: The sacraments of baptism and the Lord's Supper differ, in that baptism is to be administered but once, with water, to be a sign and seal of our regeneration and ingrafting into Christ, and that even to infants; whereas the Lord's Supper is to be administered often, in the elements of bread and wine, to represent and exhibit Christ as spiritual nourishment to the soul, and to confirm our continuance and growth in Him, and that only to such as are of years and ability to examine themselves.

Here our Catechism gives us four ways in which Baptism and the Lord's Supper differ:

(1) Baptism is to be administered once (Eph. 4:5; 1 Cor. 12:13), and the Lord's Supper is to be administered often (1 Cor. 11:26).

> The bond which then obliges us to be his holds good as long as we live, and therefore needs not to be signified, sealed, or confirmed by our being baptized a second time. But... the Lord's supper signifies our feeding or living upon Christ, and receiving daily supplies of grace from him, as our necessities require.[355]

354. Ridgeley, *Commentary on the Larger Catechism*, 2:551.
355. Ridgeley, *Commentary on the Larger Catechism*, 2:551–52.

(2) Baptism is with water (Matt. 3:11); the Lord's Supper is with bread and wine (1 Cor. 11:23, 25). Water cleanses, bread nourishes, and wine gladdens. So baptism is a sign and seal of our Spiritual cleansing; and the Lord's Supper is a sign and seal of our Spiritual nourishment in and enjoyment of Christ.

(3) Baptism is a sign and seal of our regeneration and ingrafting into Christ (Matt. 3:11, Tit. 3:5; Gal. 3:27); the Lord's Supper represents and conveys Christ as our Spiritual nourishment and confirms our continued growth in Him (1 Cor. 11:23, 24, 25, 26; 1 Cor. 10:16).

(4) Baptism is to he administered even to infants of believing parents (Gen. 17:7, 9; Acts 2:38,39; 1 Cor. 7:14); but the Lord's Supper is to be administered only to those who are "of years and ability to examine themselves" (1 Cor.11:28, 29).

The Difference According to John Calvin

The Bible presents us with "a wide difference in every respect" between baptism and the Lord's Supper.

> For if we consider the peculiar character of baptism, surely it is an entrance and a sort of initiation into the church, through which we are numbered among God's people: a sign of our spiritual regeneration, through which we are reborn as children of God. On the other hand, the Supper is given to older persons who, having passed tender infancy, can now take solid food.
>
> This distinction is very clearly shown in Scripture. For with respect to baptism, the Lord there sets no definite age. But He does not similarly hold forth the Supper for all to partake of, but only for those who are capable of discerning the body and blood of the Lord, of examining their own conscience, of proclaiming the Lord's death, and of considering its power. Do we wish anything plainer than the apostle's teaching when he exhorts each man to prove and search himself, then to eat of this bread and drink of this cup (1 Cor. 11:28)? A self-examination ought, therefore, to come first, and it is vain to expect this of infants. Again: "He who eats unwor-

> thily eats and drinks condemnation for himself, not discerning the body of the Lord" (1 Cor. 11:29). If only those who know how to distinguish rightly the holiness of Christ's body are able to participate worthily, why should we offer poison instead of life-giving food to our tender children? What is that command of the Lord: "Do this in remembrance of Me" (Luke 22:19; 1 Cor. 11:25)? What is that other command which the apostles derives from it: "As often as you eat this bread, you will proclaim the Lord's death until He comes" (1 Cor. 11:26)? What remembrance of this thing, I ask, shall we require of infants when they have never grasped it? What preaching of the cross of Christ, the force and benefit of which their minds have not yet comprehended? None of these things is prescribed in baptism. Accordingly, there is a very great difference between these two signs, as we have noted in like signs also under the Old Testament. Circumcision, which is known to correspond to our baptism, had been appointed for infants (Gen. 17:12). But the Passover, the place of which has been taken by the Supper, did not admit all guests indiscriminately, but was duly eaten only by those who were old enough to be able to inquire into its meaning (Ex. 12:26).[356]

The Difference Between Active and Passive Reception

In order for a thing to be a sacramental sign and seal of a spiritual reality, an obvious resemblance must exist in the visible sign to the spiritual reality, as we have shown in our reasons for baptizing by affusion, since the Holy Spirit is poured out on God's people. Since baptism is a sign and seal of regeneration by the Holy Spirit, wherein the recipient of regeneration is passive in the act, the regenerating work being entirely of the Holy Spirit, the recipient of water baptism is passive in the administration of the sacrament. He does nothing and contributes nothing, only receiving what is poured out on him. In the Lord's Supper, however, the recipient is fully and knowledgeably active. He is not "force-fed" the

356. Calvin, *Institutes of the Christian Religion*, 2:1352–53.

meal by another; rather, he feeds himself. He takes the bread and wine in his own hands, places them in his mouth, chews and swallows them, and digests them in his stomach. How does all this visible activity connected with the visible sign resemble the spiritual reality signified in the Lord's Supper? In this way, although the person is passive in regeneration by the Spirit, he is fully active in sanctification by the Spirit. His growth in grace and Spiritual maturation are inseparably connected with his persevering endeavors in believing the promises and obeying the commands of the Bible. So that, as the believing recipient is physically active in the sacrament, he is spiritually active in consciously receiving Christ in the sacrament, proclaiming His death, examining himself, discerning the Lord's body, and remembering Christ, in knowledge and in faith, rededicating Himself to the Lord's service. Just as the physical activity in eating the bread and wine are beyond the capacity of infants, so the spiritual activity required in the taking of the Lord's Supper is beyond the ability of infants.

The Arguments Against "Paedo-Communion"

The Larger Catechism, accurately reflecting the teaching of the Bible, states clearly that, although baptism is administered "even to infants," the Lord's Supper is administered "only to such as are of years and ability to examine themselves."

> None are to partake of the Lord's supper but those who have such a degree of knowledge that they are able to discern the Lord's body, and capable of performing that duty which the apostle recommends as necessary to the performing of it, when he says, "Let a man examine himself, and so let him eat of that bread, and drink of that cup."[357]

Some would argue that the one prerequisite for the Lord's Supper is baptism, therefore, nothing more should be required of covenant children to take the Lord's Supper than that they were baptized. They base their argument on the assumption that just as all circumcised children participated in the Passover, and since bap-

357. Ridgeley, *Commentary on the Larger Catechism*, 2:552.

tism has fulfilled circumcision, therefore all baptized children should participate in the Lord's Supper.

However, many problems exist with this viewpoint, which make it impossible for us to believe it.

The Requirements for Taking the Passover in the Old Testament

In Old Testament Israel five things could exclude a person from eating the Passover meal: (1) uncircumcision (Ex. 12:48); (2) immaturity (Ex. 12:4–5); (3) ignorance regarding the sacraments (Ex. 12:26–27); (4) ceremonial uncleanness (Num. 9:6; 5:2); and (5) a heart not consecrated to God (2 Chron. 30:8).

Circumcision

Exodus 12:43–49 makes unmistakably clear: circumcision was a prerequisite for participation in the Passover. Only those who were circumcised could take Passover. This meant, obviously, that only males were communicants in the Passover.

> According to Exodus 12:48, only an adult male stranger, mature enough himself to have children, could personally be admitted to the Passover Table (yet only without his own immature children). However, before even he himself could be admitted to the Passover, he must first comply with a number of prerequisites. First, he himself must express his desire personally to partake. Second, not just he himself but all the immature males in his home must themselves have been circumcised.... Third, he himself (but without his circumcised minor male children) must then "come near" before the Elders (and thus under their examination) Exodus 12:21 cf 18:12f. Fourth, thus becoming a Communicant, he himself... would then be admitted to the Table. No Passover for fathers with uncircumcised little boys![358]

358. Francis Nigel Lee, Ph.D., *Catechism Before Communion* (unpublished doctoral dissertation Whitefield Theological Seminary, Lakeland, FL, 1988), 39.

Maturity

Although circumcision was a prerequisite for Passover, some circumcised males could not partake, because circumcision was not the only requirement. Exodus 12 teaches us that only mature males ate the Passover. This is not so obvious in our English translations, but it is obvious in the Hebrew Bible. In Exodus 12 we learn that the first Passover was offered only by those who were mature males: "Now if the household is too small for a lamb, then *he* and *his* neighbor nearest to *his* house are to take one according to the number of persons, [*nephesh*], in them; according to what each *man*, [*ish*], should eat, you are to divide the lamb" (12:4).This verse teaches that not every "person," (*nephesh* in Hebrew), or every woman, (*ishshah*), but every "man," (*ish* in Hebrew), in the household, mature enough to have a circumcisable male offspring, was commanded to "eat" the Passover lamb.[359]

> The Passover was to be eaten sacramentarily not by the immature Israelite child, [*taf* in Hebrew], nor even by the mature woman [*ishshah* in Hebrew], but only by the mature male Israelites alias "man" [*ish* in Hebrew] (Exodus 12:3, 4, 26, 37).[360]

Furthermore, in Exodus 12:3, Moses directs his God-given commands to "all the congregation of Israel." A local Hebrew congregation consisted then, and consists today, of at least TEN MATURE MALES (Gen. 18:32; Ex. 12:3–4; 18:12–25). According to F. Nigel Lee, it is only when there are ten mature men that a local congregation of Israel can be convened. And these commands are issued to all the congregation of Israel, which, according to Keil and Delitzsch, refers to "the nation represented by its Elders." Therefore the commands are to every "man, according to their fathers' households" (12:3).

---

359. "Age and sex qualifications at the Passover, even for Israelitic manducators, also appear from Deuteronomy sixteen's inspired expansion of Exodus twelve [16:16–17]" (Lee, *Catechism Before Communion*, 50).

360. Lee, *Catechism Before Communion*, 27.

Male heads of small households took Passover together: "now if the household is too small for a lamb, then he and his neighbor nearest to his house are to take one according to the number of persons in them."

> Exodus 12:4a is thus *not* saying that the man and his wife and their children (plural!) are all to go share their passover lamb with all their next-door neighbors (plural!), according to the total number of souls altogether in both houses. No! Instead, the text specifies that the "count [number] for the lamb" is to be made according to that "number of souls" which was constituted by each mature male—alias every "man accustomed to eat." It refers to the minimum "number" of mature men (ten!) required to constitute a "Congregation of Israel,..." Indeed, it says that a lone mature man, (*ish*) is to go to the house of his neighbor. The text does not say that both the man and his whole family are to go to the homes (plural!) of their (plural!) neighbors. The sacramental principle here—where ten mature male communicants are gathered together in the Name of Jehovah—is thus the very opposite of a simple and all-inclusive non-sacramental household meal enjoyed by one whole family (or even by two whole families meeting together)![361]

It should also be pointed out that the lamb, unleavened bread and bitter herbs of the Passover were unsuitable food for infants (Ex. 12:8–10). And in Exodus 12:11 those who take the Passover are told to do so "with your loins girded, your sandals on your feet, and your staff in your hand," language hardly describing infants, young children or women.

Today godly women in the church are encouraged to partake of the Lord's Supper because of the enlargement of the New Covenant with reference to the enjoyment of the privileges and sacraments: "There is neither Jew nor Greek, there is neither slave nor free man, there is neither male nor female; for you are all one in Christ Jesus" (Gal. 3:28). Therefore, the sacraments have been changed so as not

361. Lee, *Catechism Before Communion*, 36–37.

to exclude females. For instance, because circumcision was changed to baptism, "they were being baptized, men and women alike" (Acts 8:12). And in the New Testament church, all communing members, (not under age or under discipline), including men and women, are enjoined to receive the Lord's Supper in 1 Corinthians 11:23–31. There are no references to women, or little children, partaking sacramentally of the Passover in the Old Testament. "The admission of mature women to the Holy Table occurred only when Christ reversed the fall, at His advent and death and resurrection. That is what restored woman—and advanced her!"[362]

Catechism (Knowledge)

Exodus 12:26–28 tells us that catechetical instruction in the meaning of the Passover is a prerequisite for taking the Passover: "And it will come about when your children will say to you, 'What does this rite mean to you?' that you shall say, 'It is a Passover sacrifice to the Lord who passed over the houses of the sons of Israel in Egypt when He smote the Egyptians, but spared our homes.'" In his question to his father, the covenant child uses the second person pronoun "you," not the first person pronoun "us." The point is that in asking his father about the meaning of his father's participation in the Passover, he is excluding himself as a participant. He is NOT asking, "What does this rite which WE are doing mean to US?" BUT rather, "What does this rite which YOU are doing mean to YOU?" The godly father then uses the son's inquiry to teach Him the meaning and implications of Passover. See also Exodus 13:8, 14 specifically identifies this inquiring covenant child as a covenant "son!—And you shall tell your son on that day, saying, 'It is because of what the Lord did for me when I came out of Egypt.... And it shall be when your son asks you in time to come.'"

Examination

The Levitical Examination for Cleanness

In Numbers 9 we learn that

362. Lee, *Catechism Before Communion*, 26–27.

> the Passover had a significance which required examination of the would-be participants. The Passover was to be kept when and how God Himself instituted it (v 3). But certain men had been present at a funeral, so by reason of ceremonial or Levitical uncleanness they were not permitted to keep the Passover (cf Numbers 5:2–3). Both men and women contracted ceremonial uncleanness (Numbers 5:3), so we must suppose that either (1) no women were at the funeral or (2) that women were not required to keep Passover anyway, so [their presence] at the funeral made no difference. Since women were never circumcised in Israel and only the circumcised could partake of the meal, it seems more likely that the latter is the case. In fact, if women had partaken of the Passover, we should expect roughly twenty-five per cent of the women of Israel to be approaching Moses with the same kind of question that these men had, for twenty-five per cent of the women of Israel in each of the four weeks of every month would have been unqualified to partake (if for no other reason) due to their menstrual period (Leviticus 15:19–30).... However, there is no such complaint to Moses in Numbers 9.... Now God Himself made a provision for a Passover to be held a month later for those who were ceremonially unclean on the 14th of Abib (Nisan).[363]

"It was a general principle of Old Testament Levitical cleanness that the unclean person was to be examined and then undergo whatever ritual was appropriate for his cleansing,"[364] before he would be admitted to the Passover. See Numbers 19:20 and Leviticus 13:2, 8.

The point is two-fold: (1) *the Passover was not eaten indiscriminately by every member of the holy nation of Israel*; and (2) *"a person could not simply and independently determine on his own whether or not to eat the meal."*[365]

363. Richard Bacon, *What Mean Ye By This Service? Paedocommunion in Light of the Passover* (Dallas, TX: Presbyterian Heritage Publications, 1989), 13–14.

364. Bacon, *What Mean Ye By This Service?*, 32.

365. Bacon, *What Mean Ye By This Service?*, 14. Emphasis added.

The Elders' Examination for Admittance of People to the Lord's Supper

As the Levites examined communicants regarding ceremonial cleanness in the Old Testament, so elders, the guardians and shepherds of the Lord's congregation (Acts 20:28–30), having been given the power of "the keys of the kingdom" to open and shut the kingdom (Matt. 16:19), are guardians of the Lord's Table with the responsibility to admit to that Table only those whom Christ allows.

In the Old Testament, God held Israel responsible for violations of his law in allowing the unworthy to approach his altar, *e.g.*, Lev. 23:1ff. This same principle applies to the 'altar' in the messianic age, cf. Ezekiel 44:4–9. This prophetic passage cannot have any meaning at all if it is not applied to church membership and to the Lord's Supper. (Let us remember that 1 Cor. 10:16–18, and 11:27–34 speak of the Lord's table in terms of the Old Testament altar). Therefore, it is the responsibility of the church to discipline the table.

In Ezekiel 44:4–9, God says that the new covenant Israel is responsible to discipline those who approach him.

In the Judaism of Jesus' day, Ezekiel 44 was manifested in what has come to be known as 'bar mitzvah'. God submitted Jesus to this institution before he was allowed to approach God's presence (the altar).

Under the new covenant, the church is responsible to discipline the table so as not to allow the unworthy to approach the altar, 1 Cor. 5:11–13; Matt. 18:17.

The church cannot read one's heart—all we can 'read' is one's profession. Therefore, before one approaches the table (the Lord's presence), the church must examine his profession.

What is a profession of faith? It is governed by the exercise of the keys of the kingdom. The keys were given to the church governors (elders) and not to parents (Matt. 16:19; 18:15–20). The exercise of the keys is abdicated when someone other than the governors/elders bars in church discipline a person from the Lord's Supper, or when someone other than the governors/elders admits a person to the Lord's Supper.

Church governors/elders must give account for the souls for church members, Hebrews 13:17. To allow a child to approach the table is to allow him to come under the sanction of sickness and death [1 Cor. 11:30]. God holds the church responsible for disciplining the table (Ezek. 44:4–9).

This requires an active examination of those who wish to approach the Table. This responsibility is especially pressing when the members are introduced/admitted/exposed by the exercise of the keys to the sanctions on the Lord's Supper. The governors/elders are responsible in examination to make certain the truths of the Gospel are comprehended and practiced by church members. This is seen in admitting adults to church membership. This is seen in admitting children to full communion in the Lord's Supper....

Ultimately, only Christ admits someone to His Table. The qualification is regeneration. So, in Ezekiel 44:7–11, the priests who serve at the altar in the Messiah's reign are the regenerate of the messianic age (cf. 1 Pet. 2:9). However, Christ has not designed the church in such a way that He tells His appointed rulers (the elders) what is the state of an individual's heart. Rather, He has designed it in such a way that its rulers can only hear the confession of faith on the part of those who would be admitted to the table.... In the church, the elders acting in Christ's behalf rule the church and, specifically, admit and exclude people from the church and from the Lord's table (Matt. 16:19; 18:15–20; John 20:22–23). Since it was the church in the Old Testament that granted admission to the altar to priests, and, by implication, granted to applicants admission to the altar, this establishes a principle in the church visible... a principle that is valid and assumed in the New Testament, but never explicitly discussed.

Admission to the table (*i.e.,* to the altar) in the New Testament is not automatic. It is not granted simply because one was born into a Christian family any more than children

> were admitted to the altar in the Old Testament by virtue of their parentage. Admission in both Testaments is conditioned on an applicant's conscious and willing submission to the covenant, *i.e.*, seen in New Testament terms, that he understands what it means to be born again and that he is seeking to live accordingly.[366]

A Model for Elders

At Chalcedon Presbyterian Church in Atlanta, Georgia, the elders apply the Biblical principles mentioned above in this manner: a child of church members in good standing is admitted to the Lord's Supper by the Session when the father of the child and the elder with the shepherding responsibility for that specific family agree that he/she is able to make a credible profession of faith before the congregation, with a sufficiently mature understanding of the meaning and demands of the Lord's Supper on his life and future.

Consecration

In 2 Chronicles 30:2–3, 8, 15, 17 we learn that not only ceremonial uncleanness excludes a person from the sacramental meal:

> For the king and his princes and all the assembly in Jerusalem, had decided to celebrate the Passover in the second month, since they could not celebrate it at that time, because the priests had not consecrated themselves in sufficient numbers, nor had the people been gathered to Jerusalem.... Now do not stiffen your neck like your fathers, but yield to the Lord and enter His sanctuary which He has consecrated forever, and serve the Lord your God, that His burning anger may turn away from you.... Then they slaughtered the Passover lambs on the fourteenth of the second month. And the priests and Levites were ashamed of themselves and consecrated themselves, and brought burnt offerings to the house of the Lord.... For there were many in the assembly who had

366. Leonard J. Coppes, *Daddy, May I Take Communion? Paedocommunion vs. The Bible* (Thornton, CO: Leonard J. Coppes, 1988), 23, 24, 270.

> not consecrated themselves; therefore, the Levites were over the slaughter of the Passover lambs for every one who was unclean, in order to consecrate them to the Lord.

In this passage we see that a lack of consecration to the Lord and to His service disqualified someone from taking the Passover.

> This account teaches us that something more than ceremonial uncleanness could keep an ancient Israelite from the feast. An unyielded heart also disqualified the ancient Israelite from taking the sacrament of the Passover meal, even though he had been previously circumcised. Note also the 'fencing' that took place in vv. 17–19.[367]

The Implication of These Passover Requirements for Participating in the Lord's Supper

The basis of the paedo-communionist position that baptism is the only prerequisite for communion because circumcision was the only prerequisite for Passover will not hold up in the light of the Bible. Circumcision was a prerequisite for Passover in the Old Testament, but not the only prerequisite. Thus today we may conclude that the requirements for taking the Lord's Supper are these: (1) baptism; (2) spiritual maturity; (3) catechetical instruction; (4) examination by elders and by self; and (5) avowed consecration to the Lord's service.

(For further study on this subject see: (1) *Catechism Before Communion*, an unpublished Th.D. dissertation by F. Nigel Lee; (2) *What Mean Ye By This Service? Paedocommunion in Light of the Passover* by Richard Bacon; and (3) *Daddy, May I Take Communion? Paedocommunion vs. the Bible* by Leonard J. Coppes.)

367. Bacon, *What Mean Ye By This Service?*, 14.

Chapter Thirty-Seven

The Reality of Prayer

"Prayer is the vital breath of religion in the soul…it cultivates our sense of dependence and of God's sovereignty."
~ *Robert L. Dabney*

Therefore, let everyone who is godly pray to Thee in a time when Thou mayest be found.

Psalm 32:6

The Reality of Prayer

"To tell him who believes in God, not to pray, is to command him to cease to be a man."[1]

Q. 178: What is prayer?

A:. Prayer is an offering up of our desires unto God, in the name of Christ, by the help of his Spirit; with confession of our sins, and thankful acknowledgement of his mercies.

Q. 179: Are we to pray unto God only?

A.: God only being able to search the hearts, hear the requests, pardon the sins, and fulfil the desires of all; and only to be believed in, and worshipped with religious worship; prayer, which is a special part thereof, is to be made by all to him alone, and to none other.

Q. 180: What is it to pray in the name of Christ?

A.: To pray in the name of Christ is, in obedience to his command, and in confidence on His promises, to ask mercy for his sake; not by bare mentioning of his name, but by drawing our encouragement to pray, and our boldness, strength, and hope of acceptance in prayer, from Christ and his mediation.

---

1. Robert L. Dabney, *Lectures in Systematic Theology* (Grand Rapids, MI: Zondervan Publishing House, [1878] 1975), 715.

Q. 181: Why are we to pray in the name of Christ?

A.: The sinfulness of man, and his distance from God by reason thereof, being so great, as that we can have no access into his presence without a mediator; and there being none in heaven or earth appointed to, or fit for, that glorious work but Christ alone, we are to pray in no other name but his only.

Q. 182: How doth the Spirit help us to pray?

A.: We not knowing what to pray for as we ought, the Spirit helpeth our infirmities, by enabling us to understand both for whom, and what, and how prayer is to be made; and by working and quickening in our hearts (although not in all persons, nor at all times, in the same measure) those apprehensions, affections, and graces which are requisite for the right performance of that duty.

Q. 183: For whom are we to pray?

A.: We are to pray for the whole church of Christ upon earth; for magistrates, and ministers; for ourselves, our brethren, yea, our enemies; and for all sorts of men living, or that shall live hereafter; but not for the dead, nor for those that are known to have sinned the sin unto death.

Q. 184: For what things are we to pray?

A.: We are to pray for all things tending to the glory of God, the welfare of the church, our own or others good; but not for any thing that is unlawful.

Q. 185: How are we to pray?

A.: We are to pray with an awful apprehension of the majesty of God, and deep sense of our own unworthiness, necessities, and sins; with penitent, thankful, and enlarged hearts; with understanding, faith, sincerity, fervency, love, and perseverance, waiting upon him, with humble submission to his will.

Q. 186: What rule hath God given for our direction in the duty of prayer?

A.: The whole word of God is of use to direct us in the duty of prayer; but the special rule of direction is that form of prayer which our Saviour Christ taught his disciples, commonly called The Lord's Prayer.

The Answer to Catechism Question 178, which defines prayer, is the basis of the outline for our exposition of prayer; and out of this Answer flow most of the answers of Questions 179–186.

The Nature of Prayer

[Q. 178] The Essence of Prayer:

...AN OFFERING UP OF OUR DESIRES...

[Q. 179] The Object of Prayer:

...UNTO GOD...

[Q. 180–181] The Necessity of Praying in Jesus' Name:

...IN THE NAME OF CHRIST...

[Q. 182] The Necessity of Praying with the Help of the Holy Spirit:

...BY THE HELP OF HIS SPIRIT...

[Q. 178] The Kinds of Prayer:

...WITH CONFESSION OF OUR SINS, AND THANKFUL ACKNOWLEDGEMENT OF HIS MERCIES...

The Purpose of Prayer in the Plan of God

[Q. 183–184] The Persons and Concerns for which We Are to Pray

[Q. 185] The Manner in which We are to Pray

[Q. 186] The Rule that Governs Prayer

The Essence of Prayer (*An Offering Up of Our Desires to God*)

Q. 178: What is prayer?

A.: Prayer is an offering up of our desires unto God, in the name of Christ, by the help of his Spirit; with confession of our sins, and thankful acknowledgement of his mercies.

Prayer is Talking to God

Hear my voice, O God, in my supplication (Ps. 64:1).

Prayer is talking to God. Now, when I talk to my wife, I do not limit my conversation to the start of meals, or morning or evening, beginning by saying, "Dear Dorothy..." I talk to her all day long, going and coming. The more we talk, the more we enjoy talking to each other. If I only talk to God when I am in church, at the dinner table, or in private devotions, my relationship with Him will be cold, formal and a bit awkward. If I talk to Him in the shower, at my desk as I work, while gardening, or walking, or whatever I am doing, I am much closer to Him and more familiar with Him. I have then a happy relationship in which talking to God comes easily.... When I go fishing, the first one to hear about the results is the Lord. Of course, He knows before I do. But talking to Him is life itself.[2]

Although prayer is an intimate conversation of the pious with God, yet reverence and moderation must be kept, lest we give loose rein to miscellaneous requests, and lest we

2. Rousas J. Rushdoony, *Systematic Theology*, 2 vols. (Vallecito, CA: Ross House Books, 1994), 2:1200.

crave more than God allows; further, that we should lift up our minds to a pure and chaste veneration of him, lest God's majesty become worthless for us.[3]

Prayer Is An Unburdening of the Heart Before God

Trust in Him at all times, O people; Pour out your heart before Him; God is a refuge for us (Ps. 62:8).

Prayer is the disburdening of the heart before God. It is a pouring-out of the soul with its complaints into His bosom. God's purpose in sending us affliction is that, instead of allowing hidden sorrow to eat into our hearts, we should unburden ourselves to Him in prayer and thus exercise our faith. All prayer, whether it takes the form of thanksgiving or supplication or confession, is thus an 'effusion and manifestation of internal feeling before Him who is the searcher of the heart' [Calvin]. Through this exercise God seeks to enter deeply into our hearts and to hold communion with the inward feelings of our mind. Only when we can disburden our souls thus into the bosom of God can we prevent detestable thoughts from entering deeply into our souls.[4]

Prayer is Commanded by God

Therefore, let everyone who is godly pray to Thee in a time when Thou mayest be found (Ps. 32:6).

Our warrant for praying is that God has commanded us to pray. On every page of the Bible, either explicitly or implicitly, this command to pray is found. As our Catechism says, prayer *is to be made*

---

3. John Calvin, *Institutes of the Christian Religion*, ed. by John T. McNeill, trans. by Ford Lewis Battles, 2 vols. (Philadelphia: Westminster Press, 1960), 2:872.

4. Ronald Wallace, *Calvin's Doctrine of the Christian Life* (Grand Rapids, MI: William B. Eerdmans Publishing Co., [1959] 1961), 281–82.

by all to Him (Q. 179). Therefore, "bidding us pray, by the precept itself [God] convicts us of impious obstinacy unless we obey."[5]

Prayer is Accompanied by A Promise From God

> Ask, and it shall be given to you; seek, and you shall find; knock, and it shall be opened to you (Matt. 7:7).

A divine promise is added to the divine command to pray. Prayer, then, is not only a Biblical duty, it is also a great privilege. God is a promise-making and promise-keeping Redeemer, therefore, we can be sure that when we pray to God for grace to help in time of need, He will graciously give it: "Since then we have a great high priest who has passed through the heaven, Jesus the Son of God.... Let us therefore draw near with confidence to the throne of grace, that we may receive mercy and may find grace to help in time of need" (Heb. 4:14, 16). Furthermore, since prayer is a command and a promise, "it is certain that those who try to wriggle out of coming directly to God are not only rebellious and stubborn but are also convicted of unbelief because they distrust the promises."[6]

This teaches us that prayer is a means of grace.

> It is, therefore, by the benefit of prayer that we reach those riches which are laid up for us with the Heavenly Father.... Therefore we see that to us nothing is promised to be expected from the Lord, which we are not also bidden to ask of him in prayer. So true is it that we dig up by prayer the treasures that were pointed out by the Lord's gospel, and which our faith has gazed upon.... It is by prayer that we call him to reveal himself as wholly present to us.[7]

How is God's grace conveyed to us as we pray? Prayer

> is not intended to produce a change in God, but in us.... Prayer is the vital breath of religion in the soul...it cultivates our sense

---

5. Calvin, *Institutes of the Christian Religion*, 2:866.
6. Calvin, *Institutes of the Christian Religion*, 2:866.
7. Calvin, *Institutes of the Christian Religion*, 2:851.

> of dependence and of God's sovereignty. By confessing our sins, the sense of sin is deepened. By rendering thanks, gratitude is enlivened. By adoring the divine perfections, we are changed into the same image, from glory to glory.... Prayer is a means of grace, because God has appointed it as the instrument of man's receiving His Spiritual influences.[8]

The Object of Prayer (*Prayer is An Offering Up of Our Desires unto God*)

Q. 179: Are we to pray unto God only?

A.: God only being able to search the hearts, hear the requests, pardon the sins, and fulfil the desires of all; and only to be believed in, and worshipped with religious worship; prayer, which is a special part thereof, is to be made by all to him alone, and to none other.

The Presuppositions of Prayer

The Reality of the Tri-Personal God of the Bible

> I am the LORD, and there is no other; besides Me there is no God (Isa. 45:5).

The triune God of the Bible is the God who really is there. He is the Creator and Lord of the universe, the only true and living God, besides Whom there is no other. This one true God is a personal God, a tri-personal God, and not an impersonal force. He thinks, plans, speaks, loves, cares, and takes delight in the worship and prayers of His people. He has made man in His image to glorify Him and to

---

8. Dabney, *Lectures in Systematic Theology*, 716.

enjoy Him and to commune with Him. "To tell him who believes in... God, not to pray, is to command him to cease to be a man."[9]

The Dependence and Destitution of Man

> For all have sinned and come short of the glory of God (Rom. 3:23).

As a creation of God, man is totally dependent upon God for his very existence. As a sinner he is destitute of anything good in and of himself, and he totally lacks anything that would assist him in obtaining salvation. Therefore, if he wants the resources to help him in his desperate needs, he must go outside himself and seek them in God alone, who has willingly and freely revealed Himself in Jesus Christ.

The Necessity of Faith in Christ

> Therefore having been justified by faith, we have peace with God through our Lord Jesus Christ (Rom. 5:1).

In Jesus Christ, God gives us

> all happiness in place of our misery, all wealth in place of our neediness; in him he opens to us the heavenly treasures that our whole faith may contemplate his beloved Son, our whole expectation depends upon Him, and our whole hope cleave to and rest in him.... But after we have been instructed by faith to recognize that whatever we need and whatever we lack is in God, and in our Lord Jesus Christ... It remains for us to seek in him, and in prayers to ask of him, what we have learned to be in him.[10]

Ronald S. Wallace summarizes for us the teaching of John Calvin regarding the relation of prayer and faith in Christ:

---

9. Dabney, *Lectures in Systematic Theology*, 715.
10. Calvin, *Institutes of the Christian Religion*, 2:850.

> "The principal exercise which the children of God have," says Calvin, "is to pray; for in this way they give a true proof of their faith." ... He calls prayer the "perpetual exercise of faith." Prayer is the inevitable outcome of the presence of faith in the human heart.... Prayer is nothing else but the expression of a living faith. Prayer is faith uttering the love and desire towards God which is natural to it. The same promises which give rise to faith in the heart are a constant call and challenge to prayer for their realisation, and the same Spirit who creates faith in the heart constrains the believer also to pray. The exercise of prayer is therefore sure evidence of the presence of faith but without prayer faith cannot be genuine.... "Doubtful prayer is nothing else than mere make-belief." ... We pray only because God presents Himself to us with open arms to receive us as His children.... In prayer we claim Him as our God because He has pronounced us in His Word to be His people.... The prayer of faith will thus be the prayer of self-abasement and humility. Though faith gives rise to an approach of childlike confidence to the Heavenly Father, faith is also inseparably linked up with repentance.[11]

The Only Object of Prayer is the God of the Bible

> You shall have no other gods before Me (Ex. 20:3).

The Bible makes unmistakably clear that we are to pray to the God of the Bible alone and to no one else: no other god, no angel, no human being, living or dead. We are to pray to Him alone for several reasons.

(1) Prayer is an act of worship, and we may worship only the God of the Bible: "You shall fear only the LORD your God; and you shall worship Him, and swear by His name. You shall not follow other gods, any of the gods of the peoples who surround

11. Wallace, *Calvin's Doctrine of the Christian Life*, 271–73.

you, for the LORD your God in the midst of you is a jealous God" (Deut. 6:13–15a). To pray to any creature is to

> ascribe...divine glory to a creature...[and]...to say that he is equal with God, and to rob God of that glory which is due to him alone; and to seek that from the creature which none but God can give, or to ascribe any of the perfections of the divine nature to it, is the highest affront that can be offered to the divine Majesty.[12]

(2) Only God is able to search the human heart. In Romans 8:27, He is called "He who searches the hearts," and in John 2:25, the beloved apostle writes this about Jesus: "He did not need anyone to bear witness concerning man, for He Himself knew what was in man." Many times the most sincere and most important prayers we offer to God are unspoken, offered from the heart. Furthermore, sometimes the utterances of our lips and the desires of our hearts do not agree, and for that reason also the One to whom we pray must be able to read the heart.

(3) Only God can hear our prayers, pardon our sins and fulfill the desires of our hearts.

> When we pray to God, we seek blessings which are the effects of infinite power and goodness, such as may make us completely happy, both in this and in a better world. Moreover, we are to implore forgiveness of sin from God in prayer. Now, this is a blessing which none can bestow but God.[13]

Psalm 65:2 addresses God as, "O Thou that hearest prayer." Micah 7:18 asks the question: "Who is a God like Thee, who pardons iniquity." And Psalm 145:18–19 encourages us with the words: "The LORD is near to all who call upon Him, to all who call upon Him in truth. He will fulfill the desire of those who fear Him; He will also hear their cry and will save them."

---

12. Thomas Ridgeley, *Commentary on the Larger Catechism*, 2 vols. (Edmonton, Canada: Still Waters Revival Books, [1855] 1993), 2:561.

13. Ridgeley, *Commentary on the Larger Catechism*, 2:562.

(4) Our faith is to be placed in God alone and not in anything in this creation. Psalm 146:3 instructs us: "Do not trust in princes, in mortal man, in whom there is no salvation." Prayer is heard and accepted by God when it is mixed with faith in Him. The apostle Paul asks: "How shall they call on Him in whom they have not believed?" (Rom. 10:14) "There must be a firm persuasion that he can grant us the blessings we ask for; faith addresses itself to him as God all-sufficient, and is persuaded that he will fulfil all his promises, as a God of infinite faithfulness."[14]

The Name of God: Thou Who Dost Hear Prayer

> In this noble title of God found in Psalm 65:2—"Thou who dost hear prayer"—we find one of the greatest encouragements to pray. It teaches us that "God cannot do otherwise than answer the prayers which arise out of our human need in His service and which He Himself inspires according to the Word."[15]

> The title here given to God conveys a highly important truth. Our prayers will never be in vain. For in rejecting them God would, in a way, deny His own nature. Nor does David say that hearing prayer is something God does only on occasion but that it is an abiding part of His glory, so that He can as soon deny Himself as become deaf to our petition. If we could only impress it upon our hearts that it is something peculiar [unique] to God and inseparable from Him to hear prayer, our faith in prayer would never be shaken.[16]

---

14. Ridgeley, *Commentary on the Larger Catechism*, 2:562.
15. Wallace, *Calvin's Doctrine of the Christian Life*, 290.
16. John Calvin, quoted in Wallace, *Calvin's Doctrine of the Christian Life*, 290.

The Perfections of God and Prayer

The Perfections of God as the Basis for Prayer

> From my distress I called upon the LORD; the LORD answered me.... The LORD is for me; I will not fear; what can man do to me? The LORD is for me among those who help me (Ps. 118:5–7).

Because God is for us, His chosen people, every perfection in God is for us. Every perfection in God serves as the basis for the possibility of prayer and is an encouragement to His people to pray. (1) God is omnipresent Spirit, without a body like men. He is immense, infinite and eternal. Therefore He is everywhere all the time and able to hear all the prayers of all His people. (2) He is omniscient and all-wise, and therefore has a perfect understanding of the prayers of all people, and knows the best way to answer them. (3) He is sovereign and all-sufficient, and therefore uses prayer in His plan for the universe to carry out His purposes, without being dependent upon or limited to prayer. (4) He is unchangeable and there His commands and promises regarding prayer will always be true. (5) He is righteous, so that He will never give us evil answers to our prayers. He will always answer our prayers in a way that is consistent with His holy character. (6) He is faithful, therefore He will fulfill every promise He has made to His praying people. (7) He is good and super-abundantly generous, therefore He is more willing to bless us than we are to ask for His blessing. (8) He is gracious and merciful, therefore He will not look for any merit in our prayers; but He will answer them in spite of the fact that our prayers do not deserve to be answered. (9) He is eternal, so that His ability and willingness to answer prayers never wane or grow thin. (10) He is love. Through the prayers of His people, He brings them into intimate communion with Himself in Christ.

Do God's Perfections Make Prayer Superfluous?

If God is as He has revealed Himself to be—sovereign, almighty, and all-knowing—why pray and ask Him for things? If He already has everything planned and already knows everything, why pray? Do the perfections of God make prayer superfluous? Not at all! In fact, the perfections of God are not objections to prayer, they are arguments and encouragements for prayer. The sovereign, almighty, omniscient, wise and good God has commanded us to pray. He has ordained prayer as the instrument for receiving His foreordained blessings. God is not dependent upon our prayers, but we are. God ordained prayer for our benefit, not His.

Prayer to a sovereign and omniscient God is of momentous importance: (1) It fires up our hearts "with a zealous and burning desire ever to seek, love and serve Him." (2) It keeps out of our hearts any desire or wish "of which we should be ashamed to make him a witness, while we learn to set all our wishes before his eyes, and even to pour out our whole hearts." (3) It prepares us "to receive his benefits with true gratitude of heart and thanksgiving, benefits that our prayer reminds us come from his hand." (4) Having received what we prayed for, convinced that God Himself has answered our prayer, it leads us "to meditate upon his kindness more ardently." (5) It enables us to "embrace with greater delight those things which we acknowledge to have been obtained by prayers." (6) It clarifies and confirms His providence,

> while we understand not only that he promises never to fail us, and of his own will opens the way to call upon him at the very point of necessity, but also that he ever extends his hand to help his own, not wet-nursing them with words but defending them with present help.[17]

17. Calvin, *Institutes of the Christian Religion*, 2:852.

The Necessity of Praying in Jesus' Name (*in the Name of Christ*)

Q. 180: *What is it to pray in the name of Christ?*

A.: To pray in the name of Christ is, in obedience to his command, and in confidence on His promises, to ask mercy for his sake; not by bare mentioning of his name, but by drawing our encouragement to pray, and our boldness, strength, and hope of acceptance in prayer, from Christ and his mediation.

The Meaning of Praying in the Name of Christ

> Jesus said to him... "And whatever you ask in My name, that will I do, that the Father may be glorified in the Son. If you ask Me anything in My name, I will do it" (John 14:13–14).

All true prayer must be prayed in the name of Christ, because only through Christ is prayer possible. As Jesus Himself said in John 14:6: "I am the way, the truth and the life, no one comes to the Father but by Me." Therefore God has commanded us to pray in the name of Christ (John 14:13), with confidence that God will be faithful to the promises He has made to us in Christ's name (John 14:14). If mercy is to be sought and received from God, it can only be sought and given in the name of Christ, because this divine-human person is the "one mediator also between God and men" (1 Tim. 2:5). And so Daniel prayed:

> So now, our God, listen to the prayer of Thy servant and to his supplications, and *for the sake of the Lord*, let Thy face shine on Thy desolate sanctuary. O my God, incline Thine ear and hear! Open Thine eyes and see our desolations and the city which is called by Thy name; *for we are not presenting our supplications before Thee on account of any merits of*

> *our own, but on account of Thy great compassion.* O Lord, hear! O Lord forgive! O Lord listen and take action! *For Thine own sake,* O my God, do not delay, because Thy city and Thy people are called by Thy name (Dan. 9:17–19).

To pray in Jesus' name does not mean simply that all our prayers must end with this verbal formula: "in Jesus' name," as if it were a superstitious device that manipulates God (Matt. 7:21). Rather, to pray in Jesus' name means to draw specific blessings from the "Name" of Christ, *i.e.*, from the person and work of Christ Himself, for "name" in the Bible, when used of God denotes the revelation of His character and will, the revelation of Himself. God's name is God. Those blessings that we draw from Christ's Name include: (1) Encouragement to pray; (2) Boldness in prayer; (3) Strength for prayer; and (4) Hope, *i.e.*, confident assurance, that God will hear and answer our prayer.

The Name of Christ As Encouragement

> Since then we have a great high priest who has passed through the heavens, Jesus the Son of God.... Let us therefore draw near with confidence to the throne of grace, that we may receive mercy and may find grace to help in time of need (Heb.4:14, 16).

> He who did not spare His own Son, but delivered Him up for us all, how will He not also with Him freely give us all things? (Rom. 8:32).

"It is only through the interposition of Christ that the throne of God's dreadful glory and majesty is converted into a throne of grace."[18] To come before God in the name of Christ is the entire work of faith. Faith has nothing to plead except Christ and His work. And all faith hopes to receive from God, comes through the mediatorial work of Jesus Christ. Therefore God encourages us to come before His throne of grace boldly and with confidence that we

18. Wallace, *Calvin's Doctrine of the Christian Life*, 274.

are accepted by Him in Christ. All of God's promises are fulfilled in and by Him. All God's blessings for us have been purchased by His blood. Our liberty to come to God as our Father is based on His atoning sufferings and death for our sin. He, and He alone, is the foundation of our hope that we have obtained mercy with God. Therefore we gladly and confidently make our supplications to God in the name of Christ. "*We have the heart of God as soon as we have placed before Him the name of his Son.*"[19]

The Name of Christ as Power

> May His Name endure forever; May His name increase as long as the sun shines; And let men bless themselves by Him; Let all nations call Him blessed (Ps. 72:17).

"The only fortress of salvation consists in invocation of His name."[20] By the "name" of Christ, (or of God), we are to understand: (1) Christ Himself (Ps. 22:1); (2) Christ's titles (Ex. 3:13, 14); (3) Christ's Word (Ps. 5:11; Acts 9:15); (4) Christ's works (Ps. 8:1, 5); (5) Christ's worship (Ex. 20:24); and (6) Christ's perfections (Ex. 34:6, John 17:26), which are glorious (Ps. 72:17), transcendent and incomparable (Rev. 19:16), almighty (Phil. 2:10), holy and reverent (Ps. 111:5), and eternal (Isa. 55:13). In other words,

> the "name of Jesus" signifies Jesus Himself. According to the Hebrew usage of the word, the *name* gives expression to the very being itself, and designates a person as he is, and as he reveals himself [Muller]. *Hence, to invoke the Name of Jesus is to invoke His Person, power and presence...* There is little such invocation of the Name in our time because there is little awareness of the reign and presence of the Great King, Jesus the Christ.... To ask *in His Name* means to ask in terms of His kingdom and our life in Him. To ask in His Name is to

19. John Calvin, *Commentary on the Gospel According to John*, trans. by Rev. William Pringle, 2 vols. (Edinburgh: Calvin Translation Society, 1843; reprint Grand Rapids, MI: Baker Book House, 1979), 2:158. Emphasis added.

20. John Calvin, *Institutes of the Christian Religion*, trans. by John Allen, 2 vols. (Philadelphia: Presbyterian Board of Christian Education, 1936), 2:94.

> acknowledge His Lordship over us, and His Sovereign right to give as He ordains, much, little, or nothing, and to thank Him for everything.[21]

Therefore, to pray in the name of Christ is to pray for Christ Himself to exercise His awesome power and to manifest His mighty presence in the advance of His triumphant Kingdom. (Note: Christians are not only to pray in Jesus' Name, they are also to act in Jesus' Name (Col. 3:17). All our prayers and activities must be in Jesus' Name to be effective.)

The Name of Christ as Direction

> If you ask Me anything in My name, I will do it (John 14:13–14, 15:7, 16:23).

God has manifested His Name to us in Jesus Christ (John 1:18) and in the Bible (2 Tim. 3:16–17). He has revealed to us all we need to know about Himself, His character and His will. Therefore, when we are told that we will receive from God all we ask Him in the Name of Jesus, we are being informed that whatever we ask God in accordance with the revelation of His character and His will, He will most certainly give us—If you abide in Me, and My words abide in you, ask whatever you wish, and it shall be done for you (John 15:7).

Jesus brings this out in His High Priestly Prayer found in John 17:6–8. He says that He has finished the work God gave Him of manifesting His "name" (vs. 6), which "word" (vs. 6b), His disciples have kept; and of giving them God's "words" (vs. 8). This sanctifying "word" is "truth" (vs. 17). It is obvious by the way that Jesus uses these words interchangeably that to pray "in His name" is to pray according to the Word of God, which comprises the words of God, which are the revealed Truth of God. Jesus is saying, then, that whatever we ask according to His revealed will in the Bible, God will give. This is exactly how John himself explains Jesus' promise in 1 John 5:14–15: "And this is the confidence which we have before Him, that, *if we ask anything according to His will, He hears us.* And

21. Rushdoony, *Systematic Theology*, 2:1205–07. Emphasis added.

if we know that He hears us in whatever we ask, we know that we have the request which we have asked from Him" (emphasis added).

The Name of Christ as Hope

> These things I have written to you who believe in the name of the Son of God, in order that you may know that you have eternal life. And this is the confidence which we have before Him, that, if we ask anything according to His will, He hears us. And if we know that He hears us in whatever we ask, we know that we have the requests which we have asked from Him (1 John 5:13–15).

From the name of Christ believers draw *hope of acceptance in prayer.* Believing in the name of the Son of God, we not only have eternal life, we also have the assurance that we possess eternal life in Him. Furthermore we have because of His Name "the confidence," *i.e.*, the confident hope, that our prayers are accepted with God, that He will hear us when we pray according to His will, and "we know" that He will give us what we have asked for in accordance with His revealed will.

The Reason for Prayer in the Name of Christ

Q. 181: Why are we to pray in the name of Christ?

A.: The sinfulness of man, and his distance from God by reason thereof, being so great, as that we can have no access into his presence without a mediator; and there being none in heaven or earth appointed to, or fit for, that glorious work but Christ alone, we are to pray in no other name but his only.

> Jesus said to him, "I am the way, and the truth, and the life; no one comes to the Father but by Me" (John 14:6).

> For there is one God, and one mediator between God and men, the man Christ Jesus (1 Tim. 2:5).

In this Catechism Question, we are given two reasons why it is absolutely necessary for us to offer all our prayers to God in the name of Jesus Christ. First, our sins have so separated us from God that we cannot come into His presence nor do anything to reconcile ourselves to God, and that He will not look on us with favor and blessing, but with abhorrence and anger, without a mediator, who will reconcile God and man by propitiating God and regenerating man. Second, no one else in the entire universe is qualified to be this mediator but the God-man, Jesus Christ, who reconciled God and man through His own death, and who, by His Spirit, regenerates sinful people. Therefore, we are to pray to God only in the Name of Jesus Christ, because only Jesus Christ, by God's appointment, is "an Advocate with the Father, pleading our cause before his throne, and so giving us ground of encouragement that our persons shall be accepted and our prayers answered on his account."[22]

> God is obliged in honour, as a God of infinite holiness, to separate and banish sinners from his comfortable presence, they being liable to the curse and condemning sentence of the law; by reason of which his terror makes them afraid, and his dread falls upon them. They have, however, in the gospel, not only an invitation to come, but a discovery [revelation] of that great Mediator whom God has ordained to conduct his people into his presence, and who has procured liberty of access to him.... God has, for this end, erected a throne of grace, and encouraged us to come to it, and given many great and precious promises, whereby we may hope for acceptance in his sight. Now, these promises being all established in Christ, and the blessings contained in them having been procured by his blood, and we having liberty,

22. Ridgeley, *Commentary on the Larger Catechism*, 563.

in coming, to plead what he has done and suffered, as what was designed to be the foundation of our hope of obtaining mercy, we are said to come and make our supplications to God in the name of Christ.[23]

The Necessity of Praying with the Help of the Holy Spirit (by the help of His Spirit)

Q. 182: How doth the Spirit help us to pray?

A.: We not knowing what to pray for as we ought, the Spirit helpeth our infirmities, by enabling us to understand both for whom, and what, and how prayer is to be made; and by working and quickening in our hearts (although not in all persons, nor at all times, in the same measure) those apprehensions, affections, and graces which are requisite for the right performance of that duty.

> And in the same way the Spirit also helps our weakness; for we do not know how to pray as we should, but the Spirit Himself intercedes for us with groanings too deep for words; and He who searches the hearts knows what the mind of the Spirit is, because He intercedes for the saints according to the will of God (Rom. 8:26–27).

Because of our utter weakness to do what is pleasing to God in and of ourselves, due to our sinfulness, we need the constant assistance of the Holy Spirit of God, who indwells all believers in Christ, Romans 8:9. Our weakness is especially obvious in our praying, in that we do not know how to pray as we should, either with regard to the manner in which we are to pray or the concerns for which we

---

23. Ridgeley, *Commentary on the Larger Catechism*, 2:562–63.

are to pray. The indwelling Spirit's assistance in our praying is powerful and profound. (1) He enables us to understand for whom and for what we are to pray, and how those prayers should be made; and (2) He works within us, invigorating and stimulating (*quickening*) our hearts to that frame of mind and disposition that is necessary for true prayer. For this reason, Zechariah calls the Holy Spirit poured out on the church, "The Spirit of grace and of supplications (for grace)" (Zech. 12:10). His work is to awaken in us a God-consecrated disposition and to lead the heart to prayer.

The Necessity for the Spirit's Assistance in Our Praying

> Even though prayer must be a genuine expression of the heart in its felt need and in its gratitude, it should not be dictated or inspired by merely the natural impulse of the heart. No man can pray aright through the spontaneous impulse of his own feeling. Such prayer apart from the Spirit of God is nothing more than mere heathen babble and a mockery of God. Indeed, to allow our own natural impulses to direct our prayers is to seek to make God the agent of our wicked concupiscence [evil desires], rather than to approach Him as our judge. It is dangerous, therefore, to open our lips before God "unless the Spirit instruct us how to pray aright" [Calvin]. The ability to engage in true prayer is therefore the gift of the Spirit.... It is the Spirit who moves our hearts with such fervency that they can "pierce into the very heaven" [Calvin].[24]

> For through Him [Christ] we both have our access *in one Spirit* to the Father (Eph. 2:18. Emphasis added).

This verse teaches us that the Holy Spirit is as essential to prayer as is Jesus Christ. Without the Spirit we cannot pray, for true prayer is always prayer BY or IN the Spirit THROUGH Christ. "Without the Holy Spirit prayer is mechanical, lifeless, difficult, prayer is an

24. Wallace, *Calvin's Doctrine of the Christian Life*, 286–87.

awful task; but with Him everything is changed and it becomes free and glorious and the supreme enjoyment of the soul."[25]

What does the Spirit do in our praying? Many things. He creates within us a spiritual mind. He reminds us of our sin. He shows us our need of God, His mercy and His blessing. He reveals the glory of God to our faith. He keeps our eyes and trust on the Lord Jesus Christ. He leads us into a correct understanding of the covenant promises of God. He give us joy and freedom in praying.

> *Do you enjoy prayer?* Have you ever enjoyed prayer? Is it to you a most delightful occupation? If it is not, it is because you have forgotten that the operations of the Holy Spirit are absolutely essential to prayer. Therefore, when you next engage in prayer remember this. Pray to Him, ask Him to enliven you and to quicken you. He will do so; He has already done it without your knowing it. The desire for prayer has been produced by Him.... Go to Him in your dryness, in your deadness, tell Him that you feel ashamed of yourself, tell Him that you want to know God, tell Him that you want to enjoy God, tell Him you want to know this freedom in the Spirit; and ask Him to make it possible, and go on until the answer comes. And it will come![26]

The Manner of the Spirit's Assistance in Our Praying

Without the help of the Holy Spirit prayer is impossible! We can read prayers without the Spirit. We can say prayers without the Spirit. We can repeat good phrases without the Spirit. We can kneel or raise our arms without the Spirit. But we cannot pray without the Spirit. We cannot contact God without the Spirit. We cannot commune with God without the Spirit assisting us in our praying.

Only the Spirit can give new life to someone who is spiritually dead. Only the Spirit can give a person a new heart filled with the

25. D. Martyn Lloyd-Jones, *God's Way of Reconciliation: Studies in Ephesians Chapter 2* (Grand Rapids, MI: Baker Book House, 1972), 273.

26. Lloyd-Jones, *God's Way of Reconciliation*, 277.

desire to know, obey and commune with God in prayer. In fact, the regenerated person will be

> unable to resist praying to God...it is accurate to state that if a person does not pray, he is spiritually dead. He is not a Christian. For a person that is "in the Spirit" *must* pray, just as a seed placed in fertile ground and watered must sprout. Where there is life, there must be activity. And where the Spirit of prayer is there must be prayer.[27]

How does the Holy Spirit assist us in our prayer?

(1) He helps us overcome the difficulties involved in praying, such as the difficulty of realizing the presence of God, of concentration, of developing a sense of unworthiness, of doubts. When we pray, we are besieged by all the forces of hell to distract us.

(2) He opens up to us our true needs and deficiencies, our sins and shortcomings. Self-ignorance is a great hindrance to fervent prayer.

(3) He reveals to us the rich provisions of God's abundant grace which is treasured up in Christ for us, which is a great encouragement in prayer, John 16:7–14.

> The plea of the blood of Jesus; who can estimate its power? It has shaken the kingdom of darkness until its vast foundation stones are split wide open, and the awful structure is tottering to its fall. It has quenched the wrath of God against a sinning world. It has redeemed millions upon millions of immortal sinning souls.... It has impoverished hell; it has enriched heaven a thousand-fold; it moves the Father's heart as no other power ever has or can move it.... Then take the plea of the love of God.... There is yet another plea to support our petitions, *in the glory of God....* When the Spirit, interceding in us, opens up the power of

27. Edwin Palmer, quoted in Morton Smith, *Systematic Theology*, 2 vols. (Greenville, SC: Greenville Seminary Press, 1994), 2:715.

> the great gospel pleas, the vilest of sinners may feel bold in coming to the throne of grace, as he is commanded and exhorted to do. Covered with the spotless robe of the Lord's own righteousness, he can venture nearer to the intolerable splendor of the throne of God than the most favored angel in the ranks of the heavenly hierarchy.[28]

(4) He produces in us that disposition and ignites those desires which motivate us to draw near to God.

(5) He maintains those desires and gives them stability.

(6) He strengthens and excites those spiritual fruit, gifts and graces which are essential to communion with God, such as faith, repentance, love, trust, delight in God.

(7) He either removes obstacles to prayer or else He stirs us up to watch out for them and to rise above them, such as, ignorance, unbelief, indifference, despondence, physical infirmities, business cares, the influences of society.

It is important to keep in mind this fundamental point: the Holy Spirit works in coordination with Christian activity and exertion of effort in serving Christ. As we endeavor to pray aright, He assists us. Jesus said it is those "who love ME and keep My commandments" (John 14:15), who are privileged to "ask Me anything in My name" (vs. 14).

The Holy Spirit as Our Indwelling Intercessor

Jesus Christ is our Intercessor in Heaven (Heb. 7:25–27); and the Holy Spirit is our Intercessor in our hearts:

> And in the same way the Spirit also helps our weakness; for we do not know how to pray as we should, but the Spirit Himself intercedes for us with groanings too deep for words; and He who searches the hearts knows what the mind of the

28. Curtis R. Vaughan, *The Gifts of the Holy Spirit* (Edinburgh: The Banner of Truth Trust, [1894] 1975), 345–47.

> Spirit is, because He intercedes for the saints according to the will of God" (Rom. 8:26–27).

As our Intercessor in our hearts, the indwelling Holy Spirit, helps us prepare our prayers and formulate our petitions. God hears and answers all prayers prepared by the intercessory work of the Spirit on the basis of the atonement and intercession of Jesus Christ. The Spirit produces within the believer unutterable groanings (Gal. 4:6), which are according to the Word of God, and therefore heard, understood and answered by God, even when they are mere sighs. These Spirit-produced groans and sighs are experienced only in Christians (John 17:9).

In Romans 8:26, we are told that as the Holy Spirit "intercedes for us with groanings too deep for words," God the Father, the Searcher of all hearts, "knows what the mind of the Spirit is, *because* He intercedes for the saints according to will of God." What an astounding statement! Within our renewed hearts are wishes, groans and sighs that the world knows nothing about. But God knows and understands them. The Holy Spirit Himself has created what is expressed in these groanings; and God knows the mind of the Spirit. God the Father knows what the Holy Spirit is thinking. He knows what the Spirit has said to us. He knows the meaning of what the Spirit has put in our hearts. Although we cannot express it, God knows, approves and delights in it. God can tell what the Spirit is thinking in our groanings! He sees the mind of the Holy Spirit in these spiritual sighs arising from His child and therefore, understands, approves and answers the prayer.

> As God searches the heart of the children of God He finds unuttered and unutterable groanings. Though they are thus inarticulate, there is a meaning and intent that cannot escape the omniscient eye of God—they are wholly intelligible to him. And, furthermore, they are found to be in accordance with his will. They are consonant with [in agreement with] his will because, though surpassing our understanding and utterance, they are indited [composed] by the Holy Spirit and are the ways in which his intercessions come to expression in

> our consciousness. Since they are the intercessions of the Holy Spirit, they always meet with the understanding and approval of God.[29]

The Holy Spirit, our Indwelling Intercessor, takes the desires on the heart of our Heavenly Intercessor, Jesus Christ, and plants them in our hearts, making them the petitions of our prayers. When we desire what Jesus desires, we pray for what Jesus prays. And when we pray for what Jesus prays, we receive what Jesus prays for us. Seen in this way, the intercession of Jesus Christ and the intercession of the Holy Spirit are one.

The Kinds of Prayer

(*An Offering up of Our Desires...with Confession of our Sins, and Thankful Acknowledgement of His Mercies*)

> With all prayer and petition, pray at all times in the Spirit (Eph. 6:18).

Adoration

> Who is like Thee among the gods, O LORD? Who is like Thee, majestic in holiness, awesome in praises, working wonders? (Ex. 15:11).

Adoration is the homage and entire prostration of the inner life of a person standing in awe of the splendor, majesty, holiness, blessedness, beauty and glory of the God of the Bible. It manifests this loving reverence in verbal expressions in worship to Him in whom these glorious perfections reside. This language of adoration is accompanied with praise, which arises from our consciousness of the delight we enjoy in the contemplation of these divine perfections. We adore God as we consider the revelation of Himself, His perfec-

29. John Murray, *New International Commentary on the New Testament: The Epistle to the Romans* (Grand Rapids, MI: William B. Eerdmans Publishing Co., 1959), 1:313.

tions, His will and His works in His Word. Therefore the verbal expression of adoration is largely in the titles by which the triune God is revealed in the Bible: the Lord God, the Lord our God, the Lord God Almighty, the great and dreadful God, the Lord strong and mighty, the Father of glory, the Most High, the King of kings and Lord of lords, the High and Lofty One who inhabits eternity, the Maker of heaven and earth, the Lord our righteousness, the God of peace, the God of our salvation, our Father who art in heaven, the God and Father of our Lord Jesus Christ, the only wise God, the King eternal, immortal and invisible.

But adoration is not content only with these awesome titles.

> The feeling will pour itself out with a broader flood through the vent which these may open. A few examples of Scripture may be cited here as examples of adoring worship.... 'Who is like unto thee, O LORD, among the gods? Who is like thee, glorious in holiness, fearful in praises, doing wonders?' (Ex. xv:11). 'Blessed be thou, Lord God of Israel, our Father, forever and ever. Thine, O Lord, is the greatness and the power and the glory and the victory and the majesty: for all that is in the heaven and in the earth is thine; thine is the kingdom, O Lord, and thou art exalted as Head above all. Now therefore, our God, we thank thee and praise thy glorious name.' (1 Chron. xxix:10–13). 'Bless the Lord, O my soul, O Lord my God, thou art very great: thou art clothed with honor and majesty, who coverest thyself with light as with a garment.' (Ps. civ:1, 2). 'Now unto the King eternal, immortal, invisible, the only wise God, be power and glory forever and ever. Amen.' (1 Tim. i:17):
>
> Oh! The selfishness of the thought which restricts prayer to mere petition! Shall nothing drive us to God but the pressure of want? Shall we think of him only when we are hungry, and forget him when we are full? ... Is there nothing attractive in the character of Jehovah himself to draw us with the power of a magnet? Surely it is a dull heart which does not warm to the beauty which he discloses, and whose impulse is not to

> utter its joy in these ascriptions of adoration and praise.... Or what nobler employment of the tongue, the glory of our frame, than to articulate his praise in the loftiest language which sanctified genius can inspire? ...
>
> The soul must come out of itself, and look upon Christ, who is the author of salvation; and peace flows in through the trust which ventures all upon him. Hence the profit derived from adoration. The morbid tendency to gloat over what is dark within, is checked. The eye is turned outward to gaze upon the beauty which entrances. The affections are awakened in the presence of holiness and goodness. The sickly sensibilities are toned up, and a healthy religious action takes the place of despondency which was weakening all the powers of the soul.[30]

Confession

> If we confess our sins, He is faithful and righteous to forgive us our sins and to cleanse us from all unrighteousness (1 John 1:9).

Painfully conscious that all good things from God have been forfeited by his sin, the sinner recognizes that he cannot approach God except in sackcloth and ashes, in shame and brokenness of heart, and so he begins his worship with the cry, "'Unclean! Unclean! God be merciful to me a sinner!' Such must be the language bursting from his lips, as he lies in the dust before his Judge."[31]

What does confession of sin actually involve?

First,

> it begins with a *clear perception of the nature of sin*, as seen from the inside as well as from the outside. Sin cannot be fully confessed merely in its consequences. These are dread-

30. Benjamin M. Palmer, *Theology of Prayer As Viewed in the Religion of Nature and in the System of Grace* (Jas. K. Hazen, 1894; reprint Harrisonburg, VA: Sprinkle Publications, 1980), 31–34.

31. Palmer, *Theology of Prayer*, 41.

> ful enough, but not so dreadful as the thing itself. God looks at sin in its intrinsic vileness. We make a true confession only when the eye has been opened to take the same view; not, of course, as broad and as deep as that of Jehovah, ...but a view nevertheless which is true, because it discovers the real deformity of sin as opposed to all that is beautiful and holy and excellent in the character of God.[32]

Second,

> with this conviction of the essential evil of sin, *the heart will be aroused to a proper indignation against it....* There is such a feeling in a good man's breast as a cultivated resentment, which shall pervade his whole being and arouse every faculty. There is in the soul of the true penitent a virtuous and burning hatred of that which robs God of his honor, and himself of peace.[33]

Third,

> following this holy anger against sin, *confession involves a judicial pronouncement against it before the tribunal of conscience.* God declares against it, 'the soul that sinneth, it shall die.' His justice utters the decree which it deserves; and now the sinner, arraigned before the bar of his own conscience, which is the shadow of the tribunal upon which Jehovah sits, pronounces the same condemnation. He not only perceives the fact of transgression, but feels the wrongness of it; and concurs in the justice of the penalty which the law thunders against it.[34]

Fourth,

> all this, however, would be vain *if confession did not include true repentance and abandonment of the sin which is bewailed....* In true confession all the powers of the soul are

32. Palmer, *Theology of Prayer*, 43.
33. Palmer, *Theology of Prayer*, 43.
34. Palmer, *Theology of Prayer*, 43–44.

engaged. The judgment recognizes the standard of duty, and notes the deviations from it. The conscience feels these deviations to be wrong, and fills the soul with shame. The heart kindles with a holy abhorrence of what is impure within ourselves. And the will turns from its commission 'with full purpose of, and endeavor after, new obedience.' This is the sinner purged from guilt, when his confession has been heard by him who is able to forgive.[35]

Thanksgiving

Be anxious for nothing, but in everything by prayer and supplication with thanksgiving let your requests be made known to God (Phil. 4:6).

God's whole purpose in creating us, in adorning the world with such a magnificent variety of beautiful and good things, and in watching over us with such careful providence is that we might be moved continually to render praise back to Him.... To omit such thanksgiving is to rob God of the honor due to His name.... Without thanksgiving, nothing can please God. He accepts all service only as it is an expression of grateful thanks for His mercy. Therefore thanksgiving sanctifies the rest of life and the rest of our service to God.... Thanksgiving sanctifies not only the rest of life but also the whole activity of prayer. We can pray aright only if our hearts are pervaded by a true sense of gratitude to God, since prayer must arise from a feeling of love.... Only when our feelings are regulated and our desires restrained by thanksgiving can we avoid the fretful and morose murmuring against God, and the impatience with His slowness in answering or His refusal to grant selfish wishes, which mars the prayer-life of so many. But thanksgiving is not merely a restraining influ-

35. Palmer, *Theology of Prayer*, 44.

> ence in the life of prayer. It invigorates our faith and stirs us up to a new fervour in prayer.[36]

Supplication

> Be anxious for nothing, but in everything by prayer and supplication with thanksgiving let your requests be made known to God (Phil. 4:6).

> He who is filled with disgust at the hideousness of sin, and who is fixed in his purpose to break from its control, will not rest in the impotence of simply bewailing his calamity. He will implore the divine mercy for pardon of his guilt, and the divine power for deliverance from its bondage. This is supplication, which may not differ from petition, except in the intensity of its meaning—as request may deepen into entreaty. The etymology of the word indicates at once the humility and vehemence of the prayer; being derived from the kneeling posture of the suppliant, when he pours forth his entreaties at the feet of his master.[37]

Petition and supplication spring from man the creature's total dependence upon his Creator. We petition and supplicate God when we seek from Him the blessings we need to live for His glory.

> Petition...implies a sense of need awakened in the soul. The want [lack] must not only exist, but must be felt.... It is, therefore, a law of the divine administration to supply no want [lack] which is not first felt, and so felt as to drive the creature to seek relief. Without such provision the connection would not be preserved between the creature and the Creator, and the former would perish in its helplessness.[38]

---

36. Wallace, *Calvin's Doctrine of the Christian Life*, 284–86.
37. Palmer, *Theology of Prayer*, 44–45.
38. Palmer, *Theology of Prayer*, 37.

Petition and supplication presuppose a God who has the power and the willingness to grant us what we need, and our total dependence upon Him.

> It is this which distinguishes prayer from an outcry of distress. It is the expression of intelligent hope, as well as of impassioned desire. OVER AGAINST THE INSUFFICIENCY OF THE CREATURE STANDS THE FULNESS OF THE CREATOR.... As this dependence is entire, covering the whole tract of creaturely existence and everything by which that existence may be sustained, it is easy to see how large a space petition must occupy in prayer.[39]

Intercession

> With all prayer and petition, pray at all times...for all the saints (Eph. 6:18).

> Our prayer must not be self-centred. It must arise not only because we feel our own need as a burden which we must lay upon God but also because we are so bound up in love with our fellowmen that we feel their need as acutely as our own.... To make intercession for men is the most powerful and practical way in which we can express our love for them.... Thus to every Christian Christ commits the welfare of the Church by committing to him the vital task of interceding for the Church and Kingdom. It is the presence in the midst of the Church in every age of those who come before God to make intercession that continually saves the Church in each generation from perishing through the coldness and indifference of the rest of its members. In exercising the ministry of intercession for our brethren in their need, we must feel ourselves identified with and personally involved in the need of those we pray for....

---

39. Palmer, *Theology of Prayer*, 38–39.

> Our intercession for the Church is an echo of the continued intercession of Christ. It is our expression of our unity with one another in the body of the Church and with our great High Priest and Head.... It must be asserted that our intercession within the Church is not something which we add in order to perfect or supplement the prevailing intercession of Jesus Christ. It is rather an echo within our hearts of His intercession in which we participate by the Spirit who prays within us.[40]

The Purpose of Prayer in the Plan of God

Since God has foreordained everything that happens, why has He commanded us to pray? What is God's purpose for prayer? Several wrong answers to those questions have been offered.

Some have said that the purpose of prayer is to give God input so as to help Him shape His policies. This arrogant answer is a denial of God's omniscience, sovereignty, wisdom and self-sufficiency. Romans 11:34 says: "Who has known the mind of the Lord? Or who has been His counselor?" God's eternally decreed policies are NOT being shaped by man's prayers; they were "shaped" in the mind of God before the creation of the universe. God does not submit His will to the will of man for approval or advice. "All the inhabitants of the earth are accounted as nothing, but He does according to HIS will in the host of heaven and among the inhabitants of the earth" (Dan. 4:35).

Others have said that the purpose of prayer is to change God's mind and purposes. But since God is perfect, omniscient and unchangeable, there is never any need or possibility for God to change His eternal purposes. Such an answer is an impugning of God's perfection and wisdom. It is to exalt man's goodness and knowledge above God. But, as God said: "My purpose will be established and I will accomplish all My good pleasure.... Truly I have spoken it, truly I will bring it to pass. I have planned it, surely I will do it" (Isa. 46:10–11). Furthermore, to say that God changes His mind and

---

40. Wallace, *Calvin's Doctrine of the Christian Life*, 287–89.

plans or that He can be convinced or coaxed to change His mind by man reveals a base conception of God. God describes Himself in the Bible as being "without variableness or shadow of turning" in James 1:17. Jesus Christ is described as being "the same yesterday, today and forever" in Hebrews 13:8. And God emphatically declares in Malachi 3:6: "I am the LORD, I do not change!"

Some speak of prayer as if it were a means of persuading God to do things He is really reluctant to do. This view also presupposes a low view of God and a view of man that makes him, at least, in some areas, superior to God. It is also a flat denial of the implications of God's promises that if we ask anything according to His revealed will, He will give it (1 John 5:14). Martin Luther wrote: "Prayer is not overcoming God's reluctance, but it is a laying hold of His willingness."

Still others would see prayer only as a means of spiritual growth and as a divinely appointed means of expressing our dependency upon God. Now prayer is indeed all that (Ps. 116:1); but it is much more. As high as the intent of those may be who hold this view, it still, along with the others, gives us a man-centered, hence a deficient, understanding of the purpose of prayer.

What, then, is the purpose of prayer in the eternal plan of God? *Ezekiel 36:37–38* gives us a clear answer: Thus says the LORD God, "This also I will let the house of Israel ask Me to do for them. I will increase their men like a flock.... THEN THEY WILL KNOW THAT I AM THE LORD." According to this text, the purpose of prayer is thoroughly God-centered, concerned with God's glory, God's claims, God's rights, God's promises, and God's dominion. *The purpose of prayer is to praise God and to petition Him to give us what He has promised so that humankind will know that He is the Lord.*

Arthur Pink has written on Ezekiel 36:37 in the chapter entitled "God's Sovereignty and Prayer" in his great book, *The Sovereignty of God*:

> Here then is *the* design of prayer: not that God's will may be *altered*, but that it may be *accomplished*... It is because God *has* promised certain things, that we can ask for them with the full assurance of faith. It is God's purpose that His will shall be

> brought about by His own appointed means, and that He may do His people good upon *His own* terms, and that is, by the "means" and "terms" of entreaty and supplication.[41]

So we see that the sovereignty of God does not make prayer superfluous. On the contrary, it gives prayer an important place as *the divinely decreed means of accomplishing divinely decreed purposes so that all human beings may know that God is the Lord.* Robert Haldane has written: "If indeed all things happen by a blind chance, or a fatal necessity, prayers in that case could be of no moral efficacy, and of no use; but since they are regulated by the direction of Divine wisdom, prayers have a place in the order of events."[42] God has decreed prayer as a means of accomplishing His purposes without being limited by or dependent upon prayer. The point is this: there are some things God has determined He will not do for His people except through their prayers, and even then, for His own glory, as well as for their benefit.

> Our main purpose...has been to emphasize the need for submitting, in prayer, *our wills to God's.* But it must also be added, that prayer is much more than a pious exercise, and far otherwise than a mechanical performance. Prayer is, indeed, a Divinely appointed means whereby we may obtain from God the things we ask, *providing* we ask for those things which are in accord with *His will.*[43]

---

41. Arthur W. Pink, *The Sovereignty of God* (Grand Rapids, MI: Baker Book House [1930] 1977), 212.
42. Pink, *The Sovereignty of God*, 211.
43. Pink, *The Sovereignty of God*, 218.

The People and Concerns for Which We Are to Pray

The People for Whom We Are to Pray

Q. 183: For whom are we to pray?

A.: We are to pray for the whole church of Christ upon earth; for magistrates, and ministers; for ourselves, our brethren, yea, our enemies; and for all sorts of men living, or that shall live hereafter; but not for the dead, nor for those that are known to have sinned the sin unto death.

We learn from this answer that we are to pray for the whole church of Christ on earth: "With *all* prayer and petition pray at *all* times in the Spirit, and with this in view, be on the alert with *all* perseverance and petition *for all the saints*" (Eph. 6:18); for people in places of political authority: "First of all, then, I urge that entreaties and prayers, petitions and thanksgivings, be made on behalf of all men, for kings and all who are in authority, in order that we may lead a tranquil and quiet life in all godliness and dignity" (1 Tim. 2:1–2); for ministers: "and pray on my behalf [Paul's], that utterance may be given to me in the opening of my mouth, to make known with boldness the mystery of the gospel, for which I am an ambassador in chains; that in proclaiming it I may speak boldly, as I ought to speak" (Eph. 6:19–20); "Devote yourselves to prayer, keeping alert in it with an attitude of thanksgiving; praying at the same time for us [Paul] as well, that God may open up to us a door for the word, so that we may speak forth the mystery of Christ, for which I have also been imprisoned; in order that I may make it clear in the way I ought to speak" (Col. 4:2–4); for ourselves: "Deliver me, [Jacob], I pray, from the hand of my brother, from the hand of Esau; for I fear him, lest he come and attack me, mother with children. For Thou didst say, 'I will surely prosper you, and make your descendants as the sand of the sea, which cannot be numbered for multitude'" (Gen. 32:11–12); for our brethren: "pray for one another... The effective prayer of a righteous man can accomplish much" (James 5:16); and for our enemies: "But I say to you, love your enemies, and pray for those who persecute you; in order that you may be sons of your Father who is in heaven" (Matt. 5:44–45).

> We are [also] to pray, not only for all sorts of men now living, according to what is stated in the preceding Head, but for those who *shall live hereafter.* To pray thus includes an earnest desire that the interest of Christ may be propagated from generation to generation; and that His kingdom and glory may be advanced in the world till his second coming.[44]

Jesus Himself prayed this way in John 17:20–21: "I do not ask in behalf of these alone [the apostles], but for those also who believe in Me through their word; that they may all be one." And King David also prayed for those who *shall live hereafter* in 2 Samuel 7:29: "Now therefore may it please Thee to bless the house of Thy servant, that it may continue forever before Thee. For Thou, O LORD God, hast spoken; and with Thy blessing may the house of Thy servant be blessed forever." Do you pray this way for the church? Do you pray this way for your family and descendants?

The Bible forbids us to pray for two kinds of people: (1) *The dead*; and (2) *Those that are known to have sinned the sin unto death.* The first prohibition is directed against the practice of the Roman Catholic Church; and the second is an allusion to the expressed prohibition of 1 John 5:16.

We Are Not to Pray for the Dead

This counsel is aimed at discouraging among Protestants a common practice in Roman Catholicism and High Anglicanism of praying for the dead, which practice is a logical consequence of their false doctrine of purgatory.[45] The "saved dead" do not need our

44. Ridgeley, *Commentary on the Larger Catechism,* 2:570–71. Emphasis added.

45. For an explanation and refutation of the Roman Catholic, and non-Scrip-

prayers for they are in a glorified state. The "unsaved dead" are irreversibly condemned to eternal torment, and therefore our prayers will do them no good.

> Prayers for the dead imply that their state has not yet been fixed, and that it can be improved at our request. We hold, however, that there is no change of character or of destiny after death, and that what the person is at death he remains throughout all eternity. We find an abundance of Scripture teaching to the effect that this world only is the place of opportunity for salvation, and that when this probation or testing period is past only the assignment of rewards and punishments remains. Consequently we hold that all prayers, baptisms, masses, or other rituals of whatever kind for the dead are superfluous, vain, and unscriptural.
>
> As for the righteous dead, they are in the immediate presence of Christ, in a perfect environment of holiness and beauty and glory where their every need is satisfied. They have no need of any petitions from us. They lack nothing that our prayers can supply. Their state is as perfect as it can be until the day when they and we receive our resurrection bodies. To petition God to change the status or condition of His loved ones in glory, or to suggest that He is not doing enough for them, is, to say the least, highly presumptuous, even though it may be well intended.
>
> As for the wicked dead, their state too is fixed and irrevocable. They have had their opportunity. They have sinned away their day of grace, and the uplifting and restraining influence of the Holy Spirit...has been withdrawn. It is understandable that remaining relatives and friends should be concerned about them. But the determination of their status after death is the prerogative of God alone. The holiness and justice of God are all-sufficient guarantees that while some

---

tural, doctrine of purgatory see John Calvin, *Institutes of the Christian Religion.*

> by His grace will be rewarded far above their deserts, none will be punished beyond their deserts. Consequently, the dead in Christ have no need of our prayers, and for the dead out of Christ, prayers can avail nothing.
>
> It is very significant that in Scripture we have not one single instance of prayer for the dead, nor any admonition to that end. In view of the many admonitions for prayer for those in this world, even admonitions to pray for our enemies, the silence of Scripture regarding prayer for the dead would seem to be inexplicable if it availed anything.[46]

We Are Not to Pray for Those That Are Known to Have Sinned the Sin unto Death

> If any one sees his brother committing a sin not leading to death, he shall ask and God will for him give life to those who commit sin not leading to death. There is a sin leading to death; I do not say that he should make request for this. All unrighteousness is sin, and there is a sin not leading to death (1 John 5:16–17).

The Nature of the Sin that Leads to Death

The Biblical text on which this statement in our Catechism is based is 1 John 5:16–17, quoted immediately above. These two difficult verses are impossible to understand apart from their context of 1 John 5:13–17 which makes four main points: (1) The believer can have certain knowledge that he possesses eternal life: "These things I have written to you who believe in the name of the Son of God, in order that you may know that you have eternal life" (vs. 13); (2) The believer can have certainty that his prayers will be answered: "And this is the confidence which we have be-

46. Loraine Boettner, *Roman Catholicism* (Philadelphia, PA: The Presbyterian and Reformed Publishing Co., [1962] 1976), 295–96.

fore Him, that, if we ask anything according to His will, He hears us. And if we know that He hears us in whatever we ask, we know that we have the requests which we have asked from Him" (vss. 14–15); (3) Intercessory prayer is a vital expression of brotherly love: "If any one sees his brother committing a sin not leading to death, he shall ask and God will for him give life to those who commit sin not leading to death" (vs. 16a); (4) There is a sin unto death in connection with which intercessory prayer is not commanded.: "There is a sin leading to death; I do not say that he should make request for this. All unrighteousness is sin, and there is a sin not leading to death" (vss. 16b–17).

John wants believers to be sure people so they will be bold in praying for one another. He has had much to say in 1 John about love for the brethren (2:9–11, 3:14–20, 4:7–21, 5:1–3), and now he says that if we love them we will pray for them, especially for a brother or sister who goes astray. Our intercessions for one another have limits, however, in that we are not commanded to pray for a person who is committing "a sin leading to death" (vs. 16b).

Concerning this exception in verse 16b, several observations should be made:

(1) Throughout this epistle John has taught us that true life is fellowship with Christ (1:1–5); that death is spiritual and moral separation from Him (3:14), even before physical death; and that all sins tend toward death (3:14), for they disrupt the life of fellowship with Christ.

(2) The phrase "sin leading to death," is introduced as one which was familiar with the readers of this epistle, because in Jewish tradition (Num. 18:22), some sins deserved immediate death. In their very nature they exclude one from fellowship with Christ. Death then would be exclusion from the visible body of Christ.

(3) "Sin leading to death" is literally "sin as tending to death," not necessarily involving death. Death is its natural consequence and desert, if it continues impenitently, and not its inevitable issue as a matter of fact.

(4) When we ask the question, "What is the sin that tends to death?," we must not overlook the "If anyone sees," with which verse 16 begins, emphasizing the outward and visible character of the sin. A Christian is able to see when another is not sinning unto death and when he is sinning unto death. This does not mean that our judgment is infallible, or that we may not fear that our brother sinning unto death will bring himself to death.

(5) John is addressing members of the church sharing in the privileges and joys of a common life in the visible Body of Christ. His concern is for a "brother" for whom we are to pray and a "brother" for whom we are not commanded to pray.[47]

(6) "Sin leading to death" does not refer to specific acts as such, but of acts and behavior that have a certain character. Impenitent and unconfessed sinning separates from Christ and therefore tends toward death, for "all unrighteousness is sin" (vs. 17a), and the wages of all sin is death (Rom. 6:23). Such sinning is a settled state of practicing sin and delighting in it. It manifests itself in: hatred for the brethren (3:15), refusal to walk in the light, *i.e.*, in repentance and obedience to God

47. R.S. Candlish makes the point that "his brother" "does not necessarily imply that he who sins is a true brother in the Lord. It has been already made manifest more than once in this epistle, that the relation of brotherhood, in the apostle's sense of the term, is of much wider reach and range. It arises not so much out of the character and standing of him whom you call your brother, as out of the nature of the affection with which you regard him. True, your brother, in the highest point of view, is he who, being really to God a son, is really to you on that account a brother. But whoever he may be whom you love with a brotherly love; with a love that treats him as a brother...every one so loved by you is your brother. When he sins, his sin vexes you as the sin of a brother. You cannot look on and see him sinning with indifference or amusement or contempt, as if he was a stranger...or a dog. It is your brother whom you see sinning. And therefore you speak to him as to a brother about his sin; not harshly, with sharp reproach or cutting sarcasm.... With a brother's voice, coming out of the depths of a brother's bosom, you earnestly expostulate and affectionately plead with him. Alas, he turns to you a deaf ear, and you have no power to open it. But another ear is open to you, the ear of your Father in heaven, and He can open your brother's ear. To your Father in heaven you go" (R. S. Candlish, *Exposition of I John* [Grand Rapids, MI: Associated Publishers and Authors, Inc., n.d.], 230).

> (1:7–9), unfaithfulness that denies the gospel of Christ (2:22, 4:2), idolatrous love for the seductions of this evil world (2:15–16, 5:21), impenitent disregard for living in obedience to the Law of God (2:4).

In praying for our brothers, especially those who have gone astray, we are to pray with boldness and confidence that God would restore them to the life of fellowship with Christ and His Body from which they have strayed. But in our intercessions we must remember the limit of verse 16 lest in our prayers we overstep the boundaries of propriety in our speaking to God and be over-confident, assuming that our brother's backslidden condition is not really that dangerous or that heinous in the sight of God, or that God is "duty-bound" to restore him because we have prayed for him. As R.S. Candlish has more clearly expressed it:

> But is there no risk of error? May you not be too one-sided in looking at the case [of your wayward brother], and in representing it to God? May you not be so concerned about the one terrible aspect of it, its bearing on your brother's doom, as to shut out the other aspect of it, which ought never to be lost sight of, its bearing on the Father's throne; on the holy and righteous sovereignty of His government and law? May not your sympathy with your sinning brother overbear somewhat your sympathy with Him against whom he is sinning? May you not thus be led to overstep the limits of warrantable confidence, so as to ask that life may be given to him, on any terms, at any cost, in any way, irrespectively altogether of what, in your calmer moments, you would yourself recognize as the paramount claims of the Most High? Thus your prayer for your sinning brother may slide insensibly into an apologetic pleading for indulgence to his sin. You may be tempted to represent as excusable what God regards as inexcusable; and to feel as if, whatever your brother's criminality may be there may still be favor shown to him. It is to guard you against such a frame of mind that the solemn warning is given: "*if a man see his brother sin a sin which is not unto death,*

> *he shall ask, and He shall give him life for those that do not sin unto death. There is a sin unto death: I do not say that he shall pray for it."*[48]

The Roman Catholic Distinction between Mortal and Venial Sins

A word should be said about the way Roman Catholicism uses 1 John 5:16–17 to make a distinction between mortal and venial sins. According to Rome when one commits a mortal sin, he deliberately violates the law of God in a matter of great importance, making him liable to eternal punishment. When one commits a venial sin, he transgresses God's law in a matter that is not of grave importance, and not altogether voluntary, therefore his sin is forgiven more easily, even without confession. Forgiveness for mortal sins is obtained only by the sacrament of penance.

1 John 5:16–17 and its reference to sinning not leading to death and sinning that does lead to death cannot be used by Rome to support its distinction, for verse 17 states unequivocally that "all unrighteousness is sin," and 2:4 states that "sin is lawlessness," and Romans 6:23 says that "the wages of sin is death." So then, the Roman distinction is not Biblical, for according to the Bible every sin is unrighteous and lawless and therefore merits eternal punishment.

> [Such a distinction between mortal and venial sins] has a deleterious effect in practical life, since it engenders a feeling of uncertainty, sometimes a feeling of morbid fear on the one hand, or of unwarranted carelessness on the other. The Bible does distinguish different kinds of sins, especially in connection with the different degrees of guilt attaching to them. The Old Testament makes an important distinction between sins committed presumptuously (with a high hand), and sins committed unwittingly, that is, as the result of ignorance, weakness or error, Num. 15:29–31. The former could not be atoned by sacrifice and were punished with great severity,

48. Candlish, *Exposition of I John*, 230–31.

while the latter could be so atoned and were judged with far greater leniency. The fundamental principle embodied in this distinction still applies. Sins committed on purpose, with full consciousness of the evil involved, and with deliberation, are greater and more culpable than sins resulting from ignorance, from an erroneous conception of things, or from weakness of character. Nevertheless the latter are also real sins and make one guilty in the sight of God, Gal. 6:1; Eph. 4:18; I Tim. 1:13; 5:24. The New Testament further clearly teaches us that the degree of sin is to a great extent determined by the degree of light possessed. The heathen are guilty indeed, but they who have God's revelation and enjoy the privileges of the gospel ministry are far more guilty, Matt. 10:15; Luke 12:47, 48; 23:34; John 19:11; Acts 17:30; Rom. 1:32; 2:12, I Tim. 13, 15, 16.[49]

The Concerns for Which We Should Pray

Q. 184: For what things are we to pray?

A.: We are to pray for all things tending to the glory of God, the welfare of the church, our own or others good; but not for any thing that is unlawful.

First, we are to pray for those things that concern the glory of God. Jesus taught us: "Pray, then, in this way: "Our Father who art in heaven, Hallowed [glorified, honored and worshiped] be Thy name" (Matt. 6:9).

That we may know what these are we are to inquire whether, if God should give us what we ask for, it would have a tendency to set forth any of His divine perfections, and so render him

49. Louis Berkhof, *Systematic Theology* (Grand Rapids, MI: Eerdmans, [1932] 1938), 252.

> amiable and adorable in the eyes of his creatures, so that, in answering our prayers, he would act becoming himself.[50]

Second, we are to pray continually and earnestly for the welfare, growth, faithfulness, prosperity and welfare of the Church of God; and in so praying we are to "give Him no rest until He establishes and makes Jerusalem [the church] a praise in the earth" (Isa. 62:7). The intensity of the psalmist in His prayer for the church should stir us to the importance of praying earnestly for the welfare of the church:

> If I forget you, O Jerusalem,
> May my right hand forget her skill.
> May my tongue cleave to the roof of my mouth,
> If I do not remember you,
> If I do not exalt Jerusalem
> Above my chief joy (Ps. 137:5–6).

Third, we are to pray for those things that concern our own good and the good of others: for temporal blessings, "which are the effects of divine bounty;"[51] for spiritual blessings, and for "the consolations of the Holy Ghost, arising from assurance of the love of God, whereby we may have peace and joy in believing; and for all those blessings which may make us happy in a better world."[52] The Heidelberg Catechism asks: *What has God commanded us to ask of Him? Answer: All things necessary for soul and body; which Christ our Lord has comprised in that prayer He Himself has taught us, i.e., the Lord's Prayer.*

The psalmists continually prayed for the good and welfare of the church and all of her members: "By Thy favor do good to Zion [the church]; build the walls of Jerusalem" (Ps. 51:18). Pray for the peace of Jerusalem [the church]: "'May they prosper who love you. May peace be within your walls, and prosperity within your palaces.' For the sake of my brothers and my friends, I will now say, 'May peace be with you.' For the sake of the house of the LORD our God

50. Ridgeley, *Commentary on the Larger Catechism*, 2:575.
51. Ridgeley, *Commentary on the Larger Catechism*, 2:576.
52. Ridgeley, *Commentary on the Larger Catechism*, 2:576.

I will seek your good" (Ps. 122:6–9). "Do good, O LORD, to those who are good, and to those who are upright in their hearts" (Ps. 125:4). And the encouragement God gives us to pray for the church, for each other in the church, and for ourselves is the words of Christ in Matthew 7:11: "If you then, being evil, know how to give good gifts to your children, how much more shall your Father who is in heaven give what is good to those who ask Him!"

Fourth, we are to pray for those things which are lawful for us to ask God to give us, *i.e.*, those things which are possible for us to receive, and things which God has given us reason to expect from Him in this present life: "And this is the confidence which we have before Him, that, if we ask anything according to His will, He hears us" (1 John 5:14). We are not to pray to have those things we will not receive until we die and go to heaven, such as sinless perfection, total freedom from tribulations, visions of God, etc. We must not pray that God will inflict evil on others to satisfy our own desires for revenge against those who injure us. And we must not ask for temporal blessings, "without setting bounds to our desires; nor are we to ask for them unseasonably, or for wrong ends."[53]

The Manner in Which We Are to Pray

Q. 185: How are we to pray?

A.: We are to pray with an awful apprehension of the majesty of God, and deep sense of our own unworthiness, necessities, and sins; with penitent, thankful, and enlarged hearts; with understanding, faith, sincerity, fervency, love, and perseverance, waiting upon him, with humble submission to his will.

---

53. Ridgeley, *Commentary on the Larger Catechism*, 2:576.

With an Awful Apprehension of the Majesty of God

> For thus says the High and Exalted One, who lives forever, whose Name is Holy, "I dwell on a high and holy place, and also with the contrite and lowly of spirit in order to revive the spirit of the lowly and to revive the heart of the contrite" (Isa. 57:15).

We are to pray to God with an awe-filled impression of the majestic splendor of God—His omnipotence, omniscience, holiness, spirituality, goodness, mercy, faithfulness, sovereignty *ad infinitum.* "Guard your steps as you go to the house of God.... Do not be hasty in word or impulsive in thought to bring up a matter in the presence of God. For God is in heaven and you are on earth; therefore let your words be few" (Eccl. 5:1–2). In other words, whenever you pray be conscious of the fact that you are not speaking to a figment of your imagination; you are addressing the one, true and living God, who is "majestic in holiness" and before whom "the nations are like a drop from a bucket, and are regarded as a speck of dust on the scales.... They are regarded by Him as less than nothing and meaningless" (Isa. 40:15–16).

The first rule for a proper framing of our prayers is

> that we be disposed in mind and heart as befits those who enter conversation with God. This we shall indeed attain with respect to the mind if it is freed from carnal cares and thoughts by which it can be called or led away from the right and pure contemplation of God, and then not only devotes itself completely to prayer but also, in so far as this is possible, is lifted and carried beyond itself...whoever engages in prayer should apply to it his faculties and efforts, and not, as commonly happens, be distracted by wandering thoughts. For nothing is more contrary to reverence for God than the levity that marks an excess of frivolity utterly devoid of awe. In this matter, *the harder we find concentration to be, the more strenuously we ought to labor after it.*[54]

---

54. Calvin, *Institutes of the Christian Religion*, 2:853–54. Emphasis added.

A Deep Sense of our Own Unworthiness, Necessities and Sins

> Woe is me, for I am ruined! Because I am a man of unclean lips, and I live among a people of unclean lips; for my eyes have seen the King, the LORD of hosts (Isa. 6:5).

We are to pray to God with a humble sense of our own unworthiness to come before Him. Even the seraphim around His throne covered their faces and their feet with their wings, "denoting their unworthiness to behold his glory, or to be employed by him in his service. But when we take a view of his infinite holiness, and our own impurity, we should be induced to draw nigh to him with the greatest humility."[55]

We are to pray to God with a deep sense of our total need of Him and of the heinousness of the sins which we have committed against Him.

> in our petitions we ever sense our own insufficiency, and earnestly pondering how we need all that we seek, join with this prayer an earnest—nay, burning—desire to attain it.... Now the godly must particularly beware of presenting themselves before God to request anything unless they yearn for it with sincere affection of heart, and at the same time desire to obtain it from him.... Let each one, therefore, as he prepares to pray be displeased with his own evil deeds, and (something that cannot happen without repentance) let him take the person and disposition of a beggar.[56]

With Penitent...Hearts

> Seek the LORD while He may be found; call upon Him while He is near. Let the wicked forsake his way, and the unrighteous man his thoughts; and let him return to the LORD, and

---

55. Ridgeley, *Commentary on the Larger Catechism*, 2:581.

56. Calvin, *Institutes of the Christian Religion*, 2:856, 857, 859.

> He will have compassion on him; and to our God, for He will abundantly pardon (Isa. 55:6–7).

We are to pray with repentance. To stimulate repentance within us, we should meditate on the many sins we have committed against our God, the ingratitude we have shown Him, the things we have done in our lives which fill us with shame and sorrow, and the love of God revealed in the person and redemptive work of Jesus Christ for the forgiveness of sins.

> Anyone who stands before God to pray, in his humility giving glory completely to God, [must] abandon all thought of his own glory, cast off all notion of his own worth, in fine, put away all self-assurance—lest if we claim for ourselves anything, even the least bit, we should become vainly puffed up, and perish at his presence. We have repeated examples of this submission, which levels all haughtiness, in God's servants; each one of whom, the holier he is, the more he is cast down when he presents himself before the Lord.... They depend on no assurance whatever but this alone: that, reckoning themselves to be of God, they do not despair that He will take care of them.[57]

(See Dan. 9:18–20; Ps. 143:2; Isa. 64:5–9; Jer. 14:7.) "The beginning, and even the preparation, of proper prayer is the plea for pardon with a humble and sincere confession of guilt...for unless they are founded in free mercy, prayers never reach God."[58]

With...Thankful...Hearts

> Shout joyfully to the LORD, all the earth.... Enter His gates with thanksgiving and His courts with praise (Ps. 100:1, 4).

We are to pray with thankfulness and praise, considering every blessing which God's love has lavished on us in Christ, and the gift of His Son by whom we have been purchased out of sin by God and for God. In order to be brought into a thankful state of mind

57. Calvin, *Institutes of the Christian Religion*, 2:859–60.
58. Calvin, *Institutes of the Christian Religion*, 2:860, 861.

we should meditate on the *value* of every blessing bestowed on us and the *price* that was paid that we might have them—the blood of Jesus. Consider every blessing as the result of the eternal love of God for us, the consequence of God's eternal predestination, having chosen those who are the objects of His love in Christ. Consider that God's love and grace are distinguishing and discriminating in the bestowal of mercies. God has mercy on whom He will have mercy. Why should He have mercy on you?

With...Enlarged Hearts

> Then Hannah prayed and said, "My heart exults in the LORD...my mouth speaks boldly [is enlarged] against my enemies" (1 Sam. 2:1).

An *enlarged* heart is a heart that *exults*. "Largeness" of heart is

> that state of mind in which every thing tending to contract [constrict] our affections, abate [quench] the fervency of our spirits, or hinder that importunity [urgency] which we ought to express for the best of blessings, is removed. Now, our hearts may be said to be enlarged in prayer, when we draw nigh to God in this duty with delight and earnest longing after his presence, and an interest in his love, which we reckon preferable to all other blessings; when we are affected with a becoming sense of his glorious perfections, and our own nothingness, in order to our adoring him, and coming before him with the greatest humility; when we have suitable promises given in, and are enabled to plead them with a degree of hope, arising from the goodness and faithfulness of God, that he will fulfill them, more especially as we draw nigh to him as to a covenant-God; and when our thoughts and affections are engaged without wandering, weariness, or lukewarmness, and filled with importunity [a sense of urgency], agreeable to the importance of the duty, and our absolute need of the blessings we pray for.[59]

---

59. Ridgeley, *Commentary on the Larger Catechism*, 2:587.

With Understanding

> What is the outcome then? I shall pray with the spirit and I shall pray with the mind also (1 Cor. 14:15).

Our prayers must be offered to God with understanding. Ignorance is not a spiritual gift, nor is it "the mother of devotion," rather it is an obstacle to true prayer. Prayer is not accepted with God unless it is based on grace. God's grace is manifested in connection with the knowledge of the truth of His Word. We must know something about the character and will of God, Christ and the Holy Spirit, and something about ourselves, revealed in the Bible, if our prayers are to be real prayers. Prayers merely mouthed without the concentration of the mind are no prayers at all. Such praying is superstitious and blasphemous.

1 Corinthians 14:15, quoted above, shows us the rightful place of the intellect in praying and singing. Paul is not arguing for a cold intellectualism, but is teaching us that with all our spiritual fervor, we must not neglect the importance of the mind and of understanding. Our worship of God, which includes praying and singing, must be wholehearted and "wholeminded." "All too often prayers are offered in a kind of emotional jargon, and hymns are chosen on the basis of attractive tunes rather than sound theology."[60]

With...Faith

> Therefore I say to you, all things for which you pray and ask, believe that you have received them, and they shall be granted you (Mark 11:24). "Let him ask in faith without doubting, for the one who doubts is like the surf of the sea driven and tossed by the wind" (James 1:6).

What is being affirmed in Mark 11:24 is

> God's absolute readiness to respond to the resolute faith that prays (cf Isa. 65:24). What distinguishes the faith for which

60. Leon Morris, *The First Epistle of Paul to the Corinthians: An Introduction and Commentary* (London: The Tyndale Press [1958] 1966), 195.

> Jesus calls from that self-intoxication which reduces a man and his work to a fiasco is the discipline of prayer through faith. When prayer is the source of faith's power and the means of its strength, God's sovereignty is its only restriction.... The man who bows his head before the hidden glory of God in the fulness of faith does so in the certainty that God can deal with every situation and any difficulty and that with him nothing is impossible.[61]

James 1:6 teaches us that

> prayer...is effective only when asked *in faith*; that is, with trust in God that one's request will be granted according to the divine will. The writer of Hebrews declares that "without faith it is impossible to please him [God]; for he that cometh to God must believe that he is, and that he is a rewarder of them that diligently seek him" (Heb. 11:6). Christ Himself promised, "And all things, whatsoever ye shall ask in prayer, believing, ye shall receive." (Matt. 21:22) We must draw near to God confident both of His ability and His willingness to grant our requests.[62]

But James adds: "without doubting" or "without wavering." Believing prayer does not oscillate between faith and unbelief, trust and distrust. It is not a pleading with the mouth, while the heart doubts that the prayer will be heard by God. Such a person is like "the surf of the sea driven and tossed by the wind," floating like a cork on the waves, now carried near the shore, now carried away from it. That person must not even begin to "expect that he will receive anything from the Lord, being a double-minded man, unstable in all his ways" (James 1:7–8).

> The doubting, wavering disposition is fatal to true effectiveness in prayer. Faith unlocks the divine storehouse, but unbe-

---

61. William Lane, *The Gospel According to Mark* (Grand Rapids, MI: William B. Eerdmans Publishing Co., 1974), 410.

62. Curtis Vaughan, *James: A Study Guide* (Grand Rapids, MI: Zondervan Publishing House, 1969), 23–24.

> lief bars its doors. The wavering petitioner dishonors and insults God by doubting the truth of His Word and treating Him as unworthy of confidence.... The double-minded man is a person drawn in two opposite directions...a man having two minds, one set on God, the other on the world... "Let not those who wish to pray to God have two hearts, one directed to him and one to something else." The unstable man is the vascillating man, inclined one moment to do good, the next to do evil.... The lack of constancy in the prayer life is simply an index of the man's character generally.[63]

To pray with faith implies

> an habitual disposition of soul, proceeding from a principle of regenerating grace, whereby we are led to commit ourselves and all our concerns into Christ's hands, depending on his merits and mediation for the supply of all our [needs], considering him as having purchased, and as being authorized to apply, all the benefits of the covenant of grace.... More particularly, faith exerts and discovers [reveals] itself in prayer, by encouraging the soul, and giving it an holy boldness to draw nigh to God, notwithstanding our great unworthiness.[64]

Furthermore, faith manifests itself in prayer by enabling us to plead and apply to ourselves the great promises which God has given His people in the gospel. Everything we need or ought to pray for is found in the Lord's promises in His word, which faith is encouraged to ask for. In fact, faith never prays for anything except that which glorifies God; *and so faith prays with an entire submission to the will of God. Faith knows that God knows what is best for us.*

The role of faith in prayer has been misunderstood by the charismatic/pentecostal movement. It has misapplied the promise of 1 John 5:14–15 in such a monstrous way as to make God subject to the dictates of man. The promise is this: "And this is the confidence

---

63. Vaughan, *James: A Study Guide*, 24–25.
64. Ridgeley, *Commentary on the Larger Catechism*, 2:584.

which we have before Him, that, if we ask anything according to His will, He hears us. And if we know that He hears us in whatever we ask, we know that we have the requests which we have asked from Him." The charismatic movement makes these verses say that God is "duty-bound" to give us whatever we pray for as long as we believe He will give it. "Name it and claim it," we are told. Because of this promise, God MUST give us what we pray for, because we have prayed for it. Over a century ago the great Robert L. Dabney refuted this blasphemous idea. He pointed out how 1 John 14 places practical limitations on what we can expect in answer to our prayers: "if we ask anything *according to His will* He hears us."

> All our prayers shall be specifically answered in God's time and way, but with literal and absolute accuracy, if they are believing and pious prayers, and for things according to God's will.... Here [by the Bible] the explanation of that erroneous view of the warrant of prayer, above described, is made easy and plain. It is said that if the Christian prays with right motives, and with an assured belief that he shall obtain, he will obtain; no matter what he asks, (unless it be something unlawful). Yes, but what warrant has he for the belief that he shall obtain? Faith, without an intelligible warrant, is sheer presumption. Suppose, for instance, the object of petition is the recovery of a sick friend; where does the applicant read God's pledge of a specific answer to that prayer? Certainly not in Scripture. Does he pretend a direct spiritual communication? Hardly. He has no specific warrant at all; and if he works himself up into a notion that he is assured of the answer, it is but a baseless fantasy, rather insulting than honourable to God. I know that pious biography is full of supposed instances of this kind.... These are the follies of good men; and yet God's abounding mercy may in some cases answer prayers thus blemished.
>
> We return then to Scripture and ask again, what is the extent of the warrant there found? The answer is, that God, both by promise and example, clearly holds out two classes of objects

for which Christians pray. One is the class of which an instance has just been cited—objects naturally desirable, and in themselves innocent, which yet are not essential to redemption; such as recovery from sickness, recovery of friends, good name, daily bread, deliverance from persecution, conversion of particular sinners, &c., &c. It is right to pray for such things; it is even commanded: and we have ground, in the benevolence, love, and power of God, and tender sympathy of the Mediator, to hope for the specific answer. But still the truest believer will offer those prayers with doubts of receiving the specific answer; for the simple reason that God has nowhere specifically promised to bestow it. The enlightened believer urges such petitions, perhaps warmly: but still all are conditioned upon an "if it be possible," "if it be consistent with God's secret will." And he does not know whether he shall receive or not, just because that will is still secret. But such prayers, offered with this general trust in God's power, benevolence and better wisdom, and offered in pious motives, are accepted, even though not answered, cf. 2 Cor. xii:8, with verse 9; Mat. xxvi:39, with Heb. v:7. God does not give the very thing sought, though innocent in itself; He had never promised it; but He "makes all things work together for good to the petitioner." This should be enough to satisfy every saint.

The other class of objects of prayer is, the benefits accompanying redemption; all the gifts which make up, in the elect, growth in grace, perseverance, pardon, sanctification, complete redemption. For these we pray with full assurance of a specific answer, because God has told us, that it is His purpose specifically to bestow them in answer to all true prayer. Ps. lxxxiv:11; Luke xi:13; 1 Thess. iv:3, Luke xii:32, John xv:8. So, we have a warrant to pray in faith, for the grace to do the things which God's word makes it our duty to do. In all such cases, our expectation of an answer is entitled to be as definite as was that of Apostles, when inspired with the faith of miracles. God may not give it in the shape or channel we ex-

> pected; He may choose to try our faith by unexpected delays, but the answer is sure, because definitely promised, in His own time and way.[65]

With...Sincerity...

> Hear a just cause, O LORD, give heed to my cry; give ear to my prayer, which is not from deceitful lips. (Ps. 17:1)

Our prayers must be accompanied with sincerity and honesty of heart. We will not pray with our lips, while our hearts are far from God. A sincere heart is one in which no sin has alienated it from or against God. We must not pray "from deceitful lips," *i.e.*, insincerely and dishonestly. "Feigned lips are God's abhorrence."[66]

With...Fervency

> The fervent prayer of a righteous man can accomplish much (James 5:16).

One translation of the Bible translates this verse as: "Great is the power of a good man's fervent prayer." The two conditions for powerful praying set forth here are: (1) A righteous and good character in the one praying; and (2) Earnestness and fervency in his praying. *It is the FERVENT prayer of the GODLY man that is so effective.* Another translation has it: "great is the strength of a righteous man's petition when it is urgent." *"Earnestness, fervency, energy—these are the marks of effective praying."*[67]

Our prayers, then, must be

> fired with zeal and fervency.... Prayer without fervency is like a sacrifice without a fire.... (a). Prayer without fervency is no prayer; it is speaking, not praying.... (b). Consider in what need we stand of those things which we ask in prayer. We

---

65 Dabney, *Lectures in Systematic Theology*, 722–24.

66. William S. Plumer, *Psalms: A Critical And Expository Commentary With Doctrinal & Practical Remarks* (Edinburgh: The Banner of Truth Trust, 1975), 229.

67. Vaughan, *James: A Study Guide*, 121. Emphasis added.

> come to ask the favour of God; and if we have not his love, all we enjoy is cursed to us.... (c). It is only fervent prayer that has the promise of mercy affixed to it—"Then shall you find Me, when you search for Me with all your heart" Jer. xxix:13.[68]

With...Love

> So choose life in order that you may live, you and your descendants, by loving the LORD your God, by obeying His voice, and by holding fast to Him; for this is your life (Deut. 30:19–20).

Our prayers are to be accompanied with love for God.

> This implies an earnest desire for his presence, delight in him, or taking pleasure in contemplating his perfections as the most glorious and amiable object. Desire supposes him, in some measure, withdrawn from us, or that we are not possessed of that complete blessedness which is to be enjoyed in him; and delight supposes him present, and, in some degree, manifesting himself to us. Now, love to God, in both these respects, is to be exercised in prayer. Is he in any measure withdrawn from us? We are, with the greatest earnestness, to long for his return to us, whose lovingkindness is better than life. Is he graciously pleased, in any degree, to manifest himself to us as the fountain of all we enjoy or hope for? His doing so will have a tendency to excite our delight in him, and induce us to conclude that our happiness consists in the enjoyment of him. These graces are to be exercised at all times, but more especially in prayer; for this is an offering up of our desires to God, in which we press after the enjoyment first of himself, and then of his benefits.[69]

68. Thomas Watson, *A Body of Divinity* (Grand Rapids, MI: Sovereign Grace Publishers, n.d.), 397.

69. Ridgeley, *Commentary on the Larger Catechism*, 2:586–87.

With...Perseverance

> With all prayer and petition pray at all times in the Spirit, and with this in view, be on the alert with all perseverance and petition for all the saints (Eph. 6:18).

> For a Christian to pray as he ought requires hard effort and discipline, and a firm resolve not to be discouraged by the many difficulties men experience in trying to pray. We will not pray unless we make ourselves pray, in spite of our feelings. If we were left to our own inclination in this matter our prayer-life would die out.... We must pray even though we feel no inspiration whatever to do so. We must not make it an excuse for our sloth that we are waiting for the Holy Spirit to inspire us.... We must remember that we have never any excuse for refusing to pray.... In the midst of our prayers we must struggle with wandering thoughts.[70]

Paul's exhortation to pray "with all perseverance" is as if he said to us:

> My friends, you will find such a coldness in yourselves that you will never pray to God, neither will you ever aspire to pray, unless you urge and force yourselves. For the devil will always dazzle your eyes, in order that you should not see what need you have to pray to God. And if you lie sleeping still, that will cause your God to forsake you, seeing you are so thankless as to despise his benefits, and to yield him no honour for them, no, just as if you did not know that all your welfare proceeds from him. For like villains we profane the benefits which God bestows upon us, unless we acknowledge that we hold all things at His hand, yes, even by asking all things that we need from him, and also by yielding him thanks for the things that we have received already. So then, let us to learn to link our watchfulness with all assiduity [constancy and perseverance].... It is not enough for us to

70. Wallace, *Calvin's Doctrine of the Christian Life*, 293–95.

> have prayed to God in fits and starts (as they say), but we must continue in it, and that in two ways. For first, when we have prayed to-day, both morning and evening and every hour, we must keep on and never swerve from that course, so long as we live. For our faith...must exercise itself, and this is the way in which it must do so. There is yet one other way of perseverance or holding out, which is, that when we have desired God to help us in this or that, we must repeat the same supplication not twice or three times only, but as often as we have need, a hundred and a thousand times.[71]

> Now He was telling them a parable to show that at all times they ought to pray and not to lose heart, saying, "There was in a certain city; a judge who did not fear God, and did not respect man. And there was a widow in that city, and she kept coming to him, saying, 'Give me legal protection from my opponent.' And for a while he was unwilling; but afterward he said to himself, 'Even though I do not fear God nor respect man, yet because this widow bothers me, I will give her legal protection, lest by continually coming she wear me out.'"

> And the Lord said, "Hear what the unrighteous judge said; now shall not God bring about justice for His elect, who cry to Him day and night, and will He delay long over them? I tell you that He will bring about justice for them speedily. However, when the Son of Man comes, will He find faith on the earth?" (Luke 18:1–8)

> Therefore we must never be weary in waiting for God's help. Also it is not good that we should be heard according to our own longings, because God knows what is meet and expedient for us. So then, he must govern us according to his own will. But...if we pray to him in his way and in his manner, he testifies that we shall obtain all our requests at his hand,

71. John Calvin, *Sermons on the Epistle to the Ephesians*, trans by Arthur Golding (Arthur Golding, 1577; reprint London: The Banner of Truth Trust, 1973), 682–83.

> even before we have uttered them with our mouth. Nevertheless he will sometimes hold us, as it were, in suspense, insomuch that it will seem that he is asleep when we call upon him, and that he has turned his back upon us. For this reason perseverance is required, so that if we are troubled by any distress and would gladly seek ease from it at God's hand, we must not do it once and no more, but we must return to it (oftentimes) and be (as you would say) importunate [persistent], just as we learn in the parable which our Lord Jesus tells us of the widow, who had to do with a judge who was without any fear of God, or any sense of shame. Nevertheless she obtained her suit even by being importunate [persistent]. So must we do, that is to say, we must be importunate with our God. Not that he is tardy in succouring us...but because he will try (test) the constancy of our faith. For they that come to him, and vex themselves and get angry if he does not relieve them immediately, do not pray to him, but...summon him to be at the command of their lusts.[72]

Waiting Upon Him

> But as for me, I will watch expectantly for the LORD; I will wait for the God of my salvation. My God will hear me (Mic. 7:7).

Regardless of the circumstances in which a Christian may find himself, he is to "watch expectantly for the LORD and wait for the God of my salvation," confident that God will hear and answer our prayers.

> A fixed purpose is that which more clearly characterizes the genuine Christian than any thing else. When the determination of the will is not only fixed but strong, then the soul is in a vigorous state.... Others are continually vacillating between the service of God and the world.[73]

72. Calvin, *Sermons on the Epistle to the Ephesians*, 683.

73. Archibald Alexander, *Practical Sermons To Be Read in Families and Social Meetings* (Philadelphia, PA: Presbyterian Board of Publication, 1850), 261.

The strength for such determination of will comes only from the Lord, therefore, the Christian will "wait for Him" in prayer for the strength He needs to face the circumstances around him or to be persevering as long as the circumstances remain unchanged.

> Three things are plainly implied in the expression, 'waiting on the Lord.' First, a *desire* of some benefit, with a petition for the same. Secondly, the exercise of *patience*. And thirdly, the *expectation* of receiving what is asked.... We are never more in the way of success in our waiting, than when we are conscious that we deserve nothing, and that a sovereign God, without injustice, might cast us off forever. Our hope of acceptance in waiting on the Lord is based on nothing else but the mercy of God, the merit and intercession of Christ, and the gracious declarations and promises of God.... *Perseverance* is also implied in waiting on the Lord. This, indeed, is included in the patience which has been mentioned.... But souls truly convicted of sin, persevere in waiting. *Their determination is, if they perish, to perish at the throne of grace.* No consideration will induce them to give over seeking. And all such do find mercy, and obtain from the Lord, the blessing which they seek.[74]

> Those who wait for the LORD will gain new strength; they will mount up with wings like eagles, they will run and not get tired, they will walk and not become weary (Isa. 40:31).

With Humble Submission to His Will

> And He [Jesus] went a little beyond them, and fell on His face and prayed, saying, "My Father, if it is possible, let this cup pass from Me; yet not as I will, but as Thou wilt" (Matt. 26:39).

74. Alexander, *Practical Sermons To Be Read in Families and Social Meetings*, 268–69. Emphasis added.

Without humble submission to the will of God, both revealed and unrevealed, we cannot expect our prayers to be answered. In fact, "praying" without this submission amounts to dictating to God what He should do according to our will. To pray without submission to God is to pray without faith in God, for faith trusts God to do always what is for His glory and the believer's benefit, whatever it be; and faith commits itself, or submits itself, to God's care, to God's wisdom, goodness and sovereignty.

In Matthew 26:39, we see the complete submission of Jesus in patient obedience to God the Father regarding the cross.

> Jesus' desire was conditioned upon the will of God, and he resolutely refused to set his will in opposition to the will of the Father. Fully conscious that his mission entailed submission to the horror of the holy wrath of God against human sin and rebellion, the will of Jesus clasped the transcendentally lofty and sacred will of God.[75]

If Jesus prayed *in humble submission to God's will*, even when it included pain and agony, so must we, His disciples, know a similar *humble submission* to the revealed will of God in the Bible and to the unrevealed will of God manifested in His providential dealings with us (Deut. 29:29).

Thomas Ridgeley makes these helpful comments about praying in submission to God's will, whatever it may be:

> In practising this [submission], we leave ourselves and our petitions in his hand, sensible that he knows what is best for us. The submission required does not include a being indifferent whether our prayers are heard or not; for to have this feeling would be to contradict, by the frame of our spirits, what we express with our lips. Whatever may be concluded to be lawful for us to ask, as redounding to our advantage, and as expressly promised by God, we ought to request at his hand in prayer; and if we pray for it, we cannot but desire that our prayer may be heard and answered. Now, this desire is

---

75. Lane, *The Gospel According to Mark*, 518.

> not opposed to that submission to the divine will which we are speaking of, provided we leave it to God to do what he thinks best for us, being content that the manner of his answering us, as well as the time of his bestowing those blessings which we want, together with the degree of them, especially if they are of a temporal nature, ought to be resolved into his sovereign will.[76]

The Rule that Governs Prayer: The Word of God

Q. 186: What rule hath God given for our direction in the duty of prayer?

A.: The whole word of God is of use to direct us in the duty of prayer; but the special rule of direction is that form of prayer which our Saviour Christ taught his disciples, commonly called *The Lord's Prayer.*

The Word of God As The Rule of Prayer

> And this is the confidence which we have before Him, that, if we ask anything according to His will, He hears us (1 John 5:14).

Prayer must be controlled, formed, governed and inspired by the Word of God, which is God's revealed will (Deut. 29:29).

> Though God has promised to do whatsoever his people may ask, yet he does not allow them an unbridled liberty to ask whatever may come to their minds; but he has at the same time prescribed to them a law according to which they are to

---

76. Ridgeley, *Commentary on the Larger Catechism*, 2:587.

> pray. And doubtless nothing is better for us than this restriction; for if it was allowed to every one of us to ask what he pleased, and if God were to indulge us in our wishes, it would be to provide very badly for us. For what may be expedient we know not; nay, we boil over with corrupt and hurtful desires. But God supplies a twofold remedy, lest we should pray otherwise than according to what his own will has prescribed; for he teaches us by his word what he would have us to ask, and he has also set over us his Spirit as our guide and ruler, to restrain our feelings, so as not to suffer [allow] them to wander beyond due bounds.... We ought also to ask the mouth of the Lord to direct and guide our prayers; for God in His promises has fixed for us...the right way of praying.[77]

In Ronald Wallace's discussion on Calvin's doctrine of prayer, he points out that:

> *In order to be a genuine exercise of faith, prayer must be founded upon the Word of God.* The faith that gives rise to prayer is created by the Word and is ever aroused to fresh life and vigour by listening to the promises of the Word. Through the Word, God continually acknowledges us to be His people and presents Himself so that we can lay hold of Him.... It is necessary not only that the Word of God should precede and inspire the approach to prayer but also that in its direction and in all its details our prayer should be governed and restrained by the same Word. We are not at liberty in this matter to follow the suggestions of our own minds, or to form our wishes according to our own fancy. We dare not ask for more than God would freely bestow. To do so would be to tempt God. In the exercise of faith, self-denial and self-control and obedience to the Word of God are always the ruling principles. "As nothing is more at variance with faith than the foolish and irregular desires of the flesh, it follows that

77. John Calvin, *Commentary on the Catholic Epistles: Commentary on the First Epistle of John*, trans. by John Owen (Edinburgh: Calvin Translation Society, 1843; reprint Grand Rapids, MI: Baker Book House, 1979), 266.

> those in whom faith reigns do not desire everything without discrimination, but only that which the Lord promises to give" [Calvin]. Therefore, we cannot pray in faith unless we moderate our desires and confine our prayers to what God has laid down....
>
> *The one safe rule, then, is to form our prayers only in the clear light of the Word of God, in compliance with what He has commanded, making our prayers an echo in our hearts of His promises, and not allowing ourselves to seek anything more than He has promised....* "The sole end and legitimate use of prayer...is that we may reap the fruits of God's promise" [Calvin]. *Calvin constantly recommends the actual language of Holy Scripture in the prayers we utter to God....* We must take His great promises seriously and let them encourage us to come to Him with all the greater boldness and do Him the honour of holding Him to what He has declared in His Word, and if He does not fulfil at first our demands, then, like Moses and Abraham, we must refuse to be put off, even when He seems to tell us to go away and let Him alone. "Let us learn that God in His promises is set before us as if He were our willing debtor," says Calvin. We can go to Him and with full assurance that it is not in vain require Him to behave towards us as He has promised.[78]

The Ways the Bible Can Be Used in Governing Prayer

First, we may actually pray the prayers of the Bible (*e.g.*, Ps. 90:1–2 and Ps. 130:3–4). Second, we may draw together several Bible passages into one prayer, as in Daniel 9:1–23. "Our prayers should also abound in the language of the Word of God. Our minds should be so saturated with Scripture that it flows naturally from our tongues when we approach the throne of grace."[79] Third, we may turn Bible promises and doctrines into prayers of praise and petition (*e.g.*, Ps.

78. Wallace, *Calvin's Doctrine of the Christian Life*, 276–79.

79. Michael Schneider, III, "Prayer Regulated By God's Word," *Worship in the Presence of God*, ed. by David Lachman and Frank Smith (Greenville, SC: Greenville Seminary Press, 1992), 230.

19:1 and Isaiah 2:2–4). Fourth, we may select one text of the Bible and pray through it verse by verse. The Psalms are particularly suitable for this kind of praying. Fifth, we must make sure that all our prayers are consistent with the Word of God. All our prayers must be Biblical, whether we use the actual words of the Bible, make allusions to Biblical texts, or incorporate Biblical ideas and truths in our prayers.

> All our prayers must be Scriptural prayers, in that they are instructed by the truth of God's Word.... It would be better to spend an hour in the Word discovering whether what we desire is according to God's revealed will, and five minutes praying Biblical prayer, than to spend all day assaulting heaven for something God has not promised to give. Those who pray effectual prayers are those who know the Word of God.... Our prayers, public and private, are to be regulated by God's Word.[80]

The Comprehensive Rule and The Special Rule Governing Prayer

The Comprehensive Rule: The Whole Word of God

Our Catechism (Q. 186) makes the point that *the whole word of God is of use to direct us in the duty of prayer.* It is not just the New Testament that is the rule of prayer, it is *the whole Word of God* in both the Old Testament and the New Testament. Why would our Westminster fathers make this emphasis? It was because of what they believed the Bible taught about itself. It is by His Word that He *sufficiently and effectually reveal(s) him(self) unto men for their salvation* (LCQ. 2). Both the Old Testament and the New Testament are equally *the word of God, the only rule of faith and obedience* (LCQ. 3). *The whole counsel of God, concerning all things necessary for his own glory, man's salvation, faith and life, is either expressly set down in scripture, or by good and necessary consequence may be deduced from scripture* (WCF, I, vi).

80. Schneider, "Prayer Regulated By God's Word," 231–32.

They based their belief in the comprehensive, divine and infallible authority of the whole Bible, as our only rule of faith and obedience, upon the declarations of the Bible about itself. 2 Timothy 3:16 says that "All Scripture is inspired by God," or literally, "All Scripture is God-breathed." The point is that "all" of the Bible, both Old Testament and New Testament, every word that was penned by the original human authors of the whole Bible, is the product, not of the men who wrote it, but a product of the breath of God, originating, both in its content and verbal expression, in the mind of God. Furthermore, "all" of the God-breathed Bible is "profitable for teaching, for reproof, for correction, for training in righteousness; that the man of God may be adequate, equipped for every good work" (2 Tim. 3:16–17). This entire Bible is so "profitable" to us that everything we need to be thoroughly "equipped for the good work" of prayer is to be found in its pages.

As we have seen, true prayer is the prayer of faith, and God-given faith rests upon the Word of God. *By this faith, a Christian believeth to be true WHATSOEVER IS REVEALED IN THE WORD, for the authority of God himself speaking therein; and acteth differently upon that which each particular passage thereof containeth; yielding obedience to the commands, trembling at the threatenings, and embracing the promises of God for this life and that which is to come* (WCF, XIV, ii. Emphasis added).

Since we are to ask nothing of God but what is agreeable with His revealed will, it is essential that we become well acquainted with the content of the Bible and how to make use of it properly in our prayers.

The History in the Bible

The historical sections of the Bible contain the record of the Lord's working among and in behalf of His covenant people, the sins of those people, and the virtues of those people. We can pray for God's mighty acts among His people today, for the ability to avoid the sins of God's people in the past, and for the manifestation of those virtues in our lives that were exhibited in theirs.

The Doctrines of the Bible

Throughout the Bible are revealed truths, or doctrines, a sound knowledge of which is essential to our prayer life: the Trinity of God, the perfections of God, the covenant of God, the acts of God in creation, providence, revelation and redemption, the person and work of Christ and the Holy Spirit, the order of salvation, the constitution, fallenness, restoration and purpose of human beings, etc. Knowledge of these revealed truths makes our prayers more intelligent and Biblical, giving them richness of content and fullness of faith and hope. Such knowledge also improves the manner in which we address our praise and petition to God, as well as loading us down with truths about God that we can use in prayer in the adoration of God. It also deepens and broadens our confession of sin, our thanksgivings, our intercessions and our supplications, when we realize the greatness of God and the total need of sinful human beings.

The Laws of the Bible

The Law of God in the Bible sets forth our duties, relations and responsibilities to God, to each other and to the earth. We should pray that God would give us wisdom to know how to obey His laws aright, the will-power to want to obey them, and the perseverance to obey them consistently.

The Covenant Promises of the Bible

These promises should not only encourage us to pray, they should encourage faith and hope in prayer. Furthermore, as we turn the revealed promises of God into petitions to Him, humbly beseeching Him to be faithful to what He has promised, we will be encouraged to expect distinct answers to our prayers. (See Genesis 32:7–12.)

> The promises which are contained in scripture, are also a motive and inducement to prayer. They are a declaration of God's will to give the blessings which he sees necessary for

> us; and therefore are of great use in order to our performing this duty aright.[81]

The Reproofs and Warnings of the Bible

The Bible contains many reproofs, warnings and threatenings to deter us from sin and to motivate us to faithfulness to God.

> We are induced by these reproofs and threatenings to hate sin, beg strength to subdue and mortify it, and deprecate[82] the wrath and judgments of God. We are also led by them to see our desert of punishment, while we confess ourselves to be sinners, and to bless God that he has not inflicted it upon us; especially if he has given us ground of hope that he has delivered us from the condemnation which was due to us for sin. Moreover, the reproofs of sin and threatenings against it contained in the word of God will be of use to us in prayer, as we are led by them to have an awful sense of the holiness and justice of God, and to draw nigh to him with fear and trembling, lest we should provoke his wrath by our unbecoming behavior in his presence, and so bring on ourselves a curse instead of a blessing.[83]

The Examples of True Praying by Believers in the Bible

We read of Jacob wrestling with God in prayer and of his *persistence* therein (Hos. 12:4); of Abraham's *humility* in prayer (Gen. 18:27–30); of David's *sincerity* in prayer (Ps. 17:1); of Hezekiah's *earnestness* (Isa. 38:3, 5, 19); of Jonah's *faith* (Jon. 2:2, 4); of Daniel's *reverence* and awe (Dan. 9:4, 5); of Joshua's *intercessions* (Josh. 7:6,

---

81. Ridgeley, *Commentary on the Larger Catechism*, 2:592.

82. The contemporary denotation of this word ("to criticize or demean") is not intended. When Ridgeley wrote this commentary, *deprecate* still retained a popular secondary meaning of "to undo (ward off) by prayer," which meaning is drawn directly from the root of the word itself, *precari*, meaning "to pray," from which we get the words *precatory, precative, imprecatory*, etc. The modern usage of the word probably stems from its similarity to the word *depreciate*.

83. Ridgeley, *Commentary on the Larger Catechism*, 2:599.

9); of Moses' *fervency* (Ex. 32:10, 11, 31, 32). *The book of Psalms is "a directory for prayer* to the believer, suited to every condition which he may be supposed to be in, and of praise for mercies of all kinds, whether temporal or spiritual."[84]

The Special Rule: The Lord's Prayer

After stating that the whole Bible is the comprehensive rule governing prayer, our Catechism teaches us that the Lord's Prayer in Matthew 6:9–13 is *the special rule of direction* in the duty of prayer. Why is the Lord's Prayer said to be *the special rule of direction* for our praying? "Because there is not any one portion of scripture, where the petitionary part of prayer is so comprehensively and methodically laid down, as in the Lord's prayer."[85] And it is called *the Lord's Prayer,* not because the Lord prayed it, but because He dictated it to His disciples in answer to their request: "Lord teach us to pray" (Luke 11:1).

Catechism Question 187 tells us how to use the Lord's Prayer as our model for praying, as *the special rule of direction* in praying.

> The Lord's Prayer is not only for direction, as a pattern, according to which we are to make other prayers; but may also be used as a prayer, so that it be done with understanding, faith, reverence, and other graces necessary to the right performance of the duty of prayer. (WLC, Q. 187)

A more thorough discussion of the Lord's Prayer and its uses is contained in Chapter 38.

Stonewall Jackson: Man of Prayer

The following description of General Stonewall Jackson as a man of prayer is taken from Robert L. Dabney's famous biography entitled, *Life and Campaigns of Lieutenant-General Thomas J. Jackson*:

---

84. Ridgeley, *Commentary on the Larger Catechism*, 2:600.

85. James Fisher, *The Westminster Assembly's Shorter Catechism Explained* (Philadelphia: Presbyterian Board of Publication and Sabbath-School Work, 1911), 222.

Prayer implies a Providence. For if God hath not a present means of influencing the course of natural events, it is a waste of breath to petition for His intervention. Hence it will be anticipated, that he who was so clear in his recognition of Providence was also eminently a man of prayer. This was one of the most striking traits of Jackson's religious character. He prayed much, he had great faith in prayer, and took much delight in it. While his religion was the least obtrusive of all men's, no one could know him and fail to be impressed with the regularity of his habits of private devotion. Morning and night he bent before God in secret prayer, and rare must be the exigency [crisis or duty] which could deprive him of this valued privilege. There was in him an unusual combination of courage and modesty in this duty. If the presence of others was unavoidable, it had no effect whatever, be they who they might, however great or profane, to cause him to neglect his secret orisons [prayers and supplications]. Yet, it is presumed, no one ever had the idea of ostentation suggested who witnessed one of the sacred scenes. He was accustomed, during the active campaigns [of the War between the States], to live in a common tent, like those of the soldiers. Those who passed it at early dawn and at bed-time were likely to see the shadow of his kneeling form cast upon the canvas by the light of his candle; and the most careless soldier then trod lightly and held his breath with reverent awe. Those who were sceptical of the sincerity of other men's prayers, seemed to feel that, when Jackson knelt, the heavens came down indeed into communion with earth.

This spirit of prayer was manifested by the change which it wrought in his whole manner. Everywhere else his speech was decided and curt; at the throne of grace all was different; his enunciation was soft and deliberate, and his tones mellow and supplicatory. His prayers were marked at once by profound reverence and filial confidence, and abounded much in ascriptions of praise and thanks, and the breathings of devout affections towards God. Besides his punctual observance of his private and domestic devotions, and of the weekly meetings for social prayer, he was accustomed to select from time to time some one Christian, with whom he held stated seasons of devotion, in order to avail himself of the promise "that if two of you shall agree on earth, as touching anything that they shall ask, it shall be done for them by my Father which is in heaven." And his partners in these fellowships were selected, not so much for their social as for their spiritual attractions. This narrative would be unjust to the truth, and to the memory of one of God's most honored servants, if it omitted the mention of the chief instrument for cultivating in him this spirit of prayer. When Major Jackson became a member of the [Presbyterian] congregation in Lexington, there was among its presbyters a man of God, whose memory yet smells sweet and blossoms in the dust, John B. Lyle.... It was largely due to his guidance, that Jackson attained to that thoroughness which marked all his subsequent Christian life....

This prayerfulness was a profound inward spirit yet more than it was an outward manifestation. How he compelled his own diffidence [reserve or timidity] to pray with others, under a sense of duty, has been described. But he was never forward to assume the lead of others at the throne of grace, where his station did not obviously make it proper. It has been said of him, that he was as often found leading his men in the prayer-meeting as in the field of battle.... When called on by proper authority to lead his brethren in social prayer, he always obeyed. But he loved best to mingle with his rough and hardy soldiers, in the worship of God, as a simply lay-worshipper; with them to sit in the seat of the learner, with them to sing, with them to kneel, and with them to gather around the Lord's Table. He would not pronounce the blessing over the plain food of his own mess-table, if a clergyman, or even an older Christian than himself, were present to do it....

It was in the secret communings of his heart that this spirit of prayer was most prevalent. Devotion was the very breath of his soul. Once only was he led to make a revelation of these constant aspirations, to a Christian associate peculiarly near to him; and his description of his intercourse with God was too beautiful and characteristic to be suppressed. This friend expressed to him some embarrassment in comprehending literally the precept to "pray always," and to "pray without ceasing," and asked his help in construing it. He replied that obedience ought not to be impracticable for the child of God. "But how," said the other, "can one be always praying?" He answered that if it might be permitted to him, without suspicion of religious display, he would explain by describing his own habits. He then proceeded, with several parentheses, deprecating earnestly the charge of egotism, to say that, besides the stated daily seasons of secret and social prayer, he had long cultivated the habit of connecting the most trivial and customary acts of life with a silent prayer. "When we take our meals," said he, "there is the grace. When I take a draught of water, I always pause, as my palate receives the refreshment, to lift up my heart to God in thanks and prayer for the water of life. Whenever I drop a letter into the box at the post-office, I send a petition along with it, for God's blessing upon its mission and upon the person to whom it is sent. When I break the seal of a letter just received, I stop to pray to God that He may prepare me for its contents, and make it a messenger of good. When I go to my classroom, and await the arrangement of the cadets in their places, that is my time to intercede with God for them. And so of every other familiar act of the day." "But," said his friend, "do you not often forget these seasons, coming so frequently?" "No," said he, "I have made the practice habitual to me; and I can no more forget it, than forget to drink when I am thirsty." He added that the usage had become as delightful to him as it was regular.

He had a higher and more unaffected sense of the value of the prayers of other Christians than of his own.... He never seemed to let slip an opportunity to urge Christians to prayer, for the Church and for their country. Here are examples, which only express his habitual language and spirit. Writing to a near Christian connexion, he says:

> "My dear sister,—Do not forget to remember me in prayer. To the prayers of God's people I look with more interest than to our military strength. In answer to them, God has greatly blessed us thus far, and we may sanguinely expect him to continue to do so, if we and all His people but continue to do our duty."

He usually concluded his letters to his pastor during his campaigns, thus:

> "And now, present me affectionately to all my friends and brethren, and say to them, the greatest kindness they can show me is to pray for me."

When he had completed the series of brilliant victories in the Valley of Virginia, having utterly routed five Federal generals in quick succession, he entered upon a forced march of more than a hundred miles, to join the armies below Richmond. When about half of this march was completed, he stopped to rest his army during the Sabbath; and one use which he made of the respite was to write to his pastor upon two subjects. One was the supply of chaplains for the army; and the other may be stated in his own words:

> "I am afraid that our people are looking to the wrong source for help, and ascribing our successes to those to whom they are not due. If we fail to trust in God, and to give Him all the glory, our cause is ruined. Give to our friends at home due warning on this subject."

To another friend he wrote, Dec. 5, 1862 (eight days before the great battle of Fredericksburg):

> "Whilst we were near Winchester, it pleased our ever-merciful Heavenly Father to visit my command with the rich outpouring of His Spirit. There were probably more than one hundred inquiring the way of life in my old brigade. It appears to me that we may look for growing piety and many conversions in the army: *for it is the subject of prayer.* If so many prayers were offered for the blessing of God upon any other organization, would we not expect the Answerer of prayer to hear the petitions, and send a blessing?"

And again, January 1, 1863:

> "My dear Friend,—Your last letter came safe to hand, and I am much gratified to see that your prayer-meeting for the army is still continued. Dr. White writes that in Lexington they continue to meet every Wednesday afternoon for the same purpose. I have more confidence in such organizations than in military ones as the means of an early peace, though both are necessary."

In the autumn of 1861, after the first battle of Manassas, his pastor, with another venerable minister, visited his brigade at his invitation, to preach to his soldiers, and to lodge in his quarters. They arrived at nightfall, and found the Commander-in-Chief on the spot, communicating in person some important orders. General Jackson merely paused to give them the most hurried salutation consistent with respect, and without a moment's dallying passed on to execute his duties. After a length of time he returned, all the work of the evening completed, and renewed his welcome with a beaming face, and warm *abandon* of manner, heaping upon them affectionate attentions, and inquiring after all their households. Dr. White spent five days and nights with him, preaching daily. In the General's quarters, he found his morning and evening worship as regularly held as it had been at home. Jackson modestly proposed to his pastor to lead in this worship, which he did until the last evening of his stay; when, to the usual request for prayers, he answered, "General, you have often prayed with and for me at home, be so kind as to do so tonight." Without a word of objection, Jackson took the sacred volume, and read and prayed. *"And never while life lasts," said the pastor, "can I forget that prayer.* He thanked God for sending me to visit the army, and prayed that he would own and bless my ministrations, both to the officers and privates, so that many souls might be saved. He gave thanks for what it had pleased God to do for the church in Lexington, 'to which both of us belong,' especially for the revivals He had mercifully granted to that church, and for the many preachers of the gospel sent forth from its membership. He then prayed for the pastor, and every member of his family, for the ruling elders, the deacons, and the private members of the church, such as were at home, and especially such as then belonged to the army. He then pleaded with such tenderness and fervor, that God would baptize the whole army with His Holy Spirit, that my own hard heart was melted into penitence, gratitude, and praise. When we had risen from our knees, he stood before his camp fire, with that calm dignity of mien and tender expression of countenance for which he was so remarkable, and said, 'Doctor, I would be glad to learn more fully than I have yet done, what your views are of the prayer of faith.' A conversation then commenced, which was continued long after the hour of midnight, in which, it is candidly confessed, the pastor received more instruction than he imparted."

But perhaps the most impressive exhibition of his prayerful spirit was that which was sometimes witnessed on the field of battle. More than once, as one of his favorite brigades was passing into action, he had been noticed sitting motionless upon his horse, with his right hand uplifted, while the war-worn column swept, in stern silence, close by his side, into the storm of shot. For a time, it seemed doubtful whether it was mere abstraction of thought, or a posture to relieve his fatigue. But at length those who looked more narrowly were convinced by his closed eyes and moving lips, that he was wrestling in silent prayer for them! His fervent soul doubtless swelled with the solemn thoughts of his own responsibility and his country's crisis, of the precious blood he was compelled to put in jeopardy, and the souls passing, perhaps unprepared, to their everlasting doom; and of the orphanage and widowhood which was about to ensue. Recognizing the sovereignty of the Lord of Hosts, he interceded for his veterans, that "the Almighty would cover them with His feathers, and that His truth might be their shield and buckler." The moral grandeur of this scene was akin to that when Moses, upon the Mount of God, lifted up his hands while Israel prevailed against Amalek.

The Christian reader will easily comprehend that one so conscientious, and believing, and devout, was a happy man. He had, while in Lexington, his domestic bereavements, and he felt them as every man of sensibility must; but the consolations of the gospel abounded in him at those seasons. His habitual frame was a calm sunshine. He was never desponding, and never frivolous. It is manifest, that in all the later years of his religious life, his soul dwelt continually in the blessed assurance of his acceptance through the Redeemer; and this steady spiritual joy purified and elevated all his earthly affections. It is the testimony of his pastor that he was the happiest man he ever knew.[86]

86. Robert L. Dabney, *Life and Campaigns of Lieutenant-General Thomas J. Jackson* (NC: Sterling and Albright, 1865; reprint Harrisonburg, VA: Sprinkle Publications, 1976), 103–111.

Eleven Directions for Praying by Richard Baxter, 17th Century English Presbyterian

These directions are taken from Richard Baxter's classic, *A Christian Directory*:

> *Direct.* I, See that you understand what prayer is.... True christian prayer is, the believing and serious expressing or acting of our lawful desires before God, through Jesus our Mediator, by the help of the Holy Spirit, as a means to procure of him the grant of these desires....
>
> *Direct.* II, See that you understand the ends and use of prayer.... Prayer is useful, 1. As an act of obedience to God's command. 2. As the performance of a condition, without which he hath not promised us his mercy, and to which he hath promised it. 3. As a means to actuate, and express, and increase our own humility, dependence, desire, trust, and hope in God, and so to make us capable and fit for mercy, who else should be uncapable and unfit. 4. And so, though God be not changed by it in himself, yet the real change that is made by it on ourselves....
>
> *Direct.* III, Labour above all to know that God to whom you pray...as your Maker, your Redeemer, your Regenerator; as your Owner, your Ruler, and your Father, Felicity and End....
>
> *Direct.* IV, Labour when you are about to pray, to stir up in your souls the most lively and serious belief of those unseen things that your prayers have respect to; and to pray as if you saw them all the while; even as if you saw God in his glory, and saw heaven and hell, the glorified and the damned, and Jesus Christ your Mediator interceding for you in the heavens.
>
> *Direct.* V, Labour for a constant acquaintance with yourselves, your sins and manifold [needs] and necessities.... When men are wilful strangers to themselves, and never

look backwards or inwards, to see what is amiss and [lacking], nor look forwards, to see the danger that is before them, no wonder if their hearts be dead and dull, and if they are as unfit to pray, as a sleeping man is to work.

Direct. VI, See that you hate hypocrisy, and let not your lips go against or without your hearts; but that your hearts be the spring of all your words; that you love not sin, and be not loth to leave it, when you seem to pray against it; and that you truly desire the grace which you ask, and ask not for that which you would not have: and that you be ready to use the lawful means to get the mercies which you ask....

Direct. VII, Search your hearts and watch them carefully, lest some beloved vanity alienate them from the work in hand, and turn away your thoughts or prepossess your affections, so that you [lack] them when you should use them. If the mind be set on other matters, prayer will be a heartless, lifeless thing.

Direct. VIII, Be sure that you pray for nothing that is disagreeable to the will of God, and that is not for the good of yourselves or others, or for the honour of God; and therefore take heed, lest an erring judgment, or carnal desires, or passions, should corrupt your prayers, and turn them into sin. Be especially careful therefore that your judgments and desires be sound and holy, before you offer them up to God in prayer.

Direct. IX, Come always to God in the humility that [becomes] a condemned sinner, and in the faith and [confident hope] that [becomes] a son and a member of Christ.... Hope is the life of prayer and all endeavor, and Christ is the life of hope.... And there is no hope of success, but through our powerful Intercessor. Therefore let both a crucified and glorified Christ be always before your eyes in prayer; not in a picture, but in the thoughts of a believing mind.

Direct. X, Labour hard with your hearts all the while to keep them in a reverent, serious, fervent frame, and [do not allow] them to grow remiss and cold, to turn prayer into lip-labour and lifeless formality, or into hypocritical, affected, seeming fervency, when the heart is senseless, though the voice be earnest. The heart will easily grow dull, and customary, and hypocritical, if it be not carefully watched, and diligently followed and stirred up.

Direct. XI, For the matter and order of your desires and prayers, take the Lord's Prayer as your special rule: and labour to understand it well.[87]

Ten Directions for Family Prayers by Richard Baxter

These directions are also taken from Baxter's book, *A Christian Directory*:

Direct. I, Let it be done rather by the [head] of the family himself than any other, [if possible].

Direct. II, Let prayer be suited to the case of those that join in it, and to the condition of the family; and not a few general words spoken by rote, that serve all times and persons alike.

Direct. III, Let it neither be so short as to end before their hearts can be warm and their [needs] expressed...nor yet so tedious as to make it an ungrateful burden to the family.

Direct. IV, Let not the coldness and dulness of the speaker rock the family asleep; but keep awake your own heart, that you may keep the rest awake, and force them to attention.

Direct. V, Pray at such hours as the family may be least distracted, sleepy, tired, or out of the way.

87. Richard Baxter, *The Practical Works of Richard Baxter*, 4 vols. (reprint PA: Soli Deo Gloria Publications, 1990), 1:483 –84.

Direct. VI, Let other duties concur, as oft as may be, to assist in prayer: as reading, and singing praises.

Direct. VII, Do all with the greatest reverence of God that possibly you can; not [pretended] reverence, but real; that so more of God than of man may appear in every word you speak.

Direct. VIII, The more the hearers are concerned in it, the more regard you must have to the fitness of your expressions; for before others, words must be regarded, lest they be scandalized, and God and prayer be dishonoured. And if you cannot do it competently without, use a well-composed [prayer by another].

Direct. IX, Let not family prayer be used at the time of public prayer in the church, nor preferred before it, but prefer public prayer, though the manner were more imperfect than your own.

Direct. X, Teach your children and servants how to pray themselves, that they may not be prayerless when they come among those that cannot pray.[88]

Six Directions for Secret Prayer by Richard Baxter

These six directions are taken from *A Christian Directory*:

Direct. I, Let [your prayer] be in as secret a place as conveniently as you can; that you may not be disturbed.

Direct. II, Let your voice be suited to your own help and benefit, if none else [is there] to hear you.

Direct. III, In secret let the matter of your prayers be that which is most [specifically your own concerns], or those se-

88. Baxter, *A Christian Directory*, 1:492.

cret things that are not fit for public prayer, yet never forgetting the highest interest of Christ, and the gospel, and the world and church.

Direct. IV, Be less solicitous about words in secret than with others, and lay out your care about the heart....

Direct. V, Do not through carnal unwillingness grow into a neglect of secret prayer, when you have time; nor yet do you superstitiously tie yourselves to just so long time, whether you are fit, or at leisure from greater duties, or not. But be the longer when you are most fit and vacant, and the shorter when you are not.

Direct. VI, A melancholy person who is unfit for much solitariness and heart-searchings, must be much shorter, if not also seldomer in secret prayers, than other christians that are capable of bearing it.[89]

Advice from Richard Baxter on How We May Know When Our Prayers are Heard and When They Are Not

This advice is from *A Christian Directory*:

> Two ways: sometimes by experience, when the thing itself is actually given us; and always by the promise; when we ask for that which God commandeth us to ask or promiseth to grant; for we are sure God's promises are all fulfilled. If we ask for the objects of sense (as food or raiment or health, &c), sense will tell us whether our prayers are granted in the same kind that we asked for; but if the questions be of the objects of faith, it is faith that must tell you that your prayers are granted; but yet faith and reason make use of evidences or signs. As if I pray for pardon of sin, and salvation, the promise assureth me that this prayer is granted, if I am a penitent, believing, regenerate person, otherwise not; therefore faith

89. Baxter, *A Christian Directory*, 1:492–93.

only assureth me that such prayers are granted, supposing that I discern the evidence of my regeneration, repentance, and faith in Christ. So if the question is whether my prayer for others, or for temporal mercies, be answered in some other kind, and conduce to my good some other way, faith only must tell you this from the promise, by the help of evidences. There are millions of prayers that will all be found answered at death and judgment, which we did not know to be answered any way but by believing it.[90]

90. Baxter, *A Christian Directory*, 1:490.

Chapter Thirty-Eight

The Lord's Prayer

The marvel of this prayer…is that while it is so extremely simple and brief, it fully expresses all that the Christian in this world needs.
~ *Herman Hoeksema*

Therefore, pray ye, then, in this way: "Our Father who art in heaven, Hallowed be thy name. Thy kingdom come. Thy will be done in earth, as it is in heaven. Give us this day our daily bread and forgive us our debts, as we forgive our debtors. And lead us not into temptation but deliver us from evil. For thine is the kingdom and the power and the glory forever. Amen."

Matthew 6:9–13

The Lord's Prayer

Q. 186: What rule hath God given for our direction in the duty of prayer?

A.: The whole word of God is of use to direct us in the duty of prayer; but the special rule of direction is that form of prayer which our Saviour Christ taught his disciples, commonly called *The Lord's Prayer.*

Q. 187: How is the Lord's Prayer to be used?

A.: The Lord's Prayer is not only for direction, as a pattern, according to which we are to make other prayers; but may also be used as a prayer, so that it be done with understanding, faith, reverence, and other graces necessary to the right performance of the duty of prayer.

Q. 188: Of how many parts doth the Lord's prayer consist?

A.: The Lord's prayer consists of three parts: a preface, petitions, and a conclusion.

Q. 189: What doth the preface of the Lord's prayer teach us?

A.: The preface of the Lord's prayer (contained in these words, *Our Father which art in heaven*) teacheth us, when we pray, to draw near to God with confidence of his fatherly goodness, and our interest therein; with reverence, and all other child-like dispositions, heavenly affections, and due apprehensions of his sovereign power, majesty, and gracious condescension: as also, to pray with and for others.

Q. 190: What do we pray for in the first petition?

A.: In the first petition, (which is, *Hallowed be thy name*), acknowledging the utter inability and indisposition that is in ourselves and all men to honour God aright, we pray, that God would by his grace enable and incline us and others to know, to acknowledge, and highly to esteem him, his titles, attributes, ordinances, word, works, and whatsoever he is pleased to make himself known by; and to glorify him in thought, word, and deed: that he would prevent and remove atheism, ignorance, idolatry, profaneness, and whatsoever is dishonourable to him; and, by his over-ruling providence, direct and dispose all things to his own glory.

Q. 191: What do we pray for in the second petition?

A.: In the second petition, (which is, *Thy kingdom come*), acknowledging ourselves and all mankind to be by nature under the dominion of sin and Satan, we pray, that the kingdom of sin and Satan may be destroyed, the gospel propagated throughout the world, the Jews called, the fulness of the Gentiles brought in; the church furnished with all gospel-officers and ordinances, purged from corruption, countenanced and maintained by the civil magistrate: that the ordinances of

Christ may be purely dispensed, and made effectual to the converting of those that are yet in their sins, and the confirming, comforting, and building up of those that are already converted: that Christ would rule in our hearts here, and hasten the time of his second coming, and our reigning with him for ever: and that he would be pleased so to exercise the kingdom of his power in all the world, as may best conduce to these ends.

Q. 192: What do we pray for in the third petition?

A.: In the third petition, (which is, *Thy will be done in earth, as it is in heaven*), acknowledging, that by nature we and all men are not only utterly unable and unwilling to know and do the will of God, but prone to rebel against his word, to repine and murmur against his providence, and wholly inclined to do the will of the flesh, and of the devil: we pray, that God would by his Spirit take away from ourselves and others all blindness, weakness, indisposedness, and perverseness of heart; and by his grace make us able and willing to know, do, and submit to his will in all things, with the like humility, cheerfulness, faithfulness, diligence, zeal, sincerity, and constancy, as the angels do in heaven.

Q. 193: What do we pray for in the fourth petition?

A.: In the fourth petition, (which is, *Give us this day our daily bread*), acknowledging, that in Adam, and by our own sin, we have forfeited our right to all the outward blessings of this life, and deserve to be wholly deprived of them by God, and to have them cursed to us in the use of them; and that neither they of themselves are able to sustain us, nor we to merit, or by our own industry to procure them; but prone to desire, get, and use them unlawfully: we pray for ourselves and others, that both they and we, waiting upon the providence of God from day to day in the use of lawful means, may, of his free gift, and as to his fatherly wisdom shall seem best, enjoy a competent portion of them; and have the same continued and blessed unto us in our holy and comfortable use of them, and contentment in them; and be kept from all things that are contrary to our temporal support and comfort.

Q. 194: What do we pray for in the fifth petition?

A.: In the fifth petition, (which is, *Forgive us our debts, as we forgive our debtors*), acknowledging, that we and all others are guilty both of original and actual sin, and thereby become debtors to the justice of God; and that neither we, nor any other creature, can make the least satisfaction for that debt: we pray for ourselves and others, that God of his free grace would, through the obedience and satisfaction of Christ, apprehended and applied by faith, acquit us both from the guilt and punishment of sin, accept us in the Beloved; continue his favour and grace to us, pardon our daily failings, and fill us with peace and joy, in giving us daily more and more assurance of forgiveness; which we are the rather emboldened to ask, and encouraged to expect, when we have this testimony in ourselves, that we from the heart forgive others their offences.

Q. 195: What do we pray for in the sixth petition?

A.: In the sixth petition, (which is, *And lead us not into temptation, but deliver us from evil*), acknowledging, that the most wise, righteous, and gracious God, for divers holy and just ends, may so order things, that we may be assaulted, foiled, and for a time led captive by temptations; that Satan, the world, and the flesh, are ready powerfully to draw us aside, and ensnare us; and that we, even after the pardon of our sins, by reason of our corruption, weakness, and want of watchfulness, are not only subject to be tempted, and forward to expose ourselves unto temptations, but also of ourselves unable and unwilling to resist them, to recover out of them, and to improve them; and worthy to be left under the power of them: we pray, that God would so over-rule the world and all in it, subdue the flesh, and restrain Satan, order all things, bestow and bless all means of grace, and quicken us to watchfulness in the use of them, that we and all his people may by his providence be kept from being tempted to sin; or, if tempted, that by his Spirit we may be powerfully supported and enabled to stand in the hour of temptation; or when fallen, raised again and recovered out of it, and have a sanctified use and improvement thereof: that our sanctification and salvation may be perfected, Satan trodden under our feet, and we fully freed from sin, temptation, and all evil, for ever.

Q. 196: What doth the conclusion of the Lord's prayer teach us?

A.: The conclusion of the Lord's prayer, (which is *For Thine is the kingdom, and the power, and the glory for ever. Amen.*) teacheth us to enforce our petitions with arguments, which are to be taken, not from any worthiness in ourselves, or in any other creature, but from God; and with our prayers to join praises, ascribing to God alone eternal sovereignty, omnipotency, and glorious excellency; in regard whereof, as he is able and willing to help us, so we by faith are emboldened to plead with him that he would, and quietly to rely upon him, that he will fulfil our requests. And, to testify this our desire and assurance, we say, *Amen.*

The Special Rule of Prayer

Q. 186: What rule hath God given for our direction in the duty of prayer?

A.: The whole word of God is of use to direct us in the duty of prayer; but the special rule of direction is that form of prayer which our Saviour Christ taught his disciples, commonly called *The Lord's Prayer.*

Q. 187: How is the Lord's Prayer to be used?

A.: The Lord's Prayer is not only for direction, as a pattern, according to which we are to make other prayers; but may also be used as a prayer, so that it be done with understanding, faith, reverence, and other graces necessary to the right performance of the duty of prayer.

> The Lord's Prayer is perfect in every respect; no human prayer has ever equaled it.[1]

After stating that the whole Bible is the comprehensive rule governing prayer, our Catechism teaches us that the Lord's Prayer in Matthew 6:9–13 is *the special rule of direction* in the duty of prayer. Why is the Lord's Prayer said to be *the special rule of direction* for our praying? "Because there is not any one portion of scripture, where the petitionary part of prayer is so comprehensively and methodically laid down, as in the Lord's prayer."[2] And it

---

1. R. C. H. Lenski, *The Interpretation of St. Matthew's Gospel* (Wartburg Press, 1943; reprint MN: Augsburg Publishing House, 1964), 263.

2. James Fisher, *The Westminster Assembly's Shorter Catechism Explained* (Philadelphia: Presbyterian Board of Publication and Sabbath-School Work,

is called *the Lord's Prayer*, not because the Lord prayed it, but because He dictated it to His disciples in answer to their request: "Lord, teach us to pray."

Catechism Question 187 tells us how to use the Lord's Prayer as our model for praying, as *the special rule of direction* in praying. As has been mentioned, the Lord's Prayer was not given primarily as a set form that we are to repeat in our praying without any variation, although it is appropriate to do so, as long as it is prayed *with understanding, faith, reverence and other graces necessary to the right performances of the duty of prayer*, which graces include *an awful apprehension of the majesty of God, and deep sense of our own unworthiness, necessities, and sins; with penitent, thankful, and enlarged hearts; with understanding, faith, sincerity, fervency, love, and perseverance, waiting upon him, with humble submission to his will* (WLC, Q. 185). Rather, it is a directory for prayer, teaching us the basic ingredients of adoration and petition, "leaving the suppliant himself to clothe his desires with such words as are most adapted to his present circumstances."[3]

Why do we say that this prayer is primarily a pattern for prayer and not a fixed form of prayer? First, it does not expressly contain all the elements of prayer, such as confession of sin and thanksgiving for God's blessings. Second, it is not given in the same exact expressions by Matthew and Luke (Matthew 6:9f; Luke 11:2f).[4] These two Gospel writers are in perfect harmony as to the content of the Lord's Prayer, but there is some difference between them in their mode of expression, especially in the fourth and fifth petitions. And, although Matthew includes the conclusion, Luke omits it.

> The principal thing which I would militate against, is not so much the using of the [exact] words, as dong this in a formal way, supposing that the mere recital of them does, as it were, sanctify our other prayers; which, though very agreeable to

---

1911), 222.

3. Fisher, *The Westminster Assembly's Shorter Catechism Explained*, 222.

4. "The contexts are so decidedly different that we are compelled to conclude that, as was true with regard to other sayings of Jesus, this prayer, too, was repeated by him" (Lenski, *The Interpretation of St. Matthew's Gospel*, 264).

> the sense of the Lord's prayer, are, as some suppose, so incomplete, that they will hardly be regarded by God without it. Moreover, I cannot but conclude the Papists highly to blame, who think that the frequent repetition of it...is not only necessary, but in some measure meritorious. And the practice of some ignorant superstitious persons, who think that it may be made use of as a charm, and that the words of it may be repeated, as the Jews of old did their phylacteries, as a means to drive away evil spirits, is not only to be disapproved, but is a vile instance of profaneness, very remote from the design of our Saviour in giving it.[5]

> Therefore when you say this prayer, you must well consider what you say: for it is better once said deliberately with understanding, than a thousand times without understanding: which is in very deed but vain babbling, and so more a displeasure than pleasure unto God.[6]

Above all else, the Lord's Prayer is a *SPECIAL rule of direction* for our praying because it is the one *our Savior Christ taught His disciples.* Jesus Christ, our Lord and our Savior, gave it as a gift of His love for those whom He saved from sin by the shedding of His blood on Calvary's cross. He died there so that we would and could pray this prayer from our hearts to God, knowing that because of the merits and accomplishments of His saving work in our behalf, God would hear and answer us.

The Context of the Lord's Prayer in the Sermon on the Mount

The Lord's Prayer (Matt. 6:9–13) is contained in Jesus' Sermon on the Mount (Matt. 5–7). Just prior to it is Jesus' teaching about the nature of true prayer (Matt. 6:5–8) and following it he explains forgiveness (Matt. 6:14–15), and fasting (Matt. 6:16–18).

5. Thomas Ridgeley, *Commentary on the Larger Catechism*, 2 vols. (Edmonton, Canada: Still Waters Revival Books, [1855] 1993), 2:602.

6. Hugh Latimer, *Sermons by Hugh Latimer*, ed. by Rev. George Elwes Corrie (Cambridge: The University Press, 1844), 328–29.

Matthew 6:5–8: The Nature of True Prayer

Jesus is contrasting false praying with true praying. False praying concentrates on itself and on the one who is praying. True prayer concentrates on the One to whom prayer is offered. False prayer also feels that the effectiveness of praying depends upon the length of prayers, the amount of time spent in prayer and the particular manner in which prayer is offered. False prayer is concerned with the effect of the prayer offered upon the people who hear it rather than being concerned with approaching God with reverence and godly fear. "Public prayer should be such that the people who are praying silently and the one who is uttering the words should be no longer conscious of each other, but should be carried on the wings of prayer into the very presence of God."[7]

The correct way to prayer is in the matter of approach. "The one thing that is important when we pray anywhere is that we must realize we are approaching God. That is the one thing that matters.... If only we would realize that we are approaching God everything else would be all right."[8] Approaching God means realizing who God is and what He has revealed concerning Himself in His Word. It is to remember that we are entering the audience chamber of the almighty God, who is majestic in holiness, and who is willing to hear our prayers as our Father through the Lord Jesus Christ: "But you, when you pray, go into your inner room, and when you have shut your door, pray to your Father who is in secret, and your Father who sees in secret will repay you" (Matt. 6:6).

In approaching God and realizing who He is, we must pray, not only with reverence and submission as before a great King, but also with the confidence of a child in the presence of his loving Father. As Lloyd-Jones wrote:

> I must see God as my Father who has purchased my ultimate good in Christ, and is waiting to bless me with His own fullness in Christ Jesus.... God is able to do for us exceeding

7. D. Martyn Lloyd-Jones, *Studies in the Sermon on the Mount*, 2 vols. (London: Inter-Varsity Fellowship, [1960] 1966), 2:27.

8. Lloyd-Jones, *Studies in the Sermon on the Mount*, 2:29.

abundantly above all that we can ask or think. Let us believe that and then go to Him in simple confidence.[9]

Matthew 6:14–15: The Nature of Forgiveness

After giving us His model for our prayers, which contains the petition that God would forgive us as we forgive those who have sinned against us (6:12), Jesus explains the nature of forgiveness: "For if you forgive men for their transgressions, your heavenly Father will also forgive you. But if you do not forgive men, then your Father will not forgive your transgressions" (6:14–15).

Only those who are children of God through faith in Jesus Christ (John 1:12) may pray to their Father in heaven for forgiveness of sins. And the proof that we are children of God and we are forgiven of our sins through Christ, is that we are forgiving of those who sin against us.

> If we think that our sins are forgiven by God and we refuse to forgive somebody else, we are making a mistake; we have never been forgiven. The man who knows he has been forgiven, only in and through the shed blood of Christ, is a man who must forgive others. He cannot help himself. If we really know Christ as our Saviour our hearts are broken and cannot be hard, and we cannot refuse forgiveness.[10]

Matthew 6:16–18: The Place of Fasting

Jesus finishes His exposition of true prayer with a few comments explaining the place of fasting in the Christian life. Fasting is abstinence from food for certain spiritual purposes such as prayer or meditation or seeking God's face under some exceptional circumstance. Fasting is never an end in itself, and it must never be done mechanically or merely for the sake of doing so, as if to impress God by our fasting. Fasting "is something that I do in order to

9. Lloyd-Jones, *Studies in the Sermon on the Mount*, 2:31, 32.
10. Lloyd-Jones, *Studies in the Sermon on the Mount*, 2:75.

reach that higher spiritual realm of prayer to God, or meditation, or intense intercession."[11]

Fasting is a means to an end. It is something a person should do only when he or she feels compelled or led to it by great spiritual issues.

> I must discipline myself at all times, and must fast only when I feel led by the Spirit of God to do so, when I am intent on some mighty spiritual purpose, not according to rule, but because I feel there is some peculiar need of an entire concentration of the whole of my being upon God and my worship of Him. That is the time to fast, and that is the way to approach the subject.[12]

When fasting we must not be concerned as to the effect of our fasting on others. It is between ourselves and God. Forget yourself when you pray with fasting. Be concerned only with God and with pleasing Him. Be concerned only for His honor and His glory.

The Divisions of the Lord's Prayer

Q. 188: Of how many parts doth the Lord's prayer consist?

A.: The Lord's prayer consists of three parts: a preface, petitions, and a conclusion.

> Before we set our feet across the threshold of this holy of holies, and dwell for a moment in every hall and chamber of this sanctuary, we will do well to examine the grandeur and beauty and perfection of the whole.... It certainly signifies that it is a model, the main lines of which we must always copy, and the chief principles of which we may really never violate when we approach the throne of grace with our peti-

11. Lloyd-Jones, *Studies in the Sermon on the Mount*, 2:39.
12. Lloyd-Jones, *Studies in the Sermon on the Mount*, 2:41.

> tions. And to discover these we must not be too hasty to analyze the Lord's Prayer and to expound its details; but we must rather tarry a while, to contemplate the beauty and meaning of its contents and style.[13]

The Structure of the Lord's Prayer

As our Catechism informs us, the Lord's Prayer contains three parts: a preface, six petitions and a conclusion. The first three petitions appear to be parallels to the first three commandments. Each of the first three refer to God, and then the prayer concerns itself with our earthly affairs and relations, as do the last six Commandments. The pronoun "Thy" binds the first three petitions together and distinguishes them from the rest which have the pronouns "us" and "our." The three aorist imperatives of the first three petitions strike us because all three are in the third person; the other three are in the second person.

> These first three have a mandatory sound; what they say *must* be done. God could not consent to the opposite, nor could God's children. The aorist tense helps to emphasize this: God will certainly do what he is in this striking way asked to do. For back of these imperatives is God himself. The name, the kingdom, and the will are His.[14]

The Unifying Purpose of the Lord's Prayer

In the preface, God is directly addressed—"Our Father which art in heaven," in the first petition, the goal of the entire prayer is stated—"Hallowed be Thy name" and the other six petitions set forth the means by which the goal will be reached. The conclusion is an ascription of praise to God guaranteeing that the goal of this prayer will be reached.

God's glory is the main concern of the Lord's Prayer. In the first three petitions we are specifically concerned with God's glory,

13. Herman Hoeksema, *The Triple Knowledge*, 3 vols. (Grand Rapids, MI: Reformed Free Publishing Association, 1972), 3:474.

14. Lenski, *The Interpretation of St. Matthew's Gospel*, 265–66.

without any consideration of our need or benefit. The last three petitions are concerned with what we need to be faithful servants of God. But even in these petitions, our goal is not ultimately our own benefit, but the glory of God.

> So, when we ask that God's name be hallowed, because God wills to test us whether we love and worship Him freely or for hope of reward, we must then have no consideration for our own benefit but must set before ourselves His glory, to gaze with eyes intent upon this one thing. And in the remaining petitions of this sort, it is meet to be affected in precisely the same way. And, indeed, this yields a great benefit to us, because when his name is hallowed as we ask, our own hallowing in turn also comes about. But our eyes ought, as it were, to be closed and in a sense blinded to this sort of advantage, so that they have no regard for it at all, and so that, if all hope of our own private good were cut off, still we should not cease to desire and entreat this hallowing and the other things that pertain to God's glory. In the examples of Moses and Paul, we see that it was not grievous for them to turn their minds and eyes away from themselves and to long for their own destruction with fierce and burning zeal in order that, despite their own loss, they might advance God's glory and kingdom (Ex. 32:32; Rom. 9:3). On the other hand, when we ask to be given our daily bread, even though we desire what is to our benefit, here also we ought especially to seek God's glory so as not to ask it unless it redound to his glory.[15]

The Brevity and Completeness of the Lord's Prayer

The Lord's Prayer is distinguished by simple brevity and by profound fullness. "The marvel of this prayer then is that while it is so extremely simple and brief, it fully expresses all that the Christian

15. John Calvin, *Institutes of the Christian Religion*, ed. by John T. McNeill, trans. by Ford Lewis Battles, 2 vols. (Philadelphia: Westminster Press, 1960), 2:898–99.

in this world needs."[16] It may take only seconds to repeat it, but hours can be spent meditating on it.

The Preface of the Lord's Prayer

Q. 189: What doth the preface of the Lord's prayer teach us?

A.: The preface of the Lord's prayer (contained in these words, Our Father which art in heaven) teacheth us, when we pray, to draw near to God with confidence of his fatherly goodness, and our interest therein; with reverence, and all other child-like dispositions, heavenly affections, and due apprehensions of his sovereign power, majesty, and gracious condescension: as also, to pray with and for others.

The Focus of the Preface: Speaking Face to Face to God

In praying the Lord's Prayer we must be fully and knowledgeably conscious of the fact that we are speaking directly to GOD, the Creator of the universe, face to face. Therefore, we must be careful how we address Him, because He knows the spiritual condition of our hearts.

> We come to stand before His face in the sanctuary. Then this address ["Our Father who art in heaven"] is not the thoughtless expression of what we have learned by heart, but the conscious effort to conceive Him as He is, as He revealed Himself to us in His Word, and of His relation to us. It is the spiritual exercise of faith, whereby we seek and find Him, or rather, whereby we sought and found Him, that is expressed in this address. It is the expression of that spiritual activity of

---

16. Hoeksema, *The Triple Knowledge*, 3:476.

> the mind and heart and soul whereby we are absorbed in profound contemplation of the living God, and try to penetrate the darkness that envelops us, until we gaze with adoration and wonder upon His face and all our attention is concentrated upon His glorious majesty. And thus this act of addressing God determines our whole attitude through our entire prayer. It is because He is what we declare Him to be in this address that we direct our prayer to Him, that we dare to approach Him, that we are confident that He will hear us. And it is because we gaze upon Him and keep the spiritual eyes of our faith fixed upon Him throughout our prayer that we pray as we do, and ask for the things which are briefly enumerated in the Lord's Prayer. The address, therefore, represents the indispensable preliminary of all true prayer. Expressed in spirit and in truth, it signifies that we have entered into the sanctuary of God and that we have found Him for Whom our soul is yearning.[17]

The Lord's Introduction to the Lord's Prayer

The Authorized Version of the Bible introduces the Lord's Prayer with these words: "After this manner therefore pray ye." Each word is important in understanding the prayer itself. "Therefore" indicates that this prayer is the answer to prayers that are nothing but "vain repetitions."[18] "After this manner" is William Tyndale's version of the single Greek word, "thus," referring to what follows. "Pray ye" stresses the pronoun in Greek, emphasizing that this prayer is only for the disciples of Jesus as distinguished from unbelievers, hence it can be called "The Disciples' Prayer."

---

17. Hoeksema, *The Triple Knowledge,* 3:483–84.

18. "Therefore when you say this prayer, you must well consider what you say: for it is better once said deliberately with understanding, than a thousand times without understanding: which is in very deed but vain babbling, and so more a displeasure than pleasure unto God" (Latimer, *Sermons by Hugh Latimer,* 328–29).

The Implications of Addressing God as Father

Only a true child of God through faith in Jesus Christ has the privilege of calling the Creator of the universe his Father: "But as many as received Him, to them He gave the right to become children of God, even to those who believe in His name" (John 1:12). Therefore only believers in Jesus have the authority to pray this prayer. John 8:42, 43 applies to everybody else: "Jesus said to them, 'If God were your Father, you would love Me; for I proceeded forth and have come from God, for I have not even come on My own initiative, but He sent Me. Why do you not understand what I am saying? It is because you cannot hear My word.'"

> We ought to offer all prayer to God only in Christ's name.... For in calling God "Father," we put forward the name "Christ." With what confidence would anyone address God as "Father"? Who would break forth into such rashness as to claim for himself the honor of a son of God, unless we had been adopted as children of grace in Christ?... Therefore God both calls himself our Father and would have us so address him. By the great sweetness of this name he frees us from all distrust, since no greater feeling of love can be found elsewhere than in the Father.[19]

Therefore he or she who prays and the One who hears the prayer are conscious of a Father-child relationship in Christ. The one praying is confident that he/she can approach the Creator as a little child approaches his/her Father. He trusts that God loves Him and wants to hear the desires of his heart. In and of ourselves we have no right to utter the very first words of the Lord's Prayer, without Christ. And to attempt to do so, is "sheer presumption, provocative of the fierce anger of the Lord."[20] However, until the Father enables us by His Spirit, we are even unable and unwilling to utter them sincerely, for we hate the light and love the darkness and are dead in our trespasses and sins, unwilling and unable to do anything that pleases God.

---

19. Calvin, *Institutes of the Christian Religion*, 2:899.
20. Hoeksema, *The Triple Knowledge*, 3:489.

The Implications of Calling God Our Father

The pronoun, "Our," presupposes the possession of faith in the one praying, just as the phrase, "the LORD our God" in the Old Testament presupposes faith in the one using this phrase. "Our" is a plural pronoun. In fact, plural pronouns are used throughout the Lord's Prayer. "Give US... OUR daily bread... Forgive US OUR debts as we forgive OUR debtors... Lead US not into temptation, but deliver US from the evil one." The point is that just as "Our" presupposes the possession of faith in God, it also presupposes love for all the disciples of Christ, and fellowship with all those who are believers in Christ. As the apostle John wrote: "If someone says, 'I love God,' and hates his brother, he is a liar; for the one who does not love his brother whom he has seen, cannot love God whom he has not seen" (1 John 4:20). "Your prayer must needs die on your lips if you should appear in the sanctuary of God with hatred against the brethren, or even against one brother, in your heart."[21] Or as Jesus said in the Sermon on the Mount: "If therefore you are presenting your offering at the altar, and there remember that your brother has something against you, leave your offering there before the altar, and go your way, first be reconciled to your brother, and then come and present your offering" (Matt. 5:23–24).

> This word "our" teacheth us to consider that the Father of heaven is a common Father; as well my neighbour's Father as mine; as well the poor man's Father as the rich; so that he is not a peculiar Father, but a Father to the whole church and congregation, to all the faithful. Be they never so poor, so vile, so foul and despised, yet he is their Father as well as mine: and therefore I should not despise them, but consider that God is their Father as well as mine. Here may we perceive what communion is between us; so that when I pray, I pray not for myself alone, but for all the rest: again, when they pray, they pray not for themselves only, but for me: for

21. Hoeksema, *The Triple Knowledge*, 3:479.

> Christ hath so framed this prayer, that I must needs include my neighbour in it.[22]

As John Calvin wrote:

> There is nothing in which we can benefit our brethren more than in commending them to the providential care of the best of fathers... To sum up, all prayers ought to be such as to look to that community which our Lord has established in his Kingdom and his household.[23]

The Implications of Calling God Our Father Who Art in Heaven

The God to Whom we pray is "Our Father, who art in heaven." This phrase reminds us of God's transcendent majesty, His sovereignty and holiness. As King Solomon prayed at the dedication of the Temple in Jerusalem: "O LORD, the God of Israel, there is no God like Thee in heaven above or on earth beneath, who art keeping covenant and showing lovingkindness to Thy servants who walk before Thee with all their heart.... But will God indeed dwell on the earth? Behold, heaven and the highest heaven cannot contain Thee" (1 Kings 8:23, 27). And through Isaiah the Lord said: "For thus says the high and exalted One who lives forever, whose name is Holy, 'I dwell on a high and holy place, and also with the contrite and lowly of spirit in order to revive the spirit of the lowly and to revive the heart of the contrite'" (Isa. 57:15). In these passages God is the glorious, majestic, sovereign and holy God, totally self-sufficient and self-existent, who condescends in undeserved grace to love and fellowship with the contrite. Therefore, God is to be feared as majestic sovereign, and loved, and merciful Father and Savior. Hence, Jesus taught us to address God as "Our Father," One to be loved and sought, and as Our Father "in heaven," One to be feared and worshiped.

22. Latimer, *Sermons by Hugh Latimer*, 337–38.
23. Calvin, *Institutes of the Christian Religion*, 2:901.

> That he is in heaven is added. From this we are not immediately to reason that he is bound, shut up, and surrounded, by the circumference of heaven, as by a barred enclosure. For Solomon confesses that the heaven of heavens cannot contain him (1 Kings 8:27).... But our minds, so crass are they, could not have conceived his unspeakable glory otherwise. Consequently, it has been signified to us by "heaven" for we can behold nothing more sublime or majestic than this.... Secondly, by this expression he is lifted above chance of either corruption or change. Finally, it signifies that he embraces and holds together the entire universe and controls it by his might. Therefore it is as if he had been said to be of infinite greatness or loftiness, of incomprehensible essence, of boundless might, and of everlasting immortality.... At the same time our confidence in him must be aroused, since we understand that heaven and earth are ruled by his providence and power.[24]

When God reveals Himself to us as "Father," He engenders trust in us, for if we cannot call God, "our Father," we cannot approach Him at all. When God reveals Himself as the God "who is in heaven," He engenders in us fear, awe, worship and adoring submission, for "if we cannot add 'Who art in heaven,' we make Him like unto us, drag Him down from His excellency, and pray to an idol."[25]

The Specific Teachings of Catechism Q. 189

Our Catechism Q. 189 brings out all the above points concisely. It teaches us that the preface to the Lord's Prayer—"Our Father who art in Heaven"—should do several things to us when we pray.

First, it should encourage us *to draw near to God with confidence of His fatherly goodness, and our interest therein.* As Luke 11:13 says: "If you then, being evil, know how to give good gifts to your children, how much more shall your Heavenly Father give the Holy Spirit to those who ask Him?" The point is that even an earth-

---

24. Calvin, *Institutes of the Christian Religion*, 2:902–03.
25. Hoeksema, *The Triple Knowledge*, 3:486.

ly father, even with all his sins, will not give his child useless or dangerous things instead of the necessary things of life for which his child depends on him. Therefore, how much more will our perfect Father in Heaven give His children in Christ the very things they need, when they pray to Him, especially the Holy Spirit, who is indispensable to our lives as the sons and daughters of God and in Whom all other necessary gifts are included.

> No regenerate child of God should ever doubt that when he prays to God out of real need his prayer will be answered. He who doubts this does Him the greatest dishonour, for by not believing that He will give what we really need we in fact appear to regard Him as less sympathetic and less faithful than an ordinary earthly father.... Therefore unbelief in relation to the answering of prayer is not only a weakness, but a serious sin and utter folly.[26]

Second, the preface of the Lord's Prayer should encourage us to pray *with reverence, and all other child-like dispositions, heavenly affections, and due apprehensions of his sovereign power, majesty, and gracious condescension.*

> But now, O LORD, Thou art our Father, We are the clay, and Thou our potter; And all of us are the work of Thy hand. Do not be angry beyond measure, O LORD, Neither remember iniquity forever; Behold, look now, all of us are Thy people (Isa. 64:8–9).

Great as their sin may be, the Lord remains the Father of His covenant people. Israel as clay is lowly, but God the potter, who has sovereign rights over the clay and who formed the clay into His people, remains a God of mercy. Therefore the people pray to God their Father entreating Him to be gracious and not to continue His anger toward them unabated, visiting their sins with the punishment they deserve. With the boldness of faith, the suppliant beseeches God to

---

26. Norval Geldenhuys, *The New International Commentary on the New Testament: Commentary on the Gospel of Luke* (Grand Rapids, MI: William B. Eerdmans Publishing Co., [1951] 1966), 325.

"behold, look now," *i.e.*, to give careful consideration to the fact that those who pray are His covenant people, chosen and purchased and set apart by Him. For these reason they urge Him not to forget them, but to be faithful to His covenant promises to them.

So then, we see that God's people, conscious that the LORD is their Father, pray *with reverence* to their Sovereign and with the disposition of children, confident in His love for them, beseeching Him to bless them. Other *childlike dispositions*, which should be manifested, not only when we pray, but in the whole conduct of our lives, include: humble reverence (Mal. 1:6; Heb. 12:9), patience under fatherly rebukes (Heb.12:6), grief when our Father is displeased with us, contentment with our Father's provisions (Phil. 4:11), fervent zeal for our Father's honor and the inability to bear the slightest reproach against Him, filial love, submission to our Father's will, and love for all those who are children of our Father (1 John 5:1; 3:14).

The thought that God is in Heaven should lead us to have high and *heavenly affections* and adoring thoughts of His majesty and greatness, whom all the glorious angels worship with the utmost reverence, being completely satisfied with the boundless treasure of His abundant generosity. Such truths about God should banish from our minds any low and limited views of God. As the psalmist sang: "To Thee I lift up my eyes, O Thou who are enthroned in the heavens!" (Ps. 123:1). Or as Jeremiah confessed: "We lift up our heart and hands toward God in heaven" (Lam. 3:41).

Because God is in heaven, we should pray the Lord's Prayer with *due apprehensions* (true conceptions with full appreciation) *of His sovereign power, majesty and gracious condescension.*

> Look down from heaven,
> and see from Thy holy and glorious habitation;
> Where are Thy zeal and Thy mighty deeds?
> The stirrings of Thy heart and
> Thy compassion are restrained toward me.
> For Thou art our Father, though Abraham does not know us,
> And Israel does not recognize us.
> Thou, O LORD, art our Father,
> Our Redeemer from of old is Thy name (Isa. 63:15–16).

Isaiah fully appreciates God's transcendent majesty and His gracious condescension. He understands that the "our Father" and "Redeemer from of old," lives in a "holy and glorious habitation" in Eternity; therefore He confidently and humbly calls upon Him to "look down from Heaven and see." Because of God's compassion for His covenant people, he is compassionate toward them, and Isaiah pleads for a mighty display of that compassion in Israel's behalf.

> Now it came about when I heard these words, I sat down and wept and mourned for days; and I was fasting and praying before the God of heaven. And I said, "I beseech Thee, O LORD GOD of heaven, the great and awesome God, who preserves the covenant and lovingkindness for those who love Him and keep His commandments, let Thine ear now be attentive and Thine eyes open to hear the prayer of Thy servant which I am praying before Thee now, day and night, on behalf of the sons of Israel Thy servants, confessing the sins of the sons of Israel which we have sinned against Thee; I and my father's house have sinned (Neh. 1:4–6).

As Nehemiah prays we see in him an overwhelming appreciation of the greatness, glory and holiness of "the LORD God of heaven, the great and awesome God," and of the faithfulness, mercy and grace of that God, so that in "lovingkindness" he condescends to His people to hear ("ear") and see ("eyes") them and bless them. It was Nehemiah's true conception of and loving appreciation for God's *sovereign power, majesty and gracious condescension,* not Nehemiah's fear of punishment, that moved Nehemiah to confess his sins before God and plead for forgiveness, because Israel's sins had insulted those glorious perfections.

Third, the preface of the Lord's Prayer should encourage us *to pray with and for others,* as was practiced in the apostolic church: "So Peter was kept in the prison, but prayer for him was being made fervently by the church to God" (Acts 12:5).

> We have thus a sympathy with all those who are exposed to the same wants and miseries as ourselves; we take much delight in considering them as subjects of the same common

> Lord, joining in the same profession with ourselves; and we desire and hope concerning them, that they and we shall be glorified together.... It is hence our duty to pray with as well as for others.[27]

The First Petition of the Lord's Prayer

Q. 190: What do we pray for in the first petition?

A.: In the first petition, (which is, *Hallowed be thy name*), acknowledging the utter inability and indisposition that is in ourselves and all men to honour God aright, we pray, that God would by his grace enable and incline us and others to know, to acknowledge, and highly to esteem him, his titles, attributes, ordinances, word, works, and whatsoever he is pleased to make himself known by; and to glorify him in thought, word, and deed: that he would prevent and remove atheism, ignorance, idolatry, profaneness, and whatsoever is dishonourable to him; and, by his over-ruling providence, direct and dispose all things to his own glory.

The Meaning of the Words in this Petition

The word, "hallowed," means to treat, recognize, reverence and glorify as holy. It does not imply that God's holiness should be or could be increased or that His name should be made more holy. God's character, name and revelation are what they are irrespective of us. To "hallow" or to "sanctify" means to set apart from everything common or unholy. It is to esteem, honor, reverence and adore as of supreme and infinite worth. It is the opposite of "to profane."

27. Ridgeley, *Commentary on the Larger Catechism*, 2:607.

The designation, "name," is a profound word rich in meaning. Israel commonly referred to Jehovah as "The Name," because of the importance they placed on names and naming. A person's name revealed something about that person's character. God's name is the revelation of God's character and will. It includes everything and every way God has revealed Himself to His creatures. God's name is everything that is true about Him and everything that He has revealed about Himself. The name of God in the Bible is God Himself as He has revealed Himself. "O LORD, our Lord, how majestic is Thy name in all the earth, who hast displayed Thy splendor above the heavens" (Ps. 8:1). "As is Thy name, O God, so is Thy praise to the ends of the earth" (Ps. 48:10). "This Self-revelation of God to a creature which He Himself has created with such a nature that he can know Him is God's name. This name of God, according to Scripture, is in all the works of His hands: in creation and providence, as well as in the wonders of salvation in Christ Jesus our Lord."[28] Or as our Catechism says, the name of God which we are to hallow includes *His titles, attributes, ordinances, word, works and whatsoever He is pleased to make Himself known by.* As Martin Lloyd-Jones as written: "It means God in all His attributes, God in all He is in and of Himself, and God in all that He has done and all that He is doing."[29]

"Hallowed," along with the other verbs in the first three petitions, is a third person aorist imperative verb in Greek, giving it, and the other two,

> a mandatory sound; what they say *must* be done. God could not consent to the opposite, nor could God's children. The aorist tense helps to emphasize this: God will certainly do what he is in this striking way asked to do. For back of these imperatives is God himself. The name, the kingdom, and the will are his. His name is not a mere sound, concept, thought revealed to us; it is God himself revealed to us.[30]

28. Hoeksema, *The Triple Knowledge*, 3:503.
29. Lloyd-Jones, *Studies in the Sermon on the Mount*, 2:59.
30. Lenski, *The Interpretation of St. Matthew's Gospel*, 265–66.

"Hallowed be Thy Name" is also in the passive mood. This is a request that God would make His Self-revelation in Christ and the Bible supreme in the hearts of men. This petition is also left entirely general with the verb in the third person. The point is that we are asking God to hallow His own name, to glorify His own name through us and through all things in creation. We are asking Him to

> so govern all things, the affairs of the whole world—social, economic, political, national, and international,—the affairs of the church in the world, and all things that concern us personally, and our whole life in the world, in such a way that, first of all and above all, His name may receive all glory and praise.[31]

The Point of this First Petition

We are making this request of God—"Hallowed be Thy Name"—not for God's benefit but for our own benefit. We are not asking something for God. "God has no need of our prayers for Himself. Prayer always means, and can never mean anything else than our soul drinks out of the fountain of all good."[32] In this first petition we are expressing our need and desire that God's name be hallowed, because the glory of His name is uppermost in our minds and hearts.

We are praying that God's Self-revelation will be known, loved, appreciated, acknowledged and highly esteemed by us and all people. It is as if we prayed:

> Our Father Who art in Heaven, so reveal Thyself and so let Thy Self-revelation be recognized and acknowledged by us, that Thy name alone may stand out in all the world as a name of infinite wisdom and knowledge and power, of absolute Lordship and sovereignty, of unchangeable righteousness and truth, of matchless beauty, purest love, boundless grace,

31. Hoeksema, *The Triple Knowledge*, 3:507.
32. Hoeksema, *The Triple Knowledge*, 3:501.

> abundant mercy, as the only name that is worthy of all glory and adoration and praise forever.[33]

God gives Himself many names in the Bible. He is *Elohim*, the God of great power. He is *Jehovah*, the eternally Self-existent God. *Jehovah-jireh*, which means "the Lord will provide." He is *Jehovah-ropha*, "The Lord who heals," *Jehovah-shalom*, "the Lord is our peace," *Jehovah-nissi*, "the Lord is our Banner," *Jehovah-tsidkenu*, "the Lord is our righteousness," *Jehovah-ra-ah*, "the Lord is our Shepherd," *Jehovah-shammah*, "the Lord is present." God's name stands for all this. So that Jesus is teaching us to pray in the first petition

> that the whole world may come to know God in this way, that the whole world may come to honour God like that. It is the expression of a burning and deep desire for the honour and glory of God. You cannot read the four Gospels without seeing very clearly that that was the consuming passion of the Lord Jesus Christ Himself. It is found again perfectly in that great High Priestly Prayer in John xvii when He says, "I have glorified Thee on the earth and I have manifested Thy name unto the men which Thou gavest me." He was always concerned about the glory of His Father. He said, "I have not come to seek mine own glory but the glory of Him that sent Me." There is no real understanding of the earthly life of Christ except in these terms.... This petition means just that. We should all have a consuming passion that the whole world might come to know God like that.... That is the meaning of this petition. It means a burning desire that the whole world may bow before God in adoration, in reverence, in praise, in worship, in honour, and in thanksgiving. Is that our supreme desire? Is that the thing that is always uppermost in our minds whenever we pray to God?[34]

John Calvin made the point that

33. Hoeksema, *The Triple Knowledge,* 3:505.
34. Lloyd-Jones, *Studies in the Sermon on the Mount,* 2:60–61.

> we should wish God to have the honor he deserves; men should never speak or think of him without the highest reverence...here we are bidden to request not only that God vindicate his sacred name of all contempt and dishonor but also that he subdue the whole race of mankind to reverence for it....[35] But the petition is directed also to this end: that all impiety which has besmirched this holy name may perish and be wiped out; that all detractions and mockeries which dim this hallowing or diminish it may be banished; and that in silencing all sacrileges, God may shine forth more and more in His majesty.[36]

Thomas Watson, in *A Body of Divinity* gives us several practical ways to hallow God's name. We hallow God's name by:

- Professing His Name before men
- Having a high esteem and appreciation for Him
- Setting Him in all our thoughts
- Trusting in His Name
- Mentioning His Name only in the highest reverence
- Loving His Name
- Worshipping His Name in spirit and truth
- Hallowing His day, Jer. 17:22
- Giving God the glory in all we do in His service, Ps. 96:8
- Obeying Him
- Praising His Name

---

35. "Sections 41 and 42 [in Calvin's *Institutes of the Christian Religion*, III, xx] illustrate Calvin's conception of the victory and future universality of Christ's Kingdom throughout the human race; a topic frequently introduced in the Commentaries. Cf. Comm. Ps. 2:8; 21:8, 28:57; 45:16; 47:8; 72:8; 110:2; Mat. 6:10; 12:31; John 13:31f" (footnote by Ford Lewis Battles in his edition of Calvin's *Institutes of the Christian Religion*, 2:904).

36. Calvin, *Institutes of the Christian Religion*, 2:904.

- Sympathizing with Him, Grieving when His Name is dishonored
- Giving the same honor and worship to the Father, Son, and Holy Spirit
- Standing up in defense of His revealed truths
- Leading as many people as is possible to Worship and love His Name
- Preferring the honor of God's Name before all that is dear to us
- Living a holy life[37]

To say it concisely: we are praying that God would enable us and all people to "ascribe to the LORD the glory of His name" (Ps. 96:8). It is a debt which all of us are commanded to pay: to give God the honor that is due Him in everything we say and do and are. "All conceivable honour is due to our Creator, Preserver, Benefactor, and Redeemer, and however much of zealous homage we may offer to him, we cannot give him more than his due."[38]

The Relation of This Petition to the Other Petitions

> It is one of the most prominent and striking features of this model-prayer, that it begins with God's own glory, as the great end to be sought, with the necessary means of its promotion, and then, as something secondary or subordinate, asks those things which relate to the petitioner himself. This is not to be regarded as an accidental circumstance, but as a practical lesson with respect to the comparative importance of divine and human interests, and to their relative position

37. Thomas Watson, *A Body of Divinity* (Grand Rapids, MI: Sovereign Grace Publisher, n.d.), 427–30.

38. Charles Spurgeon, *The Treasury of David,* 7 vols. (London: Passmore & Alabaster, 1882–87; reprint Grand Rapids, MI: Baker Book House, 1983), 4:339.

in our prayers, as the expression of our wishes and our governing affections.[39]

The Wise Instruction of our Catechism Q. 190 on Hallowing God's Great Name

The Reason for the First Petition

Jesus calls upon us to pray earnestly this first petition of the prayer He taught His disciples because of *the utter inability and indisposition that is in ourselves and all men to honor God aright.* It is for this reason that King David, painfully conscious of his sin, prays, "O LORD, open my lips, that my mouth may declare Thy praise" (Ps. 51:15). Left in our sin untouched by the saving grace of God, fallen man is hostile toward God, unwilling and unable to do what God commands and what is due His holy name; so that "those who are in the flesh cannot please God" (Rom. 8:6–8). Without the regenerating work of the Holy Spirit within him, fallen man is dead in his sin, loving darkness and hating light (Eph. 2:1–3; John 3:17–21). He has no desire to pray to God, for his heart is full of hatred for the God to whom we are to pray (Rom. 2:30).

The First Petition as a Prayer for Grace and the Spirit

Because we are without strength in and of ourselves to honor God aright, we must continually cry out to God that He would *by His grace enable and incline us and others* to honor Him aright. The Spirit's work in the regenerated heart enables and inclines the believer to honor the name of God (Ezek. 36:27). The prophet Zechariah calls the Holy Spirit "the Spirit of grace and supplication," or more literally, "the Spirit of grace and of pleadings for grace" (12:10). In other words, the Holy Spirit not only applies the saving grace to our hearts, He also works within us, moving us to pray for the application of that grace. He enables and inclines us to honor God

39. Joseph A. Alexander, *The Gospel According to Matthew* (NY: Charles Scribner & Co., [1860] 1867), 172.

aright. Without Christ we can do nothing; but we can do all things through Christ who strengthens us.

In praying the first petition, we are asking God

> for His grace to sanctify our hearts and minds, that we may always glorify the name of our Father in heaven. And to glorify Him implies, first of all, that we extol Him by the word of our mouth, and that we confess His glorious name.... We must praise Him as He revealed Himself.... We must adore His glorious virtues as they shine forth to us in the face of Jesus Christ our Lord, His unfathomable love, His abundant mercy, His sovereign grace. And mark you well, that to hallow His name, His holy name that stands apart from all other names, we must give Him all the glory and praise Him in all His works. We must beware, lest we divide the glory that is due unto His name between Him and ourselves. For He is God![40]

Furthermore, praying this petition implies that we will glorify God in the wholeness and in the details of our life in this world by the power of the Holy Spirit. To praise God's name in our speech and not to honor Him as our Lord in our daily walk, is worse than not glorifying Him at all. Therefore, in praying "hallowed be Thy Name," we are asking for God's Holy Spirit to continue and advance His sanctifying work within us as Christians, that we may walk faithfully in the way of His commandments for Jesus' sake.

The First Petition of the Lord's Prayer as a Prayer for the True Knowledge of God

In praying the first petition, we are praying for ourselves and for the human race that God would give us true and unadulterated knowledge of Himself as He has revealed Himself in the Bible and Jesus Christ. If we are to honor God and hallow His name, we must first *know...him, his titles, attributes, ordinances, word, works, and whatsoever he is pleased to make himself known by.* This true knowledge of God comes to us graciously by the Holy Spirit with and

40. Hoeksema, *The Triple Knowledge,* 3:511.

through the Word of God. We receive, deepen and broaden our knowledge of God through the reading, studying and meditating upon that Word of God, as well as through the preaching and teaching of it, and the instruction of ourselves and our families in it at home, in the school and in church. "The first petition of the Lord's Prayer, therefore, implies that we invoke God's indispensable blessing upon all these for the preservation and dissemination of the true knowledge of God."[41] This means that, when we pray "hallowed be Thy name," we are praying, "Our Father Who art in heaven, give us to know Thee more and more, and preserve us ever in the truth of Thy holy Word."[42]

This petition

> certainly presupposes that we are filled with an earnest desire and longing for the true knowledge of God, and that therefore we employ every means which God gives us to obtain that true knowledge. It means that we certainly are not doctrinally indifferent, but that we are zealous for the truth as revealed in the Holy Scriptures.... Indeed, this prayer requires that we live in close contact with the Word of God, and have a profound delight in the knowledge of His glorious name.[43]

> God be gracious to us and bless us,
> And cause His face to shine upon us—Selah.
> That Thy way may be known on the earth,
> Thy salvation among all nations.
> Let the peoples praise Thee, O God;
> Let all the peoples praise Thee (Ps. 67:1–3).

This psalm is a prayer for God's grace and God's blessing and God's favor upon us with the express purpose that by revealing Himself to us, we along with all the peoples of the earth may know and love Him, His ways and His salvation. We are taught here to

41. Hoeksema, *The Triple Knowledge,* 3:509.
42. Hoeksema, *The Triple Knowledge,* 3:509.
43. Hoeksema, *The Triple Knowledge,* 3:510–11.

pray that all the peoples and nations of the world may know and love the Lord, so that all the peoples on earth will praise and honor Him, and hallow His great name. Take note: they will praise Him when they know Him; and they will know Him, when God blesses them with His sovereign, almighty and prevenient grace.

An important question should be asked at this point in the light of Psalm 67:1–3. If God has instructed us to pray the specific petitions of Psalm 67:1–3, is there any doubt that God will answer the prayers He has taught us to pray? Can there be any doubt that God will make His way known savingly to all the peoples and nations of the world, and that they will praise Him, as we pray for these things to happen?

From Psalm 67, we also learn that when a person is blessed by God to *know* and honor Him as God, he will *acknowledge* His knowledge and love for God in praise and confession. They will declare openly:

> There is no one like Thee among the gods, O Lord;
> Nor are there any works like Thine.
> All nations whom Thou hast made shall come and
> worship before Thee, O Lord;
> And they shall glorify Thy name.
> For Thou art great and do wondrous deeds;
> For Thou alone art God.
> Teach me Thy way, O LORD: I will walk in Thy truth;
> Unite my heart to fear Thy name.
> I will give thanks to Thee, O Lord my God, with all my heart,
> And glorify Thy name forever (Ps. 86:8–12).

Here the psalmist is hallowing God's name by publicly, openly and enthusiastically acknowledging His loving knowledge of God in the singing of His praises and acknowledging His intention and endeavor to honor Him forever. At the same time, it is obvious that He *highly esteems* everything He knows about this God based on His Self-revelation: *his titles, attributes, ordinances, word, works, and whatsoever he is pleased to make himself known by.* Furthermore, we cannot help but notice the psalmist's confidence that someday God will savingly reveal Himself to all the world's nations so that they will know and honor His holy name, in answer to our prayer that God's name be hallowed, feared and glorified by all the world's nations.

The First Petition of the Lord's Prayer as a Prayer for the Ability to Glorify God in Thought, Word and Deed

As Psalm 86 has taught us, all those who know God are consumed with the desire to *glorify Him in thought, word and deed.* "All nations whom Thou hast made shall come and worship before Thee, O Lord; and they shall glorify Thy name" (86:9). In all that goes on in our minds, in every word we speak, and in everything we do, we are to "do all to the glory of God" (1 Cor. 10:31). Our concern must ever be that the words of our mouth and the meditations of our hearts be acceptable, glorifying, honoring and pleasing in the sight of our Lord and Redeemer.

> The LORD God of Israel declares, "...Those who honor Me, I will honor, and those who despise Me will be lightly esteemed (1 Sam. 2:30).

The Hebrew word for "honor" in this verse is *kabod,* which can also be translated "glorify." *Kabod* means "weighty" or "heavy." It refers to that which gives a person importance, and which makes a person impressive, deserving recognition and praise. The glory of God is that which makes Him impressive, and that which makes Him impressive is: (1) The revelation of Himself and all His perfections in Christ; (2) The revelation of Himself and all His perfections in the Bible; and (3) The display of Himself and all His perfections in creation and by His providence in our daily lives. The glory of the Christian, that which makes him impressive, is not of his own production; rather, it is the wealth, influence and enlightenment bestowed upon him in Jesus Christ (2 Cor. 4:3–7 and 8:9).

The Greek word for glory is *doxa* which comes from a word meaning "to form an opinion or estimate of something or someone." So then, we can say that honoring God or glorifying God involves appreciation, adoration, submission and witness.

First, appreciation. We glorify God when we recognize God's "impressiveness" in His self-revelation and have God-admiring thoughts about Him. Second, adoration. We glorify God when we praise Him and adore Him for His "impressiveness" as revealed in Christ, the Bible and creation. Third, submission. We glorify God by submitting to the supremacy and finality of His revelation in total dependence and obedience. Fourth, witness. We glorify God when we not only hold, but also when we give a good opinion of God by the witness of our lives and verbal witness to others.

> Whether you eat or drink or whatever you do, do it all for the glory of God (1 Cor. 10:31).

The principle of this classic verse is obvious: everything must be done in order to bring God praise and to please Him. And the context of this verse makes its point even more specific. Chapters 8–10 are concerned with eating and drinking—eating meat offered to idols in chapter 8; eating and making a living by preaching in chapter 9; and feasts of idols and the Lord's Supper in chapter 10. When our verse is seen in the light of these chapters its point is clear: we glorify God when we are not ultimately concerned with ourselves and our liberties but when we are concerned ultimately with whatever will manifest and promote the glory of God and extend the kingdom of Christ.

First, we eat and drink to the glory of God when we acknowledge His good gifts to us with thanksgiving (1 Cor. 10:25, 30; 1 Tim. 4:3–5).

Second, we eat and drink to the glory of God when we eat and drink with love, 8:1f; 8:13. We must put the spiritual welfare of others before the enjoyment of our own Christian liberties. Sometimes we will forego what we have the liberty in Christ to do in order to advance the gospel and build up a brother in the faith. We will avoid anything that interferes with our full effectiveness for Christ (8:9–13, 9:19–23, 10:23–29).

Third, we eat and drink to the glory of God when we eat and drink in communion with Him in Christ (10:15–17).

> And this I pray, that your love may abound still more and more in real knowledge and all discernment, so that you may

> approve the things that are excellent, in order to be sincere and blameless until the day of Christ; having been filled with the fruit of righteousness which comes through Jesus Christ, to the glory and praise of God (Phil. 1:9–11).

These verses present us with the ultimate goal of the Christian life and of our participation in the spread of the gospel (1:3, 5, 9, 11). In 1:3–11, Paul writes to the Philippians of his love for them because of their partnership with him in the evangelization of the world (1:4). He then prays for them that they will be successful in this work, 1:9f. He prays that their love, knowledge and wisdom would abound (1:9–10), and that they would be thoroughly righteous (1:11), for one all-encompassing purpose: "to the glory and praise of God" (1:11). Then in the following section (1:12–26), he defines how we are to live to the glory and praise of God by giving examples from his own life and experience.

> (1:12–14) God is glorified in us when we are content with His will, whatever it is, confident that Christ is in total control of our lives and futures, sovereignly bringing things to pass in our lives in order to advance His gospel through us.

> (1:15–18) God is glorified in us when we are rejoicing that Christ's gospel is being proclaimed regardless of who is doing it or who receives the credit for doing it.

> (1:19–26) God is glorified in us when we are being so devoted to Him and to spreading His gospel that we are willing to go to any length to please Him and to advance His kingdom, whether life or death.

The First Petition of the Lord's Prayer as a Prayer for the Conversion of the Whole World

When we pray "hallowed be Thy Name," for we are not praying only for our own personal and individual situation, we are praying for the hallowing of God's name generally and globally and universally, *that he would prevent and remove atheism, ignorance, idolatry, profaneness, and whatsoever is dishonourable to him.* Throughout the history of the church, men of God have recognized this inescapable implication of the first petition of the Lord's Prayer. If we are to pray that God would enable and incline us *and others* to know, acknowledge, highly esteem and glorify God, then we are by implication praying that God *would prevent and remove atheism.*

Remember the point Calvin made in explaining this petition:

> here we are bidden to request not only that God vindicate his sacred name of all contempt and dishonor but also that he subdue the whole race of mankind to reverence for it...the petition is directed also to this end: that all impiety which has besmirched this holy name may perish and be wiped out; that all detractions and mockeries which dim this hallowing or diminish it may be banished; and that in silencing all sacrileges, God may shine forth more and more in his majesty.[44]

Martin Bucer, the great German Reformer of the Sixteenth Century, who influenced Calvin's thought, wrote of the first petition in his commentary of the Lord's Prayer:

> Hallowed be Thy name is just as if one said: "Grant that Thou mayest be honored and glorious on earth, that all the families of the nations may worship Thee, that Thy name may be glorious and blessed among all nations, of which Psalm 8 sings."[45]

Our Catechism teaches us to pray that God *would prevent and remove atheism, ignorance, idolatry, profaneness, and whatsoever is dishonourable to him,* for three reasons: (1) Man cannot rid himself and his society of these things himself; (2) The Bible teaches us to pray for the removal of these things, because, if God's name is to be hallowed generally, all of these things must be removed; and (3) God in the Bible promises us that He will remove all these evils from us by the power of His Spirit through His Word, prayer and

44. Calvin, *Institutes of the Christian Religion*, 2:904.
45. Quoted in *Institutes of the Christian Religion: 1536 Edition*, 351.

the faithfulness of His church. (See my commentary on the Second Petition of the Lord's Prayer for more explanation.)

Our Westminster fathers looked forward to a day in the future when the church of Christ would experience extraordinary renewal and reformation by the power of the Spirit of God, surpassing the Reformation of the 16th and 17th Centuries. Under the blessing of God on the preached Word and in answer to the fervent prayers of His Church faithful to the Great Commission of Matthew 28:18–20 and the Dominion Mandate of Genesis 1:28, the Church of Christ will be equipped with qualified and faithful ministers, elders and deacons. All her congregations will return to the use of only those ordinances commanded by Christ in the Bible, which would include a removal of all ordinances, rituals and practices in the church invented by the brain of man, purged from moral and theological corruption; favored and defended by the civil magistrate, that the ordinances of the preached Word and the administration of the sacraments may be purely dispensed, which would include the removal of all non-Christian and heretical religious organizations; in order that the church may be free and effective in evangelizing the lost, in edifying and perfecting those already converted, that human societies would be leavened by the gospel, *that Christ would rule in our hearts here, and hasten the time of His second coming.*

This global reformation of the Church will lead to the Christian reconstruction of human societies (Isaiah 2 and 11) as the Spirit-empowered gospel leavens those societies, which will result in the gradual removal, from both church and culture, *of atheism, ignorance, idolatry, profaneness, and whatsoever is dishonourable to him,* as the bright light of Christ's kingdom scatters more and more of the darkness (Mark 4).

Where are we taught to expect and to pray for these things to happen as the Word of God keeps on spreading and conquering in the world?

The Removal of Atheism

> God be gracious to us and bless us,
> And cause His face to shine upon us... Selah.

> That Thy way may be known on the earth,
> Thy salvation among all nations.
> Let the peoples praise Thee, O God;
> Let all the peoples praise Thee.
> Let the nations be glad and sing for joy;
> For Thou wilt judge the peoples with uprightness,
> And guide the nations of the earth. Selah (Ps. 67:1–4).

In Psalm 67, as we have seen, we are taught to pray that God's way of salvation would be known and loved in all the nations and peoples of the earth, that all the nations and peoples would praise God, that all the nations of the globe would sing for joy, that God would intervene in history and judge the peoples with uprightness, punishing evil and protecting good men, and that He would guide the nations of the earth in His ways.

Again, God would not teach us to pray for something to happen that He does not intend to bring about through our prayers. Therefore, not only can we expect these things in Psalm 67 to come true as we pray Psalm 67, but in order for them to come, other things must happen as well. If the nations and peoples of the earth are to know and love the way of the Savior and to praise Him in worship, they must repent of their atheism, self-worship, guilty ignorance, suppression of the truth, idolatry, profaneness and whatever else is dishonoring to the Lord to whose government they will gladly submit. Therefore when we pray Psalm 67, we are praying for these very things to happen.

> For thus says the LORD, who created the heavens...
> I am the LORD, and there is none else....
> And there is no other God besides Me,
> A righteous God and a Savior;
> There is none except Me.
> Turn to Me, and be saved, all the ends of the earth;
> For I am God, and there is no other.
> I have sworn by Myself,
> The word has gone forth from My mouth in righteousness
> And will not turn back,

> That to Me every knee will bow,
> Every tongue will swear allegiance.
> They will say of Me,
> "Only in the LORD are righteousness and strength."
> Men will come to Him,
> And all who were angry at Him shall be put to shame
> (Isa. 45:18, 21–24).

Here is a powerful reason for praying for the removal of practical atheism from the church and theoretical atheism from human society: God promises that a day will come when all the ends of the earth will bow in submission and worship before Him.

It must be kept in mind that atheists are really anti-theists, who are "angry at Him", who suppress the truth about God which they cannot help but know because of the revelation of God in creation and in the human conscience, and who inexcusably deceive themselves into disbelief although they know better (Rom. 1:18–23). Atheism, therefore, is not rooted in "honest intellectual difficulties and questions" with the idea of God. Rather, it is rooted in rebellion against God, and its cure is repentance:

> The fool has said in his heart, "There is no God."
> They are corrupt, they have committed abominable deeds;
> There is no one who does good.
> The LORD has looked down from heaven
> upon the sons of men,
> To see if there are any who understand, who seek after God.
> They have all turned aside;
> together they have become corrupt;
> There is no one who does good, not even one (Ps. 14:1–3).

In other words, people try to make themselves atheists in order to escape the God who really is there, and Who they know is there, but Whom they hate in their evil hearts. No good reason exists for not believing in God.

The Removal of Ignorance

> And My holy name I shall make known in the midst of My people Israel; and I shall not let My holy name be profaned anymore. And the nations will know that I am the Lord, the Holy One in Israel. Behold, it is coming and it shall be done, declares the Lord God. That is the day of which I have spoken (Ezek. 39:7–8).

Any ignorance fallen man has of the living God is guilty, inexcusable ignorance, because man and creation are, not what fallen man thinks they are, but what God says they are:

> For the wrath of God is revealed from heaven against all ungodliness and unrighteousness of men, who suppress the truth in unrighteousness, because that which is known about God is evident within them; for God made it evident to them. For since the creation of the world His invisible attributes, His eternal power and divine nature, have been clearly seen, being understood through what has been made, so that they are without excuse. For even though they knew God, they did not honor Him as God, or give thanks; but they became futile in their speculations, and their foolish heart was darkened. Professing to be wise, they became fools, and exchanged the glory of the incorruptible God for an image in the form of corruptible man and of birds and fourfooted animals and crawling creatures (Rom. 1:18–23).

Therefore, when God condemns Israel by saying, "My people are destroyed for lack of knowledge" (Hos. 4:6a), He is not accusing them of being ignorant of sufficient true information to make the kind of decisions that will enable them to avoid destruction by their enemies. Rather, as the rest of the verse reveals, He is condemning them "because you have rejected knowledge" (Hos. 4:6b). Their lifestyle is one of rebellion against God and His Law because in their hearts they have deliberately, self-consciously, and inexcusably rejected God Himself, refusing to "know," that is, to love, Him. (In Hebrew, "know" is used interchangeably with "love" as in Genesis 4:1.)

After having said all this, we go back and look at Ezekiel 39:7–8, written above. By defeating the enemies of His Church during the reign of the Messiah, Almighty God will make His name truly known and loved in the Church and among the world's nations. Mankind will confess God's name to be literally "a name of holiness." Jeremiah also prophesies that under the New Covenant in Christ, God will not only write His law on the renewed hearts of His people enabling them to serve Him and to enjoy communion with Him, but also He prophesies that "they shall not teach again, each man his neighbor and each man his brother, saying, "Know the LORD," for they shall all know Me, from the least of them to the greatest of them, declares the LORD, for I will forgive their iniquity, and their sin I will remember no more" (Jer. 31:34). In other words, during the reign of Christ, (which began at His resurrection and is consummated at His Second Coming), a process of renewal and enlightenment has begun that will gradually eventuate in the total removal of all guilty ignorance of the living God from the human race globally. Therefore, we can and must pray earnestly for this to happen, knowing that it will gradually happen as we increasingly pray for the removal of ignorance of God from mankind.

The Removal of Idolatry

> Let all those be ashamed who serve graven images
> Who boast themselves of idols;
> Worship Him, all you gods (Ps. 97:7).

In a psalm about the LORD'S sovereignty and omnipotence, the psalmist, inspired by the Holy Spirit, petitions the Lord for two things to take place: (1) That all idolators will be ashamed of their idolatry and repent of it, and (2) That all the gods will "worship Him."

First, with reference to idolatry, William Plumer in his massive commentary on Psalms writes: "In absurdity and criminality it seems hard to conceive anything more offensive to God or destructive to the soul than idolatry, v. 7. Yet men are mad upon their idols."[46] Therefore, because idolatry is such a wicked sin, insulting

46. William S. Plumer, *Psalms: A Critical And Expository Commentary*

to God, the first two commandments in the Decalogue forbid it in any form. Both testaments make unmistakably clear that no impenitent idolator will inherit the kingdom of God (1 Cor. 6:9). In fact, public idolatry is not only a sin, it is also a capital crime, which if allowed or condoned will bring about the collapse of that society under the judgment of God (Deut. 13). Therefore, not only are idolators called upon to repent or perish; but also those who worship the one, true and living God in spirit and truth are called upon to pray fervently that all idolators will be convicted of the heinousness and odiousness of their sin and turn from it to serve the living God.

As we pray for the conversion of idolators, we can expect to see their actual conversion, because, once again, God would not teach us to pray for something that He has no intention to bring about through our prayers for that very thing. Through the prayers of the church and the evangelism of Paul, the apostle reports of many who had "turned to God from idols to serve a living and true God" (1 Thess. 1:9).

Second, we are to pray that all the gods men worship will "worship Him." To whom does "Him" refer? Hebrews 1:6 applies this verse to Jesus Christ: "And when He again brings the firstborn into the world, He says, 'And let all the angels of God worship Him.'" The writer of the book of Hebrews is quoting from the Septuagint, the Greek translation of the Hebrew Old Testament, and the difference between the Hebrew text of Psalm 27:7 and the Septuagint's translation is obvious. The first says that the gods will worship Him, *i.e.*, Christ; and the second says that the angels of God will worship Him, *i.e.*, Christ. The Septuagint interprets the Hebrew word for "gods" in verse 7, which is *elohim*, as angels. The book of Hebrews emphasizes the fact that Christ is superior to angels, as is obvious from the fact that they have been commanded to worship Him. If that is how we are to take Psalm 27:7, then the point of the petition commanded here is that we pray for the glorious exaltation and consummation of Christ's reign, when He shall come with all His holy angels, serving His purposes and singing His praise. And just

---

With Doctrinal & Practical Remarks (Edinburgh: The Banner of Truth Trust, 1975), 866.

as all the angels in heaven worship Christ, so ought we to worship Him and to pray earnestly that God would enable and incline our hearts to give Him the total worship of our hearts.

Charles Spurgeon interprets the phrase, "worship Him, all ye gods," as metaphorical. It is as if the psalmist is commanding all false gods:

> Bow down yourselves, ye fancied gods. Let Jove do homage to Jehovah, let Thor lay down his hammer at the foot of the cross, and Juggernaut remove his blood-stained car out of the road of Immanuel. If the false gods are thus bidden to worship the coming Lord, how much more shall they adore him who are godlike creatures in heaven, even the angelic spirits?... All powers are bound to recognise the chief power; since they derive their only rightful authority from the Lord, they should be careful to acknowledge his superiority at all times by the most reverent devotion.[47]

The Removal of Profaneness

> In that day there will be inscribed on the bells of the horses, "HOLY TO THE LORD." And the cooking pots in the LORD'S house will be like the bowls before the altar. And every cooking pot in Jerusalem and in Judah will be holy to the LORD of hosts; and all who sacrifice will come and take of them and boil in them. And there will no longer be a Canaanite in the house of the LORD of hosts in that day (Zech. 14:20–21).

The future of the church during the reign of Christ, according to Zechariah's prophecy, will be a happy one because it will be a holy one, and this holiness will permeate the entirety of her life and worship, extending to everything she does and to everything connected with her. Even the most trifling and insignificant things in the life of the church will be consecrated to God. And in that future, there will be no Canaanites in the house of the LORD, *i.e.*, no PRO-

47. Spurgeon, *The Treasury of David,* 4:355.

FANE persons. God promises that that day will come, therefore we are to pray for it to come, because prayer is the divinely appointed means by which God accomplishes His divinely appointed goals, without being limited to or dependent upon those means. When we so pray for whatever is in accordance with His revealed will, He hears and answers our prayers (1 John 5:14). Therefore, as we pray for the removal of the pagans from the house of the Lord, and as we pray that every cooking pot in every family in Christ's Church have inscribed on it "Holiness to the Lord," God will gradually brings these things to pass to the glory of His name.

The Removal of Whatsoever is Dishonourable to God

No utopia will exist on earth before the Second Coming of Jesus Christ and the Consummation of all things at the very end of history. Sin will always exist in human beings on earth, along with death, and all the other effects and consequences of sin, until the Day of the Lord (1 Cor. 15:50–54; 1 Pet. 3:10–12). Tares will always be present among the wheat until the day of harvest, and the tares will become increasingly evil as the wheat becomes increasingly righteous (Matt. 13:24–26).

Then, on the day of harvest at the end of the age, "the Son of Man will send forth His angels, and they will gather out of His kingdom all stumbling blocks, and those who commit lawlessness, and will cast them into the furnace of fire; in that place there shall be weeping and gnashing of teeth. Then the righteous will shine forth as the sun in the kingdom of their Father. He who has ears, let him hear" (Matt. 13:41–43). An antithesis remains between the maturing tares and the maturing wheat in God's wheat field of the world (13:38). The gradual, irresistible and triumphant growth of Christ's kingdom in size and in leavening influence of the whole world, pictured in the parables of the mustard seed and the leaven (Matt. 13:31–33), will someday at the end of history be perfected and consummated "at the end of the age, when the angels shall come forth, and take out the wicked from among the righteous, and will cast them in the furnace of fire; there shall be weeping and gnashing of teeth" (Matt. 13:49).

Now what is the point of these two parables with reference to what happens at the end of the age?

First, the parable of the wheat and tares teaches us that on the last day, *whatsoever is dishonourable to God* will be removed once and for all from the human race and the universe, both of which will be perfected at Christ's Return, as He sends the reprobate tares to hell. Everything that the wicked have placed in the path of the people of God in an evil attempt to cause them to stumble and fall into sin will someday be removed. All the allurements and seductions of the things forbidden by God's Law will be removed. The wicked people themselves will be removed from the race that will live in the home of righteousness, *i.e.*, the perfected universe (2 Pet. 3:13). When the wicked tares are eternally separated from the wheat, the righteous wheat will shine forth as the sun in the kingdom of their Father and Savior, which was prepared for them from the foundation of the world.

Second, in the parable of the dragnet and separation of the trash-fish (Matt. 13:47–52), we also read of a separation between the good and the evil that will take place at the end of the world. On that day the holy angels will make the final separation, the final removal of everything and everybody that is dishonoring to the triune God.

So then, in praying for the removal of all that is displeasing and dishonoring to God from human existence, we are praying: (1) For the sanctifying work of the Holy Spirit within us to continue to remove from our hearts and lives anything that is displeasing to God until death when we are perfected in holiness spiritually and until resurrection when we are perfected body and soul; (2) For the gradual removal of what is pleasing to God from human society by the gradual and progressive growth and increasing leavening influence of the kingdom of Christ through the preaching of the gospel; and (3) For the hastening of the perfection of everything at the return of Christ.

The First Petition of the Lord's Prayer as a Prayer that God Would by His Over-Ruling Providence, Direct and Dispose All Things to His Own Glory

Without this sovereign and almighty work of God His name would never be hallowed by His creatures. By His providence He provides for and governs His creation, wisely and powerfully directing and disposing everything that happens so that in everything He will be glorified. As the Westminster Confession of Faith, V, I testifies: *God, the great Creator of all things, doth uphold, direct, dispose, and govern all creatures, actions and things, from the greatest even to the least, by his most wise and holy providence, according to his infallible foreknowledge, and the free and immutable counsel of his own will, to the praise of the glory of his wisdom, power, justice, goodness, and mercy.* (For an exposition of the doctrine of providence and its Scriptural support see the chapter on Larger Catechism Q. 18.)

"One of the glories of providence is, that God brings good out of evil, and renders some things subservient to his interest, which in themselves have a tendency to overthrow it."[48] We see this in Psalm 76:10, where the psalmist says to God: "For the wrath of man shall praise Thee." Many illustrations of this truth can be found in the Bible and in church history, especially with reference to the persecution of Christians. "All the persecutions which the church has met with from its enemies, with a design to bring about its ruin and destruction, have been overruled for the furtherance of the gospel... the blood of the martyrs has been the seed of the church."[49]

The Implication of Praying the First Petition of the Lord's Prayer

We are praying that God would glorify His name regardless of what happens to our names (John 12:27, 28).

> In this petition we profess that we are not chiefly and first of all concerned about the question of what becomes of us and our earthly existence and life.... If we are led in ways of de-

48. Ridgeley, *Commentary on the Larger Catechism*, 2:615.
49. Ridgeley, *Commentary on the Larger Catechism*, 2:616.

pression, hunger, want, suffering, sorrow, oppression, persecution for Christ's sake, we do not rebel against the ways of the Most High, but we humbly ask Him for grace to say, "Our Father, if I must be led through these deep and difficult ways in order that Thy glorious power and grace be revealed, hallowed be Thy name."[50]

The Second Petition of the Lord's Prayer

Q. 191: What do we pray for in the second petition?

A.: In the second petition, (which is, *Thy kingdom come*), acknowledging ourselves and all mankind to be by nature under the dominion of sin and Satan, we pray, that the kingdom of sin and Satan may be destroyed, the gospel propagated throughout the world, the Jews called, the fulness of the Gentiles brought in; the church furnished with all gospel-officers and ordinances, purged from corruption, countenanced and maintained by the civil magistrate: that the ordinances of Christ may be purely dispensed, and made effectual to the converting of those that are yet in their sins, and the confirming, comforting, and building up of those that are already converted: that Christ would rule in our hearts here, and hasten the time of his second coming, and our reigning with him for ever: and that he would be pleased so to exercise the kingdom of his power in all the world, as may best conduce to these ends.

50. Hoeksema, *The Triple Knowledge,* 3:507–08.

The Optimistic Futureview of the Westminster Standards

The Westminster Standards present us with an optimistic, victory-oriented view of the future before the second coming of Christ. The Shorter Catechism Q. 26 tells us that *Christ executeth the office of a king, in subduing us to himself, in ruling and defending us, and in restraining and conquering all his and our enemies.*[51] The Larger Catechism Q. 45 adds the thought that the triumph of Christ's disciples will be evidenced in history in His *restraining and overcoming all their enemies, and powerfully ordering all things for his own glory, and their good.*[52] In Larger Catechism Q. 54, we are informed that Christ will *gather and defend his church, and subdue their enemies.*[53] And in the Larger Catechism's explanation of the first petition of the Lord's prayer, Q. 190, we are taught to pray that Christ *would prevent and remove atheism, ignorance, idolatry, profaneness, and whatsoever is dishonourable to him; and, by his over-ruling providence, direct and dispose of all things to his own glory.*[54] But the most comprehensive statement on the glorious future that awaits the kingdom of Christ is Larger Catechism Q. 191, quoted above.[55]

---

51. The Biblical support for Q. 26 is: (1) *Subduing:* Acts 15:14–16; (2) *Ruling:* Isaiah 33:22; (3) *Defending:* Isaiah 32:1–2; (4) *Restraining and conquering:* 1 Cor. 15:25, Ps. 110 throughout.

52. The Biblical support for Q. 45 is: (1) *Restraining and overcoming:* 1 Cor. 15:25; Ps. 110 throughout; (2) *Powerfully ordering:* Rom. 14:10–11; Rom. 8:28.

53. The Biblical support for Q. 54 is: Eph. 4:10–12; Ps. 110:1, and throughout.

54. The Biblical support for Q. 190 is: (1) *Prevent and remove atheism:* Ps. 67:1–4; (2) *Prevent and remove...ignorance:* Eph. 1:17–18; (3) *Prevent and remove... idolatry:* Ps. 97:7; (4) *Prevent and remove...profaneness:* Ps. 74:18–23; (5) *Prevent and remove...whatsoever is dishonourable to him:* 2 Kings 19:15–16; (6) *By his over-ruling providence, direct and dispose of all things to his own glory:* 2 Chron. 20:6–12, Ps. 83 throughout, Ps. 140:4, 8.

55. The Biblical support for Q. 191 is: (1) *Acknowledging ourselves and all mankind to be by nature under the dominion of sin and Satan:* Eph. 2:2–3; (2) *We pray, that the kingdom of sin and Satan may be destroyed:* Ps. 67:1,18; Rev. 12:10–11; (3) *The gospel propagated throughout the world:* 2 Thess. 3:1; (4) *The Jews called:* Rom. 10:1; (5) *The fullness of the Gentiles brought in:* John 17:9, 20; Rom. 11:25, 26; Ps. 67 throughout; (6) *The church furnished with all gospel-officers and ordinances:* Matt. 9:38; 2 Thess. 3:1; (7) *Purged from corruption:* Mal. 1:11; Zeph. 3:9; (8) *Countenanced and maintained by the civil magistrate:* 1 Tim. 2:1–2; (9) *That the ordinances of Christ may be purely dispensed, and made effectual to the converting of those that are yet in their sins:* Acts 4:29, 30; Eph. 6:18–20;

In the Westminster Assembly's *Directory for the Publick Worship of God*, in the *Publick Prayer before the Sermon*, the minister is encouraged to pray for several specific things, including *the propagation of the gospel and kingdom of Christ to all nations; for the conversion of the Jews, and the fulness of the Gentiles, the fall of Antichrist, and the hastening of the second coming of our Lord.*

The futureview (eschatology) of the Westminster Standards is one of the most neglected aspects of those Standards. Although they are emphatic and distinct in their understanding of what we are to expect with reference to the triumph of Christ's kingdom in history before His second coming, some scholars (and others) have left the impression that the Standards are ambiguous at best and pessimistic at worst with reference to the future of history before the second coming.

Although Reformed Christianity since the Sixteenth Century has been overwhelmingly optimistic in its futureview, controlling the mind of that period with a belief in the triumph of a Christian civilization over all other civilizations in history, the Twentieth Century has seen an eschatological pessimism replace the eschatological optimism of the Bible, the Reformed Faith, and the Westminster Standards.[56] "Hope was cut out of the heart of Christendom."[57] With that pessimism has come growing defeat and

---

Rom. 15:29–32; 2 Thess. 1:11; 2 Thess. 2:16–17; (10) *That Christ would rule in our hearts here:* Eph. 3:14–20; (11) *And hasten the time of his second coming, and our reigning with Him forever:* Rev. 22:20; (12) *And that he would be pleased so to exercise the kingdom of his power in all the world:* Isa. 64:1–2; Rev. 4:8–11.

56. Important books that explain and defend the optimistic eschatology (postmillennialism) of the Bible, the Reformed Faith, and the Westminster Standards include: (1) Ken Gentry, *He Shall Have Dominion* (Tyler, Texas: Institute for Christian Economics, 1992); (2) Iain Murray, *The Puritan Hope* (Edinburgh, Scotland: The Banner of Truth Trust, 1971); (3) R. J. Rushdoony, *God's Plan for Victory* (Fairfax, Virginia: Thoburn Press, 1980); (4) Greg Bahnsen and Ken Gentry, *House Divided* (Tyler, Texas: Institute for Christian Economics, 1989); (5) Roderick Campbell, *Israel and the New Covenant* (Philadelphia, PA: Presbyterian and Reformed Publishing Company, 1954); (6) Gary North, *Millennialism and Social Theory* (Tyler, Texas: Institute for Christian Economics); (7) Greg Bahnsen, *Victory in Jesus: The Bright Hope of Postmillennialism* (Texarkana, AR: Covenant Media Press, 1999).

57. Greg Bahnsen, *Victory in Jesus: The Bright Hope of Postmillennialism* (Texarkana, AK: Covenant Media Press, 1999), 57.

the general apostasy of the church, and the increasing irrelevancy of ostensibly Reformed and Presbyterian churches. (When an individual or institution believes in defeat, he/it will not be disappointed!)

Our prayer is that in setting forth these *old paths*, the church will return to them, and in returning to them recapture that vitality that once enabled her to be largely successful in building Christian civilizations.

> Pessimism regarding the transforming power of the gospel of Jesus Christ in history is what best *defines* pessimism. There is no pessimism in the history of man that is more pessimistic than this eschatological pessimism regarding the power of the gospel in history. The universal destruction of mankind by nuclear war—a myth, by the way—is downright optimistic compared to pessimism with regard to the transforming power of the gospel in history. This pessimism testifies that the incorrigible human heart is more powerful than God in history, that Satan's defeat of Adam in the garden is more powerful in history that Christ's defeat of Satan at Calvary. It denies Paul's doctrine of triumphant grace in history: "Moreover the law entered, that the offence might abound. But where sin abounded, grace did more abound" (Rom. 5:20). In pessimillennial theologies, grace struggles so that sin might more abound in history.[58]

To say that the Westminster Standards have a optimistic futureview is to say that they are postmillennial in their eschatology. This is the preponderant testimony of historians and theologians from the Seventeenth Century to the present. A sampling of these testimonies follows.

> Our Standards, professing to found their doctrine on the subject upon the teachings of the Scriptures, deliver the postmillennial view of the second advent of Christ.[59]

58. Gary North, *Millennialism and Social Theory* (Tyler, TX: Institute for Christian Economics, 1990), 203.

59. John L. Girardeau, *The Life Work of Girardeau*, ed. by George A. Blackburn (Columbia, SC: The State Co., 1916), 237. Girardeau was a leading Southern

> The most straightforward understanding of the eschatological outlook of the Westminster Assembly's documents, seen in their historical perspective, is postmillennialism.[60]

> The majority of Independents and Presbyterians [among the English Puritans of the Seventeenth Century] entertained a mild [post-]millennialism...That they were the largest group is evident from several sources. First, the Westminster documents reflect these views. The section entitled, *Of Publicke Prayer before the Sermon,* which was included in Westminster's *A Directory for the Publicke Worship of God,* petitioned "for the Propagation of the Gospell and Kingdome of Christ to all Nations, for the conversion of the Jewes, the fulnesse of the Gentiles, the fall of Antichrist, and the hastening of the second coming of our Lord." The *Larger Catechism,* in treating the second petition of the Lord's Prayer, gave virtually identical thoughts (Q. 191). The *Westminster Confession of Faith* identified the pope as "the man of sin," a concept which had a definitely millennial dimension for Westminster divines....In the context of the views current then, Westminster's formulation must be seen as a deliberate choice of mild [relative to the extreme versions such as the Fifth Monarchy men]...postmillennial expectations.[61]

> The great promoters of early modern postmillennialism were the Scottish Calvinists and English Puritans of the Seventeenth Century. It was they who wrote the Westminster Confession of Faith and the Larger Catechism, Answer 191 of which is postmillennial.[62]

Presbyterian scholar of the nineteenth century.

60. James R. Payton, Jr., "The Emergence of Postmillennialism in English Puritanism," *The Journal of Christian Reconstruction,* ed. by Gary North (Vallecito, CA: Chalcedon, Summer 1979: Vol. 6, no. 1), 105.

61. J. A. DeJong, *As The Waters Cover the Sea: Millennial Expectations in the Rise of Anglo-American Mission (1640–1810)* (J.H. Kok N.V. Kampen, 1970), 37, 38 (ftnt. #11).

62. North, *Millennialism and Social Theory,* 240.

> *The postmillennial hope has been the persistent viewpoint of most Reformed scholars from the sixteenth century into the early twentieth century....* The postmillennial hope of the early Reformers [Calvin, Zwingli, Bucer, Knox, THE GENEVA BIBLE] planted a seed which blossomed in the seventeenth century.... It was in the environment of this widespread Puritan [and Covenanter] postmillennialism that the Westminster Assembly met and formulated its doctrinal declarations.... Thus, the Westminster divines looked forward to the overthrow of the Roman Antichrist, the expansion of the true church by the conversion of the Jews and fullness of the Gentiles, and an age of blessing upon the church through the rule of Christ. They believed in the visible prosperity of the gospel and the future accomplishment of the Great Commission.[63]

What is postmillennialism? This label for an optimistic futureview of the triumph of Christ's kingdom in history is, in the opinion of the writer, an inadequate one. Its reference is the millennium, the thousand years mentioned in Revelation 20. "Postmillennialism" makes reference to the point that the second coming of Christ comes after (post) the millennium, as over against "premillennialism" that teaches that the second coming is before (pre) the millennium.

Now the question is: to what does the thousand years refer in Revelation 20? This is part of the problem. The Westminster Standards are silent on this issue. As Robert L. Dabney wrote: "what is the nature, and what the duration, of that millennial glory predicted in the Apocalypse? Here the [Westminster] Assembly will not dogmatize, because these unfulfilled prophecies are obscure to our feeble minds."[64] There is no unanimity of opinion on this subject, even among postmillennialists. Furthermore, the designation, post-

63. Greg Bahnsen, "The *Prima Facie* Acceptability of Postmillennialism," *The Journal of Christian Reconstruction*, ed. by Gary North (Vallecito, CA: Chalcedon, Winter, 1976–77: Vol. 3, no.2), 68–81.

64. Robert L. Dabney, "The Doctrinal Contents of the Confession," *Memorial Volume of the Westminster Assembly 1647–1897* (Richmond, VA: Presbyterian Committee of Publication, 1897), 101.

millennialism, refers only to the relation of the millennium to the second coming, it does not speak to the future of the kingdom of Christ in time before the second coming. In addition, there are various kinds of postmillennialisms: a secularized postmillennialism, historical postmillennialisms of the sixteenth and seventeenth centuries, pietistic, revivalistic postmillennialism, and theonomic postmillennialism.[65] So then, the label is an inadequate one, but we are stuck with it, therefore we must do the best we can, by the grace of God, in communicating what we mean when we use this word.

The Westminster Standards look forward to a time on earth before the second coming of Jesus Christ, when He will restrain and overcome all the enemies of Christianity, powerfully ordering everything for His own glory and the good of His church, when He will, in large part,[66] prevent and remove atheism, ignorance, idolatry, profaneness, and whatsoever is dishonorable to Him; when the gospel will be propagated throughout the world in all nations and believed by vast numbers of peoples and nations, the Jews converted, the non-Jewish nations and peoples converted, the Antichrist (*i.e.*, the papacy) fallen from power, the true church furnished with faithful gospel-officers and ordinances based only on His Word, purged from theological and moral corruption, favored and protected by the civil magistrate; and when the ordinances of Christ, viz., the preaching of the Word, the sacraments, worship and prayer,

---

65. Reformed, Theonomic Postmillennialism links together God's Law in the Bible, God's historical sanctions, *viz.*, the blessings and curses of Deuteronomy 28 and Leviticus 26, and Christ's triumphant kingdom in history as a unit. The conflict that began with Satan's tempting of Eve continues today and will continue to the Day of Judgment. "*There is a gigantic struggle in history between covenant-keepers and covenant-breakers.* We know where the struggle is headed: toward the total defeat of covenant-breakers at the end of time, [preceded by a gradual defeat in history]" (North, *Milleniallism and Social Theory*, 43). The Bible provides us with "Biblical blueprints for the reconstruction of society" (North, *Millennialism and Social Theory*, 260).

66. We say "in large part" because the Westminster fathers were not utopians. They did not believe that perfection would come to human beings until the Second Coming and life in the consummated New Heavens and New Earth. However, they did believe that sometime before the Second Coming, human society would be far more exalted morally and spiritually than it was in their day, or in ours.

are purely dispensed and made effective in converting the lost and edifying the saved.

Ken Gentry, in his masterful classic on eschatology, *He Shall Have Dominion*, has defined the basic elements of a Reformed postmillennialism in a more systematic fashion.

> First, postmillennialism is that system of eschatology which understands the Messianic kingdom to have been founded upon the earth during the earthly ministry and through the redemptive labors of the Lord Jesus Christ.[67]
>
> Second, the fundamental nature of that kingdom is essentially redemptive and spiritual rather than political and corporeal. Although it has implications for the political realm, postmillennialism is not essentially political.[68]
>
> Third, because of the intrinsic power and design of Christ's redemption, His kingdom will exercise a transformational sociocultural influence in history. This will occur as more and more people are converted to Christ, not by a minority revolt and seizure of political power.[69]
>
> Fourth, postmillennialism, thus, expects the gradual, developmental expansion of the kingdom of Christ in time and on earth. This expansion will proceed by means of the full-orbed ministry of the Word, fervent and believing prayer, and the consecrated labors of His Spirit-filled people.[70]
>
> Fifth, postmillennialism confidently anticipates a time in earth history (continuous with the present) in which the very gospel already operative in the world will have won the victory throughout the earth in fulfillment of the Great Commission. "The thing that distinguishes the biblical postmillennialist, then, from amillennialists and premillennialists is his belief that the Scripture teaches *the success of the great*

67. Kenneth Gentry, *He Shall Have Dominion: A Post-Millennial Eschatology* (Tyler, TX: Institute for Christian Economics, 1992), 70.

68. Gentry, *He Shall Have Dominion: A Post-Millennial Eschatology*, 70–71.

69. Gentry, *He Shall Have Dominion: A Post-Millennial Eschatology*, 71.

70. Gentry, *He Shall Have Dominion: A Post-Millennial Eschatology*, 71.

> *commission in this age of the church."* (Bahnsen) During that time the overwhelming majority of men and nations will be Christianized, righteousness will abound, wars will cease, and prosperity and safety will flourish.[71]
>
> "We can look forward to a great 'golden age' of spiritual prosperity continuing for centuries, or even for millenniums, during which time Christianity shall be triumphant over all the earth" [Boettner]. After this extended period of gospel prosperity, earth history will be drawn to a close by the personal, visible, bodily return of Jesus Christ.[72]

Our Westminster fathers did not invent a victory-oriented futureview. They inherited it from fifteen hundred years of church history and refined it by the written Word of God. It is still being refined and developed. Such a futureview can be found, for example, in Origen (A.D. 185–254), Eusebius (A.D. 260–340), Athanasius (A.D. 296–372), the great Augustine (A.D. 354–430),[73] Joachim of Florus (A.D., 1145–1202), Peter John Olivi (A.D., 1297), Jan Miliciz (A.D., 1367), John Calvin (1509–1564),[74] Thomas Brightman (1562–1607), William Perkins (1558–1602), John Owen (1616–1683), most of the English Puritans and Scottish Presbyterians of the sixteenth and seventeenth centuries, the New England Puritans and Presbyterians of the seventeenth through the nineteenth centuries, (such as Matthew Henry and Jonathan Edwards), the Northern and

---

71. Gentry, *He Shall Have Dominion: A Post-Millennial Eschatology*, 71.

72. Gentry, *He Shall Have Dominion: A Post-Millennial Eschatology*, 72.

73. See Augustine's *Sermon* 259:2, Book 18:31, 32, 35 in his *The City of God* and his commentary on Psalm 2.

74. See Calvin's commentaries on Isaiah 2:2–4, 65:17, Matthew 24:26, 28:18–20, Romans 11:24. For studies on Calvin's victory-oriented futureview see: (1) J. A. DeJong, *As the Waters Cover The Sea: Millennial Expectations in the Rise of Anglo-American Missions 1640–1810*, 8; (2) J. T. McNeil, ed., Calvin's *Institutes of the Christian Religion*, translated by Ford Lewis Battles, (Philadelphia: Westminster Press, 1960), 2:904; (3) Iain Murray, *The Puritan Hope* (Edinburgh: The Banner of Truth Trust, 1971), 89; (4) Greg Bahnsen, "The *Prima Facie* Acceptability of Postmillennialism," pp. 69–76, *Journal of Christian Reconstruction* 6:1 (Summer 1979); (5) James R. Payton, Jr., "The Emergence of Postmillennialism in English Puritanism," pp. 87–106, *Journal of Christian Reconstruction* 6:1 (Summer 1979); (6) Aletha Joy Gilsdorf, *The Puritan Apocalyptic: New England Eschatology in the Seventeenth Century* (NY: Garland, 1989).

Southern Presbyterians (and others) of the eighteenth, nineteenth and twentieth centuries, (such as A. A. Alexander, J. A. Alexander, Charles Hodge, A. A. Hodge, Benjamin M. Palmer, Robert L. Dabney, James H. Thornwell, W. G. T. Shedd, Augustus H. Strong, David Brown, Albert Barnes, O. T. Allis,[75] J. Gresham Machen,[76] Francis Nigel Lee, Iain Murray, John Murray,[77] Greg Bahnsen, J. Marcellus Kik, Kenneth Gentry, R. J. Rushdoony, Gary North, Lorraine Boettner, Benjamin B. Warfield, Gary DeMar, along with many others).

The Basis For the Optimistic Futureview of the Larger Catechism Q. 191

The Answer to Question 191 in the Larger Catechism presents us with a two-fold basis for its optimistic futureview: (1) Pessimism about man's abilities and accomplishments in his fallen and unregenerate condition; and (2) Optimism about the mediatorial and triumphant kingdom of Jesus Christ.

The Inability and Enslaved Condition of Fallen Human Beings

In praying, "Thy kingdom come," we must first *acknowledge ourselves and all mankind to be by nature under the dominion of sin and Satan*, and therefore totally incapable of, as well as unwilling to, free ourselves from sin, Satan and death, and therefore incapable of establishing righteous and God-honoring lives and civilizations. If man is to be free from the tyranny of sin and Satan in his personal and community life, it must be by the saving grace of God operative in the kingdom of Christ. A secularized and dechristianized postmillennialism,[78] optimistic about the progress of man, re-

75. See O. T. Allis, "Foreword" in Roderick Campbell's *Israel and the New Covenant* (1954).

76. See Machen quotes in Ned Stonehouse's *J. Gresham Machen: A Biographical Memoir* (1954), pp. 187, 245, 261.

77. See John Murray's commentary on Romans 11 in his *The Epistle to the Romans*, Vol. II, The New International Commentary on the New Testament, (Grand Rapids, Michigan: Wm. B. Eerdmans Publishing Co., 1965).

78. Jean B. Quandt, "Religion and Social Thought: The Secularization of Post-

duces "the supernatural transformation wrought by regeneration into mere humanistic moral effort,"[79] and is impotent as far as creating righteous and godly civilizations is concerned, for Jesus said, "without Me, you can do nothing."

> It was a secularized version of this Puritan vision of progress that was adopted by Enlightenment humanism: progress without God's sovereignty, authority, law, historical sanctions, or final judgment. The past was seen as being pregnant with the future. This humanist vision is not fading. Nisbet is probably correct regarding the cause of the late twentieth century's loss of faith in progress: "There is by now no single influence greater in negative impact upon the idea of progress than our far-flung and relentless jettisoning of the past."... Millions of people today are increasingly ready to abort the future, as well as abort the yet unborn who would otherwise become the future. Western society has become increasingly present-oriented, with fateful consequences for Western culture. Present-orientation is a denial of the very foundations of Western culture: respect for the past and faith in the future.[80]

The Reality of the Mediatorial and Triumphant Kingdom of Jesus Christ

The optimistic futureview of the Westminster Standards is based on the reality of the mediatorial kingship of Jesus Christ (Eph. 1:19f; Phil. 2:9f; 1 Pet. 3:21f; Dan. 7:13f). Because Jesus reigns over the universe from the right hand of God over everyone and everything that happens on earth, He cannot be defeated, His kingdom cannot be overturned, and His enemies cannot escape His defeat of them (Isa. 14:24, 27). No one and no thing can hinder Him from subduing His people to Himself, ruling and defending His church from all who would do her harm, and from restraining,

---

millennialism," *American Quarterly* 25 (Oct. 1973).

79. Gentry, *He Shall Have Dominion: A Post-Millennial Eschatology*, 447.

80. North, *Millennialism and Social Theory*, 33–34.

overcoming and conquering all our enemies, and from His *powerfully ordering all things for His own glory* and our good (Rom. 8:28).

> If the doctrine of God's sovereignty was of any practical consequence in the theology of the seventeenth century, it was when argued to its logical conclusion...the "Puritans could never insist too much on the fact that God was the Sovereign of all He had made, with the right to govern all things according to His will" [E.F. Kevan, *The Grace of Law*, p. 47].... God, the ultimate ruler of heaven and earth, must ultimately rule in His kingdom.... The New Testament portrayed Christ, not only as Redeemer and Priest but also as Lord and King, and although, as Thomas Goodwin quaintly observed, He had had "but little takings of the world yet," the time must come in the divine purpose when the earth again would be subject to her rightful master. "The world was made for him, and he will have it afore he hath done," Goodwin declared. Christ had taught the church to pray, "Thy kingdom come," and the church in seventeenth-century England looked forward to such time when He would assert His prerogative, assume the divine right to rule, and realise the hopes engendered by the Biblical assurance that the Kingdoms of earth would at last "become the kingdoms of our Lord, and of his Christ."[81]

This eternal, international, triumphant kingdom was given to the incarnate Son of God by God the Father when He raised Christ from the dead to reward Him for His humiliation for the salvation of sinners, in addition to the sovereignty He possesses eternally as the Second Person of the Holy Trinity. *Christ's mediatorial kingdom is the manifestation of the sovereign rule of God in power and grace which established a new civilization of righteousness and blessedness in history by the power of the Holy Spirit in, under and through the Lord Jesus Christ in fulfillment of God's covenant promises.* This kingdom is "so indissolubly bound up with the ministry of Christ,

---

81. Bryan W. Ball, *A Great Expectation: Eschatological Thought in English Protestantism to 1660* (Netherlands: E. J. Brill, 1975), 126.

and even identified with his person, that the gospel comes to find expression in distinctly personal terms. The decisive work of salvation is Christ's, the action of the Son of Man who "came to seek and to save the lost" (Lk xix:10)."[82] Christ's presence on earth and His victory over the works of Satan by His death and resurrection (Heb. 2:14) signal that the kingdom has actually come into human history, that it is progressing and advancing through history, and that it will continue to come in all its saving power, until it is consummated in total perfection at the second coming of Christ at the very end of the world.[83]

In his prefatory address to the King of France in his *Institutes of the Christian Religion*, John Calvin wrote:

> But our doctrine must tower unvanquished above all the glory and above all the might of the world, for it is not of us, but of the living God and his Christ whom the Father has appointed King to "rule from sea to sea, and from the rivers even to the ends of the earth." And he is so to rule as to smite the whole earth with its iron and brazen strength, with its gold and silver brilliance, shattering it with the rod of his mouth as an earthen vessel, just as the prophets have prophesied concerning the magnificence of his reign (Daniel 2:34; Isaiah 11:4; Psalm 2:9).

And based on such passages as this in Calvin's writings, Peter Toon could say of him:

> For Calvin the doctrine of Christ the King flowed from His complete victory over Satan and sin by His death, resurrection and ascension. And the Genevan Reformer confidently expected that the Gospel would make progress throughout

82. Ned B. Stonehouse, *The Witness of the Synoptic Gospels to Christ* (Grand Rapids, MI: Baker Book House, [1944] 1979), 152.

83. Some helpful books on the kingdom of Christ include: (1) Greg Bahnsen and Ken Gentry, Jr., *House Divided* (Tyler, Texas: Institute of Christian Economics, 1989); (2) Gerhardus Vos, *Biblical Theology* (Grand Rapids, Michigan: Wm. B. Eerdmans Publishing Co., 1948), 372; (3) Herman Ridderbos, *The Coming of the Kingdom* (Nutley, NJ: Presbyterian and Reformed Publishing Co., 1962).

> the whole world because of this theological basis. The English Puritans...found this doctrine most acceptable and developed it.[84]

Our Westminster fathers could pray with certainty that *the kingdom of sin and Satan may be destroyed* by the ever-advancing kingdom of Christ, because of such passages in the Bible as Psalm 67 and Psalm 110.

Psalm 67
For the choir director; with stringed instruments. A Psalm. A song.

God be gracious to us and bless us,
And cause His face to shine upon us—
Selah.
That Thy way may be known on the earth,
Thy salvation among all nations.
Let the peoples praise Thee, O God;
Let all the peoples praise Thee.
Let the nations be glad and sing for joy;
For Thou wilt judge the peoples with uprightness,
And guide the nations of the earth.
Selah.
Let the peoples praise Thee, O God;
Let all the peoples praise Thee.
The earth has yielded its produce;
God, our God, blesses us.
God blesses us,
That all the ends of the earth may fear Him.

Seventeenth century Scottish Presbyterian, David Dickson, saw in this psalm "a prophetical prayer for a blessing upon the church of the Jews for the good of the Gentiles and the enlargement of the kingdom of Christ among them."[85] He understood this psalm as a

84. Peter Toon, "The Latter-Day Glory," *Puritans, The Millennium and the Future of Israel: Puritan Eschatology 1600–1660,* ed. Peter Toon (Cambridge and London: James Clark and Co., 1970), 26.

85. David Dickson, *A Commentary on the Psalms,* 2 vols. (London: 1665; re-

hymn of praise to God by the Jews applauding Him for the conversion of all the Gentile nations in the world and for "promising to themselves, that by that means [*i.e.,* prayer], the increase of God's blessing on them shall follow, and the enlarging of the kingdom of God through all the world."[86]

According to Dickson, the church would be instrumental in the enlarging of Christ's kingdom on the earth by the global propagation of the gospel, "that Thy way may be known on the earth, Thy salvation among all nations." He said:

> The psalmist foreseeth by the revelation of God's Spirit, that the Gentiles shall be converted, and shall rejoice in God and praise him, and therefore will have the church of the Jews to welcome them, and to join with them in acclamation of praise to God, because of Christ's reigning among them and ruling them by his most holy laws.... The Spirit of God gave the church of the Jews to understand that the conversion of the Gentiles, especially the conversion of the fullness of the Gentiles, (which here is prayed for, when he saith, "*let all the peoples praise Thee*"), was to be a means or a mercy antecedent unto, or nearly joined with, the bringing in and blessing of the Jewish church, and possibly in their own land: *then shall the earth yield her increase, and God even our own God shall bless us....* When God shall be gracious to the Jews, after the conversion and bringing in of the Gentiles, and shall renew the covenant with them in Christ, it shall fare the better with true religion, and with the Christian churches among the Gentiles; it shall be to them as a resurrection from the dead, in regard both of the purity of doctrine and worship, and the multiplication of persons converted unto Christ in all places; *God shall bless us,* saith he then; and what more? *And all the ends of the earth shall fear Him.*[87]

---

print Minneapolis, MN: Klock & Klock Christian Publishers, 1980) 1:392.

86. Dickson, *A Commentary on the Psalms,* 1:392.

87. Dickson, *A Commentary on the Psalms,* 1:393–95.

It is obvious that Dickson had in mind the Pauline prophecy of the conversion of the Jews and Gentiles in Romans 11, which speaks of "the fullness of the Gentiles" in connection with the future conversion of the Jews which will mean spiritual "resurrection from the dead" for the world (Rom. 11:12–15). Furthermore, Dickson's confidence that these prophecies would certainly happen, which confidence was shared by most of the Scottish Presbyterians and English Puritans of his day was based on this belief: *God would not teach us to pray for certain things to happen unless He intended to bring those things to pass through our prayers for them.* To use Dickson's words: "It is safe to turn God's offers, promises and forms of blessing his people into prayers; we are sure so to pray according to God's will, as the church doth here."[88] So then, if God has taught us to pray that His way of salvation might be known, accepted and loved among all the nations of the earth, that all the peoples of the earth praise Him, that the earth yield her increase as God's blessing on His people, and that all the ends of the earth fear Him, then there can be no doubt that these things will come true.

> The LORD says to my Lord: "Sit at My right hand,
> Until I make Thine enemies a footstool for Thy feet."
> The LORD will stretch forth Thy strong scepter from Zion,
> Saying, "Rule in the midst of Thine enemies."
> Thy people will volunteer freely in the day of Thy power;
> In holy array, from the womb of the dawn,
> Thy youth are to Thee as the dew.
> The LORD has sworn and will not change His mind,
> "Thou are a priest forever
> According to the order of Melchizedek."
> The Lord is at Thy right hand;
> He will shatter kings in the day of His wrath.
> He will judge among the nations,
> He will fill them with corpses,
> He will shatter the chief men over a broad country.
> He will drink from the brook by the wayside;

88. Dickson, *A Commentary on the Psalms*, 1:392.

> Therefore He will lift up His head (Psalm 110).

Repeatedly the New Testament applies the enthronement and triumph of the Lord in Psalm to Jesus Christ and His present kingdom (Acts 2:29–36; Eph. 1:20–22; 1 Cor. 15:27; Heb. 10:12–14).[89] These texts refer Psalm 110 to Christ's present reign at God's right hand as a result of His death, resurrection and ascension, not to some future millennium in connection with His Second Coming.

Based on the New Testament interpretation of an Old Testament text, such as Psalm 110, Andrew Sandlin concludes:

> God predicts that he will put all enemies under Christ's feet as the result of Christ's crucifixion, resurrection, ascension, and present session at the Father's right hand. He will not postpone placing all of his enemies under Christ's feet until the second Advent. 1 Corinthians 15:23, 24 is clear: when Christ returns to earth, then comes *the end.* The kingdom will have been delivered up to the Father at the end of time, that is, the time of Christ's coming. The OT promises of Messiah's reign are fulfilled in the present interadvental age. Therefore, the kingdom of God and of Christ is a *present* reality in the earth. God is *presently* subordinating his enemies to his Son's kingdom reign. In *this*, the interadvental age, he is relentlessly advancing his kingdom.[90]

Once again David Dickson saw Psalm 110, as he saw Psalm 67, as a prophecy of the triumph of Christ's kingdom over all its enemies and its conquest of the peoples and nations of the earth before the Second Coming of Christ, but consummated at that coming. He wrote that Christ's kingdom which was "begun to be manifested among the Jews, yet was to be extended to the Gentiles with great success."[91] He saw verse two as informing us of "the means and

---

89. For documentation, see Greg Bahnsen and Ken Gentry, Jr., *House Divided: The Break-Up of Dispensational Theology*, 213–217; and William Symington, *Messiah the Prince of the Mediatorial Dominion of Jesus Christ*, especially Chapter Four.

90. Andrew Sandlin, *A Postmillennial Primer* (Vallecito, CA: Chalcedon Foundation, 1997), 36–37.

91. Dickson, *A Commentary on the Psalms*, 2:295.

manner of his conquest and governing, to wit, by the preaching of the gospel."[92] "The LORD will stretch forth Thy strong scepter from Zion, saying, 'Rule in the midst of Thine enemies.'" Dickson saw a vitally important point being made here:

> Christ wanteth [lacks] not a rod and sceptre whereby to govern, but he hath the Word of God preached for the ensign of his princely power or pre-eminence, which is the arm and power of God unto salvation to every one that believeth, and which is able to throw down every stronghold exalted against the knowledge of him: *this is the rod of Thy strength.* ... How many enemies soever shall oppose the kingdom of Christ, and how powerful soever they shall be, yet Christ shall bear rule, enjoy his kingdom, maintain his subjects, and go on in his conquests.[93]

> Jesus the King of kings is in heaven. He must stay at God's right hand until the end of history [1 Cor. 15:24f]. *His presence at God's right hand in heaven is the sign of His sovereignty over history.* He will not return physically to earth until His kingdom is fully developed in history, thereby ending history.[94]

In Psalm 110:3, we are told of the success of Christ in advancing His kingdom through His preached word in His church: "Thy people will volunteer freely in the day of Thy power; in holy array, from the womb of the dawn, Thy youth are to Thee as the dew." Dickson explains:

> the prophet showeth what success Christ shall have; for he shall have abundance of converts, who shall come to his church, offering themselves, as the free-will offerings were brought to the beautiful holy temple, and that in such multitudes and confluence, as his young converts shall be innumerable, like the dew upon the grass, which dew issueth

92. Dickson, *A Commentary on the Psalms*, 2:296.
93. Dickson, *A Commentary on the Psalms*, 2:296–97.
94. North, *Millennialism and Social Theory*, 280.

> forth as it were from the morning's womb as its daily birth.... Whatsoever course our Lord shall take, for inviting and compelling guests to come to His feast and to the society of his visible church, yet only his elect, his redeemed ones, all of them are made most willing converts by his omnipotent power effectually inclining their hearts, and making them willing: *Thy people shall be willing in the day of Thy power....* Christ's church, by the administration of holy ordinances, by setting forth the Lord's holiness, by teaching and persuading effectually to the duties of holiness, is exceedingly beautiful in the eyes of God and spiritual beholders.[95]

Our Westminster fathers, then, clearly saw in Psalm 67 and 110 the glorious truth that during the present reign of our Lord the kingdom of sin and Satan would be destroyed by the reigning and exalted Christ through the propagation of the gospel empowered by the saving omnipotence of the Holy Spirit throughout the world. John Calvin realized that Psalm 110 taught these emphases. He introduces his comments on this psalm by summarizing its main points with reference to Christ:

> in the *first* place, [the psalmist] affirms, that God conferred upon Christ supreme dominion, combined with invincible power, with which he either conquers all his enemies, or compels them to submit to him. In the *second* place, he adds, that God would extend the boundaries of this kingdom far and wide.[96]

Calvin continues:

> By these words ["until I make Thine enemies Thy footstool"] the prophet affirms that Christ would subdue all the opposition which his enemies in their tumultuous rage might employ for the subversion of his kingdom...however numerous

95. Dickson, *A Commentary on the Psalms,* 2:297.

96. John Calvin, *Commentary on the Book of Psalms,* 5 vols., trans. by Rev. James Anderson (Edinburgh: Calvin Translation Society, 1843; reprint Grand Rapids, MI: Baker Book House, 1979), 4:295.

> those enemies may be who conspire against the Son of God, and attempt the subversion of his kingdom, all will be unavailing, for they shall never prevail against God's immutable purpose, but, on the contrary, they shall, by the greatness of his power, be laid prostrate at Christ's feet.[97]

The Specifics of the Optimistic Futureview of the Larger Catechism

The Answer to Question 191 emphasizes five specifics of the Catechism's futureview regarding Christ's kingdom in time and history before the second coming of Christ: (1) The global propagation of the gospel of the kingdom of Christ, and the embracing of that gospel by a vast multitude of peoples and nations; (2) The prevention and removal from the church society of atheism, ignorance, idolatry, profaneness and whatever is dishonoring to God, in large measure; (3) The conversion of most of the Jews and most of the Gentiles; (4) The fall of the antichrist; and (5) The global reformation of the church.

The Global Propagation of the Gospel of the Kingdom of Christ

The Biblical doctrine of the faithful preaching of the Word of God produces in those who believe it great optimism in the accomplishments and success of the preached Word in history before the second coming of Christ. Isaiah makes the point time and again that it is the faithful preaching of the Word of God that God will bless in the glorious restoration of the church and its transforming effects on the whole world.

In Isaiah 2:2–4, we are told that as God exalts His church in the world, all the world's nations will stream into it crying out to the church to teach them concerning the ways of God so they can walk in His paths, "for the Law will go forth from Zion, and the Word of the LORD from Jerusalem" (vs. 3). And as the Word of God is preached among the nations, Christ will work in the nations in and

97. Calvin, *Commentary on the Book of Psalms*, 4:299.

by that preached Word, causing them to "hammer their swords into plowshares and their spears into pruning hooks. Nation will not lift up sword against nation, and never again will they learn war" (vs. 4).

It is also important to point out the central role of the *law* of God in the conversion of the *nations* prophesied in Isaiah 2:3.

> *There must be institutional conversion to God, not simply personal conversion.* "Isaiah says that it is when the nations of the world come to Christ and to the *Law of God* that we know that they have truly come to Christ... [The latter day glory of the church and world begins] when the nations of the world give up natural law.... It is when the nations of the world turn to the Law of God for their politics, their economics, their science, their everything" [Ray Sutton]. In short, "Isaiah not only describes conversions, he speaks about *Law-abiding conversions.* He not only discusses converted people, he describes converted nations with *converted laws,* converted politics, converted economics, converted education, and so forth. And, each converted sphere is known to be converted by its compliance to the *Law of God.*"[98]

In Isaiah 11:1–9, we learn what the Spirit-baptized, Messianic Son of David will accomplish in the world before the consummation of His redemptive work at the very end of the world. He will render judgment in the world in behalf of His people, oppressed by the world (vs. 4). He will destroy His wicked enemies in the earth with the rod of His mouth and with the breath of His lips (vs. 4), *i.e.,* by the Spirit-empowered Word of Christ preached by Him through His preachers. As He transforms the character of the masses of human beings from depravity to righteousness, human society will be significantly less violent and more peaceful, and by His use of the preached Word, "the earth will be full of the knowledge of the LORD as the waters cover the sea" (vs. 9).

Isaiah 45:22–24 contains the divine promise that God by His Word will cause every knee to bow before Him and every tongue to swear allegiance to Him. The LORD Himself says:

---

98. North, *Millennialism and Social Theory,* 246.

> Turn to Me, and be saved, all the ends of the earth; for I am God, and there is no other. I have sworn by Myself, the Word has gone forth from My mouth in righteousness and will not turn back, that to Me every knee will bow, every tongue will swear allegiance. They will say of Me, "Only in the LORD are righteousness and strength." Men will come to Him, and all who were angry at Him shall be put to shame.

We have no confidence in ourselves to save sinners or Christianize societies. Rather, our confidence is in the power of the Word of God that always accomplishes that purpose for which God caused it to be preached. This is the point of Isaiah 55:10–11, which says:

> For as the rain and the snow come down from heaven, and do not return there without watering the earth, and making it bear and sprout, and furnishing seed to the sower and bread to the eater; so shall My word be which goes forth from My mouth; it shall not return to Me empty, without accomplishing what I desire, and without succeeding in the matter for which I sent it.

But what does the Lord desire for His Word to accomplish when it goes forth? What does He want it to succeed in doing when He sends it forth? Isaiah answers these questions in 55:12–13, which says:

> For you will go out with joy, and be led forth with peace; the mountains and hills will break forth into shouts of joy before you, and all the trees of the field will clap their hands; instead of the thornbush the cypress will come up and instead of the nettle the myrtle will come up; and it will be a memorial to the LORD, for an everlasting sign which will not be cut off.

The Westminster Annotations and Commentary on the Whole Bible, produced by some of the Westminster divines in 1657 said of these verses that they are not exhaustively fulfilled in the restoration of the Jews to Jerusalem from the Babylonian Captivity. Rather, they saw it as describing in vivid imagery

> The flourishing estate of the church of God, in general, hereby to be intimated, as abounding in spiritual graces and comforts; those at some times also accompanied and dignified with remarkable deliverances, prosperous successes, countenance of potentates, peace, plenty and the like temporal blessings.[99]

The Prevention and Removal of Atheism, Ignorance, Idolatry, Profaneness and Whatsoever is Dishonourable to God

The Westminster fathers brought forward several Psalms as the basis of their hope that God would prevent and remove all atheism, ignorance of Him, idolatry, profaneness and whatever is dishonoring to Him in general from the church and world, in large measure, through prayer.

> God be gracious to us and bless us,
> And cause His face to shine upon us. Selah.
> That Thy way may be known on the earth,
> Thy salvation among all nations.
> Let the peoples praise Thee, O God;
> Let all the peoples praise Thee.
> Let the nations be glad and sing for joy;
> For Thou wilt judge the peoples with uprightness,
> And guide the nations of the earth. Selah (Ps. 67:1–4).

In Psalm 67 we are taught to pray that God's way of salvation would be known in all the nations on earth, that all the nations and peoples would praise God, that all the nations of the globe would sing for joy, that God would judge the peoples with uprightness, punishing evil and creating good, and that He would guide the nations of the earth in His ways.

As we have said earlier, God would not teach us to pray for something to happen that He does not intend to bring about through our

99. *The Westminster Annotations and Commentary on the Whole Bible* (facsimile), 6 vols. (Edmonton, Alberta, Canada: Still Waters Revival Books, reprint [1657]), 4: Isaiah lv.

prayers. Therefore, not only can we expect these things in Psalm 67 to come true as we pray Psalm 67, but in order for them to come, others things must happen as well. IF the nations and peoples of the earth are to know and love the way of the Savior and to praise Him in worship, they must repent of their atheism, self-worship, guilty ignorance, suppression of the truth, idolatry, profaneness and whatever else is dishonoring to the Lord to whose government they gladly submit.

In Psalm 97:7, the Lord teaches us to pray: "Let all those be ashamed who serve graven images, who boast themselves of idols." If God teaches us to pray for this to happen, surely a time will come when God will cause this to happen through our prayers. A day will come when "all" idolators will be ashamed of their idolatry and repent, turning from their idols to serve the living God.

(See extended notes on this aspect of the victory of the kingdom in my exposition of the first petition to the Lord's Prayer.)

The Conversion of the Jews and the Fullness of the Gentiles Brought In (Romans 11)

Romans 11:1–32 contains a prophecy that someday in the future the Jewish people *en masse* will receive Jesus Christ as the divine-human Messiah and enter the Christian Church. This conversion of the Jews will be accompanied with, and result in, the Spiritual resurrection and reconciliation of the whole world to Christ—global revival and reformation—the Christianization of the earth. Paul's argument is as follows.

(11:1–10) The Salvation of the Jewish Remnant

> I say then, God has not rejected His people, has He? May it never be! For I too am an Israelite, a descendant of Abraham, of the tribe of Benjamin. God has not rejected His people whom He foreknew. Or do you not know what the Scripture says in the passage about Elijah, how he pleads with God against Israel? "Lord, they have killed Thy prophets, they have torn down Thine altars, and I alone am left, and they are seeking my life." But what is the divine response to him?

> "I have kept for Myself seven thousand men who have not bowed the knee to Baal." In the same way then, there has also come to be at the present time a remnant according to God's gracious choice. But if it is by grace, it is no longer on the basis of works, otherwise grace is no longer grace. What then? That which Israel is seeking for, it has not obtained, but those who were chosen obtained it, and the rest were hardened; just as it is written, "God gave them a spirit of stupor, eyes to see not and ears to hear not, down to this very day." And David says, "Let their table become a snare and a trap, and a stumbling block and a retribution to them. Let their eyes be darkened to see not, and bend their backs forever.

Romans 11:1–10 prophesies the salvation of a Jewish *remnant* throughout history. Although God has hardened the Jewish people because of their rejection of Jesus as the Messiah, that hardening is *not total.* That prophecy has come true and continues to be true. Throughout history a *remnant* of Jews have converted to Christ, of which the apostle Paul is an example, while the *rest* or *remainder* continue to be hardened in their unbelief. This contrast between *remnant* and *rest* is particularly obvious in verses 5–7.

(11:11–15) The Salvation of the Jewish Remainder

> I say then, they did not stumble so as to fall, did they? May it never be! But by their transgression salvation has come to the Gentiles, to make them jealous. Now if their transgression be riches for the world and their failure be riches for the Gentiles, how much more will their fulfillment be! But I am speaking to you who are Gentiles. Inasmuch then as I am an apostle of Gentiles, I magnify my ministry, if somehow I might move to jealousy my fellow-countrymen and save some of them. For if their rejection is the reconciliation of the world, what will their acceptance be but life from the dead?

In verse 11, Paul asks: The rest of my hardened Jewish kinfolk did not apostatize, ("stumble"), from God totally and finally, did they? Most definitely not, he answers. This judicial hardening of Jewish people is *neither total nor final.* Not only will a *remnant* of Jews be saved throughout history, but also sometime in history, the *rest* or *the hardened remainder* of the Jewish people will be saved from their sins through faith in Jesus Christ and brought into the Christian church, as the gospel is preached to them (11:13–14). This mass, or *rest,* of the Jewish people "transgressed" by "stumbling" over Jesus in unbelief (vs. 11). This resulted in their "failure" (vs. 12), *i.e.,* their defeat, overthrow and excision from the "riches" of salvation. "What is in view is the great loss, as by overthrow in battle, sustained by Israel when the kingdom of God was taken from them. They are viewed after the figure of a defeated host and deprived of their heritage."[100]

If "their transgression," *i.e.,* the failure of the Jewish people to receive Jesus as the Messiah promised in the Old Testament, brought such "riches" of salvation in Christ (Eph. 1:7), to the whole "world" to the "Gentiles," *i.e.,* to the non-Jewish peoples; HOW MUCH MORE will be the "riches" of salvation be lavished on the Gentile world, with "their fulfillment" or "the fullness" of the Jewish people? "Their transgression" and "their fulfillment" refer to the "rest" of the hardened Jews. Their "transgression" led to their "failure" (vs. 12). If the unbelief and failure, *i.e.,* the apostasy, of the Jewish people in the first century led to such "riches for the world," how much greater riches will the world receive with "their fulfillment" or "their fullness"?

This phrase refers to the fullness of Israel as a people. The "stumbling" was theirs, the "fall" was theirs, the "transgression" was theirs, the "failure" was theirs, and so the "fulfillment" or "fullness" is to be theirs. "Fullness" in Greek denotes totality and full complement. This future condition of "fullness" stands in contrast with the unbelief and failure that characterized the Jewish people at the time Paul wrote the epistle of Romans. Someday the Jewish people will be characterized by that which is the opposite of their unbelief and failure—by faith in Jesus Christ as their Lord and Savior, thus

100. John Murray, *The New International Commentary on the New Testament: The Epistle to the Romans,* 2 vols. (Grand Rapids, MI: William B. Eerdmans Publishing Co., 1959), 2:78.

bringing their restoration to the "riches" of salvation and of the kingdom of God. And this contrast demands that the faith and restoration of the "rest" of the Jews will be as conspicuous and dramatic as their earlier unbelief and failure.

The point of verse 12 is that this "completeness," this restoration of the Jewish people to faith and salvation

> will involve for the Gentiles [*i.e.*, the rest of the world] a much greater enjoyment of gospel blessing than that occasioned by Israel's unbelief. Thus there awaits the Gentiles...gospel blessing far surpassing anything experienced during the period of Israel's apostasy, and this unprecedented enrichment will be occasioned by the conversion of Israel on a scale commensurate with that of their earlier disobedience.[101]

In verse 15, we are told of God's response to the "stumbling," "transgression" and "failure" of the mass of the Jewish people. His response has been one of "rejection." "Their rejection" has reference to God's casting them away and taking the kingdom from them: "Therefore I say to you, the kingdom of God will be taken away from you, and be given to a nation producing the fruit of it" (Matt. 21:43). Just as the "transgression" refers to the "rest," remainder, mass of Jewish people, so this "rejection" by God, and their "acceptance" by God, must refer to the "rest" as well. The point is: if God's "rejection" of apostate Israel for their unbelief brought "reconciliation" with God to the whole "world", God's future "acceptance" of the "rest" whom he previously rejected and hardened will mean "life from the dead" for the whole "world."

Because of their refusal to believe in Jesus as the Messiah, God rejected the Jewish people. He rejected them for their unbelief. But God had a purpose in their "rejection", just as He has a purpose in their future "acceptance". It was the overruling plan of God that: (1) His rejection of apostate Israel would bring reconciliation to God's favor of a world formerly alienated from Him; and (2) His acceptance of the believing mass of Jewish people in the future will bring "life from the dead" to the world. Someday

---

101. Murray, *The Epistle to the Romans*, 2:79.

the remainder of the Jewish people will be restored to God's favor by God's grace through their faith in Jesus Christ. This will have a marked beneficial effect on the rest of the world described as "life from the dead." "Whatever this result may be it must denote a blessing far surpassing in its proportion anything that was previously obtained in the unfolding of God's counsel."[102]

"Life from the dead" is that which brings "the reconciliation of the world" to climactic realization. It has a note of finality about it. This difficult phrase, "life from the dead," which will be experienced by the world when God accepts the Jewish people back into the fold, is not the ordinary phrase used in the New Testament for physical resurrection from the dead. Paul's standard expression for physical resurrection is "resurrection from the dead," and could have been easily used here, but was not. The closest parallel we have to this phrase is Romans 6:13: "present yourselves to God as those *alive from the dead*." This phrase, "alive from the dead," in Romans 6:13, refers, not to our physical resurrection at the return of Christ, but to our newness of life in Christ now by virtue of our union with Him by grace through faith (Rom. 6:1–12). Apparently, our phrase in Romans 11:15 has the same reference. For the world to receive "life from the dead" is for the world to experience Spirit-produced renewal of life through the expansion and success of the gospel of Christ. The point of the verse then is that the quickening, the bringing of new Spiritual life to the whole world will come with the dramatic conversion to Christ of the remainder of the Jewish people.

> Verse 15 resumes the theme of verse 12 but specifies what the much greater blessing is. In line with the figurative use of the terms "life" and "dead," the expression "life from the dead" could appropriately be used to denote the vivification [*i.e.*, the bringing to new life], that would come to the whole world from the conversion of the mass of Israel and their reception into the favour and kingdom of God.[103]

---

102. Murray, *The Epistle to the Romans*, 2:81–82.
103. Murray, *The Epistle to the Romans*, 2:84.

The great Reformed scholar of the early part of the twentieth century, Benjamin B. Warfield of Princeton Seminary, believed that "life from the dead" should be taken as referring to the physical resurrection at the return of Christ. His point is that with the conversion of "the fullness of the Gentiles" (vs. 25), which leads to the conversion of "the fullness of the Jews" (vs. 12), there is nothing left in the plan of God but the resurrection of the dead at the return of Christ.[104]

(11:16–32) The Basis for the Conversion of the Jews and the World: The Unity and Continuity of the Covenant

In Romans 11:16–32, we are given the basis for the future conversion of the Jewish people, and with that the Christianization of the world. That basis is the unity and continuity of God's covenant of grace. God has entered into a bond of eternal friendship with His chosen people in Christ down through their generations (Gen. 17:7). This bond was chiefly with the "seed," *i.e.*, the genetic descendants of Abraham, in the Old Testament; but, through them, God promised that He would "ingraft" believing Gentiles, while "pruning" apostate, unbelieving Jews. Eventually "all Israel will be saved" (11:26), *i.e.*, the saved remnant of the Jews, the saved rest of the Jews, and the Spiritually awakened non-Jewish people of the world, who are to be counted as the "seed" and "heirs" of Abraham, because they belong to Christ by faith, regardless of ethnic origin (Gal. 3:28–29).

The Time and Method of the Conversion of the Jews

Romans 11 also anticipates and answers two questions: HOW will Israel be saved? And, WHEN will Israel be saved? The answer to these questions is not a surprising answer. "All Israel" will be saved through the preaching of the gospel under the blessing of the Holy Spirit (Rom. 11:13, 14, 26). Both the "remnant" and the "remainder" will be saved by the same means: the preached Word. "For" in verse 15 tells us that the apostasy of Israel is not final, there-

104. See Benjamin B. Warfield, "The Prophecies of St. Paul," *Biblical and Theological Studies* (Philadelphia, PA: Presbyterian and Reformed Publishing Company, 1952 reprint), 463–502.

fore Paul continues to pursue his preaching and evangelizing ministry. Since Paul pursues that ministry to that end, his evangelizing of some Jews, no doubt, contributes to the "fulfillment," the completion and restoration of the Jewish people.

"And thus all Israel will be saved," when "the fullness of the Gentiles comes in" (Rom. 11:25–26). If we compare 11:25 with 11:12, we see that "fullness" or "fulfillment" refers to the mass or remainder of the Jewish people, not to the remnant. "The fullness of the Gentiles," then, refers to the remainder or mass of the Gentiles, *i.e.*, the non-Jewish world *en masse.* "Has come in" is the standard New Testament term for entering the kingdom of God by faith in Jesus Christ (Matt. 5:20, 7:13, 18:3). The point, then, is this: the fullness of the Gentiles mentioned in Romans 11:25 refers to the blessings of salvation for the Gentiles that are similar to those blessings on the Jewish people of completion, restoration and conversion. Massive numbers of Gentiles will enter the kingdom of Christ through faith in Him. This will set off the conversion of the remaining Jewish people in the world, which will in turn bring about "life from the dead for the world."

The unbelief of Israel was divinely ordained to promote the salvation of the Gentiles (Rom. 11:15). The faith of the Gentiles was divinely ordained to promote the salvation of the Jews (11:11). And the faith of the Jews *en masse* was divinely ordained to promote the Spiritual renewal of the rest of the people in the world (11:15). Praise God for His wisdom and sovereign mercy!

> It is very evident...that many nations, who had the gospel preached to them by the apostles, are now wholly destitute of it. And, though it is true a considerable number of the Jews at first believed in Christ; yet the greatest part of that people were cast off, and all remain, at this day, strangers and enemies to him. Hence, we cannot but suppose that those prophecies which respect their conversion, in the latter day, together with the fullness of the Gentiles being brought in, shall be more eminently accomplished than they have hitherto been.[105]

105. Ridgeley, *Commentary on the Larger Catechism*, 2:621.

The Fall of the Antichrist

For most of the English Puritans and Scottish Presbyterians of the seventeenth century, the Roman Catholic papacy[106] was the "antichrist" and "man of sin" prophesied in 2 Thessalonians 2:3–9 and Revelation 13:6–7.[107] The Westminster Confession of Faith boldly declared: *There is no other head of the church but the Lord Jesus Christ: nor can the Pope of Rome in any sense be head thereof; but is that antichrist, that man of sin, and son of perdition, that exalteth himself in the church against Christ, and all that is called God* (XXV, vi).

Whether the antichrist was the Roman papacy or the Muslim Turkish Empire, the Westminster fathers, and the majority of everyone else in their day, believed that the threat and power of the antichrist would come to a complete end in the earth, maybe in their lifetime. They based their viewpoint on their interpretation of prophecies in Daniel and Revelation. Although their hermeneutic of these books may have been flawed, nevertheless their confidence

---

106. For a defense of the view that the papacy is the "antichrist" and "man of sin" prophesied in 2 Thessalonians 2:3–9 and Revelation 13:6–7, see *Antichrist in Scripture* by F. N. Lee, (East Sussex, England: Focus Christian Ministries Trust, 1992). For a more convincing interpretation of 2 Thessalonians see Benjamin B. Warfield's, "The Prophecies of St. Paul," pp. 475–502, in *Biblical and Theological Studies*.

107. "The pre-eminent demonstration of antichristianism, however, was the uncomplicated historical fact that the Papacy had corrupted the once pure teachings of the apostolic church. Romish doctrines were, to quote William Strong, 'a mixture of God's ordinances, and carnal and heathenish superstitions'" (Ball, *A Great Expectation*, 138).

There was some disagreement, however, among the Puritans as to the identity of the antichrist. While some saw him as the papacy, others identified him as the Turkish Empire, following Luther's interpretation. Constantinople fell to the Turks in 1453. "From that time the Turks were a growing threat to the whole of Europe. Within the succeeding fifty or so years, Turkey had extended her supremacy to the Danube. After a brief respite at the beginning of the sixteenth century when she was concerned with affairs nearer home, Suleiman the Magnificent once again directed Turkish eyes to the Christian kingdoms of Europe. In 1520 Belgrade fell to Suleiman's armies. Two years later the Turks had captured Rhodes, and in 1526 the King of Hungary and his troops were decisively beaten at the battle of Mohacs, a defeat which... 'sent a wave of terror over Europe.' A new sense of urgency was given to the Mohammedan menace in 1529 with the Turkish advance on Vienna" (Ball, *A Great Expectation*, 142).

that Roman Catholicism and Islam would come to an end in human history reveals their victory-orientation toward the future of the church, religion and kingdom of Christ. Even the great Robert L. Dabney, Southern Presbyterian of the Nineteenth Century, taught at Union Seminary that "before this Second Advent, the following events must have occurred. The development and secular overthrow of Antichrist (2 Thess. ii:3–9; Dan. vii:24–26; Rev. xvii, xviii) which is the papacy."[108]

One does not have to agree with the "majority opinion hermeneutic" of the Sixteenth and Seventeenth Century Calvinists regarding the prophecies of Daniel and Revelation to believe that in history before the second coming of Christ, the church will see the global triumph of Christianity over all false religions in all nations, viz., Roman Catholicism, Arminianism, Islam and Humanism. Repeatedly the Bible prophesies that, as a result of God's blessing on the preaching of the gospel and the faithfulness of the church to her Lord, Christianity will be exalted globally in human heart and human societies (Isa. 2). This global conversion to Christ of individuals and nations will bring to an end all religions that oppose or contradict Biblical Christianity. Those passages include: Psalm 72:8–11; Psalm 67; Psalm 110; Isaiah 2:2–4; 11; Dan. 2:44–45; 7:14; Matt. 28:19, 20; and Rom. 11:12, 15, 25.

> Thus says the LORD, your Redeemer, and the one who formed you from the womb:
>
> "I, the LORD, am the Maker of all things,
> Stretching out the heavens by Myself,
> And spreading out the earth all alone,
> Causing the omens of boasters to fail,
> Making fools out of diviners,
> Causing wise men to draw back,
> And turning their knowledge into foolishness,
> Confirming the word of His servant,
> And performing the purpose of His messengers,

108. Robert L. Dabney, *Lectures in Systematic Theology* (Grand Rapids, MI: Zondervan Publishing House, [1878] 1975), 838.

> It is I who says of Jerusalem, 'She shall be inhabited!'
> And of the cities of Judah, 'They shall be built.'
> And I will raise up her ruins again.
> It is I who says to the depths of the sea, 'Be dried up!'
> And I will make your rivers dry." (Isa. 44:24–27)

In these verses the LORD identifies Himself as the Redeemer and Creator of Israel, who is the Maker of everything in the universe, and who causes the omens of boasters to fail, making fools out of the diviners, turning the alleged knowledge of the humanists into foolishness. This is the God who will sovereignly and graciously rebuild Jerusalem, using even His enemies to accomplish His purposes. God is at work overturning every false ideology, worldview and religion, exposing their emptiness and He is doing all this by "confirming the word of His servant and performing the purpose of His messengers." This reminds us of what Paul said about the effects of the preaching Word in 1 Corinthians 1:18–21:

> The preaching of the cross is...to us who are being saved... the power of God... [by which God will] destroy the wisdom of the wise.... For since in the wisdom of God the world through its wisdom did not come to know God, God was well-pleased through the foolishness of preaching to save those who believe.

The Reformation of the Church

Our Westminster fathers looked forward to a day in the future when the church of Christ would experience extraordinary renewal and reformation by the power of the Spirit of God, surpassing the Reformation of the 16th and 17th centuries. This would be "the latter day glory of the church." Under the blessing of God on the preached Word and the faithfulness of Christian individuals, families and institutions in carrying out the Dominion Mandate of Genesis 1:28 and the Great Commission of Matthew 28:18–20, the church of Christ will be equipped with qualified and faithful ministers, elders and deacons; return to the use of only those ordinances commanded by Christ in the Bible, which would include a removal of all ordinances, rituals and practices in the church invented by the brain of man; purged from moral and theological corruption; favored and defended by the civil magistrate, that the ordinances of the preached Word and the administration of the sacraments may be purely dispensed, (which will include the removal of all non-Christian and heretical religious organizations); in order that the church may be free and effective in evangelizing the lost and in edifying and perfecting those who are already converted: *that Christ would rule in our hearts here, and hasten the time of His second coming.*

Most English Puritans, Scottish Presbyterians, and New England Puritans expected this glorious future for the true church of Christ. They based their great expectation on such Biblical text as the following.

> "For from the rising of the sun, even to its setting, My name will be great among the nations, and in every place incense is going to be offered in My name, and a grain offering that is pure; for My name will be great among the nations," says the LORD of hosts (Mal. 1:11).

Malachi not only predicts the conversion to Christ of the Gentile nations of the world, he also predicts that the worship services of these converted Gentiles will be regulated by the commands and models of the Word of God "pure" and unmixed. Of course, he is using terminology that Old Testament Israel would understand, that pertained to the ceremonies of the Temple and its sacrificial system, which were shadows that were fulfilled in the reality to whom these symbols pointed, Jesus Christ. Hence, we are not to expect the church to renew the burning of incense in worship, since it was a symbolic shadow of Christ, any more that we would expect the renewal of the sacrificial system, viz. grain offerings. The point Malachi is making is that someday the worship of the church will be regulated by the Word of God alone and not by the inventions of man. Or, to use the wording of Catechism Q. 191, a day is coming when the church will be furnished with faithful church officers and ordinances, purged from corruption, with the ordinances of Christ and no other purely dispensed, *and made effectual to the converting of those that are yet in their sins, and the confirming, comforting, and building up of those that are already converted.*

> In that day there will be inscribed on the bells of the horses, "HOLY TO THE LORD." And the cooking pots in the LORD'S house will be like the bowls before the altar. And every cooking pot in Jerusalem and in Judah will be holy to the LORD of hosts; and all who sacrifice will come and take of them and boil in them. And there will no longer be a Canaanite in the house of the LORD of hosts in that day (Zech. 14:20–21).

The future of the church during the reign of Christ, according to Zechariah's prophecy, will be a happy one because it will be a holy one, and this holiness will permeate the entirety of her life and worship, extending to everything she does and everything connected with her life and mission in this world. Even the seemingly most insignificant things in the life of the church will be consecrated to God. And in that future, there will be no Canaanites, *i.e.*, no profane persons, in the house of the LORD.

> Therefore the LORD God of hosts, the Mighty One of Israel declares, "Ah, I will be relieved of My adversaries, and avenge Myself on My foes. I will also turn My hand against you, and will smelt away your dross as with lye, and will remove all your alloy. Then I will restore your judges as at the first, and your counselors as at the beginning; after that you will be called the city of righteousness, a faithful city" (Isa. 1:24–26).

She who had been a faithful wife, *i.e.*, the Old Testament church of Israel, but who had become a prostitute, will again be what she once was, "and justice which once dwelt in her should return to its old home."[109]

---

109. Joseph A. Alexander, *Commentary on the Prophecies of Isaiah*, 2 vols abridged in one (Grand Rapids, MI: Zondervan Publishing House, 1974), 93.

> Thus says the LORD God... "And kings will be your guardians, and their princesses your nurses. They will bow down to you with their faces to the earth, and lick the dust of your feet; and you will know that I am the LORD; those who hopefully wait for Me will not be put to shame (Isa. 49:22–23).

The purpose of civil government is the enforcing of God's civil laws in the administration of justice for the freedom and protection of the Church of Christ. The civil magistrate has no authority in the church, but it does have God-given authority about, or with reference to the security and welfare of the church. And a day is coming when "even the highest and most powerful rulers of the heathen nations will reverence the Church and devote to her all their wealth and power."[110] As nursing fathers and mothers, civil governments of the nations of the world will express their love for Zion and her sons (Heb. 12:22–24).

> This love rises to such an extent that these royal persons bow down to Zion and touch the ground.... These kings and queens were accustomed to have their own subjects bow down to them; now they in turn do the same thing to Zion, thus expressing their recognition that Zion is royal. It is an action of complete resignation and submission...the prophet's point is simply that the royalty of this earth will do obeisance [homage] to Zion the royal bride of Christ.[111]

Among his other criticisms of the Larger Catechism, William S. Barker writes: "One who agrees with American Presbyterianism's revisions of the Standards with regard to the civil magistrate might take exception to Questions 191's exposition...that we are praying that the church may be 'countenanced [that is, favored] and maintained by the civil magistrate.'"[112] This criticism and American

110. Edward J. Young, *The New International Commentary on the Old Testament: The Book of Isaiah*, 3 vols. (Grand Rapids, MI: William B. Eerdmans Publishing Co., 1972), 3:291.

111. Young, *The Book of Isaiah*, 3:291.

112. *The Westminster Standards: An Original Facsimile by the Assembly of Divines*, foreword by Dr. William S. Barker (Audubon, New Jersey: Old Paths Publications, [1648] 1997), x-xi.

Presbyterianism's revisions of the Standards presuppose that these words in Question 191, as well as other sections of the Confession and Catechisms, reveal an Erastian theory of the relation of church and state, *i.e.*, that that the church is an agency of the state. This charge that the original Westminster Standards are Erastian has been refuted time and again in such places as: (1) James Bannerman, *The Church of Christ*, Vol. I, pp. 171–185; (2) William Cunningham's *Historical Theology*, Vol. II, pp. 557–587; (3) Robert Shaw, *The Reformed Faith*, p. xix; (4) George Gillespie's, *Aaron's Rod Blossoming*; (5) William M. Hetherington's *History of the Westminster Divines*, p. 232–298; (6) Robert S. Paul, *The Assembly of the Lord*; (7) J. R. DeWitt, *Jus Divinum: The Westminster Assembly and the Divine Right of Church Government*; and (8) Samuel Rutherford and others, *The Divine Right of Church Government.*

The Scriptural footnotes supporting the details in Larger Catechism Question Answers 191 regarding the future reformation of the true church include several Spirit-inspired examples/models of praying for these things to take place: Matt. 9:38; 2 Thess. 3:1; 1 Tim. 2:1–2; Acts 4:29–30; Eph. 6:18–20; Rom. 15:29–32; 2 Thess. 1:11, 16, 17; Eph. 3:14–20; Rev. 22:20. The point is this: if God has given to His church explicit petitions that beseech God to give the reformation of the church, then surely God will grant us these petitions as we pray for them. As Ezekiel 36:37–38 teach us:

> Thus says the Lord God, "This also I will let the house of Israel ask Me to do for them: I will increase these men like a flock. Like the flock for sacrifices, like the flock at Jerusalem during her appointed feasts, so will the waste cities be filled with flocks of men. Then they will know that I am the LORD."

The Prayer for Christ to Rule in our Hearts Here

In praying the second petition of the Lord's Prayer we are not only praying for the advance of Christ's kingdom in human societies, we are also praying for ourselves that Christ would here and now in this life establish His reign in our hearts and govern our whole inner life.

> For this reason, I bow my knees before the Father, from whom every family in heaven and on earth derives its name, that He would grant you, according to the riches of His glory, to be strengthened with power through His Spirit in the inner man; so that Christ may dwell in your hearts through faith; and that you, being rooted and grounded in love, may be able to comprehend with all the saints what is the breadth and length and height and depth, and to know the love of Christ which surpasses knowledge, that you may be filled up to all the fullness of God (Eph. 3:14–20).

Our Westminster fathers chose this text to support their statement that we are to pray *that Christ would rule in our hearts here.* Ephesians 3:14–20 is a prayer of Paul for the Ephesian Christians. He prays that God would graciously and powerfully strengthen the heart, mind and whole inner life of believers by the Holy Spirit, so that Christ might make His presence in their lives by His Spirit known to them, for Christ's presence in believers is the abiding source of Spiritual strength and all other manifestations of our new life as Christians thereby enabling us to glorify Him and enjoy Him now and forever.

The immediate purpose of the strengthening and indwelling is so that

> believers will be firmly rooted and founded *in love*, a love for God in Christ, for the brothers and sisters in the Lord, for the neighbors, even for enemies. Moreover, this love, in turn, is necessary in order to comprehend Christ's love for those who love Him. And in the measure in which the believers' vision of that love which proceeds from Christ expands, their love for him and their ability to grasp his love for them will also increase.[113]

The ultimate purpose of this work of God in the heart is that believers might be "filled up to all the fullness of God." Chrysostom

---

113. William Hendriksen, *Exposition of Ephesians* (Grand Rapids, MI: Baker Book House, [1967] 1972), 172.

said of this statement that the fullness of God is that excellence of which God is full. It is parallel to Matthew 5:48 which says, "be perfect even as your Father in heaven is perfect," and to Ephesians 4:13, which speaks of Christians as maturing toward "the measure of the stature which belongs to the fullness of Christ." The believer, whose heart Christ governs, "is to be perfect as man, as God is perfect as God; and the perfection of man consists in his being full of God; God dwelling in him so as absolutely to control all his cognitions, feelings and outward actions."[114] Thus Paul prays that believers "may be strengthened in order to comprehend the infinite love of Christ; and that they might comprehend the love of Christ, in order that they might be filled unto the measure of God's fullness."[115]

How Does the Fulfillment of These Prophecies and the Ruling of Hearts By Christ Hasten the Time of His Second Coming, and Our Reigning with Him Forever?

This wording in the Larger Catechism does not imply that the Catechism, or the Confession for that matter, teaches the imminent, or any-moment, second physical coming of Jesus, for the Westminster Standards do not in fact teach such a doctrine. They, along with the Bible, do teach that the second coming of Christ will be sudden and unexpected, when people will think that life will continue as normal without interruption so that *they may shake off all carnal security, and be always watchful, because they know not at what hour the Lord will come; and may be ever prepared to say, Come, Lord Jesus, come quickly. Amen* (XXXIII, iii).

There are two reasons for not believing in an "any-moment" physical return of Christ to earth. (1) The Bible does not teach such a doctrine. (2) The Bible prophesies the conversion of the Jews and the Christianization of the world before the second coming of Christ.

Some have objected to the viewpoint of the Westminster Standards, saying that the triumph of the kingdom of Christ in history

---

114. Charles Hodge, *A Commentary on the Epistle to the Ephesians* (Grand Rapids, MI: William B. Eerdmans Publishing Co., n.d.), 191.

115. Hodge, *A Commentary on the Epistle to the Ephesians*, 192.

before Christ's second coming will lead to the displacement of the Christian's hope of that second coming. If the Jews are to be converted and the world Christianized before Christ's return, how can believers maintain our Biblical duty of watchfulness for Christ's appearing? How can we "watch" for an event which cannot be any moment or close at hand? As Jesus said,

> Therefore be on the alert [or watchful] for you do not know which day your Lord is coming. But be sure of this, that if the head of the house had known at what time of the night the thief was coming, he would have been on the alert and would not have allowed his house to be broken into. For this reason you be ready too; for the Son of Man is coming at an hour when you do not think He will (Matt. 24:42–44)

Several things can be said in answer to the objections stated in the previous paragraph.

First, Christ Himself taught His disciples to be ready for His coming. He also gave them a mission which could not be completed in their lifetime: to make the world's nations Christ's disciples; to grow a mustard seed into a great tree; to place leaven in the loaf until the whole loaf is leavened. "Here is an extensiveness promised which could not belong to the first century, A.D., yet Christ is conscious of no inconsistency. Though the Second Advent was not to occur in the immediate future the apostles were not relieved of the duty of watchfulness."[116]

Second, "living in expectation of the advent of Christ is *not* the same as believing the advent to be just at hand in point of time. If the latter were required of Christians, then all the generations of the Church except the last would be required to believe a deception."[117]

Third, we can see in the history of church, of evangelism and of world missions, that

116. Iain Murray, *The Puritan Hope: Revival and the Interpretation of Prophecy* (Edinburgh: The Banner of Truth Trust, [1971] 1975), 212.

117. Murray, *The Puritan Hope*, 212.

> the practical influence of the doctrine of the Second Coming is not nullified when Christians do not believe that event to be close to them in time. Simon Peter is a biblical illustration. He was distinctly told before Christ's ascension that a lengthened period of service reaching into old-age would be crowned with a martyr's death (John 21:18), yet that awareness did not hinder in his case an earnest desire for the approaching Advent, "Looking for and hasting unto the coming of the day of God" (2 Pet. 3:12).[118]

Fourth,

> the New Testament reveals why the Second Advent has a direct relevance for Christians of every generation. What is of ultimate significance is not whether Christ will come in our lifetime or later, not whether or not our death must intervene, but the truth that whether he come 'sooner' or 'later' we shall all share alike in the full redemption which that day will bring...a strong desire for Christ's coming does not depend upon our regarding it as imminent in our individual lifetime. The sanctifying power of the Advent upon our present conduct has indeed nothing to do with our being able to fix its time; it has to do rather with a true scriptural appreciation of what that event means.[119]

Fifth, in considering the issue how watchfulness for Christ's second coming is consistent with the passage of long periods of time,

> it needs to be observed that faith has a peculiar power at precisely this point. The exercise of faith can bring very near events which, chronologically considered, may lie a long way from us. Faith annihilates distance and faith finds a *present* reality and substance in things hoped for and yet not seen

118. Murray, *The Puritan Hope*, 213.
119. Murray, *The Puritan Hope*, 214–15.

(Heb. 11:1). To faith it is but "a little while" until "he that shall come will come" (Heb. 10:37).[120]

To a believer, the mere possibility, or even absolute certainty, of ages being yet to elapse before the Lord come again, ought no more to diminish the influence of that event upon his mind, and heart, and conscience, than the fact of ages having elapsed since the Lord came at first lessens the moral weight of his constant vivid sight of Christ and him crucified... I know no chronology and no chronological computation of long eras, in dealing with that Saviour, who eighteen hundred years ago trod with his blessed feet the soil of Judea, and expired on the cross of Calvary. Then why should there be any real difficulty in applying this principle in the prospect, more than in the retrospect? Does faith mounting up in the ascending series of years to the opening up of the fountain, long centuries ago, lose all sense of distance and remoteness, in the bright and vivid apprehension of the cross? And will not the same faith in its keen glance downwards and onwards along the stream of time, seize the one great and only object of its hope, and bring it near, even to the very door, ay, though ages may seem to come in between? ... These are the two events, the death of shame, the coming in glory, which faith, when rightly exercised, grasps; which I, believing, grasp. I grasp them as equally real, equally nigh. Christ dying, near and present, Christ coming, near and present. What though ages have run since that death and ages more are perhaps to run before that coming! It is nothing to me. The world's history, past and future; the Church's history, past and future; all is to me for the present as if it never had been and never were to be.... Wherever I am, whatever I am about, ought I not to be alive to my position between these two manifestations of Christ, and these alone? Behind me Christ dying; before me Christ coming.[121]

120. Murray, *The Puritan Hope*, 216.

121. Robert Candlish, "Christ Coming Quickly," quoted in Murray, *The Puritan Hope*, 216–17.

So then, to be watchful and alert with reference to the Second Coming of Jesus Christ, is to be "awaiting eagerly the revelation of our Lord Jesus Christ, who shall also confirm you to the end, blameless in the day of our Lord Jesus Christ" (1 Cor. 1:7–8). In 1 Corinthians 1:4–6, Paul is praising God for enriching the church in Corinth with Spiritual gifts so that they were "not lacking in any gift." And these gifts of the Spirit were a foretaste and pledge of those blessings and gifts of God which the church of Christ will receive in all their fullness and perfection at the second coming of Christ. Therefore the reception and operation of these Spiritual gifts led the church to anticipate, eagerly wait and long for the Revelation of Christ on the Last Day when the Spirit in all His fullness and perfection would be theirs,

> when they should enter on that inheritance of which those gifts are the foretaste and pledge. If the second coming of Christ is to Christians of the present day less an object of desire than it was to their brethren during the apostolic age, it must be because they think the Lord is 'slack concerning his promise,' and forget that with him a thousand years is as one day.[122]

Having enriched them with Spiritual gifts, God also will "confirm" them so that on the Day of Christ they will stand before Him "blameless." To "confirm" is to make steadfast and persevering in duty. Therefore, as God's people long for the Revelation of Christ, God by His Spirit will render His people steadfast and persevering in their faith in and obedience to revealed truth (2 Cor. 1:21).

> God will confirm his people so that when the day of judgment comes, which is the day of our Lord Jesus, *i.e.*, the day of his second advent, they shall stand before him blameless, not chargeable with apostasy or any other sin.... When we remember on the one hand how great is our guilt, and on the other, how great is our danger from without and from within,

---

122. Charles Hodge, *A Commentary on the First Epistle to the Corinthians* (London: The Banner of Truth Trust, [1958] 1964), 9.

> we feel that nothing but the righteousness of Christ and the power of God can secure our being preserved and presented blameless in the day of the Lord Jesus.[123]

So then, being *watchful* for the second coming includes an *eager longing* for that event to perfect what Christ has begun in us and *constancy* in faithfulness to what God demands of us in His Word.

"He who testifies to these things says, 'Yes, I am coming quickly.' Amen. Come, Lord Jesus" (Rev. 22:20). If what we have been saying is true, what does this next to the last verse of the Bible mean? The tenses of the verbs are important here. Both the indicative statement of Jesus—"I am coming quickly"—and the apostolic prayer—"Come, Lord Jesus"—contain present tense verbs. In Greek, the present tense denotes continuous action. Therefore, verse 20 can be translated: "Yes, I am continuously coming quickly. Amen. Keep on coming continuously, Lord Jesus." The point is that, whereas the apostolic church did not expect an imminent physical return of Christ to earth, they did expect an imminent, providential, non-physical coming of Christ, an intervention of Christ into history to destroy apostate Jerusalem and to deliver and exalt the church (Matt. 24:1–14). The book of Revelation is concerned with Christ's triumph over the enemies of the church in the first century, most particularly with His triumph over apostate Judaism represented in literal Jerusalem. The book closes with the promise of the risen and reigning Christ that He would "quickly" intervene in history in behalf of His church, beginning with the destruction of Jerusalem by Roman armies in 70, A.D. So then, the book ends with the earnest prayer that Jesus do what He promised, to come into history providentially, to intervene in history to destroy His enemies and to deliver-exalt His church, and to keep on intervening into history until all opposition in all areas has been put down (1 Cor. 15:24–28).

Now back to the statement in our Catechism Q. 190 that the conversion of Jews and Gentiles, the reformation of the church and the ruling of our hearts by Christ will *hasten the time of His second coming.* That is obviously alluding to 2 Peter 3:12–14, which speaks of believers as

123. Hodge, *A Commentary on the First Epistle to the Corinthians,* 10.

> looking for and hastening the coming of the day of God, on account of which the heavens will be destroyed by burning, and the elements will melt with intense heat. But according to His promise we are looking for new heavens and a new earth, in which righteousness dwells. Therefore, beloved, since you look for these things, be diligent to be found by Him in peace spotless and blameless.

This New Testament text teaches us that living "in the constant expectation of Christ's glorious appearance is both the duty of all the lovers of Him, and a special means to make them grow in holiness."[124]

Furthermore, we are not only to look forward with eagerness to the Day of the Lord at the end of history, we are to "hasten" that Day by being "diligent to be found by Him in peace spotless and blameless."

> Although the time of Christ's second coming is so fixed in the decree of God as that it cannot be altered, Acts 17:31, yet ought the Lord's people to be no less earnest in hastening their own preparation for it, and by their prayers and other means competent to them in their stations, furthering these great works to be done before, than if that day could be hastened by them: for the word in the original signifies not only our hastening toward that day but also our hastening of it; see Isa. 16:5.[125]

In 2 Peter 3:9, we are told that "the Lord is not slow about His promise [to return at the end of the world], but is patient toward you [recipients of the epistle, *i.e.*, those "chosen according to the foreknowledge of God" (1 Peter 1:1–2)], not willing for any [of you, the recipients of the epistle] to perish, but for all [of you, the recipients of the epistle] to come to repentance." In other words, the Day of the Lord will not come until all of God's chosen people are brought to repentance, because God is not willing that any of His chosen peo-

124. Alexander Nisbet, *An Exposition of 1 & 2 Peter* (Edinburgh: The Banner of Truth Trust [1982] 1995), 287.

125. Nisbet, *An Exposition of 1 & 2 Peter,* 288.

ple should perish. Accordingly, if we want to hasten the Day of the Lord, we should be busy in evangelizing the world. "When we bring the last of God's children to faith and repentance so that his house may be full (Luke 14:23),[126] then the end comes."[127]

The Prayer that Christ Would be Pleased So To Exercise the Kingdom of His Power in All the World, As May Best Conduce to These Ends

We are to pray earnestly for the advancement of Christ's kingdom in history until its perfection at the second coming of Christ,

> when the work of grace shall be brought to its utmost perfection, and all the elect, who shall have lived from the beginning to the end of time, shall be gathered together and brought into Christ's kingdom of glory...and when the highest honours shall be conferred upon them, and they shall reign with him forever and ever.... Hence, we must pray that the elect who are Christ's mystical body, may be gathered and brought in to him; and then we may be sure that he will hasten his coming. Till this is done, we are to wait patiently, as 'the husbandman waiteth for the precious fruit of the earth,' in the desired harvest [James 5:7]; and, in the mean time, we are to pray that he would be pleased to exert his power, and make the dispensations of his providence in the world conducive to the ends desired, and more particularly with respect to ourselves. Accordingly, we are to pray that we may have, not only an habitual, but an actual meetness for his heavenly kingdom; that when our Lord shall come, we may not be like those 'virgins' mentioned in the parable, who 'all slumbered and slept', but that, upon the first alarm, we may go out to meet him with joy and triumph; that, as an evidence of our meetness for his coming, we may...keep up

---

126. Luke 14:23 reads, "And the master said to the slave, 'Go out into the highways along the hedges, and compel them to come in, that my house may be filled.'"

127. Simon J. Kistemaker, *Exposition of the Epistles of Peter and of the Epistle of Jude* (Grand Rapids, MI: Baker Book House, 1987), 339.

> an intercourse with Christ, and be ready to entertain him with delight and pleasure whenever he comes, so that when he who is our life, our hope, and Saviour, as well as our King, shall appear, we may appear with him in glory.[128]

The Scriptural footnotes given by our Catechism supporting its last phrase contain a moving example of a prayer that the Lord Jesus Christ would *be pleased so to exercise the kingdom of his power in all the world, as may best conduce to these ends, i.e.,* of Christianizing the world in history and perfecting of His kingdom at the end of history.

> O that Thou wouldst rend the heavens and come down,
> That the mountains might quake at Thy presence—
> As fire kindles the brushwood, as fire causes water to boil—
> To make Thy name known to Thine adversaries,
> That the nations may tremble at Thy presence (Isa. 64:1–2).

In this prayer Isaiah earnestly beseeches God to intervene into history for the sake of His people, with such a powerful display of His glory that even His enemies will be made to know and serve Him and the world's nations tremble in fear and awe knowing that He is present with His church and world accomplishing all His purposes and fulfilling all the prophecies of His Word.

> The figure of fire is apt, for God's coming is to cause His enemies to know His Name. In the coming down God will manifest Himself and His attributes to His enemies, and they will know that He is the God of sovereign power. The Name of God, the Holy One of Israel, will bring salvation to His people but judgment to His enemies. These enemies are not merely the Babylonians, but all who oppose Him.... As mountains had quaked at His presence, so will idolatrous nations who have refused to know Him; for all the power of man, manifested in atheistic human government, will fall to pieces at His presence.[129]

---

128. Ridgeley, *Commentary on the Larger Catechism*, 2:623–24.
129. Young, *The Book of Isaiah*, 3:493.

The eighteenth century Puritan, Thomas Ridgeley, ends his exposition of the second petition of the Lord's Prayer with the following prayer:

> We adore and magnify thee, O God our Saviour, as the Governor of the world; who dost according to thy will in the armies of heaven, and amongst the inhabitants of the earth. thy power is irresistible, and thy works wonderful. But it is matter of highest astonishment, that thou shouldst exercise that gracious government in which thou condescendest to be called the King of saints. What is man that thou shouldst thus magnify him, and set thine heart upon him; that they whom thou mightest have dealt with as traitors, and enemies to thy government, and, as such, have ruled them with a rod of iron, and broken them in pieces, like a potter's vessel, should be admitted to partake of the privileges which thou are pleased to bestow on thy servants and subjects! Thou hast often invited us, by holding forth thy sceptre of grace, to come and acknowledge thee to be our Lord and Sovereign; but our hearts have been filled with rebellion against thee. We have served divers lusts and pleasures, and been in confederacy with hell and death, yielding ourselves slaves to Satan, thine avowed enemy. But now we desire to cast ourselves down before thy footstool; and, while we stand amazed at thy clemency, we, with the greatest thankfulness, accept of the overture of a pardon which thou hast made in the gospel, accounting it our highest privilege, as well as our indispensable duty, to be thy subjects. Write thy law, we beseech thee, in our hearts; bring down every high thought and imagination, which sets itself against thine interest; and make us entirely willing to be thy servants, devoted to thy fear.
>
> We also beg that thou wouldst take to thyself thy great power and reign. Let Satan's kingdom be destroyed, and thy gospel propagated throughout the world. May thine ancient people, the Jews, who now refuse that thou shouldest reign over them, be called and inclined to own thee as their King; and

may the dark parts of the earth see thy salvation. Reform thy churches; let them be constantly supplied with those who shall go in and out before them, and shall feed them with knowledge and understanding. May they be purged from those corruptions which are a reproach to thy government. Let not the commandments of men be received instead of thine holy institutions. May thine ordinances by purely dispensed, that thy people may have ground to hope for thy presence in them; and may they be made effectual for the converting of sinners, and the establishing of thy saints in their holy faith.

And let all the dispensations of thy providence in the world have a tendency to advance thy kingdom of grace, that, as thou hast in all ages appeared in behalf of thy church, so it may be preserved and carried through all the difficulties which it meets with, and be secured from the attempts or thine enemies against it, till they who rejoice in thy government here shall be received into thy heavenly kingdom hereafter.[130]

The Third Petition of the Lord's Prayer

Q. 192: What do we pray for in the third petition?

A.: In the third petition, (which is, *Thy will be done in earth, as it is in heaven*), acknowledging, that by nature we and all men are not only utterly unable and unwilling to know and do the will of God, but prone to rebel against his word, to repine and murmur against his providence, and wholly inclined to do the will of the flesh, and of the devil: we pray, that God would by his Spirit take away from ourselves and others all blindness,

130. Ridgeley, *Commentary on the Larger Catechism*, 2:624.

weakness, indisposedness, and perverseness of heart; and by his grace make us able and willing to know, do, and submit to his will in all things, with the like humility, cheerfulness, faithfulness, diligence, zeal, sincerity, and constancy, as the angels do in heaven.

The Wording of the Third Petition: Thy Will Be Done in Earth as it is in Heaven

God's "will" signifies not so much the faculty or the exercise of God's will, but the product of His will, that which He has willed for intelligent creatures, as embodied in His Law, made known by divine revelation in the Bible. As Jesus said at the conclusion of his Sermon on the Mount: "Not everyone who says to Me, 'Lord, Lord,' will enter the kingdom of heaven; but he who does the will of My Father, who is in heaven" (Matt. 7:21). "Be done" is a passive form, indicating that that revealed will which is to be performed is to be done by human beings living on earth. "As it is in heaven" indicates that human beings on earth are to do the revealed will of God as willingly, faithfully and perfectly as the angels and glorified believers do in heaven in the immediate presence of God. "As" denotes similarity rather than equality. "All that we can infer from the use of it in the petition is, that there is some analogy or resemblance between the obedience of the saints here, and that of the inhabitants of heaven."[131]

The Two Parts of the Third Petition of The Lord's Prayer

The Matter Requested: Thy Will be Done

The Manner in Which His Will is to be Done: As it is in Heaven

According to John Calvin:

---

131. Ridgeley, *Commentary on the Larger Catechism*, 2:627.

> Here is not a question of his secret will, by which he controls all things and directs them to their end.... But here God's other will is to be noted—namely, that to which voluntary obedience corresponds—and for that reason, heaven is by name compared to earth, for the angels, as is said in the psalm, willingly obey God, and are intent upon carrying out his commands (Ps. 103:20).
>
> We are therefore bidden to desire that, just as in heaven nothing is done apart from God's good pleasure, and the angels dwell together in all peace and uprightness, the earth be in like manner subject to such a rule, with all arrogance and wickedness brought to an end.
>
> And in asking this we renounce the desires of our flesh; for whoever does not resign and submit his feelings to God opposes as much as he can God's will, since only what is corrupt comes forth from us. And again by this prayer we are formed to self-denial so God may rule us according to his decision.... In sum, so we may wish nothing from ourselves but his Spirit may govern our hearts; and while the Spirit is inwardly teaching us we may learn to love the things that please him and to hate those which displease him.[132]

According to Wilhelmus á Brakel:

> Thus, the petition is that man would do that which God wishes to command, doing so for the very reason that God commands it and is pleased with man for doing so.... The petition therefore is that we may do the will of God as willingly, humbly, diligently, zealously, joyously, and steadfastly as the residents of heaven do, even though we shall not attain their perfection until we shall join them in glory.[133]

According to Rousas J. Rushdoony:

---

132. Calvin, *Institutes of the Christian Religion*, 2:906–07.

133. Brakel, *The Christian's Reasonable Service,* trans. by Bartel Elshout, 4 vols. (Pittsburgh, PA: Soli Deo Gloria, 1994), 3:526, 529.

> To pray "Thy will be done" is to hallow God's name, because it means we see our only good future in God's will, not our own. If we are prayerless, it is because we see the future, whatever our formal profession of faith, as something in our hands and for us to determine. It is an insistence on working on our own instead of under God.
>
> At the same time, formalism can pray, but without the high hope and faith of Matthew 6:9, 10, and the triple petition: "Hallowed be Thy Name. Thy Kingdom come. Thy will be done in earth, *as it is in heaven*." That last clause has an amazing audacity to it. We ourselves would never dare to ask for so much on our own, but, Christ having commanded this petition, and having supplied the words, we dare not ask for less, namely, that God's will be done on earth as it is in heaven. This is what God required of Adam in the Garden of Eden, and what the last Adam, Jesus Christ, requires of us.[134]

The Meaning of God's Will in the Third Petition

The "will" of God denotes two ideas in the Bible. The first is the sovereign will of God by which all things in creation have been foreordained. This use is seen in such phrases as "according to the good pleasure of His will" in Ephesians 1:5, which is referring to election and predestination. The second idea is God's revealed will in the Bible. Jesus used the word in this way in His statement: "My food is to do the will of Him who sent Me, and to accomplish His work" (John 4:34).

Both these two ideas come together in Deuteronomy 29:29: "The secret things belong to the LORD our God, but the things revealed belong to us and to our sons forever, that we may observe all the words of this law." God has one will. In some aspects it is "secret" and unrevealed, known only to God. Those aspects have reference to what God has sovereignly willed to happen in the future according to the good pleasure of His will. Other aspects of His one will are "revealed" in the "words of this Law," *i.e.*, Biblical revelation.

134. Rousas J. Rushdoony, *Systematic Theology*, 2 vols. (Vallecito, CA: Ross House Books, 1994), 2:1212.

We are to direct our lives and families, not by trying to second-guess God's secret will, but by obeying and believing the revealed will of God for our lives in the Bible.

> The will of God is to be considered after two sorts. First, as it is omnipotent, unsearchable, and that cannot be known unto us. Now we do not pray that his will so considered be done. For his will so considered is and ever shall be fulfilled, though we would say nay to it. For nothing, either in heaven or in earth, is able to withstand his will. Wherefore it were but folly for us to pray to have it fulfilled, otherwise than to shew thereby that we give our consent to his will, which is to us unsearchable. But there is another consideration of God's will; and in that consideration we and all faithful Christians desire that it may be done: and so considered, it is called a revealed, a manifested, a declared will; and it is opened unto us in the Bible, in the new and old testament: there God has revealed a certain will; therefore we pray that it may be done and fulfilled of us.[135]

Time and again the Bible speaks of people doing the revealed will of God in the Bible. In Hebrews 10:7, Christ is quoted as saying to God, "Lo, I come…to do Thy will." Ephesians 6:6 speaks of Christian slaves as being "slaves of Christ, doing the will of God from the heart." In Matthew 7:21, Jesus said: "Not every one who says to Me, "Lord, Lord," will enter the kingdom of heaven; but he who does the will of My Father, who is in heaven." When Jesus was asked who were His mother and brothers, He said: "For whoever does the will of God, he is My brother and sister and mother" (Mark 3:35). Christ disciples are those who do His will, therefore they are His family, hence He would teach His disciples to pray, "Thy will be done."

> It is the performance of the will of God which is decisive in determining kinship with Jesus. In the new family which Jesus calls into being there is demanded the radical obedience to God which he demonstrated in his submission to the Fa-

135. Latimer, *Sermons by Hugh Latimer*, 369.

> ther and which the disciples manifested in their response to his call. The one context which makes Jesus' word intelligible is that provided by the demands of the Kingdom of God which has drawn near in his person. Because the Kingdom is breaking in upon men there is a new urgency in the demand for obedience. At the same time this demand creates a fellowship in which the common pursuance of the will of God binds a man closely to Jesus and permits him to know another as brother, sister or mother.[136]

Thus, it is the revealed will of God by which we are to conduct ourselves in this world in all respects and in all circumstances.

> The petition is that man would do that which God wishes to command, doing so for the very reason that God commands it and is pleased with man for doing so—for we observe daily that man does not do what God commands.... Therefore the supplicant prays that God would manifest His omnipotence and goodness by granting the supplicant and others such a heart to know, love, fear, and obey Him in order that man would thereby show that God is the sole Lord, ruler, and lawgiver, who by His very nature obligates all creatures to obedience.[137]

> This is the way David prays in his Psalms: Teach me Thy statutes. Make me to understand the way of Thy precepts.... Make me walk in the path of Thy commandments, for I delight in it. Incline my heart to Thy testimonies (Ps. 119:26, 27, 35, 36).

> In this prayer, when we say, "Thy will be done," we desire of God that he will help and strengthen us, so that we may keep his holy laws and commandments. And then again we desire of him, that he will endue us with the gift of faith; so that we

---

136. William Lane, *The New International Commentary on the New Testament: The Gospel According to Mark* (Grand Rapids, MI: William B. Eerdmans Publishing Co., 1974), 148.

137. Brakel, *The Christian's Reasonable Service,* 3:526–27.

> may believe that all those things which we do contrary to his laws, be pardoned and forgiven unto us through his Son, for his passion's sake. And further, we desire him that he will fortify and strengthen us, so that we may withstand the devil's will and our own, which fight against God's will; so that we may be able to bear all tribulations and afflictions willingly and patiently, for his sake.[138]

The Wise Counsel of the Larger Catechism Q. 192

Our Catechism's exposition of the third petition, Q. 192, has two parts to it. First, it sets forth the reasons for making such a petition. Second, it explains the specific requests that we are making when we pray, "Thy will be done in earth as it is in heaven."

The Reasons for Making This Petition

By Nature We and All Men Are Not Only Utterly Unable and Unwilling to Know and Do the Will of God

> For I know that nothing good dwells in me, that is, in my flesh; for the willing is present in me, but the doing of the good is not (Rom. 7:18).
>
> But a natural man does not accept the things of the Spirit of God; for they are foolishness to him, and he cannot understand them, because they are spiritually appraised (1 Cor. 2:14).

Because of total depravity of the unregenerate and the remaining sinfulness indwelling in us as believers, in and of ourselves, without the assistance of God's Spirit, we are totally incapable and completely unwilling to know and love God and to obey His revealed will. It is only as the Holy Spirit works in us "to will and to work for His good pleasure" (Phil. 2:13), that we will gladly know and obey our God. And it is only as the Holy Spirit enlightens our

138. Latimer, *Sermons by Hugh Latimer,* 370.

minds regarding the divine authority and meaning of revealed truth, that we will believe and understand that truth, because it is "spiritually appraised."

We and All Men are Prone to Rebel Against His Word

> The mind set on the flesh is hostile toward God; for it does not subject itself to the Law of God, for it is not even able to do so; and those who are in the flesh cannot please God (Rom. 8:7–8).

These verses describe the sad plight of the total depravity and total inability of the unregenerate. And were it not for the almighty grace of God in regenerating us, we believers would still be in that hopeless condition. However, even as believers, we have the power of evil still operative within us. We are no longer slaves to sin because of the work of the Spirit liberating us from that slavery (Rom. 6–8); but we live with a constant struggle within us as Paul so painfully describes in Romans 7. He defines this inner conflict and the way to victory in it in Galatians 5:16–17: "But I say, walk by the Spirit, and you will not carry out the desire of the flesh. For the flesh sets its desire against the Spirit, and the Spirit against the flesh; for these are in opposition to one another." The point is that, although we have been Spiritually reborn and indwelt with the Holy Spirit, ferocious evil still rages within us, and it is only as we walk in the Spirit's power and according to the Spirit's written rule that we are able to get the victory over the monster within us. Therefore, we pray continually that God would enable us to do His will on earth as it is in heaven. And we sing:

O to grace how great a debtor
Daily I'm constrained to be;

Let that grace now, like a fetter,
Bind my wand'ring heart to Thee.

Prone to wander, Lord, I feel it,
Prone to leave the God I love;

Here's my heart, O take and seal it,
Seal it for Thy courts above.[139]

---

139. Robert Robinson, *Trinity Hymnal*, #400.

We and All Men are Prone to Repine and Murmur Against His Providence

> Then all the congregation lifted up their voice and cried, and the people wept that night. And all the sons of Israel grumbled against Moses and Aaron; and the whole congregation said to them, "Would that we had died in the land of Egypt! Or would that we had died in the wilderness! (Num. 14:1–2).

During Israel's wandering in the Wilderness, after their exodus from Egypt and before their entrance into Canaan, God's providence generously, and, in some instances, miraculously provided them with all they needed, guided and protected them so they were safe in His hands. But Israel murmured against God's providence time and again, not being satisfied with His directions, His will and His providence. Filled with unbelief and dissatisfaction with God and His will, they would choose either security as slaves in Egypt or the "peace" of death.

When we fail to walk by faith in God's faithful promise and to be content with His will, we will inexcusably grumble and murmur at God's providence, if things do not go the way we think they should go. Such grumbling is gross ingratitude and wickedness. Therefore because all sinners, even believing ones, are *prone to repine and murmur against His providence*, we must always be praying, especially during troublous times, that God would enable us to overcome murmuring against Him, to be content with His will and to do His will on earth as it is in heaven.

We and All Men are Wholly Inclined to Do the Will of the Flesh and of the Devil

> And you were dead in your trespasses and sins, in which you formerly walked according to the course of this world, according to the prince of the power of the air, of the spirit that is now working in the sons of disobedience (Eph. 2:1–2).

Before their conversion believers in Jesus were spiritually dead and in bondage to sin. Their daily lives were dominated by this system of evil around them and energized by Satan himself. But now, by the grace of God, we have been resurrected and liberated from all that through faith in Jesus Christ. And yet, we are not perfect yet, and we will not be perfect until we are spiritually perfected in holiness at death and physically perfected and made completely whole in resurrection at the return of Christ. Until that day we must struggle against the "flesh," *i.e.*, the remnants of evil that remain with us and which enslave the unregenerate.

It is only because of the presence and work of the Holy Spirit within us as believers that we have any inclination to do the will of God and any disinclination to do the will of sin and Satan. Therefore, we must continually pray to our Father that He will incline our hearts to serve Him and enable us to live daily according to His will and not according to our own wills or according to the seductions of sin and dictations of Satan.

The Petitions Within the Third Petition

Because all these things are true of us, our prayers that God would enable us to do His will on earth as it is in heaven, must not only be fervent and constant, they must be specific. *Knowledgeable praying is effective praying.* We should know exactly what God wants us to ask for; and then He will give us what we ask for. As we consider these specifics, we should also notice that our Catechism teaches us to petition God to do these things not only for ourselves, but also to intercede in behalf of other people that God would do the same in their hearts and lives.

That God Would by His Spirit Take Away from Ourselves and Others All Blindness, Weakness, Indisposedness and Perverseness of Heart

> For this reason I...do not cease giving thanks to you...that the God of our Lord Jesus Christ, the Father of glory, may give to you a spirit of wisdom and of revelation in the knowl-

> edge of Him. I pray that the eyes of your heart may be enlightened, so that you may know what is the hope of His calling, what are the riches of the glory of His inheritance in the saints, and what is the surpassing greatness of His power toward us who believe according to the working of the strength of His might (Eph. 1:15–19).

God wants us to pray that His Holy Spirit will take away from us any spiritual blindness and moral weakness that would hinder us from doing His will. Unbelievers have been blinded by sin and Satan (2 Cor. 4:4f), and they are completely without strength to do God's will (Rom. 5:6). On the other hand, the believer's blindness has been healed (2 Cor. 4:4), and he has been strengthened in the inner man with the power of God thus enabling Him to see and understand what the revealed will of God means and to do that will in the strength of the Lord (Eph. 6:10).

And so, in the above text, the apostle Paul prays for the Christians in Ephesus that God's Spirit would continue that work in them which began when He gave them new hearts: (1) That He would improve and perfect that new disposition He has placed in them by the "Spirit of wisdom and of revelation in the knowledge of Him." This is to pray that the Holy Spirit would give us a true knowledge of the revealed Word of God, in which "His divine power has granted to us everything pertaining to life and godliness through the true knowledge of Him who called us by His own glory and excellence" (2 Pet. 1:3); and that with that true "knowledge," He would give us "wisdom," *i.e.*, the skill to apply that knowledge practically to our everyday life. (2) That He would continue to enlighten their minds regarding their saved condition and future inheritance. (3) And that He would continue to exert "the surpassing greatness of His power" in them strengthening their faith in Christ and His Word "according to the working of the strength of His might." Therefore, we are to pray that God would remove from us any remaining spiritual blindness and moral weakness that we may do His will with all our heart.

> And He came to the disciples and found them sleeping, and said to Peter, "So, you men could not keep watch with Me for

> one hour? Keep watching and praying, that you may not enter into temptation; the spirit is willing, but the flesh is weak" (Matt. 26:40–41).

This familiar incident clearly testifies to our *indisposedness*[140] to do the will of God. The unbeliever is totally indisposed to do the will of God (Rom. 8:6–8); and the believer struggles with this *indisposedness,* because he is not yet perfect, although he can say truthfully: "I joyfully concur with the Law of God in the inner man" (Rom. 7:22). Therefore in his new heart he is disposed to do God's will, and yet in him also is a remaining *indisposedness*, as Paul said, "I see a different law in the members of my body, waging war against the law of my mind" (Rom. 7:23).

As Jesus said to His sleeping disciples, who were supposed to be alert and praying with Him so as not to enter into temptation: "the spirit is willing but the flesh is weak." The believer's "spirit," *i.e.*, his new life in Christ, is not only inclined, it is eager to do the will of God; but his "flesh," *i.e.*, the remnants of his old sinful nature that remain in him, being "weak" is disinclined, indisposed and unwilling to do the will of God. Therefore, believers must "keep watching and praying that [they] may not enter into temptation," because the "flesh" is disposed and prone to yield to the temptations of sin and the desires of Satan.

Jesus' statement to the sleepy disciples, who should have been praying, that "the spirit is willing but the flesh is weak"

> was not added by way of excuse, as some have imagined, but of warning and incentive. The fact that while the spirit is willing the flesh is weak forms a reason why we should watchfully and prayerfully strive to keep out of temptation, lest it take advantage of our weakness and overcome us. . .

140. Indispose means "to disincline; to alienate the mind and render it averse or unfavorable to any thing. A love of pleasure *indisposes* the mind to severe study and steady attention to business. The pride and selfishness of men *indispose* them to religious duties." Noah Webster, *American Dictionary of the English Language* (San Francisco, CA: Foundation for American Christian Education, [1828] 1967).

> "Do not look to the soul's readiness and be bold, but look to the flesh's weakness and be humble."[141]

> I have surely heard Ephraim grieving,
> Thou hast chastised me, and I was chastised,
> Like an untrained calf;
> Bring me back that I may be restored,
> For Thou art the LORD my God.
> For after I turned back, I repented;
> And after I was instructed, I smote on my thigh;
> I was ashamed, and also humiliated,
> Because I bore the reproach of my youth (Jer. 31:18–19).

We must also pray that God would take away completely from us any *perverseness of heart* that remains in us so that we will do God's will on earth as it is done in heaven. To be perverse is to be obstinate in what is wrong, disposed to be contrary, stubborn, and untractable. It denotes an attitude that refuses to comply to the right and acts in opposition to what is right.

The repentant people of "Ephraim," *i.e.*, northern Israel confessed their sin of *perverseness of heart*, because God turned their hearts to true repentance. And so, Israel confesses that her need for repentance was that they had acted toward God "like an untrained calf." In their impenitency they "bite and champ at the bit and bridle" in God's hand. They pull and tug to resist His control over them. They would not submit to God's yoke. They craved freedom from God's government, the license to sin, rather than the easy, light and blessed yoke of obedient love of God. Only through bitter chastisement and the inner work of the Spirit of God was Israel brought to conviction of sin, self-despair, repentance of sin, and renewed submission to God. The thought of their perverseness abashed, humiliated, and crushed Israel to the ground before the majesty of the Lord. The point is that God's covenant people win the victory over remaining *perverseness of heart* by means of the disciplinary providence of God, the preaching of the Word of God,

141. John A. Broadus, *Commentary on the Gospel of Matthew*, ed. by Alvah Hovey (Philadelphia: American Baptist Publication Society, 1886), 538.

and the inner work of the Holy Spirit bending their minds and wills to submission and teachableness and repentance before Him. So then, if we are to do God's will, we must earnestly pray that He will continue to deliver us from any remaining *perverseness of heart.*

That God Would by His Spirit and by His Grace Make Us Able and Willing to Know, Do and Submit to His Will in All Things

> Teach me, O LORD, the way of Thy statutes,
> And I shall observe it to the end.
> Give me understanding, that I may observe Thy law,
> And keep it with all my heart.
> Make me walk in the path of Thy commandments,
> For I delight in it.
> Incline my heart to Thy testimonies,
> And not to dishonest gain.
> Turn away my eyes from looking at vanity,
> And revive me in Thy ways (Ps. 119:33–37).

We must not only pray that the Holy Spirit will "mortify the flesh" that remains in us, enabling us to die more and more unto sin; but we must also pray that He will "vivify the spirit," *i.e.*, the new life He has given us, enabling us to live more and more unto righteousness. So then, we are to pray earnestly that *God would by his Spirit and his grace make us able and willing to know, do and submit to his will in all things.*

This is the very thing David does in Psalm 119:33–37. In this prayer he prays for three things. First, he prays that God Himself would *teach* Him, giving him the true "understanding" of God's Laws, because out of His love for God he has been observing them, and as a believer, he longs to obey them far more knowledgeably, consistently and whole-heartedly in the future than he has in the past. Second, he prays that God would "make" or *enable* him to live consistently in "the path of Thy commandments," that God would "incline" his heart to God's commandments rather than to materialism, because He does "delight" in those commandments, thus "reviving" Him in the whole-hearted submission to the revealed ways of God for His people. And third, he prays that God would *turn away* his eyes from desiring anything or anyone else with a greater or the same intensity that He desires his God, who is the LORD.

David knows his frailty. Although he has for a long time served God in faith and love, nevertheless, he knows that we are so frail

> that we can never come home to the mark, without God strengthen[ing] us...he beseecheth the Lord to grant him the power to persevere [in keeping God's commandments], and that he may come to the perfection thereof.... And so in the first place, when as God shall have instructed us, to make us to come to a good understanding and knowledge, he must also grant unto us a good affection and desire.... Finally after that he hath given us to will, he must also give us to perform.... O Lord... There is nothing in us but rebellion and treason against Thee, we shall never be able to walk in Thy obedience, nor never place ourselves therein, except Thou puttest to Thy hand, and inclinest our minds and hearts thereto.[142]

So then, if we are to do God's will on earth as it is done in heaven, we must pray earnestly and continuously that *God would...make us able and willing to know, do and submit to his will in all things,* and that we do His will *with the like humility, cheerfulness, faithfulness, diligence, zeal, sincerity and constancy, as the angels do in heaven.*

With the Like Humility

> He has told you, O man, what is good;
> And what does the LORD require of you
> But to do justice, to love kindness,
> And to walk humbly with your God? (Mic. 6:8).

---

142. John Calvin, *Sermons on Psalm 119* (NJ: Old Paths Publications, 1996), 87–94.

God's will is to be done *with humility.* We are "to walk humbly with our God" in fellowship with Him and obedience to Him. This is a distinctive Christian trait, for pagan cultures have no virtue corresponding to humility.

> Humility is lowliness of mind, the opposite of pride and arrogance.... [it is] "the peculiar grace of Christians, the parent and nurse of other graces, that preserves in us the light of faith and the heat of love; that procures modesty in prosperity and patience in adversity; that is the root of gratitude and obedience, and is so lovely in God's eyes, that He 'giveth grace to the humble'" [Bates]. A lowly spirit is the opposite of a lofty one. True humility is an inward grace based on a view of our own guilt, weakness, vileness, ignorance, and poverty as compared with the infinite excellence and glory of God.... It is opposed to all ostentation. It not only hides the other graces of the Christian from the gaze of self-admiration, but it hides itself also. Its aim is not to be thought humble, but to be humble.[143]

> Condemned, then, is here [Mic. 6:8] all pride, and also all the confidence of the flesh: for whosoever arrogates to himself even the least thing, does, in a manner, contend with God as with an opposing party. The true way then of walking with God is, when we thoroughly humble ourselves, yea, when we bring ourselves down to nothing; for it is the very beginning of worshipping and glorifying God when men entertain humble and low opinion of themselves.[144]

143. William Plumer, *Vital Godliness: A Treatise on Experimental and Practical Piety* (American Tract Society, 1864; reprint Harrisonburg, VA: Sprinkle Publications, 1993), 250.

144. John Calvin, *Commentaries on the Twelve Minor Prophets*, trans. by Rev. John Owen, 5 vols. (Edinburgh: Calvin Translation Society, 1843; reprint Grand Rapids, MI: Baker Book House, 1979), 3:344.

Cheerfulness

> Shout joyfully to the LORD, all the earth. Serve the LORD with gladness (Ps. 100:1, 2a).

God's will is to be done with *cheerfulness* and not grudgingly. In all aspects of our obedience to God and in all the service we give to Him, we are to serve Him "with gladness." This word, "gladness," can also be translated joy, joyfulness, mirth, pleasure. God is also to be served with fear; and the greater our fear and adoration of God, the greater our joy in serving Him and doing His will. "Reluctance in God's service is not essentially different from refusal to engage in it. Where there is no *gladness* in us, there is no acceptance with God. v. 2."[145]

Why must God's will be done with *cheerfulness*? Charles Spurgeon answers:

> To the soul that has been subdued, delivered from the bondage of its own self-dominion—the soul that is humble, teachable, weaned from the world, and changed into a little child, the thought of service has heaven in it; for such a heart remembers that in the New Jerusalem they serve God day and night, and it looks forward to perfect service as being its perfect rest. Renewed minds accept.... *I serve*, as their motto, and feel ennobled thereby.... The man who has once known, who has tasted that the Lord is gracious, and been made to enter into the Lord's covenant of mercy, and has seen under what obligations he is laid to the lovingkindness and tender mercy of Jehovah, to such a man the very thought of serving God is liberty. He delights to run in the way of God's commandments, and the statutes of the Most High are to Him sweeter than honey, or the droppings of the honeycomb.[146]

---

145. Plumer, *Psalms: A Critical And Expository Commentary With Doctrinal & Practical Remarks*, 896.

146. Charles H. Spurgeon, *The Metropolitan Tabernacle Pulpit*, 62 vols. (Pasadena, TX: Pilgrim Publications, 1979), 13:493–94.

Serving the Lord with gladness is something unregenerate people have never experienced and never will as long as they remain in their unregeneracy.

> "Serve the LORD with gladness" seems to the carnal mind to be a perfect monstrosity; and yet, mark you, this is the test between the genuine and the hypocritical professor—by this one thing shall you know who it is that fears God, and who it is that does but offer him the empty tribute of his lips.... As for the true believer in Jesus, he serves his God because he loves to serve him; he assembles with the great congregation because it is his delight to worship the Most High. To him it is the greatest of all earthly joys.[147]

Faithfulness

> Then Hezekiah turned his face to the wall, and prayed to the LORD, and said, "Remember now, O LORD, I beseech Thee, how I have walked before Thee in truth and with a whole heart, and have done what is good in Thy sight." And Hezekiah wept bitterly (Isa. 38:2–3).

God's will is to be done with *faithfulness*. King Hezekiah did God's will faithfully even in frightening and life-threatening situations. It was the habit of his life, day in and day out to walk before God "in truth and with a whole heart" and to do "what is good in Thy sight." God's will is not to be done haphazardly, spasmodically, intermittently, or lackadaisically.

When Jerusalem was under siege and threatened by the Assyrians with destruction, godly King Hezekiah turns his face to the wall to seek God's will and help without disturbance. He simply prays that God would look at his life and then do His holy will. Hezekiah "is not pleading his merits before God, as though to claim that he was deserving of salvation, but is merely pointing out the tragedy that would seem to occur if a theocratic ruler who had lived his life righteously before God should be taken without

147. Spurgeon, *The Metropolitan Tabernacle Pulpit*, 3:494–95.

heir."[148] His heart was devoted to the Lord. His obedience to God's will was not half-hearted.

Diligence

> Thou hast ordained Thy precepts, That we should keep them diligently. Oh that my ways may be established To keep Thy statutes! (Ps. 119:4–5).

God's will is to be done with *diligence, i.e.,* with steady application, constant effort, vigorous and persevering exertion of body and mind without unnecessary delay or sloth, with attentive care, assiduity, not carelessly or negligently. The psalmist not only understands that God has revealed His moral precepts and "that we should keep them diligently," he also prays to God that God would confirm and establish his "ways" so that he can and will "keep Thy statutes."

In giving us His revealed will in His Law and commanding us to obey it "diligently," God is showing to His people His great love for us and His sincere care for our welfare and life, for He knows that without His Word our lives will be dissolute and full of confusion and destruction. Knowing this we, His children by faith, earnestly desire to please our Father in heaven by doing His will diligently, and so we earnestly pray that He would so enable us to keep doing it from our hearts to His glory in all our ways, thoughts and affections. "A faithful man, after he hath known this mercy of God in guiding his life, ought to enter into himself, and think that there is neither reason nor wisdom in him how to govern himself; but that proceedeth from the good will and lovingkindness of the Lord."[149]

Zeal

> Be devoted to one another...not lagging behind in diligence, fervent in spirit, serving the Lord... (Rom. 12:10–11).

148. Young, *The Book of Isaiah,* 2:510.
149. Calvin, *Sermons on Psalm 119,* 17.

God's will is to be done with *zeal,* "not lagging behind in diligence, fervent in spirit." Zeal is "passionate ardor in the pursuit of anything...and eagerness of desire to accomplish or obtain some object."[150] One has said that "zeal is the fire of love." It is with such zeal that we are to do God's will. Fervency is warmth of devotion and pious ardor. The English word, fervency, comes from the Latin word, *ferveo,* meaning to be hot, to boil, to glow. "When discouragement overtakes the Christian and fainting in spirit as its sequel, it is because the claims of the Lord's service have ceased to be uppermost in our thought."[151]

> Nor is any thing in religion more conducive to our happiness than liveliness in the cause of God. Holy ardor is as oil to machinery; it makes every thing work smoothly. God meets him that rejoiceth and worketh righteousness. His most arduous duties refresh his spirit. He comes to them and from them not as a hireling, but as a child who delights in the law of God after the inner man.
>
> Nor should we ever forget that God abhors all services in religion where the heart is wanting. A religion without zeal is offensive to God. Duly considered, it is monstrous to all right-minded men.[152]

What makes a believer do God's will zealously and fervently? That believer's love for Jesus Christ and his devotion to glorify and enjoy Him forever.

> The highest motive which can be presented to a pious mind in favor of a life of zeal and devotedness is, that thus we do what we can to glorify our God and Saviour. To be allowed to honor the Father of our mercies, the God of all grace, and the Saviour of sinners, is one of the highest privileges ever bestowed on mortals. So the righteous have always esteemed it. The wants, the woes, the weal of mankind may properly be

150. Webster, *American Dictionary of the English Language.*
151. Murray, *The Epistle to the Romans,* 2:131.
152. Plumer, *Vital Godliness,* 566.

> thought of as motives to a life of labor and usefulness. But they are as nothing compared with the glory of Him who has made all things for himself, who is before all, above all, over all, through all, and in us all.[153]

Sincerity

> May my heart be blameless in Thy statutes,
> That I may not be ashamed (Ps. 119:80).

God's will is to be done with *sincerity.* This English word comes from the Latin word, *sincerus,* which is composed of *sine* meaning "without," and *cera,* meaning "wax," originally referring to pure honey, or to a marble statue with no nicks filled in with marble-colored wax. So that, sincerity means pure and unmixed, being in reality what a person appears or professes to be. A sincere person is a real person. To do God's will sincerely is to do it honestly, with real purity of heart, with unmixed motives, without deception or hypocrisy.

To do God's will sincerely is to do it with blamelessness of heart, as Psalm 119:80 teaches us. Because sincerity of heart results from the work of God in the heart, the psalmist, in this verse, prays that God would not only give him understanding of His will, but that He would give Him affection for it. He is praying that God would give him a pure and sincere heart that loves God's law so that he will have no other desire but to serve Him.

Constancy

> I have inclined my heart to perform Thy statutes
> Forever, even to the end (Ps. 119:112).

God's will is to be done with *constancy.* Constancy is "fixedness or firmness of mind; persevering resolution; steady, unshaken determination; particularly applicable to firmness of mind under sufferings...lasting affection; stability in love or friendship."[154]

---

153. Plumer, *Vital Godliness,* 573–74.

154. Webster, *American Dictionary of the English Language.*

When David says, "I have inclined my heart to perform Thy statutes," he is not bragging, nor is he saying that he has done so of his own moral strength. Rather he can say this because He knows that God has given him both the will and the power to keep the commandments of God: "for it is God who is at work in you, both to will and to work for His good pleasure" (Phil. 2:13). The Hebrew denotes that this inclining of His heart is a constant thing on David's part. He continually and constantly, by the power of God's indwelling Spirit, inclines his heart to do God's will. To say that David "inclined" his heart is to say that "he devoted himself with sincere affection to the observance of the law. This inclination of the heart is opposed to the wandering lusts which rise up against God, and drag us any where rather than incline us to a virtuous life."[155]

Then David adds the words, "forever, even to the end." This is *constancy.* These words show us that David "struggled manfully against all obstacles and difficulties, that they might not break his constancy; for no man perseveres in the service of God without arduous exertions."[156]

> We must not be like sudden blasts which pass by and by, but we must be constant, and that when we shall have once begun, we must pray unto God that He will continue the same our well doing which he hath begun in us, and to hold us by the hand until such time as we have finished our course.... We may alter and change our minds in other things; but we must follow unto the death, when God calleth us unto Him, being assured that in this pursuit we cannot fail to come to the true end, without to fail and err forever.[157]

As the Angels Do in Heaven

> Bless the LORD, you His angels, Mighty in strength, who perform His word, Obeying the voice of His word! (Ps. 103:20).

155. Calvin, *Commentary on the Book of Psalms,* 4:486
156. Calvin, *Commentary on the Book of Psalms,* 4:486.
157. Calvin, *Sermons on Psalm 119,* 288–89.

Having recounted all the blessings God is to His people in Christ, the psalmist concludes by calling upon God's people to join with all the holy angels in heaven in praising the Lord for His goodness to us. He also calls upon the angels themselves to "bless the LORD."

> In calling upon them to join in praising God, he teaches both himself and all the godly, that there is not a better nor a more desirable exercise than to praise God, since there is not a more excellent service in which even the angels are employed. The angels are doubtless too willing and prompt in the discharge of this duty, to stand in need of incitement from us. With what face then, it may be said, can we, whose slothfulness is so great, take it upon us to exhort them? But although these exalted beings run swiftly before us, and we with difficulty come lagging after them, yet David enjoins them to sing God's praises for our sake, that by their example he may awaken us from our drowsiness.[158]

These glorious angels of the LORD are characterized by four traits. They belong to the LORD, being "His" angels. They are "mighty in strength." They "perform His word." And they are "obeying the voice of His Word." The Lord's angels excel in strength, in the entire universe no creature equals them in power. They are doing God's will with indescribable pleasure and promptness. They wait upon His bidding as His willing and faithful servants.

This is what Jesus had in mind when He taught us to pray: "Thy will be done on earth as it is in heaven," *i.e.*, as the holy angels in heaven do God's will. "The petition therefore is that we may do the will of God as willingly, humbly, diligently, zealously, joyously and steadfastly as the residents of heaven do, even though we shall not attain their perfection until we shall join them in glory."[159]

> We are therefore bidden to desire that, just as in heaven nothing is done apart from God's good pleasure, and the an-

158. Calvin, *Commentary on the Book of Psalms*, 4:141.
159. Brakel, *The Christian's Reasonable Service*, 3:529.

gels dwell together in all peace and uprightness, the earth be in like manner subject to such a rule, with all arrogance and wickedness brought to an end.[160]

The Fourth Petition of the Lord's Prayer

Q. 193: What do we pray for in the fourth petition?

A.: In the fourth petition, (which is, *Give us this day our daily bread*), acknowledging, that in Adam, and by our own sin, we have forfeited our right to all the outward blessings of this life, and deserve to be wholly deprived of them by God, and to have them cursed to us in the use of them; and that neither they of themselves are able to sustain us, nor we to merit, or by our own industry to procure them; but prone to desire, get, and use them unlawfully: we pray for ourselves and others, that both they and we, waiting upon the providence of God from day to day in the use of lawful means, may, of his free gift, and as to his fatherly wisdom shall seem best, enjoy a competent portion of them; and have the same continued and blessed unto us in our holy and comfortable use of them, and contentment in them; and be kept from all things that are contrary to our temporal support and comfort.

160. Calvin, *Institutes of the Christian Religion*, 2:906.

The Grammar of the Fourth Petition

The verbs in the last four petitions of the Lord's Prayer are second person aorists in Greek, unlike the first three, which were in the third person. The point of this change of person is that

> the objects mentioned in these four petitions cannot be identified with God himself as were his name, kingdom and will; they are only gifts and acts of God for our various needs. The aorist imperatives are still strong because all four petitions harmonize with God's will.[161]

Luke expresses the verb of the fourth petition in the present tense, indicating continuous action: "keep on giving us day by day."

The word order of this petition, in Greek, places the emphasis, not on the verb, but on "bread." And the adjective, "daily," (appended by a second article), is a kind of climax to the emphatic noun. A literal translation of this petition could be: "our needful bread give us this day."

The Language of the Fourth Petition

"Bread" is the ordinary daily food of most human beings, the staff of life, and main staple of most nations. It refers to whatever we need to sustain our physical-spiritual life in this world. No one has explained the significance of this word "bread" as effectively as Martin Luther in his Small Catechism:

> *What is implied in the words "our daily bread"*? All things that pertain to the wants and the support of this present life; such as food, raiment, money, goods, house and land, and other property; a believing spouse and good children; trustworthy servants and faithful magistrates; favorable seasons, peace and health; education and honor; true friends, good neighbors and the like.[162]

---

161. Lenski, *The Interpretation of St. Matthew's Gospel*, 268.

162. Joseph Stump, *An Explanation of Luther's Small Catechism* (Board of Publication of the General Council, 1907; reprint Philadelphia: The United Lutheran Publication House, 1935), 129.

By asking God to "give" us this bread, we are acknowledging that our provisions for life all come to us from God.

> He is the absolute owner of all things, and divides to all men as He will. All that we have is His gift. He gives it as a blessing upon our labor; hence, we must work as well as pray. But without His blessing, our labor would be in vain. The farmer sows, but God gives the increase.[163]

As Paul tells us: "And my God shall supply all your needs according to His riches in glory in Christ Jesus" (Phil. 4:19).

We are asking God to give "us" our daily bread. In this we are taught not to pray only for ourselves, but also for others also. As the apostle Paul wrote: "with humility of mind let each of you regard one another as more important than himself; do not merely look out for your own personal interests, but also for the interests of others" (Phil. 2:3–4). "We should be concerned that they too may have their daily bread; and, when necessary, we should give them a portion of what God has first given to us, and thus become the means through which He supplies their wants."[164]

It is for "our" daily bread that we petition God. "We ask for bread which we may call our own, bread honestly gotten, bread which God intends we shall have as a reward of our labor; not someone else's bread, and not such things as God, in His wisdom, sees fit to withhold from us."[165]

We are to pray that God would give us "this day" our provisions for life. We are to pray daily, always depending entirely on the Father, for whatever we need to live for God that day; and then renew that petition every day. "When the morrow comes, if we are still alive, we are to pray again. We are to depend upon God from day to day. We are, indeed, to make a proper provision for our future, but we are not to give way to anxious, unbelieving care about it."[166]

---

163. Stump, *An Explanation of Luther's Small Catechism*, 130.
164. Stump, *An Explanation of Luther's Small Catechism*, 130.
165. Stump, *An Explanation of Luther's Small Catechism*, 130.
166. Stump, *An Explanation of Luther's Small Catechism*, 130.

Linguists are not agreed on the derivation and precise meaning of the Greek word, επιουσιον translated "daily." J. A. Alexander speaks of it as "one of the most doubtful and disputed words in Scripture."[167] Interpreters are divided mainly over two meanings, either of which is suitable for understanding our text. The first meaning denotes essence or substance, that which is required for support. Hence the petition would be: "give us this day our needful or substantial bread, needed to support life." The second meaning is coming or coming on, an elliptical expression for the coming or ensuing day. Hence the translation: "give us our bread day by day." It is obvious that, though the translations differ, in reality there is little difference between them. Each of them give us a good and appropriate sense of the meaning of the petition. J. A. Alexander concludes: "The bread for which we pray is of course that which supports us, and of which we stand in daily need."[168]

The Reasons Behind the Fourth Petition of the Lord's Prayer

Larger Catechism Q. 193 gives us several reasons explaining why we must continually pray to God: "Give us this day our daily bread."

In Adam, and By Our Own Sin, We Have Forfeited Our Right to All the Outward Blessings of this Life, and Deserve to Be Wholly Deprived of Them by God, and to Have Them Cursed to Us in the Use of Them

Because Adam was our representative and covenant head before God in the Covenant of Works, we, as the entire race, have experienced the consequences of his act of disobedience in eating of the forbidden fruit. In fact, Romans 5:12 tells us that "all sinned" in Adam. This verb, in Greek, is in the aorist tense, denoting at a specific point in the past all of Adam's descendents sinned. That point was when Adam our covenant head sinned, as Romans 5:12–19 goes on to ex-

167. Alexander, *The Gospel According to Matthew,* 173–74.
168. Alexander, *The Gospel According to Matthew,* 174.

plain. Therefore, what sin did to him it does to us, because we are not only charged with his guilt, we have inherited from him a sinful human nature, and we are accountable for our own sins as well as the original sin. Hence, our sins have separated us from God and robbed us of any kind of blessings, spiritual or "outward," *i.e.*, material, for the wages of sin are only and always death were it not for God's grace. In forfeiting life we have forfeited any enjoyment and use of the material blessings that sustain life.[169] Jeremiah 5:23–25 says it well:

> But this people has a stubborn and rebellious heart;
> They have turned aside and departed.
> They do not say in their heart,
> "Let us now fear the LORD our God,
> Who gives rain in its season,
> Both the autumn rain and the spring rain,
> Who keeps for us The appointed weeks of the harvest."
> Your iniquities have turned these away,
> And your sins have withheld good from you.

Our sin turns all of creation against us. God uses the energies of creation to bless us, but when we rebel against Him, He turns them against us. So then, our sin turns away from us the blessings of God, and move God to withhold the ordinary temporal and material, as well as spiritual, blessings from us.

When Adam sinned, God said: "Cursed is the ground for your sake; in sorrow you shall eat of it all the days of your life" (Gen. 3:17). So then, we not only deserve *to be wholly deprived* of life and all its blessings, because of our sin, they have been *cursed to us in the use of them*. The curse of God rests on all that is important to the sinner, (unless he is saved from that curse through Christ)—his vocation, his family and on every other aspect of his life, as long as he is disobedient to God. Everything about the rebel's life shrivels up. As Deuteronomy 28:15–19 warns us:

---

169. Larger Catechism Q. 193 speaks of our forfeiting *our right to all the outward blessings of this life*, but it is questionable whether man has ever had a "right" to those material gifts of God's grace.

> But it shall come about, if you will not obey the LORD your God, to observe to do all His commandments and His statutes which I charge you today, that all these curses shall come upon you and overtake you. Cursed shall you be in the city, and cursed shall you be in the country. Cursed shall be your basket and your kneading bowl. Cursed shall be the offspring of your body and the produce of your ground, the increase of your herd and the young of your flock. Cursed shall you be when you come in, and cursed shall you be when you go out.

Neither They of Themselves are Able to Sustain Us

> And He humbled you and let you be hungry, and fed you with manna which you did not know, nor did your fathers know, that He might make you understand that man does not live by bread alone, but man lives by everything that proceeds out of the mouth of the LORD (Deut. 8:3).

As delightful as *the outward blessings of this life* may be, and regardless of how many of them we have been given, in and of themselves, they do not have the power to sustain our lives in this world, without the providence of God providing, governing and using these blessings as His instruments by which He sustains us and enhances our lives in this world. The above passage teaches us that in Israel's "wilderness experience," when the people were hungry, God fed them manna miraculously, to teach them the fundamental principle of their existence in the world as God's covenant people: the source of life in every respect is the Lord God, the provisions of His providence and the strength and direction of His Word, *i.e.*, "by everything that proceeds out of the mouth of the LORD."

> This principle did not mean that the Israelites were to expect at all times the miraculous provision of food, as in the instance when God provided manna. Normal circumstances would involve the normal acquisition of food supplies. But if the command of God directed the people to do something or

> go somewhere, the command should be obeyed; shortage of food and water, lack of strength, or any other excuse would be insufficient, for the command of God contained within it the provision of God.[170]

Nor We to Merit, or By Our Own Industry to Procure Them

> And Jacob said, "O God of my father Abraham and God of my father Isaac, O LORD, who didst say to me, "Return to your country and to your relatives, and I will prosper you," I am unworthy of all the lovingkindness and of all the faithfulness which Thou hast shown to Thy servant (Gen. 32:9–10).

In praying that the Lord would deliver him from the approaching Esau and his army, Jacob pled the covenant promises of God as the basis of his petition for deliverance. And yet, Jacob, made no audacious demands on God, for he quickly confessed that he was totally unworthy of all the material and social blessings of this life which God had poured out on him in an overwhelming display of his "lovingkindness" and "faithfulness." As our Catechism says, we have not merited any of the outward blessings of this life, all of which are gifts of God's grace to us. Furthermore, it is not simply or directly because of our ingenuity and labor that we have acquired these material possessions, but solely because of the "lovingkindness" and "faithfulness" of God to His promises to His covenant people.

> Beware lest you forget the LORD your God by not keeping His commandments...lest, when you have eaten and are satisfied, and have built good houses and lived in them, and when your herds and your flocks multiply, and your silver and gold multiply, and all that you have multiplies, then your heart becomes proud and you forget the LORD your God who brought you out from the land of Egypt, out of the house

170. Peter Craigie, *The New International Commentary on the Old Testament: The Book of Deuteronomy* (Grand Rapids, MI: William B. Eerdmans Publishing Co., 1976), 185.

> of slavery.... Otherwise, you may say in your heart, "My power and the strength of my hand made me this wealth." But you shall remember the LORD your God, for it is He who is giving you power to make wealth, that He may confirm His covenant which He swore to your fathers, as it is this day (Deut. 8:11–14, 17–18).

It cannot be said more clearly or unequivocally. It is not by man's power or ingenuity that he possesses and enjoys the outward blessings of this life, including all the wealth that many times goes with them. "You shall remember the LORD your God, for it is HE who is giving you power to make wealth." His providence causes you to eat and be satisfied. He enabled you to build beautiful houses and live in them. He multiplied your flocks and herds. He made your silver and gold increase. If you forget that and begin congratulating yourself, then you will return to slavery. But if you remember it, God will graciously and generously "confirm His covenant" with you and cause you to receive the best of His blessings on everything that is important to you all your life. Therefore, fear God, work hard in your calling, and in recognition of your dependence on His gifts, constantly pray "give us this day our daily bread."

We Are Prone to Desire, Get and Use Them Unlawfully

> For from the least of them even to the greatest of them,
> Every one is greedy for gain ("given to covetousness" KJV)
> And from the prophet even to the priest
> Every one deals falsely (Jer. 6:13).

God's severe treatment of His covenant people in the Old Testament ought not to seem strange or overbearing to us, for contempt for God, along with every other kind of evil, permeated every level and every rank of the entire national community. Everyone from the most powerful to the most disadvantaged "covet covetousness," are addicted to coveting and "greedy for gain." Even the prophets and priests were so addicted to coveting material possession that "everyone deals falsely" to get what they want. Were it not for the grace of God all of us would be dominated by the evil *desire* to obtain material wealth and power and we would seek to obtain those things by whatever way accomplished our purposes regardless of its morality or immorality.

> A merchant, in whose hands are false balances,
> He loves to oppress (Hos. 12:7).

Some people will stop at nothing, and be however deceitful they need to be, to exert oppressive power and control over other people, because they love to oppress others. They love the sense of power and they love the advantage over them that enables them to profit from them and so satisfy their hunger for wealth and power. Whatever outward blessings of life they may *have*, they *get* them unlawfully, *i.e.*, in total disregard to justice and compassion.

> You ask and do not receive, because you ask with wrong motives, so that you may spend it on your pleasures (James 4:3).

James earlier informed his readers that they often lack things they need to live simply because in an attitude of self-sufficiency they fail to ask God to give them what they need (4:2). But now he is warning them by explaining that the reason they ask for what they need from God and still do not receive those things is precisely because they have ungodly motives and they would *use* those blessings in an ungodly manner: "because you ask with wrong motives, so that you may spend it on your own pleasures."

> Their requests were legitimate, but the reason for making them was illegitimate. They wanted only to satisfy their own cravings, pamper their own passions. God's glory, God's service, consideration for other people—none of these things entered into their thinking. Such prayers are an insult to God.[171]

171. Curtis Vaughan, *James: A Study Guide* (Grand Rapids, MI: Zondervan Publishing House, 1969), 85.

The Specific Requests of the Fourth Petition

We Pray for Ourselves and Others, That Both They and We...Enjoy a Competent Portion of All the Outward Blessings of This Life.

> Here is what I have seen to be good and fitting: to eat, to drink and enjoy oneself in all one's labor in which he toils under the sun during the few years of his life which God has given him; for this is his reward. Furthermore, as for every man to whom God has given riches and wealth, He has also empowered him to eat from them and to receive his reward and rejoice in his labor; this is the gift of God. For he will not often consider the years of his life, because God keeps him occupied with the gladness of his heart (Eccl. 5:18–20).

In the Fourth Petition we are asking God not simply to give us those material things we need to exist in this world, but, more importantly, we are asking Him to enable us to *enjoy a competent portion* of the material, physical and social blessings of life on earth. No Neoplatonist can consistently make this prayer, for he believes that material, "worldly" things are base and lowly, and that only the spiritual and heavenly are good and wholesome. He believes that to be a good Christian, one must deny and suppress physical desires, eschew material wealth and disassociate himself from social, political and profit-making concerns, spending all his time thinking about and preparing himself for dying and going to Heaven. The Neoplatonist realizes that he does need a measure of material provisions to survive physically in this life, and so he asks for them, but the thought that we are to ask God to help us ENJOY the material blessings and earthly pleasures of this life is repugnant to him.

And yet that is what Ecclesiastes 5:18–20 teaches us. Whatever measure of material blessings and earthly pleasures God in His wisdom sees fit to give us in this life, with that we will be truly grateful and content, for we know we deserve nothing good from Him. And we are to pray that God would give us the ability and freedom to *enjoy* life in the enjoyment of the material blessings and earthly pleasures He gives us.

Notice how Ecclesiastes 5:18–20 makes this point. First, it says that it is "good and fitting," (or "beautiful") to take pleasure in eating and drinking and to "enjoy oneself in all one's labor." Second, although life is short, life is to be received as a gracious gift from God. Third, if one has the privilege of possessing "riches and wealth," he must recognize gratefully that they are all gifts of God to him. Fourth, God Himself has "empowered" the hard-working, grateful man to benefit from his vocation, and to "rejoice in his labor; this is the gift of God." The point here is not that wealth itself is a gift of God, which it is, but rather that the gift of God is the ability to benefit from and delight in the benefits of his vocation and hard work. And fifth, because God so fills his life "with the gladness of his heart" in his enjoyment of the material and social, as well as spiritual blessings of this life, the hard-working, contented person does "not often consider the years of his life," that they are brief and passing swiftly. "God keeps him occupied with the gladness of his heart!" If a person develops an enjoyable and grateful use of the gifts of this life which God gives him, "God would let the resultant joy drive out the anxious thoughts that might otherwise fill the heart, and so life would pass swiftly, and the passing days would scarcely be remembered."[172] Or as Delitzsch has put it: "Over this enjoyment he forgets the frailty and the darkened side of this life.... Such an one, permitted by God to enjoy this happiness of life, is thereby prevented from tormenting himself by reflections regarding its transitoriness."[173]

172. H. C. Leupold, *Exposition of Ecclesiastes* (The Wartburg Press, 1957; reprint Grand Rapids, MI: Baker Book House, 1968), 132.

173. Franz Delitzsch, *Commentary on the Song of Songs and Ecclesiastes*, trans. by Rev. M. G. Easton (Grand Rapids, MI: William B. Eerdmans Publishing Co., 1970), 303.

We Pray for Ourselves and Others, That Both They and We…Have The Outward Blessings of This Life Blessed Unto Us in Our Holy and Comfortable Use of Them.

> But the Spirit explicitly says that in later times some will fall away from the faith, paying attention to deceitful spirits and doctrines of demons, by means of the hypocrisy of liars seared in their own conscience as with a branding iron, men who forbid marriage and advocate abstaining from foods, which God has created to be gratefully shared in by those who believe and know the truth. For everything created by God is good, and nothing is to be rejected, if it is received with gratitude: for it is sanctified by means of the word of God and prayer (1 Tim. 4:1–5).

Material possessions, physical appetites, vocational success, loving human relationships, and earthly pleasures are all blessings from God graciously bestowed upon His people in Christ. But false teachers in Paul's day, and in ours, try to confuse Christians about this wonderful truth and make them feel guilty about enjoying, or even possessing these earthly pleasures. These teachers have apostatized from the Faith. These hypocrites are instigated by the devil, and their consciences are seared as with a red-hot iron. And what exactly are these "doctrines of demons" which they try to impose upon the consciences of weak and unsuspecting Christians? They argue that because worship and godliness are defined by external observances, rituals and prohibitions, and therefore the physical and material are base and lowly distractions from the spiritual, which alone are good and holy, it must follow that physical desires and enjoyments are to be suppressed. Earthly life is to be lived in severe austerity, for all that matters is the spiritual life and preparation for the heavenly life, they say. Therefore, these apostates, for those reasons, "forbid marriage and advocate abstaining from foods," *e.g.*, wine. The suppression of the sexual drives, the exaltation of celibacy over the married state, and the prohibition of certain foods on certain days and of feasting and celebrations of the earthly joys and relations of this life enable a person to live on a higher plane of holiness and godliness. This, says Paul under the inspiration of the Holy Spirit, is a "doctrine of demons" that reveals apostasy.

Paul refutes such false doctrine because it is insulting to God, destructive of true worship and detrimental to the daily life of the believer in Jesus. His argument is powerful.

First, God created earthly joys and relations "to be gratefully shared in by those who believe and know the truth." God created the blessings of this life to be enjoyed by those who believe in Jesus and who understand the revealed truth of God regarding creation and redemption. These blessings yield "inconceivable joy to all the godly, when they know that all the kinds of food which they eat are put into their hands by the Lord, so that the use of them is pure and lawful. What insolence is it in men to take away what God bestows!"[174]

It should be observed that, to be rightly enjoyed, the blessings of this life must be "gratefully shared in" so that "it is a beastly way of eating, when we sit down at table without any prayer, and, when we have eaten to the full, depart in utter forgetfulness of God."[175] And that they were created by God to be enjoyed "by those who believe and know the truth."

> Properly speaking, God has appointed to His children alone the whole world and all that is in the world. For this reason, they are called the heirs of the world.... And since all things are subject to Christ, we are fully restored by His mediation [as lords of the earth], and that through faith; and therefore all that unbelievers enjoy may be regarded as the property of others, which they rob or steal.... By ingrafting us into His Son, [God] constitutes us anew to be lords of the world, that we may lawfully use as our own all the wealth with which he supplies us.[176]

174. John Calvin, *Commentaries on the Epistles to Timothy, Titus and Philemon*, trans. by Rev. William Pringle (Edinburgh: Calvin Translation Society, 1843; reprint Grand Rapids, MI: Baker Book House, 1979), 103.

175. Calvin, *Commentaries on the Epistles to Timothy, Titus, and Philemon*, 105.

176. Calvin, *Commentaries on the Epistles to Timothy, Titus, and Philemon*, 103–105.

Second, "everything created by God is good, and nothing is to be rejected, if it is received with gratitude." This is an obvious allusion to God's assessment of His universe and everything in it, immediately upon its creation: "And God saw all that He had made, and behold, it was very good" (Gen. 1:31). That settles it. Every worldview that includes the idea that the material, physical world is base and low and in conflict with the spiritual and heavenly, which are good and holy, is a contradiction of God's assessment and therefore is indeed a "doctrine of demons." Because earthly joys and relations created by God are good, none of them is to be rejected as evil in and of themselves. They are all to be enjoyed to the glory of God and in thankfulness to Him for His kind and gracious earthly gifts.

Third, Paul makes the point that, if these earthly blessings are to be properly enjoyed, they must be "sanctified by means of the word of God and prayer." Three points are being made here. (1) God has consecrated ("sanctified") the good things of creation for the use and enjoyment of His people in Christ, whom He has made to be lords and masters of the earth in Christ and under His rule. We are not worthy to enjoy one morsel of this world's bread because of our sin, and we are such sinners that we should be banished from this earth. But by God's grace in Christ we are heirs of the world. Therefore, we learn here that

> meats serve to the salvation of our souls, and though their proper use be to maintain our bodies in this world, yet God leads us further, and fully assures us of His love He bears us, and that He takes us for His children, and so our salvation is confirmed by this temporal nourishment, which He gives us, and we receive of Him.[177]

This means that "for the Christian, eating and drinking are no secular activities (1 Cor. 10:31). While, before partaking of food, *he* utters his petition and thanksgiving, *God* at the same time pronounces his word of blessing (cf. Deut. 8:3)."[178] (2) God consecrates

177. John Calvin, *Sermons on Epistles of Timothy and Titus* (London: 1579; reprint Edinburgh: The Banner of Truth Trust, 1983), 369. Language modernized.

178. William Hendriksen, *Exposition of the Pastoral Epistles* (Grand Rapids,

these blessings to us "by means of the word of God." How? By His promises to us that He made the earth and all the good things in it not merely for Himself, for He had no need of it, but for our benefit and enjoyment. "True it is that His goodness reaches even to the wild beasts, even to asses, to horses and to dogs, but yet the beasts themselves are made for man."[179] But if this word is to be the means by which we enjoy God's blessings, we must embrace that Word by faith. (3) God consecrates these blessings to us "by means of... prayer." Faith in the Word of God and prayer cannot be separated. It is a contradiction for us to be persuaded that by His Word God will nourish and sustain us and then not to go to Him to ask Him for that nourishment and sustenance. "If we will pray to God aright, we must be instructed in His Word."[180]

We Pray That We Might be Blessed With Contentment in a Competent Portion of All the Outward Blessings of This Life that God Chooses to Give Us.

> But godliness actually is a means of great gain, when accompanied by contentment. For we have brought nothing into the world, so we cannot take anything out of it either. And if we have food and covering, with these we shall be content (1 Tim. 6:6–8).

These words of the Apostle Paul come in a wider context of 1 Timothy 6:6-12, the concern of which is to set forth the value of contentment (6:6–8), and the evil of covetousness (6:9–12). In saying that "godliness actually is a means of great gain," he is not saying that we should try hard to be godly because, if we do, we will benefit materially and financially. That is a low and sinful attitude. But he is saying that godliness is a means of great gain in the blessings of this life—material and otherwise—if, and only if, it is "accompanied with con-

---

MI: Baker Book House [1957] 1979), 148.

179. Calvin, *Sermons on Epistles of Timothy and Titus*, 369. Language modernized.

180. Calvin, *Sermons on Epistles of Timothy and Titus*, 373. Language modernized.

tentment," "that is, godliness cultivated for its own sake, not as a stepping-stone to wealth or worldly consideration."[181]

Verse seven gives us a reason for the statement in verse six we have just considered:

> the real good for man lies in what he is as a rational and moral being, not in the outward means and possessions he may gather into his lot: *for we brought nothing into the world, because neither are we able to take anything out of it*...the apostle not merely says that we both enter and leave the world in a state of destitution as to worldly goods, but that the one is ordered with a certain respect to the other: we brought nothing with us of earthly treasure when we were ushered into life here, because neither could we take aught with us when we leave it; thus have a lesson embodied in our very birth, in order that we might keep in view the solemn exemplification it was to find at the hour of death. If we do so, we shall live in the habitual recollection that all we can accumulate of the things of earth during our sojourn in it, is adventitious merely—of the nature of a temporary appendage—and not, therefore, for a moment to be compared with the state of the soul itself in reference to God and righteousness. Here, and here alone, lie the essential elements of our well-being.[182]

Then, in verse eight we are informed that "if we have food and covering, with these we shall be content." If we have these two essentials for physical life, we have all the material things we need to live contentedly in this present life.

But what is contentment? It is an inner attitude in which we rest satisfied with the will of God regarding what measure He in His infinite wisdom and goodness has seen fit to give us of material blessings and earthly pleasures. We submissively receive whatever God gives without murmuring or complaining. We thankfully en-

---

181. Patrick Fairbairn, *Commentary on the Pastoral Epistles:* (T & T Clark, 1874; reprint Grand Rapids, MI: Zondervan Publishing House, 1956), 235.

182. Fairbairn, *Commentary on the Pastoral Epistles: I & II Timothy and Titus*, 236–37.

joy all of God's gifts to us and we leave the future in the hands of our loving and wise God. There is no stoicism in Christian contentment, nor bluntness of emotion or desire.

We may learn more about the true nature of Christian contentment by considering what it is not.

- Contentment is not envy. It never grows sick when the success of others is greater than our own.
- Contentment is not worry about our life in this world. It casts all its cares upon the Lord, knowing that He cares for us (1 Pet. 5:7).
- Contentment is not covetousness. The New Testament has two words for covetousness: one literally means "the love of money," and the other means "a desire for more," or "greed." As one has said, "if a man is not content in that state he is in, he will not be content in any state he would be in."[183]
- Contentment is not pride. "Humility is the mother of contentment.... They that deserve nothing should be content with any thing."[184]
- Contentment is not murmuring and complaining against God's providence, rather it "dwells with her sisters gratitude, submission, resignation."[185]
- Contentment is not distrust of God or despondence regarding how He has ordered your circumstances by His providence.

We Pray That We Would Be Kept From All Things That Are Contrary to Our Temporal Support and Comfort.

Two things I asked of Thee,
Do not refuse me before I die:
Keep deception and lies from me,

183. Quoted in Plumer, *Vital Godliness*, 458.
184. Quoted in Plumer, *Vital Godliness*, 459.
185. Plumer, *Vital Godliness*, 460.

> Give me neither poverty nor riches,
> Feed me with the food that is my portion,
> Lest I be full and deny Thee and say,
> "Who is the LORD?"
> Or lest I be in want and steal,
> And profane the name of my God (Prov. 30:7–9).

This prayer is an honest expression of the holy desires of Agur's heart. He beseeches God to deliver him from everything and anything that is not only *contrary to our temporal support and comfort,* but from everything and anything that "deadens the heart and eclipses the glory of the Savior." He asks God to deliver him from anything that would woo his heart from Christ as its chief love and delight. It is as if he said: "Give me, O Lord, what You think I need, nothing more and nothing less. Keep me from any circumstance of life that would be a temptation for me."

We must be willing to leave the assignment of our daily provisions entirely with God. Both riches and poverty are from God (1 Kings 3:13; Deut. 15:11; Job 1:21). As Bishop Hall said, "Whithersoever God gives, I am both thankful and indifferent; so as, while I am rich in estate, I may be poor in spirit; and while I am poor in estate, I may be rich in grace."[186]

Agur does not trust his own heart. He knows himself and his sinful frailty. He fears that if God made him rich, he would be arrogant, and if God made him poor, he would murmur at God's providence, and so he prays that God would give him just what he needs to live in this world for Him. He does not say, "lest I be rich and cumbered with care," or "lest I be poor and cumbered with work," but "lest I be rich *and sin,*" and "lest I be poor *and sin.*" "Sin is that which a good man is afraid of in every condition and under every event (Nehemiah 6:13)."[187]

---

186. Quoted in Charles Bridges, *An Exposition of Proverbs* (Marshallton, DE: The National Foundation for Christian Education, n.d.), 598.

187. Matthew Henry, *Matthew Henry's Commentary on the Whole Bible,* 6 vols. (Peabody, MA: Hendrickson Publishers, [1991] 1992), 3:795.

The Manner in Which the Fourth Petition Must be Made to God

Waiting Upon the Providence of God from Day to Day in the Use of Lawful Means

> Let him who steals steal no longer; but rather let him labor, performing with his own hands what is good, in order that he may have something to share with him who has need (Eph. 4:28).

Trusting God's providence to give us "our daily bread" does not justify laziness, passivity and inactivity on our part, as if all we have to do is sit and wait for God to drop whatever blessings we need in our laps. Such an attitude is totally contrary to the Word of God. As we wait patiently and trustingly for God to provide for us in His own time as He sees fit, we are to persevere in well-doing. As we cast all our cares upon Him, we are to take care that we are doing what He has commanded us to do in working to provide for ourselves and our families, for the Bible says that he who does not provide for his household is worse than an infidel: "But if any one does not provide for his own, and especially for those of his household, he has denied the faith, and is worse than an unbeliever" (1 Tim. 5:8).

In fact, living in idleness without labor in a vocation, when one is able, as a parasite on others, is viewed by God as theft, and the Bible's exhortation is clear: "If anyone will not work, neither let him eat" (2 Thess. 3:10). Therefore, if we do not want to be condemned as thieves by God, we must labor in a vocation, "performing with our own hands, what is good," not only because God created us in His image to work as He works, but also "in order that (we) might have something to share with him who has need." So then, as God provides us with "our daily bread" by using our efforts at providing for ourselves and our families in His strength, He also uses our labor and the benefits of our labor to provide the "daily bread" of those who are in need unable to provide for themselves.

> For even when we were with you, we used to give you this order: If anyone will not work, neither let him eat. For we hear that some among you are leading an undisciplined life, doing no work at all, but acting like busybodies. Now such persons we command and exhort in the Lord Jesus Christ to work in quiet fashion and eat their own bread (2 Thess. 3:10–12).

Paul repeatedly exhorted the Thessalonians to follow his own example and to work hard in their callings. He told them time and again that a person who *can* work, but deliberately and habitually *refuses* to work, should not be allowed to eat.[188]

In verse eleven Paul directs his comments to a specific situation in the Thessalonian church. He has heard that some in the church are "leading an undisciplined life, doing no work at all, but acting like busybodies." "These people were not simply idle, they were meddling in the affairs of others."[189] We can deduce the reason for this from the theme and purpose of 1 and 2 Thessalonians. They were acting like parasites on others and trying to get others to share their eschatology that because the second coming of Christ would happen any moment, there is no use in working.

Therefore, in verse twelve, Paul directly exhorts the "busybodies," although tactfully because he wants to secure repentance from them and win them back into the fellowship of the church.[190] He urges them "in the Lord Jesus Christ to work in quiet fashion and eat their own bread." Their view of the any-moment return of Christ had made them excitable and restless which led to their idle waiting for it to happen. And so Paul "directs them to that calmness of dis-

---

188. The words "will not work" in 2 Thessalonians 3:10 is the present continuous tense denoting habitual attitude. The phrase "neither let him eat" is not an indicative statement of fact, it is an imperative, and should not be translated "neither will he eat."

189. Leon Morris, *The New International Commentary on the New Testament: The First and Second Epistles to the Thessalonians* (Grand Rapids, MI: William B. Eerdmans Publishing Co., 1959), 256.

190. They may have been excommunicated from the church due to the sin mentioned. He speaks of them as people "among you" in verse 11, rather than as people "of you."

position which ought to characterize those whose trust is in Christ. They are to earn their living."[191]

Receive The Outward Blessings of This Life as His Free Gift, and As His Fatherly Wisdom Shall Seem Best.

> The rich and the poor have a common bond, the LORD is the Maker of them all (Prov. 22:2).

Prosperity and poverty are both sent by God to accomplish His purposes. Those who prosper have no grounds for pride and self-confidence. Those who are in financial stress have no grounds for despair, or to be envious, for their lives and condition are in God's hands. Therefore, we must be content with God's providence and perfect will, for He does all things well (Rom. 8:28; Phil. 4:11–13). Our Father in Heaven knows what is best for us.

> For this reason I say to you, do not be anxious for your life, as to what you shall eat, or what you shall drink; nor for your body, as to what you shall put on. Is not life more than food, and the body than clothing? Look at the birds of the air, that they do not sow, neither do they reap, nor gather into barns; and yet your heavenly Father feeds them. Are you not worth much more than they? And which of you by being anxious can add a single cubit to his life's span? And why are you anxious about clothing? Observe how the lilies of the field grow; they do not toil neither do they spin, yet I say to you that even Solomon in all his glory did not clothe himself like one of these. But if God so arrays the grass of the field, which is alive today and tomorrow is thrown into the furnace, will He not much more do so for you, O men of little faith? Do not be anxious then, saying, "What shall we eat?" or "What shall we drink?" or "With what shall we clothe ourselves?" For all these things the Gentiles eagerly seek; for your heavenly Father knows that you need all these things. But seek first His

191. Morris, *The First and Second Epistles to the Thessalonians*, 256.

> kingdom, and His righteousness; and all these things shall be added to you (Matt. 6:25–33).

This beloved section of Jesus' Sermon on the Mount is self-explanatory. It cannot be made any clearer or more forceful. The believer in Jesus is not to worry about any aspect of his life in this world, not his health, his strength, his success, his daily bread, nor what is going to happen to him. Rather than being consumed with anxieties about food, drink and clothing, the Christian, trusting God for everything, is to be consumed with seeking above all else God's kingdom and God's righteousness, knowing that as we do, everything else we need will be provided for us.

As Martyn Lloyd-Jones said: "If I am guilty of being worried and anxious about these matters of food and drink and clothing, and about my life in this world, and certain things which I lack—if these dominate me and my life, then I am really living and behaving as a heathen."[192] Rather, the Christian must live in faith, seeking earnestly and intensely and constantly the kingdom and righteousness of God, giving that goal absolute priority over everything else, assured that as he faithfully pursues that goal, His Father in heaven will give to him whatever he needs to live out his life in this world.

> Put God, His glory and the coming of His kingdom, and your relationship to Him, your nearness to Him and your holiness in the central position, and you have the pledge word of God Himself through the lips of His Son, that all these other things, as they are necessary for your well-being in this life and world, shall be added unto you.... Be unlike the heathen; remember that God knows all about you as your Father, and is watching over you. Therefore seek to be more like Him and to live your life nearer to Him.... If you want to seek anything, if you want to be anxious about anything, be anxious about your spiritual condition, your nearness to God and your relationship to Him. If you put that first, worry will go; that is the result. This great concern about your relationship

192. Lloyd-Jones, *Studies in the Sermon on the Mount,* 2:136.

to God will drive out every lesser concern about food and clothing.[193]

The Fifth Petition of the Lord's Prayer

Q. 194: What do we pray for in the fifth petition?

A.: In the fifth petition, (which is, *Forgive us our debts, as we forgive our debtors*), acknowledging, that we and all others are guilty both of original and actual sin, and thereby become debtors to the justice of God; and that neither we, nor any other creature, can make the least satisfaction for that debt: we pray for ourselves and others, that God of his free grace would, through the obedience and satisfaction of Christ, apprehended and applied by faith, acquit us both from the guilt and punishment of sin, accept us in the Beloved; continue his favour and grace to us, pardon our daily failings, and fill us with peace and joy, in giving us daily more and more assurance of forgiveness; which we are the rather emboldened to ask, and encouraged to expect, when we have this testimony in ourselves, that we from the heart forgive others their offences.

John Calvin wrote: "To sum up: the beginning, and even the preparation, of proper prayer is the plea for pardon with a humble and sincere confession of guilt."[194]

---

193. Lloyd-Jones, *Studies in the Sermon on the Mount*, 2:145.
194. Calvin, *Institutes of the Christian Religion*, 2:860.

The Position of the Fifth Petition in the Lord's Prayer

This Fifth Petition occupies a perfect position in the Lord's Prayer.

> If we have understood the real meaning and implications of all the preceding petitions, the very exercise of sending them to the throne of grace must have awakened within us a deep sense of our imperfections and our sins, and therefore must have deepened our feeling of need for the forgiveness of our sinful condition and of our actual transgressions.
>
> This was true emphatically when we prayed the first three petitions of the Lord's Prayer.... As we were praying, we felt deeply in our hearts that often we do seek things quite different from those we professed to seek in the first three petitions.., and we realized that there is but a small beginning of the new obedience within us, and that all the rest is still sinful....
>
> But this does not only apply to the first three petitions. Also while we stammered the prayer for bread, we felt our lack of faith and confidence, our sinful anxiety for the morrow, as well as our lusting after the things of this present world. We felt indeed that if our Father in heaven would literally hear our prayer and give us nothing but bread for this day, we would not be content, but rather be filled with anxiety.
>
> And therefore, if we have uttered these petitions in the sanctuary before the face of God in spirit and in truth, we should be quite ready now to pray: "And forgive us our debts." Do not remember, our Father in heaven, even the sins that characterized and marred my prayer before Thy face.[195]

It is also important to note that the petition for forgiveness follows the petition for daily bread. These two petitions are connected because we cannot expect God to give us the good things of this life, which have been forfeited by us because of our sins, unless He

195. Hoeksema, *The Triple Knowledge*, 583–84.

is pleased to forgive those sins that provoke Him to withhold His blessings from us.

> Nor can we take comfort in any outward blessings, while our consciences are burdened with a sense of the guilt of sin, and we have nothing to expect, as the consequence of it, but to be separated from his presence. Hence, we are taught to pray that God would "forgive us our sins."[196]

The fact that the petition for forgiveness is followed by the petition for grace against temptation and deliverance from evil. The second will always follow the first because justification must needs precede sanctification; and sanctification will always follow justification.

> We must have the forgiveness of sins before we can even have the right to be delivered from the bondage of sin and from the dominion of the evil one. On the other hand, even while we pray for forgiveness, we already have in mind the petition for deliverance from sin that immediately follows. We could not possibly pray sincerely for remission of our transgressions unless there were in our hearts the sincere longing for complete deliverance from all evil and for spiritual perfection.[197]

John Calvin explains the relation of this Fifth Petition with the Sixth Petition:

> With this and the following petition, Christ briefly embraces all that makes for the heavenly life, as the spiritual covenant that God has made for the salvation of his church rests on these two members alone: "I shall write My laws upon their hearts," and, "I shall be merciful toward their iniquity," (Jer. 31:33 cf. 33:8). Here Christ begins with forgiveness of sins, then presently adds the second grace: that God protect us by

196. Ridgeley, *Commentary on the Larger Catechism*, 2:633.
197. Hoeksema, *The Triple Knowledge*, 3:584.

> the power of his Spirit and sustain us by his aid so we may stand unvanquished against all temptations.[198]

The Language of the Fifth Petition

The Fifth Petition begins with the conjunction, "and." This should not be overlooked. It teaches us that we cannot enjoy *a competent portion of the good things of this life*, unless our sins are forgiven and we are accepted with God through Jesus Christ.

"Forgive" is literally "dismiss" or "send away" or "remit." "Debts" means "obligations" before God. It speaks of what we owe Him. Luke uses the word "sins." Our sins make us indebted to God, for they deserve eternal punishment from His hand.

> A sin is a legal offense before God, and a debt is a legal debt to a man. The cancellation of either sin or debt is a legal fact. To *forgive* is thus not an antinomian fact but a legal and moral one. The word *apheimi* [remit] in classical Greek was used, among other ways, to describe a divorce, a canceling of a marriage, and, *to release from a legal bond....* Restitution is basic to forgiveness; the debt is canceled because in some real and specific way amends have been made.[199]

"Forgive" is in the aorist tense denoting definite, final remission. What sinners need is complete and definitive remission of all their debts with God so as to live before Him, which includes the removal of the due punishment and the assurance of divine favor. This prayer for forgiveness is

> a very bold and amazing request. It means that we implore God to dismiss our debts, to cancel them.... And this implies, in the first place, that He dismisses them from His own heart and mind, so that He will never recall them again, never make mention of them any more, that He completely obliterates them from His book of remembrance.... It means...that

198. Calvin, *Institutes of the Christian Religion*, 2:910.
199. Rushdoony, *Systematic Theology*, 2:1216, 1217.

> God will never hold it against us that we have always missed the mark.[200]

"As" (ωσ) in the phrase, "as we forgive our debtors," is not causal, that is, it does not give the reason or basis for God's forgiveness of us, and so the limiting clause may not be translated, "because we forgive our debtors." Rather the Greek word for "as" denotes a correlative or complementary relationship. In other words, God gives us the grace of forgiveness, not because we forgive others, but as we forgive others. "Our forgiving others is the evidence that God's grace has really wrought faith in us and made us his children."[201]

The record of the Lord's Prayer in Matthew 6:12 reads: "Forgive us our debts." We are praying that God would totally liquidate our debt to Him, *i.e.*, the eternal punishment we owe Him because we have not loved Him with all our hearts. In Luke 11:4 we read: "And forgive us our sins." The word for sin means to miss the mark. The important connection between these two accounts to notice is that both "debts" and "sins" are plural nouns. "The plural denotes that we have many sins, and besides, all kinds of sins, sins of our whole being, of our entire nature and life."[202]

The identity of the pronoun "us" is crucial to the correct interpretation of this text. In other words, who is the person who can pray, "And forgive us our debts, as we forgive our debtors"? He or she is the person who knows God as "our Father in heaven." And the only person who has the privilege of calling God, Father, are those who are believers in Jesus Christ: "But as many as received Him, to them He gave the right to become children of God, even to those who believe in His name" (John 1:12). It is for this reason that the Lord's Prayer has been called "the Children's Prayer," because it is not a prayer for everybody, but only for those who have become God's children through faith in Christ. "It is the relationship of the child to the Father, and the moment we realize we have offended, or

200. Hoeksema, *The Triple Knowledge*, 3:589.
201. Lenski, *The Interpretation of St. Matthew's Gospel*, 270.
202. Hoeksema, *The Triple Knowledge*, 3:591.

grieved or sinned against the Father, we confess it and ask to be forgiven, and we are sure that we are forgiven."[203]

The Reasons for the Fifth Petition

We and Others Are Guilty Both of Original and Actual Sin

The New Testament is unequivocal regarding the sinful condition of all human beings: we are sinners, having disregarded and transgressed God's Law, and are therefore guilty before Him and under His condemnation. "What then? Are we better than they? Not at all; for we have already charged that both Jews and Greeks are all under sin" (Rom. 3:9). The Law of God condemns all human beings for their infractions of it, "that every mouth may be closed, and all the world may become accountable to God" (Rom. 3:19). To be "under sin" is to be under the tyranny of sin, and the pervasiveness of the corruption of sin is demonstrated in the series of indictments set forth in Romans 3:10–18, which cover the whole range of human character and activity proving that from whatever angle human beings may be viewed, the verdict of the Bible is of universal and total depravity. Furthermore, the guilt which each human being bears results from *"original sin," i.e.*, the guilt we have inherited from the original sin of Adam, who acted as our covenant representative (Rom. 5:18), and from the *"actual sins"* which human beings commit every day (Rom. 3:23; 6:23). Therefore, we are in need of forgiveness of sin, and should pray the Fifth Petition of the Lord's Prayer continually, because our sins alienate us from God: "Your iniquities have made a separation between you and your God, and your sins have hid His face from you, so that He does not hear" (Isa. 59:2).

We and Others Are Debtors to the Justice of God

Because of our guiltiness before God for disregarding and transgressing His Law, all human beings are *debtors to the justice of God.* God's justice demands that all sin be punished: "the wages of sin is death" (Rom. 6:23). Why? God's justice is *"that perfection of*

203. Lloyd-Jones, *Studies in the Sermon on the Mount*, 2:73.

God by which He maintains Himself over against every violation of His holiness, and shows in every respect that He is the Holy One.... Divine justice is originally and necessarily obliged to punish evil... Luke 17:10; 1 Cor. 4:7; Job 41:11."[204]

Sin is a real "debt." It is an offense and insult to the holiness of God. It is a violation of His holy Law, making us deserving of everlasting punishment. We owe God the "debt" of complete obedience to God's Law which God demands of all intelligent creatures. We failed in our obedience to Him, therefore God's Law denounces us and threatens us with punishment. Thus, we owe God the "debt" of eternal punishment.

Therefore, we should pray the Fifth Petition of the Lord's Prayer continually, because, as we shall see, we cannot pay the debt we owe God. If it is not fully paid, we will perish eternally in our sins, because "the wrath of God is revealed from heaven against all ungodliness and unrighteousness of men" (Rom. 1:18). And without forgiveness of sin by God, each day of our lives we are "storing up wrath [for ourselves] in the day of wrath and revelation of the righteous judgment of God, who will render to every man according to his deeds" (Rom. 2:5–6).

Neither We Nor Any Other Creature Can Make the Least Satisfaction for That Debt

Human beings can not in any way, in and of themselves, *make the least satisfaction* of God's justice for their *debt* to God. Because the value of the person sinned against determines the heinousness of the crime, and because the heinousness of the crime determines the severity of punishment, sin against the infinitely holy God is infinitely heinous deserving of infinite punishment (Lev. 24:20). We have inexcusably lost any ability to obey God perfectly in this life, and any punishment we would endure, would require eternity to pay; therefore, we can not *make the least satisfaction for that debt* our sin has incurred: "If Thou, LORD, shouldst mark iniquities, O Lord, who could stand?" (Ps. 130:3).

204. Louis Berkhof, *Systematic Theology* (Grand Rapids, MI: William B. Eerdmans Publishing Co., [1932] 1938), 74-75.

> If the sinner makes an overture to pay the debt, he must either yield sinless obedience, which is impossible from the nature of the thing, or bear the stroke of justice, and suffer the punishment due to him; and if he is content to do the latter, he knows now that it is to fall into the hands of the living God, or to be plunged into an abyss of endless misery. If he think that he shall be secure by fleeing from justice, he will find every attempt to flee from it vain; for God is omnipresent, and "there is no darkness nor shadow of death, where the workers of iniquity may hide themselves" [Job 34:22]. Nothing therefore remains but that he make supplication to his Judge, that he would pass by the crimes he has committed, without demanding satisfaction. But to do this is to desire that he would act contrary to the holiness of his nature; which would be such a blemish on his perfections, that he is obliged to reject the suit, or else must cease to be God. What would his pardoning crime without satisfaction be, but to relinquish his throne, deny his sovereignty, and act contrary to his own Law, which is the rule of his government? … But is there no intercessor who will plead the sinner's cause, or appear for him in the court of heaven? There can be no such intercessor but one who is able to make an atonement, and thereby secure the glory of divine justice, by having the debt transferred or placed to his account, and giving a full satisfaction for it. But this work belongs to none but our Lord Jesus Christ, who has obtained redemption and forgiveness through his blood. Now, no one can take encouragement from what He has done but he who addresses himself to God by faith.[205]

We are as the debtor in Jesus' parable, who was unable to settle his account with his king for ten thousand talents: "Since he did not have the means to repay, his lord commanded him to be sold, along with his wife and children and all that he had, and repayment to be made" (Matt. 18:24). Therefore, our only hope is that God will graciously grant us full and free forgiveness, as the king in the parable did to his unworthy debtor: "And the lord of that slave felt compassion and released him and forgave him the debt" (Matt. 18:27). And, should God choose to hear

205. Ridgeley, *Commentary on the Larger Catechism*, 2:634.

our prayer and forgive us, may we never be as the ungrateful debtor and refuse to forgive those who sin against us, for if we show such ingratitude, our Lord will do to us as the king did to his unmerciful debtor: "And his lord, moved with anger, handed him over to the torturers until he should repay all that was owed him" (Matt. 18:34).

> Beware, oh sinner, whoever you are, for God is just! Do not imagine that you will be able to satisfy God by praying, "O God, be merciful to me a sinner" or by doing your utmost to refrain from evil and to practice virtue. To imagine such is to be on the broad way to eternal destruction, and causes millions, who live under the ministry of the gospel, to perish.... The justice of God, which cannot be compromised to the least degree, of necessity demands the punishment of the sinner. God cannot deny Himself, and thus grace does not negate His justice. Grace is not incompatible with justice, but confirms it. This is the grace of God so highly exalted in His Word—that God, without finding anything in man, yes, contrary to his desert, gave His Son as a Surety. He transferred the sins of the elect from their account to His and by bearing the punishment justly due upon their sin, satisfied the justice of God on their behalf. This is grace, namely, that God offers Jesus as Surety in the gospel. It is grace when God grants faith to a sinner to receive Jesus and to entrust his soul to Jesus. It is grace when God converts a sinner, granting him spiritual life. It is grace when God permits a sinner to sensibly experience His favor. It is grace when God sanctifies a sinner, leading him in the way of holiness to salvation.[206]

The Point and Implication of the Fifth Petition

> The Christian lives through forgiveness. This is what justification by faith is all about. We could have no life or hope with God at all, had God's Son not borne the penalty of our sins so that we might go free. But Christians fall short still, and forgiveness is needed each day.... Christians must be

206. Brakel, *The Christian's Reasonable Service*, 1:129.

> willing to examine themselves and let others examine them for the detecting of day-to-day shortcomings.... The discipline of self-examination, though distasteful to our pride, is necessary because our holy Father in heaven will not turn a blind eye to his children's failings, as human parents so often (and so unwisely) do. So what he knows about our sins we need to know too, so that we may repent and ask pardon for whatever has given offense.[207]

The Basis and Prerequisites for a Prayer for Forgiveness

The Free Grace of God

> For all have sinned and come short of the glory of God, being justified as a gift by His grace through the redemption which is in Christ Jesus (Rom. 3:23–24).

Without the free and sovereign grace of God, there can be no forgiveness of sins. God was under no obligation to provide a way of salvation from sin for sinners. In perfect justice He could have sentenced us all to eternal perdition. But, He sovereignly and graciously chose to save a vast portion of the human race from all their sins through the redemptive work of Christ. That choice was of sheer, unmerited, undeserved and unearned grace. Our text says that, although "all have sinned and come short of the glory of God" nevertheless all believers in Jesus are "justified as a gift by His grace." This phrase, "as a gift" can also be translated "freely." The Greek word, δωρεαν, is also used in John 15:25, where Jesus says: "They hated Me *without a cause*." The phrase, "without a cause," is the Greek word, δωρεαν. The point is that there was (and is) nothing in Jesus that would justify their hatred of Him. So then, Romans 3:24 could also be translated: "justified without a cause by His grace." Nothing in the believer, either in his character, motives or behavior,

207. J. I. Packer, *I Want To Be A Christian* (Wheaton, IL: Tyndale House Publishers, Inc., [1977] 1983), 211, 213.

is the cause of his justification. Nothing in him makes him worthy or deserving of justification. Salvation is "by His grace" alone.

> The combination of the terms "freely" and "by his grace" has the effect of emphasizing the completely unmerited character of God's justifying act.... No element in Paul's doctrine of justification is more central than this—God's justifying act is not constrained to any extent or degree by anything we are or do which could be esteemed as predisposing God to this act.... This action on God's part derives its whole motivation, explanation, and determination from what God himself is and does in the exercise of free and sovereign grace.... It is the glory of the gospel of Christ that it is one of free grace.[208]

The Obedience and Sacrifice of Jesus Christ

> Being justified freely by His grace *through the redemption which is in Christ Jesus* (Rom. 3:24. Emphasis added).

The accent in this verse on the freeness and graciousness of God's grace does not eliminate the necessity for the means through which this free grace is operative in our lives. Once God chose to be gracious to sinners, the only way open to Him was through the redemptive mediation of His Son. This emphasizes: "(1) The costly price at which this justification was procured; (2) The price at which it was procured does not negative but enhances the gracious character of the act."[209] To "redeem" is to pay the ransom price necessary to deliver those held in bondage. And that ransom price is nothing less than "the ransom secured by Christ in the shedding of His blood and the giving of His life."[210] In other words, expiation is impossible without propitiation. Before forgiveness of sins can be forgiven, the penalty of sin must be paid; and Jesus did that by taking God's wrath, which our sin deserved, upon Himself bearing it away, for "without shedding of blood there is no forgiveness" (Heb. 9:22).

208. Murray, *The Epistle to the Romans*, 1:115.
209. Murray, *The Epistle to the Romans*, 1:115.
210. Murray, *The Epistle to the Romans*, 1:116.

However, our catechism points out that a prerequisite for forgiveness is not only the *sacrifice* of Christ on the cross, it also includes the *obedience* of Christ to God's Law. As we have repeatedly emphasized, the basis of our salvation is laid in the obedience and sacrifice of Christ, because of what God demands of any person who is to be forgiven and accepted into His family. First, He demands of them a life of perfect obedience to His Law. Second, He demands of them punishment for all sins committed against that Law.

These two demands place salvation entirely beyond the achievement of human beings. But, by God's grace, Christ has acted as the substitute for His people in both. He lived a life of perfect obedience to God's Law in our behalf and in our place: "For as through the one man's disobedience the many were made sinners, even so through the obedience of the One the many will be made righteous" (Rom. 5:19). And He sacrificed Himself as our substitute on the cross in our behalf and in our place, taking upon Himself the punishment our sins deserved: "He Himself bore our sins in His body on the cross" (2 Pet. 2:24).

The Necessity of Faith

> For I am not ashamed of the gospel, for it is the power of God for salvation to every one who believes, to the Jew first and also to the Greek. For in it the righteousness of God is revealed from faith to faith; as it is written... "But the righteous man shall live by faith" (Rom. 1:16–17).

This text could be said to be the theme of the epistle to the Romans. It teaches us that the saving power of God is operative through the gospel in the lives of all those who believe that gospel and place their faith in Jesus Christ. Paul is emphatic here that salvation has no reality, validity or meaning apart from faith in Christ. "Wherever there is faith, *there* the omnipotence of God is operative unto salvation. This is a law with no exceptions."[211]

211. Murray, *The Epistle to the Romans*, 1:28.

Our text repeatedly emphasizes the necessity of faith if salvation from sin is to be received: "to every one who believes...from faith to faith...by faith." In fact, this is a continuing emphasis throughout the entire epistle to the Romans. For example in Romans 3:22, Paul speaks of "the righteousness of God through faith in Jesus Christ unto all who believe."

> The apostle must have some purpose in what seems to us repetition. And the purpose is to accent the fact that not only does the righteousness of God bear savingly upon us *through faith* but also that it bears savingly upon *everyone* who believes. It is not superfluous to stress both. For the mere fact that the righteousness of God is through faith does not of itself as a proposition guarantee that faith always carries with it this effect.... "From faith" points to the truth that only "by faith" are we the beneficiaries of this righteousness... "To faith" underlines the truth that every believer is the beneficiary whatever his race or culture or the degree of his faith. Faith *always* carries with it the justifying righteousness of God.... The appeal to Habakkuk 2:4 is for the purpose of confirmation from the Old Testament.... The truth being established by the apostle is that the righteousness of God is by faith—the emphasis rests upon the way in which man becomes the beneficiary of this righteousness.[212]

The Petitions Implied in the Fifth Petition

What are we petitioning God to do for us when we ask Him to forgive us our debts?

That God Would Acquit Us Both From the Guilt and Punishment of Sin

> For all have sinned and fall short of the glory of God, being justified as a gift by His grace through the redemption which

212. Murray, *The Epistle to the Romans*, 1:32–33.

> is in Christ Jesus; whom God displayed as a propitiation in His blood through faith. This was to demonstrate His righteousness, because in the forbearance of God He passed over the sins previously committed; for the demonstration, I say, of His righteousness at the present time, that He might be just and the justifier of the one who has faith in Jesus (Rom. 3:23–26).

In asking God to forgive us of our sin-debts, we are expressing our earnest desire to Him that He

> would not lay those sins to our charge which we daily commit, or that he would not, as the psalmist says, "enter into judgment with us," and, in consequence, that he would not punish us as our iniquities deserve. We thus pray for the application of Christ's righteousness, as the ground and foundation of our claim to forgiveness.[213]

Therefore, believing in Christ alone for justification from God, the believer, in praying the Fifth Petition, is pleading with God, for Christ's sake, to continue to remove from him both the guilt of his sins and to deliver him from the punishment he deserves as a guilty sinner. He is praying for acquittal in the court of God because of the redemptive work of Christ in his behalf and in his place.

That God Would Accept Us in the Beloved

> He predestined us to adoption as sons through Jesus Christ to Himself, according to the good pleasure of His will, to the praise of the glory of His grace, which He freely bestowed on us in the Beloved. In Him we have redemption through His blood, the forgiveness of our trespasses, according to the riches of His grace (Eph. 1:5–7).

The believer prays for acquittal because what he wants is full acceptance with God "in the Beloved," *i.e.*, by virtue of His union and communion with the dearly beloved Son of God. He is pray-

213. Ridgeley, *Commentary on the Larger Catechism*, 2:636.

ing for the experience of what is promised in Romans 5:1–2 as a consequence of his justification by faith in Christ: "Therefore having been justified by faith, we have peace with God through our Lord Jesus Christ, through whom also we have obtained our introduction by faith into this grace in which we stand; and we exult in the hope of the glory of God." The believer craves constant communion with the living God, therefore he does not want any sin in his life to interrupt that communion. And so, he prays earnestly for forgiveness, and cleansing, and for the assurance that he has been accepted with God, that Christ does in fact love him, and that He has washed him from his sins in His own blood, *i.e.*, that he is *accepted in the Beloved.*

That God Would Continue His Favor and Grace to Us

> Grace and peace be multiplied to you in the knowledge of God and of Jesus our Lord (2 Pet. 1:2).

In praying the Fifth Petition, believers are praying that God would *continue His favor and grace to us.* But, we as believers know that because of God's grace we have been restored to His favor. So, why do we pray for the continuance of these blessings we know we already possess?

> I answer, that there are many privileges which God does or certainly will bestow upon his people, which they are, nevertheless, to pray for; otherwise they who are in a state of grace, are not to pray for perseverance in grace, because they are assured that it shall be maintained unto salvation, according to God's promise. Indeed, whatever promises are contained in the covenant of grace, a believer ought not, according to this objection, to pray that God would apply them to him, and so glorify his faithfulness in accomplishing them, since he is certainly persuaded that he will do it. Yet, all allow that we are to pray for the fulfillment to us of these promises. Hence, even if we have a full assurance that God has forgiven our sins, yet, as we daily contract guilt, we are daily to pray

> that he would not lay it to our charge, or deal with us as our iniquities deserve.[214]

The recipients of Peter's two epistles were believers in Jesus Christ, saved by God's grace (1 Pet. 1:1–2; 2 Pet. 1:1–3), and yet the apostle Peter could pray for them that "grace and peace be multiplied to you in the knowledge of God and of Jesus our Lord." The work of "grace" is advanced in us and God's "peace" increases in us as we grow in "the knowledge of God and of Jesus our Lord." As they do so our assurance of God's favor toward us also becomes stronger and brighter. Therefore, since God has determined to do some things in us and for us only as we pray and ask for these things, we should pray that as God forgives us our sins, we will continue in His favor and grace. "Ask and you shall receive; seek and you shall find; knock and it will be opened to you" (Matt. 7:7).

That God Would Pardon our Daily Failings

As sinners, we are both already in arrears to God's justice, and every day increasing our debt. We sin every day, which means that every day we deserve only to be condemned for our sin. Every day our debt grows greater. Therefore, every day we must rejoice in the salvation we have in Jesus Christ by God's sheer grace. Every day we should seek forgiveness for our daily sins.

> Return, O Israel, to the LORD your God,
> For you have stumbled because of your iniquity.
> Take words with you and return to the LORD.
> Say to Him,
> "Take away all iniquity,
> And receive us graciously,
> That we may present the fruit of our lips.
> Assyria will not save us,
> We will not ride on horses;
> Nor will we say again, 'Our god,'
> To the work of our hands;
> For in Thee the orphan finds mercy" (Hos. 14:1–3).

---

214. Ridgeley, *Commentary on the Larger Catechism*, 2:637.

> Although our iniquities testify against us,
> O LORD, act for Thy name's sake!
> Truly our apostasies have been many,
> We have sinned against Thee (Jer. 14:7).

It is of great significance that Matthew 6:12 reads: "And forgive us our *debts*." The focus is on plural "debts," not on one "debt." The plural denotes that day and day out we have many sins, all kinds of sins, secret and public sins, daily sins. The point is that in our prayers for forgiveness of sin we are not dealing with

> an abstract notion of sin, but with very concrete sins, which are known to us and which we confess in this prayer before God with sorrow of heart. O, it is so easy to approach the throne of grace and ask that God will forgive all our iniquity and all our sin in general. Then we deal with the general concept *sin*, without any specific content. Then there is nothing personal in our prayer. We do not bring our own personal, individual corruptions before the throne of grace and ask concretely for forgiveness. But such is not the meaning of the fifth petition. It presupposes that we have clearly before our mind our concrete, individual transgressions, which we have committed and still do commit when we utter this fifth petition before the face of God. When we bow our heads in prayer and utter this fifth petition, it is well that we elaborate upon it somewhat, and instead of referring to the general concept *sin*, we say: 'Our Father in heaven, please forgive the evil thoughts that arose in my mind and still arise within me; the evil desires of murder and adultery and theft and rebellion of which I am now conscious, as I bow before Thy throne; the evil speech, the evil words which I spoke against Thee and against the brethren; and all the evil deeds which I have committed. Forgive them all, our Father, and remember them nevermore. Dismiss them from Thy mind, for they all make me worthy of Thy wrath. And give me grace to believe that in spite of them all, even as I am sorry for my sins, I am righteous before Thee in Jesus Christ my Lord.[215]

---

215. Hoeksema, *The Triple Knowledge*, 592–93.

That God Would Fill Us with Peace and Joy, In Giving us Daily More and More Assurance of Forgiveness

> Purify me with hyssop, and I shall be clean;
> Wash me, and I shall be whiter than snow.
> Make me to hear joy and gladness,
> Let the bones which Thou hast broken rejoice.
> Hide Thy face from my sins,
> And blot out all my iniquities.
> Create in me a clean heart, O God,
> And renew a steadfast spirit within me.
> Do not cast me away from Thy presence,
> And do not take Thy Holy Spirit from me.
> Restore to me the joy of Thy salvation,
> And sustain me with a willing spirit.
> Then I will teach transgressors Thy ways,
> And sinners will be converted to Thee (Ps. 51:7–12).

> Now may the God of hope fill you with all joy and peace in believing, that you may abound in hope by the power of the Holy Spirit (Rom. 15:13).

Believers in Jesus not only desire forgiveness of sins, we also crave the assurance that we possess it.

> We long to know and be assured that God has so forgiven, dismissed, cancelled [our] debts, and so clothed [us] with eternal righteousness that [we are] still the object of that blessing of the forgiveness of sins *now*, at once, in this world, while we are still in the flesh, in which everything testifies against us, condemns us, speaks of wrath and death and hell. We desire to have it, not as something that will deliver us from the guilt of sins that we have committed in the past, but even while we are still sinful, while we are still sinning. That is the amazing wonder and boldness of this petition. We do not say: "Father, last week we sinned," or, "Yesterday we sinned," or, "This morning we sinned; please forgive." But we

> say: "Father, we are sinning all the time. We are sinning at this very moment, while we are praying. Please dismiss our debts from Thy book, and clothe us with righteousness in Thy judgment. And Father, we must have an answer. Please give us the unspeakably blessed assurance and peace of forgiveness in our hearts."[216]

Hoeksema has not overstated the truth as the two texts quoted above testify. In Psalm 51, David not only prays earnestly for forgiveness of his hideous sins (vs. 2 and 7), he just as earnestly prays: "Make me to hear joy and gladness" (vs. 8). He not only prays that God would blot out his iniquities (vs. 9), and create in him a new heart (vs. 10), he also prays: "Restore to me the joy of Thy salvation" (vs. 12), *i.e.*, the joy of knowing that his sins have been fully forgiven and blotted out and that salvation from sin is truly his. Furthermore, Paul, in Romans 15:13, speaks of the "joy and peace in believing" which "the God of hope" freely gives. When a person believes the gospel of Jesus Christ, he not only receives the promises of the gospel into his own life, *e.g.*, the forgiveness of sins and adoption into the family of God; he also receives joy and peace in the assurance of his reception of salvation and the hope that these gospel promises will always be his.

The Encouragement to Pray for Forgiveness: We are... Emboldened to Ask [For Forgiveness], and Encouraged to Expect [Forgiveness], When we Have This Testimony in Ourselves, That We From the Heart Forgive Others Their Offences.

> Only the forgiving are forgiven. Those who hope for God's forgiveness, said Jesus, must be able to tell Him that they too have forgiven their debtors. This is not a matter of earning forgiveness by works, but of qualifying for it by repentance. Repentance—change of mind—makes mercy and forbearance central to one's new life-style. Those who live by God's

216. Hoeksema, *The Triple Knowledge,* 2:594.

> forgiveness must imitate it; one whose only hope is that God will not hold his faults against him forfeits his right to hold others' faults against them.... It is true that forgiveness is by faith in Christ alone, apart from works, but repentance is faith's fruit, and there is no more reality in a profession of faith than there is reality of repentance accompanying it.[217]

In other words, *the proof that we have been forgiven is that we forgive others.*

This in no way implies that we make ourselves worthy of forgiveness by being forgiving. Our forgiving of one another is not meritorious. In fact, it is so inconsistent and insincere that it is worthy of divine condemnation were it not for our acceptance with God because of Christ. God's forgiveness of our sins is forever based upon the perfect life and sacrificial death of the Lord Jesus Christ. But after saying this, we must still take the Fifth Petition with extreme seriousness.

> You probably ask whether it means that God will not forgive my sins if I do not forgive the brother that sinned against me? And the answer to this question is an emphatic "Yes." It means exactly that. It means nothing else. God gives us the grace of forgiveness only, not on the ground or on condition that, but *as* we forgive one another.[218]

Jesus emphasizes this repeatedly in His teaching ministry.

> If therefore you are presenting your offering at the altar, and there remember that your brother has something against you, leave your offering there before the altar, and go your way, first be reconciled to your brother, and then come and present your offering (Matt. 5:23–24).

In Matthew 5:21–26, which is a section in the Sermon on the Mount, Jesus is explaining the true meaning of the commandment,

217. Packer, *I Want To Be A Christian*, 214.
218. Hoeksema, *The Triple Knowledge*, 598.

"You shall not commit murder." In verses 23 and 24, He is teaching us that

> not only are we not to harbour murder and evil thoughts in our heart against another; but the commandment not to kill really means we should take positive steps to put ourselves right with our brother.... We must not only repress these unkind and unworthy thoughts [mentioned in verses 21 and 22].... We must actually take steps to remove the cause of the trouble [between ourselves and another].... We have to reach the stage in which there shall be nothing wrong even in spirit between our brother and ourselves.... This matter, He tells us, is so important, that, even if I find myself at the altar with a gift I am going to offer to God, and there suddenly remember something I have said or done, something which is causing another person to stumble or go wrong somehow; if I find that I am harbouring unkind and unworthy thoughts about him or in any way hindering his life, then our Lord tells us (may I put it thus with reverence), we should, in a sense, even keep God waiting rather than stay. We must get right with our brother and then come back and offer the gift. In the sight of God there is no value whatsoever in an act of worship if we harbor a known sin.[219]

> For if you forgive men for their transgressions, your heavenly Father will also forgive you. But if you do not forgive men, then your Father will not forgive your transgressions (Matt. 6:14–15).

When Jesus tells us to ask God for forgiveness of our sins "as we also have forgiven our debtors," he is not telling us to feel free to ask God for forgiveness because we have forgiven our debtors. He says "as" not "because." In other words, we are to ask God for forgiveness of our sins, as we are forgiving others of their sins against us. Forgiveness on our part must be the context, not the basis, for our prayers to God for forgiveness.

219. Lloyd-Jones, *Studies in the Sermon on the Mount*, 1:227–28.

> The proof that you and I are forgiven is that we forgive others. If we think that our sins are forgiven by God and we refuse to forgive somebody else, we are making a mistake; we have never been forgiven. The man who knows he has been forgiven, only in and through the shed blood of Christ, is a man who must forgive others. He cannot help himself. If we really know Christ as our Saviour our hearts are broken and cannot be hard, and we cannot refuse forgiveness.... Pray to God and say, 'Forgive me O God as I forgive others because of what Thou hast done for me. All I ask is that Thou shouldst forgive me in the same manner; not to the same degree, because all I do is imperfect. In the same way, as it were, as Thou hast forgiven me, I am forgiving others. Forgive me as I forgive them because of what the cross of the Lord Jesus Christ had done in my heart.' ... True forgiveness breaks a man, and he must forgive. So that when we offer this prayer for forgiveness we test ourselves in that way. Our prayer is not genuine, it is not true, it is of no avail, unless we find there is forgiveness in our heart.[220]

> Then Peter came and said to Him, "Lord, how often shall my brother sin against me and I forgive him? Up to seven times?" Jesus said to him, "I do not say to you, up to seven times, but up to seventy times seven. For this reason the kingdom of heaven may be compared to a certain king who wished to settle accounts with his slaves. And when he had begun to settle them, there was brought to him one who owed him ten thousand talents. But since he did not have the means to repay, his lord commanded him to be sold, along with his wife and children and all that he had, and repayment to be made. The slave therefore falling down, prostrated himself before him, saying, "Have patience with me, and I will repay you everything." And the lord of that slave felt compassion and released him and forgave him the debt.

220. Lloyd-Jones, *Studies in the Sermon on the Mount*, 2:75–76.

> But that slave went out and found one of his fellow-slaves who owed him a hundred denarii; and he seized him and began to choke him, saying, "Pay back what you owe." So his fellow-slave fell down and began to entreat him, saying, "Have patience with me and I will repay you." He was unwilling however, but went and threw him in prison until he should pay back what was owed. So when his fellow-slaves saw what had happened, they were deeply grieved and came and reported to their lord all that had happened. Then summoning him, his lord said to him, "You wicked slave, I forgave you all that debt because you entreated me. Should you not also have had mercy on your fellow-slave, even as I had mercy on you?" And his lord, moved with anger, handed him over to the torturers until he should repay all that was owed him. So shall My heavenly Father also do to you, if each of you does not forgive his brother from your heart (Matt. 18:21–35).

The story of this parable of the unmerciful servant is plain enough. And its point is obvious: The disciples of Christ must show to others the forgiveness they themselves have received from God.

> The deepest secret of this love which characterizes realized discipleship is that they have learn[ed] how to forgive. They extend to others the divine forgiveness which they have experienced, a forgiveness which passes all understanding.... "Where God's forgiveness produces a readiness to forgive, there God's Mercy grants forgiveness of debts again at the Last Judgment; but he who abuses God's gift, faces the full severity of Judgment."[221]

> This vivid story, told in colorful detail, accentuates the contrast between God's infinite love and mercy and man's stingy behavior which he attempts to justify on the basis of law. Jesus uses this parable to tell Peter something about the mag-

221. Joachim Jeremias, *The Parables of Jesus*, trans. by S.H. Hooke (NY: Charles Scribner Sons, 1963), 210, 214.

> nitude of God's forgiving love toward sinful man. Man's sin is so great that God has to forgive him infinitely more than the numerical count of seventy-seven times. The depth of God's mercy simply cannot be measured. It can only be approximated, and vaguely at that, by telling the story of the public servant who owed his master a sum which ran into the millions.[222]

Forgiven of an enormous debt by the king, the king's servant refuses to forgive a debt owed to him. He demanded justice without mercy. This was a serious mistake, for as James says: "judgment without mercy will be shown to anyone who has not been merciful" (James 2:13).

> The servant refused to reflect the compassion his master had shown him. Because he did not show mercy to his fellowman, but demanded justice, he had to face his master the king once more.... What the servant had done to his debtor, the master now does to him; justice is administered without mercy. The servant has cast himself into everlasting misery. God cannot overlook a refusal to show mercy, for this is contrary to his nature, his Word, and his testimony. God pardons by accepting the sinner as if he had never sinned at all. God forgives the sinner's debt and he remembers his sin no more (Ps. 103:12 and Jer. 31:34). And God expects the forgiven sinner to do the same. He is therefore God's representative in showing the divine characteristic of pardoning grace.[223]

We should carefully note one element in this parable. The servant's debt to the king was absolutely unpayable. In today's figures, it amounted to between 15 and 20 million dollars. But God forgives the debt of His people in and through Jesus Christ.

> This is the fundamental character of the kingdom of heaven. It is a kingdom in which God the eternal King forgives His

---

222. Simon Kistemaker, *The Parables of Jesus* (Grand Rapids, MI: Baker Book House, 1980), 66–67.

223. Kistemaker, *The Parables of Jesus,* 70.

people and gives to them the righteousness of the cross of Christ. This forgiveness is, from the viewpoint of God's counsel, eternal. When Balaam was asked by Balak, king of Moab, to curse Israel, God changed his cursings into blessings. He was forced to say, among many other things: "He hath not beheld iniquity in Jacob, neither hath he seen perverseness in Israel: the Lord his God is with him, and the shout of a king is among them" (Num. 23:21). The idea is that God *never* sees iniquity in His people.

This is possible only because God sees His people as those who belong to Christ. Their forgiveness was historically realized on the cross of Christ. Christ assumed responsibility for the debt which His people owed to God, taking upon Himself the payment of that debt. He did this because the punishment of eternal hell was endured by Him when He suffered and died. Though each sin we commit deserves eternal hell, and though the number of the people of God is very great, Christ paid back all that debt when He endured the horrors of hell on the cross. And He paid the debt because, while He suffered the anguish and torments of hell, He still loved God, served Him and glorified His Father. When the dark and dreadful waves of God's fierce wrath swept over His soul, He still loved God with a perfect heart. And thus He paid the debt for all God's people. It is paid so completely that not one small particle of that debt remains to be paid....

This forgiveness becomes our forgiveness in the way of confession of sin. We become conscious of this great blessing when we carry the burden of our sin and guilt to Calvary and confess at the foot of the cross our own unworthiness. We find the assurance of forgiveness when we, by faith, lay hold on Christ and His perfect sacrifice. Then we actually come to know that this great debt is taken away.

This great forgiveness of God must be manifested in our lives.... When we sin, this sin is committed not only against God, it is also often against our fellow saints. We offend our fellow saints by our sins, do harm to them, and put ourselves in debt to them by the sins we commit.... It is always true that in the Church we stand in debt to one another.... All our sins, in one way or another, are sins that affect our relationships with our fellow saints. And we must live in this consciousness that we continually put ourselves in debt to those with whom we live. Or, to put it in the form in which the parable brings this to our attention, our fellow saints put themselves continually in debt to us by their sins.

Hence, the point of the parable is clear. If we experience the forgiveness of God for the sins which we commit against Him, we will surely forgive our fellow saints also. This follows in the nature of the case. If we know our sins, we are overwhelmed with the consciousness of the staggering debt we owe to God. But when we experience the wonder that God has forgiven us, then this can only fill us with awe and thanksgiving.... And this mercy is completely undeserving. God does not need to forgive us. He is under no obligation to forgive our debt. We have, in no way, made ourselves worthy of forgiveness. If God would refuse to cancel our debt, and if He would punish us forever in hell, we could raise not one word of complaint. We would receive what is justly our due. How can we ever be grateful enough for such a great wonder? ...

If we experience God's forgiving mercy and understand even a little of the astonishing wonder of it, then there is no problem at all in forgiving our brother. Then we do not forgive him three times, or, in generosity, seven times; but there cannot possibly be any end to such forgiveness. God forgives us again and again. How can we do anything less? ...

If we fail to forgive our brother, it is only because we have not been forgiven by God. And when we fail we shall never experience forgiveness ourselves.... Therefore, only in the way of forgiving our brothers will we experience the blessed peace of forgiveness.... And forgiving one another, we will live in

> the rich blessedness of the communion of saints who together have salvation in the cross of Jesus Christ.[224]

Rushdoony makes a practical application of this point to culture and society in *Systematic Theology*. He says that in this Fifth Petition we have

> a standard for social order. In Christ we have the forgiveness of sins, a release from a legal bond, the death penalty for our rebellion against God and His law. We are now in Him a community of grace and law; we delight in God's word instead of rebelling against it. Having received grace, we manifest it one to another. Being now within the law instead of outlaws, we seek to do God's will and to extend the circle of God's grace and law.... This transforms forgiveness from the empty, humanistic meaning it now has to a manifestation of both God's law and God's grace. Instead of an emotional feeling with no content, it becomes a transforming power in society.... Forgiveness in the Biblical sense is basic to social order and personal peace. We are therefore commanded to pray for it. Prayer, after all, is a privilege, the privilege of access to God through Jesus Christ.[225]

What does it mean to "forgive" another person who asks us for forgiveness? We are to forgive as God has forgiven us: "Be kind one to the other, tenderhearted, forgiving one another, just as God, for Christ's sake has forgiven you" (Eph. 4:32). Our forgiveness of others must be gracious, because forgiveness is never deserved, it is always granted out of mercy; and it never has the ulterior motive of getting some benefit for oneself. Furthermore, forgiveness from God or from one human being to another is a declaration of the cancellation of a debt, as God promises to us: "I will forgive their iniquity, and their sin I will remember no more" (Jer. 31:34).

---

224. Herman Hanko, *The Mysteries of the Kingdom: An Exposition of the Parables* (Grand Rapids, MI: Reformed Free Publishing Association, 1975), 67–71.

225. Rushdoony, *Systematic Theology*, 2:1217.

> When you forgive another, you declare that you are canceling his debt, removing his guilt, and promising that you will never again bring up his guilt...[or]...bring up his offences to use against him. The promise involved three things: (1). I will not bring the matter up to you. (2). I will not bring the matter up to another. (3). I will not bring the matter up to myself.[226]

Why Should A Christian Repeatedly Pray for Forgiveness of Sins if Christ's Death on the Cross Was a Perfect Atonement for Our Sins Once-For-All?

This is a reasonable question. If Christ has made atonement for our sins once and for all on Calvary, and if God has justified and forgiven us eternally through Him, if the debt we had with God has been paid in full by Christ, then why are we commanded in the Bible to pray repeatedly and daily for forgiveness of our sins? How does the need for a prayer for daily forgiveness square with the fact that in justification God pardons all sins, past, present and future, which involves the complete removal of all guilt and of every penalty?

Justified believers continue to sin (1 John 1:8). Jesus taught His disciples to pray daily for the forgiveness of sins (Matt. 6:12). Old Testament believers plead for pardon (Ps. 32:5; 51:1–4; 130:3, 4). How does this harmonize with the fact that in justification ALL of the believer's sins are forgiven?

> In justification God indeed removes the guilt, but not the culpability [responsibility] of sin, that is, He removes the sinner's just amenability [liability and susceptibility] to punishment, but not the inherent guiltiness of whatever sins he may continue to perform. The latter remains and therefore always produces in believers a feeling of guilt, of separation from God, of sorrow, of repentance, and so on. Hence they feel the need of confessing their sins.... The believer who is really conscious of his sin feels within him an urge to confess it and to seek the comforting assurance of forgiveness. More-

226. Jay Adams, *From Forgiven To Forgiving* (Amityville, NY: Calvary Press, 1994), 82.

> over, such confession and prayer is not only a subjectively felt need, but also an objective necessity. Justification is essentially an objective declaration respecting the sinner in the tribunal of God, but it is not merely that; it is also a...passing into the consciousness of the believer. The divine sentence of acquittal is brought home to the sinner and awakens the joyous consciousness of the forgiveness of sins and of favor with God. Now this consciousness of pardon and of a renewed filial relationship is often disturbed and obscured by sin, and is again quickened and strengthened by confession and prayer, and by a renewed exercise of faith.[227]

On one hand, justification is a once-for-all and complete change of legal standing before God, but two distinctions must be made:

> one between the completeness of title [to eternal salvation], and completeness of possession as to the benefits of our justification; the other between our justification in God's breast, and our own sense and consciousness thereof. On the latter distinction, we may remark: as our faith strengthens, so will the strength of our apprehension of a justified state grow with it. The former also may, to some extent, be affected by the increase of our faith. God may make that increase the occasion of manifesting to the soul larger measures of favour and grace. But the soul is not one whit more God's accepted child then, than when it first believed. We have seen that the thing which, strictly speaking, is imputed, is the title to all the legal consequences of Christ's righteousness, *i.e.*, title to pardon and everlasting adoption, with all the included graces. Now, the acknowledged and legitimate son of a king is a prince, though an infant. His status and inheritance are royal, and sure; though he be for a time under tutors and governors, and though he may gradually be put into possession of one and another, of his privileges, till his complete majority. So the gradual possession of the benefits of justification does not imply that our acquisition of the title is gradual. These views may assist us in the

227. Berkhof, *Systematic Theology*, 515.

intricate subject of the relation which justification bears to the believer's future sins. On the one hand these things are evident; that there is not a man on the earth who does not offend, James iii: 2, that sin must always be sin in its nature, and as such, abhorrent to God, by whomsoever committed; and even more abhorrent in a believer, because committed against greater obligations and vows; and that sins committed after justification need expiation, just as truly as those before. On the other hand, the proofs above given clearly show, that the justified believer does not pass again under condemnation when betrayed into sin. Faith is the instrument for continuing, as it was for originating our justified state. This is clear from Romans xi:20 ["you stand only by your faith"], Heb. x:38 ["But My righteous one shall live by faith; and if he shrinks back, My soul has no pleasure in him."], as well as from the experience of all believers, who universally apply afresh to Christ for cleansing, when their consciences are oppressed with new sin. In strictness of speech, a man's sin must be forgiven after it is committed. Nothing can have a relation before it has existence, so that it is illogical to speak of sin as pardoned before it is committed. How, then, stands the sinning believer, between the time of a new sin and his new application to Christ's cleansing blood? We reply: Justification is the act of an immutable God, determining not to impute sin, through the believer's faith. This faith, though not in instant exercise at every moment, is an undying principle in the believer's heart, being rendered indefectible only by God's purpose of grace, and the indwelling of the Holy Ghost. So God determines, when the believer sins, not to impute guilt for Christ's sake, which determination also implies this other, to secure in the believer's heart, the unfailing actings of faith and repentance, as to all known sin. So that his justification from future sins is not so much a pardoning of them before they are committed, as an unfailing provision by God both of the meritorious and instrumental causes of their pardon, as they are committed.[228]

228. Dabney, *Lectures in Systematic Theology*, 644–45.

Appendix: How To Forgive

Luke 17:1–10

> And He said to His disciples, "it is inevitable that stumbling blocks should come, but woe to him through whom they come! It would be better for him if a millstone were hung around his neck and he were thrown into the sea, than that he should cause one of these little ones to stumble. Be on your guard! If your brother sins, rebuke him; and if he repents, forgive him. And if he sins against you seven times a day, and returns to you seven times, saying, 'I repent,' forgive him."
>
> And the apostles said to the Lord, "Increase our faith!" And the Lord said, "If you had faith like a mustard seed, you would say to this mulberry tree, 'Be uprooted and be planted in the sea'; and it would obey you. But which of you having a slave plowing or tending sheep, will say to him when he has come in from the field, 'Come immediately and sit down to eat'? But will he not say to him, 'Prepare something for me to eat, and properly clothe yourself and serve me until I have eaten and drunk; and afterward you will eat and drink'? He does not thank the slave because he did the things which were commanded, does he? So you too, when you do all the things which are commanded you, say, 'We are unworthy slaves; we have done only that which we ought to have done.'"

Jesus says that we must be willing to forgive others, and he accepts no excuses for failing to be forgiving. We may not say, "I'll forgive when I feel like it" or "When I get more faith" or "When the person asking me for forgiveness shows definite improvement." Jesus tells us to forgive because He commands it.[229]

---

229. For an extended study of forgiveness by Jay Adams, see: (1) *More Than Redemption*, pp. 184–232; (2) *From Forgiven to Forgiving*; and (3) *The Christian Counselor's Manual*, pp. 63–70.

Luke 17:1–2 warns us about the danger of being stumbling blocks to other people, particularly to the young and the weak. We become stumbling blocks by discouraging others, by leading others into sin, by being unwilling to forgive, and by being unwilling to repent and ask forgiveness.

Luke 17:3–4 presents us with the duty of forgiveness. It is a two-step process: (1) If a brother sins, lovingly rebuke him; and (2) If a brother sins and repents, forgive him.

One brother's correction of a fallen or wayward brother must always be with the awareness of common guilt and willingness to forgive, and in terms of Galatians 6:1: "Brethren, even if a man is caught in any trespass, you who are spiritual, restore such a one in a spirit of gentleness, looking to yourself, lest you too be tempted." If compassionate rebuke is refused then Matthew 18:15–17 is to be followed faithfully and patiently. Church discipline is a means of grace.[230]

If your rebuke works and the sinning brother repents, forgive him. To do this properly a person must have a Biblical understanding of the nature of forgiveness and of repentance.

Forgiveness is a promise that can be made and kept regardless of feeling. As God says to us in forgiving us: "I will remember your sins against you no more" (Jer. 31:34). Therefore, forgiveness means that: (1) You will not bring up that sin again to the person you have forgiven; (2) You will not bring it up to other people; and (3) You will not allow yourself to dwell on it again.

The repentance required for forgiveness in Luke 17 is obviously a minimal repentance and confession in order for forgiveness to be given (Matt. 18:21–22; 1 Cor. 13:4–5). As Jay Adams has explained: "It is certain, then, that Jesus does not condition the granting of forgiveness upon the behavior of the offender after forgiveness, but rather hangs the granting of forgiveness upon the brother's verbal testimony."[231]

---

230. Helpful Proverbs on the power and nature of loving rebuke: Proverbs 12:1, 5–6, 25; 15:4, 5, 23, 31–32; 17:9, 10; 19:29; 20:18.

231. Jay Adams, *The Christian Counselor's Manual* (Grand Rapids, MI: Baker Book House, [1973] 1981), 68–69.

> Christ is not saying, do not forgive in any sense unless there is repentance anymore than he is saying allow others to make a mockery of you by empty words. Christ is not giving permission to refuse pardon. Sins are forgiven in two ways: (1). If injured, put aside feelings of revenge and do not cease to love him and repay him with good instead of injury, Romans 12:21; and (2). When we receive a brother into our favor in such a way as to think well of him and be convinced that the memory of his fault is wiped out before God, should we blindly believe anyone who comes saying he repents? When anyone is suspect of levity, we can still forgive him when he asks for pardon in such a way that we keep an eye on his behavior in the future, lest he should make a mockery of our kindness.[232]

Jay Adams has wisely pointed out that

> the Biblical concept of forgiving and forgetting often has been misrepresented. The Bible speaks of "fruits appropriate to repentance." One forgives, but he does not immediately forget; rather, he remembers and looks for the *fruit* or the *results* that eventually accompany true repentance. It takes time for fruit to grow. When fruit is discerned, forgetting *then* becomes possible. Perhaps the most evident fruit and one that does as much as any other to facilitate forgetting is the desire and willingness of the forgiven offender to build a new relationship with the one who has forgiven.[233]

Three helpful principles should be kept in mind in forgiving another person:

(1) When you forgive, each offense is not the fifth or the seventh—it is always the first! That is the point of Jesus statement that upset the apostles: "If he sins against you seven

232. John Calvin, *Commentary on the Harmony of the Evangelists, Matthew, Mark, and Luke*, trans by Rev. William Pringle, 4 vols. (Edinburgh, Calvin Translation Society, 1843; reprint Grand Rapids, MI: Baker Book House, 1979), 2:364.

233. Adams, *The Christian Counselor's Manual*, 65 (ftnt. #6).

times a day, and returns to you seven times, saying, 'I repent,' forgive him."

(2) Forgiveness should develop into full reconciliation, where hostility and alienation are replaced by peace and fellowship.

> Reconciliation is a change of relationship between persons (God and man; man and man) that involves at least three elements: (1). *confession* of sin to God and to any others who have been offended; (2). *forgiveness* by God and by the one who has been offended; (3). the establishment of *a new relationship* between the offender and God and between the offender and the offended party (parties). In reconciliation, enmity and alienation are replaced by peace and fellowship.[234]

(3) Forgiveness does not demand restitution first. What does the Bible teach about restitution? (a) Restitution means the returning to the rightful owner what has been taken illegally from him. It also means to make amends by doing something or by paying something to make up for losses or injury incurred. (b) It is a civil punishment administered by the civil magistrate (Ex. 22:1, 4, 7; Lev. 6:5; Num. 5:7; 2 Sam. 12:6). (c) It was a ceremonial rite, in reference to offering the reparation offering to Jehovah, which pointed to Jesus Christ and was fulfilled in Him, who alone could make restitution to God for us and in our place (1 Pet. 2:24; Luke 7:36–50). (d) The desire to make restitution to those whom you have offended is an evidence of true and genuine conversion (Luke 19:8–9; Matt. 5:23–24; Phil. 18–19). (e) Restitution in everyday (non-civic) relationships is not to be demanded in every instance of injury or loss. On some occasions, for the benefit of the Kingdom of God, we allow ourselves to be defrauded (1 Cor. 6:1–8). The offended need not feel obligated to demand restitution as a prerequisite to forgiveness (Matt. 5:38–44). Matthew 18:23–27 sets the tone for the Christian's dealing with those who might cause injury or loss (Eph. 4:32). This is

234. Adams, *The Christian Counselor's Manual*, 63.

> not to be interpreted so as to forbid the Christian's ever taking to court those who commit a crime against him, if the occasion requires it (1 Cor. 6:1f; Acts 25:11; Deut. 16:18–17:13).

What are the motives for forgiving those who have sinned against us? We forgive because we ourselves are forgiven by God. We forgive because we are forgiven people. How many times has God forgiven us? And, we forgive out of love for Christ, gratitude to Him and the desire to honor Him.

In *Luke 17:5–6* we see the response of the disciples to Jesus' command to forgive: "We need more faith!" To which Jesus said, in effect, "No. It is not the greatness of faith; but the object on which faith rests, from which faith draws its strength to forgive. In forgiveness, a mustard-seed-faith will do."

> The problem is much more straight-forward, uncomplicated, and simple. [It is not a problem of weak faith,] it is a problem of obedience. Christ told them what to do and they were to obey.... What one must do is to commit himself to the *hard* task of promising not to raise the matter of the offence again. That is the essence of granting forgiveness.[235]

APPENDIX:

THE WORDS FOR "FORGIVENESS" IN THE BIBLE

The Hebrew words for forgiveness in the Old Testament

Salach: "to lighten by lifting," (Num. 14:19, 20; Neh. 9:17; Ps. 103:3, 4; Isa. 55:7; Jer. 31:34). "It is used to describe God lightening a person's life by lifting the load of guilt from his shoulders."[236] It also

235. Adams, *The Christian Counselor's Manual*, 69.

236. Jay Adams, *More Than Redemption: A Theology of Christian Counseling* (Grand Rapids, MI: Baker Book House, 1979), 186.

denotes the restoration of a sinner to Divine favor by atonement (Leviticus 4:20, 26, 31; 5:10, 15, 18).

Nasa: "to take away by lifting off" (Gen. 50:17; Ex. 34:6, 7; Ps. 32:1, 5; Hosea 1:6). It focuses on the taking away and carrying off the sin.

The Greek words for forgiveness in the New Testament

Aphiemi: "to let go, release, remit" (Matt. 18:27, 37; 6:12; Col. 1:14; Mark 3:29; Acts 5:31; 13:38; 26:18; Luke 4:18). It is primarily used when speaking of sins as debts that are "cancelled" or "remitted" or "paid in full." Sins are liabilities. Sin is a debt to God. Forgiveness is viewed as the release, remission and relief of this liability.

Charizomai: "to bestow favor freely" (Eph. 4:32; Col. 2:13; 3:13; Luke 7:42, 43). Forgiveness is always undeserved by the one who receives it.

The multi-dimensional meaning of forgiveness

Mark 3:28–30: A forgiven person is one who is no longer held liable for his sin, no longer held guilty. He can no longer be held accountable for it (Rom. 3:19). The liability of punishment has been removed.

Acts 7:60: Forgiveness is the condition in which one's sins are no longer charged against him. (Contrast 2 Chron. 24:21, 22.)

> The result of forgiveness is...freedom from liability. A new outlook on life comes to the forgiven person [Jer. 50:20; Ps. 103:12]. All remembrances, traces of liability are gone. The forgiven person has a brand new record—freed completely from his past. Unforgiven persons carry the past as a part of their present...The future belongs to forgiven people; others drag their contaminating past into the future, wherever they go, and destroy it for themselves.[237]

Hosea 8:13; 9:9: "Remembering," "visiting" and "punishing" in these texts all speak of God's judgment. For the forgiven person

---

237. Adams, *More Than Redemption*, 191–92.

these are lifted away and no longer are threats.

The Sixth Petition of the Lord's Prayer

Q. 195: What do we pray for in the sixth petition?

A.: In the sixth petition, (which is, *And lead us not into temptation, but deliver us from evil*), acknowledging, that the most wise, righteous, and gracious God, for divers holy and just ends, may so order things, that we may be assaulted, foiled, and for a time led captive by temptations; that Satan, the world, and the flesh, are ready powerfully to draw us aside, and ensnare us; and that we, even after the pardon of our sins, by reason of our corruption, weakness, and want of watchfulness, are not only subject to be tempted, and forward to expose ourselves unto temptations, but also of ourselves unable and unwilling to resist them, to recover out of them, and to improve them; and worthy to be left under the power of them: we pray, that God would so over-rule the world and all in it, subdue the flesh, and restrain Satan, order all things, bestow and bless all means of grace, and quicken us to watchfulness in the use of them, that we and all his people may by his providence be kept from being tempted to sin; or, if tempted, that by his Spirit we may be powerfully supported and enabled to stand in the hour of temptation; or when fallen, raised again and recovered out of it, and have a sanctified use and improvement thereof: that our sanctification and salvation may be perfected, Satan trodden under our feet, and we fully freed from sin, temptation, and all evil, for ever.

The Wording of the Sixth Petition

> And lead us not into temptation, but deliver us from evil.

Although some Bible teachers separate these two clauses into two petitions, giving the Lord's Prayer seven rather than six petitions, it would appear that in these two clauses we have really only one request. They form one sentence connected by the conjunction "but." It is parallel to the fifth petition, which also consists of two clauses. Furthermore, a close relation exists between

> preservation in and from temptation and deliverance from evil.... Must we conceive of the relation between the two parts of this sixth petition to be such that in the first part we ask for the same blessing of grace as in the second, the first clause expressing the thing asked for negatively and in the midst of our present life, where the world, the devil, and our own flesh also tempt us to evil, while the last part expresses the same thought positively.[238]

However, although referring to the same issue, the second clause does express more than the first clause.

> For preservation in and from temptation leaves us nevertheless still in this world, and therefore it cannot be final. The Christian cannot rest content with a state in which he must be continually preserved against the temptation of the flesh, the world, and the devil. He wants more. He longs for protection, for the state in which preservation against temptation is no longer necessary. He looks forward to the complete victory which will come in the state of perfection, in the day of our Lord Jesus Christ. In final analysis it is for that victory

238. Hoeksema, *The Triple Knowledge*, 3:607–08.

> that he prays in the second part of this sixth petition, "...but deliver us from evil." ... The one part asks for preservation, the other for perfect deliverance.[239]

A close connection also exists between this petition and the fifth petition, as the "and" at the beginning of the Sixth Petition indicates. The Fifth Petition asks for forgiveness of sins and the Sixth Petition asks for victory over sin now and forever. The Sixth Petition looks forward to a better and more blessed state in which prayers for forgiveness will never be necessary.

The relationship of the Fifth and the Sixth Petitions is theological.

First, the Fifth Petition is basic for the Sixth Petition. "Justification is the basis of sanctification.... We are justified in order that we may be delivered from sin and death. We are pardoned in order that we may be liberated. We are forgiven in order that we may be freed from the power and pollution of sin."[240]

Second,

> in the experience of the believer and in the application of these blessings [of justification and sanctification] to the elect, the two are most intimately related and can never be separated. In the life and consciousness of the Christian justification never exists alone, without sanctification. He that believes that he is justified is already in principle delivered from evil.... The prayer for forgiveness of sins cannot be his final request with respect to sin. As long as he is in need of the prayer of remission, he has not reached perfection. He is still sinful, and he still transgresses the good commandments of his God in thought, word, and deed. With this condition he can never be satisfied. The very same sorrow after God that makes him bemoan his sins and impels him to cry out for forgiveness also causes him to hate sin, to realize the danger of falling into temptation while he is in this world, to seek strength to fight against the powers of evil within him

239. Hoeksema, *The Triple Knowledge,* 608–09.
240. Hoeksema, *The Triple Knowledge,* 3:610.

> and round about him, and to long and pray for the state in which he will be completely delivered from the dominion and corruption of sin and serve his Father in heaven in perfect righteousness. Hence, the petition for forgiveness of sins already looks forward to, and must needs to be followed by this other prayer, "And lead us not into temptation, but deliver us from evil."[241]

"Lead," εισφερω, means "to carry or bring in, to convey." When used in the Lord's Prayer it means that we pray not to be brought into temptation, or that God would not cause it to happen. "Temptation," πειρασμοσ, means "a test, temptation, or experience." In the Lord's Prayer what is at issue is not a test (Ps. 139:23), but the experience of being tempted to sin by evil powers. "Deliver," ρυομαι, means "to save, protect, guard, or ward off." This word takes on an eschatological sense in the Sixth Petition.

> Salvation is ultimately eternal preservation. Eschatological salvation rests on present deliverance from sin and from the power that rules in this sinful age. Prayer is made for final preservation...but with the confidence that God is the Lord who impresses even evil into his service, so that in the very prayer for deliverance evil is overcome by the divinely conferred affirmation of God's will.[242]

"Evil," πονηροσ, means "morally bad, harmful, and morally reprehensible. This word is either a masculine adjective or a neuter adjective in Greek. If masculine it could be translated "the evil one," with reference to Satan. If neuter it is a request for deliverance for all evil, moral and eschatological.

A word should be said about the fact that the word, πειρρασμοσ, should be translated "temptation" and not "trial" in the Sixth Petition, although it can mean both depending upon the context. In

241. Hoeksema, *The Triple Knowledge,* 3:611.

242. *Theological Dictionary of the New Testament,* abridged in one volume, eds. Gerhard Kittel and Gerhard Friedrich, trans. Geoffrey W. Bromiley (Grand Rapids, MI: Eerdmans; United Kingdom, The Paternoster Press Ltd., [1985] 1988), 989.

James 1:2–3, it is properly translated not "temptations" but "trials" that "test the faith of the believer, [giving] to that faith a tried character, and thus bear the fruit of the spiritual grace of patience."[243] But other passages properly translate the word "temptations" in the evil sense of the word, as in James 1:13, 14 and Matthew 4:1. The context in which the word is used must be allowed to determine how it will be translated.

Trials and temptations are closely related. God does send trials to test and strengthen faith, as He did with Abraham throughout his life. But Satan tries to turn those trials into temptations to sin. All trials are temptations and all temptations are trials for the people of God. However, there is also a great difference between these two words. What is a trial of the faith of believers is at the same time a temptation to the indwelling sin remaining in them. "When, for instance, a believer is threatened with the loss of a profitable position in the world unless he in some way becomes unfaithful and denies his Lord, his faith is being tried; but the same situation is an appeal to his sinful nature to deny Christ and keep his position."[244]

Another difference between trials and temptations is this:

> trial always presents the truth; temptation is always a lie. Temptation always presents the way of sin and iniquity, of backsliding and unfaithfulness, of denying Christ and violating the covenant of God, as something desirable, as a good that is worth striving for, as preferable to the way of obedience, righteousness, holiness, and faithfulness to Christ.[245]

A third difference between trials and temptations is with reference to motives and purpose. The motives of temptation are hatred for God and that which is good and love for sin. The purpose of Satan, the tempter, is always to dishonor God and to destroy the believer. Trials are motivated by love for God, each other and whatever is pleasing to God; and their purpose is the benefit and salvation of God's people.

243. Hoeksema, *The Triple Knowledge,* 3:612.
244. Hoeksema, *The Triple Knowledge,* 3:613.
245. Hoeksema, *The Triple Knowledge,* 3:614.

The great English Puritan, John Owen, defined temptation as

> in general...any thing, state, way or condition that, upon any account whatever, hath a force or efficacy to seduce, to draw the mind and heart of a man from its obedience which God requires of him, into any sin, in any degree of it whatever. In particular, that is a temptation to any man, which causes or occasions him to sin, or in any thing to go off from his duty, either by bringing evil into his heart, or drawing out that evil that is in his heart, or any other way diverting him from communion with God, and that constant, equal, universal obedience, in matter and manner, that is required of him.[246]

The implications of the word, "Lead," should be carefully noted. Christ teaches His disciples to pray, "Lead us not into temptation." We are not asking simply that God would never allow us ever to be tempted, for it is impossible to escape temptation in this world. Nor are we asking only that God may preserve us in the midst of temptations. This obviously is implied in the petition. The Sixth Petition means far more. By it we are turning to the God of our salvation in Christ, who called us out of the darkness of sin into His marvelous light, and we are praying:

> Our Father who art in heaven, hold my hand. Give me grace. Uphold me by Your almighty power. Give me light and understanding, that I may always know Your way; and always sanctify my heart by Your Spirit and Word, in order that I may not suffer defeat, but have the victory in the midst of my enemies.[247]

But, the Sixth Petition means still more. To ask God "Lead us not into temptation" is

> an acknowledgement of the absolute sovereignty of God even with respect to sin and evil, even over the devil, the world,

246. John Owen, *The Works of John Owen,* 24 vols., ed. by Thomas Russell (London: Richard Baynes, 1826), 7:443.

247. Hoeksema, *The Triple Knowledge,* 3:619.

> and our own sinful flesh, so that we cannot be overcome by temptation unless God Himself leads us into it.... The child of God, praying from the depths of his regenerated heart, knows that above them all [the world, flesh and devil], and that too, as their absolute Lord stands his Father in heaven, Who employs the devil, the world and even his own sinful flesh for His adorable, sovereign purpose.... And deeply conscious of this sovereignty of God with respect to all temptations, he does not pray that he may never meet with temptation, nor only that in the midst of temptation his Father in heaven may preserve him, but very positively, "*Lead* me not into temptation."[248]

> Although the weakness of the flesh cannot prevail against the power of God, who confirms and preserves true believers in a state of grace, yet converts are not always so influenced and actuated by the Spirit of God, as not in some particular instances sinfully to deviate from the guidance of divine grace, so as to be seduced by, and comply with the lusts of the flesh; they must, therefore, be constant in watching and prayer, that they be not led into temptation. When these are neglected, they are not only liable to be drawn into great and heinous sins, by Satan, the world and the flesh, but sometimes by the righteous permission of God actually fall into these evils. This, the lamentable fall of David, Peter and other saints described in Holy Scripture, demonstrates.[249]

Of course, this is not at all to imply that God is the author of sin, or that God makes people sin:

> Let no one say when he is tempted, "I am being tempted by God"; for God cannot be tempted by evil, and He Himself does not tempt anyone. But each one is tempted when he is carried away and enticed by his own lust. Then when lust has

248. Hoeksema, *The Triple Knowledge*, 3:620.
249. The Canons of Dordt, V, 4.

> conceived, it gives birth to sin; and when sin is accomplished, it brings forth death (James 1:13–15).

The Point of the Sixth Petition

When the believer prays the two clauses of this Sixth Petition, he is expressing his deep abhorrence of all sin, his sincere desire to fight against it, and his great love for God and holiness. He earnestly prays that God would protect and strengthen him in the power of the Holy Spirit against all the assaults of sin and Satan so that he will not be overcome by evil in this present spiritual struggle. And he also prays that God will enable him constantly and strenuously to resist all his evil enemies until at last he obtains a total victory. And so he prays: "Lead me not into the traps of temptation, but on the contrary, deliver me completely from evil." As we have suggested, deliverance from evil has a wider significance than being preserved in temptation.

> The praying child of God has not fully disemburdened his heart before his Father in heaven as far as his relation to the dominion and power of sin is concerned by the prayer for preservation against the temptations that encompass him on all sides in this world. He must say more.... He cannot be satisfied until the final goal is reached. He longs for the day when his enemies shall be no more, the dangers of sin and death no longer threaten him, the day of complete salvation and perfect victory. To that final state of perfection he looks forward to when he prays, "Deliver me from evil."[250]

How does God answer this prayer for preservation and deliverance in this life?

> Our Father in heaven hears this prayer even now, while we are still in the body of this death. And when He does hear this prayer, the firstfruit is that we increase in that grace whereby we may cast an even deeper glance into the inner recesses of our own existence, and discover more and more

250. Hoeksema, *The Triple Knowledge,* 3:623–24.

sins and more corruptions in our sinful nature. Sins we never noticed before then come to stand clearly before our consciousness. Secondly, the answer to this prayer results too in our growing more sensitive, so that we begin to consider sinful what formerly we approved, and so that we begin spontaneously to approve that which is excellent. Further, the answer to this prayer reveals itself in this, that we become more deeply sorry for our sin and our sinful condition, bemoan them in sackcloth and ashes before our God, and that we more earnestly seek and find the blessedness of His forgiving grace. Still more: in answer to this prayer God gives us grace to fight the battle against sin. He gives us the knowledge of "that good, and acceptable, and perfect will of God," and instills into our hearts a deeper and greater love of that perfect will. He causes us to watch and pray, and gives us more abundant grace to put off the old man and his deeds, and to put on the new man, as the elect of God, "bowels of mercies, kindness, humbleness of mind, meekness, longsuffering" and "charity, which is the bond of perfectness," Col. 3:12, 14. In short, He gives us grace to put on the whole armor of God, that we may fight the good fight of faith, and that in this fight we may not be defeated and overcome, but persevere even unto the end, that no one take our crown. And thus, being replenished by His grace daily, we continue to pray, and indeed cry more fervently as our prayer is heard: "Our Father Who art in heaven, deliver us from evil."

Yet, the final answer to this prayer will not be heard until we arrive at perfection in eternal glory.... O, indeed, our Father in heaven hears this prayer even while we are still in the flesh and in this present world, in the midst of all kinds of temptations. Nevertheless, He will not deliver us to the utmost until death comes to open the door for us into the heavenly perfection. This prayer is heard, first of all, when the earthly house of this tabernacle is dissolved, and we enter into the house of God not made with hands, eternal in the heavens. But in the

> last analysis, final perfection and deliverance from the evil one and from all evil, from all sin and corruption and from all the effects of sin, does not come until the day of the Lord, when He shall raise our corruptible and mortal bodies into the glory of incorruptibility and immortality, and give us our place forever in the heavenly tabernacle of God in the new creation. In last analysis it is to that perfection that this prayer looks forward.[251]

As we explain the point of the Sixth Petition, it becomes clear that only the regenerated people of God can pray this prayer. In other words, the pronoun "us" in this petition refers to true believers in Jesus Christ. Only those who know God as "Our Father who art in heaven," who have been regenerated into His image and adopted in His family will even have the desire to pray this prayer. No unregenerate, unbelieving rebel against God, dead in his sin, would ever hate sin so much that he would pray to God to protect him and strengthen him in the face of temptation to resist its seductions. And no unregenerate person, who loves the darkness and hates the light, would ever cry out to God for deliverance from evil. The spiritual disposition required of a person if he is to pray this Sixth Petition is a

> disposition in which we earnestly long for complete perfection. It implies a deep and growing spiritual knowledge of our sinful condition, a profound consciousness of our sin. It presupposes a deeply rooted hatred and abhorrence of sin, of all sin, and that too, because sin is contrary to the will of God and dishonors His holy name. It presupposes that he who utters this prayer is moved by a strong resolution to fight against all evil and to keep all the commandments of God. For how shall one bring this prayer before the face of the Holy One as long as there is even one sin which he nourishes and presses to his bosom? There is, moreover, in this prayer the expression of a deep consciousness of our utter dependence upon the grace of God, and of the truth of the words of

251. Hoeksema, *The Triple Knowledge*, 634–35.

> Jesus, "Without Me you can do nothing." As long as we imagine that in any sense we can deliver ourselves from evil, this prayer has no room in our hearts. And so, this last petition is motivated by the love of the bride for the Bridegroom and by the desire to be like Him at His coming.[252]

The Necessity for the Sixth Petition

The Larger Catechism gives us three reasons for praying the Sixth Petition.

The Sovereignty of God

> Acknowledging, that the most wise, righteous, and gracious God, for divers holy and just ends, may so order things, that we may be assaulted, foiled, and for a time led captive by temptations.

God is a sovereign Lord who has foreordained whatsoever comes to pass according to the good pleasure of His own will, for His own glory and for the benefit of His chosen people. Although we cannot always understand the purpose in His dealings with us, nevertheless we can always trust Him to never act out of character. He is *most wise,* therefore none of His dealings with us will be unwise, however they may appear to us. He is *righteous,* therefore none of His dealings with us will be unjust, unfair, overly harsh or too severe, however they appear to us. He is *gracious,* therefore in all His dealings with us He is concerned for the welfare, happiness and holiness of His people, and will cause everything that happens to us to work together for our good, as we love Him (Rom. 8:28). He does not deal with His people as our sins deserve, but rather He blesses us in Christ without regard for demerits or lack of worth.

This sovereign God may so order and orchestrate things for perfectly *holy and just* reasons and purposes that seem good to Him, that His dearly beloved people *may be assaulted, foiled, and for a time led captive by temptations.* We see this truth illustrated in

252. Hoeksema, *The Triple Knowledge,* 636.

the life of Hezekiah: "And even in the matter of the envoys of the rulers of Babylon, who sent to him [Hezekiah] to inquire of the wonder that had happened in the land, God left him alone only to test him, that He might know all that was in his heart" (2 Chron. 32:31).

What does this text mean when it says that "God left him"? Obviously this leaving is in a relative sense, because God does not leave or forsake His children absolutely. Sometimes God causes us to lose our awareness of His presence and nearness, as David experienced in Psalm 73. Other times God withholds, to a degree, but not totally, His restraint on our sin to help us see our deep sinfulness, as He did to King David in 2 Samuel 24. He also increases and intensifies our trials and sufferings in order to test us, as He did to Israel in the wilderness (Deut. 8). Furthermore, He sometimes brings sickness and other calamities as He did with Job, Hezekiah, and Paul (Job 1:1–20; 19:25; 2 Chron. 32; 2 Cor. 12).

What was the attitude of these men as God "left" them? Job said: "I know that my Redeemer lives, and at the last He will take His stand on the earth. Even after my skin is flayed, yet in my flesh I shall see God" (Job 19:25). He also said: "though He slay me, yet will I trust Him" (13:15). It is said of Hezekiah that he "humbled the pride of his heart" (2 Chron. 32:26). And Paul declared,

> And He [Christ] has said to me, "My grace is sufficient for you, for power is perfected in weakness." Most gladly, therefore, I will rather boast about my weaknesses, that the power of Christ may dwell in me. Therefore I am well content with weaknesses, with insults, with distresses, with persecutions, with difficulties, for Christ's sake, for when I am weak, then I am strong" (2 Cor. 12:9–10).

The Westminster Confession of Faith deals with this subject with greater detail.[253]

> *The most wise, righteous, and gracious God, doth oftentimes leave for a season his own children to manifold temptations,*

253. See our exposition of Larger Catechism Question 18 in *The Reality of Providence.*

> *and the corruptions of their own hearts, to chastise them for their former sins, or to discover [reveal] to them the hidden strength of corruption, and deceitfulness of their hearts, that they may be humbled; and to raise them to a more close and constant dependence for their support upon himself, and to make them more watchful against all future occasions of sin, and for sundry other just and holy ends* (WCF, V, v).

So then, why does God ever *order things* so that His people may be *assaulted, foiled and for a time led captive by temptations*? The Westminster Confession defines some of those *divers holy and just ends*: (1) *To chasten them for their former sins*; (2) *To discover* [reveal] *unto them the hidden strength of corruption and deceitfulness of their hearts;*[254] (3) *That they may be humbled*; (4) *To raise them to a more close and constant dependence for their support upon Himself*; and (5) *To make them more watchful against all future occasions of sin.*

> There may be several reasons, but a very common one is that He desires to teach us a lesson, that we may be cured of our own pride and conceit and self-confidence. Perhaps we have a deeply rooted personal weakness or sin of character, and God lets us go all the way of that sin, in order that we may learn to abhor it. Perhaps we are proud, and God causes us to stumble over our own pride, that we may be humbled. Perhaps we are forever walking on the very edge of the world, and God lets us slip right into the world, that we may be cured of our carelessness, and be sanctified. Perhaps we are playing with the fire of worldly pleasures, and God causes us to burn ourselves badly, that we may learn to keep our garments clean. The apostle Peter was inclined to trust in self and to boast in his own strength. And the Lord warned him. But the more he was warned, the more loudly he boasted that

254. God does these things so that "a man shall see that it is God alone who keeps from all sin. Until we are tempted, we think we live on our own strength. Though all men do this or that, we will not. When the trial comes, we quickly see, whence is our preservation by standing or falling. So was it in the case of Abimeleck, Gen. xxiii:6" (Owen, *The Works of John Owen,* 7:440).

> he was ready to go with Jesus into prison and into death, and that he would never be offended. And God prepared all the circumstances for Peter's temptation. He let him climb the full height of his self-confidence, in order then to withdraw His grace and Spirit from him, though not entirely, and expose his utter lack of strength, by leading him into the trap of temptation when he denied his Lord. And thus the Lord sanctifies and reforms His children in a pedagogical way, that they may be saved. But the sincere child of God is deathly afraid of this extreme remedy. He dreads it. He hopes that it may never by necessary. And therefore he prays, "Lead us not into temptation."[255]

The Power of Evil

> Acknowledging...that Satan, the world, and the flesh, are ready powerfully to draw us aside, and ensnare us.

This statement of our Catechism is anything but an exaggeration. *Satan* is always ready to trap us and destroy us: "Then Satan stood up against Israel and moved David to number Israel" (1 Chron. 21:1). This *world* of evil people is full of traps and seductions for the believer, and we are always in great danger of being overcome by them: "Be on guard, that your hearts may not be weighted down with dissipation and drunkenness and the worries of life, and that day come on you suddenly like a trap; for it will come upon all those who dwell on the face of all the earth" (Luke 21:34–350). And the remaining, indwelling sin in the believer, *i.e.*, the *flesh*, is always working against the believer to destroy him: "Each one is tempted when he is carried away and enticed by his own lust" (James 1:14).

The Weakness of Man

> Acknowledging...that we, even after the pardon of our sins, by reason of our corruption, weakness, and want [lack] of

255. Hoeksema, *The Triple Knowledge*, 3:621–22.

> watchfulness, are not only subject to be tempted, and forward to expose ourselves unto temptations, but also of ourselves unable and unwilling to resist them, to recover out of them, and to improve them; and worthy to be left under the power of them.

Even true believers in Jesus, who have experienced regeneration and forgiveness of sins, sill have remaining in us moral *corruption,* a host of *weaknesses* and withal a frequent lack or *want of watchfulness*[256] regarding sin and its avoidance: "For the flesh sets its desire against the Spirit, and the Spirit against the flesh; for these are in opposition to one another, so that you may not do the things that you please" (Gal. 5:17). Because of this indwelling sin described in Romans 7, we are *not only subjected to be tempted,* and ready, quick, eager and *forward to expose ourselves into temptations* (As Peter in Matthew 26:69f and Galatians 2:11f, and Jehoshaphat in 2 Chronicles 18:3f and 19:2f), but we *of ourselves* are *unable and unwilling to resist them, to recover out of them, and to improve them*: "but I see a different law in the members of my body, waging war against the law of my mind, and making me a prisoner of the law of sin which is in my members. Wretched man that I am! Who will set me free from the body of this death?" (Rom. 7:23–24) (as David in 1 Chronicles 12:1f, and Asa in 2 Chronicles 16:7f). There we are *worthy to be left under the power of* the temptations of the world, the flesh and the devil, but for the grace of God!: "But My people did not listen to My voice; and Israel did not obey Me. So I gave them over to the stubbornness of their heart, to walk in their own devices" (Ps. 81:11–12).

The Content of the Sixth Petition

The Larger Catechism explains the content of the Sixth Petition with four points.

---

256. Matthew 26:41: Keep watching and praying, that you may not enter into temptations; the spirit is willing, but the flesh is weak.

That We Might be Kept From Temptation

> We pray, that God would so over-rule the world and all in it, subdue the flesh, and restrain Satan, order all things, bestow and bless all means of grace, and quicken us to watchfulness in the use of them, that we and all his people may by his providence be kept from being tempted to sin.
>
> We are to pray that he would keep us from falling by temptation, that it may be like a wave dashing against a rock, which remains unmoved, or like a dart shot against a breastplate of steel, which only blunts its point, and returns it back without receiving injury.[257]

The Goal of This Petition: To be Kept from Temptation

> I do not ask Thee to take them out of the world, but to keep them from the evil one (John 17:15).

The fact that Christ's disciples are not "of the world," (James 4:4, 1 John 2:15–17), is no reason to pray that they should be removed "out of the world." They are to remain as shining lights "in the world" (Phil. 2:15). Jesus makes it clear in His High Priestly Prayer that He does not want His disciples "raptured" out of this evil world.

> Their place is still in the world. It would be...disastrous for the world to have them taken out of the world.... The place of God's people is in the world, though, of course, not of it.... His prayer is...that they should be kept [guarded, protected] from evil.... They have a task to do in the world so it is important that they should be in the world. But it is equally important that they should be kept from evil, for evil is fatal to the discharge of their task.[258]

---

257. Ridgeley, *Commentary on the Larger Catechism*, 2:661.

258. Leon Morris, *The New International Commentary on the New Testament: The Gospel According to John* (Grand Rapids, MI: William B. Eerdmans Publishing Co., 1971), 730.

Earlier in His Prayer, Jesus petitions the Father: "Holy Father, keep them in Thy name, the name which Thou hast given Me, that they may be one, even as We are" (John 17:11). Jesus is praying that God would keep His disciples from evil by keeping them in His Name, *i.e.*, by keeping them under the direction and saving power of "the name which is above every name" (Phil. 3:9). God raised Jesus from the dead and seated Him at His own right hand "far above all rule and authority and power and dominion, and every name that is named, not only in this age, but also in the one to come" (Eph. 1:21). Therefore, "there is salvation in no one else; for there is no other name under heaven that has been given among men, by which we must be saved" (Acts 4:12).

So then, Jesus is praying that God would keep His disciples *under the saving power of His Name*, delivering us daily from the power, deceit, pressures, attractions, temptations and tyranny of sin, and *under the governing authority of His Name*, enabling us to walk faithfully in His ways regardless of our emotional state. Verse eleven concludes with the reason for Jesus' petition. He prays that God would keep us in His name so that we would be kept in Christian unity, because we are so vulnerable, so susceptible to temptation, so prone to wander when we stand alone, besides the fact that we are so easily scattered.

Christ's prayer that God would protect His disciples from evil in all its forms is inseparable from His prayer that God would consecrate them to Himself: "Sanctify them in Thy truth; Thy word is truth" (John 17:17). With this petition Jesus prays that His disciples might be "more and more delivered from the power of sin in all its forms, and more and more conformed to the will and image of God, and that this might be effected by means of God's truth."[259]

The Means By Which This Goal will be Reached

God will keep His people from temptation in at least seven ways.

259. John Brown, *An Exposition of Our Lord's Intercessory Prayer* (William Oliphant, 1866; reprint Minneapolis, MN: Klock & Klock Christian Publishers, 1978), 93.

By God's Over-Ruling of the World

> I do not ask Thee to take them out of the world, but to keep them from evil (John 17:15).

This verse is a petition of prayer by Jesus to His Father. Its implication is that the sovereign God is in total control of His creation, including Satan and all evil forces, having foreordained whatever comes to pass for His own glory and the benefit of His people. Therefore, Jesus is asking God to over-rule the evil designs of Satan, the evil intentions of the world, and the desires of the "flesh" so that none of them will accomplish their objectives in the lives of His chosen people. As Jesus said to Peter, "Simon, Simon, behold, Satan has demanded permission to sift you like wheat; but I have prayed for you, that your faith may not fail" (Luke 22:31–32).

By God's Subduing of the Flesh

> Create in me a clean heart, O God,
> And renew a steadfast spirit within me (Ps. 51:10).

> Establish my footsteps in Thy word,
> And do not let any iniquity have dominion over me
> (Ps. 119:133).

Only God can subdue, hold in check, and finally destroy indwelling sin, or what Paul calls "the flesh." In the conclusion of his description of the ferocious struggle that goes on in him as a Christian between his Spiritually renewed heart and the remnants of his fallen nature, Paul cries out: "Wretched man that I am! Who will set me free from the body of this death? Thanks be to God through Jesus Christ our Lord!" (Rom. 7:24–25). He hates his sinfulness. He hates himself for sinning. He loves His Lord and Savior; and he loves the Law of his Lord and Savior. And yet, remaining a sinner until death, he continues to sin and to do the things that, in his new heart, he does not want to do. At the same time, because of his remaining sinfulness, he finds it difficult to do consistently the things his new heart desires to do, *i.e.*, worship, serve and obey God completely. Therefore, he rejoices that any victory he has over sin in his life, any subduing of the evil desires that originate in his "flesh," are the result of the work of Jesus Christ for him, in his death and resurrection, and in him by the sanctifying power of the Spirit of Christ (Rom. 8:1–14; Gal. 5:16–25).

We see this attitude of Paul also expressed in the words of the psalmist. In confessing his sins with Bethsheba to the Lord, David also prays, in his own words, that God would "subdue his flesh" that made adultery with her so easy, so that he would not be tempted to such heinous crimes again. He prayed: "Create in me a clean heart, O God, and renew a steadfast spirit within me." This petition is a confession of his sinfulness and of his dependence on God's almighty power and sovereign grace for the removal of that sinfulness. A "clean heart" signifies affections and motives free from sin's pollution. "Create" indicates the necessity of the intervention of Almighty God. "In me" is more literally "for or to me," suggesting that this work of God is a gift of grace. The prayer for the renewal of "a steadfast spirit within me" is a prayer for a firm, stable, unwavering spirit free from fickleness and cowardice. "Renew" implies

> a previous possession of it, derived not from nature but from grace, and interrupted by his yielding to temptation. Though his faith and love could not utterly fail, his fixedness of purpose was destroyed for the time, and could only be recovered by a new conversion.[260]

Later in Psalm 119:133, when David prays for God to "establish" his footsteps in His word and not to let "any iniquity have dominion" over him, he is praying that God would cause him to walk safely and firmly in the path of His Law and to subdue within him the remaining power of corruption so that it will not oppress him. In other words, in the two clauses of this verse David is praying that God would conform him to his Word, and give him the power to withstand all temptations by the work of God's Spirit within him overcoming and bridling the "flesh."

---

260. Joseph A. Alexander, *The Psalms Translated and Explained* (Grand Rapids, MI: Baker Book House, [1873] 1975), 232.

We can do nothing at all, except God governeth us by his holy spirit. So then, it is not enough that we have the word of God preached to us, to hear it, and to be exercised in the reading thereof: But it is God that must put to His helping hand over and besides: he it is that must make the preaching of it effectual, and pierce our ears, to the end we might understand that which is set down unto us, and open our eyes when we read, and that altogether by his Holy Spirit.... And besides, it is not enough to have the knowledge of the will of God, and to understand the right way to salvation: But God also must lead us himself, and hold us by the hand even unto the end. And why so? For we will never cease drawing backward, when as God shall have faithfully instructed us, if so be he himself doth not still conduct us, and always holdeth us with a strong and mighty arm: because that our rebellious nature will never cease to withdraw us clean contrary....

David goeth forward and saith, *Suffer not any iniquity to have dominion over me.* To what end, and purpose saith he this? For he had before desired God to order his steps, to the end he might serve him in true and faithful obedience. Forsooth [*in truth*] it is, because that when God hath bestowed his grace upon us, to be desirous to cleave unto him, yet shall we never come to the full end thereof without great afflictions, having so mighty an enemy to stand against us as we have. It is very true that we desire nothing else but to be made teachable of God, and to suffer ourselves to be governed by the great Pastor and Shepherd, Jesus Christ: this already one good step: but let us a little better consider, wherefore such grace profiteth us not. It is because the Devil cometh soon after to set it on fire, for always findeth good store of wood in us according as we are stored with many vices and imperfections in our nature, until such time as God shall have wholly taken us from out of this flesh. For all our lusts and affections are so many rebellions against God, as that we never cease to fight against him, that if at anytime on the one side we go about to do good, we are on the other side carried to do evil.

What must we then do? We had need to have God to array us with a power and constancy, to resist all these contrarieties and wicked lusts which are in us: that we be not only teachable, and governed by him, but also that we be fenced with such armor and weapon, as are needed to fight against Satan and all his crafty sleights and strengths, to the end our enemy might have no hold of us.... And when as we shall be thus armed, then to see how we ought wholly and fully cleave unto God....

So then, it is not without cause, that David here [Ps. 119:133] joineth these two things together, to be guided by the majesty of God, and above all to be so mightily strengthened, as that no iniquity could have dominion over him but that he was well able to overcome all the temptations wherewith Satan any way could assail him.[261]

By God's Restraining of Satan

And because of the surpassing greatness of the revelations, for this reason, to keep me from exalting myself, there was given me a thorn in the flesh, a messenger of Satan to buffet me—to keep me from exalting myself. Concerning this I entreated the Lord three times that it might depart from me (2 Cor. 12:7–8).

John Owen has pointed out that

Satan tempts sometimes singly by himself, without taking advantage from the world, the things, or persons of it, or ourselves. So he deals in his injection of evil and blasphemous thoughts of God, into the hearts of the saints.... These fiery darts are prepared in the forge of his own malice, and shall

261. Calvin, *Sermons on Psalm 119*, 342–45.

> with all their venom and poison be turned into his own heart for ever.[262]

And the believer cannot overcome the "fiery darts" Satan hurls at him except *by God's restraining of Satan.* How does He do it?

First, God restrains Satan by His sovereign will and omnipotence, which Satan cannot resist, frustrate or overturn. *God from all eternity did, by the most wise and holy counsel of his own will, freely and unchangeably ordain whatsoever comes to pass* (Westminster Confession of Faith, III, i). And according to His eternal decree, "God causes all things to work together for good to those who love God, to those who are called according to His purpose" (Rom. 8:28). Therefore, we do not need to fear Satan, because "the very hairs of your head are all numbered" by God (Matt. 10:30), and "not a hair of your head will perish" without His will (Luke 21:18). In other words, our Father's sovereignty and omnipotence restrain Satan.

Second, Jesus triumphed over Satan in His death on the cross and in so doing greatly curtailed Satan's power and influence in the lives of God's people: "Since the children share in flesh and blood, He Himself likewise also partook of the same, that through death He might render powerless him who had the power of death, that is, the devil; and might deliver those who through fear of death were subject to slavery all their lives" (Heb. 2:14–15). "At the cross, the place of death, the decisive encounter between God and Satan occurred. The Son came into the world precisely for this purpose, that *through death,* his death, he might render ineffective our enemy *the devil* who wields *the power of death.*"[263] The redemptive work of Christ undoes and renders inoperative the enslaving work of Satan over those for whom Christ died. They are set free from their bondage to his tyranny. As John wrote: "the one who practices sin [habitually] is of the devil... The Son of God appeared for this purpose, that He might destroy the works of the devil" (1 John 3:8). Therefore, he can say this to believers: "You are from God, little children,

262. Owen, *The Works of John Owen,* 7:442.

263. Philip E. Hughes, *A Commentary on the Epistle to the Hebrews* (Grand Rapids, MI: William B. Eerdmans Publishing Co., 1977), 111.

and have overcome them; because greater is He who is in you than he who is in the world" (1 John 4:4).

When Jesus cast out the demons from a demon-possessed man, the Pharisees said that He could do that only because He was in league with Satan (Matt. 12:24). His answer is an irrefutable one: "And if Satan casts out Satan, he is divided against himself; how then shall his kingdom stand? And if I by Beelzebul cast out demons, by whom do your sons cast them out? Consequently they shall be your judges" (Matt. 12:26–27). He then explains what His power to expel demons means: "But if I cast out demons by the Spirit of God, then the kingdom of God has come upon you. Or how can anyone enter the strong man's house and carry off his property, unless he first binds the strong man? And then he will plunder his house" (12:28–29). Jesus came to bind the strong man restraining him from his overpowering influence on us who are believers in Jesus Christ.

> Let Christians rejoice, that if a subtle, cruel, active, and powerful enemy is continually prowling about, the eye of infinite wisdom and love rests ever on them, the arm of never-tiring omnipotence is around them to protect and defend them. The lion of hell is a chained lion, a muzzled lion, to the Christian. He may alarm, but he shall never devour them. His chain is in the hand of his conqueror and their Lord.[264]

Third, because of the believer's union with Christ, he can triumph over Satan's schemes in his daily life. Before his conversion, the believer was "energized" by Satan (Eph. 2:1–2), but he is now "energized by the Holy Spirit," who has set him free from the power of sin and death. He is in a position in Christ to "crush Satan" under his feet by the power of the preached Word and a faithful Christian life (Rom. 16:20). Now in Christ by the power of the Holy Spirit, the believer is victorious over Satan's influences, temptations and seductions. Therefore, Peter can exhort us: "Be of sober spirit, be on the alert. Your adversary, the devil, prowls about like a roaring lion, seeking someone to

---

264. John Brown, *Expository Discourses on 1 Peter*, 2 vols. (Edinburgh/ Pennsylvania: The Banner of Truth Trust, 1975), 2:571.

devour. But resist him, firm in your faith, knowing that the same experiences of suffering are being accomplished by your brethren who are in the world" (1 Pet. 5:8–9). And James can exhort us: "Submit therefore to God. Resist the devil and he will flee from you. Draw near to God and He will draw near to you. Cleanse your hands, you sinners; and purify your hearts, you double-minded." (James 4:7–8).

Now, the question is how is the Christian to resist Satan in his life?

First, he must resist Satan's attacks on himself in the form of temptations. He must

> carefully keep out of the way of temptation, avoid every thing that can be avoided in consistency with duty, which may afford an opportunity to the great enemy or his agents to assail him with solicitations to sin.... When the Christian is attacked, he must not flee, he must not yield himself up into the hands of his enemy; he must resist, he must oppose him. He must not comply with his solicitations.... He must not allow himself to deliberate on a proposal which involves in it the denial of truth, the neglect of duty, or the commission of sin, by whatever plausibilities and apparent advantages it may be recommended, but immediately, and with abhorrence, reject it.[265]

Second, he must attack Satan.

> Non-compliance with the suggestions of the wicked one is, however, but a part of the Christian duty of resistance. The Christian must oppose the wicked one. He must not merely stand on the defensive; he must attack the enemy.... He must so resist the devil as that he shall flee from him. In plain words, he must make solicitations to sin occasions and means of progress in holiness. For example, when tempted to fretfulness under affliction, instead of yielding to the temptation, he must 'glorify God in the fires,' by more than ever possessing his soul in patience.... When tempted to be

265. Brown, *Expository Discourses on 1 Peter,* 2:573.

> ashamed of Christ or his cause, he must seize that opportunity of making his conduct proclaim more loudly than ever, 'God forbid that I should glory, save in the cross of our Lord Jesus Christ.' ... Let temptations to carelessness produce increased vigilance, and to indolence increased diligence.[266]

Third, He must resist Satan's attacks on the cause of Christ. Satan is

> constantly engaged in endeavoring to corrupt the truth as it is in Jesus; to introduce, and maintain, and extend error, and superstition, and fanaticism, and schism, and bigotry, and disorder and impurity into the churches of Christ, and to oppose the exertions which are making to diffuse the knowledge and the influence of the truth and grace which came by Jesus Christ. The Christian is to fight against Satan, not only in his own heart, but in the church and the world.[267]

Fourth, he must be "of sober spirit" and "on the alert," or as the KJV has it to be "sober and vigilant." He sees things as they really are, in the light of God's Word, and he is not intoxicated by this evil world. His priorities are straight. He understands that God is more excellent than man, that heaven is better than earth, and far better than hell, and that time is shorter than eternity. He is always watchful and on guard against Satan's attacks, keeping his heart with all diligence, for out of it are the issues of life (Prov. 4:25, 26).

> He must, like a watchful sentinel, take good heed, that through none of the external senses, the gates, as [John] Bunyan represents them, of the good town Mansoul, the great adversary, under any disguise, finds his way to the citadel of the heart. He must be watchful, for his enemy is so.[268]

Fifth, he must be "firm" and "steadfast in the faith." Having believed "the faith," *i.e.*, the system of revealed truth in the Bible, he

266. Brown, *Expository Discourses on 1 Peter,* 2:573–74.
267. Brown, *Expository Discourses on 1 Peter,* 2:575.
268. Brown, *Expository Discourses on 1 Peter,* 2:581.

must continue believing it, keeping it habitually before his mind, meditating on it, ever increasing his understanding of it and improving his application of it in his life. "Let him lose sight of the truth...and, like Samson shorn of his locks, he is weak as another man. Whenever he staggers through unbelief, he becomes powerless in resisting the great adversary."[269]

Sixth, he must "submit to God." "To set ourselves under [submit to] God is to subordinate ourselves to Him, to bring our wills under His control, to yield cordial obedience to His commands."[270]

Seventh, he must "draw near to God." James was probably thinking of Psalm 145:18: "The LORD is near to all who call upon Him, to all who call upon Him in truth." "The closer we live to God, the more we know of His comfort, support, and power, and the easier it is to resist the devil."[271]

Eighth, he must live a pure life, inside and out: "Cleanse your hands...purify your hearts." "To profess to be seeking the Divine forgiveness and favour while cherishing and practicing consciously, willfully what he hates, is mockery,—an insult to the Majesty of heaven, a profanation of the mercy-seat."[272]

By God's Ordering All Things

> Therefore let him who thinks he stands take heed lest he fall. No temptation has overtaken you but such as is common to man; and God is faithful, who will not allow you to be tempted beyond what you are able; but with the temptation will provide the way of escape also, that you may be able to endure it (1 Cor. 10:12–13).

God orders and orchestrates everything that happens in our lives so that: (1) Believers will experience no temptation to sin that is not "common to man." (2) Believers will never experience a temptation to sin that is greater than they can resist as they are trusting

---

269. Brown, *Expository Discourses on 1 Peter,* 2:583.
270. Vaughan, *James: A Study Guide,* 89.
271. Vaughan, *James: A Study Guide,* 90.
272. John Adam, quoted in Vaughan, *James: A Study Guide,* 91.

in Him. (3) When temptations do come God will always provide a way of escape for us, *i.e.*, a true and working solution in the Word of God, so that we will not be forced to give in to the temptation. And the believer can be certain of these things because "God is faithful."

This verse presupposes the sovereignty and omnipotence of God, who is able to do all His holy will and perform all He decrees. It presupposes that God is in total control of all of creation. As God said: "I am the LORD, and there is no other, the One forming light and creating darkness, causing well-being and creating calamity; I am the LORD who does all these" (Isa. 46:6–7).

By God's Blessing All Means of Grace

> Now the God of peace, who brought up from the dead the great Shepherd of the sheep through the blood of the eternal covenant, even Jesus our Lord, equip you in every good thing to do His will, working in us that which is pleasing in His sight, through Jesus Christ; to whom be the glory forever and ever. Amen (Heb. 13:20–21).

We have learned from our study of Larger Catechism Q. 154 that *the outward and ordinary means whereby Christ communicates to his church the benefits of his mediation, are all his ordinances; especially the word, sacraments, and prayer; all which are made effectual to the elect for their salvation.* Here we saw three truths. First, God has ordained the means of grace, *i.e.*, whatever God has commanded of us in His Word as to how He wants to be worshiped and served, especially prayer, the preaching of the Word and the sacraments of baptism and the Lord's Supper. Second, as means of saving grace, through them God communes with His Church and conveys into the lives of His people the benefits purchased for them by the life and death of the Mediator of the New Covenant, Jesus Christ. Third, these ordinances, or means of grace, do not convey the blessings of God's grace automatically into our lives merely by our physical partaking of them. They are *made effectual to the elect for their salvation* by the work of the Holy Spirit, as Larger Catechism Q. 155 and Q. 161 taught us.[273]

273. Larger Catechism Q. 155: *The Spirit of God maketh the reading, but es-*

The point of this brief summary of the doctrine of the means of grace is this: God keeps us from temptation and delivers us from evil by blessing all his ordinances to be real means of grace in our lives, conveying God's all-sufficient grace to us that we might stand against temptation effectively.

Hebrews 13:20–21 is essentially a prayer for God to bless His means of grace, "working in us that which is pleasing in His sight through Jesus Christ" in order that we who are the sheep of the great Shepherd and who are in covenant with Him because of His blood through faith, might be equipped "in every good thing to do His will." The text contains several important truths that should be carefully studied: (1) God Himself brings and establishes His peace in our lives and in all our relationships. (2) The price paid for that peace was the shed blood of Jesus purchasing God's covenant promises for us. (3) The proof of God's acceptance of Christ's sacrifice in our behalf is Christ's resurrection and exaltation. (4) God establishes His peace in us Spiritually by working into us the desire and will-power to do what is pleasing to Him. (5) This enables believers in Jesus Christ to will what God wills and to live for His glory. "Thus in Christ the lifeline which connects the creature to the Creator and His eternal purposes is restored."[274]

By God's Quickening Us to Watchfulness in The Use of the Means of Grace

> Keep watching and praying, that you may not enter into temptation: the spirit is willing, but the flesh is weak (Matt. 26:41).

What does it mean to "enter into temptation"? It is not merely to be tempted and it is not to be conquered by temptation, *i.e.*, to commit the sin we are tempted to commit. A person may "enter into temptation" and yet not do what he is tempted to do. "God can make

---

pecially the preaching of the Word, an effectual means of enlightening. Larger Catechism Q. 161: *The sacraments become effectual means of salvation...only by the working of the Holy Ghost, and the blessing of Christ.*

274. Hughes, *A Commentary on the Epistle to the Hebrews*, 591.

a way for a man to escape, when he is in, he can break the snare, tread down Satan, and make the soul more than a conqueror, though it have entered into temptation."[275]

To "enter into temptation" is, as Paul said, "fall into temptation" (1 Tim. 6:9).

> As a man falls into a pit or a deep place, where are gins [traps] and snares, wherewith he is entangled, the man is not presently killed and destroyed, but he is entangled and detained, he knows not how to get free, or be at liberty. So it is expressed again to the same purpose in 1 Cor. x:13, 'no temptation hath taken you'; that is, to be taken by a temptation, and to be tangled with it, held in its cords, not finding at present a way to escape. Thence saith 2 Peter ii:9—'The Lord knoweth how to deliver the godly out of temptations': they are entangled with them, God knows how to deliver them out of them. When we suffer a temptation to enter into us, then we enter into temptation: whilst it knocks at the door, we are at liberty; but when any temptation comes in, and parlies with the heart, reasons with the mind, entices and allures the affections, be it long or a short time, do it thus insensibly and imperceptibly, or do the soul take notice of it, we enter into temptation.

So then, unto our entering into temptation is required,

(1) That by some advantage, or on some occasion, Satan be more earnest than ordinary in his solicitations to sin, by affrightments or allurements, by persecutions or seductions, by himself or others; or that some lust or corruption by his instigation, and advantages of outward objects provoking, as in prosperity, or terrifying, as in trouble, do tumultuate more than ordinary within us....

(2) That the heart be so far entangled with it, as to be put to dispute, and argue in its own defense, and yet not be wholly able to eject or cast out the poison, and leaven that which hath

275. Owen, *The Works of John Owen,* 7:444–45.

> been injected; but is surprised, if be never so little off its watch, into an entanglement not easy to be avoided; so that the soul may cry, and pray, and cry again, and yet not be delivered; as Paul sought the Lord thrice for the departure of his temptation and prevailed not. The entanglement continues.[276]

Now the question arises: what are the means of preventing our entering into temptation? Jesus answers: "keep watching and keep praying."

To "watch" is to be on guard, to be alert, considering all the ways and means by which temptation can sneak up on us and attack us. In other words, "Don't be caught off-guard!"

> A universal carefulness, and diligence, exercising itself in, and by all ways and means, prescribed by God, over our hearts and ways, the baits and methods of Satan, the occasions and advantages of sin in the world, that we be not entangled, is that which in this word is pressed on us.[277]

Or as the book of Proverbs exhorts us: "Keep your heart with all diligence for out of it flow the issues of life."

As we keep a watchful eye on ourselves and on the world around us, we are to continue to "pray," to cry out to God to keep us from entering into temptation because it is only by His all-sufficient grace that we are kept from falling.

> Watch *yourselves,* and pray *yourselves.* Watch and pray against this present temptation to drowsiness and security; *pray* that you may *watch*; beg of God by his grace to keep you awake, now that there is occasion.... Watch and pray against the further temptation you may be assaulted with; *watch and pray* lest this sin prove the inlet of many more.[278]

---

276. Owen, *The Works of John Owen,* 7:445–46.
277. Owen, *The Works of John Owen,* 7:449.
278. Henry, *Matthew Henry's Commentary on the Whole Bible,* 5:323.

> The manner of resistance [to temptation] which is here enjoined is, not to draw courage from reliance on our own strength and perseverance, but, on the contrary, from a conviction of our weakness, to ask arms and strength from the Lord. Our *watching*, therefore, will be of no avail without *prayer*.[279]

The reason Jesus gives us for watching and praying that we enter not into temptation is this: "the spirit is willing but the flesh is weak." The believer in Jesus has been Spiritually regenerated (1 John 5:1). He is a "new creation" (2 Cor. 5:17), with new desires and affections. God's Holy Spirit has implanted within him a seed of new life and a willingness to love and obey God, so that the believer "joyfully concurs with the Law of God in the inner man" (Rom. 7:22). God's Spirit within him enables him to walk in God's statutes with great carefulness (Ezek. 36:27). And yet, remnants of that old fallen human nature that once dominated his life still remain within him. He struggles against this old "flesh," with its old desires, habits and tendencies (Rom. 7). It constantly struggles against the Spirit of God indwelling him (Gal. 5:17), and the Spirit constantly wages war against that flesh. And victory in this battle comes only through faith in Christ (Rom. 7:24–25) and living in the Spirit of God (Gal. 5:16f).

This "weakness" of the "flesh" that characterizes the believer's life in this world is real and dangerous. The spirit, *i.e.*, his Spiritually new life in Christ, is eager to endure and overcome temptation, but the indwelling sin within the believer is weak, utterly helpless in temptation, "a drag and a terrible handicap to the spirit in us. By calling on the disciples to watch and to pray Jesus seeks to rouse their spirit into full activity. By sleeping and giving way to sleep-producing sorrow of heart they were yielding to the flesh."[280, 281]

---

279. Calvin, *Commentary on the Harmony of the Evangelists, Matthew, Mark, and Luke*, 3:235–36.

280. Lenski, *The Interpretation of St. Matthew's Gospel*, 1042.

281. It should be pointed out again that no neo-platonism is implied here. To say that within the believer is a war between the spirit and the flesh is not to say that that battle is the spiritual side of man versus his physical side. The Bible attributes no such dichotomy to human beings, whom God created and pronounced good, body and soul. The war is between the Spirit of God within the believer and

In and of ourselves, we are weakness itself. In ourselves,

> we have no strength, no power to withstand. Confidence of any strength in us, is one great part of our weakness.... And, which is worse, it is the worst kind of weakness that is in us; a weakness from treachery; a weakness arising from that party which every temptation hath in us. If a castle or fort be never so strong and well fortified, yet if there be a treacherous party within, that is ready to betray it on every opportunity, there is no preserving it from the enemy. There are traitors in our hearts, ready to take part, to close, and side with every temptation, and to give up all to them; yea, to solicit and bribe temptations to do the work; as traitors incite an enemy. Do not flatter yourselves that you shall hold out; there are secret lusts that lie lurking in your hearts, which perhaps now stir not, which as soon as any temptation befalls you, will rise, tumultuate, cry, disquiet, seduce and never give over, until they are either killed or satisfied.[282]

> This admonition relates properly to believers, who, being regenerated by the Spirit of God, are desirous to do what is right, but still labour under the *weakness of the flesh*; for though the grace of *the Spirit* is vigorous in them, they are *weak* according to the *flesh*. And though the disciples alone have their weakness here pointed out to them, yet, since what Christ says of them applies equally to all, we ought to draw from it a general rule, that it is our duty to keep diligent *watch* by *praying*; for we do not yet possess the power of *the Spirit* in such a measure as not to fall frequently through the *weakness of the flesh*, unless the Lord grant his assistance to raise up and uphold us. But there is no reason why we should tremble with excessive anxiety; for an undoubted remedy is held out to us, which we will neither have far to seek nor to seek in vain; for Christ promises that all who, being earnest

---

the sin that remains within him. Paul uses the word "flesh," for man's fallen and sinful human nature in this world.

282. Owen, *The Works of John Owen*, 7:454.

in *prayer*, shall perseveringly oppose the slothfulness of the flesh, will be victorious.[283]

By God's Providence Keeping Us From Being Tempted to Sin

> Also keep back Thy servant from presumptuous sins;
> Let them not rule over me (Ps. 19:13).

In fulfilling His promise in Romans 8:28 that He would cause everything that happens to those who love Him in Christ to work together for their good, God makes this additional promise:

> No temptation has overtaken you but such as is common to man; and God is faithful, who will not allow you to be tempted beyond what you are able; but with the temptation will provide the way of escape also, that you may be able to endure it (1 Cor. 10:13).

Therefore, David can pray, asking God to "keep back Thy servant from presumptuous sins; let them not rule over me." David is praying for God's restraining and supporting grace, and for God in His providence to keep him from facing temptations to sin that are too powerful for him to resist. Calvin said that by "presumptuous sins," "he means known and evident transgressions accompanied with proud contempt and obstinacy."[284] "Presumptuous sins are here personified as tyrants who strive to bring the servant of God into unbecoming subjection to them. That the Lord alone can keep from this servitude, discovers the depth of human corruption."[285]

---

283. Calvin, *Commentary on the Harmony of the Evangelists, Matthew, Mark, and Luke*, 3:236.

284. Plumer, *Psalms: A Critical And Expository Commentary With Doctrinal & Practical Remarks*, 260.

285. Hengstenberg, quoted in Plumer, *Psalms: A Critical And Expository Commentary With Doctrinal & Practical Remarks*, 261.

That We Might be Kept in Temptation

> We pray that...if tempted, that by his Spirit we may be powerfully supported and enabled to stand in the hour of temptation.

> For this reason, I bow my knees before the Father, from whom every family in heaven and on earth derives its name, that He would grant you, according to the riches of His glory, to be strengthened with power through His Spirit in the inner man (Eph. 3:14–16).

> Now may our God and Father Himself and Jesus our Lord direct our way to you; and may the Lord cause you to increase and abound in love for one another, and for all men, just as we also do for you; so that He may establish your hearts unblamable in holiness before our God and Father at the coming of our Lord Jesus with all His saints (1 Thess. 3:11–13).

> Now to Him who is able to keep you from stumbling, and to make you stand in the presence of His glory blameless with great joy, to the only God our Savior, through Jesus Christ our Lord, be glory, majesty, dominion and authority, before all time and now and forever. Amen (Jude 24–25).

These three passages are prayers that essentially are asking God to strengthen and keep His people from falling when facing temptation, that *if tempted...by his Spirit we may be powerfully supported and enabled to stand in the hour of temptation.* In Ephesians 3:14–16, quoted above, Paul prays that God would strengthen the believers in Ephesus with His power through His Spirit in their hearts and minds, so that when temptation came they would "be strong in the Lord, and in the strength of His might" that they "may be able to stand firm against the schemes of the devil" (Eph. 6:10, 11). Therefore, having put on the "whole armor of God," and strengthened by the Spirit in their "inner man," believers are "able to resist in the evil day, and having done everything, to stand firm" (Eph. 6:13).

In 1 Thessalonians 3:11–13, Paul prays that God would cause the believers in Thessalonica to abound in love toward one another, "so that He may establish your hearts unblamable in holiness before our God and Father at the coming of our Lord Jesus with all His saints." The word "establish" has the idea of buttressing, supporting, encouraging. And so, he prays that God would support and encourage the hearts of the believers so that they will be "unblamable in holiness before our God" in their daily lives—not just blamelessness in total self-surrender to God before men, but blamelessness in total self-surrender to God "before God." "The believer does not simply live uprightly. He belongs to God; he is set apart entirely for God's service."[286] And, to be blameless in holiness before God, the believer would have to be "established," "buttressed," "supported," and "encouraged" by God in the midst of temptation so he would not cave in to it.

Jude's ascription of praise to God focuses on two things: (1) God's omnipotent ability to "keep you from stumbling and to make you stand in the presence of His glory blameless with great joy;" and (2) God's majestic glory and saviorhood revealed in Jesus Christ: "to the only God our Savior, through Jesus Christ our Lord, be glory, majesty, dominion and authority." We are such sinners that only God can save us and keep us saved. Only God can keep us from "stumbling," *i.e.*, sinning (James 2:10). Only God can keep us standing in "blamelessness and great joy" in the midst of temptations. Therefore only God can keep us from giving in to temptation; hence, we must earnestly and continually pray: "O Lord, keep us from stumbling. Keep us standing with blamelessness and joy in the midst of temptations."

That We Might be Recovered from Temptation

> We pray that...when fallen, raised again and recovered out of it, and have a sanctified use and improvement thereof.

286. Morris, *The First and Second Epistle to the Thessalonians,* 114.

Although Christians are no longer slaves to sin (Rom. 6:17), they are sinners, new creations in Christ, but sinners nevertheless. They are no longer "in sin," but sin remains in them. They were "dead in sin" and they are now "alive in God," but they struggle with the indwelling sin remaining in them until they die, and their only victory in this struggle is in and by Christ (Rom. 7). Because true believers often do not do the good they really want to do, and do sinful things they really do not want to do, they sometimes will yield to temptations and sin against God. When this happens they need for God to do two things for them: (1) To raise them out of temptation and bring them to spiritual recovery; and (2) To enable them to learn from the temptation they fell into and to use it to their spiritual advantage.

That, When Fallen, We Might Be Raised Again and Recovered Out of Temptation

> Restore to me the joy of Thy salvation,
> And sustain me with a willing spirit (Ps. 51:12).

When Christians fall into temptation, it does not mean that they throw the previous victories over sin away and must start all over again from zero in their Christian walk. Rather, confessing their sin and turning from it, rejoicing in Christ's perfect redemptive work for them, they can be recovered from it and continue their Christian lives where they left off before they sinned. But, just as only God could save them from sin in the first place, so only God can recover them out of temptation. And He does that by His grace for His people. David knew that, and so, after falling into the sin of adultery and being convicted of his sin, he cries out to God to restore to him "the joy of Thy salvation" by restoring him to godly living: "sustain me with a willing spirit." Sin interrupts the believer's fellowship with God, destroying his joy and weakening his assurance of his favor. Therefore, in his prayer for forgiveness of sin, and longing for the return of that fellowship and assurance of God's presence in his life, he beseeches God to lift him out of the pit into which he had fallen by renewing and sustaining within him "a spirit of spontaneous conformity to God's will."[287] David prays that God would "sustain" him, *i.e.*, hold him up and preserve him from falling into temptation as he had done before.

That We Might Have A Sanctified Use and Improvement of the Temptation

> Be of sober spirit, be on the alert. Your adversary, the devil, prowls about like a oaring lion, seeking someone to devour. But resist him, firm in your faith, knowing that the same experiences of suffering are being accomplished by your brethren who are in the world. And after you have suffered for a little, the God of all grace, who called you to His eternal glory in Christ, will Himself perfect, confirm, strengthen, and establish you. To Him be dominion forever and ever. Amen (1 Pet. 5:8–11).

> If we have fallen by a temptation, we are farther to pray that God would overrule it to his own glory and our spiritual advantage. Though there is nothing good in sin, yet God can bring good out of it. This He does when he humbles the sinner for it, makes him afraid of going near the brink of the pit into which he fell, and inclines him to be more watchful, that he may not, by indulging some sins, lay himself open to temptations which would lead him to the commission of many others. God's overruling a believer's fall for his good, will also induce him to depend on Christ by faith, sensible of his inability to resist the least temptation without him. It will likewise excite in him the greatest thankfulness to God, who has found a way for his escape out of the snare in which he was entangled; so that he will receive abundant advantage, and God will be greatly glorified.[288]

287. Alexander, *The Psalms Translated and Explained,* 233.
288. Ridgeley, *Commentary on the Larger Catechism*, 2:662.

1 Peter 5:8–11 tells those who are resisting Satan, with alertness, diligence and steadfastness of faith: "after you have suffered for a little, the God of all grace, who called you to His eternal glory in Christ, will Himself perfect, confirm, strengthen and establish you." We must suffer trials and temptations in this life but

> God will, notwithstanding, and even by means of these afflictions, promote your spiritual improvement, and add to your real happiness...through the preaching of God's word, the influence of his Spirit, and the overruling power of his providence, these afflictions should work together for [our] good, in the most extensive sense of the word, for making [us] really and ultimately completely holy and happy, in entire conformity to the holy, holy, holy ever-blessed One.[289]

More specifically the Word, Spirit and Providence of God will "perfect," complete, and fully equip us for faithful service to God in and by our suffering. God will "confirm" us through suffering trials and temptations. He will make and keep us firm, steadfast and unbending in the face of evil. He will "strengthen" us, enabling us "not only to stand, but to withstand; not only to keep [our] ground, but to press forward; not merely to defend [our] selves, but to attack [our] enemies."[290] And He will "establish" us. The Greek word for establish denotes "to make to rest securely as a building on its foundation."

> Afflictions both prove the soundness of the foundation, leading the Christian more narrowly to examine it, and prove, too, that he is really built on the foundation. The Christian who is enabled to triumph over temptation, is stronger than if he had never been tempted.... This is the great object of God to settle His people on the foundation, the rock Christ.... Never will we find safety, heart peace, and progress in holiness, till we are driven from everything in ourselves, to make [Christ] all our strength... to do nothing, to attempt nothing,

289. Brown, *Expository Discourses on 1 Peter,* 2:590.
290. Brown, *Expository Discourses on 1 Peter,* 2:593.

> to hope for nothing, but in him. Then shall we find his fullness and all-sufficiency, and be "more than conquerors through Him who hath loved us." Few things in Christian experience are more employed by God to bring His people into this state of settledness on the rock Christ, than the afflictions rising out of the assaults of the evil one, and that resistance to those assaults, which are accomplished in the whole Christian brotherhood in the world. Thus can God bring good out of evil; strengthen faith by what was meant to overthrow it; increase the holiness and comfort of His people by what was meant to involve them in guilt, and depravity, and misery.[291]

> "He shall perfect (that no defect may remain in you), he shall stablish (that ye may be guilty of no backsliding), he shall strengthen (that ye may overcome every adverse power), and thus he shall settle you" [Bengel], establish you more firmly than ever on the foundation, by those very means which were intended to remove you from it.[292]

That Our Sanctification and Salvation May Be Perfected

> We pray...that our sanctification and salvation may be perfected, Satan trodden under our feet, and we fully freed from sin, temptation, and all evil, forever.

When we pray the Sixth Petition of the Lord's Prayer, we are not only praying for deliverance from sin and evil in this life, we are praying for total, complete and unqualified deliverance from temptation and evil in all their forms and consequences forever. What a glorious day that will be! As believers we will experience the progressive perfection of our sanctification and salvation, for "He who began a good work in [us] will keep on perfecting it until the day of Christ Jesus" (Phil. 1:6), on which day this progressive work of sanc-

291. Brown, *Expository Discourses on 1 Peter,* 2:594–95.
292. Brown, *Expository Discourses on 1 Peter,* 2:595–96.

tification by God is completely consummated and we will be *fully freed from sin.* As believers we are able to be "serpent-treaders" in this life in getting victories over Satan's assaults, but at the Second Coming of Christ, Satan will be fully and eternally *trodden under our feet,* by being cast into hell forever (Rev. 20:10). And as believers we are freed from the power of sin and death by the regenerating power of the Holy Spirit, so that we are no longer slaves to sin, we are strengthened to resist temptation, and we are liberated from the debilitating and soul-destroying effects of all evil. But on the Last Day, when we are perfected totally as glorified human beings, we will be *fully freed from sin, temptation and all evil forever.*

> Now we pray to God that you do no wrong; not that we ourselves may appear approved, but that you may do what is right, even though we should appear unapproved. For we can do nothing against the truth, but only for the truth. For we rejoice when we ourselves are weak but you are strong; this we also pray for, that you be made complete (2 Cor. 13:7–9).

What is meant by the perfecting of sanctification and salvation in believers? It means that the lifelong process of sanctification and program of salvation from the punishment and power of sin in believers is brought to completion and is consummated. All the purposes and goals of God's saving plan for His people are reached—all of His people are saved totally and to the uttermost in the fullest sense of the words. Sanctification is concluded and perfected in glorification:

> For whom He foreknew, He also predestined to become conformed to the image of His Son, that He might be the firstborn among many brethren; and whom He predestined, these He also called; and whom He called, these He also justified; and whom He justified, these He also glorified (Rom. 8:29–30).

According to these verses the glorification of believers is inseparable from the glorification of Christ Himself. In Romans 8:17, we are told that believers and Christ are glorified together: "if indeed we suffer with Him in order that we may also be glorified with

Him." In fact, our glorification is connected with the glorification of the whole creation: "the creation itself also will be set free from its slavery to corruption into the freedom of the glory of the children of God" (Rom. 8:21).

> In Romans 8:29–30 it is apparent that the glorification spoken of in verse 20 is the realization of the predestinating purpose spoken of in verse 29, namely, conformity to the image of God's Son, that he might be the firstborn [preeminence and supereminence] among many brethren.... The glory bestowed upon the redeemed is derived from the relation they sustain to the "firstborn." But the specific character involved in being the "firstborn" is derived from the relation he sustains to the redeemed in that capacity. Hence they must be glorified *together.*[293]

Glorification is the completion of the whole process of salvation. It is

> the attainment of the goal to which the elect of God were predestinated in the eternal purpose of the Father and it involves the consummation of the redemption secured and procured by the vicarious work of Christ.... It is the complete and final redemption of the whole person when in the integrity of body and spirit the people of God will be conformed to the image of the risen, exalted and glorified Redeemer, when the very body of their humiliation will be conformed to the body of Christ's glory (*cf.* Phil. 3:21).[294]

It should also be pointed out that salvation is not perfected at the death of the believer. At that point he is made perfect in holiness as he enters immediately into the glorious presence of God, when "the spirits of just men [are] made perfect" (Heb. 12:23). But, how-

293. John Murray, *Collected Writings of John Murray,* 4 vols. (Edinburgh/Pennsylvania: The Banner of Truth Trust, 1977), 2:315.

294. John Murray, *Redemption Accomplished and Applied* (Grand Rapids, MI: William B. Eerdmans Publishing Co., 1955), 174.

ever glorious death may be for the believer, it is not the goal of his hope and expectation nor the goal of salvation.

> The redemption which Christ has secured for his people is redemption not only from sin but also from all its consequences. Death is the wages of sin and the death of believers does not deliver them from death.... Hence glorification has in view the destruction of death itself. It is to dishonour Christ and to undermine the nature of the Christian hope to substitute the blessedness upon which believers enter at death for the glory that is to be revealed when "this corruptible will put on incorruption and this mortal will put on immortality." ... Preoccupation with the event of death indicates a deflection of faith, of love, and of hope. We who have the firstfruits of the Spirit "groan without ourselves," the apostle reminds us, 'waiting for the adoption, the redemption of our body' (Rom. 8:23). That is the glorification.... This truth that glorification must wait for the resurrection of the body advises us that glorification is something upon which all the people of God will enter *together* at the same identical point in time.[295]

The believer's sanctification and salvation are perfected not in an individualistic manner, but in a covenantal manner. His sanctification and salvation are advanced to perfection as the whole body of Christ, of which he is a member, is brought by the Spirit to "the unity of the faith, and of the knowledge of the Son of God, to a mature man, to the measure of the stature which belongs to the fullness of Christ" (Eph. 4:13). Therefore, the perfection of the believer must be defined in terms of the perfection of the Body of Christ, the Family of God, the Covenant Community, the Church of Jesus Christ.

2 Corinthians 13:7–9 is a difficult passage to interpret. It is Paul's prayer for the Corinthian Church, and his concern is the perfection or completion of the Church. The Greek word for "be made complete" in verse 9 denotes "a correct articulating of limbs and

---

295. Murray, *Redemption Accomplished and Applied,* 174–75.

joints in the body, a resetting of what has been broken and dislocated, and hence a restoration of harmonious and efficient functioning."[296] Therefore, by praying for their perfection and completion, Paul is expressing his longing "to see them [the individual members that were at odds with each other] fully integrated in the communion of the Church as their proper sphere of life and function, harmoniously and fruitfully articulated as members together in the body of Christ."[297]

This union and solidarity of God's people in the process of sanctification in this life does not change in the perfection of their sanctification in glorification, as we have seen above.

> There is much for our instruction in this fact that the final act of the application of redemption is one that affects all alike at the same moment of time in the final accomplishment of God's redemptive design. It is as a body that the whole company of the redeemed will be glorified.... It is union with Christ that binds together all the phases of redemptive love and grace.... The glorification of the elect will coincide with the final act of the Father in the exaltation and glorification of the Son.[298]

That Satan Be Trodden Under Our Feet

> And the God of peace will soon crush Satan under your feet. The grace of our Lord Jesus be with you (Rom. 16:20).

This verse is obviously an allusion to God's word to Satan after the Fall of man into sin recorded in Genesis 3:15: "And I will put enmity between you and the woman, and between your seed and her seed; He shall bruise you on the head, and you shall bruise him on the heel." In this first gospel promise of the Bible, God promises the de-

---

296. Philip E. Hughes, *The New International Commentary on the New Testament: Paul's Second Epistle to the Corinthians* (Grand Rapids, MI: William B. Eerdmans Publishing Co., 1962), 484.

297. Hughes, *Paul's Second Epistle to the Corinthians*, 484.

298. Murray, *Redemption Accomplished and Applied*, 176–77.

feat of evil in this world subjectively and objectively. God sovereignly asserts that He "will put enmity between you and the woman, and between your seed and her seed." This means that He will reverse the effects of the Fall and of evil in the hearts of His chosen people. He will remove the enmity that exists in the sinner's heart for God and replace it with love for Him. Furthermore, He will remove the love for evil in the sinner's heart and replace it with enmity toward evil. This is the goal of regeneration and sanctification. But, God also promises to destroy evil and Satan objectively, historically and finally. He promises that the seed of the woman will "bruise" Satan's head, as Satan bruises His heal. This is an obvious reference to the Messiah, Jesus, who in His death on the cross, bruised by sin and Satan, in reality defeated Satan, crushing Satan's skull on Golgotha: "Since then the children share in flesh and blood, He Himself likewise also partook of the same, that through death He might render powerless him who had the power of death, that is, the devil" (Heb. 2:14). Therefore, Jesus could say with reference to the purpose of His death: "Now judgment is upon this world; now the ruler of this world shall be cast out. And I, if I be lifted up from the earth, will draw all men to Myself" (John 12:31–32). The apostle John, who recorded these words of Jesus explains them in 1 John 3:8: "The Son of God appeared for this purpose, that He might destroy the works of the devil."

It is in the light of this truth of the defeat of Satan in the death of Christ and because of that defeat that we must interpret Paul's promise to the Roman Christians in Romans 16:20: "And the God of peace will soon crush Satan under your feet." Every word in this promise is important. (1) God Himself will bring peace to His people and world by crushing Satan. (2) God will defeat Satan in history by using His Church, *i.e.*, under the feet of faithful believers. (3) He will do this "speedily."

> The promise of a victorious issue undergirds the fight of faith. The final subjugation of all enemies comes within the horizon of this promise (*cf.* 1 Cor. 15:25–28). But we may not exclude the conquests which are the anticipations in the present of the final victory, 1 John 2:14; 4:4.[299]

299. Murray, *The Epistle to the Romans*, 2:237.

> The prediction of Genesis 3:15 has also a long-range historical scope. It means that throughout history, and culminating in the grand triumph before the end, Christ's people and Kingdom shall crush Satan's head, *i.e.*, destroy his power. There is thus a local, a progressive, and a culminating fulfillment.[300]

This conquest of Satan by Christ and His Church is vividly and figuratively presented in Revelation 12:7–11:

> And there was war in heaven, Michael and his angels waging war with the dragon. And the dragon and his angels waged war, and they were not strong enough, and there was no longer a place found for them in heaven. And the great dragon was thrown down, the serpent of old who is called the Devil and Satan, who deceives the whole world; he was thrown down to the earth, and his angels were thrown down with him. And I heard a loud voice in heaven, saying, "Now the salvation, and the power, and the kingdom of our God and the authority of His Christ have come, for the accuser of our brethren has been thrown down, who accuses them before our God day and night. And they overcame him because of the blood of the Lamb and because of the word of their testimony, and they did not love their life even to death.

Many good reasons can be brought forward to commend the view that "Michael" is a symbolic representation of Christ,[301] a name

---

300. Rousas J. Rushdoony, *Romans and Galatians* (Vallecito, CA: Ross House Books, 1997), 302.

301. This "Captain of the angelic host is a symbol for the Seed of the Woman, the Son of God—represented now not as a Child [Rev. 12:1–6], but as Michael, the great Warrior-Protector who leads the armies of heaven in battle against the demons.... The name 'Michael' (meaning *Who is like God?*) occurs elsewhere in the Scriptures only in Daniel and Jude. Michael is portrayed in Daniel as 'the great Prince' who stands as the special Protector of the people of God" (David Chilton, *The Days of Vengeance: An Exposition of the Book of Revelation* [Ft. Worth, TX: Dominion Press, 1987], 311). In Daniel 10:5–6, he is described with language that is used by John to describe the exalted Christ in Revelation 1:13f.

that emphasizes His divine nature and power; and that the "angels"[302] who accompany "Him are His apostles."[303]

David Chilton's comments on this text are to the point:

> This defensive action by the forces of evil proved an utter failure.... For the forces of evil, the battle is lost. This is exactly what Jesus prophesied about the prospects for His Church Militant: "The gates of hell shall not prevail against it" (Matt. 16:18). Jesus pictures the Church, not as a city under siege by the forces of evil, but rather as a great army, besieging the capital city and headquarters of the enemy; and it is the forces of evil that succumb to the onslaught of the Church. The people of God are the aggressors: They take the initiative in the warfare, and are successful in their assault on the gates of hell.... The outcome of the Holy War is this: The Kingdom has arrived! The power of God and the authority of Christ have come, have been made manifest in history....
>
> This great apocaplyptic battle, the greatest fight in all history, has already been fought and won by the Lord Christ, St. John says, and the Dragon has been overthrown. Moreover, the martyrs who spent their lives in Christ's service did not die in vain; they are partakers in the victory: They conquered the Dragon by the blood of the Lamb—by means of His definite, once-for-all victory—and by the word of their testimony. The martyrs' faithfulness to Christ is demonstrated in that they did not love their life even to death, knowing that "he who loves his life loses it; and he who hates his life in this world shall keep it to life eternal" (John 12:25).
>
> The Holy War between Michael and the Dragon therefore cannot possibly be a portrayal of the final battle of history at the end of the world.... It is not a battle to take place at the Second Coming. The victory over the Dragon, according to

302. The Greek word for "angel" (*angelos*) also means "messenger."

303. For exegetical support of this view see David Chilton's *The Days of Vengeance*, 311–315.

St. John, does not take place by means of a cataclysmic event at the end of history, but by means of *the* cataclysmic event that took place in the middle of history: the sacrifice of the Lamb.... The cosmic victory over the Dragon takes place through the Gospel, and the Gospel alone—the Gospel in its objective aspect (the work of Christ), and the Gospel in its subjective aspect (the proclamation of the work of Christ).

When, therefore, did Satan fall from heaven? He fell, definitively, during the ministry of Christ, culminating in the atonement, the resurrection, and the ascension of the Lord to His heavenly throne.... He [Christ] went on the offensive, entering history to do battle with the Dragon, and immediately the Dragon counterattacked, fighting back with all his might, wreaking as much havoc as possible [with numerous outbreaks of demonism].... As Michael leading the angels, Christ led His apostles against the Dragon, driving him out of his position. The message of the Gospels is that in the earthly ministry of Christ and His disciples, Satan lost his place of power and fell down to earth [in defeat]:

And the seventy [preachers sent out by Jesus] returned with joy, saying, "Lord, even the demons are subject to us in Your name." And He said to them, "I was watching Satan fall from heaven like lightning. Behold, I have given you authority to tread upon serpents and scorpions, and over all the power of the enemy, and nothing shall injure you. Nevertheless, do not rejoice in this, that the spirits are subject to you, but rejoice that your names are recorded in heaven" (Luke 10:17–20).[304]

That We Be Fully Freed From Sin, Temptation, and All Evil, For Ever

I do not ask Thee to take them out of the world, but to keep them from evil (John 17:15).

304. Chilton, *The Days of Vengeance*, 313–316.

> Now may the God of peace Himself sanctify you entirely; and may your spirit and soul and body be preserved complete, without blame at the coming of our Lord Jesus Christ (1 Thess. 5:23).

In His High Priestly Prayer in John 17, Jesus prays to the Father and asks Him not to take His disciples out of this world, but as long as He sees fit to keep them in this world, to "keep them from evil," that they might be freed from the tyranny of sin, the defeat of temptation, and the soul-destroying effects of evil.

> The place of God's people is in the world, though, of course, not of it. The church has often sought to contract out, to become a kind of holy club. But this is not the prayer of the Master. His prayer is rather that they should be kept from evil.... They have a task to do in the world so it is important that they should be in the world. But it is equally important that they should be kept from evil, for evil is fatal to the discharge of their task.[305]

Jesus prays that His disciples be kept from all forms of evil, including "the evil one," so that the name of the triune God might be effectively born throughout the world and proclaimed to all nations (John 17:11, 12, 18). To be "kept from evil" is not only to be kept from Satan, the evil one, *i.e.*, "to be preserved from or enabled to rise above his temptations," it also means

> to be preserved from the evil of sin—the contagion of the sinful tempers and habits of the present evil world.... It was by being thus kept—in reference to the name of the Father—kept from evil—that the apostles were to obtain that oneness with the Father and the Son, in reference to the great work of displaying the glory of God in the salvation of men.[306]

But now, after saying all this, our prayer to be delivered from evil is not exhausted when we pray to be kept from evil in this life.

305. Morris, *The Gospel According to John*, 730.
306. Brown, *The Intercessory Prayer of Our Lord Jesus Christ*, 91–92.

The ultimate goal and intention of our prayer is to be *FULLY freed from sin temptation and ALL evil FOREVER.*

> The praying child of God has not fully disemburdened his heart before his Father in heaven as far as his relation to the dominion and power of sin is concerned by the prayer for preservation against the temptations that encompass him on all sides in this world. He must say more.... He cannot be satisfied until the final goal is reached. He longs for the day when his enemies shall be no more, the dangers of sin and death no longer threaten him, the day of complete salvation and perfect victory. To that final state of perfection he looks forward when he prays, "Deliver me from evil."[307]

In 1 Thessalonians 5:23, the apostle Paul prays for the Thessalonian Christians that God would "sanctify them entirely" and that their "spirit and soul and body be preserved complete, without blame at the coming of our Lord Jesus Christ." The Spirit-wrought processes of sanctification and preservation are already in progress in the Christian's life in this world. At the second coming of Christ those processes will be consummated, and believers will be perfectly and completely sanctified in both body and soul in absolute blamelessness forever.

And so, the final answer to our prayer to be delivered from temptation, sin and all evil

> will not be heard until we arrive at perfection in eternal glory.... O, indeed, our Father in heaven hears this prayer even while we are still in the flesh and in this present world, in the midst of all kinds of temptations. Nevertheless, He will not deliver us to the utmost until death comes to open the door for us into the heavenly perfection. This prayer is heard, first of all, when the earthly house of this tabernacle is dissolved, and we enter into the house of God not made with hands, eternal in the heavens. But in the last analysis, final perfection and deliverance from the evil one and from

---

307. Hoeksema, *The Triple Knowledge,* 2:624.

all evil, from all sin and corruption and from all the effects of sin, does not come until the day of the Lord, when He shall raise our corruptible and mortal bodies into the glory of incorruptibility and immorality, and give us our place forever in the heavenly tabernacle of God in the new creation. In last analysis it is to that perfection that this prayer looks forward.[308]

Conclusion

It is the great duty of all believers to use all diligence in the ways of Christ's appointment, that they fall not into temptation. I know God is able to deliver the godly out of temptation. I know He is 'faithful, not to suffer us to be tempted above what we are able, but will make a way for our escape,' yet I dare say...that it is our great duty and concernment to use all diligence, watchfulness and care that we enter not into temptation.[309]

The Conclusion of the Lord's Prayer

Q. 196: What Doth the Conclusion of the Lord's Prayer Teach Us?

A.: The conclusion of the Lord's prayer, (which is *For Thine is the kingdom, and the power, and the glory for ever. Amen.*) teacheth us to enforce our petitions with arguments, which are to be taken, not from any worthiness in ourselves, or in any other creature, but from God; and with our prayers to join praises, ascribing to God alone eternal sovereignty, omnipotency, and glorious

---

308. Hoeksema, *The Triple Knowledge,* 3:635.
309. Owen, *The Works of John Owen,* 7:450.

excellency; in regard whereof, as he is able and willing to help us, so we by faith are emboldened to plead with him that he would, and quietly to rely upon him, that he will fulfil our requests. And, to testify this our desire and assurance, we say, *Amen.*

The Language of the Conclusion of the Lord's Prayer

The conclusion of the Lord's Prayer begins with the word, "For," indicating that it is giving the reason and basis for the whole prayer: "We ask all these six petitions because Thine is the kingdom." It is also an ascription of praise to our Father in heaven, so that the prayer begins and ends in the adoration of God.

"Thine" has reference to "Our Father who art in heaven." It means "belonging to You, as Your right, and as Your actual possession" is the kingdom, power and glory. And the article "the" that precedes the three nouns in the conclusion is significant. Ultimately God's is THE only kingdom and THE only power and THE only glory. Neither man's nor Satan's claims to any of these things rivals God's. The kingdoms and power and glories of man and Satan are subordinate to and under the control of and work to accomplish the purposes of God's kingdom, power and glory.

"Kingdom" refers to God's absolute and total sovereignty over the entire creation and everything in it. "The kingdom" means that His sovereignty is undisputed, exclusive and eternal. God governs everything according to the good pleasure, so that nothing ever happens in all creation without His will. As He said in Isaiah 46:10–11: "My purpose will be established, and I will accomplish all My good pleasure.... Truly I have spoken; truly I will bring it to pass. I have planned it, surely I will do it."

"Power" is the ability to carry out one's will. When applied to God, power refers to His omnipotence, His ability to do whatever He wills: "Our God is in the heavens; He does whatever He pleases" (Ps. 115:3). The only limits to His omnipotence are His own righteous nature and sovereign will. In other words, God is able to accomplish all His holy will: "For the LORD of hosts has planned, and who can frustrate it? And as for His stretched-out hand, who can turn it back?" (Isa. 14:27). His is "the power," or as Psalm 62:11 says: "Once God has spoken; twice I have heard this: that power belongs to God." To say "Thine is THE power" "is not the same thing as saying that God is very powerful, that He is more powerful than any other being, or even that He is supremely powerful." It means that He is all-powerful, for the simple reason that all power is strictly His. Not only the power that is within God is His, but also the force and ability of the creature is from Him and is His. And without Him there is no power anywhere in all this wide creation.

God's "glory" is the radiant manifestation of the fullness and sum of all God's perfections: His infinity, blessedness, all-sufficiency, eternity, unchangeableness, incomprehensibility, omnipresence, omnipotence, omniscience, wisdom, holiness, justice, love, mercy, grace, long-suffering, goodness, truth, faithfulness. His "glory" shines brightly in all creation: "The heavens are telling of the glory of God" (Ps. 19:1). Jesus is the incarnation of the "glory" of God: "And the Word became flesh, and dwelt among us, and we beheld His glory, glory as of the only begotten from the Father, full of grace and truth" (John 1:14). When God makes a person a Christian it is by healing his mind of unbelief so that he might "see the light of the gospel of the glory of Christ, who is the image of God.... For God, who said, "Light shall shine out of darkness," is the One who has shone in our hearts to give the light of the knowledge of the glory of God in the face of Christ" (2 Cor. 4:4–6). Furthermore, God's is "the glory." All glory that shines forth in creation is God's glory, not man's: "Worthy art Thou, our Lord and our God, to receive glory and honor and power; for Thou didst create all things, and because of Thy will they existed, and were created" (Rev. 4:11). "It is all the radiation of the infinite goodness of God...there is no glory anywhere that is not of God."[310] Therefore, as the Larger Catechism begins: *Man's chief and highest end is to glorify God, and fully to enjoy him for ever.*

310. Hoeksema, *The Triple Knowledge*, 3:645–46.

God's kingdom, power and glory are "forever." This refers to past, present and future. God always rules. God always exerts power. God always displays glory. His kingdom, power and glory are of infinite, unchangeable and eternal duration.

The Authority of the Conclusion of the Lord's Prayer

> This doxology [conclusion] is wanting [lacking] in some ancient codices.., and omitted in quotation by some ancient writers, which has led the modern critics to regard it as an addition from some old church liturgy. Its great antiquity, however, and its constant use for ages, make it safer to retain it till some light is thrown upon the four centuries, or more, which intervene between the date of this gospel and the oldest extant manuscript.[311]

The Point of the Conclusion of the Lord's Prayer

> The prayer finishes with a doxology. That devotion that begins with prayer ends in praise. All rule, and might, and honor, belong to God; only to him let them for ever be ascribed. His is "the *kingdom*," or right to rule; "the *power*," or the might to uphold his authority; and "the *glory*," or the honor that comes out of his government."[312]

> The doxology tells us *why* we can pray, and why we can be confident in prayer.... The doxology is a confession that God is God.[313]

As we have pointed out, the word, "for," with which the conclusion of the Lord's Prayer is introduced indicates that in this conclusion we are given the reason and basis for the six petitions of the Lord's Prayer. It contains the "arguments" we may humbly present to God as to why He should answer theses petitions. "This doxology also expresses the reason why the believer prayed as he did, and why

311. Alexander, *The Gospel According to Matthew*, 175–76.
312. Charles Spurgeon, quoted in Rushdoony, *Systematic Theology*, 2:1220.
313. Rushdoony, *Systematic Theology*, 2:1220.

he presented before the throne of grace the petitions of this perfect prayer, and that too, in the order in which they occur."[314]

The Explanation of the Larger Catechism

Our Larger Catechism tells us that the purpose of this conclusion to the Lord's Prayer is to teach us several things:

- To enforce our petitions with arguments, which are to be taken, not from any worthiness in ourselves, or in any other creature, but from God
- To join praises with our prayers, ascribing to God alone eternal sovereignty, omnipotency, and glorious excellency
- As God is able and willing to help us, so we by faith are emboldened to plead with him that He would, and quietly to rely upon him, that he will fulfill our requests [Or, as our Shorter Catechism puts it concisely, it teaches us "to take our encouragement in prayer from God only, and in our prayers to praise Him, ascribing kingdom, power and glory to Him."]
- And, in testimony of our desire, and assurance to be heard, we say, "Amen."

The Enforcing of Petitions With Arguments

The Propriety of Humble Argument in Prayer

> Now I urge you, brethren, by our Lord Jesus Christ and by the love of the Spirit to strive together with me in your prayers to God for me (Rom. 15:30).

Someone has said that in prayer "God loves to be won over by the power of argument." This, of course, is not literally true and can be easily misunderstood. God is more willing to give than we are to ask; and He knows what we need before we ask. But nevertheless

314. Hoeksema, *The Triple Knowledge,* 3:647.

this statement makes an important point: God does want us to enforce our petitions in prayer with arguments and reasons as to why we think He should answer our petitions. Our "arguments" should be given humbly and with a submissive and grateful spirit regarding however He chooses to answer our prayers.

Jacob prayed in this way when he heard that Esau was coming with an army to kill him for stealing his birthright from him. His words were:

> O God of my father Abraham and God of my father Isaac, O LORD, who didst say to me, "Return to your country and to your relatives, and I will prosper you." I am unworthy of all the lovingkindness and of all the faithfulness which Thou hast shown to Thy servant; for with my staff only I crossed this Jordan, and now I have become two companies. Deliver me, I pray, from the hand of my brother, from the hand of Esau; for I fear him, lest he come and attack me, mother with children. For Thou didst say, "I will surely prosper you, and make your descendants as the sand of the sea, which cannot be numbered for multitude" (Gen. 32:9–12).

God heard Jacob's prayer and brought a measure of reconciliation between the two brothers.

But, it should be carefully observed how Jacob prayed. He petitioned God to rescue him from Esau, and then he gave "arguments" or reasons why he thought God should answer his prayer: (1) God is the covenant God of his grandfather and father, Abraham and Isaac; (2) God made him a promise that He would cause him to prosper; and (3) God made him a promise that his descendants would be more numerous than the sand of the sea. "Dead men cannot prosper or bear children. Therefore, O LORD, I humbly beseech you to save me from Esau in faithfulness to Your covenant promises to me."

In Romans 15:30, quoted above, the apostle Paul is urging the Roman Christians to pray for him and his ministry. He enforces his plea to them to comply with his request with two phrases: "by our Lord Jesus Christ and by the love of the Spirit." His plea is urged on the basis of who and what Christ is and does, and of the love of the

Holy Spirit for Christ's Church. And, just as Paul enforces his plea to the Romans "to strive together with me in your prayers to God for me," so we are to enforce our prayers to God with reasons urging God to answer our earnest prayers.

Furthermore, the conclusion of the Lord's Prayer also is the presentation of arguments to God as to why He should answer the six petitions of the Lord's Prayer as we pray them.

> Father, cause Your name to be honored, your kingdom to come and your will to be done, because Yours alone is the kingdom, power and glory. Father, provide us with our daily bread, forgive us our sins, save us from temptation and deliver us from all evil, for Yours alone is the kingdom, power and glory. Nothing in all creation, neither human nor demonic, can prevent you from answering the prayers You Yourself have taught us to pray.

The Source of Our Arguments in Prayer

> And I prayed to the LORD my God and confessed and said, "Alas, O Lord, the great and awesome God, who keeps His covenant and lovingkindness for those who love Him and keep His commandments, we have sinned, committed iniquity, acted wickedly, and rebelled, even turning aside from Thy commandments and ordinances.... Righteousness belongs to Thee, O Lord, but to us open shame...because of their unfaithful deeds which they have committed against Thee.... To the LORD our God belong compassion and forgiveness, for we have rebelled against Him.... O Lord, in accordance with all Thy righteous acts, let now Thine anger and Thy wrath turn away from Thy city, Jerusalem.... So now, our God listen to the prayer of Thy servant and to his supplications, and for Thy sake, O Lord, let Thy face shine on Thy desolate sanctuary. O my God, incline Thine ear and hear! *Open Thine eyes and see our desolations...for we are not presenting our supplications before Thee on account of any merits of our own, but on account of Thy great compassion.* O

> Lord, hear! O Lord, forgive! O Lord, listen and take action! For Thine own sake, O my God, do not delay, because Thy city and Thy people are called by Thy name (Dan. 9:4–19. Emphasis added).

Daniel's prayer is a model for humbly "arguing" with God. He offers God petitions from his heart and then gives God reason after reason why he thinks God should answer his prayer. But now, a question must be asked: From where are these arguments and reasons to be taken? The answer is found in Jacob's prayer, Daniel's prayer, Paul's prayer and the Lord's Prayer.

In Jacob's prayer in Genesis 32, he bases his argument on the promises of the Covenant God of his fathers. Daniel enforces his pleas with the perfections and promises of God peppered through his prayer in chapter 9:

> O Lord, the great and awesome God, who keeps His covenant and lovingkindness... Righteousness belongs to Thee... To the LORD our God belong compassion and forgiveness...in accordance with all Thy righteous acts...for Thy sake, O Lord...on account of Thy great compassion...for Thine own sake, O My God...because Thy city and Thy people are called by Thy name.

In Paul's urging of the Romans to pray for him in 15:30, he pleads "by our Lord Jesus Christ and the love of the Spirit." And the arguments in the conclusion of the Lord's Prayer enforcing the six petitions are the perfections of God: "the kingdom, power and glory forever."

The point is that all these prayers we have just mentioned enforce their petitions *with arguments, which are to be taken, not from any worthiness in ourselves, or in any other creation, but from God* as He has revealed Himself in the Bible. Daniel said it well: "Open Thine eyes and see our desolations...for we are not presenting our supplications before Thee on account of any merits of our own, but on account of Thy great compassion" (Dan. 9:18).

> God would surely respond to this plea because He was and is a God who "delights in mercy" (Mic. 7:18). The covenant God is

> a Father. By His covenant He brings us into His family. As a Father He takes pleasure in the requests of His children when they appeal to His covenant character. Just as a father finds delight in his child's appeals to his honesty or generosity or faithfulness or love, so our God "delights in mercy." Daniel knew that. He did not forget for a moment that he was in the presence of the Great King. That memory, however, made his appeal for mercy all the more poignant and all the more welcome by the Father. In seeking mercy from the God of heaven Daniel knew that he was touching the deep places of his covenant God. In His covenant God had promised to be merciful. Daniel prayed He would be so.[315]

The Joining of Praise to Petition

> Be anxious for nothing, but in everything by prayer and supplication with thanksgiving let your requests be made known to God (Phil. 4:6).

> And let the peace of Christ rule in your hearts...and be thankful. Let the word of Christ richly dwell within you... with thankfulness in your hearts to God. And whatever you do in word or deed, do all in the name of the Lord Jesus, giving thanks through Him to God the Father (Col. 3:15–17).

The chief element of prayer is praise. The Lord's Prayer begins and ends with the praise and adoration of the Father. The conclusion is an ascription of praise to God in which we adore God.

> And this is after all the essence, the deepest meaning, of all prayer. The highest purpose of prayer is not to receive something for ourselves. O, this is true too: in prayer we desire something, we ask something from God. Principally we always ask for His grace, and we long to enter into His covenant fellowship. But the chief purpose always is that we may

315. Sinclair Ferguson, *Mastering the Old Testament: Daniel*, ed. by Lloyd Ogilvie (Dallas/ London/ Vancouver/ Melbourne: Word Publishing, 1988), 195.

> adore Him and glorify His holy name. In prayer we desire grace to know Him, in order that we may taste Him as the sole fountain of all good, and thus ascribe all praise and honor and glory to Him alone. Only conceived of in this light can we understand that prayer is the chief part of thankfulness. In prayer we desire to receive in our own consciousness an impression of the goodness, of all the wonderful virtues and glory of the Most High. And having become deeply conscious of the wonders of His Being, we then adore Him and express His wonders before one another and before the whole world, but also, and principally, before His face. And such adoration is the highest expression of gratitude.... All we can do is ascribe praise to Him, and adore the wonderful virtues of His being.... To glorify and adore the Most High is the sole proper way of thanksgiving for His benefits.[316]

> Such is the idea of this doxology at the close of the Lord's Prayer. It still addresses the Lord, our God, our Father Which is in heaven; yet not any more in humble petition, but in adoration. The believer here tells the Lord something. He praises Him in His face, and in exultation declares that His is the kingdom, His is the power, His is the glory, and that too, forever.[317]

Adoration is the homage and entire prostration of the inner life of a person standing in awe of the splendor, majesty, holiness, blessedness and glory of the God of the Bible. It manifests this loving reverence in verbal expressions in worship to Him in whom these glorious perfections reside. This language of adoration is accompanied with praise, which arises from the consciousness of the delight we enjoy in the contemplation of these divine perfections. We adore God as we consider the revelation of Himself, His perfections, His will and His works in His Word.

> Oh! The selfishness of the thought which restricts prayer to mere petition! Shall nothing drive us to God but the pressure

316. Hoeksema, *The Triple Knowledge*, 3:640–41.
317. Hoeksema, *The Triple Knowledge*, 3:641.

> of want? Shall we think of him only when we are hungry, and forget him when we are full? ... Is there nothing attractive in the character of Jehovah himself to draw us with the power of a magnet? Surely it is a dull heart which does not warm to the beauty which he discloses, and whose impulse is not to utter its joy in these ascriptions of adoration and praise.... Or what nobler employment of the tongue, the glory of our frame, than to articulate his praise in the loftiest language which sanctified genius can inspire? ...
>
> The soul must come out of itself, and look upon Christ, who is the author of salvation; and peace flows in through the trust which ventures all upon him. Hence the profit derived from adoration. The morbid tendency to gloat over what is dark within, is checked. The eye is turned outward to gaze upon the beauty which entrances. The affections are awakened in the presence of holiness and goodness. The sickly sensibilities are toned up, and a healthy religious action takes the place of the despondency which was weakening all the powers of the soul.[318]

Paul points out the centrality of praise in prayer in Philippians 4:6, quoted above: "in everything by prayer and supplications *with thanksgiving* let your requests be made known to God."

> The recalling of God's goodness and mercy will save us from the many pitfalls which await the ungrateful soul, *e.g.*, over-concern with our immediate problems, forgetfulness of God's gracious dealings with us in the past, disregard of the needs of others who are more unfortunate than we are.[319]

(Three times in three consecutive verses, (Col. 3:15–17), Paul urges his readers to pray with thanksgiving.)

---

318. Palmer, *Theology of Prayer*, 32–34.

319. Ralph P. Martin, *The Epistle of Paul to the Philippians: An Introduction and Commentary* (Grand Rapids, MI: William B. Eerdmans Publishing Co., [1959] 1965), 169–70.

A perfect example of a prayer of adoration and praise, *ascribing to God alone eternal sovereignty, omnipotency, and glorious excellency,* is found in 1 Chronicles 29:10–13:

> So David blessed the LORD in the sight of all the assembly; and David said, "Blessed art Thou, O LORD God of Israel our father, forever and ever. Thine, O LORD, is the greatness and the power and the glory and the victory and the majesty, indeed everything that is in the heavens and the earth; Thine is the dominion, O LORD, and Thou does exalt Thyself as head over all. Both riches and honor come from Thee, and Thou dost rule over all, and in Thy hand is power and might; and it lies in Thy hand to make great, and to strengthen everyone. Now therefore, our God, we thank Thee, and praise Thy glorious name.

The Encouragement to Prayer

As the sovereign, omnipotent and all-glorious God, He is fully *able and willing to help us,* His people: "Now to Him who is able to do exceeding abundantly beyond all that we ask or think." (Eph. 3:20). In fact God is more willing to help His people than we are to ask for help:

> ask, and it shall be given to you; seek, and you will find; knock, and it shall be opened to you. For everyone who asks receives; and he who seeks finds; and to him who knocks it shall be opened. Now suppose one of you fathers is asked by his son for a fish; he will not give him a snake instead of a fish, will he? Or if he is asked for an egg, he will not give him a scorpion, will he? If you then, being evil, know how to give good gifts to your children, *how much more* shall your Heavenly Father give the Holy Spirit to those who ask Him?" (Luke 11:9–13. Emphasis added).

Believing this about God, *by faith* in His Word, believers *are emboldened to plead with Him that He would* [help us], *and quietly to rely upon Him, that He will fulfill our requests.*

Then Jehoshaphat stood in the assembly of Judah and Jerusalem, in the house of the LORD before the new court, and he said,

> O LORD, the God of our fathers, art Thou not God in the heavens? And art Thou not ruler over all the kingdoms of the nations? Power and might are in Thy hand so that no one can stand before Thee. Didst Thou not, O our God, drive out the inhabitants of this land before Thy people Israel, and give it to the descendants of Abraham Thy friend forever?... Behold how they [Judah's enemies] are rewarding us, by coming to drive us out from Thy possession which Thou hast given us as an inheritance. O our God, wilt Thou not judge them? For we are powerless before this great multitude who are coming against us; nor do we know what to do, but our eyes are on Thee" (2 Chron. 20:5–12).

Here we see King Jehoshaphat of Judah boldly praying for God's protection against the enemies of Judah, confident that God would answer his prayer and come to their aid, because he knows He is willing to do so as "LORD, the God of our fathers," and that He is able to do so as "God in the heavens, ...ruler over all the kings of nations," who has "power and might" in His "hand" so that "no one can stand before" Him. Because God acted in behalf of His people in driving out the inhabitants of Canaan under Joshua and giving the land to the children of God, surely He will act in destroying those who are "coming to drive us out from Thy possession which Thou has given us as an inheritance." Jehoshaphat is confident as he prays that Jehovah will not desert His covenant friends, the seed of "Abraham Thy friend forever." Therefore, because we have "a great high priest who has passed through the heavens, Jesus the Son of God," who sympathizes with us in our weaknesses having been "tempted in all things as we are, yet without sin.... Let us therefore draw near with confidence [and boldness] to the throne of grace, that we may receive mercy and may find grace to help in time of need" (Heb. 4:14–16). "'This is nothing less than a revolution in the fundamental conception of religion and one of the most important revelations of the epistle'...for 'only Christianity can give sinful creatures the boldness to present themselves before God.' (Spicq)"[320]

> Now Zerah the Ethiopian came out against them with an army of a million men and 300 chariots, and he came to Mareshah. So Asa went out to meet him, and they drew up in battle formation in the valley of Zephathah at Mareshah. Then Asa called to the LORD his God, and said, "Lord, there is no one besides Thee to help in the battle between the powerful and those who have no strength; so help us, O LORD our God, for we trust in Thee, and in Thy name have come against this multitude, O LORD, Thou art our God; let not man prevail against Thee." So the LORD routed the Ethiopians before Asa and Judah, and the Ethiopians fled (2 Chron. 14:9–12).

In this incident, King Asa of Judah, believing that Jehovah is everything He has revealed Himself to be, *by faith...quietly relies upon Him, that He will fulfill our requests.* This battle was won before it began. It was won when Asa prayed. Vastly outnumbered, King Asa calmly prays for divine assistance. He confesses that Judah in and of herself does not have the resources to defeat the great Ethiopian army. He describes the battle to the LORD as "the battle between the powerful [Ethiopians] and those who have no strength [Judah]." However, this description does not discourage Asa. In confident "trust" in the Lord, Asa faces the Ethiopians knowing that, because "O LORD, Thou art our God," *i.e.*, because Jehovah is the Covenant Lord and Savior of Judah, He will not let man "prevail" against Him. Therefore, in covenant mercy and covenant faithfulness, Jehovah fulfills Asa's requests, as he *quietly* trusted in and relied upon Him.

The Point of The "Amen" After the Conclusion of the Lord's Prayer

We add "Amen" to *testify this our desire and assurance.* By concluding the Lord's Prayer with "Amen," we are testifying that what

320. Spicq, quoted in Hughes, *A Commentary on the Epistle to the Hebrews*, 174.

we have prayed in the Lord's Prayer is the sincere desire of our hearts and that we are assured that God will grant our petitions, since Jesus Himself placed those petitions in our hearts and mouths.

The word, "Amen," is used extensively in worship in both the Old Testament and the New Testament. Jesus also used the word frequently. It comes from a Hebrew word meaning "to strengthen."

> Hence it is used as a word of confirmation by which a statement is firmly underscored by the speaker, or complete acceptance is indicated by the hearer. In either case the one who says, "Amen," lends his personal weight to what is said, whether by stressing that he means what he says, or by assuring others that he welcomes and concurs with the statement which has been made.[321]

The Three Closely Related Meanings of "Amen" in the Old Testament

First, "Amen" has the nature of swearing an oath in the name of God (Num. 5:11–31; Deut. 27:11–26; Neh. 5:13).

Second, "Amen" is "the confirming of a commission by declaring that it is in accordance with the will of God ... 1 Kings 1:36."[322]

Third, "Amen" denotes "agreement accompanied with praise... 1 Chron. 16:36; Neh. 8:6; Ps. 14:41; 72:19."[323]

The "Amen" in the New Testament

First, Jesus used the word frequently before many of His claims, commands and promises, although it is difficult to see that in our English translations, where His word, "Amen" is usually translated, "Verily." For example, in John's Gospel, He says, "Amen, Amen, I say to you" (John 1:51; 3:3, 5, 11; 5:19, 24, 25; 6:26, 32). This usage makes the words that follow doubly emphatic.

---

321. Herbert M. Carson, *Hallelujah! Christian Worship* (England: Evangelical Press, 1980), 148.

322. K. Deddens, *Where Everything Points to Him*, trans. by Theodore Plantinga (Alberta, CA/ Caledonia, MI: Inheritance Publications, 1993), 154.

323. Deddens, *Where Everything Points to Him*, 155.

Second, Paul often uses "Amen" in his Epistles. In 2 Corinthians 1:20, He writes that "For as many as may be the promises of God, in Him they are yes; wherefore also by Him is our Amen to the glory of God through us." Our "Amen" to God's promises is the echo of Christ's "Yes" to those promises. Christ is the Guarantee of the promises of God.

Third, on the isle of Patmos, John saw a vision of the glorified Christ, whose redemptive work is finished. He is our pledge that the promises of God will be fully realized in us. John makes this point by referring to Jesus as "The Amen, the faithful and true Witness" in Revelation 3:14. He is given this title, because "He embodies in His own person the emphatic 'Amen' of God that no word of promise will fail."[324]

Fourth, "Amen" is used as a congregational response in the worship of service: "Otherwise if you bless in the spirit only, how will the one who fills the place of the ungifted say the "Amen" at your giving of thanks, since he does not know what you are saying?" (1 Cor. 14:16). (See also Rev. 5:14.)

Fifth, "Amen" is used after prayers, and especially after doxologies (Rom. 16:27; Rom. 1:25; 9:5; 11:36; Gal. 1:5; Eph. 3:21; Phil. 4:20; 1 Tim. 1:17; Rev. 1:6; 7:12). When the congregation hears the praise of God read aloud, it ought to respond with the "Amen," representing its acceptance of that which is heard.

> At the end [of the Lord's Prayer] is added, "Amen." ... By it is expressed the warmth of desire to obtain what we have asked of God. And our hope is strengthened that all things of this sort have already been brought to pass, and will surely be granted to us, since they have been promised by God, who cannot deceive. And this agrees with the form of prayer we previously set forth: "Do, O Lord, for thy name's sake, not on account of us or our righteousness" (*cf* Dan. 9:18–19). By this the saints not only express the end of their prayers but confess themselves unworthy to obtain it unless God seeks the

---

324. Carson, *Hallelujah! Christian Worship*, 149.

> reason from himself, and that their confidence of being heard stems solely from God's nature.[325]

The Use of the "Amen" By the Congregation of the Lord

God has spoken. God has acted. God has come to us in Jesus Christ. He has taken the gracious initiative in creation, redemption, reconciliation and revelation. Our response to Him is faith which "utters its grateful 'Amen' to all that God has said and done."[326]

Giving Assent to the Word of God

"Amen" is to be used to give assent to the declaration of the Word of God. Moses told Israel that after they crossed into the Land of Promise the people were to gather at Mount Gerizim and Mount Ebal, and proclaim the covenant blessings and curses of the Lord. After each sentence of judgment the congregation answered, "Amen," (Deut. 27:16, 17; Neh. 5:13).

> The people in acknowledgement of their sinful failure [in the days of Moses and Nehemiah] pledged obedience; and as a token of their fidelity to the pledge they unitedly joined in the "Amen" which, because it was an open response to the Word of God, issued in praise.[327]

Giving Expression to Our Unity with the Speaker in Prayer and Praise

"The usage of 'Amen' in prayer and praise is a characteristic feature of the worshipping church, and it is rooted in biblical practice."[328] In 1 Corinthians 14, Paul is dealing with the issue of tongue speaking in the church in Corinth. He insists that an interpretation must be given or else the speaker is to be silent.

---

325. Calvin, *Institutes of the Christian Religion*, 2:916.
326. Carson, *Hallelujah! Christian Worship*, 149.
327. Carson, *Hallelujah! Christian Worship*, 150.
328. Carson, *Hallelujah! Christian Worship*, 150.

> His argument is that the congregation must be able to participate in the prayer which is being offered. So he puts the issue firmly—how can the man who does not know the tongue say "the Amen" at the giving of thanks? [1 Cor.14:16] Clearly Paul envisages the utterance of this "Amen" as being the normal practice of the church. It is the believers' affirmation before God that they are united in spirit with the one who is leading them in prayer. It is no mere mechanical or routine performance for it involves an intelligent grasp of what is being said.[329]

After David's great hymn of praise to God was sung (1 Chron. 16:7–36), "then all the people said, "Amen," and praised the LORD."

> It is in the realm of praise that the Amen rings out so powerfully and so frequently both in the Old Testament and in the New. Believers cannot listen to praise being offered to God and remain dumb. They are not spectators watching someone else perform, nor hearers listening to another's words. Such is their own grateful response to the glory of God that they must participate. The praise which one believer offers is theirs as well, and their fervent "Amen" is their own glad affirmation of their indebtedness to the grace of God.[330]

The Heidelberg Catechism Q. 129 tells us that *"'Amen' signifies, it shall truly and certainly be: for my prayer is more assuredly heard of God, than I feel in my heart that I desire these things of Him.* In Hebrew "Amen" is derived from a verb that denotes "to make firm and unmovable."

> When, therefore, we thus close our prayers, we do a very serious thing. For then we declare, first of all, before the face of God that in our prayers we were true, that we did not lie when we prayed, that we did not play the hypocrite, but that we are sure that the things we prayed for are the objects of the desire of our inmost heart.... By that little word ["Amen"] we express

329. Carson, *Hallelujah! Christian Worship*, 150.
330. Carson, *Hallelujah! Christian Worship*, 151.

that we honestly and sincerely asked for and desired, in the first place, the things concerning God: the glory of His name, the coming of His kingdom, grace that I may do His will.... By that closing word we express that we are sure that we are quite satisfied with bread for today, that we long for forgiveness of sins and that we earnestly desire to forgive one another. By 'Amen' we express that we dread the temptations...that we desire to be delivered from evil, and long for final perfection. In other words, 'Amen' signifies that I uttered my prayer in true faith.... Hence, at the close of our prayer we say: 'Amen.' O Father, Who knowest the hearts... Thou knowest that my prayer was in truth, and that I earnestly desire these things of Thee. And I am assured that Thou wilt grant unto me exactly the contents of my petitions.[331]

331. Hoeksema, *The Triple Knowledge*, 3:651–52.

Bibliography

Aalders, Gerhard Charles. *Bible Student's Commentary: Genesis*. 2 vols. trans. William Heynen. Grand Rapids, MI: Zondervan, 1981.

Adams, James E. *War Psalms of the Prince of Peace: Lessons from the Imprecatory Psalms*. Phillipsburg, NJ: Presbyterian & Reformed Publishing Co., 1991.

Adams, Jay E. "Afterword: The Influence Of Westminster." *To Glorify And Enjoy God*, ed. John L. Carson and David W. Hall. Edinburgh: The Banner of Truth Trust, 1994.

__________. *The Biblical View of Self-Esteem, Self-Love, Self-Image*. Eugene, OR: Harvest House Publishers, 1986.

__________. *The Christian Counselor's Commentary: Proverbs*. Woodruff, SC: Timeless Texts, 1997.

__________. *The Christian Counselor's Manual*. Grand Rapids, MI: Baker Book House [1973] 1981

__________. *From Forgiven To Forgiving*. Amityville, NY: Calvary Press, 1994.

__________. *More Than Redemption: A Theology of Christian Counseling*. Grand Rapids, MI: Baker Book House, 1979.

Adeney, Walter F. *Ezra and Nehemiah*. Minneapolis, MN: Klock & Klock Christian Publishers, Inc. 1980.

Alexander, Archibald. *Practical Sermons To Be Read in Families and Social Meetings*. Philadelphia, PA: Presbyterian Board of Publication, 1850.

Alexander, Joseph A. *The Acts of the Apostles*. Edinburgh: The Banner of Truth Trust, [1857] 1991.

_______________. *The Gospel According To Matthew*. New York: Charles Scribner and Company, 1867.

_______________. *The Prophecies of Isaiah*. 2 vols. unabridged in 1. Grand Rapids, MI: Zondervan Publishing House, 1974.

_______________. *The Psalms Translated and Explained*. Grand Rapids, MI: Baker Book House, [1873] 1975.

Alighieri, Dante. *The Vision* or *Hell, Purgatory and Paradise of Dante Alighieri*. trans. Rev. Henry Francis Cary. London and New York: Frederick Warne & Co., 1892.

Allis, Oswald T. *Prophecy and The Church*. Nutley, N.J.: Presbyterian and Reformed Publishing Company, 1972.

Ames, William. *The Marrow of Theology*. ed. John D. Eusden. Durham, NC: The Labyrinth Press, [1968] 1983.

Anthony, Mark. "Is Baptismal Regeneration Being Taught in the Reformed Community?" *The Counsel of Chalcedon* (July/August 2002).

Armstrong, John. "The Authority of Scripture." *Sola Scriptura*. ed. Don Kestler. Morgan, PA: Soli Deo Gloria Publications, 1995.

Armstrong, Karen. *A History of God: The 4,000-Year Quest Of Judaism, Christianity and Islam*. New York: Ballentine Books, 1993.

Arnot, William. *Studies in Proverbs: Laws From Heaven for Life on Earth*. Grand Rapids, MI: Kregel Publications, [1884] 1978.

Augustine, Aurelius. *Augustine: Later Works*. ed. John Burnaby. Philadelphia, PA: Westminster Press, 1955.

__________________. *The City of God*. trans. Marcus Dods, George Wilson, J. J. Smith. New York: Random House, 1950.

Bacon, Richard. *What Mean Ye By This Service? Paedocommunion in Light of the Passover*. Dallas, TX: Presbyterian Heritage Publications, 1989.

Bahnsen, Greg L. *Always Ready: Directions for Defending the Faith*. Nacogdoches, TX: Covenant Media Press, [1996] 2008.

______________. *A Biblical Introduction To Apologetics*. Auburn, CA: Covenant Tape Ministry.

______________. *By This Standard*. Tyler, TX: Institute for Christian Economics, [1985] 1998.

______________. "Christ in the World of Thought." *Chalcedon Report* 103 (March, 1974).

______________. "The Comprehensive Scope of Salvation." *Penpoint* 3/4 (July 1992).

______________. "The Concept and Importance of Canonicity." *Antithesis* I/5 (September/October 1990): 42–45.

______________. "The Person, Work and Present Status of Satan." *The Journal of Christian Reconstruction* 1:2 (Winter, 1974): 11–43.

______________. "The *Prima Facie* Acceptability of Postmillennialism." *Journal of Christian Reconstruction* 6/1 (Summer 1979): 69–76.

______________. *Theonomy in Christian Ethics.* Nutley, NJ: The Craig Press, 1977.

______________. *Victory in Jesus: The Bright Hope of Postmillennialism.* Texarkana, AR: Covenant Media Press, 1999.

______________. "The Westminster Assembly and the 'Equity of the Judicial Law.'" *Penpoint* 4/7 (October, 1993).

Bahnsen, Greg L., and Gentry, Kenneth, Jr. *House Divided: The Break-up of Dispensational Theology.* Tyler, TX: Institute for Christian Economics, 1989.

Baldwin, Joyce. *1 & 2 Samuel: An Introduction and Commentary.* Downer's Grove, IL: InterVarsity Press, 1988.

Ball, Bryan W., *A Great Expectation: Eschatological Thought in English Protestantism to 1660.* (Netherlands: E. J. Brill, 1975).

Bannerman, Douglas. *The Scripture Doctrine of the Church.* Stoke-on-Trent: Tentmaker Publications, [1887] 2006.

Bannerman, James. *The Church of Christ,* 2 vols. Canada: Still Waters Revival Books, [1869] 1991.

Barnes, Albert. *Notes: Critical, Explanatory, and Practical on the Book of the Prophet Isaiah.* Boston: Crocerk & Brewster, [1860] digitized 2007.

____________. *Notes on the New Testament Explanatory and Practical: Matthew-Mark.* ed. Robert Frew. Grand Rapids, MI: Baker Book House, 1974.

Barnes, Roland. *Selecting God's Men.* Cumming, GA: Triumphant Publications.

Bavinck, Herman. *The Doctrine of God.* trans. William Hendriksen. Grand Rapids: Eerdmans, [1951] 1991.

______________. *Our Reasonable Faith.* tr. Henry Zylstra. Grand Rapids, MI: Baker Book House, [1956] 1977.

Baxter, Richard. *The Practical Works of Richard Baxter.* 4 vols. Ligonier, PA: Soli Deo Gloria, [1673] 1990.

Beare, F. W. *The First Epistle of Peter.* Oxford: Basil Blackwell, 1961.

Beattie, Francis R. *The Presbyterian Standards: An Exposition of the Westminster Confession of Faith and Catechisms.* Richmond, VA: The Presbyterian Committee of Publication, 1896.

Beeley, Ray. *Amos: Introduction and Commentary.* London: The Banner of Truth Trust, [1969] 1970.

Beisner, E. Calvin. *Prospects for Growth: A Biblical View of Population, Resources, and The Future.* Westchester, IL: Crossway Books, 1990.

_______________. *Psalms of Promise.* Colorado Springs, CO: NavPress, 1988.

Bennett, Arthur, ed. *Valley of Vision: A Collection of Puritan Prayers and Devotions.* Edinburgh: Banner of Truth Trust, 1975.

Berkhof, Louis. *Systematic Theology.* Grand Rapids, MI: Eerdmans, [1932] 1996.

Berkhouwer, G. C. *The Conflict with Rome.* trans. David H. Freeman. Philadelphia, PA: The Presbyterian and Reformed Publishing Co., 1958.

_______________. *Faith and Justification.* Grand Rapids, MI: Wm. B. Eerdmans Publishing Co., 1954.

_______________. "General and Special Divine Revelation." *Revelation and the Bible,* ed. Carl F. Henry. Philadelphia, PA: Presbyterian and Reformed Publishers, 1958.

_______________. *The Return of Christ,* trans. James Van Oosterom, ed. Marlin J. Van Elderen. Grand Rapids, MI: William B. Eerdmans Publishing Co., 1972.

_______________. *Studies in Dogmatics: The Church,* trans. James E. Davison. Grand Rapids, MI: Wm. B. Eerdmans Publishing Co., 1976.

Bird, W. R. *The Origin of Species Revisited: The Theories of Evolution and of Abrupt Appearance.* 2 vols. NY: Philosophical Library, 1989.

Blaikie, W. G. *The First Book of Samuel: The Expositor's Bible.* ed. W. Robertson Nicoll. NY: Funk & Wagnalls Co., 1900.

Blair, S. Ray. "According to the Pattern Shown in the Mount—Exodus 25:40." *The Biblical Doctrine of Worship: A Symposium.* Reformed Presbyterian Church of North America, 1974.

Blake, William. "Education," *Foundations of Christian Scholarship.* ed. Gary North. Vallecito, CA: Ross House Books, 1976.

Blamires, Harry. *The Christian Mind.* London: S.P.C.K., 1963.

Boer, Jeff. "Regardless of What You Have Heard, Overeating is Not the Sin of Gluttony." *Christianity and Society* 5/1 (January 1995).

Boettner, Loraine. *Roman Catholicism.* Philadelphia, PA: The Presbyterian and Reformed Publishing Co., [1962] 1976.

______________. *Studies in Theology*. Philadelphia, PA: The Presbyterian and Reformed Publishing Co., [1947] 1967.

Bogue, Carl. *Jonathan Edwards and the Covenant of Grace*. Cherry Hill, NJ: Mack Publishing Co., 1975.

Booth, Randy. *Children of the Promise: The Biblical Case for Infant Baptism*. Phillipsburg, NJ: Presbyterian and Reformed Publishing Co., 1995.

Boston, Thomas. *The Beauties of Boston*. Inverness, Scotland: Christian Focus Publications, 1979.

______________. "The Necessity of Repentance." *Repentance*. MacDill AFB, FL: Tyndale Bible Society, n.d.

Boyd, James Oscar. "Echoes of the Covenant with David," *Princeton Theological Review* XXV (1927).

Brakel, Wilhelmus à. *The Christian's Reasonable Service*. 4 vols. Morgan, PA: Soli Deo Gloria Publications, 1992.

Breck, Carrie E. *The Baptist Hymnal*. Nashville, TN: Convention Press, 1991.

Bridges, Charles. *The Christian Ministry*. London: The Banner of Truth Trust, [1830] 1967.

______________. *An Exposition of Proverbs*. Marshallton, DE: The National Foundation for Christian Education, n.d.

Broadus, John A. *Commentary on the Gospel of Matthew*, ed. Alvah Hovey. Philadelphia: American Baptist Publication Society, 1886.

Brooks, Thomas. *Heaven on Earth*. London: The Banner of Truth Trust, [1654] 1961.

Broomall, Wick. "Type, Typology." *Baker's Dictionary of Theology*. Grand Rapids, MI: Baker Book House, [1960] 1966.

Brown, John. *Analytical Exposition of the Epistle of Paul the Apostle to the Romans*. Grand Rapids, MI: Baker Book House, [1857] 1981.

__________. *Expository Discourses on I Peter*. 2 vols. Edinburgh: The Banner of Truth Trust, [1848] 1975.

__________. *Hebrews*. London: The Banner of Truth Trust, [1862] 1972.

__________. *The Intercessory Prayer of Our Lord Jesus Christ*. Minneapolis, MN: Klock & Klock Christian Publishers, [1866] 1978.

Bruce, F. F. *New International Commentary on the New Testament: The Book of the Acts*. Grand Rapids, MI: William B. Eerdmans [1954]

1964.

Bruner, Frederick Dale. *A Theology of the Holy Spirit: The Pentecostal Experience*. Grand Rapids, MI: William B. Eerdmans Publishing Co., [1970] 1977.

Buchanan, James. *The Holy Spirit*. London: The Banner of Truth Trust, [1843] 1966.

_____________. *Not Guilty*. prepared by John Appleby. London: Grace Publication Trust, [1990] 1995.

Buis, Harry. *The Doctrine of Eternal Punishment*. Philadelphia, PA: Presbyterian and Reformed Publishing Co., 1957.

Bunyan, John. "Reprobation Asserted." *The Works of John Bunyan*. 3 vols. Grand Rapids, MI: Baker Book House, [1875] 1977.

Burton, Ernest De Witt. *A Critical and Exegetical Commentary on the Epistle to the Galatians, ICC*. Edinburgh: T&T Clark, [1921] 1968.

Bush, George. *Notes on Exodus*. 2 vols. Minneapolis, MN: James Family Christian Publishers, [1852] 1979.

Calamy, Edmund. *The Godly Man's Ark*. London: James Nisbet and Co., [1865] 2006.

Calvin, John. *Calvin's Commentaries*. 22 vols. trans. Rev. James Anderson. Grand Rapids, MI: Baker Book House, 1979.

__________. *Concerning the Eternal Predestination of God*. London: James Clarke & Co., 1961.

__________. *Institutes of the Christian Religion*. 2 vols. ed. John T. McNeill, trans. Lewis Ford Battles. Philadelphia: The Westminster Press, 1940.

__________. *Sermons From Job*. Grand Rapids, MI: Baker Book House, 1952.

__________. *Sermons on Deuteronomy*. trans. Arthur Golding. Edinburgh/Pennsylvania: The Banner of Truth Trust [1593] facsimile reprint 1987.

__________. *Sermons on Galatians*. Audubon, NJ: Old Paths Publications [1574] 1995.

__________. *Sermons on Melchizedek and Abraham: Justification, Faith and Obedience*. Willow Street, PA: Old Paths Publications, [1592] 2000.

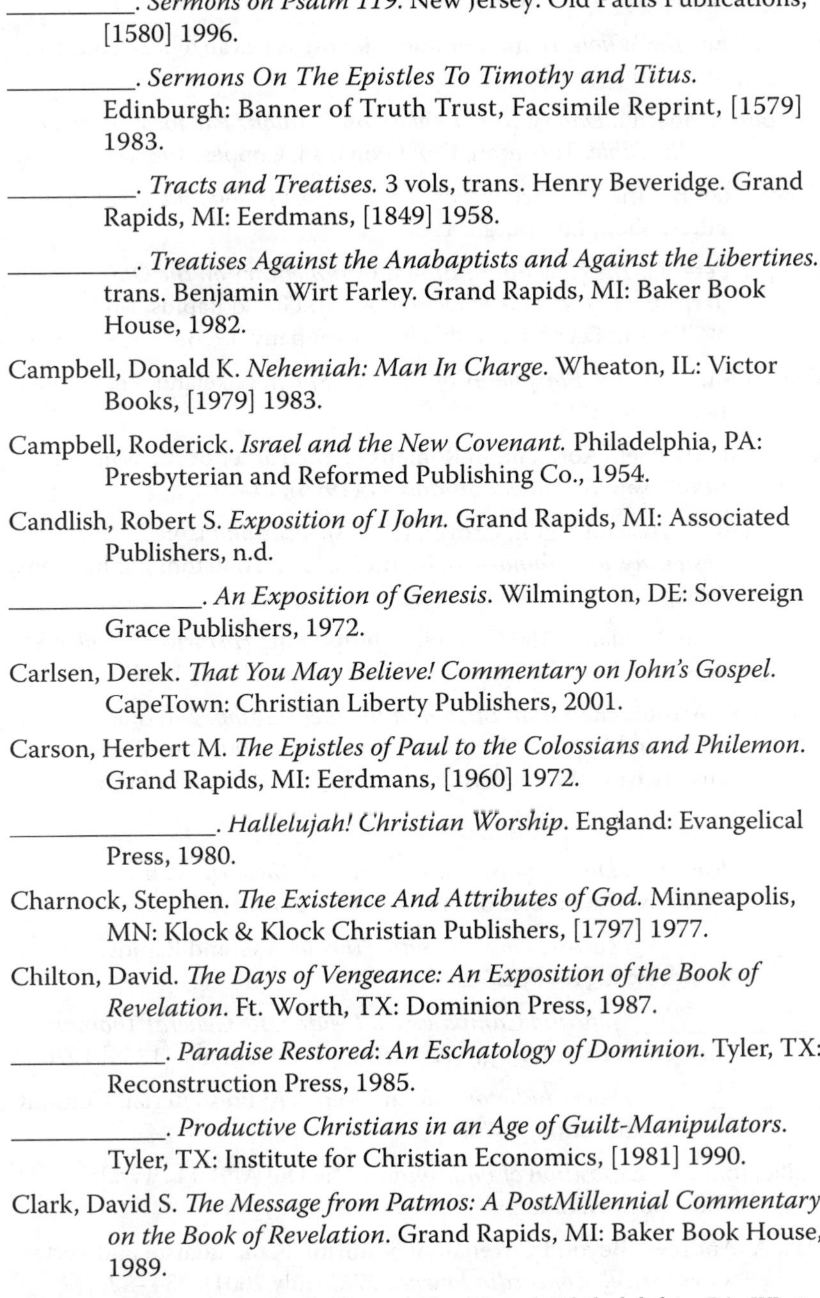

__________. *Sermons on Psalm 119.* New Jersey: Old Paths Publications, [1580] 1996.

__________. *Sermons On The Epistles To Timothy and Titus.* Edinburgh: Banner of Truth Trust, Facsimile Reprint, [1579] 1983.

__________. *Tracts and Treatises.* 3 vols, trans. Henry Beveridge. Grand Rapids, MI: Eerdmans, [1849] 1958.

__________. *Treatises Against the Anabaptists and Against the Libertines.* trans. Benjamin Wirt Farley. Grand Rapids, MI: Baker Book House, 1982.

Campbell, Donald K. *Nehemiah: Man In Charge.* Wheaton, IL: Victor Books, [1979] 1983.

Campbell, Roderick. *Israel and the New Covenant.* Philadelphia, PA: Presbyterian and Reformed Publishing Co., 1954.

Candlish, Robert S. *Exposition of I John.* Grand Rapids, MI: Associated Publishers, n.d.

______________. *An Exposition of Genesis.* Wilmington, DE: Sovereign Grace Publishers, 1972.

Carlsen, Derek. *That You May Believe! Commentary on John's Gospel.* CapeTown: Christian Liberty Publishers, 2001.

Carson, Herbert M. *The Epistles of Paul to the Colossians and Philemon.* Grand Rapids, MI: Eerdmans, [1960] 1972.

_______________. *Hallelujah! Christian Worship.* England: Evangelical Press, 1980.

Charnock, Stephen. *The Existence And Attributes of God.* Minneapolis, MN: Klock & Klock Christian Publishers, [1797] 1977.

Chilton, David. *The Days of Vengeance: An Exposition of the Book of Revelation.* Ft. Worth, TX: Dominion Press, 1987.

__________. *Paradise Restored: An Eschatology of Dominion.* Tyler, TX: Reconstruction Press, 1985.

___________. *Productive Christians in an Age of Guilt-Manipulators.* Tyler, TX: Institute for Christian Economics, [1981] 1990.

Clark, David S. *The Message from Patmos: A PostMillennial Commentary on the Book of Revelation.* Grand Rapids, MI: Baker Book House, 1989.

Clowney, Edmund. *By God's Grace...The Church.* Philadelphia, PA: Westminster Theological Seminary, 1971.

Cole, R. Alan. *Exodus*. Downers Grove, IL: Inter-Varsity Press, 1973.

Cook, Paul. *The Whole Truth*. London: The British Evangelical Council and Evangelical Press, n.d.

Coppes, Leonard J. *Daddy, May I Take Communion? Paedocommunion vs. The Bible*. Thornton, CO: Leonard J. Coppes, 1988.

Cowan, Ian B. "The Five Articles of Perth." *Reformation and Revolution*. ed. D. Shaw, Edinburgh, 1967.

Craigie, Peter C. *The New International Commentary on the Old Testament: The Book of Deuteronomy*. Grand Rapids, MI: William B. Eerdmans Publishing Company, 1976.

Crampton, Gary. *The Blasphemy of the Holy Spirit*. Lakeland, FL: Whitefield Press, 1987.

Cranford, Michael. "Abraham in Romans 4: The Father of All Who Believe." *New Testament Studies* 41 (1995): 71–88.

Crenshaw, Curtis and Gunn, Grover, III. *Dispensationalism, Today, Yesterday, and Tomorrow*. Memphis, TN: Footstool Publications, 1985.

Cunningham, William. "The Council of Jerusalem." *Historical Theology*. 2 vols. London: The Banner of Truth Trust, [1862] 1969.

Custance, Arthur. *The Virgin Birth and the Incarnation*. 2nd online ed. Grand Rapids, MI: Zondervan, [1976] 2001. http://www.custance.org/Library/Volume5/Part_VIII/Chapter1.html

Dabney, Robert L. *Discussions: Evangelical and Theological*. 5 vols. London: The Banner of Truth Trust, [1890] 1967.

_______________. *Lectures in Systematic Theology*. Grand Rapids, MI: Zondervan, [1878] 1972.

_______________. *Life and Campaigns of Lieutenant-General Thomas J. Jackson*. Harrisonburg, VA: Sprinkle Publications, [1865] 1976.

_______________. *Sacred Rhetoric*. Richmond, VA: Presbyterian Committee of Publication, 1870.

Daille, John. *An Exposition of Philippians*. MacDill AFB, FL: Tyndale Bible Society, n.d.

Das, A. Andrew. "Beyond Covenantal Nomism: Paul, Judaism and Perfect Obedience." *Concordia Journal* 27/3 (July 2001): 234–52.

The Daughters of St. Paul. *Basic Catechism*. Boston, MA: St. Paul Books and Media, [1987] 1993.

Davidheiser, Bolton. *Evolution and Christian Faith*. Nutley, NJ: Presbyterian and Reformed, 1969.

______________. *Science and the Bible*. Grand Rapids, MI: Baker Book House, 1971.

Davis, John J. *Moses and the Gods of Egypt: Studies in the Book of Exodus*. Grand Rapids, MI: Baker Book House, [1972] 1979.

Deddens, K. *Where Everything Points to Him*. trans. Theodore Plantinga. Alberta, CA and Caledonia, MI: Inheritance Publications, 1993.

DeJong, J. A. *As The Waters Cover the Sea: Millennial Expectations in the Rise of Anglo-American Mission. 1640–1810*. Kampen: J. H. Kok, 1970.

DeMar, Gary. "Denying SOLA SCRIPTURA." *Biblical Worldview* 9/12 (December 1993).

DeRidder, Richard R. *Discipling the Nations*. Grand Rapids, MI: Baker Book House, [1971] 1975.

Dick, John. *Lectures on Theology*. 2 vols. Philadelphia: J. Whetham, 1836.

Dickson, David. *A Commentary on the Psalms*. 2 vols. London: 1665; reprint Minneapolis, MN: Klock & Klock Christian Publishers, 1980.

____________. *The Elder and His Work*. Dallas, TX: Presbyterian Heritage Publications, 1990.

Douma, J. *The Ten Commandments: Manual for the Christian Life*. trans. Nelson D. Kloosteman. Phillipsburg, NJ: Presbyterian and Reformed Publishers, 1996.

Durham, Deanna. *Life Among The Moonies: Three Years in the Unification Church*. Plainfield, NH: Logos International, 1981.

Dwight, Timothy. *Theology: Explained and Defended in a Series of Sermons*. 5 vols. Middletown, CT: Clark & Lyman, 1819.

Dyrness, F. Seth. "Types of Satanic Intervention." *The Journal of Christian Reconstruction* 1/2 (1974): 44–62.

Eadie, John. *Commentary on the Epistle of Paul to the Colossians*. Grand Rapids, MI: Zondervan Publishing House, [1856] 1957.

Edwards, Jonathan. *Heaven: A World of Love*. Amityville, NY: Calvary Press, [Banner of Truth Trust 1969] 1992.

Erdman, Charles. *The Acts*. Philadelphia: The Westminster Press, 1919.

______________. *The Epistle of Paul to the Philippians*. Philadelphia: The Westminster Press, 1932.

Erickson, Millard J. *God In Three Persons: A Contemporary Interpretation of the Trinity*. Grand Rapids, MI: Baker Books, 1995.

Eyres, Lawrence. *The Elders of the Church*. Philadelphia: Presbyterian and Reformed Publishers, 1975.

Fairbairn, Patrick. *Commentary on the Pastoral Epistles: I & II Timothy, Titus*. Grand Rapids, MI: Zondervan Publishing House, [1874] 1956.

______________. *An Exposition of Ezekiel*. Grand Rapids, MI: Sovereign Grace Publishers, 1971.

Falwell, Jerry, ed., *Liberty Bible Commentary.* 2 vols. Lynchburg, VA: The Old-Time Gospel Hour, 1982.

Fee, Gordon. *New International Commentary on the New Testament The First Epistle to the Corinthians*. Grand Rapids, MI: William B. Eerdmans, [1973] 1987.

Fergusson, James. *An Exposition of the Epistles of Paul to the Galatians, Ephesians, Philippians, Colossians, Thessalonians*. Indiana: Sovereign Grace Publishers, n.d.

Ferguson, Sinclair. *John Owen on the Christian Life*. Edinburgh, The Banner of Truth Trust, 1987.

______________. *Mastering the Old Testament: Daniel*. ed. Lloyd J. Ogilvie. Dallas: Word Publishing, 1988.

Findlay, G. G. *The Epistle to the Galatians, The Expositor's Bible*. New York: Funk & Wagnalls Co., 1900.

Fisher, Edward. *Fisher's Catechism*. Presbyterian Board of Publishing and Sabbath School Work, 1911.

Fisher, James. *The Westminster Shorter Catechism Explained*. Philadelphia, PA: Presbyterian Board of Publication and Sabbath-School Work [1753] 1911.

Flavel, John. *The Fountain of Life*. London: The Religious Tract Society, 1671.

__________. *The Method of Grace*. Grand Rapids, MI: Baker Book House, 1977.

Foulner, Martin. *Theonomy and the Westminster Confession of Faith*. Marpet Press, 1997.

Frame, John M. *The Doctrine of the Knowledge of God.* Philipsburg, NJ: Presbyterian and Reformed Publishing Co., 1987.

Fraser, J. Cameron. "The Occasional Elements of Worship." *Worship in the Presence of God.* eds. David Lachman and Frank J. Smith. Greenville, SC: Greenville Seminary Press, 1992.

Gaffin, Richard, Jr., *The Centrality of the Resurrection.* Grand Rapids, MI: Baker Book House, 1978.

_______________. "A Reformed Critique of the New Perspective." *Modern Reformation* (March/April 2002).

Geisler, Norman and MacKenzie, Ralph. "What Think Ye of Rome? Part Four: The Catholic-Protestant Debate on Papal Infallibility." *Christian Research Journal* (Fall 1994).

Geldenhuys, Norval. *New International Commentary on the New Testament: The Commentary on the Gospel of Luke.* Grand Rapids, MI: Wm. B. Eerdmans, [1951] 1966.

Gentry, Kenneth, Jr., *The Charismatic Gift of Prophecy.* Memphis, TN: Footstool Publications, 1989.

_______________. *The Greatness of the Great Commission.* Tyler, Texas: Institute for Christian Economics, 1990.

_______________. *He Shall Have Dominion: A Post-Millennial Eschatology.* Tyler, TX: Institute for Christian Economics, 1992.

Gerstner, John H. *Repent or Perish.* Ligonier, PA: Soli Deo Gloria Publications, 1990.

_______________. *The Theology of the Major Sects.* Grand Rapids, MI: Baker Book House, 1960.

Gill, John. *Body of Divinity.* Atlanta, GA: Turner Lassetter, [1839] 1965.

Gillespie, George. *Aaron's Rod Blossoming.* Harrisonburg, VA: Sprinkle Publications, [1646] 1985.

_______________. *A Dispute Against the English Popish Ceremonies Obtruded Upon the Church of Scotland.* ed. Christopher Coldwell. Dallas, TX: Naphtali Press, [1630, 1844] 1993.

Gilsdorf, Aletha Joy. *The Puritan Apocalyptic: New England Eschatology in the Seventeenth Century.* NY: Garland, 1989.

Girardeau, John L. *Calvinism and Evangelical Arminianism.* Harrisonburg, VA: Sprinkle Publications.

______________. The Doctrine of Adoption." *Discussions of Theological Questions*. Harrisonburg, VA: Sprinkle Publications, [1905] 1986.

______________. *The Life Work of Girardeau*. ed. by George A. Blackburn. Columbia, SC: The State Co., 1916.

Godfrey, W. Robert. "Back to Basics: A Response to the Robertson-Fuller Dialogue." *Presbuterion* 9/1–2 (1983).

________________. "The Westminster Larger Catechism." *To Glorify and Enjoy God*. ed. John Carson and David Hall. Edinburgh, Scotland: The Banner of Truth Trust, 1994.

________________. " What do we Mean by Sola Scriptura?" *Sola Scriptura*. ed. Don Kistler. Morgan, PA: Soli Deo Gloria Publications, 1995.

Graham, Billy. *How To Be Born Again*. Canada: Word Publishing, [1977] 1989.

Graham, Henry G. *Where We Got the Bible*. Rockford, IL: Tan Books and Publishers, Inc., 1911.

Greaves, Richard. *Theology and Revolution in the Scottish Reformation: Studies in the Thought of John Knox*. Grand Rapids, MI: Christian University Press, 1980.

Green, William H. *The Argument of the Book of Job Unfolded*. Minneapolis, MN: Klock & Klock Christian Publishers, [1874] 1979.

Greenhill, William. *An Exposition of Ezekiel*. Edinburgh; Pennsylvania: The Banner of Truth Trust, [1645–1667] 1994.

Gundry, Robert. "Grace, Works, and Staying Saved in Paul." *BIBLICA* 66 (1985).

Haldane, Robert. *An Exposition of the Epistle to the Romans*. MacDill AFB, FL: MacDonald Publishing, n.d.

Hall, David W. "Appendix B: Parliamentary Background of the Assembly." *To Glorify and Enjoy God*, ed. John L. Carson and David W. Hall. Edinburgh, Scotland: The Banner of Truth Trust, 1994.

Hall, David W., ed., *Jus Divinum Regiminis Ecclesiastici, or, The Divine Right of Church-Government, written by sundry ministers in London, several of whom were Westminster Divines, including Samuel Rutherford, in 1646*. Dallas, TX: Naphtali Press, 1995.

Hanko, Herman. "The Fear of the Lord in Worship." *Worship in the Presence of God*, ed. David Lachman and Frank J. Smith. Greenville, SC: Greenville Seminary Press, 1992.

______________. *The Mysteries of the Kingdom: An Exposition of the Parables*. Grand Rapids, MI: Reformed Free Publishing Co., 1975.

Hanson, Buddy. *God's Ten Words: A Commentary on the Ten Commandments*. Tuscaloosa, AL: The Hanson Group, 2002.

Harris, Jack. *Freemasonry: The Invisible Cult in Our Midst*. Towson, MD: Jack Harris, 1983.

Harris, R. Laird, and Gleason L. Archer, Jr., eds., *Theological Wordbook of the Old Testament*, 2 vols. Chicago: Moody Press, 1980.

Harrison, Everett F., ed., *Baker's Dictionary of Theology*. Grand Rapids, MI: Baker Book House, [1960] 1966.

Hastings, James. *A Dictionary of the Bible*. Edinburgh: Charles Scribner's Sons, T&T Clark, 1908.

Hendriksen, William. *New Testament Commentary*. 12 vols. Grand Rapids, MI: Baker Book House

Hengstenberg, E. W. *Christology of the Old Testament*. 2 vols. MacDill AFB, FL: MacDonald Publishing Co., n.d.

_________________. *The Works of Hengstenberg*. 7 vols. Cherry Hill, NJ: Mack Publishing Co., n.d.

Henry, Carl F. H., ed. *Revelation and the Bible*. Philadelphia, PA: Presbyterian and Reformed, 1958.

Henry, Matthew. *Matthew Henry's Commentary on the Whole Bible*. 6 vols. Peabody, MA: Hendrickson Publishers, 1992.

Herter, Theophilus J. *The Abrahamic Covenant in the Gospels*. Cherry Hill, NJ: Mack Publishing Co., [1966] 1972.

Hesselink, I. John. *Calvin's First Catechism: A Commentary*. Louisville, KY: Westminster/ John Knox Press, 1997.

Hetherington, William M. *History of the Westminster Assembly of Divines*. Canada: Still Waters Revival Books, [1856] 1993.

Hill, Christopher. *The English Bible And The Seventeenth-Century Revolution*. London, England: Penguin Books, 1994.

Hodge, Archibald A. *The Confession Of Faith*. London: The Banner of Truth Trust, [1958] 1964.

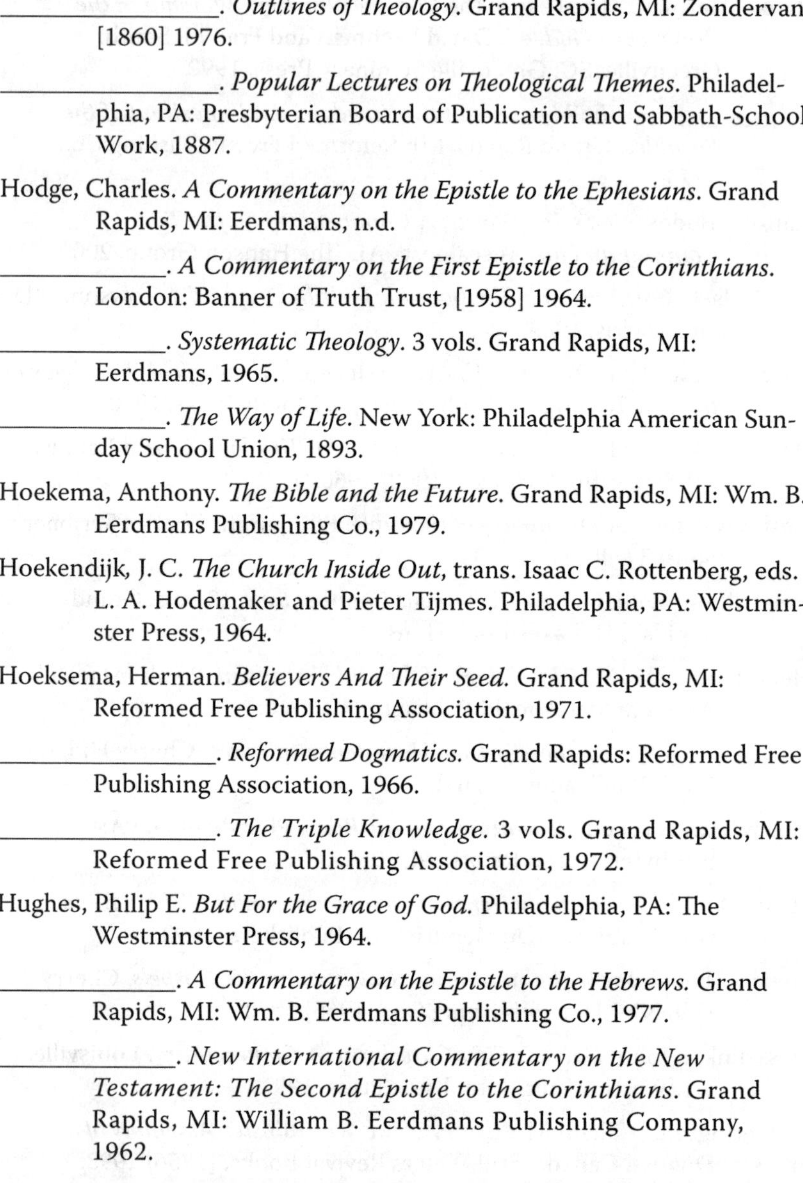

________. *Outlines of Theology*. Grand Rapids, MI: Zondervan, [1860] 1976.

________. *Popular Lectures on Theological Themes*. Philadelphia, PA: Presbyterian Board of Publication and Sabbath-School Work, 1887.

Hodge, Charles. *A Commentary on the Epistle to the Ephesians*. Grand Rapids, MI: Eerdmans, n.d.

________. *A Commentary on the First Epistle to the Corinthians*. London: Banner of Truth Trust, [1958] 1964.

________. *Systematic Theology*. 3 vols. Grand Rapids, MI: Eerdmans, 1965.

________. *The Way of Life*. New York: Philadelphia American Sunday School Union, 1893.

Hoekema, Anthony. *The Bible and the Future*. Grand Rapids, MI: Wm. B. Eerdmans Publishing Co., 1979.

Hoekendijk, J. C. *The Church Inside Out*, trans. Isaac C. Rottenberg, eds. L. A. Hodemaker and Pieter Tijmes. Philadelphia, PA: Westminster Press, 1964.

Hoeksema, Herman. *Believers And Their Seed*. Grand Rapids, MI: Reformed Free Publishing Association, 1971.

________. *Reformed Dogmatics*. Grand Rapids: Reformed Free Publishing Association, 1966.

________. *The Triple Knowledge*. 3 vols. Grand Rapids, MI: Reformed Free Publishing Association, 1972.

Hughes, Philip E. *But For the Grace of God*. Philadelphia, PA: The Westminster Press, 1964.

________. *A Commentary on the Epistle to the Hebrews*. Grand Rapids, MI: Wm. B. Eerdmans Publishing Co., 1977.

________. *New International Commentary on the New Testament: The Second Epistle to the Corinthians*. Grand Rapids, MI: William B. Eerdmans Publishing Company, 1962.

Hunt, Susan, and Peggy Hutcheson. *Leadership for Women in the Church*. Atlanta, GA: Christian Education and Publications, 1991.

Hunter, Archibald M. *Interpreting the Parables*. Philadelphia: The Westminster Press, 1960.

Hurst, Kerry W. "The Administration of the Sacraments." *Worship in the Presence of God*. ed. David Lachman and Frank J. Smith. Greenville, SC: Greenville Seminary Press, 1992.

Hutchson, George. *The Gospel of John*. London: The Banner of Truth Trust, [1657] 1972.

Jenkyn, William. *Exposition of the Epistle of Jude*, revised by Rev. James Sherman. Minneapolis, MN: James & Klock Publishing Co., reprint 1976.

Jeremias, Joachim. *The Parables of Jesus*. trans. S. H. Hooke. NY: Charles Scribner Sons, 1963.

Johnson, Dennis E. *The Message of Acts in the History of Redemption*. Phillipsburg, NJ: Presbyterian and Reformed Publishers, [1973] 1997.

Jones, Douglas. "Issue and Interchange." *Antithesis* 1/5 (September/ October 1990): 46–59.

Jones, Douglas, and Douglas Wilson. *Angels in the Architecture: A Protestant Vision for Middle Earth*. Moscow, ID: Canon Press, 1998.

Jones, Norman L. *Study Helps on the Heidelberg Catechism*. Eureka, SD: Publications Committee of the Eureka Classics, 1981.

Jordan, James B. "Biblical Absolutism, II: The Chronology of the Bible." Unpublished Manuscript.

____________. "The Dietary Laws of Scripture: Their Meaning for Today." Unpublished paper.

____________. *The Law of the Covenant: An Exposition of Exodus 21–23*. Tyler, TX: Institute for Christian Economics, 1984.

Junkin, George. *Commentary Upon the Epistle to the Hebrews*. Philadelphia: Smith, English & Co.; NY: Robert Carter & Brothers, 1873.

Kaiser, Walter C., Jr. "The Blessing of David: The Charter for Humanity." *The Law and the Prophets*. ed. John H. Skilton. Presbyterian and Reformed Publishing Co., 1974.

________________. *Ecclesiastes: Total Life*. Chicago: Moody Press, [1979] 1981.

________________. *Toward Old Testament Ethics*. Grand Rapids, MI: Academie Books/ Zondervan, 1983.

Keddie, Gordon J. *Triumph of the King: The Message of 2 Samuel.* Durham, England: Evangelical Press, 1990.

Keil, C. F., and F. Delitzsch. *Biblical Commentary on the Old Testament.* 25 vols. trans. James Martin. Grand Rapids, MI: Eerdmans, 1971.

Kellogg, Samuel. *The Book of Leviticus.* MN: Klock & Klock, [1899] 1978.

Kelly, Douglas. "The Westminster Shorter Catechism." *To Glorify and Enjoy God,* ed. John L. Carson and David W. Hall. Edinburgh: The Banner of Truth Trust, 1994.

Kennedy, D. James. *A Nation in Shame.* Ft. Lauderdale, FL: Coral Ridge Ministries, 1985.

Kevan, Ernest. *The Grace of Law: A Study in Puritan Theology.* Grand Rapids, MI: Guardian Press, 1976.

___________. *The Moral Law. God's Law.* Pennsylvania: Sovereign Grace Publishers, 1963.

Kidner, Derek. *The Message of Ecclesiastes.* Downers Grove, IL: Inter-Varsity Press, 1976.

Kik, J. Marcellus. *Eschatology of Victory.* Phillipsburg, NJ: Presbyterian and Reformed Publishing Co., 1971.

Kim, Young Oon. *Unification Theology.* New York, NY: The Holy Spirit Association for the Unification of World Christianity, 1980.

Kistemaker, Simon J. *Exposition of the Epistles of Peter and of the Epistle of Jude.* Grand Rapids, MI: Baker Book House, 1987.

_________________. *The Parables of Jesus.* Grand Rapids, MI: Baker Book House, 1980.

Kittel, Gerhard, and Gerhard Friedrich, eds., *Theological Dictionary of the New Testament.* Abridged in One Volume. trans. Geoffrey W. Bromiley. Grand Rapids, MI: Wm. B. Eerdmans, [1985] 1988.

Kline, Meredith. *By Oath Consigned: A Reinterpretation of the Covenantal Signs of Circumcision and Baptism.* Grand Rapids, MI: William B. Eerdmans Publishing Co., 1968.

_____________. *Treaty of the Great King: The Covenantal Structure of Deuteronomy.* Grand Rapids, MI: Wm. B. Eerdmans Publishing Co.,

Knight, George W., III. "Separation from Unbelief." Pamphlet distributed by *The Presbyterian Guardian.*

Knox, John. *Selected Writings of John Knox.* ed. David Laing; Dallas, TX: Presbyterian Heritage Publications, [1895] 1995.

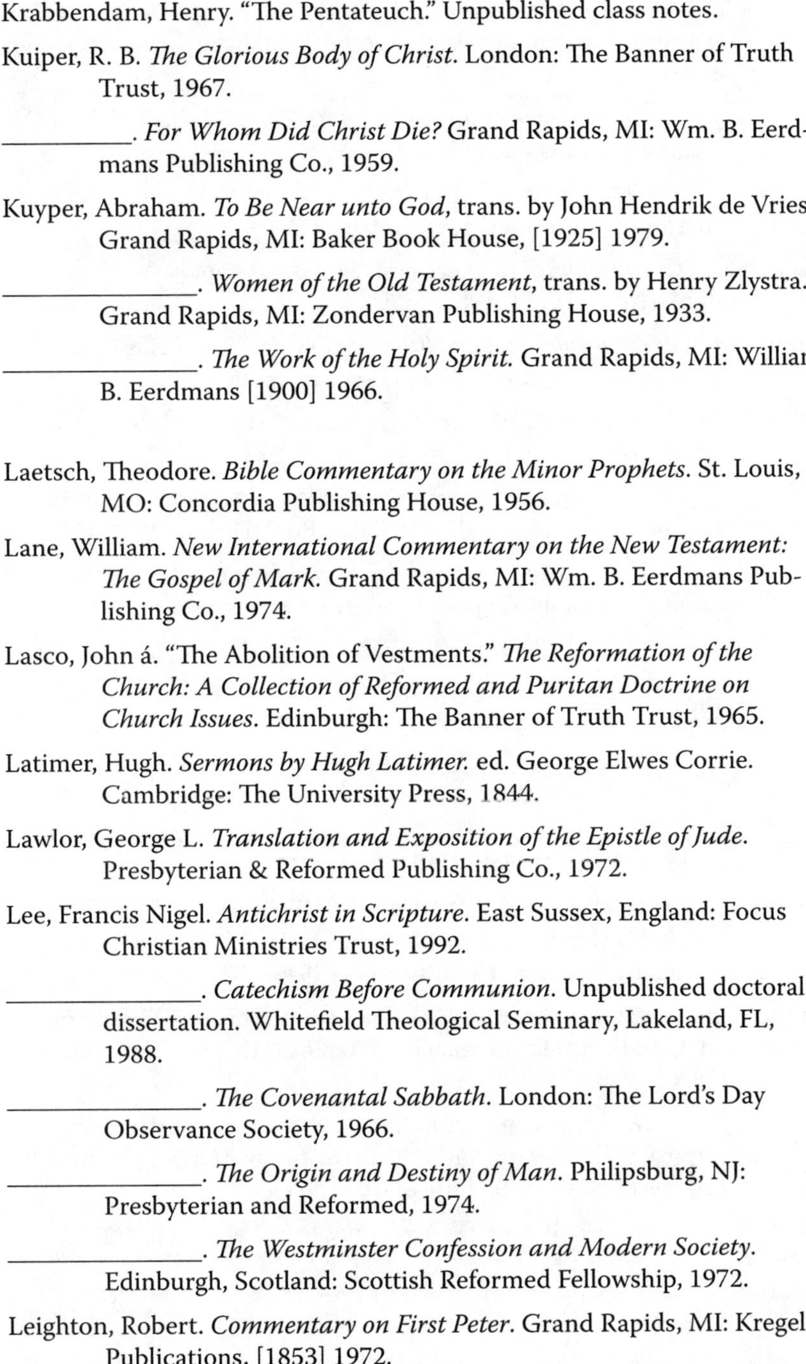

Krabbendam, Henry. "The Pentateuch." Unpublished class notes.

Kuiper, R. B. *The Glorious Body of Christ*. London: The Banner of Truth Trust, 1967.

__________. *For Whom Did Christ Die?* Grand Rapids, MI: Wm. B. Eerdmans Publishing Co., 1959.

Kuyper, Abraham. *To Be Near unto God*, trans. by John Hendrik de Vries. Grand Rapids, MI: Baker Book House, [1925] 1979.

__________. *Women of the Old Testament*, trans. by Henry Zlystra. Grand Rapids, MI: Zondervan Publishing House, 1933.

__________. *The Work of the Holy Spirit*. Grand Rapids, MI: William B. Eerdmans [1900] 1966.

Laetsch, Theodore. *Bible Commentary on the Minor Prophets*. St. Louis, MO: Concordia Publishing House, 1956.

Lane, William. *New International Commentary on the New Testament: The Gospel of Mark*. Grand Rapids, MI: Wm. B. Eerdmans Publishing Co., 1974.

Lasco, John á. "The Abolition of Vestments." *The Reformation of the Church: A Collection of Reformed and Puritan Doctrine on Church Issues*. Edinburgh: The Banner of Truth Trust, 1965.

Latimer, Hugh. *Sermons by Hugh Latimer*. ed. George Elwes Corrie. Cambridge: The University Press, 1844.

Lawlor, George L. *Translation and Exposition of the Epistle of Jude*. Presbyterian & Reformed Publishing Co., 1972.

Lee, Francis Nigel. *Antichrist in Scripture*. East Sussex, England: Focus Christian Ministries Trust, 1992.

__________. *Catechism Before Communion*. Unpublished doctoral dissertation. Whitefield Theological Seminary, Lakeland, FL, 1988.

__________. *The Covenantal Sabbath*. London: The Lord's Day Observance Society, 1966.

__________. *The Origin and Destiny of Man*. Philipsburg, NJ: Presbyterian and Reformed, 1974.

__________. *The Westminster Confession and Modern Society*. Edinburgh, Scotland: Scottish Reformed Fellowship, 1972.

Leighton, Robert. *Commentary on First Peter*. Grand Rapids, MI: Kregel Publications, [1853] 1972.

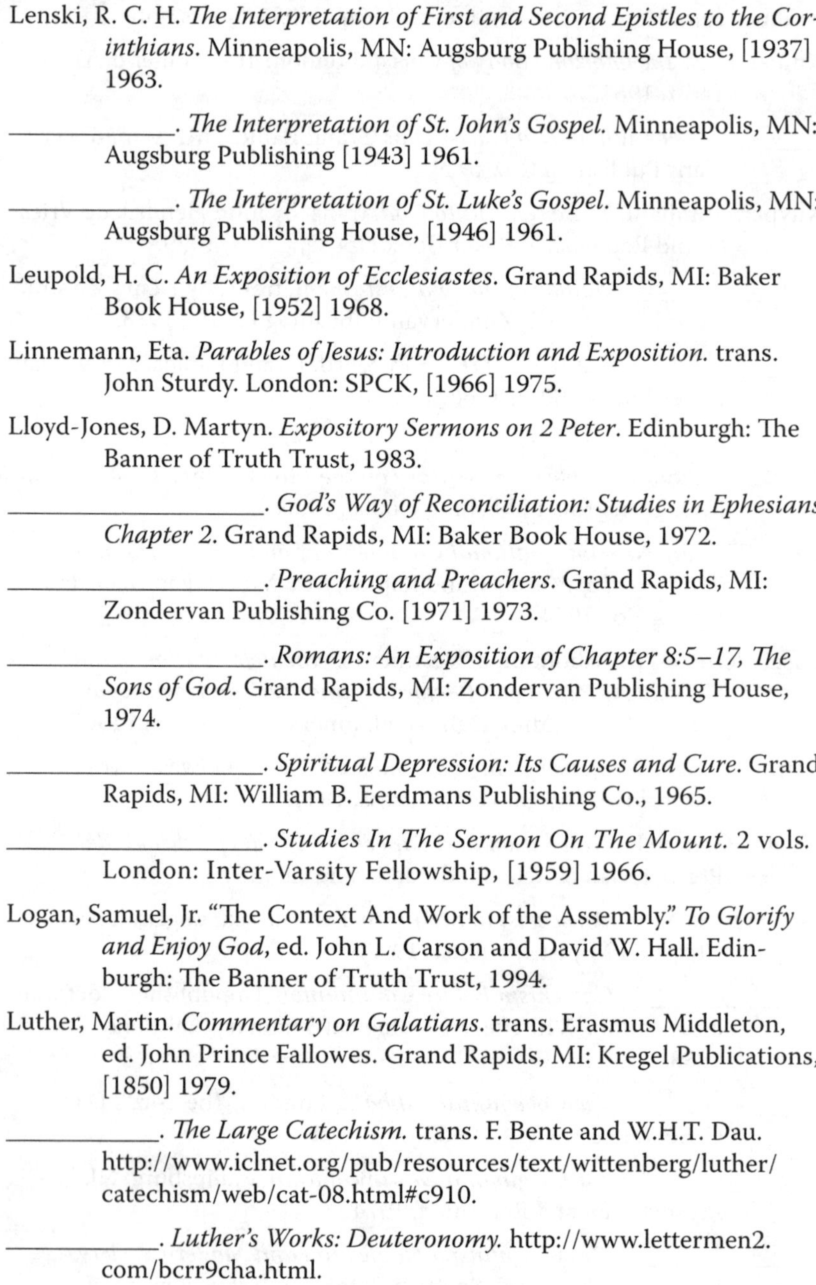

Lenski, R. C. H. *The Interpretation of First and Second Epistles to the Corinthians*. Minneapolis, MN: Augsburg Publishing House, [1937] 1963.

____________. *The Interpretation of St. John's Gospel.* Minneapolis, MN: Augsburg Publishing [1943] 1961.

____________. *The Interpretation of St. Luke's Gospel.* Minneapolis, MN: Augsburg Publishing House, [1946] 1961.

Leupold, H. C. *An Exposition of Ecclesiastes*. Grand Rapids, MI: Baker Book House, [1952] 1968.

Linnemann, Eta. *Parables of Jesus: Introduction and Exposition.* trans. John Sturdy. London: SPCK, [1966] 1975.

Lloyd-Jones, D. Martyn. *Expository Sermons on 2 Peter*. Edinburgh: The Banner of Truth Trust, 1983.

____________________. *God's Way of Reconciliation: Studies in Ephesians Chapter 2.* Grand Rapids, MI: Baker Book House, 1972.

____________________. *Preaching and Preachers.* Grand Rapids, MI: Zondervan Publishing Co. [1971] 1973.

____________________. *Romans: An Exposition of Chapter 8:5–17, The Sons of God*. Grand Rapids, MI: Zondervan Publishing House, 1974.

____________________. *Spiritual Depression: Its Causes and Cure.* Grand Rapids, MI: William B. Eerdmans Publishing Co., 1965.

____________________. *Studies In The Sermon On The Mount.* 2 vols. London: Inter-Varsity Fellowship, [1959] 1966.

Logan, Samuel, Jr. "The Context And Work of the Assembly." *To Glorify and Enjoy God*, ed. John L. Carson and David W. Hall. Edinburgh: The Banner of Truth Trust, 1994.

Luther, Martin. *Commentary on Galatians*. trans. Erasmus Middleton, ed. John Prince Fallowes. Grand Rapids, MI: Kregel Publications, [1850] 1979.

____________. *The Large Catechism.* trans. F. Bente and W.H.T. Dau. http://www.iclnet.org/pub/resources/text/wittenberg/luther/catechism/web/cat-08.html#c910.

____________. *Luther's Works: Deuteronomy.* http://www.lettermen2.com/bcrr9cha.html.

M 'Crie, Thomas, "On the Right of Females to Vote," *Miscellaneous Writings*. Edinburgh: John Johnstone, Hunter Square, 1841.

______________. *Unity of the Church*. Dallas, TX: Presbyterian Heritage Publications, [1821] 1989.

MacArthur, John, Jr. "The Sufficiency of The Written Word." *Sola Scriptura*. ed. Don Kistler. Morgan, PA: Soli Deo Gloria Publications, 1995.

Machen, J. Gresham. *The Christian Faith in the Modern World*. Grand Rapids, MI: Eerdmans, [1936] 1968.

______________. *The Virgin Birth of Christ*. Grand Rapids, Michigan: Baker Book House, 1967.

______________. *What Is Faith*. Grand Rapids, MI: Wm. B. Eerdmans Publishing Co., [1925] 1965.

Mack, Edward. *The Christ of the Old Testament*. Richmond, VA: Presbyterian Committee of Publication, 1926.

______________. *The Preacher's Old Testament*. Fleming H. Revell Company, 1923.

Mack, Wayne. *The Role of Women in the Church*. Cherry Hill, NJ: Mack Publishing, [1972] 1973.

MacLeod, Donald. *The Place of Women in the Church*. London: The Banner of Truth Trust, 1970.

______________. *Rome and Canterbury: A View From Geneva*. Ross-Shire, Scotland and Houston, TX: Christian Focus Publications, 1989.

Manton, Thomas. *An Exposition of John 17*. Wilmington, DE: Sovereign Grace Publishers, 1972.

Marcel, Pierre C. *The Biblical Doctrine of Infant Baptism*. trans. Phillip E. Hughes. London: James Clark and Co., Ltd., [1953] 1959.

______________. *The Relevance of Preaching*. trans. Rob Roy McGregor. Grand Rapids, MI: Baker Book House, 1963.

Martens, Elmer A. *God's Design: A Focus on Old Testament Theology*. Grand Rapids, MI: Baker Book House, 1981.

Martin, Paul. "An Exposition of Leviticus 10:1-3." *The Biblical Doctrine of Worship: A Symposium*. Reformed Presbyterian Church of North America, 1974.

Martin, Ralph P. *Tyndale Commentaries: The Epistle of Paul to the Philippians: An Introduction and Commentary*. Grand Rapids, MI: William B. Eerdmans Publishing Co., [1959] 1965.

Matatics, Gerald. "Issue And Interchange." *Antithesis* 1/5 (September/ October 1990): 46–59.

McCoy, Charles S., and J. Wayne Baker, *Fountainhead of Federalism: Heinrich Bullinger And The Covenantal Tradition*. Louisville, KY: Westminster/ John Knox Press, 1991.

McCracken, Robert B. "An Exposition of II Chronicles 26:16-21." *The Biblical Doctrine of Worship: A Symposium*. Reformed Presbyterian Church of North America, 1974.

McKnight, William J. *The Apocalypse of Jesus Christ: A Reappearance*. 4 vols. Boston, MA: Hamilton Bros. Publishers, 1927.

Meek, James A. "The New Perspective on Paul: An Introduction for the Uninitiated." *Concordia Journal* 27/3 (July 2001): 208–33.

Miller, C. John. *Repentance and 20th Century Man*. Ft. Washington, PA: Christian Literature Crusade, [1975] 1980.

Miller, Samuel. *Presbyterianism: The Truly Primitive and Apostolical Constitution of the Church of Christ*. Philadelphia: Presbyterian Board of Publication, 1835.

____________. *The Ruling Elder*. Dallas, TX; Jackson, MS: Presbyterian Heritage Publications, 1987.

Mitchell, Alexander. *The Westminster Assembly Its History and Standards*. Canada: Still Waters Revival Books, [1883] 1992.

Moore, Thomas V. *A Commentary On Haggai and Malachi*. Edinburgh: The Banner of Truth Trust, [1856] 1958.

________________. *A Commentary on Zechariah*. Edinburgh: The Banner of Truth Trust, [1856] 1958.

Morecraft, Joe, III. *How God Wants Us To Worship Him*. San Antonio, TX: Vision Forum, 2004.

Morgan, Edmund S. *The Puritan Family: Religion and Domestic Relations in Seventeenth-Century New England*. NY: Harper & Row Publishers, [1944] 1966.

Morgan, Ray. *When Two Become One: A Diamond in the Making*. AuthorHouse, 2007.

Morris, Henry M. *The Beginning of the World*. Denver, CO: Accent Books, 1977.

_______________. *The Twilight of Evolution*. Grand Rapids, MI: Baker Book House, 1963.

Morris, Leon. *The Apostolic Preaching of the Cross*. Grand Rapids, MI: Wm. B. Eerdmans Publishing Co., [1955] 1965.

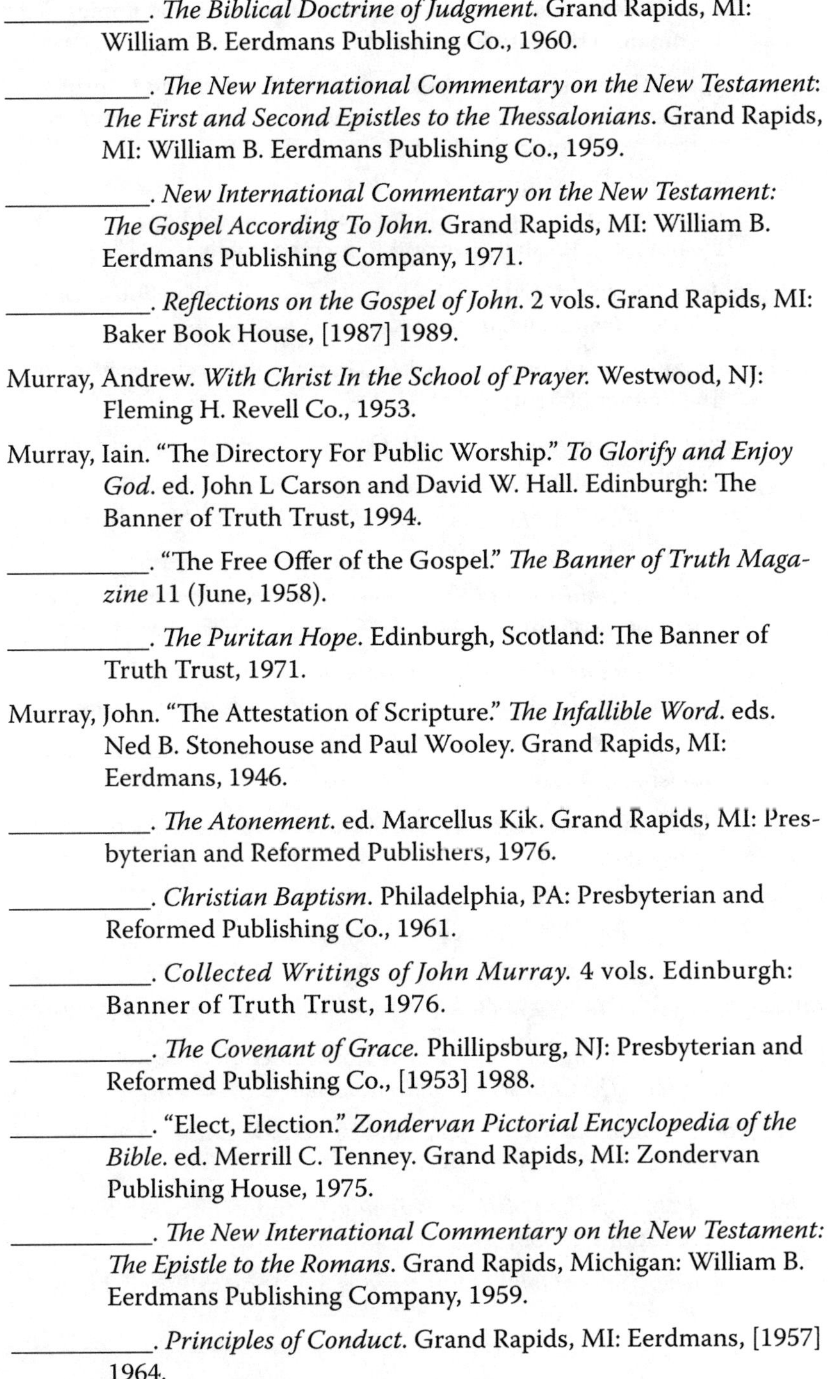

__________. *The Biblical Doctrine of Judgment.* Grand Rapids, MI: William B. Eerdmans Publishing Co., 1960.

__________. *The New International Commentary on the New Testament: The First and Second Epistles to the Thessalonians.* Grand Rapids, MI: William B. Eerdmans Publishing Co., 1959.

__________. *New International Commentary on the New Testament: The Gospel According To John.* Grand Rapids, MI: William B. Eerdmans Publishing Company, 1971.

__________. *Reflections on the Gospel of John.* 2 vols. Grand Rapids, MI: Baker Book House, [1987] 1989.

Murray, Andrew. *With Christ In the School of Prayer.* Westwood, NJ: Fleming H. Revell Co., 1953.

Murray, Iain. "The Directory For Public Worship." *To Glorify and Enjoy God.* ed. John L Carson and David W. Hall. Edinburgh: The Banner of Truth Trust, 1994.

__________. "The Free Offer of the Gospel." *The Banner of Truth Magazine* 11 (June, 1958).

__________. *The Puritan Hope.* Edinburgh, Scotland: The Banner of Truth Trust, 1971.

Murray, John. "The Attestation of Scripture." *The Infallible Word.* eds. Ned B. Stonehouse and Paul Wooley. Grand Rapids, MI: Eerdmans, 1946.

__________. *The Atonement.* ed. Marcellus Kik. Grand Rapids, MI: Presbyterian and Reformed Publishers, 1976.

__________. *Christian Baptism.* Philadelphia, PA: Presbyterian and Reformed Publishing Co., 1961.

__________. *Collected Writings of John Murray.* 4 vols. Edinburgh: Banner of Truth Trust, 1976.

__________. *The Covenant of Grace.* Phillipsburg, NJ: Presbyterian and Reformed Publishing Co., [1953] 1988.

__________. "Elect, Election." *Zondervan Pictorial Encyclopedia of the Bible.* ed. Merrill C. Tenney. Grand Rapids, MI: Zondervan Publishing House, 1975.

__________. *The New International Commentary on the New Testament: The Epistle to the Romans.* Grand Rapids, Michigan: William B. Eerdmans Publishing Company, 1959.

__________. *Principles of Conduct.* Grand Rapids, MI: Eerdmans, [1957] 1964.

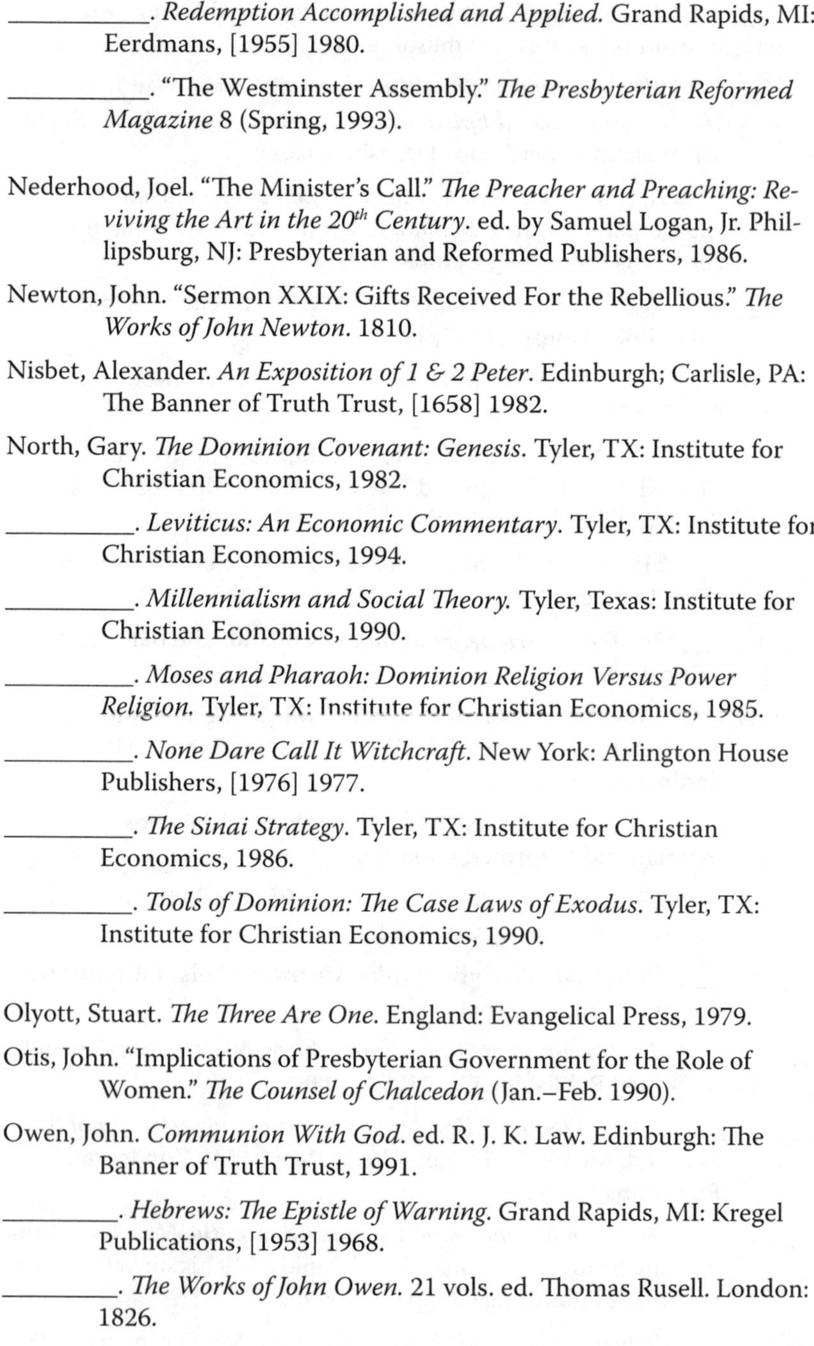

__________. *Redemption Accomplished and Applied.* Grand Rapids, MI: Eerdmans, [1955] 1980.

__________. "The Westminster Assembly." *The Presbyterian Reformed Magazine* 8 (Spring, 1993).

Nederhood, Joel. "The Minister's Call." *The Preacher and Preaching: Reviving the Art in the 20th Century*. ed. by Samuel Logan, Jr. Phillipsburg, NJ: Presbyterian and Reformed Publishers, 1986.

Newton, John. "Sermon XXIX: Gifts Received For the Rebellious." *The Works of John Newton*. 1810.

Nisbet, Alexander. *An Exposition of 1 & 2 Peter*. Edinburgh; Carlisle, PA: The Banner of Truth Trust, [1658] 1982.

North, Gary. *The Dominion Covenant: Genesis*. Tyler, TX: Institute for Christian Economics, 1982.

__________. *Leviticus: An Economic Commentary*. Tyler, TX: Institute for Christian Economics, 1994.

__________. *Millennialism and Social Theory.* Tyler, Texas: Institute for Christian Economics, 1990.

__________. *Moses and Pharaoh: Dominion Religion Versus Power Religion.* Tyler, TX: Institute for Christian Economics, 1985.

__________. *None Dare Call It Witchcraft*. New York: Arlington House Publishers, [1976] 1977.

__________. *The Sinai Strategy*. Tyler, TX: Institute for Christian Economics, 1986.

__________. *Tools of Dominion: The Case Laws of Exodus*. Tyler, TX: Institute for Christian Economics, 1990.

Olyott, Stuart. *The Three Are One*. England: Evangelical Press, 1979.

Otis, John. "Implications of Presbyterian Government for the Role of Women." *The Counsel of Chalcedon* (Jan.–Feb. 1990).

Owen, John. *Communion With God*. ed. R. J. K. Law. Edinburgh: The Banner of Truth Trust, 1991.

__________. *Hebrews: The Epistle of Warning*. Grand Rapids, MI: Kregel Publications, [1953] 1968.

__________. *The Works of John Owen*. 21 vols. ed. Thomas Rusell. London: 1826.

Ozmont, Steven. *When Fathers Ruled: Family Life in Reformation Europe.* Cambridge, MA: Harvard University Press, 1983.

Packer, J. I. *Evangelism and the Sovereignty of God.* Downers Grove, IL: InterVarsity Press, 1961.

_________. *I Want To Be A Christian.* Wheaton, IL: Tyndale House Publishers, Inc., [1977] 1983.

_________. "Introduction." *The Death of Death in the Death of Christ.* London: The Banner of Truth Trust, [1852] 1963.

_________. *Knowing God.* Dowers Grove, IL: Inter Varsity Press, 1973.

_________. *A Quest for Godliness.* Wheaton, IL: Crossway Books, 1990.

_________. "The Puritan Approach to Worship." *Antithesis* 2/1 (Jan/Feb 1991).

Palmer, Benjamin. "Perpetuity of the Divine Law." *The Counsel of Chalcedon* 14/ 2 (April, 1992).

_______________. *Sermons by Rev. B. M. Palmer, Volumes I and II.* Harrisonburg, VA: Sprinkle Publications, [1875] 2002.

_______________. *Theology of Prayer As Viewed in the Religion of Nature and In the System of Grace.* Harrisonburg, VA: Sprinkle Publications, [1894] 1980.

Palmer, Edwin. *The Holy Spirit.* Philadelphia, PA: Presbyterian and Reformed, [1958] 1964.

Pas, Arend J. Ten *The Lordship of Christ.* Vallecito, CA: Ross House Books, 1978.

Paterson, Alexander. *A Concise System Of Theology on the Basis of the Shorter Catechism.* New York: Obert Carter and Brothers, 1856.

Paxton, Geoffrey. *The Shaking of Adventism.* Grand Rapids, MI: Baker Book House, 1977.

Payne, Franklin E. *Biblical/Medical Ethics: The Christian and the Practice of Medicine.* Milford, MI: Mott Media, Inc., 1985.

Payton, James R., Jr. "The Emergence of Postmillennialism in English Puritanism." *The Journal of Christian Reconstruction* 6/1 (Summer 1979).

Pink, Arthur W. *The Attributes of God.* Swengel, PA: Reiner Publications, n.d.

____________. *The Doctrines of Election and Justification*. Grand Rapids, MI: Baker Book House, [1974] 1976.

____________. *The Doctrine of Sanctification*. Swengel, PA: Reiner Publications, 1966.

____________. *The Sovereignty of God*. Grand Rapids, MI: Baker Book House [1930] 1977.

Pipa, Joseph. *The Lord's Day*. Great Britain: Christian Focus Publications, 1997.

Plumer, William S. *Hints And Helps In Pastoral Theology*. New York: Harper and Brothers, 1874.

______________. "How Stands My Case With God?" *The Counsel of Chalcedon*. Dunwoody, GA: Chalcedon Presbyterian Church, Feb/Mar 1998.

______________. *The Law of God As Contained in the Ten Commandments, Explained and Enforced*. Philadelphia, PA: Presbyterian Board of Education, 1864.

______________. *Psalms: A Critical and Expository Commentary With Doctrinal & Practical Remarks.* Edinburgh: The Banner of Truth Trust, 1975.

______________. *Vital Godliness: A Treatise on Experimental and Practical Piety*. Harrisonburg, VA: Sprinkle Publications, [1864] 1993.

Plummer, Alfred. *A Critical and Exegetical Commentary on The Gospel According to S. Luke*. Edinburgh: T & T Clark, [1896] 1969.

Pollard, Jeff. *Christian Modesty*. Pensacola, FL: Mt. Zion Publications, n.d.

Postman, Neil. *Amusing Ourselves to Death: Public Discourse in the Age of Show Business*. NY: Viking, 1985.

____________. *Teaching As A Conserving Activity.* NY: Delacorte Press, 1979.

Poythress, Vern. *Understanding Dispensationalists*. Grand Rapids, MI: Zondervan Publishing House, 1993.

Pratt, Richard L., Jr. *Every Thought Captive: A Study Manual for the Defense of Christian Truth.* Phillipsburg, NJ: Presbyterian and Reformed Publishers, 1979.

Presbyterian Church in America. "Preface." *The Book of Church Order of the Presbyterian Church in America.* Office of the Stated Clerk of the General Assembly of the Presbyterian Church in America,

[1990] with 1995 Amendments.

Pusey, E. B. *Pusey on the Old Testament*. 2 vols. Grand Rapids, MI: Baker Book House, [1950] 1974.

Quandt, Jean B. "Religion and Social Thought: The Secularization of Postmillennialism." *American Quarterly* 25 (Oct. 1973).

Ramm, Bernard. *Them He Glorified*. Grand Rapids, MI: William B. Eerdmans Publishing Co., 1963.

____________. *The Witness of the Spirit*. Grand Rapids, MI: William B. Eerdmans Publishing Company, 1959.

Reid, James. "Appendix." *Memoirs of the Westminster Divines*. Edinburgh: The Banner of Truth Trust, [1811] 1982.

Reisinger, Ernest. "The Lordship Controversy and Repentance." *Founders Journal* 14 (Fall 1993).

Reymond, Robert L. *The Justification of Knowledge: An Introductory Study of Apologetic Methodology*. Nutley, NJ: Presbyterian and Reformed, 1976.

_______________. *A New Systematic Theology of the Christian Faith*. Nashville, TN: Thomas Nelson Publishers, 1998.

Ridderbos, Herman. *The Coming of the Kingdom*. Philadelphia, PA: Presbyterian And Reformed Publishing, [1962] 1975.

_______________. *New International Commentary on the New Testament: The Epistle of Paul to the Churches of Galatia*. Grand Rapids, MI: Wm. B. Eerdmans Publishing Co., [1953] 1965.

_______________. *Paul: An Outline of His Theology*. trans. John Richard DeWitt. Grand Rapids, MI: Wm. B. Eerdmans, 1975.

Ridderbos, J. *Bible Student's Commentary: Deuteronomy*. Grand Rapids, MI: Regency Reference Library and Zondervan, 1984.

Richardson, John R. *What Happens After Death?* Houston, TX: St. Thomas Press, 1981.

Ridgeley, Thomas. *Commentary on the Larger Catechism*. 2 vols. Canada: Still Waters Revival Books, [1855] 1993.

Ripley, F. J. *This is the Faith: Catholic Theology for Laymen*. New York: Guild Press, 1960.

Robertson, O. Palmer. *The Christ of the Covenants*. Phillipsburg, NJ: Presbyterian and Reformed, 1980.

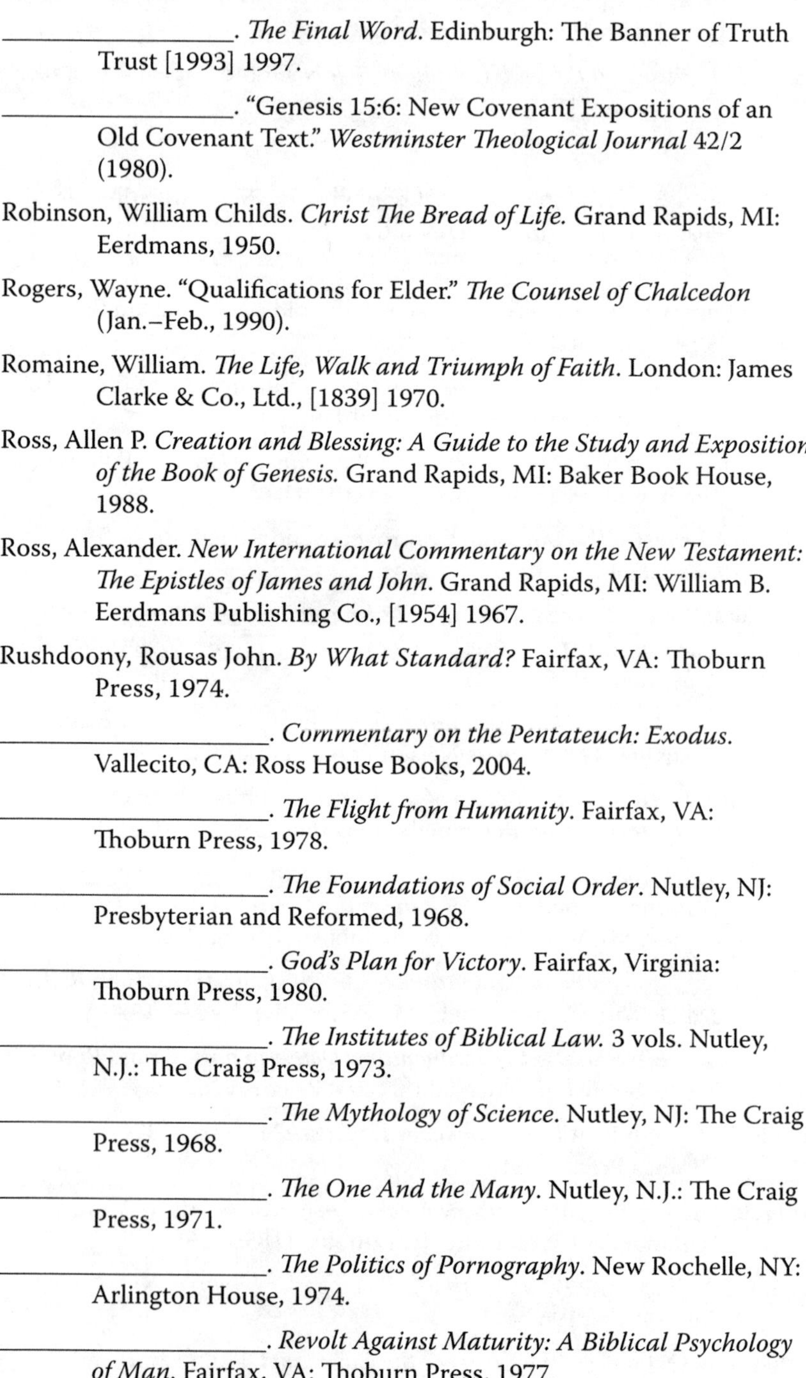

________. *The Final Word.* Edinburgh: The Banner of Truth Trust [1993] 1997.

________. "Genesis 15:6: New Covenant Expositions of an Old Covenant Text." *Westminster Theological Journal* 42/2 (1980).

Robinson, William Childs. *Christ The Bread of Life.* Grand Rapids, MI: Eerdmans, 1950.

Rogers, Wayne. "Qualifications for Elder." *The Counsel of Chalcedon* (Jan.–Feb., 1990).

Romaine, William. *The Life, Walk and Triumph of Faith.* London: James Clarke & Co., Ltd., [1839] 1970.

Ross, Allen P. *Creation and Blessing: A Guide to the Study and Exposition of the Book of Genesis.* Grand Rapids, MI: Baker Book House, 1988.

Ross, Alexander. *New International Commentary on the New Testament: The Epistles of James and John.* Grand Rapids, MI: William B. Eerdmans Publishing Co., [1954] 1967.

Rushdoony, Rousas John. *By What Standard?* Fairfax, VA: Thoburn Press, 1974.

________. *Commentary on the Pentateuch: Exodus.* Vallecito, CA: Ross House Books, 2004.

________. *The Flight from Humanity.* Fairfax, VA: Thoburn Press, 1978.

________. *The Foundations of Social Order.* Nutley, NJ: Presbyterian and Reformed, 1968.

________. *God's Plan for Victory.* Fairfax, Virginia: Thoburn Press, 1980.

________. *The Institutes of Biblical Law.* 3 vols. Nutley, N.J.: The Craig Press, 1973.

________. *The Mythology of Science.* Nutley, NJ: The Craig Press, 1968.

________. *The One And the Many.* Nutley, N.J.: The Craig Press, 1971.

________. *The Politics of Pornography.* New Rochelle, NY: Arlington House, 1974.

________. *Revolt Against Maturity: A Biblical Psychology of Man.* Fairfax, VA: Thoburn Press, 1977.

____________________. *Romans and Galatians*. Vallecito, CA: Ross House Books, 1997.

____________________. *Salvation and Godly Rule*. Vallecito, CA: Ross House Books, 1983.

____________________. *Systematic Theology*. 2. Vols. Vallecito, CA: Ross House Books, 1994.

____________________. *Thy Kingdom Come: Studies in Daniel and Revelation*. Phillipsburg, NJ: Presbyterian and Reformed, 1971.

____________________. *Toward A Christian Marriage*. ed. Elizabeth Fellersen. Nutley, NJ: Presbyterian and Reformed, 1975.

Rutherford, Samuel. *Rutherford's Catechism*. Edinburgh: Blue Banner Productions, [1886] 1998.

Ryle, J. C. *Expository Thoughts on the Gospels*. 7 vols. New York: The Baker & Taylor Co., 1873.

Ryken, Leland. *Redeeming the Time: A Christian Approach to Work and Leisure*. Grand Rapids, MI: Baker Books, 1995.

Sandlin, Andrew. *A Postmillennial Primer*. Vallecito, CA: Chalcedon Foundation, 1997.

Schaeffer, Francis. *Genesis In Space and Time: The Flow of Biblical History*. Downers Grove, IL: InterVarsity Press, 1972.

________________. *Joshua and The Flow of Biblical History*. Downers Grove, IL: InterVarsity Press, 1975.

________________. *Pollution and The Death of Man: The Christian View of Ecology*. Wheaton, IL: Tyndale House, 1970.

Schaff, Philip, ed. *The Creeds of Cristendom*. 3 vols. Grand Rapids, MI: Baker Book House, [1931] 1998.

Schenck, Lewis Bevens. *The Presbyterian Doctrine of Children in the Covenant*. Phillipsburg, NJ: Presbyterian and Reformed, [1940] 2001.

Schilder, Klaas. *Christ in His Suffering*. trans. Henry Zylstra. Grand Rapids, MI: Baker Book House, [1938] 1979.

Schlossberg, Herbert. *Idols for Destruction: Christian Faith and Its Confrontation with American Society*. New York: Thomas Nelson Publishers, 1983.

Schnell, William J. *Thirty Years A Watchtower Slave*. Grand Rapids, MI: Baker Book House, 1956.

Schneider, Michael, III. "Prayer Regulated By God's Word." *Worship in the Presence of God.* ed. David Lachman and Frank Smith. Greenville, SC: Greenville Seminary Press, 1992.

Schwertley, Brian M. *A Historical and Biblical Examination of Women Deacons.* Southfield, MI: Reformed Witness, 1998.

Scott, Thomas. *The Articles of the Synod of Dordt.* Harrisonburg, VA: Sprinkle Publications, 1993.

Shaw, Robert. *The Reformed Faith.* Inverness, Scotland: Christian Focus Publications, 1974.

Shedd, W. G. T. *Calvinism: Pure and Unmixed.* Edinburgh: Banner of Truth Trust, [1893] 1986.

_____________. *A Critical and Doctrinal Commentary on the Epistle of St. Paul to the Romans.* Grand Rapids, MI: Zondervan Publishing Co., [1879] 1967.

_____________. *Dogmatic Theology.* 3 vols. Nashville: Thomas Nelson Publishers, 1980.

_____________. *Sermons to the Spiritual Man.* London: The Banner of Truth Trust, [1884] 1972.

Shepherd, Norman. *The Call of Grace.* Phillipsburg, New Jersey: Presbyterian and Reformed Publishing Company, 2000.

Shroeder, H. J., trans. *Canons and Decrees of the Council of Trent.* Rockford, IL: Tan Books and Publishers, 1978.

Silva, Moises. "The Law and Christianity: Dunn's New Synthesis." *Westminster Theological Journal* 53 (1991).

Simpson, E. K., and F. F. Bruce. *New International Commentary on the New Testament: Commentary on The Epistles to the Ephesians and the Colossians.* Grand Rapids, MI: William B. Eerdmans Publishing, [1957], 1965.

Skilton, John H., ed. *The New Testament Student and Theology, Vol. III.* Nutley, N.J.: Presbyterian and Reformed Publishing Company, 1976.

Small, Dwight H. *The Biblical Basis for Infant Baptism.* Grand Rapids, MI: Baker Book House, [1959] 1968.

_____________. *Christian, Celebrate Your Sexuality.* Ada, MI: Fleming H. Revell Co., 1974.

Smalley, Gary, and John Trent. *The Gift of Honor.* NY: Pocket Books, 1987.

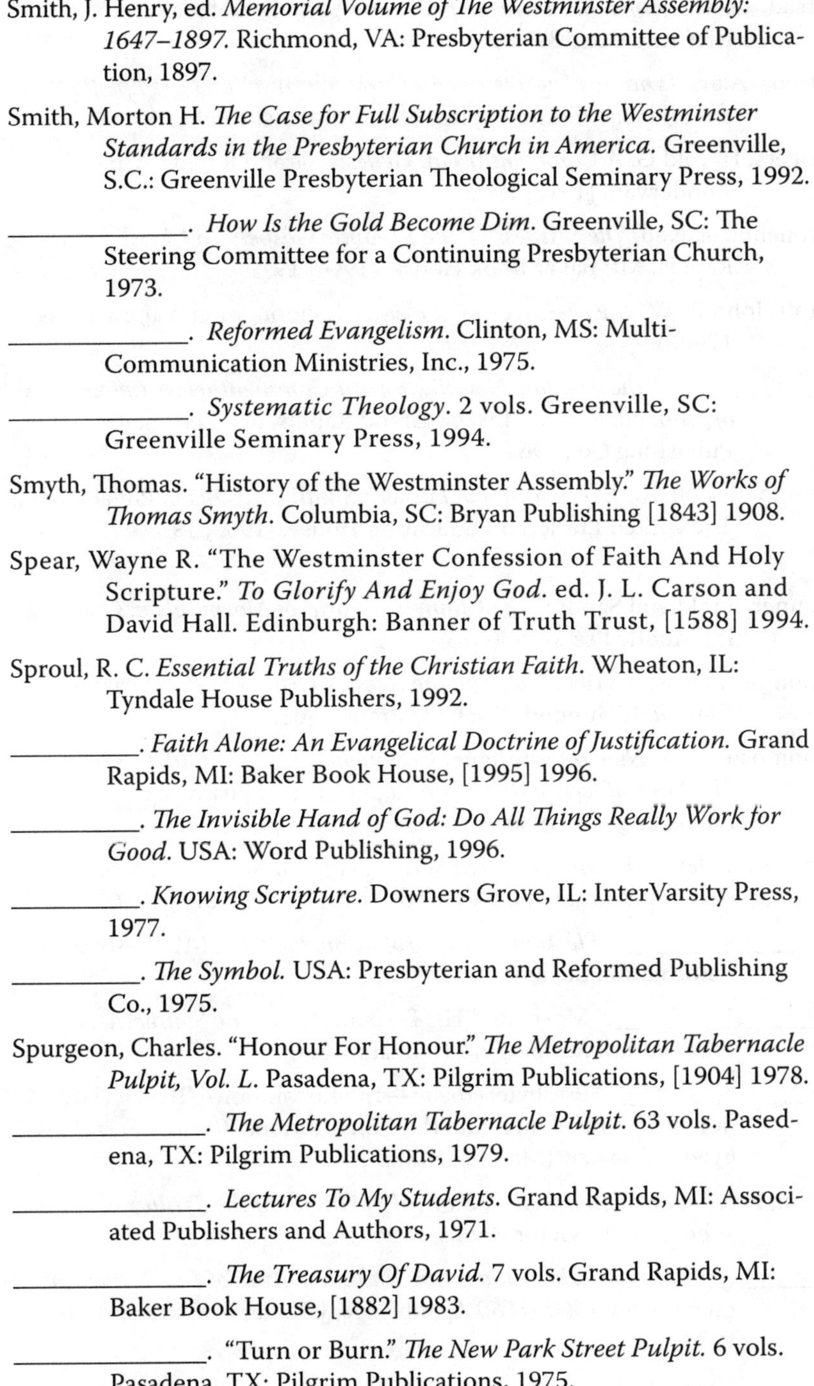

Smith, J. Henry, ed. *Memorial Volume of The Westminster Assembly: 1647–1897.* Richmond, VA: Presbyterian Committee of Publication, 1897.

Smith, Morton H. *The Case for Full Subscription to the Westminster Standards in the Presbyterian Church in America.* Greenville, S.C.: Greenville Presbyterian Theological Seminary Press, 1992.

______________. *How Is the Gold Become Dim.* Greenville, SC: The Steering Committee for a Continuing Presbyterian Church, 1973.

______________. *Reformed Evangelism.* Clinton, MS: Multi-Communication Ministries, Inc., 1975.

______________. *Systematic Theology.* 2 vols. Greenville, SC: Greenville Seminary Press, 1994.

Smyth, Thomas. "History of the Westminster Assembly." *The Works of Thomas Smyth.* Columbia, SC: Bryan Publishing [1843] 1908.

Spear, Wayne R. "The Westminster Confession of Faith And Holy Scripture." *To Glorify And Enjoy God.* ed. J. L. Carson and David Hall. Edinburgh: Banner of Truth Trust, [1588] 1994.

Sproul, R. C. *Essential Truths of the Christian Faith.* Wheaton, IL: Tyndale House Publishers, 1992.

__________. *Faith Alone: An Evangelical Doctrine of Justification.* Grand Rapids, MI: Baker Book House, [1995] 1996.

__________. *The Invisible Hand of God: Do All Things Really Work for Good.* USA: Word Publishing, 1996.

__________. *Knowing Scripture.* Downers Grove, IL: InterVarsity Press, 1977.

__________. *The Symbol.* USA: Presbyterian and Reformed Publishing Co., 1975.

Spurgeon, Charles. "Honour For Honour." *The Metropolitan Tabernacle Pulpit, Vol. L.* Pasadena, TX: Pilgrim Publications, [1904] 1978.

_______________. *The Metropolitan Tabernacle Pulpit.* 63 vols. Pasedena, TX: Pilgrim Publications, 1979.

_______________. *Lectures To My Students.* Grand Rapids, MI: Associated Publishers and Authors, 1971.

_______________. *The Treasury Of David.* 7 vols. Grand Rapids, MI: Baker Book House, [1882] 1983.

_______________. "Turn or Burn." *The New Park Street Pulpit.* 6 vols. Pasadena, TX: Pilgrim Publications, 1975.

Stead, W. T. *Hymns that have Helped*. New York: Doubleday and McClure Co., 1897.

Stibbs, Alan. *Tyndale New Testament Commentary: The First Epistle General of Peter*. Grand Rapids, MI: Eerdmans, 1959.

Stigers, Harold G. *A Commentary on Genesis*. Grand Rapids, MI: Zondervan, [1917] 1976.

Stonehouse, Ned. *The Witness of The Synoptic Gospels To Christ*. Grand Rapids, MI: Baker Book House, [1944] 1979.

Stott, John R. W. *The Message of Galatians*. London: Inter-Varsity Press, 1968.

____________. *The Tyndale New Testament Commentaries: The Epistles of John*, ed. R. V. G. Tasker. Grand Rapids, MI: Eerdmans Publishing Co., 1964.

Stump, Joseph. *An Explanation of Luther's Small Catechism*. Philadelphia: The United Lutheran Publication House, [1907] 1935.

Tanner, Jerald and Sandra. *The Changing World of Mormonism*. Chicago, IL: Moody Press, 1980.

Thompson, Ernest Trice. *Through The Ages: A History of the Christian Church*. Richmond, VA: CLC Press, 1965.

Thompson, J. A. *New International Commentary on the Old Testament: The Book of Jeremiah*. Grand Rapids, MI: William B. Eerdmans Publishing Co., 1980.

Thornwell, James H. *The Collected Writings of James Henley Thornwell*. 4 vols. Edinburgh: The Banner of Truth Trust, [1875] 1986.

________________. *Election and Reprobation*. Jackson, MI: Presbyterian Reformation Society, 1961.

________________. "Moses and His Dispensation." *The Southern Presbyterian Review* 12/4 (January, 1860).

________________. "Presbyterianism—The Revolution—The Declaration of Independence, and the Constitution." *The Southern Presbyterian Review* (March, 1848).

Toon, Peter. *Our Triune God: A Biblical Portrayal of the Trinity*. Wheaton, IL: Victor Books, 1996.

__________. *Puritans, The Millennium and the Future of Israel: Puritan Eschatology 1600–1660*. Cambridge, UK: James Clark and Co., 1970.

Torrance, Thomas F. *Calvin's Doctrine of Man.* Grand Rapids, MI: Eerdmans, 1957.

Torrey, R.A., "The Certainty and Importance of the Bodily Resurrection of Jesus Christ from the Dead," *The Fundamentals*, Vol. 2. Bible Institute of Los Angeles, 1917.

Tripp, Tedd. *Shepherding a Child's Heart.* Wapwallopen, PA: Shepherd Press, 1995.

Turretin, Francis. *Institutes of Elenctic Theology.* 3 vols. trans. George Musgrave Giger. Phillipsburg, New Jersey: Presbyterian and Reformed, 1992.

Van Reenen, G. *The Heidelberg Catechism—Sermons.* Netherlands Reformed Congregations, 1955.

Van Til, Cornelius. *Christianity in Conflict: Syllabus for Course in History of Apologetics.* Philadelphia, Westminster Theological Seminary, 1962.

______________. *Common Grace and Witness-Bearing.* Phillipsburg, NJ: Lewis Grotenhuis, 1954.

______________. *The Doctrine of Scripture.* Philadelphia, PA: den Dulk Christian Foundation, 1967.

______________. *An Introduction To Systematic Theology.* Philadelphia, PA: Westminster Theological Seminary, 1971.

______________. *A Christian Theory of Knowledge.* Philadelphia, PA: Presbyterian and Reformed Publishing, 1969.

______________. "The Doctrine of Creation and Christian Apologetics." *Journal of Christian Reconstruction* 1/1 (Summer 1974).

Vassady, Bela. *Christ's Church: Evangelical, Catholic and Reformed.* Grand Rapids, MI: Wm. B. Eerdmans Publishing Co., 1965.

Vaughan, Clement R. *The Gifts of the Holy Spirit.* Edinburgh: The Banner of Truth Trust, [1894] 1975.

Vaughan, Curtis. *James: A Study Guide.* Grand Rapids, MI: Zondervan, 1969.

Veith, Gene Edward. *Reading Between the Lines.* Wheaton, Illinois: Crossway Books, 1990.

Venn, Henry. *The Complete Duty of Man.* New York: American Tract Society, n.d.

Venning, Ralph. *The Plague of Plagues.* Edinburgh, Scotland: Banner of Truth, [1669] 1965.

Visscher, Gerhard H. "New Views Regarding Legalism and Exclusivism in Judaism: Is There a Need to Reinterpret Paul?" *Koinonia* 18/2 (Fall 1999).

Vos, Geerhardus. *Biblical Theology*. Grand Rapids, MI: Eerdmans, 1948.

_____________. *Redemptive History and Biblical Interpretation*. Phillipsburg, NJ: Presbyterian and Reformed Publishing Co., 1980.

Vos, Johannes. *The Westminster Larger Catechism: A Commentary*. ed. by G.I. Williamson. Phillipsburg, NJ: P&R Publishing, 2002.

Walker, Williston. *A History of the Christian Church*. New York: Charles Scribner's Sons, 1959.

Wallace, Ronald. *Calvin's Doctrine of the Word and Sacrament*. Edinburgh: Oliver and Boyd LTD., 1953.

_____________. *The Ten Commandments: The Study of Ethical Freedom*. Grand Rapids, MI: William B. Eerdmans Publishing Co., 1965.

Walvoord, John F. *The Millenial Kingdom*. Grand Rapids, MI: Zondervan, 1983.

Warfield, Benjamin B. *Biblical and Theological Studies*. ed. by Samuel G. Craig. Philadelphia, PA: Presbyterian and Reformed, 1952.

__________________. *Calvin and Augustine*. ed. Samuel G. Craig. Philadelphia, PA: Presbyterian and Reformed, 1956.

__________________. *Faith And Life*. Edinburgh: Banner of Truth, [1916] 1974.

__________________. *The Lord of Glory*. Grand Rapids, MI: Baker Book House, [1907] 1974.

__________________. *The Person and Work of Christ*. ed. by Samuel G. Craig. Philadelphia, PA: Presbyterian and Reformed, 1950.

__________________. *The Plan of Salvation*. Grand Rapids, MI: Wm. B. Eerdmans Publishing Co., 1955.

__________________. *Selected Shorter Writings of Benjamin B. Warfield*. Nutley, N.J.: Presbyterian and Reformed Publishing Co., [1893] 1973.

__________________. *The Westminster Assembly And Its Work*. Cherry Hill, NJ: Mack Publishing Company, n.d.

Watson, Thomas. *Body Of Divinity*. Grand Rapids, Michigan: Sovereign Grace Publishers, n.d.

______________. *A Divine Cordial: An Exposition of Romans 8:28.* Grand Rapids, MI: Baker Book House, [1663] 1981.

Weaver, Richard M. *The Southern Tradition At Bay.* Washington, D.C.: Regnery Gateway, 1989.

Webb, Robert A. *Christian Salvation Its Doctrine and Experience.* Harrisonburg, VA: Sprinkle Publications, [1921] 1985.

Webster, Noah. *Noah Webster's First Edition of an American Dictionary of the English Language.* San Francisco, CA: Foundation for American Christian Education, [1828] 1967.

Webster, William. *The Church of Rome at the Bar of History.* Edinburgh: The Banner Of Truth Trust, 1995.

Wells, Tom. *Faith: The Gift of God.* Edinburgh: The Banner of Truth Trust, 1983.

Wenham, Gordon J. *New International Commentary on the Old Testament: The Book of Leviticus.* Grand Rapids, MI: William B. Eerdmans Publishing Co., 1979.

Whitcomb, John C., Jr. *The Early Earth.* Nutley, NJ: Presbyterian and Reformed Publishing Co., 1972.

Whitcomb, John C., Jr., and Henry M. Morris, *The Genesis Flood: The Biblical Record and its Scientific Implications.* Philadelphia, PA: Presbyterian and Reformed, 1968.

White, James. "*Sola Scriptura* and the Early Church." *Sola Scriptura.* ed. Don Kistler. Morgan, PA: Soli Deo Gloria Publications, 1995.

Whyte, Alexander. *The Shorter Catechism.* Edinburgh: T & T Clark, 1961.

Wilkins, Steve. "The Legacy of the Half-Way Covenant." Lecture delivered at the Auburn Avenue Pastors Conference, Winter, 2002.

Williams, Jonathan W. "The Contribution of Presbyterian Theology and Government on Early American History." *The Counsel of Chalcedon* (Aug.–Oct. 1986).

Williamson, G. I. *The Westminster Confession of Faith For Study Classes.* Philadelphia, PA: Presbyterian and Reformed, 1964.

Wilson, Augusta Evans. *A Speckled Bird.* New York: G.W. Dillingham Co., 1902.

Wilson, Daniel. *The Divine Authority and Perpetual Observance of the Lord's Day.*

Wilson, Douglas. *Fidelity: What It Means to be a One-Woman Man.* Moscow, ID: Canon Press, 199.

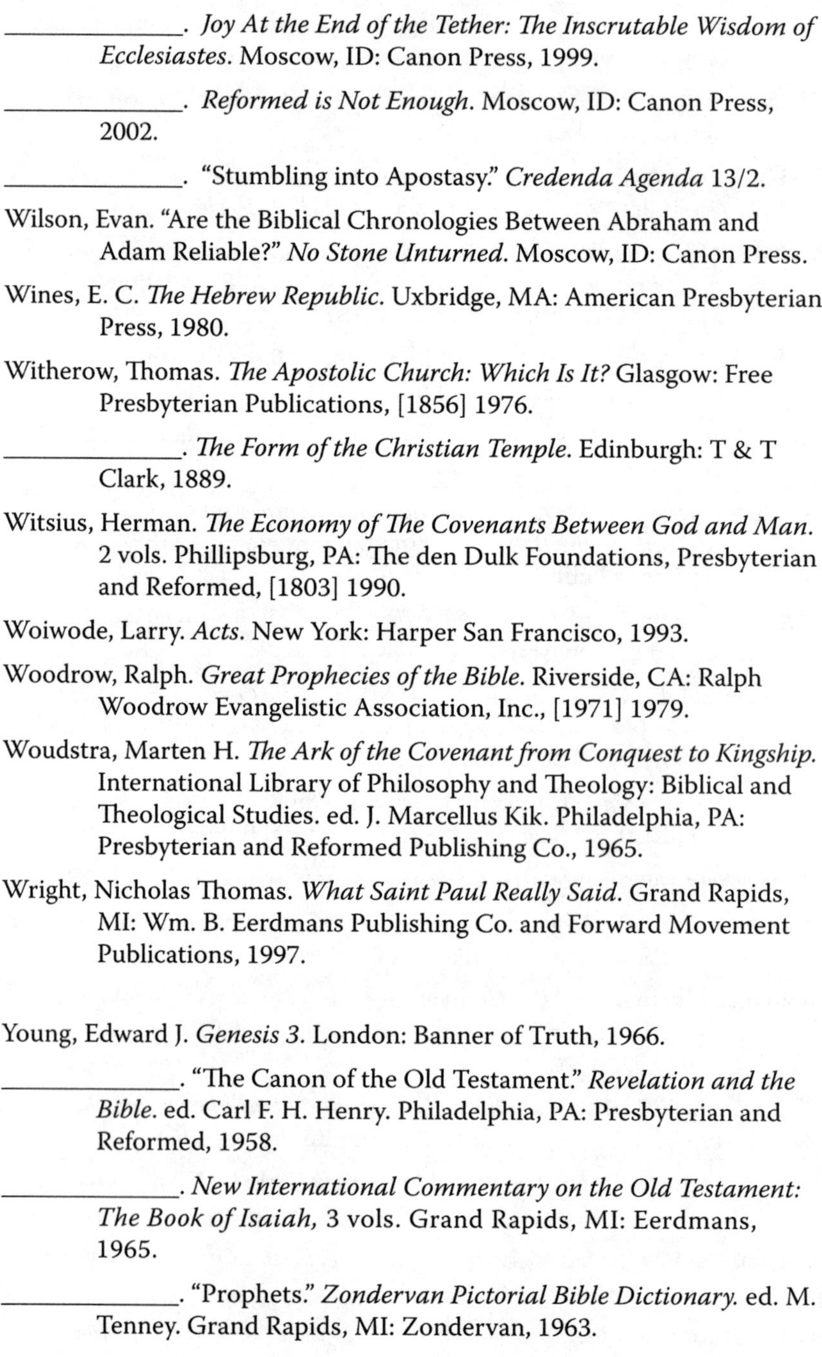

______________. *Joy At the End of the Tether: The Inscrutable Wisdom of Ecclesiastes*. Moscow, ID: Canon Press, 1999.

______________. *Reformed is Not Enough*. Moscow, ID: Canon Press, 2002.

______________. "Stumbling into Apostasy." *Credenda Agenda* 13/2.

Wilson, Evan. "Are the Biblical Chronologies Between Abraham and Adam Reliable?" *No Stone Unturned*. Moscow, ID: Canon Press.

Wines, E. C. *The Hebrew Republic*. Uxbridge, MA: American Presbyterian Press, 1980.

Witherow, Thomas. *The Apostolic Church: Which Is It?* Glasgow: Free Presbyterian Publications, [1856] 1976.

______________. *The Form of the Christian Temple*. Edinburgh: T & T Clark, 1889.

Witsius, Herman. *The Economy of The Covenants Between God and Man*. 2 vols. Phillipsburg, PA: The den Dulk Foundations, Presbyterian and Reformed, [1803] 1990.

Woiwode, Larry. *Acts*. New York: Harper San Francisco, 1993.

Woodrow, Ralph. *Great Prophecies of the Bible*. Riverside, CA: Ralph Woodrow Evangelistic Association, Inc., [1971] 1979.

Woudstra, Marten H. *The Ark of the Covenant from Conquest to Kingship*. International Library of Philosophy and Theology: Biblical and Theological Studies. ed. J. Marcellus Kik. Philadelphia, PA: Presbyterian and Reformed Publishing Co., 1965.

Wright, Nicholas Thomas. *What Saint Paul Really Said*. Grand Rapids, MI: Wm. B. Eerdmans Publishing Co. and Forward Movement Publications, 1997.

Young, Edward J. *Genesis 3*. London: Banner of Truth, 1966.

______________. "The Canon of the Old Testament." *Revelation and the Bible*. ed. Carl F. H. Henry. Philadelphia, PA: Presbyterian and Reformed, 1958.

______________. *New International Commentary on the Old Testament: The Book of Isaiah,* 3 vols. Grand Rapids, MI: Eerdmans, 1965.

______________. "Prophets." *Zondervan Pictorial Bible Dictionary*. ed. M. Tenney. Grand Rapids, MI: Zondervan, 1963.

______________. *Thy Word Is Truth*. Grand Rapids, MI: Eerdmans, 1957.

Young, William. "The Second Commandment: The Principle that God is to be Worshipped Only in Ways Prescribed in Holy Scripture and that the Holy Scripture Prescribes the Whole Content of Worship." *The Biblical Doctrine of Worship: A Symposium*. Reformed Presbyterian Church of North America, 1974.